9, 10, 1

15, 16, 18, 36, 50
17, 19, 20, 28

MEDIEVAL ENGLAND

READINGS IN MEDIEVAL CIVILIZATIONS AND CULTURES: VI
series editor: Paul Edward Dutton

MEDIEVAL ENGLAND,

1000-1500

A READER

edited by

EMILIE AMT

broadview press

Canadian Cataloguing in Publication Data

Main entry under title:
 Medieval England 1000-1500: a reader

(Readings in medieval civilisations and cultures; 6)
Includes index.
ISBN 1-55111-244-2

1. Great Britain – History – Medieval period, 1066-1485 – Sources.   2. England – Civilization – 1066-1485 – Sources. I. Amt, Emilie, 1960- .
II. Title. III. Series.

DA170.M42 2000   942.03   C00-931838-0
Broadview Press Ltd., is an independent, international publishing house, incorporated in 1985.

North America:
P.O. Box 1243, Peterborough, Ontario, Canada K9J 7H5
3576 California Road, Orchard Park, NY 14127
TEL: (705) 743-8990; FAX: (705) 743-8353;
E-MAIL: customerservice@broadviewpress.com

United Kingdom: Turpin Distribution Services Ltd.,
Blackhorse Rd., Letchworth, Hertfordshire SG6 1HN
TEL: (1462) 672555; FAX (1462) 480947; E-MAIL: turpin@rsc.org

Australia: St. Clair Press, P.O. Box 287, Rozelle, NSW 2039
TEL: (02) 818-1942; FAX: (02) 418-1923

www.broadviewpress.com

Book design and composition by George Kirkpatrick.
PRINTED IN CANADA

TABLE OF CONTENTS

INTRODUCTION

Medieval English history is rich in source material, and this book is intended to provide a sampling of those sources for students and other readers. To encompass five centuries of English history in 85 documents is, of course, impossible. Instead, I have tried both to convey some of the wonderful variety found in the written record and to supply pieces that will complement the textbooks and monographs that history students are likely to be reading in their courses. Some constitutional highlights and standard texts such as Magna Carta and Froissart are included here, but many of the contents are less well known because they have been less readily available. My emphases have been on political history and social history, and I have chosen pieces in part for their readability, therefore including, for example, a great deal of narrative material and very few record sources (charters, financial accounts, and so on), because the latter tend to be less useful to the non-specialist. I have also largely excluded literary sources, which are well represented in their own anthologies and other widely available editions; the focus here is on the sources we call "historical" because they purport to record the reality of national events and people's lives. The coverage of historical events and time periods is of necessity uneven: some significant political developments, for example, have been omitted, but I hope that readers will benefit from the clusters of documents on certain other topics, such as Anglo-Saxon monarchy, the Black Death, and late medieval commercial life.

In approaching medieval sources, the modern reader needs to maintain a critical stance which takes into account the nature of medieval society. Literacy was very limited throughout this time period; most of those who wrote were male clerics working either within the church or on behalf of the secular authorities, and most literate clerics themselves came from a noble or wealthy background. For all these reasons, medieval sources have a pervasive bias: they represent the perspective of the elite, usually the ecclesiastical or monastic elite, and overwhelmingly the male elite. Even when writers record the testimony of common men and women, as for example in the coroners' rolls (doc. 45) or the records of a manorial court (doc. 54), a filter of officialdom still stands between the commoner's experience and the written record. The reader must be constantly aware of this, and alert to other potential limitations, if she or he is to benefit as fully as possible from these sources.

On the other hand, some attempt to understand medieval viewpoints — to enter into medieval mindsets — is crucial to understanding these documents and the stories they tell. I do not want to suggest that there is a single such viewpoint. The acceptance of hierarchy and authority, the importance of personal bonds, the pervasiveness of hardship, the tenuousness of life itself, the basic homogeneity of religious culture, the general acceptance of supernatural intervention in earthly matters, and the literalness with which people regarded both secular and sacred ritual were some of the elements that contributed to an experience shared by all levels of society. Yet it is a serious mistake to think of any human society, or even a group within that society, as monolithic. My students often want to know "what people thought" in the Middle Ages about some aspect or other of life. Quite apart from the obvious risk of generalizing about hundreds of years of human experience and opinion, the historian of any period needs to look for differences as much as for consensus. Queen Emma (doc. 6) and Queen Edith (doc. 7) presented themselves as fulfilling very different ideals of royal womanhood. English Jews had many persecutors but also some protectors (docs. 26, 38). Everyone seemed to accept villeinage as the proper condition of the majority of the population — until John Ball preached against it and helped touch off the Peasants' Revolt (doc. 62). While political and intellectual historians have long focused on controversies within the medieval elite, recent generations of medieval historians have also begun to reveal that the fabric of society was a much richer tapestry than has traditionally been thought. Anyone who studies the past must bear in mind both the variety of human conditions and the wide spectrum of human reactions even in similar situations. Such an approach is not just a matter of reading a variety of texts; it is a matter of exploring the richness of a single text. I hope that the documents collected here will be read in such a way.

My thanks are due to many colleagues and friends for their assistance in the preparation of this volume, among them Paul Dutton for first suggesting the project and for his encouragement and guidance throughout its execution. The shape and contents of the book owe a great deal to the expertise and advice of Robert Stacey and John Shinners; its shortcomings are of course my own. Hood College's interlibrary loan service and the unfailing help of Anne Thayer, Cynthia Feher, and Darylyne Provost made the project possible. William Tubbs and Katherine Rabenstein have also helped me locate and secure sources. Lisa Algazi graciously agreed to produce for this book the first English translation of the section of *L'Histoire de Guillaume le Maréchal* included here. Special thanks to Martha Amt for technological support; to Courtney Becker and Erin Passwater for a great deal of technical assistance and especially for compiling the index; and to all my family and friends for patiently bearing with me in periods of intensive anthologizing.

MEDIEVAL ENGLISH MONEY

Throughout most of the period covered in this book, the standard units of English money were the pounds (£), shillings (s.), and pence (d. for the Latin *denarius*) that appear over and over in the documents printed here. Twelve pence made a shilling, and twenty shillings (or 240 pence) made a pound. Another unit frequently used in accounting was the mark, which consisted of thirteen shillings and four pence. In some of the Anglo-Saxon documents below, the *ora*, equal to sixteen pence, is the standard unit of account.

A penny was not an insubstantial amount of money. While it is impossible to convert medieval amounts into modern monetary equivalents, some idea of the value of money may be had from examining wages and prices. In the twelfth century, for example, an ordinary laborer who worked for money (though most people did not) might earn a few pence daily; a knight could earn eight pence a day. Many ordinary purchases cost less than a penny, hence the common practice of physically cutting the silver coins into half-pennies and quarter-pennies, or "farthings." A single sheep cost between four and nine pence to buy, and as part of a wool-producing flock it produced for its owner a profit of two or three pence annually. A riding horse cost one pound, but a warhorse cost £20 — as much as the annual income from a good-sized manor. These are just a few examples. A number of the documents in this book list various wages and prices, and the reader can easily draw further comparisons from them.

CHAPTER ONE

THE ELEVENTH CENTURY

Fig. 1: A nineteenth-century copy of an Anglo-Saxon manuscript illustration showing men and women at work picking grapes and pressing them to extract the juice to make wine.

1. ÆLFRIC'S COLLOQUY

Providing a glimpse of the activities of ordinary people that is rare for the eleventh century, this educational text is part of an ancient tradition of such dialogues, intended as tools for teaching Latin. The author, Ælfric of Canterbury (d. 1006), gained prominence as an abbot, homilist, and educator. The students in this dialogue are depicted as boys living in a monastery school, whose way of life is further illuminated later in the chapter.

Source: trans. A. F. Leach, *Educational Charters and Documents, 598 to 1909* (Cambridge: Cambridge University Press, 1911), pp. 37-47; revised, with additional material trans. E. Amt from *Ælfric's Colloquy*, ed. G. N. Garmonsway (London: Methuen & Co., Ltd., 1939), pp. 21-47.

Boys: Master, we children ask you to teach us to speak correctly, for we are unlearned and speak corruptly.

Master: What do you want to say?

Boys: What do we care what we say, so long as we speak correctly and say what is useful, not old-womanish or improper?

Master: Are you willing to be flogged while learning?

Boys: We would rather be flogged while learning than remain ignorant; but we know that you will be kind to us and not flog us unless you are obliged.

Master: I ask you what you were saying to me. What work do you do?

First boy: I am a professed monk and I sing seven times a day with the brethren and I am busy with reading and singing; and meanwhile I want to learn to speak Latin.

Master: What do these companions of yours know?

First boy: Some are plowmen, others shepherds, some are cowherds, some too are hunters, some are fishermen, some hawkers, some merchants, some shoemakers, some salters, some bakers of the place.

Master: What do you say, plowman, how do you do your work?

Plowman: Oh, sir, I work very hard. I go out at dawn to drive the oxen to the field, and yoke them to the plow; however hard the winter I dare not stay at home for fear of my master; and having yoked the oxen and made the plowshare and coulter fast to the plow, every day I have to plow a whole acre or more.

Master: Have you anyone with you?

Plowman: I have a boy to drive the oxen with the goad, and he is now hoarse with cold and shouting.

Master: What more do you do in the day?

Plowman: A great deal more. I have to fill the oxen's bins with hay, and give them water, and carry the dung outside.

Master: Oh, it is hard work.

Plowman: Yes, it is hard work, because I am not free.

Master: What do you say, shepherd? Do you have any work?
Shepherd: Yes, I have. First thing in the morning I drive my sheep to pasture, and I stand over them with dogs, in heat and cold, so that wolves do not devour them; and I lead them back to the sheepfolds, and I milk them twice a day. And I move their folds, and besides this I make cheese and butter. And I am faithful to my lord.

Master: O oxherd, what do you do?
Oxherd: My lord, I have a great deal of work. When the plowman unyokes the oxen, I lead them to pasture, and I stand over them all night watching for thieves, and early in the morning I hand them over again to the plowman well fed and watered.

Master: Is this man one of your companions?
Boys: Yes, he is.
Master: Do you know anything?
Huntsman: One craft only.
Master: What is it?
Huntsman: I am a hunter.
Master: Whose?
Huntsman: The king's.
Master: How do you practice your craft?
Huntsman: I weave my nets and put them in the right place, and I train my dogs to chase wild animals, until they suddenly come to the nets and thus are trapped, and I cut their throats in the nets.
Master: Don't you know how to hunt without nets?
Huntsman: I can also hunt without nets.
Master: How?
Huntsman: I chase the wild animals with swift dogs.
Master: What kind of wild animals do you usually catch?
Huntsman: I catch stags and boars and deer and goats and sometimes hares.
Master: Did you go hunting today?
Huntsman: No, because it is Sunday, but I went hunting yesterday.
Master: What did you catch?
Huntsman: Two stags and one boar.
Master: How did you catch them?
Huntsman: I caught the stags in nets, and I slew the boar.
Master: How did you dare to slay a boar?

Huntsman: The dogs drove him toward me, and standing in front of him I suddenly cut his throat.

Master: That was very brave of you.

Huntsman: A huntsman must not be fearful, because many kinds of beasts live in the woods.

Master: What do you do with your game?

Huntsman: I give the king everything I catch, because I am his huntsman.

Master: What does he give you?

Huntsman: He clothes me well and feeds me; sometimes he gives me a horse or an arm-ring, so that I will more willingly exercise my craft.

Master: What craft do you know?

Fisherman: I am a fisherman.

Master: What do you receive from your craft?

Fisherman: Food and clothing and money.

Master: How do you catch fish?

Fisherman: I board a boat and put my nets in the river, and I cast my hooks and fishtraps, and I take up whatever they catch.

Master: What if the fish are unclean?

Fisherman: I throw the unclean ones out, and I take up the clean ones for myself for food.

Master: Where do you sell your fish?

Fisherman: In the city.

Master: Who buys them?

Fisherman: The citizens. I can't catch as many as I can sell.

Master: What kinds of fish do you catch?

Fisherman: Eels and pike, minnows and burbots, trout and lampreys, and whatever swims in the river. And sprat.

Master: Why don't you fish in the sea?

Fisherman: Sometimes I do, but rarely, because I need a large boat on the sea.

Master: What do you catch in the sea?

Fisherman: Herring and salmon, dolphin and sturgeon, oysters and crabs, mussels, winkles, cockles, flounder, sole, lobster, and so on.

Master: Do you want to catch a whale sometime?

Fisherman: No, I don't.

Master: Why?

Fisherman: Because catching a whale is a dangerous business. It is safer for me to go to the river with my hook, than to go whaling with many ships.

Master: Why is that?

Fisherman: Because I would rather catch a fish that I can kill than one which can drown or kill not only me but also my companions with a single blow.

Master: All the same, many do catch whales and escape the dangers, and they get a high price for them.

Fisherman: You speak the truth, but I do not dare, because of the timidity of my mind.

Master: What do you say, fowler? How do you ensnare birds?

Fowler: I ensnare birds in many ways: sometimes with nets, sometimes with snares, sometimes with lime, sometimes with whistling, sometimes with a hawk, sometimes with traps.

Master: Do you have a hawk?

Fowler: Yes, I have.

Master: Do you know how to tame them?

Fowler: Yes, I do. What good would they be to me unless I knew how to tame them?

Huntsman: Give me a hawk.

Fowler: I will gladly give you one, if you will give me a swift dog. What kind of hawk do you wish to have, larger or smaller?

Huntsman: Give me the larger one.

Master: How do you feed your hawks?

Fowler: They feed themselves and me in the winter, and in the spring I send them flying free in the woods. Then I catch the young ones for myself in the autumn, and tame them.

Master: And why do you let the tamed ones fly away from you?

Fowler: Because I don't want to feed them in the summer, because they eat too much.

Master: Still, many people feed their tame hawks over the summer, so as to have them ready again.

Fowler: Yes, they do, but I don't want to work so hard on them, because I know I can catch others — not just one, but many more.

Master: What do you say, merchant?

Merchant: I say that I am useful to the king and to the nobles, and to the rich, and to all people.

Master: How so?

Merchant: I board a ship with my goods, and I sail across the seas and sell my stuff. And I buy precious things which are not made in this land, and bring them back here for you, at great peril on the sea, and sometimes I am shipwrecked and barely escape with my life.

Master: What kinds of things do you bring us?

Merchant: Purple cloth and silk, precious stones and gold, various clothing and perfume, wine and oil, ivory and brass, copper and tin, sulfur and glass and similar things.

Master: Do you wish to sell these things here for what you bought them for there?

Merchant: No. What good would all my work do me then? I want to sell them here for more than I bought them for there, so that I get some money, with which to feed myself and my wife and my children.

Master: You, cobbler, what do you do that's useful to us?

Cobbler: Indeed my craft is very useful to you, and necessary.

Master: How?

Cobbler: I buy skins and hides, and I prepare them by my craft, and from them I make footwear of many kinds, shoes, clogs, and boots, and buckets, and bridles and harness, and flasks and bottles, spurs and halters, bags and purses; and not one of you wants to go through a winter without the help of my craft.

Master: O saltmaker, what good does your craft do for us?

Saltmaker: My craft is of great benefit to everyone. Not one of you will take delight in lunch or dinner, unless my craft is a guest there too.

Master: How so?

Saltmaker: What person really enjoys pleasant food without a taste of salt? Who fills up the cellar or storehouse without my art? Look: every butter and cheese is lost to you unless I am there to guard it, and you do not enjoy even your vegetables without me.

Master: What do you say, baker? Whom does your craft benefit, or can we lead life without you?

Baker: You would be able to live for some time without my craft, but not for long and not very well: for without my craft every table seems empty, and without bread every food becomes loathsome. I make people's hearts stronger, I am the vigor of men, and not even children want to go without me.

Master: What shall we say about the cook, if we want something of his craft?

Cook: If you expel me from your company, you will eat your vegetables uncooked, and your meat raw, and you won't even be able to have a rich soup without my craft.

Master: We do not care for your craft, and it is not necessary for us, because we ourselves can cook what needs to be cooked, and roast what needs to be roasted.

Cook: If for that reason you dismiss me, and you do what you've said, then you will all be cooks, and none of you will be the chief, and without my craft you will not eat.

Master: O monk, you who spoke to me, look: I have shown that you have good and very necessary companions. Now who are these other men?

Boy: I have smiths here — the blacksmith, the goldsmith, the silversmith, the coppersmith, the carpenter, and many other workers of various crafts.

Master: Do you have some wise counselor?

Boy: Yes, I have. How can our congregation be governed without a counselor?

Master: What do you say, counselor? Which craft seems to you foremost among all these?

Counselor: I tell you, the service of God seems to me to hold first place among all these crafts, as the evangelist writes: "Seek ye first the kingdom of God and his righteousness, and all these things will be added unto you."

Master: And which among the secular arts seems to you to keep first place?

Counselor: Agriculture, because the plowman feeds all of us.

Smith: Where does the plowman get his plowshare and coulter? He wouldn't even have his goad if not for my craft. Where does the fisherman get his hook, the cobbler his awl, the tailor his needle? Don't they all come from my work?

Counselor: What you say is true, but all of us would rather be the plowman's guest than yours, because the plowman gives us bread and drink; you, what do you give us in your workshop but iron sparks and the sound of pounding hammers and blowing bellows?

Carpenter: Which of you does not benefit from my craft, when houses and all sorts of containers and even ships are all made by me?

Smith: O carpenter, why do you speak so, when you wouldn't even be able to make a single hole without my craft?

Counselor: Oh, all you good fellows and good workers, let us end this dispute and have peace and harmony among us, and let each help the other by his craft, and let us all meet at the plowman's, where we find food for ourselves and fodder for our horses. And this is the advice I give all workmen, that each of them should do his work as well as he can, as the man who neglects his work is dismissed from his work. Whether you are a priest or a monk, a layman or a soldier, apply yourself to that, and be what you are, as it is a great loss and shame for a man not to be what he is and what he ought to be.

Master: Now, children, how do you like this speech?

Boys: We like it very much, but what you say is too deep for us, and is beyond our age. But talk to us in a way we can follow so that we may understand what you are talking about.

Master: Well, I ask you why you are learning so diligently?

Boys: Because we do not want to be like beasts, who know nothing but grass and water.

Master: And what do you want?

Boys: We want to be wise.

Master: In what wisdom? Do you want to be crafty in lies, with a thousand shapes, artful in speeches, sly, deceitful, speaking good and thinking evil, given to sweet words, nourishing deceit within, like a whited sepulcher, full of uncleanness?

Boys: We do not want to be wise in that way, for he is not wise who deceives himself with pretense.

Master: But how do you want to be wise?

Boys: We want to be simple and without hypocrisy, and wise so that we turn away from evil and do good. But so far you have spoken with us more profoundly than our age can understand; so talk to us so that we can understand, not so profoundly.

Master: Well, I will do what you ask. You, boy, what did you do today?

Boy: I did many things. At night when I heard the bell, I got out of bed and went to church and sang the nocturn with the brethren. Then we sang the martyrology and lauds; after that, prime and the seven psalms with litanies and first mass; next tierce, and did the mass of the day; after that we sang sext, and ate and drank and slept; and then we got up again and sang nones, and now here we are before you ready to listen to what you tell us.

Master: When will you sing vespers or compline?

Boy: When it's time.

Master: Were you flogged today?

Boy: I was not, because I was very careful.

Master: And how about the others?

Boy: Why do you ask me that? I daren't tell you our secrets. Each one knows whether he was flogged or not.

Master: What do you eat each day?

Boy: At this time I eat meat, for I am a boy living under the rod [that is, a novice monk who has not yet taken vows].

Master: What else do you eat?

Boy: I eat vegetables and eggs, fish and cheese, butter and beans and all fitting things, giving thanks.

Master: You are very voracious to eat everything that is given you.

Boy: I am not so gluttonous that I can eat all kinds of food in one meal.

Master: So how?

Boy: Sometimes I eat these foods, and sometimes others, in moderation, as befits a monk, not voraciously, for I am not a glutton.

Master: And what do you drink?

Boy: Ale, if I have it, or water if I don't have ale.

Master: Don't you drink wine?

Boy: I'm not rich enough to buy myself wine; and wine is not the drink of children or of the foolish, but of old and wise men.

Master: Where do you sleep?

Boy: In the dormitory with the brethren.

Master: Who calls you to nocturns?

Boy: Sometimes I hear the bell, and get up; sometimes my master wakes me with a ground-ash.

Master: All you good children and clever scholars, your teacher exhorts you to keep the commandments of God, and behave properly everywhere. Walk quietly when you hear the church bells and go into church, and bow to the holy altars, and stand quietly and sing in unison, and ask pardon for your sins, and go out again without playing, to the cloister or to school.

Questions: What can be learned about everyday life and economic conditions in Anglo-Saxon England from this dialogue? What does it tell us about the relationships between the craftspeople and their customers, or those who benefit from their work? How do the monastic schoolboys in this piece compare with those who figure in Lanfranc's Constitutions (doc. 12) and in Orderic Vitalis' autobiographical passage (doc. 13)?

2. THE RIGHTS OF VARIOUS PERSONS

A less idealized picture of Anglo-Saxon life emerges from this technically precise description of the obligations and rights of people of different ranks and occupations. Written in the first half of the eleventh century as a guide to estate management, it summarizes the legal conditions with which its author was most familiar but recognizes the existence of a great variety of such customs across the kingdom.

Source: trans. A.E. Bland, P.A. Brown, and R.H. Tawney, *English Economic History: Select Documents* (London: G. Bell and Sons, Ltd., 1914), pp. 5-9; revised.

The Thegn's Law. The thegn's law is that he be worthy of his book-right [that is, the right conferred on him by charter], and that he do three things for his land, fyrdfare [that is, military service], burhbote [that is, repair of fortified towns], and bridge-work. Also from many lands a greater land-service arises at the king's command, such as the deer-hedge at the king's abode and provision of warships and sea-ward and head-ward [that is, guarding the king] and fyrd-ward, almsfee and churchscot, and many other diverse things.

Fig. 2: Field Workers A nineteenth-century copy of a detail from the famous eleventh-century Anglo-Saxon manuscript known as the Harley Psalter, showing men at work in the fields plowing (bottom center), sowing (lower right), and at harvest supper (upper right).

The Geneat's Service. Geneat-service is diverse according to the custom of the estate. On some he must pay land-gafol [that is, rent] and grass-swine [that is, fee for pasturing pigs] yearly, and ride and carry and lead loads, work, and feast the lord, and reap and mow and cut the deer-hedge and maintain it, build and hedge the burh, bring strange wayfarers to the town, pay churchscot and alms-fee, keep head-ward and homeward, go errands far and near whithersoever he be told.

The Cotter's Service. The cotter's service is according to the custom of the estate. On some he must work for his lord each Monday throughout the year and for three days each week in harvest. On some he works through the whole harvest every day and reaps an acre of oats for a day's work, and he shall have his sheaf which the reeve or lord's servant will give him. He ought not to pay land-gafol. It befits him to have 5 acres; more, if it be the custom of the estate; and if it be less, it is too little, because his work shall be oft required; he shall pay his hearth-penny on Holy Thursday, as all free men should; and he shall defend his lord's inland, if he be required, from sea-ward and the king's deer-hedge and from such things as befit his degree; and he shall pay his churchscot at Martinmas [November 11].

The Gebur's Services. The gebur's services are diverse, in some places heavy, in others moderate; on some estates he must work two days at week-work at such work as is bidden him every week throughout the year, and in harvest three days at week-work, and from Candlemas [February 2] to Easter three. If he do carrying, he need not work while his horse is out. He must pay on Michaelmas day [September 29] 10 gafol-pence, and on Martinmas day 23 sesters of barley and two henfowls, at Easter a young sheep or two pence; and from Martinmas to Easter he must lie at the lord's fold as often as his turn comes; and from the time of the first plowing to Martinmas he must plow an acre every week and himself fetch the seed in the lord's barn; also 3 acres at boonwork and 2 for grass-earth [that is, pasture-land]; if he need more grass, he shall earn it as he shall be allowed; for his gafol-earth [that is, rent] he shall plow 3 acres and sow it from his own barn; and he shall pay his hearth-penny; two and two they shall feed a hunting-hound; and every gebur shall pay 6 loaves to the lord's swineherd when he drives his herd to mast [that is, pasture for pigs]. On the same lands where the above customs hold good, it belongs to the gebur that he be given for his land-stock 2 oxen and 1 cow and 6 sheep and 7 acres sown on his yardland; wherefore after that year he shall do all the customs that befit him; and he shall be given tools for his work and vessels for his house. When death befalls him, his lord shall take back the things which he leaves.

This land-law holds good on some lands, but, as I have said before, in some places it is heavier, in others lighter, for all land-customs are not alike. On some lands the gebur must pay honey-gafol, on some meat-gafol, on some ale-gafol.

Let him who keeps the shire take heed that he knows what are the ancient uses of the land and what the custom of the people.

Of Those Who Keep the Bees. It belongs to the bee-churl, if he keep the gafol-hives, that he give as is customary on the estate. Among us it is customary that he give 5 sesters of honey for gafol; on some estates more gafol is wont to be rendered. Also he must be oft ready for many works at the lord's will, besides boon-plowing and bedrips [that is, reaping] and meadow-mowing; and if he be well landed, he must have a horse that he may lend it to the lord for carrying or drive it himself whithersoever he be told; and many things a man so placed must do; I cannot now tell all. When death befalls him, the lord shall have back the things which he leaves, save what is free.

Of the Swineherd. It belongs to the gafol-paying swineherd that he give of his slaughter according to the custom of the estate. On many estates the custom is that he give every year 15 swine for sticking, 10 old and 5 young, and have himself what he breeds beyond that. To many estates a heavier swine-service belongs. Let the swineherd take heed also that after sticking he prepare and singe well his slaughtered swine; then is he right worthy of the entrails, and, as I said before of the bee-keeper, he must be oft ready for any work, and have a horse for his lord's need. The unfree swineherd and the unfree bee-keeper, after death, shall be worthy of one same law.

Of the Serf-Swineherd. To the serf swineherd who keeps the inherd [that is, the lord's herd] belong a sucking-pig from the sty and the entrails when he has prepared bacon, and further the customs which befit the unfree.

Of Men's Board. To a bondservant belong for board 12 pounds of good corn and 2 sheep-carcasses and a good meat-cow, and wood, according to the custom of the estate.

Of Women's Board. To unfree women belong 8 pounds of corn for food, one sheep or 3d. for winter fare, one sester of beans for Lent fare, in summer whey or 1d.

To all serfs belong a midwinter feast and an Easter feast, a plowacre [that is, an acre for plowing] and a harvest handful [that is, a sheaf from each acre], besides their needful dues.

Of Followers [that is, free but landless retainers]. It belongs to the follower that in 12 months he earn two acres, the one sown and the other unsown; he shall sow them himself, and his board and provision of shoes and gloves belong to him; if he may earn more, it shall be to his own profit.

Of the Sower. It belongs to the sower that he have a basketful of every kind of seed when he have well sown each sowing throughout the year.

Of the Ox-herd. The ox-herd may pasture 2 oxen or more with the lord's herd in the common pastures by witness of his ealdorman [that is, reeve]; and thereby may earn shoes and gloves for himself; and his meat-cow may go with the lord's oxen.

Of the Cow-herd. It belongs to the cow-herd that he have an old cow's milk for seven days after she has newly calved, and the beestings [that is, first milk after calving] for fourteen nights; and his meat-cow shall go with the lord's cow.

Of Sheep-herds. The sheep-herd's right is that he have 12 nights' manure at midwinter and 1 lamb of the year's increase, and the fleece of 1 bellwether and the milk of his flock for seven nights after the equinox and a bowlful of whey or buttermilk all the summer.

Of the Goat-herd. To the goat-herd belongs his herd's milk after Martinmas day and before that his share of whey and one kid of the year's increase, if he have well cared for his herd.

Of the Cheese-maker. To the cheese-maker belong 100 cheeses, and that she make butter of the wring-whey [that is, residue from cheese-pressing] for the lord's table; and she shall have for herself all the buttermilk save the herd's share.

Of the Barn-keeper. To the barn-keeper belong the corn-droppings in harvest at the barn-door, if his ealdorman give it him and he faithfully earn it.

Of the Beadle. It belongs to the beadle that for his office he be freer from work than another man, for that he must be oft ready; also to him belongs a strip of land for his toil.

Of the Woodward. To the woodward belongs every windfall tree.

Of the Hayward. To the hayward it belongs that his toil be rewarded with land at the ends of the fields that lie by the pasture meadow; for he may expect that if he first neglects this, to his charge will be laid damage to the crops; and if a strip of land be allowed to him, this shall be by folk-right next the pasture meadow, for that if out of sloth he neglect his lord, his own land shall not be well defended, if it be found so; but if he defend well all that he shall hold, then shall he be right worthy of a good reward.

Land-laws are diverse, as I said before, nor do we fix for all places these customs that we have before spoken of, but we show forth what is accustomed there where it is known to us; if we learn anything better, that will we gladly cherish and keep, according to the customs of the place where we shall then dwell; for gladly should he learn the law among the people, who wishes not himself to lose honor in the country. Folk-customs are many; in some places there belong to the people winter-feast, Easter-feast, boon-feast for harvest, a drinking feast for plowing, rick-meat [that is, a feast after making the hay-rick], mowing reward, a wainstick [that is, a measure of wood] at wood-loading, a stack-cup [that is, a feast] at corn-loading, and many things that I cannot number. But this is a reminder for men, yea, all that I have set forth above.

Questions: If gebur-status was the most common condition of peasants (with cotters being another large group), what does this document reveal about the workload on estates and the economic condition of lords? How much of his or her time and effort did a person owe to the lord? Of the specialized occupations on the estate, which ranked high and which low? What were the perks of specific jobs? Who is missing from this document?

3. ANGLO-SAXON WILLS

Anglo-Saxon law allowed great testamentary latitude to both men and women; those who were wealthy enough to compose wills could dispose quite freely of real estate and moveable goods. The wills printed here are those of two laymen (Ælfhelm and Ketel), a laywoman (Ælfflæd), and a churchman (Ælfric); they represent a small sample of the seventy or so wills that survive from pre-Conquest England.

Source: trans. D. Whitelock, *Anglo-Saxon Wills* (Cambridge: Cambridge University Press, 1930), pp. 31-35, 39-43, 53-55, 89-91.

The Will of Ælfhelm (975-1016)

Herein is the declaration of how Ælfhelm has disposed of his property and his goods in fulfilment of his duties both to God and men. First to his lord a hundred mancuses of gold and two swords and four shields and four spears and four horses, two of them harnessed and two unharnessed.

And for his soul he grants to St. Etheldreda's the estate at Wratting except the two hides which Ethelric has. And I grant the estate at Brickendon to St. Peter's at Westminster, but it is my wish that when there is mast, two hundred pigs be fed for my wife's sake, to benefit whatever foundation she pleases.

And I grant to my son Ælfgar the estate at Whepstead and that at Walton for his lifetime, and after his death they are to go wherever he pleases, for the souls of both of us. And I declare what I gave to my wife as a marriage-gift, namely, Baddow and Burstead and Stratford and the three hides at Enhale. And when we first came together, I gave her the two hides at Wilbraham, and Rayne and whatever pertains to it. And I grant her Carlton and I grant her the chief messuage [that is, dwelling] at Gestingthorpe, and all the possessions that are on it, including produce and men; but I grant to Godric and my daughter half the woodland and open land, except that which I grant to my priest. And I grant to my wife and my daughter half the estate at Conington, to divide between them, except the four hides which I grant to Æthelric and Ælfwold, and the half hide which I grant to my servant Osmær.

And I grant to Ælfmaer and his brother Ælfstan, to divide between them the two estates, Hatley and Potton, except what I grant to Osgar. And I grant to Godhere what I bought from Wimund. And I grant Littlebury to Leofsige after my death, on condition that the agreement which we concluded before the ealdorman shall hold good. And I grant to him and his wife the estate at Stockton for a hundred mancuses of gold, and I wish that the gold be given to my lord in payment of my heriot [that is, death tax].

And I grant to be divided among my three brothers the estate at Troston, except that I grant to Ælfwold that which Æthelric had. And I grant Ælfhelm the hide at Ickleton and the property at Maworth. And I grant Wulfmær what I had at Barnham.

And for my soul's sake I grant my long-ship to Ramsey, half for the abbot, and half for the community. And I grant to my wife half the stud at Troston, and half to my companions who ride with me. And my wife is to succeed to half of what is on the woodland, and my daughter to half. And I wish that my wife shall in all cases receive half the stock at each village, whoever may succeed to the land, as it was granted to her.

Now I pray you, dear lord, that my will may stand, and that you will not permit it to be wrongfully altered. God is my witness that I was as obedient to your father as ever I could be, and thoroughly loyal in thought and in deed, and was ever faithful to you with perfect loyalty and devotion; of this God is my witness.

That man who shall alter my will (unless it be you, Sire, and I am confident that you will not), may God drive him from his kingdom, unless he will quickly alter it back again; and may God and all his saints maintain each of those who give their support that the will may stand.

Endorsed. If anyone ever alters or removes anything in this will, may God's grace and his eternal reward be taken from him for ever; and may he never be found in his favor, but be excommunicated from the society of all Christ's chosen companies, both now and in eternity, unless he will quickly desist from that and also make full restitution.

The Will of Ælfflæd (1000-2)

Ælfflæd declares in this document how she wishes to have her property disposed of, in fulfilment of her duties to God and to men.

First I grant to my lord after my death the eight estates, namely Dovercourt, Beaumont, Alresford, Stanway, Barton, Lexden, Elmset and Buxhall; and two armlets of two pounds in weight, and two drinking-cups and a silver vessel. And I humbly pray you, Sire, for God's sake and for the sake of my lord's [that is, husband's] soul and for the sake of my sister's soul, that you will protect the holy foundation at Stoke in which my ancestors lie buried, and the property which they gave to it as an immune right of God for ever: which property I grant exactly as my ancestors had granted it, that is the estate at Stoke to the holy foundation with everything that belongs to the village there, and the wood at Hatfield which my sister and my ancestors gave. Then these are the estates which my ancestors bequeathed to it after my sister's lifetime and after mine: Stratford, Freston, Wiston, Lavenham, Balsdon, Polstead, Withermarsh, Greenstead, Peldon, Mersea and the woodland at Totham which my father granted to Mersea, and Colne and Tey.

Then these are the estates which my ancestors bequeathed to other holy places: namely the estate at Eleigh to Christchurch at Canterbury for the use of the community; and the estate at Hadham to St. Paul's minster at London as episcopal property, and the estate at Heybridge for the use of the community at St. Paul's minster; and the estate at Baythorn for the use of the community at Barking.

And I grant Woodham after my death to Ælfthryth, my lord's mother, and after her death it is to go to St. Mary's foundation at Barking just as it stands, with the produce and with the men. And I grant for the use of the community at St. Edmund's the two estates Chelsworth and Cockfield, just as my ancestors have granted them, and the estate at Nedging after the death of Crawe my kinswoman. And I grant to Mersea after my death everything that my lord and my sister granted, that is Fingringhoe and the six hides on which the minster stands. And I grant after Crawe's death the estate at Waldingfield to St. Gregory's at Sudbury according to the agreement my sister made about it.

And I grant to St. Peter and St. Etheldreda and St. Wihtburg and St. Sexburg and St. Eormenhild, at Ely, where my lord's body lies buried, the three estates which we both promised to God and his saints; namely, Rettendon, which was my marriage gift, Soham and Ditton, just as my lord and my sister have granted it; and the one hide at Cheveley, which my sister obtained, and the pair to the ring which was given as burial fee for my lord.

And I grant to the ealdorman Æthelmær the estate at Lawling after my death, with its produce and its men, just as it stands, on condition that during my life he shall be a true friend and advocate to me and to my men, and after my death, be a true friend and advocate of the holy foundation at Stoke, where my ancestors lie buried, and its property. And I grant the estate at Liston to Æthelmær my [lord's kinsman?] with the produce and with the men just as it stands, and humbly pray him that he will be my true friend and protector during my life, and after my death will help to secure that my will and my ancestors' wills may stand.

These are the boundaries of Balsdon: from the stream at *Humelcyrre*; from *Humelcyrre* to *Heregeresheafod*; from *Heregeresheafod* along the old hedge to the green oak; then on until one comes to the paved road; from the paved road along the shrubbery until one comes to Acton; from Acton until one comes to Roydon; from Roydon back to the stream. And there are five hides of land.

These are the boundaries of Withermarsh and Polstead: from *Loppandun* to Shelley; from Shelley to the Brett; along the Brett to the Stour; along the Stour to Leofman's boundary; along Leofman's boundary to the *Amalburn*; from the *Amalburn* to *Northfield*; then on to *Bindhæcc*; from *Bindhæcc* to *Tudanhæcc*; from *Tudanhæcc* to Giffords Hall; from Giffords Hall to Nurstead, from Nurstead to *Hwitingho*; from *Hwitingho* to *Wudemannestun*; from *Wudemannestun* to Kersey boundary; from Kersey boundary to Hadleigh boundary; from Hadleigh boundary to Layham boundary; from Layham boundary back to *Loppandun*.

The Will of Archbishop Ælfric (1003-4)

Here it is made known how Archbishop Ælfric drew up his will. First as his burial fee, he bequeathed to Christchurch the estates at Westwell and Bourne, and Risborough. And he bequeathed to his lord his best ship and the sailing tackle with it, and sixty helmets and sixty coats of mail. And if it were his lord's will, he wished that he would confirm to St. Alban's the estate at Kingsbury, and himself retake possession of *Eadulfington* in return.

And he bequeathed to Abingdon the estate at Dumbleton, and three hides of it to Ælfnoth for his life, which afterwards [are to belong] to Abingdon with the rest. And he bequeathed him ten oxen and two men, and they are to be subject to the lordship to which the land belongs. And he bequeathed the estate which he bought at Wallingford to Ceolweard, and after his death to Cholsey.

And he bequeathed to St. Alban's the estate at Tew, and the terms were to remain unchanged between the abbot and Ceolric which had been agreed upon with the Archbishop; namely that Ceolric was to hold the portion of the estate which he has for his life, and also that portion which the Archbishop let to him in return for his money; that was seven and a half hides for five pounds and fifty mancuses of gold; and after his day all of it together is to go to St. Alban's. And their terms were that Osney also should go to that monastery after Ceolric's day. And he bequeathed to St. Alban's the estate in London which he bought with his money, and all his books he also bequeathed there and his tent.

And he arranged that what money there was should be taken and first every debt paid, and afterwards what was due was to be provided for his heriot. And he granted a ship to the people of Kent and another to Wiltshire. And as regards other things besides these, if there should be any, he bade that Bishop Wulfstan and Abbot Leofric should act as seemed best to them. And the estates in the west, at Fiddington and Newton, he bequeathed to his sisters and their children. And the land of Ælfheah, Esne's son, is always to remain in his family.

And he bequeathed to Archbishop Wulfstan a pectoral cross, and a ring and a psalter; and to Bishop Ælfheah a crucifix. And in accordance with God's will he forgave the people of Kent the debt which they owed him, and the people of Middlesex and Surrey the money which he paid on their behalf. And it is his will that after his day every penally enslaved man who was condemned in his time be set free.

If anyone change this, may he have it to account for with God. Amen.

The Will of Ketel (1052–66)

Here in this document is Ketel's will: namely, that I grant Stisted to Christchurch after my time, for the sake of my father's soul and for Sæflæd's. And it is my will that all my men shall be free, and that my reeve, Mann, shall occupy the free land which I have given over into his possession, for ever freely during his life, and after his death that estate is to go with the other. And I grant to the church the land which Wihtric had in his possession, and Leofwine and Siric and Goding, to where the fence reaches Leofric's hedge; and [I enjoin] that no one shall refuse him egress. And I desire that all the men to whom I grant freedom shall have all things which are in their possession except the land.

And I grant to Archbishop Stigand, my lord, the estate at Harling just as it stands, except that the men shall all be free, and that I grant ten acres to the church. And if I do not come back again, I grant to him as my heriot a helmet and a coat of mail and a horse with harness and a sword and a spear. And I desire that in accordance with the agreement Edwin and Wulfric shall after my time succeed to everything which is mine everywhere in that village, except so much as I grant to the church; namely, the land let for services which my man Ælfwold holds; and he is to occupy the other during his lifetime. And afterwards all the land which comes into his possession is to go with the other to the church.

If Edwin my uncle will maintain the partnership with me and my uncle Wulfric with regard to the estate at Melton, if we outlive him we are to succeed to the estate at Thorpe, on condition that after the death of both of us, the estate at Melton shall go to St. Benedict's at Holme, for our ancestors' souls and for our own souls: and the estate at Thorpe to Bury St. Edmunds.

And this is the agreement between me and my sister Bote: if I end my life before her, that she is to succeed to the estate at Ketteringham and a mark of gold or the equivalent: and if I outlive her, then I shall have the land at Somerleyton. And my sister Gode and I have made a similar agreement: if she survive me, she is to take possession of the estate at Walsingham, except ten acres, which are to go to the church: and if I live longer than she, then I shall have the estate at Preston.

And I grant to my brother Godric the estate at Hainford just as it stands in my possession, and Coggeshall. And for the land at Stratton (?) he shall give Ælfwig my servant two pounds. And I and my stepdaughter Ælfgifu have made an agreement about the estate at Onehouse that whichever of us shall live the longer, is to have as much land as the two of us have there. And if death befall us both on the way to Rome, the estate is to go to Bury St. Edmunds for me and for Sæflæd and for Ælfgifu, but the men are all to be free.

And I grant to Earl Harold after my time the half estate at *Moran*, as fully and completely as I rightfully acquired it with my wife in the witness of God and many men: and I have since neither lost it by lawsuit (?) nor forfeited it. And I beseech you by the Lord who created you and all creatures, that if I do not come back, you will never let it be possessed after my time by my enemies who wrongfully occupy it and make use of it to my continual injury. And I grant the estate at Frating according to the agreement which you yourself and Archbishop Stigand my lord made. And I grant to Ælfric, my priest and relation, the estate at Rushford. And if anyone be so foolish as to wish to detract from my will, may God and all his saints destroy him on the Day of Judgment.

Questions: What kinds of possessions were bequeathed, and to whom? Who is the richest, and who the poorest? What do we learn of less rich and powerful people than the authors? What purposes do the authors of these wills seem to have in mind? How does the archbishop's will differ from those of the lay individuals? How does the woman's will differ from the men's? What similarities unite them?

4. LAWS OF CNUT

Anglo-Saxon England has left us many law codes. In this one, issued by King Cnut (1016-40), English traditions and terminology stand side-by-side with reminders of the Scandinavian presence, a legacy first of the Viking invasions (in the ninth and tenth centuries) and then of the invasion and rule of Danish kings. One important concept in Anglo-Saxon law was the "wergeld" (see §36) or "wer" (§74), the sum of money which expressed the worth of an individual for purposes of compensation or penalty. This code also refers to the Anglo-Saxon "gemot," the regular assembly of a given community. The laws printed here are only part of Cnut's code; his extensive ecclesiastical legislation has largely been omitted.

Source: trans. B. Thorpe, *Ancient Laws and Institutes of England* (London: Record Commission, 1840), vol. I, pp. 377-391, 399-409, 413-42; revised.

This then is the secular ordinance which, by the counsel of my witan, I will that it be observed over all England.

1. That is then the first that I will; that just laws be established, and every unjust law be carefully suppressed, and that every injustice be weeded out and rooted up, with all possible diligence, from this country. And let God's justice be exalted; and henceforth let every man, both poor and rich, be esteemed worthy of folk-right, and let just judgments be given to him.

2. And we instruct, that though anyone sin and deeply destroy himself, let the correction be regulated so that it be becoming before God and tolerable before the world. And let him who has power of judgment very earnestly bear in mind what he himself desires, when he thus says: "And forgive us our sins, as we forgive." And we command that Christian men be not condemned to death, on any account, for altogether too little: but rather let gentle punishments be decreed, for the benefit of the people; and let God's handiwork, and his own purchase which he dearly bought, not be destroyed for little.

3. And we command, that Christian men be not too readily sold out of the land; and especially be not brought into heathendom; but let it be carefully guarded against, that those souls be not made to perish which Christ bought with his own life.

4. And we command, that ye undertake diligently to cleanse the country on every side, and everywhere to desist from evil deeds: and if witches or diviners, workers of secret death or adulteresses, be anywhere found in the land, let them be diligently driven out of this country; or let them totally perish in the country, unless they desist and the more thoroughly amend.

And we command, that adversaries and outlaws of God and men retire from the country, unless they submit and the more earnestly amend: and let thieves and public robbers forthwith perish, unless they desist.

Of Heathenism

5. And we earnestly forbid every heathenism: heathenism is, that men worship idols; that is, that they worship heathen gods, and the sun or the moon, fire or rivers, water-wells or stones, or forest trees of any kind; or love witchcraft, or promote the working of secret death in any way, or make sacrifices to idols ... or perform anything pertaining to such illusions.

6. Let manslayers and perjurers, violators of holy orders and adulterers, submit and make amends; or with their sins retire from the country.

7. Let cheats and liars, robbers and reavers, have God's anger, unless they desist, and the more thoroughly amend: and whoever will lawfully cleanse the country, and suppress injustice, and love righteousness, then must he diligently correct such things, and shun the like....

8. Let ... one money pass over all the nation, without any counterfeit, and let no man that refuse; and he who after this shall make false money, let him

forfeit the hands with which he wrought that false money, and not redeem them with any thing, neither with gold nor with silver: and if anyone accuse the reeve, that he wrought that false by his leave, let him clear himself with a threefold purgation, and if the purgation then fail, let him have the same judgment as he who wrought the false.

9. And let weights and measures be carefully rectified, and every species of injustice henceforth abstained from.

10. And let repairing of fortresses and of bridges, and equiping of fleets, be diligently set about; and army service also, whenever it is requisite, for our common need.

11. And be it constantly inquired, in every way, how counsel may most especially be devised for the benefit of the nation; and orthodox Christianity most exalted, and unjust laws most diligently abolished: because through this it shall turn to some good in the country, that injustice be put down, and justice loved, before God and before the world. Amen.

12. These are the fines to which the king is entitled from all men in Wessex: that is, for breach of peace and house-breaking, assault, and harboring fugitives, and failure to serve in the army, unless the king honors someone by conceding these rights to him.

Outlawries

13. And whoever does a deed of outlawry, let the king have power over him. And if he holds land by charter, let that be forfeited into the king's hand, no matter whose man he is. And take notice, whoever may feed or harbor the fugitive shall pay five pounds to the king, except he shall clear himself that he knew not of his being a fugitive.

14. And in Mercia he enjoys all as is here before written, over all men.

15. And by Danish law he enjoys [similar rights.] And if anyone keep or harbor an unpledged man, let him make amends for it, as the law formerly was. And he who shall henceforth set up unjust law, or make unjust judgment, for hatred or bribery, let him be liable to the king for 120 shillings, by English law, unless he dare to prove on oath that he knew nothing more just; and let him ever forfeit his thaneship, unless he repurchase it from the king, and as he will allow him. And by Danish law, let him be guilty of *lah-slit* [that is, a fine in Danish law], unless he clear himself, that he knew no better. And he who denies just law and just judgment, let him be liable unto him who is entitled to it: either to the king for 120 shillings, or to an earl for 60 shillings, or to the hundred for 30 shillings; so with every one of them, if it so happen, by English law: and he who by Danish law shall corrupt just law, let him pay *lah-slit*.

16. And he who shall accuse another wrongfully, so that he be the worse

either in substance or advancement, if then the other can show to be false that which one would charge upon him; let him be liable in his tongue, unless he redeem himself with his wergeld.

17. And let no one apply to the king, unless he may not be entitled to any justice within his hundred; and let the hundred-*gemot* be applied to, under penalty of the *wite* [that is, a fine under English law], so as it is right to apply to it.

18. And thrice a year let there be a *burh-gemot*, and twice a year a shire-*gemot*, under penalty of the *wite*, as is right; unless there be need oftener. And let there be present the bishop of the shire and the ealdorman; and there let both expound the law of God as well as the secular law....

That Every Man Shall Be in a Tithing

20. And we will, that every freeman be brought into a hundred, and into a tithing, who wishes to be entitled to purgation or to wergeld, in case anyone shall slay him after he is 12 years of age; or let him not afterwards be entitled to any free rights, be he householder or be he follower. And that every one be brought into a hundred and in surety; and let the surety hold and lead him to every plea. Many a powerful man will, if he can and may, defend his man in whatever way it seems to him that he may the more easily defend him; whether as a freeman or a *theow* [that is, unfree person]. But we will not allow that injustice.

Of Thieves

21. And we will, that every man above twelve years make oath that he will neither be a thief nor cognizant of theft.

22. And let every true man who has not been of bad reputation and has failed neither in oath nor ordeal within his hundred, be entitled to a single purgation. And for an untrue man, let a single oath be chosen in three hundreds, and a threefold oath as far as it belongs to the *burh*; or let him go to the ordeal, and let a single purgation be preceded by a single fore-oath, and a threefold purgation by a triple fore-oath. And if a thane have a true man to take the fore-oath for him, be it so. If he have not, let him begin his suit himself: and let no fore-oath ever be remitted.

23. And let no man be entitled to any vouching to warranty, unless he have true witness whence that came to him which is attached with him; and let the witness declare, by the favor of God and his lord, that he is a true witness for him, as he saw with his eyes and heard with his ears that he rightfully obtained it.

24. And let no one buy any thing above the value of four pence, either living or lying, unless he have the true witness of four men, be it within a *burh*, or be it up in the country. For if it then be attached, and he have no such witness, let there be no vouching to warranty; but let his own be rendered to the proprietor; and the *æfter-gild*, and the *wite*, to him who is entitled thereto. And if he have witness, as we have here before ordained, then let it be thrice vouched to warranty: at the fourth time, let him keep possession of it, or render it to him who owns it. And it seems right to us, that no man should hold possession where there is witness, and it can be known that it had been abstracted: and that no man ought to claim possession, at the earliest, before six months after it had been stolen....

Of a False Oath

36. And if anyone swear a false oath on a relic, and he be convicted, let him forfeit his hands, or half his wergeld; and let that be divided between lord and bishop. And let him not be thenceforth oath-worthy, unless he the more thoroughly before God make amends, and find him surety that he will ever after abstain from the like.

Of False Witness

37. And if anyone stand openly in false witness, and he be convicted, let not his witness afterwards stand for aught, but let him pay to the king, or to the lord of the land, according to his *heals-fang* [that is, a portion of his wergeld].

38. At no time is injustice allowed; and yet at festival-tides, and fast-tides, and in festival-places, one ought most earnestly to take care. And always as a man is mightier or of greater degree, so ought he the more thoroughly to avoid injustice, before God and before the world. And let divine amends be earnestly and constantly sought, according as the books prescribe; and let secular amends be sought according to secular law.

39. If anyone kill a servant of the altar, let him be an outlaw to God and to men, unless he the more thoroughly make amends through exile, and also to the kindred, or clear himself by a purgation; and within thirty days let him set about amends, both to God and to men, on peril of all he possesses.

40. And if anyone wrong a man in holy orders, or a foreigner, through any means, as to money or as to life, then shall the king be unto the victim in the place of a kinsman and of a protector, unless he have another lord besides. And let amends be made to the king as it may be fitting; or let him avenge the deed very deeply. It belongs very rightly to a Christian king that he avenge God's anger very deeply, according as the deed may be.

Of Men in Holy Orders

41. If a servant of the altar commit homicide, or else work iniquity very enormously, let him then forfeit both degree and country, and go in exile as far as the pope shall prescribe to him, and earnestly do penance. And if he will clear himself, let him clear himself with a three-fold purgation; and unless he begin the amends within 30 days, to God and to men, let him be an outlaw....

44. If a man who has committed a crime worthy of death desire confession, let it never be denied him: and if anyone deny it him, let him make amends for that to the king with 120 shillings, or clear himself; let him select five [oath-helpers], and be the sixth himself....

Of Adultery

51. If anyone commit adultery, let him make amends for it as the deed may be. It is a wicked adultery when a married man lies with a single woman, and much worse, with another's wife, or with one in holy orders.

Of Incest

52. If anyone commit incest, let him make amends for it, according to the degree of kin, with wergeld as well as with *wite*, and with all his possessions. It is by no means alike whether a man lie with a sister, or if it were a distant relative.

Of Widows and Maids

53. If anyone ravish a widow, let him make amends for it with his wergeld. If anyone ravish a maid, let him make amends for it with his wergeld.

That No Woman Commit Adultery

54. If, during her husband's life, a woman lie with another man, and it become public, let her afterwards be for a worldly shame as regards herself, and let her lawful husband have all that she possessed; and let her then forfeit both nose and ears: and if it be a prosecution, and the purgation fail, let the bishop use his power, and judge severely.

55. If a married man lie with his own maid-servant, let him forfeit her, and make amends for himself to God and to men: and he who has a lawful wife, and also a concubine, let no priest administer to him any of those rites which ought to be administered to a Christian man before he desist, and so deeply make amends as the bishop may teach him; and let him ever desist from the like.

56. If foreigners will not correct their fornications, let them retire from the land, with their possessions and sins.

57. If there be open working of death, so that a man be murdered, let the slayer be delivered up to the kinsmen, and if there be a prosecution, and he fail at the purgation, let the bishop judge.

Of Plotting against a Lord

58. If anyone plot against the king, or his lord, let him be liable in his life, and in all that he owns, unless he go to the threefold ordeal....

Of Him Who Fights in the King's Household

60. If anyone fight in the king's household, let him forfeit his life, unless the king will be merciful to him.

In Case Anyone Disarm Another

61. If anyone unlawfully disarm a man, let him compensate with his *heals-fang*; and if he bind him, let him compensate with half his wergeld....

Of the Heriot

71. And if anyone depart this life intestate, be it through his neglect, or be it through sudden death, then let not the lord draw more from his property than his lawful heriot. And, according to his direction, let the property be distributed very justly to the wife, and children, and relations; to every one, according to the degree that belongs to him.

72. And let the heriots be as it is fitting to the degree. An earl's such as thereto belongs, that is: eight horses, four saddled and four unsaddled, and four helmets, and four coats of mail, and eight spears, and as many shields, and four swords, and two hundred mancuses of gold. And after that, a king's thane's, from those who are nearest to him: four horses, two saddled and two unsaddled, and two swords, and four spears, and as many shields, and a helmet, and a coat of mail, and fifty mancuses of gold. And of the medial thanes: a horse and his trappings, and his arms; or his *heals-fang* in Wessex; and in Mercia, two pounds; and in East Anglia, two pounds. And the heriot of a king's thane among the Danes, who has his privilege from the king, four pounds. And if he have further relation to the king: two horses, one saddled and the other unsaddled, and one sword, and two spears, and two shields, and fifty mancuses of gold: and he who is of less means, two pounds.

73. And where the husband dwelt without claim or contest, let the wife and the children dwell in the same, unassailed by litigation. And if the husband, before he was dead, had been cited, then let the heirs answer, as he himself should have done if he had lived.

Of a Widow: That She Continue Twelve Months Husbandless

74. And let every widow continue husbandless a twelve-month: let her then choose what she herself will; and if she, within the space of a year, choose a husband, then let her forfeit her morning-gift [given by her husband when they married], and all the possessions which she had through the first husband; and let the nearest kinsmen take the land and the possessions that she had before. And let the husband be liable for his *wer* to the king, or to him to whom he may have granted it. And though she be taken forcibly, let her forfeit the possessions, unless she be willing to go home again from the man, and never again be his. And let not a widow take the veil too precipitately. And let every widow pay the heriots, *wite*-less, within twelve months, unless it be convenient to her earlier.

75. And let no one compel either woman or maiden to marry him whom she herself mislikes, nor for money sell her; unless he is willing to give anything voluntarily....

Of Stolen Property

77. And if any man bring a stolen thing home to his cottage, and he be detected [by the owner]; it is just that the owner have what he went after. And unless it has been brought under his wife's key-lockers, let her be clear; for it is her duty to keep the keys of them; namely, her treasury, and her chest, and her boxes. If it be brought under any of these, then she is guilty. And no wife may forbid her husband to put into his house what he will. Before now, the child which lay in the cradle, though it had never tasted meat, was held by the covetous to be equally guilty as if it had discretion. But henceforth I most strenuously forbid it, and also very many things that are very hateful to God.

Of Him Who Flees from His Lord

78. And the man who shall flee from his lord, or from his comrade, by reason of his cowardice, be it in the fleet, or be it in the army, let him forfeit all that he owns, and his own life, and let the lord seize his possessions, and his land, which he previously gave him: and if he holds land by charter, let that go into the king's hands.

Of Him Who Falls before His Lord

79. And if a man fall before his lord in the army, be it within the land, or be it without the land, let the heriots be forgiven; and let the heirs succeed to the land and the property, and divide it very justly....

Of Hunting

81. And I will that every man be entitled to his hunting, in wood and in field, on his own possession. And let every one forego my hunting: take notice where I will have it untrespassed on, under penalty of the full *wite*....

84. And he who violates these laws, which the king has now given to all men, be he Danish or be he English, let him be liable in his wergeld to the king: and if he again violate them, let him pay twice his wergeld: and if he be then so daring that he violate them a third time, let him forfeit all that he possesses....

Questions: Using these laws in conjunction with Ælfric's Colloquy (doc. 1) and The Rights of Various Persons (doc. 2), how would you describe the life of an ordinary Anglo-Saxon man or woman? What values and concerns are expressed in the laws? What kinds of penalties are most common? What crimes are considered most serious? How are ranks and conditions of people distinguished? What evidence is there here for how laws are made? What do we learn of the status of women?

5. CNUT'S LETTER TO THE ENGLISH PEOPLE

In 1027 King Cnut made a European tour that was somewhat unusual for the time. He reports on his activities and explains his future plans in the letter below.

Source: trans. T. Forester, *The Chronicle of Florence of Worcester* (London: Henry G. Bohn, 1854), pp. 137-139; revised.

Cnut, king of all England, and of Denmark, Norway, and part of Sweden, to Ethelnoth, [archbishop of Canterbury], and Aelfric, archbishop of York, and to all the bishops and prelates, and to the whole nation of the English, both the nobles and the commons, greeting.

I notify you that I have lately taken a journey to Rome, to pray for the forgiveness of my sins, and for the welfare of my dominions, and the people under my rule. I had long since vowed this journey to God, but I have been hitherto prevented from accomplishing it by the affairs of my kingdom and other causes of impediment. I now return most humble thanks to my God Almighty for suffering me in my lifetime to visit the sanctuary of his apostles, Saints Peter and Paul, and all others which I could find either within or without the city of Rome, and there in person reverentially worship according to my desire. I have performed this chiefly, because I have learnt from wise men that St. Peter the apostle has received from God great power in binding and loosing, and carries the keys of the kingdom of heaven; and therefore I esteemed it very profitable to seek his special patronage with the Lord.

Be it known to you that, at the celebration of Easter, a great assembly of nobles was present with our lord, the pope John, and Conrad the emperor; that is to say, all the princes of the nations from Mount Garganus to the neighboring sea. All these received me with honor and presented me with magnificent gifts; but more especially was I honored by the emperor with various gifts and valuable presents, both in gold and silver vessels, and in palls and very costly robes. I spoke with the emperor himself, and the lord pope, and the princes who were there, in regard to the wants of my people, English as well as Danes; that there should be granted to them more equal justice and greater security in their journeys to Rome, and that they should not be hindered by so many barriers on the road, nor harassed by unjust tolls. The emperor assented to my demands, as well as King Rodolph [of Burgundy], in whose dominions these barriers chiefly stand; and all the princes made edicts that my people, the merchants as well as those who go to pay their devotions, shall pass to and fro in their journeys to Rome in peace, and under the security of just laws, free from all molestation by the guards of barriers or the receivers of tolls. I made further complaint to my lord the pope, and expressed my high displeasure, that my archbishops are sorely aggrieved by the demand of immense sums of money, when, according to custom, they resort to the apostolical see to obtain the pallium [that is, the archbishop's stole]; and it is decreed that it should no longer be done. All things, therefore, which I requested for the good of my people from my lord the pope, and the emperor, and King Rodolph, and the other princes through whose territories our road to Rome lies, they have most freely granted, and even ratified their concessions by oath; to which four archbishops, twenty bishops, and an innumerable multitude of dukes and nobles who were there present, are witnesses. Wherefore I return most hearty thanks to Almighty God for my having successfully accomplished all that I had desired, as I had resolved in my mind, and having satisfied my wishes to the fullest extent.

Be it known therefore to all of you, that I have humbly vowed to the Almighty God himself henceforward to amend my life in all respects, and to rule the kingdoms and the people subject to me with justice and clemency, giving equitable judgments in all matters; and if, through the intemperance of youth or negligence, I have hitherto exceeded the bounds of justice in any of my acts, I intend by God's aid to make an entire change for the better. I therefore adjure and command my counselors to whom I have entrusted the affairs of my kingdom, that henceforth they neither commit themselves, nor suffer to prevail, any sort of injustice throughout my dominions, either from fear of me, or from favor to any powerful person. I also command all sheriffs and magistrates throughout my whole kingdom, as they tender my regard and their own safety, that they use no unjust violence to any man, rich or poor, but that all, high and low, rich or poor, shall enjoy alike impartial law; from which they are never to deviate, either on account of royal favor, respect of person in the great, or for the sake of amassing money wrongfully, for I have no need to accumulate wealth by iniquitous exactions.

I wish you further to know, that, returning by the way I went, I am now going to Denmark to conclude a treaty for a solid peace, all the Danes concurring, with those nations and peoples who would have taken my life and crown if it had been possible; but this they were not able to accomplish, God bringing their strength to naught. May he, of his merciful kindness, uphold me in my sovereignty and honor, and henceforth scatter and bring to naught the power and might of all my adversaries. When, therefore, I shall have made peace with the surrounding nations, and settled and reduced to order all my dominions in the East, so that we shall have nothing to fear from war or hostilities in any quarter, I propose to return to England as early in the summer as I shall be able to fit out my fleet. I have sent this epistle before me in order that my people may be gladdened at my success; because, as you yourselves know, I have never spared, nor will I spare, myself or my exertions, for the needful service of my whole people. I now therefore command and adjure all my bishops and the governors of my kingdom, by the duty they owe to God and myself, to take care that before I come to England all dues belonging to God, according to the old laws, be fully discharged; namely, plow-alms, the tithe of animals born in the current year, and the pence payable to St. Peter at Rome, whether from towns or vills; and in the middle of August the tithes of corn; and at the feast of St. Martin the first-fruits of grain [payable] to everyone's parish church, called in English *ciric-sceat*. If these and such-like dues be not paid before I come, those who make default will incur fines to the king, according to law, which will be strictly enforced without mercy. Farewell.

Questions: What conception did Cnut have of his royal position, as expressed here and in his laws? How accurately might such a letter reflect his personal piety? What was the relationship of the king of England with other European powers? What were the relationships between the English government, the English church, and the church at Rome?

6. PRAISE OF QUEEN EMMA

Queen Emma's colorful, even shocking, career is only partially described in the biograph-
ical work excerpted here. The daughter of Duke Richard of Normandy, in 1002 she mar-
ried King Ethelred of England, with whom she had two sons, Alfred and the future
King Edward the Confessor (1042-66). When Ethelred was driven from the throne in
1014 by the invading Swein of Denmark, Emma fled to her homeland; after Swein's and
Ethelred's deaths she joined the other side, as it were, by agreeing to return and marry
Swein's son King Cnut (here "Knútr"), who had been Ethelred's implacable enemy.
This is the point at which The Praise of Queen Emma *introduces her, tactfully mak-*
ing no explicit reference to her first marriage. The biography, commissioned by Emma
herself and putting her actions in the best possible light, was written in 1041-42, by
which time Emma and her family had suffered further trauma and tragedy. She had then
achieved political eminence through her son by Cnut, who was reigning in England as
King Hörthaknútr (or Harthcnut, 1040-2). Later, when Emma's son Edward succeeded
his half-brother, Emma would find her relations with her son somewhat strained and her
own position again precarious.

Source: trans. A. Campbell, *Encomium Emmae Reginae* (London: The Royal Historical Society,
1949), pp. 5-7, 33-35, 39-53.

Prologue

May our Lord Jesus Christ preserve you, O Queen, who excel all those of your
sex in the admirability of your way of life.

I, your servant, am unable to show you, noble lady, anything worthy in my
deeds, and I do not know how I can be acceptable to you even in words. That
your excellence transcends the skill of anyone speaking about you is apparent
to all to whom you are known, more clearly than the very radiance of the sun.
You, then, I esteem as one who has deserved of me to such a degree, that I
would sink to death unafraid, if I believed that my action would lead to your
advantage. For this reason, and, furthermore, in accordance with your injunction, I long to transmit to posterity through my literary work a record of deeds,
which, I declare, touch upon the honor of you and your connections....

Sveinn, king of the Danes, mighty alike in courage and arms and also in
counsel, brought the English kingdom under his rule by force, and, dying,
appointed his son Knútr to be his successor in the same kingdom....

Book II

16. Everything having been thus duly settled, [Knútr] the king lacked nothing
except a most noble wife; such a one he ordered to be sought everywhere for

him, in order to obtain her hand lawfully, when she was found, and to make
her the partner of his rule, when she was won. Therefore journeys were undertaken through realms and cities and a royal bride was sought; but it was with
difficulty that a worthy one was ultimately found, after being sought far and
wide. This imperial bride was, in fact, found within the bounds of Gaul, and to
be precise in the Norman area, a lady of the greatest nobility and wealth, but
yet the most distinguished of the women of her time for delightful beauty and
wisdom, inasmuch as she was a famous queen. In view of her distinguished
qualities of this kind, she was much desired by the king, and especially because
she derived her origin from a victorious people, who had appropriated for
themselves part of Gaul, in despite of the French and their prince. Why should
I make a long story of this? Wooers were sent to the lady, royal gifts were sent,
furthermore precatory messages were sent. But she refused ever to become the
bride of Knútr, unless he would affirm to her by oath, that he would never set
up the son of any wife other than herself to rule after him, if it happened that
God should give her a son by him. For she had information that the king had
had sons by some other woman; so she, wisely providing for her offspring,
knew in her wisdom how to make arrangements in advance, which were to be
to their advantage. Accordingly the king found what the lady said acceptable,
and when the oath had been taken, the lady found the will of the king acceptable, and so, thanks be to God, Emma noblest of women, became the wife of
the very mighty King Knútr. Gaul rejoiced, the land of the English rejoiced
likewise, when so great an ornament was conveyed over the seas. Gaul, I say,
rejoiced to have brought forth so great a lady, and one worthy of so great a
king, the country of the English indeed rejoiced to have received such a one
into its towns. What an event, sought with a million prayers, and at length
barely brought to pass under the Savior's favoring grace! This was what the
army had long eagerly desired on both sides, that is to say that so great a lady,
bound by a matrimonial link to so great a man, worthy of her husband as he
was worthy of her, should lay the disturbances of war to rest. What greater or
more desirable thing could be wished than that the accursed and loathsome
troubles of war should be ended by the gentle calm of peace, when equals were
clashing with equals in might of body and boldness of heart, and when now
the one side and now the other was victorious, though at great loss to itself, by
the changing fortunes of war?

17. But when by the divine dispensation they at length after frequent and
protracted interchange of emissaries decided to be joined by the marital link, it
is hard to credit how vast a magnitude of delight in one another arose in them
both. For the king rejoiced that he had unexpectedly entered upon a most
noble marriage; the lady, on the other hand, was inspired both by the excellence of her husband, and by the delightful hope of future offspring. Both
armies also rejoiced indescribably, looking forward to increasing their posses-

sions by joining forces, which was how events afterwards turned out. For very many peoples were subdued in war, and very many nations extremely diverse in habits, customs and speech were permanently compelled to pay annual tribute to the king and to his royal issue. But what wonder if so great a king as we describe should conquer in war those resisting him, since he brought under his sway very many peoples of their own free will, partly by his munificent bounty, and partly because they desired his protection? None indeed, for the divine grace bestows its favor where the scale of justice and uprightness is evenly adjusted.

18. But why should I protract the matter? I have said that there was great joy at the union of such great persons; but I declare that there was much greater at the achievement of the advantage of a male offspring. For indeed soon afterwards it was granted by the Savior's grace that the most noble queen bore a son. The two parents, happy in the most profound and, I might say, unparalleled love for this child, sent in fact their other legitimate sons [that is, Edward and Alfred, Emma's sons by Ethelred] to Normandy to be brought up, while keeping this one with themselves, inasmuch as he was to be the heir to the kingdom. And so they washed this very dear child, as is the custom of all Christians, in the sacred baptismal font, and gave him a name which conveyed in a measure an indication of his future excellence. For indeed he was called Hörthaknútr, which reproduced his father's name with an addition, and if the etymology of this is investigated in Germanic, one truly discerns his identity and greatness. "Harde," indeed, means "swift" or "strong," both of which qualities and much more could be recognised in him above all others, for he excelled all the men of his time by superiority in all high qualities....

Book III

1. When Knútr was dead and honorably buried in the monastery built at Winchester in honor of St. Peter, the lady, Queen Emma, remained alone in the kingdom, sorrowing for the bitter death of her lord and alarmed at the absence of her sons. For one of them, namely Hörthaknútr, whom his father had made king of the Danes, was in his own kingdom, and two others were residing with their relative Robert, for they had been sent to the country of Normandy to be brought up. And so it came to pass that certain Englishmen, forgetting the piety of their lately deceased king, preferred to dishonor their country than to ornament it, and deserted the noble sons of the excellent Queen Emma, choosing as their king one Haraldr, who is declared, owing to a false estimation of the matter, to be a son of a certain concubine of the above-mentioned King Knútr; as a matter of fact, the assertion of very many people has it that the same Haraldr was secretly taken from a servant who was in childbed, and put in the

chamber of the concubine, who was indisposed; and this can be believed as the more truthful account. Soon after being chosen, this man, fearing for the future, summoned Archbishop Æthelnoth, a man gifted with high courage and wisdom, and commanded and prayed to be consecrated king, and that the royal scepter, which was committed to the archbishop's custody, should be given to him together with the crown, and that he should be led by the archbishop, since it was not legal that this should be done by another, to the lofty throne of the kingdom. The archbishop refused, declaring by oath that while the sons of Queen Emma lived he would approve or consecrate no other man as king: "Them Knútr entrusted to my good faith; to them I owe fidelity, and with them I shall maintain faith. I lay the scepter and crown upon the holy altar, and to you I neither refuse nor give them; but by my apostolic authority, I forbid all bishops that any one of them should remove these things, or give them to you or consecrate you. As for you, if you dare, lay hands upon what I have committed to God and his table." He, wretched man, did not know what to do or whither to turn. He used threats and it did not avail him, he promised gifts and sorrowed to gain nothing, for that apostolic man could not be dislodged by threats or diverted by gifts. At length he departed in despair, and so despised the episcopal benediction, that he hated not only the benediction itself, but indeed even turned from the whole Christian religion. For when others entered church to hear mass, as is the Christian custom, he either surrounded the glades with dogs for the chase, or occupied himself with any other utterly paltry matters, wishing only to be able to avoid what he hated. When the English observed his behavior they sorrowed, but since they had chosen him to be their king, they were ashamed to reject him, and accordingly decided that he should be their king to the end.

2. But Emma, the queen of the kingdom, silently awaited the end of the matter, and for some little time was in her anxiety daily gaining God's help by prayer. But the usurper was secretly laying traps for the queen, since as yet he dared not act openly, but he was allowed to hurt her by nobody. Accordingly, he devised an unrighteous scheme with his companions, and proposed to kill the children of his lady, that henceforth he might be able to reign in security and live in his sins. He would, however, have effected nothing whatever in this matter if, helped by the deceit of fraudulent men, he had not devised what we are about to narrate. For having hit upon a trick, he had a letter composed as if from the queen to her sons, who were resident in Normandy, and of this I do not hesitate to subjoin a copy:

3. "Emma, queen in name only, imparts motherly salutation to her sons, Eadweard and Ælfred. Since we severally lament the death of our lord, the king, most dear sons, and since daily you are deprived more and more of the kingdom, your inheritance, I wonder what plan you are adopting, since you are

aware that the delay arising from your proscrastination is becoming from day to day a support to the usurper of your rule. For he goes round hamlets and cities ceaselessly, and makes the chief men his friends by gifts, threats and prayers. But they would prefer that one of you should rule over them, than that they should be held in the power of him who now commands them. I entreat, therefore, that one of you come to me speedily and privately, to receive from me wholesome counsel, and to know in what manner this matter, which I desire, must be brought to pass. Send back word what you are going to do about these matters by the present messenger, whoever he may be. Farewell, beloved ones of my heart."

4. This forgery, when it had been composed at the command of Haraldr the tyrant, was sent to the royal youths by means of deceitful couriers, presented to them as being from their unwitting mother, and received by them with honor, as a gift from their parent. They read its wiles in their innocence, and alas too trustful of the fabrication, they unwisely replied to their parent that one of them would come to her, and determined upon day and time and place for her. The messengers, accordingly, returned and told the foes of God what answer had been made to them by the most noble youths. And so they awaited the prince's arrival, and schemed what they should do to him to injure him. Now on the fixed day Ælfred, the younger prince, selected companions with his brother's approval, and beginning his journey came into the country of Flanders. There he lingered a little with Marquis Baldwin, and when asked by him to lead some part of his forces with him as a precaution against the snares of the enemy, was unwilling to do so, but taking only a few men of Boulogne, boarded ship and crossed the sea. But when he came near to the shore, he was soon recognised by the enemy, who came and intended to attack him, but he recognised them and ordered the ships to be pushed off from that shore. He landed, however, at another port, and attempted to go to his mother, deeming that he had entirely evaded the bane of the ambush. But when he was already near his goal, Earl Godwine met him and took him under his protection, and forthwith became his soldier by averment under oath. Diverting him from London, he led him into the town called Guildford, and lodged his soldiers there in separate billets by twenties, twelves and tens, leaving a few with the young man, whose duty was to be in attendance upon him. And he gave them food and drink in plenty, and withdrew personally to his own lodging, until he should return in the morning to wait upon his lord with due honor.

5. But after they had eaten and drunk, and being weary, had gladly ascended their couches, behold, men leagued with the most abominable tyrant Haraldr appeared, entered the various billets, secretly removed the arms of the innocent men, confined them with iron manacles and fetters, and kept them till the morrow to be tortured. But when it was morning, the innocent men were led

out, and were iniquitously condemned without a hearing. For they were all disarmed and delivered with their hands bound behind their backs to most vicious executioners, who were ordered, furthermore, to spare no man unless the tenth lot should reprieve him. Then the torturers made the bound men sit in a row, and reviling them beyond measure, followed the example of that murderer of the Theban Legion, who first decimated guiltless men, though more mercifully than they did. For that utterly pagan ruler spared nine of the Christians and killed the tenth, but these most profane and false Christians killed nine of the good Christians and let the tenth go. That pagan, though he massacred Christians, nevertheless ordered that they should be beheaded on an open plain unfettered by bonds, like glorious soldiers. But these, though they were in name Christians, were nevertheless in their actions totally pagan, and butchered the innocent heroes with blows from their spears bound as they were, like swine. Hence all ages will justly call such torturers worse than dogs, since they brought to condemnation the worthy persons of so many soldiers not by soldierly force but by their treacherous snares. Some, as has been said, they slew, some they placed in slavery to themselves; others they sold, for they were in the grip of blind greed, but they kept a few loaded with bonds to be subjected to greater mockery. But the divine pity did not fail the innocent men who stood in such peril, for I myself have seen many whom it snatched from that derision, acting from heaven without the help of man, so that the impediments of manacles and fetters were shattered.

6. Therefore, since I am dealing briefly with the sufferings of the soldiers, it remains that I should curtail the course of my narrative in telling of the martyrdom of their prince, that is to say the glorious Ælfred, lest perchance if I should choose to go over all that was done to him in detail, I should multiply the grief of many people and particularly of you, Lady Queen. In this matter I beg you, lady, not to ask more than this, which I, sparing your feelings, will briefly tell. For many things could be told if I were not sparing your sorrow. Indeed there is no greater sorrow for a mother than to see or hear of the death of a most dear son. The royal youth, then, was captured secretly in his lodging, and having been taken to the island called Ely, was first of all mocked by the most wicked soldiery. Then still more contemptible persons were selected, that the lamented youth might be condemned by them in their madness. When these men had been set up as judges they decreed that first of all both his eyes should be put out as a sign of contempt. After they prepared to carry this out, two men were placed on his arms to hold them meanwhile, one on his breast, and one on his legs, in order that the punishment might be more easily inflicted on him. Why do I linger over this sorrow? As I write my pen trembles, and I am horror-stricken at what the most blessed youth suffered. Therefore I will the sooner turn away from the misery of so great a disaster, and touch

upon the conclusion of this martyrdom as far as its consummation. For he was held fast, and after his eyes had been put out was most wickedly slain. When this murder had been performed, they left his lifeless body, which the servants of Christ, the monks, I mean, of the same Isle of Ely, took up and honorably interred. However, many miracles occur where his tomb is, as people report who even declare most repeatedly that they have seen them. And it is justly so: for he was martyred in his innocence, and therefore it is fitting that the might of the innocent should be exercised through him. So let Queen Emma rejoice in so great an intercessor, since him, who she formerly had as a son on earth, she now has as a patron in the heavens.

7. But the queen, smitten by so unheard-of a crime, considered in silent thought what it was needful that she should do. And so her mind was carried this way and that in uncertainty, and she was chary of trusting herself further to such perfidy, for she was dazed beyond consolation with sorrow for her murdered son, although she derived comfort in a much greater degree from his assured rest. And so she was, as we have said, distressed for a twofold reason, that is to say, because of misery and sadness at her son's death, and also because of uncertainty concerning what remained of her own life and her position. But perchance at this point some one, whom ill-will towards this lady has rendered spiteful and odious, will protest to me: "Why did she refuse to die the same death, since she in no way doubted that her son, who had been slain under these conditions of treachery, enjoyed eternal rest?" To rebut this I consider that one must use such a reply as: "If the persecutor of the Christian religion and faith had been present, she would not have shrunk from encountering mortal danger. On the other hand it would have appeared wrong and abominable to all the orthodox, if a matron of such reputation had lost her life through desire for worldly dominion, and indeed death would not have been considered a worthy end to the fortunes of so great a lady." Keeping these and similar arguments in mind, and considering advantageous to her fortunes that authentic injunction of the Lord's exhortation, in which, to wit, He says to the elect, "If they should persecute you in one city, flee into another," she acted upon a hope of saving what was left of her position, which was under the circumstances in which she was placed sufficiently sound, and at length followed a sagacious plan by the grace of the divine regard. She believed it expedient for her to seek foreign nations, and she brought this decision to consummation with shrewd judgment. However, she did not find that those nations which she sought were to be foreign to her, for while she sojourned among them she was honored by them in a most proper manner, just as she was by her own followers. And so she assembled as many nobles who were faithful to herself as she could, in view of the circumstances and the time. When these were present, she told them her inmost thoughts. When they had proceeded to approve the

plan put in train by their lady, their ships' supplies [were] prepared for exile. And so, having enjoyed favorable winds, they crossed the sea and touched at a certain port not far from the town of Bruges. The latter town is inhabited by Flemish settlers, and enjoys very great fame for the number of its merchants and for its affluence in all things upon which mankind places the greatest value. Here indeed she was, as she deserved, honorably received by Baldwin, the marquis of that same province, who was the son of a great and totally unconquered prince, and by his wife Athala (a name meaning "most noble"), daughter of Robert, king of the French, and Queen Constance. By them, furthermore, a house in the above-named town, suitable for royal outlay, was allotted to the queen, and in addition a kind offer of entertainment was made. These kindnesses she partly accepted with the greatest thanksgiving, partly she showed that up to a point she did not stand in need.

8. And so, being placed in such great security, she sent messengers to her son Eadweard to ask that he should come to her without delay. He obeyed them, mounted his horse and came to his mother. But when they had the opportunity for discussion, the son declared that he pitied his mother's misfortunes, but that he was able in no way to help, since the English nobles had sworn no oath to him, a circumstance indicating that help should be sought from his brother. Thereupon Eadweard returned to Normandy, and the queen still hesitated in her mind as to what she ought to do. After her son's departure, she dispatched messengers to her son Hörthaknútr, who then held sway over the Danes, and through them revealed to him her unheard-of sorrow, and begged him to hasten to come to her as soon as possible. The horror of so great a crime made his ears tremble, and first of all as he deliberated his spirits sank stunned by intolerable sorrow. For he burned in his heart to go and avenge his brother's injuries, nay more, to obey his mother's message.

9. Accordingly, providing for either eventuality, he got ready the greatest forces he could of ships and soldiers, and assembled the greater number of them in a certain inlet of the sea, to come to his support if on his journey the opportunity to give battle or the need for defense should befall him. For the rest, he set out accompanied by not more than ten ships to go to his mother, who was laboring under the very great distress of sorrow. When, therefore, they were absorbed in their prosperous voyage, and were not only eagerly plowing the salt foam with brazen prows, but also raising their topsails to the favorable winds, whereas the surface of the sea is never dependable, but is always found to be unreliable and faithless, suddenly a murky tempest of winds and clouds was rolled up from behind, and the surface of the sea forthwith was agitated by overtaking south winds. And so the anchors were dropped from the prows, and caught in the sands of the bottom, which is what is wont to be done in such desperate straits. This incident, although it was distressing to them

at the time, is not believed to have taken place without the consent of God, who disposes all things, as the issue of the affair afterwards proved, when the limbs of all yielded to quiet rest and sleep. For on the next night, when Hörthaknútr was at rest in his bed, by divine providence a vision appeared, which comforted and consoled him and bade him be of good cheer. Furthermore, it exhorted him not to desist from his undertaking, for after a space of a few days the unjust usurper of his kingdom, Haraldr, would perish, and the kingdom conquered by his father's strength would return safely by most rightful succession to himself, the rightful heir.

10. The dreamer accordingly, when he awoke, was enlightened by the signs described above, and returned thanks to Almighty God for such great consolation, and had at the same time not the slightest doubt about the coming events which the vision above described had foretold. Thereupon, the wrath of the sea having subsided, and the storm having dropped, he spread his bellying sails to the favorable winds; and thus, having enjoyed a successful voyage, he touched at Bruges. Here, having moored his ships with anchors and rods, and having commissioned sailors to look after them, he betook himself directly with chosen companions to the lodging of his mother. What grief and what joy sprang up at his arrival, no page shall ever unfold to you. There was no little pain when his mother beheld with some stretch of her imagination, the face of her lost one in his countenance; likewise she rejoiced with a great joy at seeing the survivor safe in her presence. And so she knew that the tender mercy of God had regard to her, since she was still undeprived of such a consolation. And soon afterwards, while the son was lingering with his mother expecting the events promised by the vision above described, messengers arrived bearing glad tidings, and announced, to wit, that Haraldr was dead, reporting furthermore that the English nobles did not wish to oppose him, but to rejoice together with him in jubilation of every kind; therefore they begged him not to scorn to return to the kingdom which was his by hereditary right, but to take counsel for both his own position and their safety with regard to the comnmon good.

11. Encouraged by these things, Hörthaknútr and his mother decided to return to the shores of the ancestral realm. When word of this matter smote the ears of the people, soon you would have seen pain and grief to be universal. For the rich mourned her departure, with whom they had ever enjoyed pleasant converse; the poor mourned her departure, by whose continual generosity they were relieved from the burden of want; the widows mourned with the orphans, whom she had freely enriched when they were taken from the holy baptismal font. Therefore I do not know with what praises to exalt her, who never failed to be immediately present with those being re-born in Christ. Her faith clearly calls for praise and at the same time her kindness is in every way to be extolled. If I should propose to discuss this matter with regard to her indi-

vidual good deeds, I believe that my time would be exhausted before my subject, so I hasten to return to the course of our narrative.

12. While preparations were being made for the return of the queen and her son, the whole shore was perturbed by lamentation and groaning, and all raised angry right hands to the sky. They wept, in short, that she, whom during her whole exile they had regarded as a fellow citizen, was leaving them. She had not been a burdensome guest to any of the rich, nor had she been oppressive to the poor in any matter whatever. Therefore you would have thought that all were leaving their native soil, you would have said that all the women intended to seek foreign lands along with her. Such was the lamentation on the whole shore, such was the wailing of all the people standing by. Although they rejoiced with her to some extent at her recovery of her old position, nevertheless the matrons could not let her go with dry eyes. At last love of the homeland prevailed, and having kissed all severally and having said a tearful farewell to them, she sought the deep sea with her son and her followers after a great abundance of tears had been shed on both sides.

13. Under these circumstances the English nobles, lacking confidence in the legation previously sent, met them before they crossed the sea, deeming that the best course was for them to make amends to the king and queen, and to place themselves devotedly under their dominion. When Hörthaknútr and his mother had been apprised by these men, and when he had at length reached a port on the other side of the sea, he was most gloriously received by all the inhabitants of that country, and thus by the grace of the divine favor the realm which was properly his was restored. After the events described, he arranged all his affairs in the calm of peace, and being gripped by brotherly love, sent messengers to Eadweard and asked him to come and hold the kingdom together with himself.

14. Obeying his brother's command, he was conveyed to England, and the mother and both sons, having no disagreement between them, enjoy the ready amenities of the kingdom. Here there is loyalty among sharers of rule, here the bond of motherly and brotherly love is of strength indestructible. All these things were granted them by Him, who makes dwellers in a house be of one mind, Jesus Christ, the Lord of all, who, abiding in the Trinity, holds a kingdom which flourishes unfading. Amen.

Questions: Given the author's avowed intent to produce a flattering picture of Emma and her actions, what alternative interpretations could be placed on the facts recorded here? Does the text include any hints that some contemporaries did have a less positive view of her? What was expected of a woman in Emma's position, and how did such a woman win approval? How was political power gained and wielded in Anglo-Saxon England?

7. THE LIFE OF KING EDWARD WHO RESTS AT WESTMINSTER

Emma's son Edward soon succeeded his younger half-brother and became the king known as Edward "the Confessor" (1042-66) for his conspicuous piety. After his death his wife Edith, daughter of Godwin, the powerful earl of Wessex, commissioned the biography of Edward which is excerpted here. Like Praise of Queen Emma, *it presents a glowing picture of its patroness, but here the focus is on her husband. Among its themes are the king's religious devotion and ongoing power struggles involving the queen's brothers.*

Source: trans. F. Barlow, *The Life of King Edward who rests at Westminster, attributed to a monk of Saint-Bertin*, 2nd ed. (Oxford: Oxford Medieval Texts, 1992), pp.61-73, 75-77, 79-83, 91-97, 117-121, 123-127.

[Book 1]

6. And so, with the kingdom made safe on all sides by these nobles, the most kindly King Edward passed his life in security and peace, and spent much of his time in the glades and woods in the pleasures of hunting. After divine service, which he gladly and devoutly attended every day, he took much pleasure in hawks and birds of that kind which were brought before him, and was really delighted by the baying and scrambling of the hounds. In these and such like activities he sometimes spent the day, and it was in these alone that he seemed naturally inclined to snatch some worldly pleasure. Otherwise this man, of his free will devoted to God, lived in the squalor of the world like an angel and "at the accepted time" he zealously showed how assiduous he was in practising the Christian religion. What tongue or what page could unfold, in accordance with reality and true accounting, how kindly he received religious abbots and monks, above all foreign, whom he knew to be very devout and strict in their service to God, how humbly he joined in their conversation, and, at their departure, with what generosity he lavished himself on them? This he used to do throughout his reign; and since the news spread widely that such was his pleasure, he kept hospitality of this kind not only frequently but all the time. Moreover, like a good father, he exhibited such men as models to the abbots and monks of his own kingdom, for monastic discipline had come to these more recently, and was on that account less strict. He used to stand with lamb-like meekness and tranquil mind at the holy offices of the divine mysteries and masses, a worshipper of Christ manifest to all the faithful; and at these times, unless he was addressed, he rarely spoke to anyone. Moreover, it was quietly, and only for the occasion — in any case, it should be distinctly said, with no

mental pleasure — that he displayed the pomp of royal finery in which the queen obligingly arrayed him. And he would not have cared at all if it had been provided at far less cost. He was, however, grateful for the queen's solicitude in these matters, and with a certain kindness of feeling used to remark on her zeal most appreciatively to his intimates. He stooped with great mercy to the poor and infirm, and fully maintained many of these not only daily in his royal court but also at many places in his kingdom. Finally, his royal consort did not restrain him in those good works in which he prepared to lead the way, but rather urged speedier progress, and often enough seemed even to lead the way herself. For while he would give now and then, she was prodigal, but aimed her bounty to such good purpose as to consider the highest honor of the king as well. Although by custom and law a royal throne was always prepared for her at the king's side, she preferred, except in church and at the royal table, to sit at his feet, unless perchance he should reach out his hand to her, or with a gesture of the hand invite or command her to sit next to him. I say she was a woman to be placed before all noble matrons or persons of royal and imperial rank as a model of virtue and integrity for maintaining both the practices of the Christian religion and worldly dignity. Although in the earthly kingdom great prosperity smiled upon them, occasionally, however, in the plots of certain insurgents adversity struck with force. But not such as could cripple a realm ruled by so great a king; indeed, the kingdom, employing the brother earls mentioned before as its protectors, most quickly either assuaged it or with military valor stamped it out.

There rose, for example, almost at the same time, on this side Gruffydd, king of the West Britons, and on the other the king of the Scots with an outlandish name [that is, Macbeth]. The former, however, with Earl Harold directing the English army, was often defeated, and in the end was killed. But we deliberately reserve this story for a more faithful treatment in the future. It is rather protracted and complicated, and can be explained better in a longer report. Besides, the man whom we, impressed by the burden of the labor he undertook and his unusual industry, have undertaken to describe in this book (but not without uneasiness of mind), cannot be portrayed with slight effort or in a short essay to the satisfaction of those readers who want to know in more detail about things done with great love and labor.

The Scottish king, too, was first defeated with the destruction of almost all his men by Earl Siward and forced to take to shameful flight. Then, when Earl Tostig ruled the earldom, the Scots, since they had not yet tested him and consequently held him more cheaply, harassed him often with raids rather than war. But this irresolute and fickle race of men, better in woods than on the plain, and trusting more to flight than to manly boldness in battle, Tostig, sparing his own men, wore down as much by cunning schemes as by martial courage and military campaigns. And as a result they and their king preferred to serve him and King Edward than to continue fighting, and, moreover, to confirm the peace by giving hostages.

But this story also we refrain from writing now until a surer investigation and a suitable time gives us the opportunity to unfold it. We cannot, however, while life lasts, entirely disregard these two episodes which reflect honor and glory on both these earls, for, owing to their surpassing merit, we are greatly in their debt. But now let us turn again to King Edward and his royal consort Edith — the illustrious mistress whom we chiefly serve in this present account — and display with all the power and understanding we have, and with the aid of God's grace and favor, with what zeal they showed their devout faith in the church of Christ.

Outside the walls of London, upon the River Thames, stood a monastery [that is, Westminster Abbey] dedicated to St. Peter, but insignificant in buildings and numbers, for under the abbot only a small community of monks served Christ. Moreover, the endowments from the faithful were slender, and provided no more than their daily bread. The king, therefore, being devoted to God, gave his attention to that place, for it both lay hard by the famous and rich town and also was a delightful spot, surrounded with fertile lands and green fields and near the main channel of the river, which bore abundant merchandise of wares of every kind for sale from the whole world to the town on its banks. And, especially because of his love of the Prince of the Apostles, whom he worshipped with uncommon and special love, he decided to have his burial place there. Accordingly he ordered that out of the tithes of all his revenues should be started the building of a noble edifice, worthy of the Prince of the Apostles; so that, after the transient journey of this life, God would look kindly upon him, both for the sake of his goodness and because of the gift of lands and ornaments with which he intended to ennoble the place. And so at the king's command the building, nobly begun, was made ready, and there was no weighing of the cost, past or future, as long as it proved worthy of, and acceptable to, God and St. Peter. The house of the principal altar, raised up with most lofty vaulting, is surrounded by dressed stone, evenly jointed. Moreover, the circumference of that temple is enclosed on both sides by a double arch of stones, with the structure of the work strongly consolidated from different directions. Next is the crossing of the church, which is to hold in its midst the choir of God's choristers, and, with its twin abutments, from either side support the high apex of the central tower. It rises simply at first with a low and sturdy vault, swells with many a stair spiraling up in artistic profusion, but then with a plain wall climbs to the wooden roof which is carefully covered with lead. And indeed, methodically arranged above and below, are chapels to be consecrated through their altars to the memory of apostles, martyrs, confessors, and virgins. Moreover, the whole complex of this enormous building is set at a sufficient distance from the east end of the old church to allow not only the brethren dwelling there to continue with their service to Christ but also some part of the nave, which is to lie in between, to advance a good way.

But so that the king should not labor alone, the queen, his worthy spouse, was drawn to emulate that project of his, so pleasing to God. She instantly imitated the king's love with her own, and demonstrated her own heart's devotion for the holy church in the place of her up-bringing. For at Wilton at that time, although there was a convent of the handmaidens of Christ, a choir, too, of the greatest antiquity, and her namesake saint, adequately housed, was worshiped there — Edith, from whose stock King Edward himself was descended — the church was still of wood. And she judged no place more deserving her devoted labor and zeal than that which, she recalled, had taken pains with her education, and where above all she had learned those virtues which deservedly made her seem suitable to become queen of the English. Also, nowhere did she believe alms would be better bestowed than where the weaker sex, less skilled in building, more deeply felt the pinch of poverty, and was less able by its own efforts to drive it away. Benignly she planned this herself, as one abounding in the bowels of mercy through the Holy Spirit, and began here royally to build a monastery in stone. Impetuously she urged the workmen to make haste. Thus here the king and there the queen strove in a contest which was pleasing to God and not disagreeable to them. But the prudent queen's building, because it was more modestly planned, was completed more quickly. No delays she wove for this undertaking; and when a few years had slipped by it was finished nobly with all things necessary to, and becoming, such a work and also royal honor and glory. In having a speedy dedication performed the woman blessed by God would suffer no delay. Indeed, she warned in advance Herman, the famous and well-educated bishop of the diocese, for this task, and prepared most earnestly all the things that would be required on the appointed day for the ceremony. When lo! "the envious devil, the enemy of all good intentions," sought to upset what had been well done so that it should not come to completion. For, a short time before the appointed day, he set fire to the town, and all that had been prepared there, together with almost all the houses, except for this church, was burned in one vast conflagration. But this diabolical mockery did not affright this faithful woman's mind, nor did it deter her from completing the divine project she had planned. She made haste with other preparations of even greater splendor, and, with a multitude of bishops, abbots, monks, and clerks and a concourse of all the faithful, she devoutly performed the ceremony of dedication, then bestowed on the new bride of God new gifts worthy of her royal highness....

7. The consecration of this church in honor of St. Benedict, the father and instructor of monks, performed in the year 1065, was followed, to the distress of the whole country, by a disturbance in the kingdom. At this time the earl of the Northern Angles, whom we have often mentioned,[the queen's brother] Tostig, was at the king's court; and he stayed with him for some time, detained by his love of the king and while he dealt with some palace business which had been put on him. Meanwhile, a party of nobles, whom he had repressed with the heavy yoke of his rule because of their misdeeds, conspired among themselves against him.... King Edward, a man worthy of God, thinking to appease the untamed mob with his usual wisdom, sent them through messengers goodly orders, that is to say, to desist from the madness they had begun and receive right and justice for every injury which they could prove against him. But those in revolt against their God and king rejected the conciliatory message, and replied to the king that either he should straightway dismiss that earl of his from his person and the whole kingdom, or he himself would be treated as an enemy and have all them as enemies. And when the most gracious king had a second and third time through messengers and by every kind of effort of his counselors tried to turn them from their mad purpose, and failed, he moved from the forests, in which he was as usual staying for the sake of regular hunting, to Britford, a royal manor near the royal town of Wilton. And when he had summoned the magnates from all over the kingdom, he took counsel there on what was to be done in this business. Not a few charged that glorious earl with being too cruel; and he was accused of punishing disturbers more for desire of their property which would be confiscated than for love of justice. It was also said, if it be worthy of credence, that they had undertaken this madness against their earl at the artful persuasion of his brother, Earl Harold (which heaven forbid!). But I dare not and would not believe that such a prince was guilty of this detestable wickedness against his brother. Earl Tostig himself, however, publicly testifying before the king and his assembled courtiers, charged him with this; but Harold, rather too generous with oaths (alas!), cleared this charge too with oaths.

When the rebels, after many negotiations with the king through messengers, would not agree, but rather raged more furiously in their mad purpose, Edward stirred up the whole population of the rest of England by a royal edict and decided to crush their impudent contumacy by force. But because changeable weather was already setting in from hard winter, and it was not easy to raise a sufficient number of troops for a counter offensive, and because in that race horror was felt at what seemed civil war, some strove to calm the raging spirit of the king and urged that the attack should not be mounted. And after they had struggled for a long time, they did not so much divert the king from his desire to march as wrongfully and against his will desert him. Sorrowing at this, he fell ill, and from that day until the day of his death he bore a sickness of the mind. He protested to God with deep sorrow, and complained to Him, that he was deprived of the due obedience of his men in repressing the presumption of the unrighteous; and he called down God's vengeance upon them.

The queen was, on the one hand, confounded by the quarrel of her brothers and, on the other, bereft of all support by the powerlessness of her husband, the king. And when her counsels came to naught — and by God's grace she shone above all in counsel if she were heard — she plainly showed her foreboding of future evils by her tears. And when she wept inconsolably, the whole palace went into mourning. For when misfortunes had attacked them in the past, she had always stood as a defense, and had both repelled all the hostile forces with her powerful counsels and also cheered the king and his retinue. Now, however, when, owing to sin, things had turned against them, all men deduced future disasters from the signs of the present. But the king, the beloved of God, when he could not save his earl, graciously heaped on him many gifts and then let him depart, profoundly distressed at the powerlessness that had come upon him. And a short time after, Tostig took leave of his sorrowing mother and some of his friends, and with his wife and infant children, and a goodly company of his thegns crossed the Channel and came to that old friend of the English people, Count Baldwin.... This happened a few days before Christmas; and soon, within the festal days, King Edward, the beloved of God, languishing from the mental illness he had contracted, died indeed to the world, but was joyfully taken up to live with God....

[Book 2]

1. And so, as we got so far as to record the death of this glorious king, let us first briefly say something about his earlier life. King Edward of happy memory was chosen by God before the day of his birth, and consequently was consecrated to the kingdom less by men than, as we have said before, by heaven. He preserved with holy chastity the dignity of his consecration, and lived his whole life dedicated to God in true innocence. God approved this as an acceptable burnt offering, and with profound love made him dear to men and worshipful among the citizens of heaven. For, as we have learnt from the joint testimony of good and fitting men, God glorified him in this life of corruption by these signs.

2. A certain young woman, already provided with a husband, but gladdened with no fruit of the marriage, had an infection of the throat and of those parts under the jaw which, from their likeness to an acorn, are called glands. These had so disfigured her face with an evil smelling disease that she could scarcely speak to anyone without great embarrassment. She was advised in a dream that

if she were washed in water by King Edward she would be cured of this most dreadful infection. She then, with the certainty of faith, revealed the dream's instructions. And when the king heard of it, he did not disdain to help the weaker sex, for he had the sweetest nature, and was always charming to all suitors. A dish of water was brought; the king dipped in his hand; and with the tips of his fingers he anointed the face of the young woman and the places infected by the disease. He repeated this action several times, now and then making the sign of the cross. And believe in wonder one about to relate wonders! Those diseased parts that had been treated by the smearing of the king softened and separated from the skin; and, with the pressure of the hand, worms together with pus and blood came out of various holes. Again the good king kneaded with his holy hand and drew out the pus. Nor did he shrink from enduring the stench of the sick woman until with his healing hand he had brought out all that noxious disease. Then he ordered her to be fed daily at the royal expense until she should be fully restored to health. And hardly had she been at court a week, when, all foulness washed away, the grace of God moulded her with beauty. And she, who formerly through this or some other sickness had been barren, in that year became pregnant by the same husband, and lived henceforth happily enough with all around her. Although this seems new and strange to us, the Franks aver that Edward had done this often as a youth when he was in Neustria, now known as Normandy.

Likewise a certain blind man was going about claiming that he had been advised in sleep, that if his blind face were washed in the water with which the king rinsed his hands, he would both overcome the blindness and restore his lost sight. When Edward heard of this from his domestic servants, at first he contradicted them and blamed them for believing it to be true. But when they demanded urgently that he should not resist God's will, at length he courteously agreed. It was then, as they say for certain, the day of the vigil of the festival of All Saints, when the king, having made his morning ablutions, entered the chapel. Meanwhile his servants washed the blind man with the same water, and conducted him after the king into the house of prayer. When the king left after the canonical offices had been solemnly sung in honor of all the saints, word was brought to him by his domestics that he who was blind now saw. The king, therefore, with pious curiosity, came unto him in the chapel, and, calling him to him, inquired whether he could indeed see. This the man began to affirm and gave thanks to God. To test the truth of the words, however, the king, as pure as a dove, stretched forth the palm of his hand, and asked for an account of his action. "You are stretching out your hand, O my lord king," the man replied. Once more the king, sticking his forefinger and middle finger like a pair of horns before the man's face, asked what he did. And the man answered what he saw. Also, a third time, the king, grasping his beard in his hand, again asked what he did. And the man furnished correctly the information that was sought. Then the king considered that he had been sufficiently examined, and went forward for a little while to pray; and, having thrice bowed his knee before the altar, he gave thanks to God and entrusted the man to his servants to be maintained as long as he lived at the royal charge. The man lived for a long time at court, a witness to the virtue that he had received by the glory of God.

11. ...When King Edward, replete with faith, perceived that the power of the disease was forcing him to his end, with the commendation and prayers of the most important of God's faithful he resigned himself to the funeral rites. For, indeed, being now freed by the protection of the spirit of God from the affairs of a secular ruler, he could through heavenly contemplation enjoy more easily a vision of the future. While his frail body was being sustained by the hands of the devout awaiting his death, becoming drowsy because of his body's heaviness, he was instructed infallibly about those things which we for our sins bear at the present time. While he slept those in attendance felt in his sleeping body the travail of his unquiet soul, and, woken by them in their terror, he spoke these words. (Up till then, for the last two days or more, weakness had so tired him that when he spoke scarcely anything he said had been intelligible.) "O eternal God," he said, "if I have learnt those things which have now been revealed to me from you, grant also the strength to tell them. But if it was only an illusion, let my former sickness burden me according to your will." And then, as they who were there testify, he used such resources of eloquence that even the healthiest man would have no need of more.

"Just now," he said, "two monks stood before me, whom I had once known very well when I was a young man in Normandy, men of great sanctity, and for many years now relieved of earthly cares. And they addressed me with a message from God. 'Since,' they said, 'those who have climbed to the highest offices in the kingdom of England, the earls, bishops, and abbots, and all those in holy orders, are not what they seem to be, but, on the contrary, are servants of the devil, within a year and a day after the day of your death God has delivered all this kingdom, cursed by him, into the hands of the enemy, and devils shall come through all this land with fire and sword and the havoc of war.' Then I said this to them, 'I will show God's designs to the people, and the forgiveness of God shall have mercy upon the penitents. For he had mercy on the people of Nineveh, when they repented on hearing of the divine indignation.' But they said, 'These will not repent, nor will the forgiveness of God come to pass for them.' 'And what,' I asked, 'shall happen? And when can a remission of this great indignation be hoped for?' 'At that time,' they answered, 'when a green tree, if cut down in the middle of its trunk, and the part cut off carried the space of three furlongs from the stock, shall be joined again to its trunk, by itself and without the hand of man or any sort of stake, and begin once more to push leaves and bear fruit from the old love of its uniting sap, then first can a remission of these great ills be hoped for.'"

When those who were present had heard these words — that is to say, the queen, who was sitting on the floor warming his feet in her lap, her full brother, Earl Harold, and Rodbert, the steward of the royal palace and a kinsman of the king, also Archbishop Stigand and a few more whom the blessed king when roused from sleep had ordered to be summoned — they were all sore afraid as men who had heard a speech containing many calamities and a denial of the hope of pity. And while all were stupefied and silent from the effect of terror, the archbishop himself, who ought to have been the first either to be afraid or to give a word of advice, with folly at heart whispered in the ear of the earl that the king was broken with age and disease and knew not what he said. But the queen, and those who had been wont to know and fear God in their hearts, all pondered deeply the words they had heard, and understood them quite otherwise, and correctly. For these knew that the Christian religion was chiefly dishonored by men in holy orders, and that both the Pope of Rome by means of legates and letters and the king and queen by frequent admonition had often proclaimed this. But there were some men, irreparably attracted to the devil by riches and worldly glory, who had so neglected the conduct of their lives that they did not fear to fall into the wrath of God which then was already threatening them. For though this should take vengeance for a time on the flocks of harmless sheep, it is not to be hidden from the pastors and those of us who have sinned that, if we are not punished in this world and in purgatory, it is greatly to be feared that vengeance for our sins will be reserved for us in eternity....

But leaving this sorrow for a while, let us return to the other, and describe how this gem of God stripped off the corruption of his earthly body and obtained a place of eternal splendor in the diadem of the heavenly king. When he was sick unto death and his men stood and wept bitterly, he said, "Do not weep, but intercede with God for my soul, and give me leave to go to Him. For He will not pardon me so that I shall not die who would not pardon Himself so that He should not die." Then he addressed his last words to the queen, who was sitting at his feet, in this wise: "May God be gracious to this my wife for the zealous solicitude of her service. For certainly she has served me devotedly, and has always stood close by my side like a beloved daughter. And so from the forgiving God may she obtain the reward of eternal happiness." And stretching forth his hand to his governor, her brother, Harold, he said, "I commend this woman and all the kingdom to your protection. Serve and honor her with faithful obedience as your lady and sister, which she is, and do not despoil her, as long as she lives, of any due honor got from me. Likewise I also commend those men who have left their native land for love of me, and have up till now served me faithfully. Take from them an oath of fealty, if they should so wish, and protect and retain them, or send them with your safe conduct safely across the Channel to their own homes with all that they have acquired in my service. Let the grave for my burial be prepared in the minster in the place which shall be assigned to you. I ask that you do not conceal my death, but announce it promptly in all parts, so that all the faithful can beseech the mercy of Almighty God on me, a sinner." Now and then he also comforted the queen, who ceased not from lamenting, to ease her natural grief. "Fear not," he said, "I shall not die now, but by God's mercy regain my strength." Nor did he mislead the attentive, least of all himself, by these words, for he has not died, but has passed "from death to life," to live with Christ.

And so, coming with these and like words to his last hour, he took the viaticum from the table of heavenly life and gave up his spirit to God the Creator on the fourth of January, foreshowing a funereal and mournful head, if we may use the expression, of the new year, on account of which we should be obliged to observe the whole body of months become weak with tribulation and manifold slaughter. Then could be seen in the dead body the glory of a soul departing to God. For the flesh of his face blushed like a rose, the adjacent beard gleamed like a lily, his hands, laid out straight, whitened, and were a sign that his whole body was given not to death but to auspicious sleep. And so the funeral rites were arranged at the royal cost and with royal honor, as was proper, and amid the boundless sorrow of all men. They bore his holy remains from his palace home into the house of God, and offered up prayers and sighs and psalms all that day and the following night. Meanwhile, when the day of the funeral ceremony dawned, they blessed the office of the interment they were to conduct with the singing of masses and the relief of the poor. And so, before the altar of St. Peter the Apostle, the body, washed by his country's tears, is laid up in the sight of God. They also caused the whole of the thirty days following to be observed with the celebration of masses and the chanting of psalms, and expended many pounds of gold for the redemption of his soul in the alleviation of different classes of the poor. Having revealed him as a saint while still living in the world, as we wrote before, at his tomb likewise merciful God reveals by these signs that he lives with Him as a saint in heaven. For at the tomb through him the blind receive their sight, the lame are made to walk, the sick are healed, the sorrowing are refreshed by the comfort of God, and for the faith of those who call upon Him, God, the King of kings, works the tokens of his goodness.

Questions: For what does the author admire Edward? What is the relation between the king and his subjects? With what kinds of problems does a king have to cope? For what does the author admire Edith, and how does this compare with the picture of Emma in the previous work? Edward and Edith had no children; how does the author nevertheless portray their marriage as successful? What is the meaning of the deathbed scene?

8. WULFSTAN'S LAWS FOR NORTHUMBRIAN PRIESTS

Like many of the leading churchmen of his day, Archbishop Wulfstan of York (1002-23) saw the enforcement of law and morality as one of his chief duties. To this end he composed law codes that were issued by both Ethelred and Cnut (see the Laws of Cnut, doc. 4), and he also wrote the following regulations for the clergy of Northumbria, a northern territory with a tradition of independence. The ora, mentioned frequently here, is an amount of money equal to 16 Saxon pence, or one-fifteenth of a pound.

Source: trans. B. Thorpe, *Ancient Laws and Institutes of England* (London: Record Commission, 1840), vol. II, pp. 291-303; revised.

1. If anyone offer any wrong to any priest, let all the brethren, with the bishop's succor, zealously see to the atonement; and let them be, in every case of right, as it is written, "as one body and one spirit."

2. And we, God's messenger, forbid that any priest either buy or accept another's church, unless anyone shall undo himself with a capital crime, so that he thenceforth be not worthy of the altar-service; and if any priest do otherwise, let him forfeit his reverence, and the friendship of his brethren; and let him nowhere celebrate mass, ere he has it who rightfully owns it. And let him who did the wrong pay twenty *ores* to the bishop; twelve *ores* to the priest whom he displaced from his church; twelve *ores* to all the brethren: and let him also forfeit the money, if he unlawfully gave any for the church of another priest: and let every priest find for himself twelve bondsmen, that he will rightly observe the priestly law.

3. And if any priest sin, and he, against the bishop's command, celebrate mass, let him pay for [breaking] the command twenty *ores*, and in addition thereto, let him make amends for the sin he previously committed.

4. If a priest decline obedience to the bishop's own edict, let him pay twenty *ores*.

5. If a priest commit to laymen a judgment that he should commit to ecclesiastics, let him pay twenty *ores*.

6. If a priest decline obedience to the archdeacon's edict, let him pay twelve *ores*.

7. If a priest be criminal, and he celebrate mass against the archdeacon's command, let him pay twelve *ores*.

8. If a priest refuse baptism or confession, let him make amends for that with twelve *ores*, and, above all, earnestly pray for pardon to God.

9. If a priest at proper time do not fetch chrism, let him pay twelve *ores*.

10. We enjoin, that every child be baptized within nine days, under penalty of six *ores*; and if a child, within nine days, die a heathen, through negligence, let them make amends before God, without secular penalty. And if it be over nine days, let them make amends before God, and pay twelve *ores* for the hardness through which he was a heathen so long.

11. If a priest misguide the people respecting festival or fast, let him make amends to God, and pay twelve *ores*.

12. If a priest unlawfully, out of his district, obtain orders, let him pay twelve *ores*; and a deacon six *ores*; and forfeit his orders, unless the bishop of the district will grant him the orders.

13. If a priest in an unhallowed house celebrate mass, let him pay twelve *ores*.

14. If a priest without a hallowed altar celebrate mass, let him pay twelve *ores*.

15. If a priest consecrate the bread in a wooden chalice, let him pay twelve *ores*.

16. If a priest celebrate mass without wine, let him pay twelve *ores*.

17. If a priest neglect the eucharist, let him pay twelve *ores*.

18. If a priest in one day celebrate mass oftener than thrice, let him pay twelve *ores*.

19. If a man break the peace of a church, let him make amends according to the rank of the church, and according as its protection may be.

20. If anyone traffic with a church, let him make amends according to *lah-slit* [that is, a customary fine imposed on Danes].

21. If anyone reduce a church to servitude, let him make amends according to *lah-slit*.

22. If anyone unlawfully turn a priest out of a church, let him make amends according to *lah-slit*.

23. If anyone wound a priest, let him make amends for the wound, and as altar-*bot* [that is, atonement] for his order, give twelve *ores*; for a deacon, six *ores* as altar-*bot*.

24. If anyone slay a priest, let him make compensation for him according to his full *wer* [that is, his legal monetary worth]; and to the bishop, twenty-four *ores*, as altar-*bot*: for a deacon twelve *ores* as altar-*bot*.

25. If a priest dishonor a church, from which all his dignity is to proceed, let him make amends for it.

26. If a priest place unbecoming things in a church, let him make amends for it.

27. If a priest turn out anything of the church, let him make amends for it.

28. If a priest of his own will leave the church to which he was ordained, let him make amends for it.

29. If a priest despise or insult another, with word or with deed, let him make amends for it.

30. If a priest fight with another, let him make amends to him and to the bishop.

31. If a priest be aiding to another in wrong, let him make amends for it.

32. If a priest refuse another lawful succor, let him make amends for it.

33. If a priest leave another unwarned of that which he knows will harm him, let him make amends for it.

34. If a priest neglect the shaving of beard or of locks, let him make amends for it.

35. If a priest forsake a woman, and take another, let him be excommunicated.

36. If a priest, at the appointed time, do not ring the hours, or sing the hours, let him make amends for it.

37. If a priest come with weapons into a church, let him make amends for it.

38. If a priest misorder the annual services of the church, by day or by night, let him make amends for it.

39. If a priest misconduct an ordeal, let him make amends for it.

40. If a priest enwrap his tonsure, let him make amends for it.

41. If a priest love drunkenness, or become a wandering minstrel or a singer of tales, let him make amends for it....

43. If a priest let the yearly dues pass unreminded, let him make amends for it.

44. If a priest shun the synod, let him make amends for it.

45. If a priest will not submit to law, but opposes the bishop's ordinance, let him make amends for it; or let him be sundered from the clerical community, and forfeit both his fellowship and every dignity; unless he submit and the more deeply make amends.

46. If anyone corrupt the law of God, or the law of the people, let him diligently make amends for it.

47. We are all to worship and love one God, and zealously observe one Christianity, and every heathenship totally renounce.

48. If then anyone be found that shall henceforth practice any heathenship, either by sacrifice or by [superstition], or in any way love witchcraft, or worship idols, if he be a king's thane, let him pay ten half-marks; half to Christ, half to the king.

49. If it be any other man owning land, let him pay six half-marks; half to Christ, and half to the landlord.

50. If it be a ceorl, let him pay twelve *ores*.

51. If a king's thane make denial, then let twelve [oath-helpers] be named to him, and let him take twelve of his kinsmen, and twelve Celts; and if it fail, then let him pay a fine of ten half-marks.

52. If a land-owning man make denial, then let be named to him of his equals as many Celts as to a king's thane; if it fail him, let him pay a fine of six half-marks.

53. If a ceorlish man make denial, then let be named to him of his equals as many Celts as to the others; if it fail him, let him pay a fine of twelve *ores*.

54. If there be a pagan sanctuary on anyone's land, about a stone, or a tree, or a well, or any folly of such kind, then let him who made it pay a fine; half to Christ, half to the landlord: and if the landlord will not aid in levying the fine, then let Christ and the king have it.

55. Sunday's traffic we forbid everywhere, and every folk-mote [that is, meeting], and every work, and every journeying, whether in a wagon, or on a horse, or with a burden.

56. He who shall do any of these, let him pay the [English] fine: a freeman twelve *ores*; an unfree man, with his hide; except travelers, who may, in case of need, convey food; and on account of war, anyone may, on the eve of a festival, if needful, travel between York and a distance of six miles.

57. He who breaks a festival or lawful fast, let him pay a fine of twelve *ores*; and we will that every Rome-penny be paid by Peter's mass to the episcopal seat; and we will, that in every wapentake [that is, subdivision of a shire] there be named two true thanes, and one mass-priest, who shall collect it, and afterwards render it, so that they dare swear to it.

58. If a king's thane, or any landlord, withhold it, let him pay ten half-marks; half to Christ, half to the king.

59. If any townsman conceal or withhold any penny, let the landlord pay the penny, and take an ox from the man; and if the landlord neglect it, then let Christ and the king take a full fine of twelve *ores*.

60. If anyone withhold his tithe, and he be a king's thane, let him pay ten half-marks; a land-owner, six half-marks; a ceorl, twelve *ores*.

61. And we prohibit, with God's prohibition, that any man have more wives than one, and let her be lawfully betrothed and given; and let no man marry among kin more near than outside the fourth degree, nor any man marry among his spiritual kin; and if anyone do so, let him not have God's mercy, unless he abstain, and make amends as the bishop may prescribe.

62. But if in that unlawfulness he die, let him forfeit a hallowed grave, and God's mercy.

63. If anyone lie with a nun, let both be liable for their *wer*, both he and she; and if they die in that sin, without abstaining, let them forfeit a hallowed grave and God's mercy.

64. If anyone forsake his lawful wife, as long as she lives, and unlawfully wed another woman, let him not have God's mercy, unless he make amends.

65. But let everyone lawfully keep his wife, as long as she lives, unless they both choose, with the bishop's counsel, to separate, and will thenceforth observe chastity.

66. If any man henceforth shall corrupt just law, let him make amends earnestly.

67. We are all to love and worship one God, and strictly hold one Christianity, and totally renounce all heathenship: and we will that land purchase, and law-giving, and wisdom, and true witness, and righteous judgment, and [various legal procedures], stand fast; and customary taxation, and the lord's accustomed dues, and, above all, one Christianity, and one kingship, for ever in the nation.

Questions: What are the similarities and differences between these rules and the secular laws of Cnut? What are the duties of priests? What problems seem to arise among the clergy? Which infractions are regarded as most serious? How are the clergy to be disciplined?

9. THE ANGLO-SAXON CHRONICLE ON THE NORMAN CONQUEST

From the late ninth century into the twelfth, the Anglo-Saxon Chronicle provides a contemporary record of events in England, updated annually by monks whose identities are unknown to us. The excerpt below tells the story, some of it in alliterative verse, of the momentous Norman Conquest, from the perspective of the conquered.

Source: trans. J. Ingram, *The Anglo-Saxon Chronicle* (New York: E.P. Dutton, 1912), pp. 144-154, 162-168; revised.

A.D. 1065   ... About midwinter [December 25] King Edward came to Westminster, and had the minster there consecrated, which he had himself built to the honor of God, and St. Peter, and all God's saints. This church-hallowing was on Childermas day [December 28]. He died on the eve of twelfth-day [that is, on January 5]; and he was buried on twelfth-day in the same minster; as it is hereafter said.

> Here Edward king,
> of Angles lord,
> sent his steadfast
> soul to Christ.
> In the kingdom of God
> a holy spirit!
> He in the world here

abode awhile,
in the kingly throng
of council sage.
Four and twenty
winters wielding
the scepter freely,
wealth he dispensed.
In the tide of health,
the youthful monarch,
offspring of Ethelred!
ruled well his subjects;
the Welsh and the Scots,
and the Britons also,
Angles and Saxons —
relations of old.
So apprehend
the first in rank,
that to Edward all
— the noble king —
were firmly held
high-seated men.
Blithe-minded aye
was the harmless king;
though he long ere,
of land bereft,
abode in exile
wide on the earth;
when Cnut o'ercame
the kin of Ethelred,
and the Danes wielded
the dear kingdom
of Engle-land.
Eight and twenty
winters' rounds
they wealth dispensed.
Then came forth
free in his chambers,
in royal array,
good, pure, and mild,
Edward the noble;
by his country defended —

by land and people.
Until suddenly came
the bitter Death
and this king so dear
snatched from the earth.
Angels carried
his soul sincere
into the light of heaven.
But the prudent king
had settled the realm
on high-born men —
on Harold himself,
the noble earl;
who in every season
faithfully heard
and obeyed his lord,
in word and deed;
nor gave to any
what might be wanted
by the nation's king.

This year also was Earl Harold hallowed to king; but he enjoyed little tranquillity therein the while that he wielded the kingdom.

A.D. 1066 This year came King Harold from York to Westminster, on the Easter succeeding the midwinter when the king (Edward) died. Easter was then on [April 16,] the sixteenth day before the calends of May. Then was over all England such a token seen as no man ever saw before. Some men said that it was the comet-star, which others denominate the long-haired star. It appeared first on [April 25,] the eve called *Litania major,* that is, on the eighth before the calends of May; and so shone all the week. Soon after this came in Earl Tostig from beyond sea into the Isle of Wight, with as large a fleet as he could get; and he was there supplied with money and provisions. Thence he proceeded, and committed outrages everywhere by the sea-coast where he could land, until he came to Sandwich. When it was told King Harold, who was in London, that his brother Tostig was come to Sandwich, he gathered so large a force, naval and military, as no king before collected in this land; for it was credibly reported that Earl William from Normandy, King Edward's cousin, would come hither and gain this land; just as it afterwards happened. When Tostig understood that King Harold was on the way to Sandwich, he departed thence, and took some of the boatmen with him, willing and unwilling, and went north into the Humber with sixty skips; whence he plundered in Lindsey, and there slew many good men. When the Earls Edwin and Morkar understood that, they came hither, and drove him from the land. And the boatmen forsook him. Then he went to Scotland with twelve smacks; and the king of the Scots entertained him, and aided him with provisions; and he abode there all the summer. There met him Harald, king of Norway, with three hundred ships. And Tostig submitted to him, and became his man. Then came King Harold to Sandwich, where he awaited his fleet; for it was long ere it could be collected: but when it was assembled, he went into the Isle of Wight, and there lay all the summer and the autumn. There was also a land force everywhere by the sea, though it availed naught in the end. It was now the nativity of St. Mary [September 8], when the provisioning of the men began; and no man could keep them there any longer. They therefore had leave to go home: and the king rode up, and the ships were driven to London; but many perished ere they came thither. When the ships were come home, then came Harald, king of Norway, north into the Tyne, unawares, with a very great sea-force — no small one; that might be, with three hundred ships or more; and Earl Tostig came to him with all those that he had got; just as they had before said: and they both then went up with all the fleet along the Ouse toward York. When it was told King Harold in the south, after he had come from the ships, that Harald, King of Norway, and Earl Tostig were come up near York, then went he northward by day and night, as soon as he could collect his army. But, ere King Harold could come thither, the Earls Edwin and Morkar had gathered from their earldoms as great a force as they could get, and fought with the enemy. They made a great slaughter too; but there was a good number of the English people slain, and drowned, and put to flight: and the Northmen had possession of the field of battle. It was then told Harold, king of the English, that this had thus happened. And this fight was on [September 20,] the eve of St. Matthew the apostle, which was Wednesday. Then after the fight went Harald, king of Norway, and Earl Tostig into York with as many followers as they thought fit; and having procured hostages and provisions from the city, they proceeded to their ships, and proclaimed full friendship, on condition that all would go southward with them, and gain this land. In the midst of this came Harold, king of the English, with all his army, on the Sunday, to Tadcaster; where he collected his fleet. Thence he proceeded on Monday throughout York. But Harald, king of Norway, and Earl Tostig, with their forces, were gone from their ships beyond York to Stamford Bridge; because it was given them to understand, that hostages would be brought to them there from all the shire. Thither came Harold, king of the English, unawares against them beyond the bridge; and they closed together there, and continued long in the day fighting very severely. There was slain Harald the Fair-haired, king of Norway, and Earl Tostig, and a multitude of people with them, both of Norwegians and English; and the

Norwegians that were left fled from the English, who slew them hotly behind; until some came to their ships, some were drowned, some burned to death, and thus variously destroyed; so that there was little left: and the English gained possession of the field. But there was one of the Norwegians who withstood the English folk, so that they could not pass over the bridge, nor complete the victory. An Englishman aimed at him with a javelin, but it availed nothing. Then came another under the bridge, who pierced him terribly inwards under the coat of mail. And Harold, king of the English, then came over the bridge, followed by his army; and there they made a great slaughter, both of the Norwegians and of the Flemings. But Harold let the king's son, Edmund, go home to Norway with all the ships. He also gave quarter to Olave, the Norwegian king's son, and to their bishop, and to the earl of the Orkneys, and to all those that were left in the ships; who then went up to our king, and took oaths that they would ever maintain faith and friendship unto this land. Whereupon the king let them go home with twenty-four ships. These two general battles were fought within five nights. Meantime Earl William came up from Normandy into Pevensey on [September 28,] the eve of St. Michael's mass; and soon after his landing was effected, they constructed a castle at the port of Hastings. This was then told to King Harold; and he gathered a large force, and came to meet him at the estuary of Appledore. William, however, came against him unawares, ere his army was collected; but the king, nevertheless, very hardly encountered him with the men that would support him: and there was a great slaughter made on either side. There was slain King Harold, and Leofwin his brother, and Earl Girth his brother, with many good men: and the Frenchmen gained the field of battle, as God granted them for the sins of the nation. Archbishop Aldred and the corporation of London were then desirous of having the child Edgar to king, as he was quite natural to them; and Edwin and Morkar promised them that they would fight with them. But the more prompt the business should ever be, so was it from day to day the later and worse; as in the end it all fared. This battle was fought on the day of Pope Calixtus [October 14]: and Earl William returned to Hastings, and waited there to know whether the people would submit to him. But when he found that they would not come to him, he went up with all his force that was left and that came since to him from over sea, and ravaged all the country that he overran, until he came to Berkhampstead; where Archbishop Aldred came to meet him, with the child Edgar, and Earls Edwin and Morkar, and all the best men from London; who submitted then for need, when the most harm was done. It was very ill-advised that they did not so before, seeing that God would not better things for our sins. And they gave him hostages and took oaths: and he promised them that he would be a faithful lord to them; though in the midst of this they plundered wherever they went. Then on midwinter's day [December 25] Archbishop

Aldred hallowed him as king at Westminster, and gave him possession with the books of Christ, and also had him swear, berfore he would set the crown on his head, that he would so well govern this nation as any before him best did, if they would be faithful to him. Nevertheless he laid very heavy tribute on men, and in Lent went over sea to Normandy, taking with him Archbishop Stigand, and Abbot Aylnoth of Glastonbury, and the child Edgar, and the Earls Edwin, Morkar, and Waltheof, and many other good men of England. Bishop Odo and Earl William lived here afterwards, and wrought castles widely through this country, and harassed the miserable people; and ever since has evil increased very much. May the end be good, when God will! In that same expedition [against William] was Leofric, Abbot of Peterborough; who sickened there, and came home, and died soon after, on the night of Allhallow-mass [November 1]. God honor his soul! In his day was all bliss and all good at Peterborough. He was beloved by all; so that the king gave to St. Peter and him the abbey at Bur-ton, and that at Coventry, which the Earl Leofric, who was his uncle, had for-merly made; with that of Croyland, and that of Thorney. He did so much good to the minster of Peterborough, in gold, and in silver, and in shroud, and in land, as no other ever did before him, nor anyone after him. But now was Gilden-borough become a wretched borough. The monks then chose for abbot Provost Brand, because he was a very good man, and very wise; and sent him to Edgar Etheling, for that the land-folk supposed that he should be king: and the etheling received him gladly. When King William heard say that, he was very wroth, and said that the abbot had renounced him: but good men went between them, and reconciled them; because the abbot was a good man. He gave the king forty marks of gold for his reconciliation; and he lived but a little while after — only three years. Afterwards came all wretchedness and all evil to the minster. God have mercy on it!

A.D. 1067 This year came the king back again to England on St. Nicholas's day [Decem-ber 6]; and the same day was burned the church of Christ at Canterbury. Bishop Wulfwy also died, and is buried at his see in Dorchester. The child Edric and the Welsh were unsettled this year, and fought with the castlemen at Hereford, and did them much harm. The king this year imposed a heavy geld on the wretched people; but, notwithstanding, let his men always plunder all the country that they went over; and then he marched to Devonshire, and beset the city of Exeter eighteen days. There were many of his army slain; but he had promised them well, and performed ill; and the citizens surrendered the city because the thanes had betrayed them.... This year went out Githa, Harold's mother, and the wives of many good men with her, to the Flat-Holm, and there abode some time; and so departed thence over sea to St. Omer. This Easter came the king to Winchester.... Soon after this came [King William's

60

wife] the Lady Matilda hither to this land; and Archbishop Aldred hallowed her as queen at Westminster on Whit Sunday [May 27]. Then it was told the king, that the people in the north had gathered themselves together, and would stand against him if he came. Whereupon he went to Nottingham, and wrought there a castle; and so advanced to York, and there wrought two castles; and the same at Lincoln, and everywhere in that quarter. Then Earl Gospatric and the best men went into Scotland. Amidst this came one of Harold's sons from Ireland with a naval force into the mouth of the Avon unawares, and plundered soon over all that quarter; whence they went to Bristol, and would have stormed the town; but the people bravely withstood them. When they could gain nothing from the town, they went to their ships with the booty which they had acquired by plunder; and then they advanced upon Somersetshire, and there went up; and Ednoth, master of the horse, fought with them; but he was there slain, and many good men on either side; and those that were left departed thence.

A.D. 1068   This year King William gave Earl Robert the earldom over Northumberland; but the landsmen attacked him in the town of Durham, and slew him, and nine hundred men with him. Soon afterwards Edgar Etheling came with all the Northumbrians to York; and the townsmen made a treaty with him: but King William came from the south unawares on them with a large army, and put them to flight, and slew on the spot those who could not escape; which were many hundred men; and plundered the town. St. Peter's minster he made a profanation, and all other places also he despoiled and trampled upon; and the etheling went back again to Scotland. After this came Harold's sons from Ireland, about midsummer [June 24], with sixty-four ships into the mouth of the Taft, where they unwarily landed: and Earl Breon came unawares against them with a large army, and fought with them, and slew there all the best men that were in the fleet; and the others, being small forces, escaped to the ships: and Harold's sons went back to Ireland again.

A.D. 1069   This year died Aldred, Archbishop of York; and he is there buried, at his see. He died on the day of Protus and Hyacinthus [September 11], having held the see with much dignity ten years wanting only fifteen weeks. Soon after this came from Denmark three of the sons of King Sweyne with two hundred and forty ships, together with Earl Esborn and Earl Thurkill, into the Humber; where they were met by the child Edgar, and Earl Waltheof, and Merle-Sweyne, and Earl Gospatric with the Northumbrians, and all the landsmen; riding and marching full merrily with an immense army: and so all unanimously advanced to York; where they stormed and demolished the castle, and won innumerable treasures therein; slew there many hundreds of Frenchmen, and led many with them to the ships; but, ere that the shipmen came thither, the Frenchmen had burned the city, and also the holy minster of St. Peter had they entirely plundered, and destroyed with fire. When the king heard this, then went he northward with all the force that he could collect, despoiling and laying waste the shire withal; whilst the fleet lay all the winter in the Humber, where the king could not come at them. The king was in York on Christmas Day, and so all the winter on land, and came to Winchester at Easter. Bishop Egelric, who was at Peterborough, was this year betrayed, and led to Westminster; and his brother Egelwine was outlawed. This year also died Brand, abbot of Peterborough, on the fifth before the calends of December [November 27].

A.D. 1070 This year Lanfranc, who was abbot of Caen, came to England; and after a few days he became archbishop of Canterbury. He was invested on the fourth before the calends of September [August 29] in his own see by eight bishops, his suffragans. The others, who were not there, by messengers and by letter declared why they could not be there. The same year Thomas, who was chosen Bishop of York, came to Canterbury, to be invested there after the ancient custom. But when Lanfranc craved confirmation of his obedience with an oath, he refused; and said, that he ought not to do it. Whereupon Archbishop Lanfranc was wroth, and bade the bishops, who were come thither by Archbishop Lanfranc's command to do the service, and all the monks to unrobe themselves. And they by his order so did. Thomas, therefore, for the time, departed without consecration. Soon after this, it happened that the Archbishop Lanfranc went to Rome, and Thomas with him. When they came thither, and had spoken about other things concerning which they wished to speak, then began Thomas his speech: how he came to Canterbury, and how the archbishop required obedience of him with an oath; but he declined it. Then began the Archbishop Lanfranc to show with clear distinction, that what he craved he craved by right; and with strong arguments he confirmed the same before Pope Alexander, and before all the council that was collected there; and so they went home. After this came Thomas to Canterbury; and all that the archbishop required of him he humbly fulfilled, and afterwards received consecration....

A.D. 1085 In this year men reported, and of a truth asserted, that Cnut, king of Denmark, son of King Sweyne, was coming hitherward, and was resolved to win this land, with the assistance of Robert, Earl of Flanders; for Cnut had married Robert's daughter. When William, king of England, who was then resident in Normandy (for he had both England and Normandy), understood this, he went into England with so large an army of horse and foot, from France and Brittany, as never before sought this land; so that men wondered how this land could feed all that force. But the king left the army to shift for themselves through all this land amongst his subjects, who fed them, each according to his

BILLETING

quota of land. Men suffered much distress this year; and the king caused the land to be laid waste about the seacoast; that, if his foes came up, they might not have anything on which they could very readily seize. But when the king understood of a truth that his foes were impeded, and could not further their expedition, then he let some of the army go to their own land; but some he held in this land over the winter. Then, at the midwinter, was the king in Gloucester with his council, and held there his court five days. And afterwards the archbishop and clergy had a synod three days. There was Mauritius chosen Bishop of London, William of Norfolk, and Robert of Cheshire. These were all the king's clerks. After this the king had a large meeting, and very deep consultation with his council, about this land; how it was occupied, and by what sort of men. Then he sent his men over all England into each shire; commissioning them to find out how many hundreds of hides were in the shire, what land the king himself had, and what stock upon the land; or, what dues he ought to have by the year from the shire. Also he commissioned them to record in writing, how much land his archbishops had, and his diocesan bishops, and his abbots, and his earls; and though I may be prolix and tedious, what, or how much, each man had, who was an occupier of land in England, either in land or in stock, and how much money it were worth. So very narrowly, indeed, did he commission them to trace it out, that there was not one single hide, nor a yard of land, nay, moreover (it is shameful to tell, though he thought it no shame to do it), not even an ox, nor a cow, nor a swine was there left, that was not set down in his writ. And all the recorded particulars were afterwards brought to him.

A.D. 1086 This year the king wore his crown, and held his court, in Winchester at Easter; and he so arranged, that he was by the Pentecost [May 24] at Westminster, and dubbed his son Henry a knight there. Afterwards he moved about so that he came by Lammas [August 1] to Salisbury; where he was met by his councilors; and all the landsmen that were of any account over all England became this man's vassals as they were; and they all bowed themselves before him, and became his men, and swore him oaths of allegiance that they would against all other men be faithful to him. Thence he proceeded into the Isle of Wight; because he wished to go into Normandy, and so he afterwards did; though he first did according to his custom; he collected a very large sum from his people, wherever he could make any demand, whether with justice or otherwise. Then he went into Normandy; and Edgar Etheling, the relation of King Edward, revolted from him, for he received not much honor from him; but may the Almighty God give him honor hereafter. And Christina, the sister of the etheling, went into the monastery of Romsey, and received the holy veil. And the same year there was a very heavy season, and a troublesome and sorrowful year in England, in murrain of cattle, and corn and fruits did not grow, and so much untowardness in the weather, as a man may not easily think; so tremendous was the thunder and lightning, that it killed many men; and it continually grew worse and worse with men. May God Almighty better it whenever it be his will.

How tough it was,

A.D. 1087 After the birth of our Lord and Savior Christ, 1087 winters; in the 21st year after William began to govern and direct England, as God granted him, was a very heavy and pestilent season in this land. Such a sickness came on men, that full nigh every other man was in the worst disorder, that is, in the diarrhea; and that so dreadfully, that many men died in the disorder. Afterwards came, through the badness of the weather as we before mentioned, so great a famine over all England, that many hundreds of men died a miserable death through hunger. Alas! how wretched and how rueful a time was there! When the poor wretches lay full nigh driven to death prematurely, and afterwards came sharp hunger, and dispatched them withal! Who will not be penetrated with grief at such a season? Or who is so hardhearted as not to weep at such misfortune? Yet such things happen for folks' sins, because they will not love God and righteousness. So it was in those days, that little righteousness was in this land with any men but with the monks alone, wherever they fared well. The king and the head men loved much, and overmuch, covetousness in gold and in silver; and recked not how sinfully it was got, provided it came to them. The king let his land at as high a rate as he possibly could; then came some other person, and bade more than the former one gave, and the king let it to the man that bade him more. Then came the third, and bade yet more; and the king handed it over to the man that offered him most of all: and he cared not how very sinfully the stewards got it from wretched men, nor how many unlawful deeds they did; but the more men spake about right law, the more unlawfully they acted. They erected unjust tolls, and many other unjust things they did, that are difficult to reckon. Also in the same year, before harvest, the holy minster of St. Paul, the episcopal see in London, was completely burned, with many other minsters, and the greatest part, and the richest of the whole city. So also, about the same time, almost every major port in all England was entirely burned. Alas! rueful and woeful was the fate of the year that brought forth so many misfortunes. In the same year also, before the Assumption of St. Mary [August 15], King William went from Normandy into France with an army, and made war upon his own lord Philip, the king, and slew many of his men, and burned the town of Mantes, and all the holy minsters that were in the town; and two holy men that served God, leading the life of anchorites, were burned therein. This being thus done, King William returned to Normandy. Rueful was the thing he did; but a more rueful befell him. How more rueful? He fell sick, and it dreadfully ailed him. What shall I say? Sharp death, which passes by neither rich men nor poor, seized him also. He died in Normandy, on

[September 9,] the next day after the nativity of St. Mary, and he was buried at Caen in St. Stephen's minster, which he had formerly reared, and afterwards endowed with manifold gifts. Alas! how false and how uncertain is this world's weal! He that was before a rich king, and lord of many lands, had not then of all his land more than a space of seven feet! and he that was formerly enshrouded in gold and gems, lay there covered with mould! He left behind him three sons: the eldest, called Robert, who was earl in Normandy after him; the second, called William, who wore the crown after him in England; and the third, called Henry, to whom his father bequeathed immense treasure. If any person wishes to know what kind of man he was, or what honor he had, or of how many lands he was lord, then will we write about him as well as we understand him: we who often looked upon him, and lived sometime in his court. This King William then that we speak about was a very wise man, and very rich; more splendid and powerful than any of his predecessors were. He was mild to the good men that loved God, and beyond all measure severe to the men that gainsayed his will. On that same spot where God granted him that he should gain England, he reared a mighty minster, and set monks therein, and well endowed it. In his days was the great monastery in Canterbury built, and also very many others over all England. This land was moreover well filled with monks, who modeled their lives after the rule of St. Benedict. But such was the state of Christianity in his time, that each man followed what belonged to his profession — he that would. He was also very dignified. Thrice he wore his crown each year, as oft as he was in England. At Easter he bare it in Winchester, at Pentecost in Westminster, at midwinter in Gloucester. And then were with him all the rich men over all England; archbishops and diocesan bishops, abbots and earls, thanes and knights. So very stern was he also and hot, that no man dared do anything against his will. He had earls in his custody, who acted against his will. Bishops he hurled from their bishoprics, and abbots from their abbacies, and thanes into prison. At length he spared not his own brother Odo, who was a very rich bishop in Normandy. At Bayeux was his episcopal stall; and he was the foremost man of all to aggrandize the king. He had an earldom in England; and when the king was in Normandy, then was he the mightiest man in this land. Him he confined in prison. But amongst other things is not to be forgotten that good peace that he made in this land; so that a man of any account might go over his kingdom unhurt with his bosom full of gold. No man dared slay another, had he never so much evil done to the other; and if any churl lay with a woman against her will, he soon lost the limb that he played with. He truly reigned over England; and by his capacity so thoroughly surveyed it, that there was not a hide of land in England that he knew not who had it, or what it was worth, and afterwards set it down in his book. The land of the Welsh was in his power; and he wrought castles therein; and ruled Anglesey withal. So also he subdued Scotland by his great strength. As to Normandy, that was his native land; but he reigned also over the earldom called Maine; and if he might have yet lived two years more, he would have won Ireland by his valor, and without any weapons. Assuredly in his time had men much distress, and very many sorrows. Castles he let men build, and miserably oppress the poor. The king himself was so very rigid; and extorted from his subjects many marks of gold, and many hundred pounds of silver; which he took of his people, for little need, by right and by unright. He was fallen into covetousness, and greediness he loved withal. He made many deer-parks; and he established laws therewith; so that whosoever slew a hart, or a hind, should be deprived of his eyesight. As he forbade men to kill the harts, so also the boars; and he loved the tall deer as if he were their father. Likewise he decreed by the hares, that they should go free. His rich men bemoaned it, and the poor men shuddered at it. But he was so stern, that he recked not the hatred of them all; for they must follow withal the king's will, if they would live, or have land, or possessions, or even his peace. Alas! that any man should presume so to puff himself up, and boast over all men. May the Almighty God show mercy to his soul, and grant him forgiveness of his sins! These things have we written concerning him, both good and evil; that men may choose the good after their goodness, and flee from the evil withal, and go in the way that leadeth us to the kingdom of heaven....

After his death his son, called William also as the father, took to the king-dom, and was blessed as king by Archbishop Lanfranc at Westminster [on Sep-tember 26,] three days before Michaelmas day. And all the men in England submitted to him, and swore oaths to him. This being thus done, the king went to Winchester, and opened the treasure house, and the treasures that his father had gathered, in gold, and in silver, and in vases, and in palls, and in gems, and in many other valuable things that are difficult to enumerate. Then the king did as his father bade him before he was dead: he there distributed treasures for his father's soul to each monastery that was in England; to some ten marks of gold, to some six, to each upland church sixty pence. And into each shire were sent a hundred pounds of money to distribute amongst poor men for his soul. And before he departed, he bade that they should release all the men that were in prison under his power. And the king was in London at midwinter.

Questions: How does the author present Kings Edward, Harold, and William? How did the Norman Conquest affect England, according to this source? Are there any indica-tions of the author's political sympathies? What events other than national political ones are of interest to the chronicler?

10. THE TEXT OF THE BAYEUX TAPESTRY

The Bayeux Tapestry is a unique pictorial narrative, a series of scenes embroidered on linen with a running commentary above. It tells a Norman version of the story of King Harold and William the Conqueror. The entire text, and some of the scenes, are reproduced here. In this translation, brief phrases that simply identify a place or person are placed in parentheses.

Source: trans. E. Amt from *The Bayeux Tapestry*, ed. D.M. Wilson (New York: Alfred A. Knopf, 1985), plates 1–73.

(King Edward.) (*figure 3*) Where Harold, duke of the English, and his knights are riding to Bosham church (*figure 4*). Where Harold sails the sea (*figure 5*) and, with sails full of wind, comes to the land of Count Guy [of Ponthieu]. (Harold.) Where Guy is arresting Harold and has led him to Beaurain and has held him there. Where Harold and Guy are conversing.

Here Duke William's messengers have come to Guy. (Turold.) (William's messengers.) Here a messenger has come to Duke William. Here Guy has brought Harold to William, duke of the Normans. Here Duke William has come to his palace with Harold (*figure 6*). (Where a certain clerk and Ælf-gyva....) Here Duke William and his army have come to Mont-St-Michel. And here they have crossed the River Couesnon. Here Duke Harold has pulled them out of the sands. And they have come to Dol [to attack Duke Conan of Brittany], and Conan turns and flees. (Rennes.) Here Duke William's knights are fighting against Dinan, and Conan has offered them the keys. Here William has given Harold arms. Here William comes to Bayeux, where Harold takes an oath to Duke William (*figure 7*).

FIG. 3

FIG. 4

FIG. 4

FIG. 5

FIG. 6

FIG. 7

FIG. 8

Here Duke Harold has returned to the land of England and comes to King Edward (*figure 8*). Here King Edward, on his deathbed, addresses his trusty friends. And here he has died (*figure 9*). Here the body of King Edward is carried to the church of St. Peter the apostle [that is, Westminster Abbey] (*figure 10*). Here they have given the king's crown to Harold.

Here sits Harold (*figure 11*), king of the English. (Archbishop Stigand.) These men are marveling at the star [that is, Halley's Comet]. (Harold.) Here an English ship comes to the land of Duke William. Here Duke William has ordered ships to be built (*figure 12*).

Here they are dragging the ships to the sea. These men are carrying arms to the ships. And here they are pulling a cart with wine and arms (*figure 13*). Here Duke William, in a great ship, has crossed the sea and comes to Pevensey (*figure 14*).

FIG. 9

FIG. 10

FIG. 11

FIG. 12

FIG. 13

FIG. 14

FIG. 15

FIG. 16

FIG. 17

FIG. 18

FIG. 19

FIG. 20

Here the horses are getting out of the ships. And here the knights hurry to Hastings to seize supplies. Here is Wadard. Here meat is being cooked. And here the servants have been preparing, and here they have served, the midday meal (*figure 15*). And here the bishop [that is, William's brother Odo, bishop of Bayeux] blesses the food and drink (*figure 16*). (Bishop Odo. William. Robert.) This man has ordered that a castle be constructed at Hastings. Here reports about Harold have been brought to William. Here a house is being burned.

Here the knights have left Hastings and have come to the battle against King Harold. Here Duke William asks Vital whether he has seen Harold's army.

This man reports to Harold about Duke William's army. Here Duke William exhorts his knights to prepare themselves manfully and wisely for battle against the English army (*figures 17, 18*).

Here Leofwine and Gyrth, King Harold's brothers, have been killed.

Here English and French together have been killed in battle (*figure 19*).

Here Bishop Odo, holding a staff, encourages the young men. Here is Duke William [showing his face to the troops] (*figure 20*). (Eustace.) Here the French are fighting.

And those who were with Harold have been killed. Here King Harold has been killed (*figure 21*). And the English have turned in flight.

Questions: Why does the story include Harold's adventures in Normandy? How is the Norman viewpoint evident? Compare this account with that in the Anglo-Saxon Chronicle (doc. 9). What does the Tapestry reveal about eleventh-century warfare? What do the images in the Tapestry reveal about everyday life and material culture?

FIG. 21

11. DOMESDAY BOOK

In 1086 William the Conqueror ordered a far-reaching census to be taken of the lands and resources in England (as described above in the Ango-Saxon Chronicle entry for the year 1085, the anomaly in years being due to different ways of calculating the "new year" in the Middle Ages). The resulting returns were condensed and compiled into the large volume known to later generations as the "Domesday Book," because its testimony as to certain historical matters of status and tenure was the final authority and judgment. For historians, William's census is an incomparable snapshot of almost the entire kingdom, providing a wealth of statistical detail that we have for no other part of Europe at this time.

Source: trans. E. Amt from *Domesday Book 15. Gloucestershire*, ed. J. S. Moore (Chichester: Phillimore, 1982), sections 162a G, 162d [1], 166c 28, 167a,b 34.

Gloucestershire

In the time of King Edward the city of Gloucester paid £36 (in counted coin), twelve sesters of honey (by the measure of that borough), 36 dickers of iron, 100 iron rods for nails for the king's ships, and certain other minor customary payments in the king's hall and chamber. Now the city itself pays the king £60 at the rate of twenty pence per *ora*. And the king receives £20 from the mint.

In the demesne land of the king, Roger de Berkeley holds one house and one fishery in the town itself, and it is outside the king's hand. Baldwin held this in the time of King Edward.

Bishop Osbern holds the land and dwellings which Edmar held; he pays 10s. with another customary payment.

Geoffrey de Mandeville holds six dwellings. In the time of King Edward these paid 6s. 8d. with another customary payment.

William Baderon holds two dwellings at 30d.

William the scribe holds one dwelling at 51d.

Roger de Lacy holds one dwelling at 26d.

Bishop Osbern holds one dwelling at 41d.

Berner holds one dwelling at 14d.

William Bald holds one dwelling at 12d.

Durand the sheriff holds two dwellings at 14d.

The same Durand holds one dwelling at 26d. and also one dwelling which renders no customary payment.

Hadwin holds one dwelling which pays rent but keeps back another customary payment.

Gosbert holds one dwelling; Dunning holds one dwelling; Widard holds one dwelling.

Arnulf the priest holds one dwelling which pays rent and keeps back another customary payment.

All these dwellings paid the royal customary payments in the time of King Edward. Now King William receives nothing from them, nor does Robert his official. These dwellings were in King Edward's farm [that is, his assets producing a fixed income] on the day he was alive and dead. But now they have been removed from the farm and from the king's customary payments.

In the time of King Edward the king's demesne in the city supplied all lodging and clothing. When Earl William took it into his farm it continued to supply clothing.

Sixteen houses used to be where the castle stands; now they are gone. And in the borough of the city fourteen houses have been destroyed....

The King's Land

King Edward held Cheltenham. There were eight and a half hides. One and a half hides belong to the church; Reinbald holds them. In demesne were three plows, and twenty villeins and ten bordars and seven slaves with eighteen plows. The priests had two plows. There were two mills at 11s. 8d. King William's reeve added to this manor two bordars and four villeins and three mills, of which two are the king's and the third the reeve's, and one additional plow there. In the time of King Edward it paid £9 5s., and 3000 loaves of bread for dogs. Now it pays £20, twenty cows, 20 pigs, and 16s. for loaves of bread.

In King's Barton King Edward had nine hides. Of these, seven were in demesne, where there are three plows, and fourteen villeins and ten bordars with nine plows. There are seven slaves. Two free men hold two hides from this manor and have there nine plows. They cannot separate themselves or their land from the manor. There was a mill at 4s. King William's reeve added eight bordars and two mills and one plow. In the time of King Edward it paid £9 5s., and 3000 loaves of bread for dogs. Now it pays £20, twenty cows, 20 pigs, and 16s. for loaves of bread.

Archbishop Ældred leased Brawn, a part of this manor. There were three virgates of land and three men there. Miles Crispin holds it now.

Alwin the sheriff leased another part, by the name of Upton. There was one hide of land and there are four men. Humfrey holds it now.

The same Alwin leased another part, by the name of Murrells. There are three virgates of land there. Nigel the physician holds it now....

In Botloe Hundred:

King Edward held Dymock. There were twenty hides and two plows in demesne there, and 42 villeins and ten bordars and eleven freedmen having 41 plows. There is a priest holding twelves acres there. There are four *radknights* [that is, tenants owing escort duty] with four plows. There is woodland three leagues long and one league wide. The sheriff paid what he wished from this manor in the time of King Edward. King William held it in his demesne for four years. After that Earl William and his son Roger had it; on what terms, the men of the county do not know. Now it pays £21....

Earl Hugh's Land

In Bisley Hundred:

Earl Hugh hold Bisley, and Robert holds it from him. There are eight hides there. In demesne there are four plows, and twenty villeins and twenty-eight bordars with twenty plows. There are six male slaves and four female slaves. There are two priests and eight *radknights* who have ten plows, and twenty-three other men who pay 44s. and two sesters of honey. There are five mills there at 16s. and woodland at 20s. And in Gloucester there are eleven burgesses who pay 66d. It was worth £24; now it is worth £20.

In Longtree Hundred:

The same earl holds Westonbirt. Alnoth held it in the time of King Edward. There are three hides there which pay geld. In this hundred Leofwin held one hide.

In the same place the earl himself holds one hide at Througham. Leofnoth held it from King Edward and could go where he wished. This land pays geld. There are four bordars there with one plow and four acres of meadow. It is worth 20s.

In the same place the earl himself holds half a hide which Roger de Lacy claims at Edgeworth, as the county testifies. It is worth 10s. and pays geld.

In Witley Hundred:

The earl himself holds Chipping Camden. Earl Harold held it. Fifteen hides pay geld there. In demesne are six plows, and fifty villeins and eight bordars with twenty-one plows. There are twelve slaves and two mills at 6s. 2d. There are three female slaves there. It was worth £30; now it is worth £20.

In Longtree Hundred:

The earl himself holds two manors of four hides which pay geld, and two of his men hold them from him. Alnoth and Leofwin held them in the time of King

Edward. There was no one who could answer for these lands, but they are valued by the men of the county at £8....

Land of William Goizenboded

In Chelthorn Hundred:
William Goizenboded holds Pebworth from the king. Wulfgeat and Wulfward held it in the time of King Edward as two manors. There are six hides and one virgate there. In demesne there is one plow, and one bordar and one slave. It was worth £7; now it is worth £4 10s.

The same William holds Ullington. One thegn held it in the time of King Edward. There are five hides there. In demesne are two plows, and two villeins and one Frenchman hold one and a half hides with one plow. Earl Algar made this manor part of Pebworth. It was worth 100s.; now it is worth 40s.

In Holmford Hundred:
The same William holds Farmcote. Alwin held it. There are three hides which pay geld there. In demesne there are two plows, and four villeins with four plows, and thirteen male and female slaves. Geoffrey holds it from William. It was worth £10; now it is worth £3.

The same William holds Guiting Power. King Edward held it and leased it to Alwin his sheriff to have for his lifetime. But he did not give it as a gift, as the county testifies. When Alwin died, King William gave his wife and lands to a young man named Richard. Now Richard's successor William holds this land thus. There are ten hides, of which nine pay geld. In demesne there are four plows, and four villeins and three Frenchmen and two *radknights* and a priest, with two bordars; all the men have five plows between them. There are eleven male and female slaves and two mills at 14s. Five salt-houses there pay twenty loads of salt. In Winchcombe two burgesses pay 11s. 4d. It was worth £16; now it is worth £6.

Questions: How is the Domesday Book organized? How are people classified? What differences between towns and the countryside are evident? Which properties are most valuable? What kinds of revenue do the king and lords receive? What changes have occurred since the time of King Edward?

12. LANFRANC'S CONSTITUTIONS

In addition to bringing a whole new class of French lords to England, William the Conqueror also replaced most of the leaders of the English church with men from the continent of Europe. William appointed the eminent Lanfranc of Pavia, whose interests included monastic reform, to be the new archbishop of Canterbury and head of the English church. In the Constitutions below, written for the monks of Canterbury's cathedral, Lanfranc incorporated elements from the written rules of several well-regarded monasteries in Normandy and other parts of France.

Source: trans. D. Knowles, *The Monastic Constitutions of Lanfranc* (New York: Oxford University Press, 1951), pp. 72-5, 82-3, 85-90, 99-101, 104-107, 110-113; and trans. A.F. Leach, *Educational Charters and Documents, 598 to 1909* (Cambridge: Cambridge University Press, 1911), pp. 63-67, revised.

In the election of an abbot all, or at least the larger and more weighty part of the community, must agree upon their choice. If the abbot-elect is blessed away from home, he shall be received with a solemn procession on his return. At the two halting-places he shall lie prostrate, and when at the second halt the chant is done the bishop, if present, or his representative shall set the abbot in his stall and place. When this is done the prior (in the absence of the bishop) shall intone the *Te Deum*, and while this is being sung all the brethren shall approach in order to the kiss of peace, genuflecting before and after the kiss. Henceforward the abbot is to be treated with especial honor everywhere.

On his first attendance at chapter all who have obediences [that is, official positions] in the monastery and keep the goods of the house shall lay before his feet their keys of office; if the abbot has decided to make no change he shall entrust the offices to them again. When he bows after beginning an antiphon all the community shall bow, as also when he is named in the list in chapter (if he be present) and when he does penance for a fault in psalmody, or any other fault in choir. When he goes to read, or returns from reading, the whole community rises. When he passes through the cloister or any other place, all before whom he passes shall rise until he be past. When he enters the chapter-house and the brethren are already seated, all shall descend the steps until he is seated. Wherever he be, strict order and discipline should be kept; therefore, wherever he be, either within or without the cloister, if he take a brother to task for acting or speaking contrary to good order, he who is reprimanded shall at once humbly do penance as in chapter, and stand before him until he bid him be seated. And if the brother see him to be in anger he shall make satisfaction, doing penance before him, until he be appeased. But the abbot shall take care that he do not this before seculars.

Whenever the abbot is seated no one shall presume to sit by him unless bidden; when told to be seated the brother shall bow down to the abbot's knees and kiss them, and so humbly sit by him. Whosoever gives him anything or receives anything from him shall kiss his hand. When he enters the refectory two of the brethren shall wait upon him with water and towel. When he is in choir none shall dare to punish the children save at his bidding.

In the early morning no one shall dare to make a sound so long as he is in bed asleep. If the master of the children see that the hour is passing at which the signal is wont to be given by the prior, he should rise and rouse the children as quietly as may be, simply touching with his rod their bedclothes. This done, they shall leave the dormitory, wash and comb their hair, and after the usual prayers return to their school, sitting in silence till the abbot rises.

When he is making a stay outside the monastery, and sends the community greeting or asks for prayers, all in chapter shall bow, bending their knees to the footpace. The pope and the king are saluted in this manner also, but for other persons only a profound bow is made. When the abbot sends a command to any brother, whenever the message reaches him he is straightway to do obeisance kneeling....

Saving the reverence due in all things to the abbot, the prior, who is called the provost in the Rule, is to be honored above the other servants of God's house. He alone of the other officials takes precedence of his side of the choir in choir and chapter and refectory. He alone is incensed by the priest after the abbot at Vespers and Lauds, whensoever the choir is incensed at those hours. He shall also dispose of external matters in the abbot's absence. If the abbot be far away, he may depose from office those whom he learns to be handling their business in a way contrary to the profit of the monastery. When need arises he holds, or causes to be held, a chapter of all servants who work in the offices of the monastery, and punishment is inflicted at his order according to the deserts of those culpable. When he enters the chapter-house all rise and stand on the footpace till he sits down. If he is late and the claustral prior be already seated in the chief place, he shall not enter. If there be a matter which cannot, or should not, be put off, the claustral prior shall on his coming take the first place on the other side of the chapter-house. When he passes through the cloister or the choir those whom he passes do not rise; should he wish to sit in the cloister with the other brethren those only rise with whom he wishes to sit; but when he finds brethren seated outside the cloister they all rise....

The sacrist's office is to keep all the ornaments and utensils and furnishings of the church, and to see that the horarium is kept. On feasts of twelve lessons, after the gospel has been read in the third nocturn and during festal octaves he shall uncover the altar, and then take to the vestry the gospel book for the priest to carry when at the words *per singulos dies* he proceeds to the altar. When the priest returns from the altar to the lectern he waits upon him with a lantern and candle, and when the collect is done he receives the lantern from him and then places the gospel book upon the altar.

His task it is to ring the bells, or to instruct others how they are to be rung. He need ask permission to ring for the hours on no occasion, save only for Prime and the collation, and for Terce and Vespers, when the abbot is sitting and talking in the cloister with the brethren. He distributes candles throughout the household offices according to need, and as the abbot or prior may bid. He takes charge of the burial both of monks and laymen; he sees to what is to be done, and decides the place of burial.

It is his task twice a week, or more often if need be, to wash the chalices, and before Easter and as often as may be necessary at other times to wash the corporals [that is, communion cloths] — that is, if he be a priest or deacon. If he be not, he should tell the prior or abbot, and with his permission entrust the task to someone with the requisite order. All possible care shall be taken in washing the corporals; vessels of bronze, used for no other purpose, shall be employed, and the water in which they are washed shall be thrown into a special place like that from the chalices. While they are drying, every care shall be taken to prevent any dirt lighting upon them....

And since the sacrist's office, both in the matters mentioned and in many others which are not written here, is manifold and complicated, it should be entrusted not to one only but to many; but one shall be in command over the rest, who shall act according to his direction, reserving important decisions to the abbot or prior.

The chamberlain has the task of procuring all garments and shoes and beds and bedding which are needful for the brethren and allowed them by the Rule. He also provides razors and scissors and towels for shaving; also the towels hanging in the cloister, and the towels and handcloths and all the vessels for [Maundy Thursday]. He sees to the glazing and repairing of the dormitory windows; he provides the horseshoes for the horses of abbot and prior and those guests to whom the abbot and prior shall order that horseshoes be given. To brethren about to go on a journey he shall give capes, gaiters and spurs. Once a year he causes the straw to be renewed in all the beds, and at the same time cleans out the dormitory.

To the cellarer's office it belongs to procure all things necessary for the brethren in the way of bread and drink and all kinds of food according to the circumstances of the neighborhood. He shall provide utensils for the cellar and kitchen, and flagons and tankards and other vessels for the refectory, as well as all necessary furniture for these three places. He should be the father of the whole community, and should have a care both for the sound and still more for the sick. He shall do nothing in important affairs without taking counsel of the abbot or prior.

He should ask the cantor to give him several days' warning and acquaint him of the day when the passage in the rule referring to him is to be read in chapter, so that he may on that day make the brethren a seemly feast in the refectory; the tables of the refectory shall not however be covered for the occasion. After the aforementioned passage has been read in chapter and expounded, and when the prior has said "Let us now speak of matters of discipline," he shall at once prostrate himself in the usual place and say: "I confess that I handle this office that has been laid upon me carelessly and slackly and far otherwise than I should, and in the course of it I offend God and our elders in many things, I confess. And so for this I beg absolution of you and of the elders." When he has said this the president of the chapter shall absolve him of these offenses that he has mentioned, and of all others that he has committed, and when all have answered with all earnestness at the end, as is the custom, "Amen," he shall go to the feet of him who presides and then shall be bidden to go to his seat. When the chapter is done, and the *Verba mea* has been said, if it is to be said on that day, the brethren shall say the fiftieth psalm for the cellarer; that done, with its *Gloria* and *Pater noster* the hebdomadarian shall say *Et ne nos inducas*; *Salvum fac servum tuum*; *Dominus vobiscum*; *Oremus: Omnipotens sempiterne Deus, miserere famulo tuo*, and the rest. If they have received a death notice on that day, and are going to the church chanting *Verba mea*, they say the forementioned psalm for the cellarer with its chapters and collect before they go. But if the passage in the Rule occur for reading on a day when a feast cannot be made, as on ember days [that is, days of fasting and prayer in each season of the year] and the like; the cellarer shall ask permission of the prior and chapter to put off the feast to another day when it may be kept more adequately in seemly wise.

The brother who is appointed to receive guests should have ready in the guest-house beds, chairs, tables, towels, cloths, tankards, plates, spoons, basins and such-like — firewood also. Bread and drink and other provisions he receives of the cellarer for his guests by means of the servants at his disposal.

Whosoever wishes to speak with the abbot, prior or any monk of the cloister shall use the guestmaster as his ambassador, and he, without making a sign to anyone, shall tell the abbot or prior of the guest's wish, and then do what the superior may decide. If permission is granted to a monk of the cloister to speak with a guest, whether a relative or a stranger, it is the guest-master's business to take the monk from the cloister to the guest. If the abbot or prior is not willing that they should talk together, he must not say a word or make a sign or give the slightest nod to the brother concerned, so that he may not be able to gather at all what has happened.

It is his particular task to watch the brethren carefully when they return from obediences, to see whether they have servants of the right kind and the saddle as required by rule and if they behave with due restraint in the courtyard, so that if they do anything irregular he may accuse them of it in chapter.

If visiting clerks say they would like to dine in the refectory, it is his office to tell the abbot or prior of their desire, and if their request is granted he instructs them carefully how to behave in the refectory, and, after instructing them, when the gong is beaten he shall take them to the parlor, where the abbot, or the prior if the abbot is away, shall pour water over their hands; after this the aforesaid brother shall lead them to the abbot's table. When dinner is over and the community leaves the refectory, their guide remains alone with them after the abbot or prior has gone, and follows the procession with them until it goes out of the refectory, when he shall lead them out of the cloister saying with them in an ordinary tone of voice the psalm *Miserere*.

It is his duty also to lead strange monks who do not know the place through the cloister into the church for prayer. Death bills shall be given by him to the master of the children, and incoming ones shall be brought by him into chapter. It is his duty also to introduce into chapter seculars who are to receive confraternity. His also it is to show the buildings to those who wish to see them, taking care that the community is not then sitting in the cloister; he shall not introduce into the cloister under any circumstances anyone wearing riding-boots or spurs, nor anyone who goes barefoot or has only drawers on his legs. Finally it is his task to lead into chapter novices coming from the world, and to teach them how to make their first petition.

The almoner, either himself if occasion serve, or by means of reliable and truthful servants, shall take great pains to discover where may lie those sick and weakly persons who are without means of sustenance. If he himself goes forth to seek and visit the indigent, he shall take two servants with him, and before he enters the house to which he is going he shall cause any women who may be there to leave it. Entering the house he shall speak kindly and comfort the sick man, and offer him the best of what he has that may be needful for him. If the sick man ask for something else he shall do what he can to obtain it. He shall never enter houses in which sick or infirm women are lying, but shall send to them all necessaries that he can by means of one of his servants. But before he gives any help of the kind mentioned above he shall tell the abbot or prior, and apportion the alms of the monastery according to their decision.

The brother to whom the care of the infirmary is given, and who is set to serve the sick, shall have his own cook and separate kitchen, if the plan of the buildings and the resources of the house allow, so that he may be able to prepare what is necessary for the sick at the right times. He himself shall place before the sick brethren all the dishes prepared for them.

Every day after Compline he shall sprinkle holy water over the beds of all the sick. When the three prayers before nocturns have been said, he shall take a dark lantern and go round the beds of all the sick, seeing carefully that no one who is capable of rising shall remain in bed. It is his special duty to disclose and accuse in chapter the negligences of all who abide in the forementioned infirmary.

When he perceives a sick man is now nearing his end, it is his duty to instruct his servants to heat water to wash the body. It is his business, and that of his servants, to keep the hearse and bring it out when necessary, and to provide the board which the prior strikes once, according to custom, when the washing of the body is done. When a brother has died and has been borne into the church, he shall wash the place in which he lay and spread fresh straw or rushes.

The abbot or prior shall take every care that nothing necessary for the infirmarian's office shall ever be lacking in the infirmary....

When the penalty due for a light fault has been assigned to a brother, he eats apart from the rest at the ninth hour, if the brethren dined at the sixth, and at Vespers, if the brethren dined at the ninth hour, but he may have the same meat and drink as they, unless it has been explicitly forbidden him.

In church and chapter he shall be either in his usual place, or last of all, or somewhere between the two, according to the measure of his fault and the command of the abbot. In church he shall not celebrate Mass, nor read Epistle, Gospel or lesson; he shall not sing a responsory nor begin an antiphon, nor do anything of the kind save along with all the others; he shall not carry a candle or thurible vested; he shall not go up to make an offertory or receive the kiss of peace.

At the end of an office in choir, by day or by night, when *Kyrie eleison* is intoned, he shall prostrate himself before the step where the monks stand to receive blessings, and shall lie there until the words *Qui tecum vivit*. If a feast of twelve lessons occur, he shall cease from this penance until an ordinary day returns. While the brethren are eating in the refectory he shall be in the church.

When the abbot wishes to release him from this penance and is himself in church with the community, he shall send one of the seniors about him to the brother as he lies prostrate, who shall give him a sign from the abbot to rise. Rising at once he shall bow humbly to the abbot and go to his place. If the abbot is in chapter and the brethren make intercession, he shall say to the brother "You are released from your penance for a light fault," or something of the kind, and the brother shall rise at once and go to the feet of the abbot, and then return to his place. If the abbot be on a journey, the prior, or whoever is superior at the time, may do all this.

If a brother (which God forbid) commit a grave fault, and this become commonly known so that it cannot well be amended by private penance, the offense shall be examined before the abbot in chapter by the brethren, and the brother who is condemned by the judgment of all shall suffer severe corporal punishment, and be ordered to do penance as for a grave fault. When he has been scourged and has put on his clothing and girdle, he shall lay aside his knife, put up his hood and go in absolute silence to the place appointed, led by the brother who keeps the key. Then the abbot shall appoint one of the seniors, to whom he may safely entrust the task of guarding him; he shall lead him to the hours, and after the hours shall take him back again to his own place. After chapter this senior shall ask the abbot in private what shall be the condition of the brother's confinement, and what he shall have to eat, and when. The brother shall speak to his warden and to any others the abbot may appoint, but no one else shall associate with the penitent or speak to him.

When the bell rings for office he shall come to the church door, led by his warden and with his hood up, and if the community have not yet gone in he shall lie there prostrate until they have all entered; if they have already entered he shall stand there, bowing and kneeling as do the brethren in choir while the office is chanted; if any pass by him he shall bow humbly to them. If he see the abbot about to go by he shall prostrate himself while he passes. When the office is done he shall cover his head and prostrate himself at the feet of those who leave the church until all have passed. As they pass they shall say to him in a whisper, "God have mercy upon thee." When all are out he shall return to the place whence he came, led by his warden and with his head covered.

He shall come into chapter on days fixed by the abbot, led by the aforesaid warden, and undergo corporal punishment with humility and patience. A reasonable allowance of food and drink shall be made him, lest he be overcome by excessive hardship, and fall into melancholy. This shall be his treatment until he win pardon by his humility, patience and promise of amendment, added to the intercession of the brethren....

When anyone turns from the world to the monastic life he shall first be received like other guests in the guest-house, and when his desire is known the brother in charge of the guest-room shall report the matter to the abbot or, in the abbot's absence, to the superior for the time being. Then the abbot or prior or some spiritual brother chosen for the purpose shall speak with him, and if he see that the newcomer's desire is from God, the matter shall be made known to the brethren in chapter, and, when their counsel has been given, if the abbot deems that he should be received, he shall come into chapter on a day fixed, led by the aforesaid guest-master, who shall have instructed him in the form of the petition he is to make. Prostrating in the usual place, when he is asked what he would say, he shall answer in the most humble wise, and make petition in these or similar words: "I ask for the mercy of God, and to be of your company and to be accounted a brother of this house, and I desire to become a monk of this monastery, and to serve God here." The abbot, or he who presides in his stead, shall answer: "May almighty God grant you the fellowship and company of his chosen ones," and the whole community shall answer "Amen." Then he shall be bidden to rise, and shall be told of all things hard and harsh which those who wish to live a devout and regular life endure in this estate, as well as the things harder and harsher which may befall them if they bear themselves disorderly. If, when he has heard this, he still stands fast in his intent, and promises that he will be ready to endure still harder and harsher things, he who presides at chapter shall answer him: "May the Lord Jesus Christ so make perfect in you what you promise for His love, that you may win His grace and life eternal." To this all shall answer "Amen," and he shall continue: "And we for the sake of His love grant you on such conditions what you ask with such humility and constancy." On this the novice shall go and humbly kiss his feet. Then at his command the novice-master shall lead him into the church, and there he shall sit by an altar outside the choir and wait till the chapter is done.

After that his aforesaid master shall lead him into the chamberlain's cell, or some other room more convenient for what is to be done. Before this, however, he shall receive the tonsure, if he is a layman, with its accompaniment of blessings with antiphons and psalms and collects as ordained. This shall be done either in church before the introit of the Mass on the step where the brethren ordinarily receive blessings, or in the chapel of the infirmary, or in the abbot's chapel, according as the abbot think fit. Then the novice, whether clerk or layman, shall be led to the place aforesaid and there shall be shorn and shaved in monastic fashion; then he shall put off his secular clothes and put on the regular monastic habit, save for the cowl, including the hood sewn to the tunic. While this is being done, the seven penitential psalms shall be said in monotone by brethren who have been appointed to do this. Thus dressed, he shall be taken to the community: if he is a clerk, he shall sit last among the clerks; if a layman, last among the lay monks; and in processions likewise. In chapter and refectory he shall take his place according to the time of his conversion.

He shall sleep in the cell of the novices, or, if the monastery have no such special cell, in the dormitory. He shall not read in public, nor sing anything alone, nor make offering at Mass, nor receive the kiss of peace. In the cloister he shall sit apart with his master, in a place appointed for the novices, and none shall speak to him or make a sign to him without leave of his master; this master shall be such a one as may by the example of his life and by the words of his teaching give him good advice for his soul and teach him our way of life....

When many days have passed, if the brethren approve of his behavior and he of their way of life, he is to be told by his master to ask the prior and some of the elders to intercede for him with the abbot that he may be blessed and make profession. If the abbot is willing to bless him, on the day fixed, when the sermon in chapter is done, he shall prostrate in the usual place and, thus lying, shall make petition to be blessed. After he has been bidden to rise, he shall again be told of all the hard and difficult things in our way of life that have been appointed by the holy fathers. If he answer that he is ready to endure all these things, and harder still if need be, the abbot shall ask the brethren who sit with him what they think, and whether they grant that his prayers should be heard. When they reply that they grant this willingly, he shall say "And I too grant it in the name of the Lord." ...

If a child is to be offered to the monastery he shall be tonsured, and then, bearing in his hands a host and chalice with wine in it, as is the custom, he shall be offered by his parents after the Gospel to the priest celebrating Mass. When his offering has been received by the priest, his parents shall wrap the child's hands in the cloth which covers the altar and which hangs down in front, and then the abbot shall accept him. When this is done the parents shall straightway promise before God and his saints that the child shall never abandon the monastic life through their agency or that of anyone representing them, and that they will never knowingly give him anything that might lead to his ruin. This promise shall have been previously written down and witnessed, and now they shall make it verbally and then place it on the altar.

When this is done the abbot shall bless a cowl and, taking off the child's cloak or tippet of fur or any other kind of smock he may be wearing, shall say, "May the Lord strip thee of the old man," as above, and, clothing him with the cowl, shall continue, "May the Lord clothe thee with the new man," and the rest. Then the child shall be taken to be shaven and clad in the monastic fashion. When he has grown up and is to make his profession, all is done as described previously for the case of one coming into the monastery from the world, save that the part which has been done already should not be repeated.

When each day the smallest bell begins to ring for chapter, all the brethren sitting in choir shall at once rise and stand facing the east and waiting, while the brethren elsewhere in the monastery shall enter the choir. No one at that time shall hold a book, nor read nor look at a book; no one shall for any reason whatever remain seated in the cloister; but when the bell ceases to ring all in order shall follow their leader out of church.

When the brethren are seated in chapter the superior gives a sign, and the reader, after asking a blessing, reads and gives out the customary lesson and notices. Then, after the sermon, the superior says, "Let us now speak of matters of discipline." If anyone is accused who bears a name common to one or more others, and the accuser does not make it absolutely definite beyond doubt, then all of that name shall at once arise and humbly offer themselves for penance, until the accuser says clearly whom he means to accuse. This he shall do by specifying, if possible, the dignity in order or office, as follows: "Dom Edward the priest," or "deacon," or "subdeacon," or "sacristan," or "master of the children or juniors," or something of the sort; he shall not say "Dom Edward the archdeacon," or "of London," or any surname that he bore in the world.

The accuser shall not, during the chapter in question, inflict punishment on him he accuses. The brother who is lying prostrate shall, when questioned in the usual way, answer *mea culpa*, save when he is asking for confraternity, or is resigning office, or when one is asking prayers for a relative, father, mother, brother or sister, who has died recently, and since he entered the monastery, or when one or more intercede for a brother doing penance for a grave fault, or when a brother is departing for a long journey, or when something great and difficult and beyond his powers is put upon a brother. In this, and similar cases, he should answer, "I ask the mercy of God, and your mercy, and I beseech etc.," as circumstances require.

He who is to undergo punishment shall be scourged either with a single stout rod while he lies in his shift on the ground, or with a bundle of finer rods while he sits with his back bare. In each case he is punished at the discretion of the superior, who should consider the degree and the magnitude of the fault. While he is being scourged all the brethren should bow down with a kindly and brotherly compassion for him. No one should speak, and no one look at him save for the seniors who may make intercession for him. No one who is accused may in the same chapter accuse his previous accuser. The abbot or prior shall appoint him who is to administer punishment, taking care that neither child, nor junior, nor novice is bidden.

No one shall speak privately in chapter with another, or with several. Whatever is said shall be heard by the superior and the whole community. Only matters of utility and pertaining to the religious life shall be discussed; while one is speaking the rest shall keep silence; no one shall interrupt a speaker save the president, who may bid a speaker have done if it seem to him that his words are too many or to no purpose. When the president begins to speak, even if one is already speaking he shall cease, and absolute silence shall be preserved by all present....

The prior ought to make a noise to waken the brethren at such hour in the morning as the boys when they have said their several prayers can see to read in the cloister, and when they begin to read let them for some time read aloud, sitting separate from each other, so that one cannot touch another with his hands or clothes. No child shall dare to make a sign or say a word to another except in the sight and hearing of the master; nor get up from the place in which he sits unless told or given leave to do so.

Wherever the children go there should be a master between every two of them. When they pass in front of the brethren they should bow to them, and the brethren remaining seated should do the same. One lantern should serve for two; if there are three, the third should carry a second lantern; if there are more, the same arrangement should be observed.

They should not put anything into anyone's hand or take anything from anyone's hand, except in the case of the abbot, the senior prior, or their own master, and that not everywhere but only in proper places, where it cannot or ought not to be otherwise. The precentor, too, when he is in their school may give or take from them a book from which to sing or read. If they are serving at the altar, too, they can give or take as their orders require.

They should be flogged in a chapter of their own, as their elders are in the great chapter. When they go to confession they should go to the abbot or prior or those specially assigned for the purpose by the abbot. While one confesses another should sit on the steps, and the master should sit close by outside the chapter-house.

If they go into the refectory after the verse which is said before food, or into choir at the hours after the Gloria of the first psalm, they are to go to their places and bow as usual, while their master is to go to the place set apart for those who are tardy: but the boy who waits at the abbot's table is not to have any abstinence from food or drink imposed on him except by the abbot's orders. But if by his orders it is imposed, either he must be pardoned or he must be removed from the abbot's table.

In choir, if the abbot is there, no one may strike them, no one order them out except by his direction. When he is away, the precentor may chastise them for things to do with his office, and the prior for other things, in which they behave childishly. Wherever they are, no one except the persons above-mentioned may make signs to them, no one may smile at them. No one shall go into their school, no one shall speak to them anywhere, unless leave to go in or to talk to them has been given by the abbot or prior.

They are never to read or do anything else in bed at midday but to cover themselves up and keep quiet. A monk of more than ordinary gravity and discretion shall be master over the other masters, one who may know how, when he has heard any charge against them, to inflict punishment in moderation on those who are at fault or to let them off. When they go to bed the masters shall stand by them at night with lighted candles until they are covered up.

Young men, whether those who have been brought up in the monastery or those coming in from the outside world, who are given in charge to masters, shall be looked after in most things as is before provided with regard to the boys. They shall, as is above said, sit separate from each other; shall never leave the place in which they are kept, except with the monk who has charge of them; shall carry lanterns in pairs; and shall make confession to no one but the abbot or prior, unless by special arrangement.

At the midday rest they shall not read or write, or do any work; but cover themselves up and keep quiet; they shall have their beds before or between their masters' beds. If they have to get up, they shall first wake their master, then light a lantern, if it is night, and go to the necessarium with their master.

No one shall be allowed to sit in the place assigned to them except the abbot, the prior and their masters; nor make any communication to them by words or signs, except with the leave of the abbot or prior; and when leave is given the master ought to sit between the youth and the one who is talking to him. No youth is to talk to another, except so that the master may hear and understand what is said by both of them. The masters ought to sit between them or in front of them, so as to be able to see them, if they want to. When they go to bed the masters ought to stand in front of them until they lie down and are covered over, and at night, with lighted candles.

In the monastery, in chapter, refectory and processions they are to be mixed up with the elder monks, and, if necessary, without regard to the order of their admission. If they read at table, or are serving in the kitchen, when the brethren get up from table they shall go with them into the monastery, and when "And lead us not into temptation" has been said shall return with their keepers to the refectory. No two or more [ordinary brothers] of the convent shall stay with them, if possible; but if the scarcity of older monks or the greater numbers of the young ones require it, a sufficient number shall be assigned to take charge of them.

But if the method of taking care of the youths which prevails in some monasteries is preferred, that, namely, they shall sit singly in different and separate places about the cloister, each custodian shall have his separate charge, one or more together, if their number is so great as to demand it, and each singly shall carry a lantern at night. A custodian shall never leave his charge, without confiding him to another of the brethren in whom he has full confidence. In a word all the care shall be shown them as above described....

Questions: Who are the officials of the monastery, and what are their duties? How do the Constitutions express the monks' vows of poverty, chastity, and obedience? How do these practical rules facilitate worship, prayer, and contemplation? What was life like for the younger members of the community? How would monastic life compare with life in the secular world?

13. ORDERIC VITALIS'S ACCOUNT OF HIS LIFE

Orderic Vitalis (1075-c.1142), one of the great historians of the Anglo-Norman world, ended his lengthy history with the following brief account of his own life. It is included here as an example of the experience of a child born after the Conquest, to an English mother and Norman father, and of a common type of monastic career, that of a child oblate, in the last quarter of the eleventh century.

Source: trans. M. Chibnall, *The Ecclesiastical History of Orderic Vitalis* (Oxford: Oxford University Press), vol. VI, pp. 551-557.

Now indeed, worn out with age and infirmity, I long to bring this book to an end, and it is plain that many good reasons urge me to do so. For I am now in the sixty-seventh year of my life and service to my Lord Jesus Christ, and while I see the princes of this world overwhelmed by misfortunes and disastrous setbacks I myself, strengthened by the grace of God, enjoy the security of obedience and poverty…. I give thanks to thee, supreme King, who didst freely create me and ordain my life according to thy gracious will. For thou art my King and my God, and I am thy servant and the son of thine handmaid, one who from the beginning of my life has served thee as far as I was able. I was baptized on Holy Saturday at Atcham, a village in England on the great river Severn. There thou didst cause me to be reborn of water and the Holy Spirit by the hand of Orderic the priest, and didst impart to me the name of that priest, my godfather. Afterwards when I was five years old I was put to school in the town of Shrewsbury, and performed my first clerical duties for thee in the church of St. Peter and St. Paul the apostles. There Siward, an illustrious priest, taught me my letters for five years, and instructed me in psalms and hymns and other necessary knowledge. Meanwhile thou didst honor this church on the river Meole, which belonged to my father, and didst build a holy monastery there through the piety of Earl Roger. It was not thy will that I should serve thee longer in that place, for fear that I might be distracted among kinsfolk, who are often a burden and a hindrance to thy servants, or might in some way be diverted from obeying thy law through human affection for my family. And so, O glorious God, who didst command Abraham to depart from his country and from his kindred and from his father's house, thou didst inspire my father Odelerius to renounce me utterly, and submit me in all things to thy governance. So, weeping, he gave me, a weeping child, into the care of the monk Reginald, and sent me away into exile for love of thee and never saw me again. And I, a mere boy, did not presume to oppose my father's wishes, but obeyed him willingly in all things, for he promised me in thy name that if I became a monk I should taste of the joys of Paradise with the Innocents after my death. So with this pact freely made between me and thee, for whom my father spoke, I abandoned my country and kinsfolk, my friends and all with whom I was acquainted, and they, wishing me well, with tears commended me in their kind prayers to thee, O almighty God, Adonai. Receive, I beg thee, the prayers of these people and, O compassionate God of Sabaoth, mercifully grant what they asked for me.

And so, a boy of ten, I crossed the English Channel and came into Normandy as an exile, unknown to all, knowing no one. Like Joseph in Egypt, I heard a language which I did not understand. But thou didst suffer me through thy grace to find nothing but kindness and friendship among strangers. I was received as an oblate monk in the abbey of Saint-Évroul by the venerable Abbot Mainer in the eleventh year of my age, and was tonsured as a clerk on Sunday, 21 September. In place of my English name, which sounded harsh to the Normans, the name Vitalis was given me, after one of the companions of St. Maurice the martyr, whose feast was being celebrated at that time. I have lived as a monk in that abbey by thy favor for fifty-six years, and have been loved and honored by all my fellow monks and companions far more than I deserved. I have labored among thy servants in the vineyard of the choice vine, bearing heat and cold and the burden of the day, and I have waited knowing that I shall receive the penny that thou hast promised, for thou dost keep faith. I have revered six abbots as my fathers and masters because they were thy vicars: Mainer and Serlo, Roger and Warin, Richard and Ralph. These men have all been lawfully appointed to rule the abbey of Saint-Évroul, they have carefully and diligently guided internal and external affairs, knowing that they must render account for me and all the others, and by thy help and guidance they have provided for all our needs. On 15 March, when I was sixteen years old, at the command of Serlo, abbot elect, Gilbert, bishop of Lisieux, ordained me subdeacon. Then two years later, on 26 March, Serlo, bishop of Séez, laid the stole of the diaconate on my shoulders, and I gladly served thee as a deacon for fifteen years. At length in my thirty-third year William, archbishop of Rouen, laid the burden of priesthood on me on 21 December. On the same day he also blessed two hundred and twenty priests, with whom I reverently approached thy holy altar, filled with the Holy Spirit; and I have now loyally performed the sacred offices for thee with a joyful heart for thirty-four years....

Questions: How does Orderic's account of his life reflect the times he lived in and his profession? What is his attitude toward his childhood? Does this account give a different impression of the life of child oblates from that in Lanfranc's Constitutions?

CHAPTER TWO

THE TWELFTH CENTURY

Fig. 22: The Seal of Henry I A nineteenth-century engraving of the great seal of King Henry I (1100-1135). Seals were used by medieval kings, and increasingly by other individuals, to authenticate documents, much as signatures are used today. In a pattern typical of the Norman kings, Henry is shown enthroned as king of England on the front and mounted as duke of Normandy on the reverse.

14. HENRY I'S CORONATION CHARTER

To help secure his slightly shaky claim to the throne by enlisting the good will of barons and church, Henry I (1100-35) issued at the time of his coronation a document often known as the Charter of Liberties. Capitalizing on the unpopularity in church circles of his brother and predecessor, William II (1087-1100), Henry promised to abandon William's high-handed practices and be in every way a good king by following the good customs of the past. The Coronation Charter was not innovative in its content, but it established a tradition for Henry's successors, who found that they were expected to issue similar documents when they took the throne, and eventually it was one of the precedents contributing to Magna Carta.

Source: trans. G.C. Lee, *Source-Book of English History: Leading Documents* (New York: Henry Holt and Company, 1900), pp. 125-127; revised.

In the year of the incarnation of the Lord 1101, Henry, son of King William, after the death of his brother William, by the grace of God, king of the English, to all faithful, greeting:

1. Know that by the mercy of God, and by the common counsel of the barons of the whole kingdom of England, I have been crowned king of the same kingdom; and because the kingdom has been oppressed by unjust exactions, I, from regard to God, and from the love which I have toward you, in the first place make the holy church of God free, so that I will neither sell nor place at rent, nor, when archbishop, or bishop, or abbot is dead, will I take anything from the domain of the church, or from its men, until a successor is installed into it. And all the evil customs by which the realm of England was unjustly oppressed will I take away, which evil customs I partly set down here.

2. If any of my barons, earls, or others who hold from me shall have died, his heir shall not redeem his land as he did in the time of my brother, but shall relieve it by a just and legitimate relief. Similarly also the men of my barons shall relieve their lands from their lords by a just and legitimate relief.

3. And if any one of the barons or other men of mine wishes to give his daughter in marriage, or his sister or niece or relation, he must speak with me about it, but I will neither take anything from him for this permission, nor forbid him to give her in marriage, unless he should wish to join her to my enemy. And if, when a baron or other man of mine is dead, a daughter remains as his heir, I will give her in marriage according to the judgment of my barons, along with her land. And if when a man is dead his wife remains, and is without children, she shall have her dowry and right of marriage, and I will not give her to a husband except according to her will.

4. And if a wife has survived with children, she shall have her dowry and right of marriage, so long as she shall have kept her body legitimately, and I will

not give her in marriage, except according to her will. And the guardian of the land and children shall be either the wife or another one of the relatives as shall seem to be most just. And I require that my barons should deal similarly with the sons and daughters or wives of their men.

5. The common tax on money which used to be taken through the cities and counties, which was not taken in the time of King Edward, I now forbid altogether henceforth to be taken. If anyone shall have been seized, whether a moneyer or any other, with false money, strict justice shall be done for it.

6. All fines and debts which were owed to my brother, I remit, except my rightful rents, and except those payments which had been agreed upon for the inheritances of others or for those things which more justly affected others. And if anyone for his own inheritance has stipulated anything, this I remit, and all reliefs which had been agreed upon for rightful inheritances.

7. And if any one of my barons or men shall become feeble, however he himself shall give or arrange to give his money, I grant that it shall be so given. Moreover, if he himself, prevented by arms, or by weakness, shall not have bestowed his money, or arranged to bestow it, his wife, or his children or his parents, and his legitimate men shall divide it for his soul, as to them shall seem best.

8. If any of my barons or men shall have commited an offense he shall not give security to the extent of forfeiture of his money, as he did in the time of my father, or of my brother, but according to the measure of the offense so shall he pay, as he would have paid from the time of my father backward, in time of my other predecessors; so that if he shall have been convicted of treachery or of crime, he shall pay as is just.

9. All murders moreover before that day in which I was crowned king, I pardon; and those which shall be done henceforth shall be punished justly according to the law of King Edward.

10. The forests, by the common agreement of my barons, I have retained in my own hand, as my father held them.

11. To those knights who hold their land by military service, I yield of my own gift the lands of their demesne plows free from all payments and from all labor, so that as they have thus been favored by such a great alleviation, so they may readily provide themselves with horses and arms for my service and for the defense of my kingdom.

12. A firm peace in my whole kingdom I establish and require to be kept from henceforth.

13. The law of King Edward I give to you again with those changes with which my father changed it by the counsel of his barons.

14. If anyone has taken anything from my possessions since the death of King William, my brother, or from the possessions of anyone, let the whole be

immediately returned without alteration, and if anyone shall have retained anything thence, he upon whom it is found will pay it heavily to me. Witnesses
Maurice, bishop of London, and Gundulf, bishop, and William, bishop-elect,
and Henry, earl, and Simon, earl, and Walter Giffard, and Robert de Montfort,
and Roger Bigod, and Henry de Port, at London, when I was crowned.

*Questions: What message is the king trying to send with this document? Why does he
refer several times to King Edward? What are the main areas of tension between the
king and the church? Between the king and his barons?*

15. EADMER'S ACCOUNT OF
QUEEN EDITH-MATILDA

*Another of Henry I's moves to strengthen his hand at the beginning of his reign was his
marriage to Edith, a princess of the Scottish and Anglo-Saxon royal families. But there
was a problem: Edith was living in the convent of Wilton — perhaps as a nun. The following account of the matter was written by a close associate of Archbishop Anselm.
Released from the nunnery, Edith changed her name to the Norman "Matilda" upon her
marriage to the king.*

Source: trans. G. Bosanquet, *Eadmer's History of Recent Events in England: Historia Novorum in Anglia*
(London: The Cresset Press, 1964), pp. 126-131.

A few days after this Matilda, the daughter of Malcolm, most noble king of the
Scots and of Margaret, who is known to have been descended from the old
kings of the English, married this Henry, king of England. Now Margaret herself was a daughter of Edward, son of King Edmund, who was a son of King
Ethelred, son of that glorious King Edgar of whom mention was made at the
very beginning of this work. Although the matter of this union has, as some
may perhaps think, no bearing on the intended purpose of this work, yet, as it
was handled by Anselm, for he both married them with his blessing and also
consecrated her as queen, I think I ought briefly to describe how this came
about. I am particularly anxious to do this because quite a large number of
people have maligned Anselm saying, as we have ourselves heard them do, that
in this matter he did not keep to the path of strict right. Now it is true that this
Matilda was brought up from early childhood in a convent of nuns and grew
up there to womanhood, and many believed that she had been dedicated by
her parents to God's service as she had been seen walking abroad wearing the
veil like the nuns with whom she was living. This circumstance, when, long
after she had discarded the veil, the king fell in love with her, set the tongues of
very many wagging and held back the two from embracing one another as

Fig. 23: Edith Matilda King Henry I's queen, whose decision to leave a convent in order to marry the king is described by Eadmer, is shown here in a nineteenth-century engraving drawn from a statue in the west doorway of Rochester Cathedral.

they desired. Accordingly, as all were looking for a sign from Anselm on this question, the girl herself went to him and humbly besought his advice and help in the matter. He, alluding to the rumor which was going about, declared that he was not to be induced by any pleading to take from God his bride and join her in marriage to an earthly husband. She replied denying absolutely that she had been so dedicated. She denied too that she had ever at any time been veiled with her own consent and declared that, if it was necessary to convince him, she would prove it at the judgment seat of the whole English church. "But, that I did wear the veil," she said, "I do not deny. For, when I was quite a young girl and went in fear of the rod of my Aunt Christina, whom you knew quite well, she to preserve me from the lust of the Normans which was rampant and at that time ready to assault any woman's honor, used to put a little black hood on my head and, when I threw it off, she would often make me smart with a good slapping and most horrible scolding, as well as treating me as being in disgrace. That hood I did indeed wear in her presence, chafing at it and fearful; but, as soon as I was able to escape out of her sight, I tore it off and threw it on the ground and trampled on it and in that way, although foolishly, I used to vent my rage and the hatred of it which boiled up in me. In that way, and only in that way, I was veiled, as my conscience bears witness. And if anyone says that I was dedicated, of that too the truth may be gathered from the fact, which is known to many persons still living, that my father, when by chance he saw me veiled snatched the veil off and tearing it in pieces invoked the hatred of God upon the person who had put it on me, declaring that he had rather have chosen to marry me to Count Alan than consign me to a house of nuns. That is my answer to the slanders which are spread abroad about me. This I ask your Wisdom to consider and to do for me as your Fatherhood knows should be done." To cut the story short, Anselm refrained from giving an immediate decision and declared that the case ought to be determined by the judgment of the chief persons of religion in the kingdom. So at his bidding on an appointed day the bishops, the abbots, and all the nobles and the leading men of the religious profession assembled in the manor of St. Andrew of Rochester, named Lambeth, to which he himself had then come for the treatment of this question.

In due order the case was brought up for discussion. From various sources credible witnesses came forward declaring that the simple truth supported the girl's story. Besides these came two archdeacons, William of Canterbury and Hambald of Salisbury, whom Father Anselm had sent to Wilton where the girl had been brought up to make enquiries to see what was known with certainty on this matter. They declared in the hearing of the whole assembly that they had made most careful enquiries of the sisters and that they had not been able to gather from them anything at all which was inconsistent with the account given. Accordingly Anselm warned them and charged them all by their Christian duty of obedience that no one of them should let favor or fear pervert his judgment but that each one, realizing that it was indeed God's cause, should to the best of his ability give help to secure that the matter should be rightly decided "lest," he said, "and God forbid that it should be so, there go forth a judicial sentence such that it may be a precedent in the future for either depriving anyone unfairly of his liberty or of wrongly defrauding God of what is rightly his." They all with acclamation signified that this was what should be done and promised that they would not fail to do so. The father then withdrew from the assembly by himself. This representative assembly of the church of England then discussed the question of the decision which should be pronounced. When this had been done Anselm was reverently escorted back into the assembly and what was the finding upon the matter on which they were all agreed, was then declared. They said that having looked carefully into the matter it seemed to them established, and of this they stated they were prepared to provide proof, that under the circumstances of her case the girl could not rightly be bound by any decision to prevent her being free to dispose of her person in whatever way she legally wished to do so. "Although," they said, "we should have no difficulty in proving this by simple reasoning, yet, since this is unnecessary, we refrain from doing so, holding, as we do, that more reliable than any reasons of ours is a like decision pronounced in a similar case by your predecessor of revered memory, our father and master, Lanfranc. When the great Duke William first conquered this land, many of his men, pluming themselves on so great a victory and considering that everything ought to yield and submit to their wishes and lusts, began to do violence not only to the possessions of the conquered but also where opportunity offered to their women, married and unmarried alike, with shameful licentiousness. Thereupon a number of women anticipating this and fearing for their own virtue betook themselves to convents of sisters and taking the veil protected themselves in their company from such infamy. Thus when after a time this violence had quieted down and, considering the nature of the times, comparative peace had been restored in the land, the question was asked of that Father Lanfranc what view he took of the treatment of those who had safeguarded their chastity by taking such refuge, that is, whether or not they should be bound to remain in the convent and keep the veil which they had taken. This question he with the advice of a general Council resolved by giving judgment that to those women who had by their conduct so clearly testified their devotion to virtue should be accorded the honor due to them for their chastity rather than that they should be forced to keep to the life of the convent, unless they chose it of their own free will." The speakers added: "We took part in these proceedings and have also heard this judgment approved by men of wisdom. We are anxious that this decision should hold good in the present case and ask that it be confirmed. Though we realize that her case is less serious than theirs, seeing that, while all wore the veil for the like cause, they did so of their own accord, she under compulsion; yet, that no one may think that we are influenced by favor towards anyone, we do not want in giving judgment to go further but are content to rest our decision on this alone, that what held good in the more serious case should hold good in the less serious."

Then Anselm referring to these findings said: "You know the warning and the charge which I gave you and the promise that you made. Seeing then that you have unanimously given judgment as seemed to you to be most just, as you assure me you have, I do not reject your judgment, I accept it with all the more confidence, as I am told that it is supported by the authority of so great a Father." Then the girl was brought into the assembly. Calmly she hears and appreciates what has taken place and petitions that she be given audience to make a brief statement. Then speaking aloud she offered to prove by oath or by any other process of ecclesiastical law that her story as already described was in accordance with the real truth of the matter. This she declared that she would do, not as thinking that they did not believe her, but to cut away any opportunity for ill-affected persons to utter any scandal in the future. They replied that there was no need for any such thing, as, if an evil man out of the evil treasure of his heart brought forth evil things, he would immediately be silenced, as the truth had been proved and established by the consensus of opinion of so many persons of position. After this, having obtained an interview with Anselm and his blessing, she departed and a few days later became, as I have said, wife and queen.

When this union was due to be made and established in accordance with the ritual of the church and all the nobility of the realm and the people of lesser degree were come together for this ceremony and were crowding round the king and the maid in front of the doors of the church, Father Anselm himself standing raised up above the crowd instructed them all how the girl's case, about which there had been so much talk, had been enquired into and determined by the bishops and persons of the kingdom professed in religion. He then on divine authority gave them warning and charged them that if anyone was on this matter aware of anything contrary to what the judgment had decided, so that it could be shown that according to the Christian law this union ought not to be made, he should without any hesitation and without incurring the displeasure of anyone openly declare it. At this they all cried out with one accord that the matter had been rightly decided and that there was now no ground on which anyone, unless possibly actuated by malice, could properly raise any scandal. Thereupon the pair were joined together in lawful matrimony with the dignity befitting king and queen.

So there, as my conscience truly bears witness, I have described in due sequence what took place, as I being myself present heard and saw it all, have described it without inclining to either side, simply setting out the girl's story without asserting whether it was true or not. If then anyone still chooses to say that in this matter Anselm did anything which was not right, let him beware. We at any rate who have known his inmost heart in this and many other difficulties bear him witness that, as he himself used to say, he had not at that time either the knowledge or the ability to enable him to act more rightly or more justly than he in fact did.

Questions: What does Edith-Matilda's testimony tell us of conditions immediately after the Norman Conquest? What was her adolescence like, and how did she escape from that world? What does the story reveal about attitudes toward the monastic life and toward marriage? What were the concerns of the investigators? What is the author's intent?

16. WILLIAM OF MALMESBURY'S HISTORY OF RECENT EVENTS

Although he had literally dozens of illegitimate children, Henry I left no legitimate son, and after his death his daughter and heir Matilda was shouldered aside by her cousin Stephen (1135-54), against whom she then waged a lengthy civil war. The following account, by one of twelfth-century England's finest chroniclers, was dedicated to Matilda's illegitimate half-brother Robert, earl of Gloucester, who emerges as the hero in this version. This excerpt covers the period in which Matilda came closest to deposing Stephen and becoming England's first queen regnant. (Matilda is known as "the empress" because her first marriage was to the German emperor; after his death, she married Count Geoffrey of Anjou.)

Source: trans. J.A. Giles, *William of Malmesbury's Chronicle of the Kings of England, from the Earliest Period to the Reign of King Stephen* (London: Henry G. Bohn, 1847), pp. 481-483, 490-493, 498, 505-507, 509-511, 515-525; revised.

In the twenty-seventh year of his reign, in the month of September, King Henry came to England, bringing his daughter [the empress Matilda] with him. But, at the ensuing Christmas, convening a great number of the clergy and nobility at London, ... he turned his thoughts on a successor to the kingdom. On which subject, having held much previous and long-continued deliberation, he now at this council compelled all the nobility of England, as well as the bishops and abbots, to make oath, that, if he should die without male issue, they would, without delay or hesitation, accept his daughter Matilda, the former empress, as their sovereign: observing how, prejudicially to the country, fate had snatched away his son William, to whom the kingdom by right had pertained: and that his daughter still survived, to whom alone the legitimate succession belonged, from her grandfather, uncle, and father, who were kings; as well as from her maternal descent for many ages back.... All therefore, in this council, who were considered as persons of any note, took the oath: and first of all William, archbishop of Canterbury; next the other bishops, and the abbots in like manner. The first of the laity who swore was David, king of Scotland, uncle of the empress; then Stephen, earl of Mortain and Boulogne, nephew of King Henry by his sister Adala: then Robert the king's son, who was born to him before he came to the throne, and whom he had created earl of Gloucester, bestowing on him in marriage Mabel, a noble and excellent woman; a lady devoted to her husband, and blessed in a numerous and beautiful offspring. There was a singular dispute, as they relate, between Robert and Stephen, contending with rival virtue, which of them should take the oath first; one alleging the privilege of a son, the other the dignity of a nephew....

[After King Henry's death in 1135,] Stephen earl of Mortain and Boulogne, nephew of King Henry, as I have before said, who, after the king of Scotland, was the first layman that had sworn fidelity to the empress, hastened his return into England by Whitsand. The empress, from certain causes, as well as her brother, Robert earl of Gloucester, and almost all the nobility, delayed returning to the kingdom. However, some castles in Normandy, the principal of which was Domfront, espoused the party of the heiress. Moreover, it is well known, that, on the day on which Stephen disembarked in England, there was, very early in the morning, contrary to the nature of winter in these countries, a terrible peal of thunder, with most dreadful lightning, so that the world seemed well-nigh about to be dissolved. He was received, however, as king, by the people of London and of Winchester, and gained over also Roger bishop of Salisbury, and William Pont de l'Arche, the keepers of the royal treasures. Yet, not to conceal the truth from posterity, all his attempts would have been vain, had not his brother, Henry bishop of Winchester, who is now legate of the papal see in England, granted him his entire support: allured indeed by the fullest expectation that Stephen would follow the example of his grandfather William in the management of the kingdom, and more especially in the strictness of ecclesiastical discipline. In consequence, when Stephen was bound by the rigorous oath which William archbishop of Canterbury required from him, concerning restoring and preserving the liberty of the church, the bishop of Winchester became his pledge and surety. The written tenor of this oath, I shall be careful hereafter to insert in its proper place.

Stephen, therefore, was crowned king of England on Sunday [December 22,] the eleventh before the kalends of January, the twenty-second day after the decease of his uncle, A.D. 1135, in the presence of three bishops, that is, the archbishop, and those of Winchester and Salisbury; but there were no abbots, and scarcely any of the nobility. He was a man of activity, but imprudent: strenuous in war; of great mind in attempting works of difficulty; mild and compassionate to his enemies, and affable to all. Kind, as far as promise went; but sure to disappoint in its truth and execution. Whence he soon afterwards neglected the advice of his brother, befriended by whose assistance, as I have said, he had supplanted his adversaries and obtained the kingdom....

In the same year, after Easter, Robert earl of Gloucester, of whose prudence Stephen chiefly stood in awe, came to England. While he was yet resident in Normandy, he had most earnestly considered, what line of conduct he should determine upon in the present state of affairs. If he became subject to Stephen, it seemed contrary to the oath he had sworn to his sister; if he opposed him, he saw that he could nothing benefit her or his nephews, though he must grievously injure himself. For the king, as I said before, had an immense treasure, which his uncle had been accumulating for many years. His coin, and that of the best quality, was estimated at a hundred thousand pounds; besides which, there were vessels of gold and silver, of great weight, and inestimable value, collected by the magnificence of preceding kings, and chiefly by Henry. A man possessed of such boundless treasures could not want supporters, more especially as he was profuse, and, what by no means becomes a prince, even prodigal.... Stephen, indeed, before he came to the throne, from his complacency of manners, and readiness to joke and sit, and regale, even with low people, had gained so much on their affections, as is hardly to be conceived: and already had all the nobility of England willingly acknowledged him. The most prudent earl therefore was extremely desirous to convince them of their misconduct, and recall them to wiser sentiments by his presence; for he was unable to oppose Stephen's power, from the causes aforesaid: indeed he had not the liberty of coming to England, unless, appealing as a partaker of their revolt, he dissembled for a time his secret intentions. He did homage to the king, therefore, under a certain condition; namely, so long as he should preserve his rank entire, and maintain his engagements to him; for having long since scrutinized Stephen's disposition, he foresaw the instability of his faith....

In the year 1139, the venom of malice, which had long been nurtured in the breast of Stephen, at length openly burst forth. Rumors were prevalent in England, that earl Robert was on the very eve of coming from Normandy with his sister: and when, under such an expectation, many persons revolted from the king, not only in inclination but in deed, he avenged himself for this injury, at the cost of numbers. He, also, contrary to the royal character, seized many at court, through mere suspicion of hostility to him, and obliged them to surrender their castles, and accede to any conditions he prescribed....

[In late September of that year], Earl Robert, having at length surmounted every cause of delay, arrived with the empress his sister in England, relying on the protection of God and the observance of his lawful oath; but with a much smaller military force than any other person would have required for so perilous an enterprise; for he had not with him, at that time, more than one hundred and forty horsemen.... [and] proceeded through the hostile country to Bristol accompanied, as I have heard, by scarcely twelve horsemen, and was joined in the midst of his journey by Brian Fitz-Count of Wallingford.... [He] committed the empress to Henry bishop of Winchester and Waleran earl of Meulan for safe conduct, a favor never denied to the most inveterate enemy, by honorable soldiers. Waleran, indeed, declined going farther than Calne, but the bishop continued his route. The earl, therefore, quickly collecting his troops, came to the boundary appointed by the king, and placed his sister in safe quarters at Bristol. She was afterwards received into Gloucester by Miles, who held the castle of that city under the earl in the time of King Henry, doing him homage and swearing fidelity to him; for this is the chief city of his county....

The whole country then around Gloucester to the extremity of Wales, partly by force, and partly by favor, in the course of the remaining months of that year, gradually espoused the party of their sovereign the empress. The owners of certain castles, securing themselves within their fastnesses, awaited the outcome of events. The city of Hereford was taken without difficulty; and a few soldiers, who, determined on resistance, had thrown themselves into the castle, were blocked up. The king drew nigh, to devise means for their assistance, if possible; but frustrated in his wishes, he retired with disgrace. He also approached Bristol, and going beyond it, burnt the neighborhood around Dunstore, leaving nothing, as far as he was able, which could minister food to his enemies, or advantage to anyone....

The whole of this year [1140] was embittered by the horrors of war. There were many castles throughout England, each defending their neighborhood, but, more properly speaking, laying it waste. The garrisons drove off from the fields both sheep and cattle, nor did they abstain either from churches or church-yards. Seizing such of the country people as were reputed to be possessed of money, they compelled them, by extreme torture, to promise whatever they thought fit. Plundering the houses of the wretched husbandmen, even to their very beds, they cast them into prison; nor did they liberate them, except upon their giving every thing they possessed or could by any means scrape together for their release. Many calmly expired in the midst of torments inflicted to compel them to ransom themselves, bewailing, which was all they could do, their miseries to God. And, indeed, at the instance of the earl, the legate, with the bishops, repeatedly excommunicated all violators of church-yards and plunderers of churches, and those who laid violent hands on men in holy or monastic orders, or their servants: but this his attention profited but little. It was distressing, therefore, to see England, once the fondest cherisher of peace and the single receptacle of tranquillity, reduced to such a pitch of misery, that not even the bishops, nor monks, could pass in safety from one town to another. Under King Henry, many foreigners, who had been driven from home by the commotions of their native land, were accustomed to resort to England, and rest in quiet under his fostering protection: in Stephen's time, numbers of free-booters from Flanders and Brittany flocked to England, in expectation of rich pillage. Meanwhile, the earl of Gloucester conducted himself with caution, and his most earnest endeavors were directed to gaining conquests with the smaller loss to his adherents. Such of the English nobility as he could not prevail upon to regard the obligation of their oath, he held it sufficient if he could so restrain, that, if they did not assist, they would not injure the cause: being willing, according to the saying of the comic writer, "To do what he could, when he could not do what he would." But when he saw the opportunity present itself, he strenuously performed the duty both of soldier and of general: more especially, he valiantly subdued those strongholds which were of signal detriment to the cause he had espoused; that is to say, Harptree, which king Stephen had taken from certain soldiers of the earl before he came to England, and many others: Sudley, Cerney, which the king had garrisoned, as I have said; and the castle which Stephen had fortified over against Wallingford, he leveled to the ground. He also, in these difficult times, made his brother Reginald earl of Cornwall. Nor indeed did the king show less spirit in performing the duties of his station; for he omitted no occasion of repeatedly beating off his adversaries, and defending his own possessions. But he failed of success, and all things declined, for lack of justice. Dearth of provisions, too, increased by degrees, and the scarcity of good money was so great, from its being counterfeited, that sometimes, out of ten or more shillings, hardly a dozen pence would be received. The king himself was reported to have ordered the weight of the penny, as established in King Henry's time, to be reduced because, having exhausted the vast treasures of his predecessor, he was unable to provide for the expense of so many soldiers. All things, then, became venal in England: and churches and abbeys were no longer secretly, but even publicly exposed to sale.

During this year, in Lent, on [March 20,] the thirteenth before the kalends of April, at the ninth hour of the fourth day of the week, there was an eclipse throughout England, as I have heard. With us, indeed, and with all our neighbors, the obscuration of the sun was so remarkable, that persons sitting at table, as it then happened almost everywhere, for it was Lent, at first feared that chaos was come again: afterwards learning its cause, they went out, and beheld the stars around the sun. It was thought and said by many, not untruly, that the king would not continue a year in the government....

At length, on [February 2,] the day of the Purification of the blessed Mary, [the earl of Gloucester and his army] arrived [in Lincolnshire] at the river flowing between the two armies, called the Trent, which, from its springs, together with floods of rain, had risen so high, that it could not possibly be forded. Here, at last, disclosing his intention to his son-in-law, who had joined him with a strong force, and to those he had brought with him, he added that he had long since made up his mind, never to be induced to fly, be the emergency what it might; if they could not conquer, they must die or be taken. All encouraged him to hope the best; and, wonderful to hear, though on the eve of hazarding a battle, he swam over the rapid river I have mentioned, with the whole of his party. So great was the earl's ardor to put an end to calamity, that he preferred risking extremities to prolonging the sufferings of the country. The king, too, with many earls, and an active body of cavalry, abandoning the siege, courageously presented himself for battle. The royalists began the prelude to the fight, which they call the "joust," as they were skilled in that exercise: but when they saw that the earl's party, if they may be so called, did not attack from a distance with lances, but at close quarters with swords, and broke the king's ranks with violent and determined onset, the [king's] earls, to a man, for six of them had entered the conflict, together with the king, attempted to ensure their safety by flight. A few barons, of laudable fidelity and valor, who would not desert him, even in his necessity, were made captive. The king, though he by no means wanted spirit to defend himself, being at last attacked on every side by the earl of Gloucester's soldiers, fell to the ground by a blow from a stone; but who was the author of this deed is uncertain. Thus, when all around him were either taken or dispersed, he was compelled to yield to circumstances and become a captive. On which the truly noble earl of Gloucester commanded the king to be preserved uninjured, not suffering him to be molested even with a reproach; and the person, whom he had just before fiercely attacked when dignified with the sovereignty, he now calmly protected when subdued: that the tumults of anger and of joy being quieted, he might show kindness to his relation, and respect the dignity of the diadem in the captive. The citizens of Lincoln were slaughtered on all sides by the just indignation of the victors....

The king, according to the custom of such as are called captives, was presented to the empress, at Gloucester, by her brother, and afterwards conducted to Bristol. Here, at first, he was kept with every mark of honor, except the liberty of going at large: but in succeeding time, through the presumption of certain persons, who said openly and falsely, that it did not behove the earl to treat the king otherwise than they chose; and also because it was reported that having either eluded or bribed his keepers, he had been found, more than once, beyond the appointed limits, more especially in the night-time, he was confined with fetters.

In the meanwhile, both the empress and the earl dealt by messengers with the legate his brother, that he should forthwith receive her [as queen] into the church, and to the kingdom, as the daughter of King Henry, to whom all England and Normandy had sworn allegiance.... By means of negotiators on either side, the business was so far forwarded, that they agreed to meet in conference, on an open plain on this side of Winchester. They assembled therefore on the third Sunday in Lent [March 2], a day dark and rainy, as though the fates would portend a woeful change in this affair. The empress swore, and pledged her faith to the bishop, that all matters of importance in England, and especially the bestowing of bishoprics and abbeys, should await his decision, if he, with the holy church, would receive her as sovereign, and observe perpetual fidelity towards her. Her brother Robert, earl of Gloucester, swore as she did, and pledged his faith for her, as did also Brian fitzCount, lord marcher of Wallingford, and Miles of Gloucester, afterwards earl of Hereford, with some others. Nor did the bishop hesitate to receive the empress as sovereign of England,

and, together with certain of his party, to pledge his faith that, so long as she did not infringe the covenant, he would observe his fidelity to her. On the morrow, which was the fifth before the nones of March [March 3], a splendid procession being formed, she was received in the cathedral of Winchester: the bishop-legate conducting her on the right side, and Bernard, bishop of St. David's, on the left. There were present also Alexander, bishop of Lincoln, Robert of Hereford, Nigel of Ely, Robert of Bath: the abbots Ingulf of Abingdon, Edward of Reading, Peter of Malmesbury, Gilbert of Gloucester, Roger of Tewkesbury, and some others. In a few days, Theobald, archbishop of Canterbury, came to the empress at Winchester, by invitation of the legate: but he deferred promising fidelity to her, deeming it beneath his reputation and character to change sides, till he had consulted the king. In consequence, he, and many other prelates, with some few of the laity, were allowed to visit Stephen and converse with him: and, graciously obtaining leave to submit to the exigency of the times, they embraced the sentiments of the legate. The empress passed Easter, which happened on [March 30,] the third before the kalends of April, at Oxford; the rest returned to their respective homes.

On [April 8,] the day after the octaves of Easter, a council began, with great parade, at Winchester, consisting of Theobald, archbishop of Canterbury, all the bishops of England, and many abbots: the legate presiding. Such as were absent, accounted for it by messengers and letters. As I was present at the holding of this council, I will not deny posterity the truth of every circumstance; for I perfectly remember it. On the same day, ... the legate called the bishops apart, and discoursed with them in secret of his design; then the abbots and, lastly, the archdeacons were summoned. Of his intention nothing transpired publicly, though what was to be done engrossed the minds and conversation of all....

On the fourth day of the week the Londoners came: and being introduced to the council, urged their cause, so far as to say, that they were sent from the fraternity, as they call it, of London, not to contend, but to entreat that their lord the king might be liberated from captivity: that all the barons, who had long since been admitted to their fellowship, most earnestly solicited this of the lord legate and the archbishop, as well as of all the clergy who were present. The legate answered them copiously and clearly: and, that their request might be the less complied with, his speech of the preceding day [in favor of making the empress queen] was repeated, with the addition, that it did not become the Londoners, who were considered as the chief people of England, in the light of nobles, to side with those persons who had deserted their lord in battle; by whose advice the king had dishonored the holy church: and who, in fact, only appeared to favor the Londoners, that they might drain them of their money.

In the meantime, a certain person, whose name, if I rightly remember, was Christian, a clerk belonging to the queen, as I heard, rose up, and ... read [a] letter in their hearing: of which this was the purport. "The queen earnestly entreated the whole clergy assembled, and especially the bishop of Winchester, the brother of her lord, to restore the said lord to his kingdom, whom abandoned persons, and even such as were under homage to him, had cast into chains." To this suggestion, the legate answered to the same effect as to the Londoners....

It was now a work of great difficulty to soothe the minds of the Londoners: for though these matters, as I have said, were agitated immediately after Easter, yet was it only a few days before the nativity of St. John [June 24] that they would receive the empress. At that time a great part of England readily submitted to her government.... The lord legate, too, appeared of laudable fidelity in furthering the interests of the empress. But, behold, at the very moment when she imagined she should get possession of all England, every thing was changed. The Londoners, ever suspicious and murmuring among themselves, now burst out into open expressions of hatred: and, as it is reported, even laid in wait for their sovereign and her nobles. Aware of and escaping this plot, they gradually retired from the city, without tumult and in a certain military order.... The Londoners, learning their departure, flew to their residence and plundered every thing which they had left in their haste.

Not many days after, a misunderstanding arose between the legate and the empress which may be justly considered as the melancholy cause of every subsequent evil in England.... Offended at [her refusal to take his advice], he kept from her court many days; and though repeatedly sent for, persisted in refusing to go thither. In the meanwhile, he held a friendly conference with the queen, his brother's wife, at Guildford, and being wrought upon by her tears and concessions, bent his mind to the liberation of Stephen. He also [spoke against the empress:] that she wished to seize his person; that she observed nothing which she had sworn to him; that all the barons of England had performed their engagements towards her, but that she had violated hers, as she knew not how to use her prosperity with moderation.

To allay, if possible, these commotions, the earl of Gloucester, with a retinue not very numerous, proceeded to Winchester; but, failing in his endeavors, he returned to Oxford, where his sister had for some time established her residence. She therefore understanding, as well from what she was continually hearing, as from what she then learned from her brother, that the legate had no friendly dispositions towards her, proceeded to Winchester with such forces as she could muster.... [Meanwhile the legate] sent for all such as he knew were well-disposed to the king. In consequence almost all the earls of England came; for they were full of youth and levity, and preferred military enterprise to peace. Besides, many of them were ashamed at having deserted the king in battle, as has been said before, and thought to wipe off the ignominy of having fled, by attending this meeting. Few, however, attended the empress ... [and] the roads on every side of Winchester were watched by [King Stephen's] queen and the earls who had come with her, lest supplies should be brought in to those who had sworn fidelity to the empress. The town of Andover also was burned. On the west, therefore, necessities were procured but scantily and with difficulty, ... the Londoners lending every possible assistance [to the legate], and omitting no circumstance which might distress [the empress]. The people of Winchester were, though secretly, inclined to her side, regarding the faith they had before pledged to her, although they had been in some degree compelled by the bishop to such a measure. In the meanwhile combustibles were hurled from the bishop's castle on the houses of the townspeople, who, as I have said, rather wished success to the empress than to the bishop, which caught and burned the whole abbey of nuns within the city, and the monastery which is called Hyde without the walls.... The abbey of nuns at Wherwell was also burned by one William de Ypres, an abandoned character who feared neither God nor man, because some of the partisans of the empress had secured themselves within it.

In the meantime, the earl of Gloucester, though suffering, with his followers, by daily contests with the royalists, and though circumstances turned out far beneath his expectation, yet ever abstained from the burning of churches, notwithstanding he resided in the vicinity of St. Swithun's. But unable to endure any longer the disgrace of being, together with his party, almost besieged, and seeing fortune inclining towards the enemy, he deemed it expedient to yield to necessity; and, having marshaled his troops, he prepared to depart. Sending his sister, therefore, and the rest, in the vanguard, that she might proceed without interruption, he himself retreated gradually, with a chosen few, who had spirit enough not to be alarmed at a multitude. The earls immediately pursuing him, as he thought it disgraceful, and beneath his dignity to fly, and was the chief object of universal attack, he was made captive. The rest, especially the chiefs, proceeded on their destined journey, and, with the utmost precipitation, reached Devizes.... [The earl] never consented to negotiate his liberation, except with the knowledge of his sister. At last the affair was thus decided: that the king and himself should be liberated on equal terms: no condition being proposed except that each might defend his party, to the utmost of his abilities, as before.... [On the appointed] day, the king, released from his captivity, left his queen, and son, and two of the nobility at Bristol, as sureties for the liberation of the earl; and came with the utmost speed to Winchester, where the earl, now brought from Rochester, whither he had first been taken, was at this time confined. The third day after, when the king came to Winchester, the earl departed, leaving there on that day his son William, as a pledge, till the queen should be released. Performing with quick despatch the journey to Bristol, he liberated the queen, on whose return, William, the earl's son, was set free from his detention. It is, moreover, sufficiently well known that, although, during the whole of his captivity and of the following months till Christmas, he was enticed by numberless and magnificent promises to revolt from his sister, yet he always deemed his fraternal affection of greater importance than any promise which could be made him. For leaving his property and his castles, which he might have quietly enjoyed, he continued unceasingly near the empress at Oxford, where, as I have said before, fixing her residence, she held her court....

Questions: What factors caused the civil war of Stephen's reign? How does the author describe the conditions of warfare? What rules of noble conduct do we see in operation here? How does the author defend the earl of Gloucester's actions? How are King Stephen and Matilda the empress depicted here? Why, when Matilda had come so close to the throne, did she lose her chance?

17. FOUNDATION DOCUMENTS OF GODSTOW ABBEY

The founding of monastic houses, including communities for women, was a prominent feature of the twelfth century and continued uninterrupted during the long civil war of Stephen's reign. The first document below is from a fifteenth-century English version of the records of Godstow Abbey in Oxfordshire, translated for the nuns because they were then unable to read the Latin and French originals. The charters which follow are among the most typical medieval records, preserved by monasteric communities to prove their rights to properties bestowed on them by their benefactors. John de St. John is generally thought to have been Ediva's most important ally in founding Godstow. The final document printed here is an unusually full example of an entrance charter, recording the dedication of new nuns and the dowries they brought with them.

Source: Chronicle modernized from *The English Register of Godstow Nunnery, Near Oxford*, ed. A. Clark (London: Early English Text Society, 1905), pp. 26-27; charters trans. E. Amt from *Monasticon Anglicanum*, ed. W. Dugdale (London, 1846), vol. 4, pp. 362-364.

Godstow Chronicle

In Winchester there was a lady born of the worthiest blood of this realm; she was called Dame Ediva. Her father and mother had no other children, but only her, and because of that, she was more loved and cherished. She was fair and comely, and was well with the King Almighty; and later was married to a knight, Sir William Launcelene. By the grace of God they had three children together, who were very fair and graceful, one son and two daughters; the son was abbot of Abingdon.

Now of the lady I shall tell you, in what manner and in what way she lived in God's service. After the death of her husband it often came to her by a vision that she should go near to the city that was called Oxford, and there she should abide until she should see a sign from the King Almighty, showing how and in what way she should build a place for God's service. To Binsey [near Oxford] this lady came, as had been shown to her in a vision during her prayers; there she dwelt and lived a very holy life. Then one night she heard a voice, which said to her what she should do: "Ediva, Ediva, arise, and go without delay, there where the light of heaven alights on earth from the firmament, and there ordain nuns to the service of God, twenty-four of the finest gentlewomen that you can find." And thus was this abbey first founded. Now this lady next went to the king, Henry I, and showed him everything that God had sent her in a vision. When the king had heard all that she would say, between them they discussed how and in what way they might bring this good deed to completion. And so they were busy in God's service, [working out] how they might best build a church for the worship of God, and of our Lady, and St. John the Baptist.

Now is this lady, Dame Ediva, the abbess in her church, and twenty-four ladies with her. Of her two daughters, the eldest — Dame Emma was her name — was the prioress of this house; and Dame Hawise, the second daughter, was the second prioress as long as she lived. Now they are commended to God, of the Mother born, who for us sinners would vouchsafe to die. May he grant us, if it please him, to come to his joy.

Charter from John de St. John, c. 1135

To Alexander, bishop of Lincoln, and all the barons of Oxfordshire, both clerical and lay, John de St. John sends greetings. Let it be known to you that I have granted to the nun Ediva, and to all the nuns of her congregation dwelling there, or to their successors, the land of Godstow, and all that belongs to it, firmly and peacefully, in perpetual alms, for the souls of my father and mother, and for the souls of my ancestors, who acquired that land. And after the death of the said Ediva let the nuns have no abbess in that place except one from the same congregation. Witnesses: Alexander, bishop of Lincoln; Robert d'Oilli; Walter the archdeacon; William the dean; Master R.; Q. the chaplain; A. the priest; Walchevius; Warin; R. Hareng; G. de Mont; G. Lovell; Hugh Talmage; Ralph the clerk. And this was confirmed in the presence of the bishop of Salisbury.

Confirmation Charter from the Bishop of Lincoln, c. 1138

Alexander, by God's grace bishop of Lincoln, to all faithful members of the holy church, greetings. Blessed be God, whose name is glorious throughout all ages, who, just as he always multiplies his church with new fruit, so illuminates it in our time with the new light of holy religion when new churches are founded by the growing devotion of the faithful, to his own praise, since every soul blesses and praises God in every place of his dominion. Though he is always and everywhere marvelous in his saints, marvels declare the working of his virtue in the venerable convent of holy women who, wearing the holy habit, live in Godstow by the foresight and under the rule of a remarkable matron devoted to God, Ediva, who prudently built the church of that place, from the first stone onwards, at her own expense and labor and with the collected alms of the faithful, in honor of the holy Virgin Mary, mother of God, and of the blessed St. John the Baptist, and with the help of God brought it to conclusion. But if there is joy — or rather, because there certainly is joy — among God's angels over one sinner who repents, much more is it so over the innumerable aforementioned handmaidens of Christ, present and future, whose whole life will be repentance, wholly fixed on God; their life is on earth but their manner of living is that of heaven. They, living in the flesh but beyond flesh, have eternally vowed themselves to Christ the bridegroom, and crucifying their fleshly desires either have no experience of the vices of the flesh or avoid them through resistance. To the dedication of this church, celebrated in the year 1138 A.D., in the fourth year of the reign of the most pious King Stephen in England, came the aforesaid king and his wife Queen Matilda, and earls and barons and also bishops, Theobald, archbishop of Canterbury, Roger, bishop of Salisbury, Simon, bishop of Worcester, Robert, bishop of Exeter, Robert, bishop of Bath, and Algar, bishop of Constance, from amongst whom I, Alexander (who, at God's command, was in charge of governing that general parish of St. Mary, the mother church of Lincoln, being the third bishop in that seat, and the aforesaid brothers being my suffragans), as minister, with the help and grace of the Holy Spirit, completed the dedication of the convent. And since we cannot deny the testimony of truth to those things which were done in our presence, by the evidence of these present letters we make known to all, present and future, that the things written below, which the same church holds as dowry, were offered, given, and granted by the faithful with such devotion that the example of those going before might cause the minds of those following to be moved. The king gave from his own demesne 100 shillings' worth of land in the neighborhood which is called Walton, and his wife Queen Matilda gave ten marks, and Eustace their son gave 100s. in money until he has land; and Theobald, archbishop of Canterbury, gave 100 shillings' worth of land. And

I, Alexander, bishop of Lincoln, gave 100s. from the tolls of Banbury. And Robert, bishop of Exeter, gave 40s. in two churches, that is 20s. in the church of St. Mary in Gloucester, and 20s. in Faringdon. And Roger, bishop of Salisbury, gave a certain mill which is called Boy Mill, with the land which lies next to it. And the abbot of Westminster gave 60s. And Ingulf, abbot of Abbingdon, gave 60s., and John de St. John gave one mill worth £4 in Wolvercote and the tenements of two men with appurtenances, and a piece of land in front of the gate of the said church in the island which lies between two waters, and half of a meadow called Lambey. Robert d'Oilli gave the other half of the same meadow, namely Lambey, and one measure of grain each year, and Miles, constable of Gloucester, gave 20 shillings' worth of land. And the citizens of Oxford gave the land in Port Meadow which Sagrun held. Robert, earl of Leicester, and his wife Countess Amice gave 60 shillings' worth of land in Halse. And Hugh of Tew gave nine shillings' worth of land in Oxford. And Sevarus gave seven shillings' worth in the same vill and nine shillings' worth in London, in East Cheap. And Roger de Almari gave the sowing of 25 acres each year in Bletchingdon, and the same amount of fallow. And Walter of Perry gave one virgate of land and five acres in the same vill. And Reginald de St. Valéry gave and granted Herringsham and Boyham and one fishpond with appurtenances, and the whole island between the two bridges and the aforesaid things which John de St. John gave at the dedication of the aforesaid church. And Elwin son of Godegose gave the church of St. Giles which is outside Oxford, and from the other part of the same vill towards Abingdon he gave 18 shillings' worth of land. Robert of Wytham gave a piece of meadow next to the church of Godstow. Ralph son of Roger gave five shillings' worth of land in Shipton, Nicholas Basset gave one hide of land in Rissington, and Simon of Odell gave half of the church of Pateshull with appurtenances. King Stephen also granted them [permission to hold] a three-day fair at the festival of St. John the Baptist [August 29]. And Walter, archdeacon of Oxford, gave them a tithe of his demesne in Cutteslowe. All these things Lord Alberic, bishop of Ostia, who then acted as legate of the holy Roman church in England, sanctioned with apostolic authority. These things King Stephen strengthened with the privilege of royal power. These things Archbishop Theobald and our whole gathering of bishops confirmed with episcopal authority, and thus we all, by equal consent, equal vow, and one voice, decided that whoever shall by rash enterprise presume to encroach upon, take away, diminish or change for the worse any of the benefits with which the aforesaid church shall have been endowed or by which it shall yet be, by God's will, canonically enriched in the future, will lie under anathema, unless he shall do suitable penance. By apostolic exchange, Lord Alberic the legate granted pardon from one year of penance to the donors of the aforesaid benefits, and forty days' penance each year to all who shall visit the same church with devout heart on the day of St. Prisca the virgin [January 18] or on the nativity of St. John the Baptist [June 24]. And we, the canons of St. Mary the mother church of Lincoln, subscribing to the letters of our bishop, Alexander, bless God for his gifts, and we grant the prayers of our humility to all who shall visit that church during the aforesaid festivals for the pious love of God and shall with the support of their gifts comfort the aforesaid handmaids of Christ serving God.

Charter from Vincent of Wytham, c. 1160

May all people present and future know that I, Vincent of Wytham, have granted and by this my present charter confirmed to God and to the church of St. Mary and St. John the Baptist at Godstow, and to the nuns serving God there, the land called Medley, which my father Robert gave to the said church in perpetual alms with his three daughters to be nuns in that church. Moreover I, Vincent, with the assent and consent of my wife Matilda and of my heirs, have given and granted to God and the aforesaid church, with my two daughters consecrated to God there, five acres of meadow from my own inheritance, which meadow is called Revenere, with all its appurtenances, freely and peacefully, for the redemption of my soul and of my ancestors, in perpetual alms. These are the witnesses: Thomas and Eustace and Ralph the priests; Richard the parson of Wytham; John the clerk; Robert, William, and John, my sons; Richard de Vallibus; William of Baghurst; Robert son of Goldwin; Lawrence de Clera; and many others.

Questions: Is Ediva's family a typical one? What are the concerns and motivations of the individuals granting the charters? What are the roles of women and men in the establishment of Godstow? What kind of relationships do women and men have in these documents?

18. GERALD OF WALES'S DESCRIPTION OF HENRY II

One of the dominant figures in twelfth-century Europe, Henry II (1154-1189), son of the Empress Matilda, left multiple legacies to England: in law and justice, in finance and administration, and in relations between the king and his vassals and between the royal government and the church. Here the historian Gerald of Wales, who knew him, describes the king.

Source: trans. E.P. Cheyney, *Readings in English History Drawn from the Original Sources* (Boston: Ginn and Company, 1922), pp. 137-139, with additional material trans. E. Amt from *Giraldi Cambrensis Opera*, ed. J.F. Dimock (London: Longmans, Green, Reader, and Dyer, 1867), pp. 303-306.

Henry II, king of the English, was a man of ruddy complexion, large, round head, piercing, blue-gray eyes, fierce and glowing red in anger, with fiery face and a harsh voice. He was short of neck, square of chest, strong of arm, and fleshy in body. By nature rather than from over-indulgence he had a large paunch, yet not such as to make him sluggish. For he was temperate in food and drink, sober and inclined to be prudent in all things so far as this is permitted to a leader. And that he might overcome this unkindness on the part of nature by diligence, and lighten the fault of the flesh by greatness of spirit, often by an internal warfare, as it were conspiring against himself, he exercised his body with unbounded activity. Besides, wars frequently occurred; in these he was pre-eminent in action and gave himself not a moment of rest. In times of peace as well, he took no rest or quiet for himself. Immoderately devoted to hunting, he went out at early dawn on a swift horse. Now descending into the valleys, now penetrating the forests, now ascending the peaks of mountains, he spent his days in activity; when he returned to his home in the evening, either before or after the meal one rarely saw him seated. Then after such strenuous exertion on his part he used to weary the whole court by continual marches. But since this is most useful in life: "nothing to excess," and no remedy is purely good, so he accelerated other problems in his body with frequent swelling of his hands and feet, increased by abuse to these limbs sustained in riding; and if nothing else, he certainly hastened old age, the mother of all ills.

He was a man of medium height, a thing which could not be said of any of his sons — the two elder a little exceeding medium height, while the two younger remained below that stature. Setting aside the activities of his mind and his impulse to anger, he was chief among the eloquent, and — a thing which is most conspicuous in these times — he was most skilled in letters; a man easy to aproach, tractable, and courteous; in politeness second to none. A leader so strong in sense of duty that, as often as he conquered in arms, he himself was more often conquered by his sense of justice. Strenuous in war, in

Fig.24: Effigies of Henry II and Eleanor of Aquitaine King Henry II (1154-89) and Queen Eleanor are shown here in nineteenth-century engravings drawn from their tomb effigies at the abbey of Fontévrault in Anjou. From the time of William the Conqueror until the early thirteenth century, most English kings were buried in religious establishments in their French, rather than their English, territories. Eleanor brought Henry her inheritance, the large and rich duchy of Aquitaine in southern France, when she married him in 1152 after divorcing the French king, Louis VII.

peace he was cautious. Often in martial affairs he shrank from the possible disasters of war, and tried wisely all things before resorting to arms. He wept over those lost in the line of battle more than their leader; he was more gentle to the dead soldier than to the living, mourning with much greater grief over the dead than winning the living with his love. When disasters threatened, none was kinder; when security was gained, no one was more severe. Fierce towards the unconquered, merciful towards the conquered; strict towards those at home, easy towards strangers; in public lavish, prudent in private. If he had once hated a man, rarely afterwards would he be fond of him, scarcely ever would he hate one whom he had once loved. He was especially fond of hawking; he was equally delighted with dogs, which followed wild beasts by sagacity of scent, taking pleasure as well in their loud sonorous barkings as in their swift speed. Would that he had been as much inclined to devotion as he was to hunting!

After the grave enmity with his sons, instigated, it is said, by their mother, he was a public violator of his marriage vows. With a natural inconstancy, he often and freely broke his word. For whenever matters became difficult, he preferred to break his promise rather than turn from what he was doing, and he would sooner hold his words invalid than abandon his deeds. In all his actions he was prudent and moderate; and on account of this, the remedy going somewhat too far, he was dilatory in doing right and justice, and, to the great harm of his people, he was slow to respond in such matters. And justice should be freely granted, according to God, but justice which is priceless came at a price, and everything available was for sale at a high price and for a profit, so that both the kingdom and the church were heirs of Gehazi.

He was a most diligent maker and keeper of peace; he was incomparable in giving alms, especially for the support of the land of Palestine. He was a lover of humility, an enemy of fame and pride. "He filled the hungry with good things, and the rich he sent empty away. He exalted the meek and cast down the mighty from their seats."

He presumed detestably to usurp things which are God's; zealous for justice, though not from knowledge, he joined the rights of the kingdom to those of the church, gathering both to himself. Although he was a son of the church and had drawn from her the honor of his position, either unmindful or inattentive to the holy power which had been conferred upon him, he devoted scarcely any time to divine services; and even this little time, perhaps on account of great affairs of state and for the sake of the public welfare, he consumed more in plans and talk than in true devotion. The revenues of the vacant sees he diverted into the public treasury. The mass became corrupted by the working of the leaven, and while the royal purse kept receiving that which Christ demands as his own, new troubles kept arising. In the meantime he kept pouring out the universal treasure, giving to a wicked soldiery what ought to have been given to the priesthood.

Very wisely he planned many things, arranging them carefully. These affairs did not always result successfully — in fact, they often turned out quite the opposite. But never did any great disaster occur which did not spring from causes connected with his family. As a father he enjoyed the childhood of his children with natural affection; through their elder years, however, looking at them more as a stepfather. And although great and famous sons were his, nevertheless they were a hindrance to his perfect happiness. Perhaps this was according to his deserts, since he always pursued his successors with hatred. And since human prosperity is neither permanent nor perfect, by extreme ill fortune, where he ought have found joy, he found conflict; where security, strife; where peace, ruin; where fortitude, ingratitude; where rest and tranquility, the greatest disquiet and disturbance. Whether because of some fault in marriage, or as punishment for some parental misdeed, there was never peace between the father and his sons or among the sons themselves. But having summarily subdued the foes of the kingdom and the disturbers of peace, brothers and sons, natives and foreigners, he saw all that followed go according to his will. If only he had also, by the proper service of good works, finally recognized this ultimate divine favor.

Whomsoever he once had carefully observed, although surrounded daily by so great a number, he never afterwards forgot. Whatever he heard anywhere which was worthy of being remembered, he never allowed to slip from his memory. He thus had at hand ready knowledge on almost all historical subjects, and experience in almost all affairs. And to conclude these remarks by a few additional words, if he had been finally elected by God, and would finally turn himself to allegiance to him, among the leaders in the world he would be incomparable on account of his many gifts of nature.

Questions: Which elements of this portrait seem to be standard traits associated with any king? Which have the ring of reality? What does Gerald admire in the king, and what does he criticize? Why? What aspects of Henry's character would most appeal to the twelfth-century public?

19. THE CONSTITUTIONS OF CLARENDON

One of Henry II's projects was the standardization of legal procedures, and to this end he wished to assert more authority over the church, whose system of ecclesiastical courts were felt to offer excessive protection to clergy who broke the law. In 1164 Henry sought the agreement of church leaders to the Constitutions of Clarendon, which had been drafted by royal officials and which Henry, somewhat disingenuously, claimed were merely a restatement of well-established customs governing relations between the English church and government. But Thomas Becket, archbishop of Canterbury, balked at approving the Constitutions, and thus began his famous quarrel with the king.

Source: trans. H. Gee and W.G. Hardy, *Documents Illustrative of the History of the English Church* (London: Macmillan, 1910), pp. 68-72; revised.

In the year 1164 from our Lord's Incarnation, the fourth of the pontificate of Alexander, the tenth of Henry II, most illustrious king of the English, in the presence of the same king, was made this remembrance or acknowledgment of a certain part of the customs, liberties, and dignities of his ancestors, that is of King Henry his grandfather, and of others, which ought to be observed and held in the realm. And owing to strifes and dissensions which had taken place between the clergy and justices of the lord king and the barons of the realm, in respect of customs and dignities of the realm, this recognition was made before the archbishops and bishops and clergy, and the earls and barons and nobles of the realm. And these same customs recognized by the archbishops and bishops, and earls and barons, and by those of high rank and age in the realm, Thomas, archbishop of Canterbury, and Roger, archbishop of York, and Gilbert, bishop of London, and Henry, bishop of Winchester, and Nigel, bishop of Ely, and William, bishop of Norwich, and Robert, bishop of Lincoln, and Hilary, bishop of Chichester, and Jocelyn, bishop of Salisbury, and Richard, bishop of Chester, and Bartholomew, bishop of Exeter, and Robert, bishop of Hereford, and David, bishop of St. David's, and Roger, elect of Worcester, conceded, and by word of mouth steadfastly promised on the word of truth, to the lord king and his heirs, should be kept and observed in good faith and without evil intent, these being present: Robert, earl of Leicester, Reginald, earl of Cornwall, Conan, earl of Brittany, John, earl of Eu, Roger, earl of Clare, Earl Geoffrey de Mandeville, Hugh, earl of Chester, William, earl of Arundel, Earl Patrick, William, earl of Ferrers, Richard de Luci, Reginald de St. Valery, Roger Bigot, Reginald de Warenne, Richer de Aquila, William de Braose, Richard de Camville, Nigel de Mowbray, Simon de Beauchamp, Humphry de Bohun, Matthew de Hereford, Walter de Mayenne, Manser Biset the steward, William Malet, William de Courcy, Robert de Dunstanville, Jocelin de Balliol, William de Lanvallei, William de Caisnet, Geoffrey de Vere, William de Hastings, Hugh de Moreville, Alan de Neville, Simon son of Peter, William Maudit the chamberlain, John Maudit, John Marshall, Peter de Mara, and many other magnates and nobles of the realm, as well clerical as lay.

Now of the acknowledged customs and dignities of the realm a certain part is contained in the present document, of which part these are the chapters:

1. If controversy shall arise between laymen, or clergy and laymen, or clergy, regarding advowson and presentation to churches, let it be treated or concluded in the court of the lord king. *HIGH COURT*

2. Churches belonging to the fee of the lord king [that is, churches on the royal demesne] cannot be granted in perpetuity without his own assent and grant. *ULTIMATE CROWN CONTROL*

3. Clerks cited and accused of any matter shall, when summoned by the king's justice, come into his own court to answer there concerning what it shall seem to the king's court should be answered there, and in the church court for what it shall seem should be answered there; yet so that the king's justice shall send into the court of holy church to see in what way the matter is there treated. And if the clerk be convicted, or shall confess, the church must not any longer protect him. *LAY AND CLERICAL CRIME*

4. Archbishops, bishops, and parish clergy of the realm are not allowed to leave the kingdom without licence of the lord king; and if they do leave, they *treason* shall, if the king so please, give security that neither in going nor in staying nor in returning, will they seek the ill or damage of the lord king or realm.

5. Excommunicate persons are not to give pledge for the future, nor to take oath, but only to give security and pledge of abiding by the church's judgment that they may be absolved.

6. Laymen are not to be accused save by proper and legal accusers and witnesses in the presence of the bishop, so that the archdeacon does not lose his right nor anything due to him thence. And if the accused be such that no one wills or dares to accuse them, the sheriff, when requested by the bishop, shall cause twelve lawful men from the neighborhood or the town to swear before the bishop that they will show the truth in the matter according to their conscience. *JURY*

7. No one who holds of the king in chief, and none of his demesne officers are to be excommunicated, nor the lands of any one of them to be put under an interdict unless first the lord king, if he be in the country, or his justice if he be outside the kingdom, be applied to in order that he may do right for him; and so that what shall appertain to the royal court be concluded there, and that what shall belong to the church court be sent to the same to be treated there.

8. In regard to appeals, if they shall occur, they must proceed from the archdeacon to the bishop, and from the bishop to the archbishop. And if the archbishop fail in showing justice, they must come at last to the lord king, that by his command the dispute be concluded in the archbishop's court, so that it must not go further without the assent of the lord king.

9. If a dispute shall arise between a clerk and a layman, or between a layman and a clerk, whether a given tenement is held in free alms or as a lay fee, it shall be concluded by the consideration of the king's chief justice on the award of twelve lawful men, whether the tenement is held in free alms or as a lay fee, before the king's justiciar himself. And if the award be that it is held in free alms, it shall be pleaded in the church court, but if to the lay fee, unless both claim under the same bishop or baron, it shall be pleaded in his own court, so that for making the award he who was first seised [that is, in possession] lose not his seisin until the matter be settled by the plea.

10. If anyone of a city, or castle, or borough, or a demesne manor of the lord king, be cited by archdeacon or bishop for any offense for which he ought to answer them, and refuse to give satisfaction at their citations, it is well lawful to place him under interdict; but he must not be excommunicated before the chief officer of the lord king of that town be applied to, in order that he may adjudge him to come for satisfaction. And if the king's officer fail in this, he shall be at the king's mercy, and thereafter the bishop shall be able to restrain the accused by ecclesiastical justice.

11. Archbishops, bishops, and all persons of the realm who hold of the king in chief, have their possessions from the lord king as a barony, and are answerable therefor to the king's justices and ministers, and follow and do all royal rights and customs, and like all other barons, have to be present at the trials of the court of the lord king with the barons until it comes to a judgment of loss of limb, or death.

12. When an archbishopric or bishopric is vacant, or any abbey or priory of the king's demesne, it must be in his own hand, and from it he shall receive all revenues and rents as demesne. And when it is time to install a clergyman in the church, the lord king must cite the chief clergy of the church, and the election must take place in the chapel of the lord king himself, with the assent of the lord king, and the advice of the persons of the realm whom he shall have summoned to do this. And the person elected shall there do homage and fealty to the lord king as to his liege lord for his life and limbs and earthly honor, saving his order, before he be consecrated.

13. If any of the nobles of the realm forcibly prevent the archbishop or bishop or archdeacon from doing justice in regard of himself or his people, the lord king must bring them to justice. And if perchance anyone should deforce the lord king, the archbishops and bishops and archdeacons must judge him, so that he gives satisfaction to the lord king.

14. The goods of those who are under forfeit of the king, no church or cemetery is to detain against the king's justice, because they belong to the king himself, whether they be found inside churches or outside.

15. Pleas of debts due under pledge of faith or without pledge of faith are to be in the king's justice.

16. Sons of villeins ought not to be ordained without the assent of the lord on whose land they are known to have been born.

Now the record of the aforesaid royal customs and dignities was made by the said archbishops and bishops, and earls and barons, and the nobles and elders of the realm, at Clarendon, on the fourth day before the Purification of the Blessed Mary [January 29], ever Virgin, the lord Henry the king's son with his father the lord king being present there. There are moreover many other great customs and dignities of holy mother church and the lord king and the barons of the realm, which are not contained in this writing. And let them be safe for holy church and the lord king and his heirs and the barons of the realm, and be inviolably observed.

Questions: What are the potential areas of disagreement here? What are the implications of the king's assertions of authority over the church? What precedents have you encountered, in earlier documents, for the king's position? What are the implications of Becket's resistance to the Constitutions?

20. THE MURDER AND MIRACLES OF THOMAS BECKET

The quarrel between Henry II and Archbishop Thomas Becket, in which the Constitutions of Clarendon featured prominently, quickly escalated and resulted in Becket's exile overseas. Years of bitter argument and tense negotiation followed. In 1170 a compromise allowed the archbishop to return home, which he did in December, the point at which the excerpt below takes up the story. The author of the biographical extract below was an eyewitness to and participant in the events at Canterbury, though not those at the royal court in France.

Source: Grim trans. W.H. Hutton, *S. Thomas of Canterbury, An Account of his Life and Fame from the Contemporary Biographers and other Chroniclers* (London: David Nutt, 1899), pp. 233-245, revised; additional material trans. E. Amt from *Materials for the History of Thomas Becket*, ed. J.C. Robertson (London: Rolls Series, 1875-83), vol. I, pp. 145, 147, 154, 207, 213-214, 326, 362, 393; vol. II, pp. 428-430; miracles trans. E.P. Cheyney, *Readings in English History Drawn from the Original Sources* (Boston: Ginn and Company, 1922), pp. 160-164, revised.

Edward Grim's Life of Thomas Becket

Having returned, therefore, with the highest purity and devotion of spirit, the archbishop celebrated the holy nativity of the Savior, cheerfully reminding his people that his own way did not lie among men. On the day of the Lord's nativity, as soon as he had finished his sermon to the people, with a terrible sentence he condemned [Robert Broc,] one of the king's men, who, the day before, had attacked some of the archbishop's servants and, to insult them, shamefully cut off their horses' tails. And he laid a similar penalty on Ralph de Broc too, who was [Robert's] blood relative and no gentler in character, the originator of all malice, who raged like a wild beast against the archbishop's men and household. And he made it clear to the people that the three bishops [of York, Salisbury, and London] lay under the same sentence, lest anyone communicate with such men, who had dared to challenge the injunction of kings, against the ancient statutes of Christ Church, Canterbury. In conclusion he declared, "Whoever sows hatred and discord between me and my lord the king, let them be accursed by Jesus Christ, and let the memory of them be blotted out from the assembly of the saints." But those whom malice had already armed against the Lord's anointed were not at all afraid of the declaration of this terrible sentence.

Then the above-named bishops, choosing to entrust themselves to the indignation of the king rather than to the judgment of God and the church, and quickly crossing the sea, went to the king, and bowing at his feet, with enough complaining speech to turn a hard heart, they deplored their suspension, telling how they had been treated by their lord of Canterbury, whose industry and talent were deeply divided from the priestly office, to the disgrace of the king and the kingdom. The accusers added that he would dare even more than he had so far, if the king were to bear such presumption patiently. Beset by such things, as if driven mad, scarcely containing himself in his frenzy, and not realizing what he was exclaiming, the king in the midst of repeated exchanges is said to have spoken thus: "I have nourished and promoted in my realm sluggish and wretched knaves who are faithless to their lord, and permit him to be tricked thus infamously by a low clerk!" He spoke, and withdrew from the midst of the colloquy, seeking a private place, to see whether solitude might ameliorate the madness he had conceived, and reflection might better cast out the raging poison he had swallowed. But his words were heard by four knights, distinguished in birth and members of the king's own household; and fatally did they interpret the import of what the king had said. Permitting no delay, and certainly urged on by one who was a murderer from the beginning, they conspired with one accord for the death of an innocent. And he who inspired the deed made it easy to perpetrate. For, leaving the king utterly ignorant, and embarking on a ship, at their prayer by favorable winds they were transported to England, landing at the "port of dogs" [at Dover], and from then on they should be called miserable dogs, not knights. But the king did not know that the knights had departed, supposing that they would quickly turn back from any evil after he sent them. But with such speed were they carried across that they could not be recalled or caught by messengers before the sin was committed. It is clear enough from the consequences that their accursed and rash action was against the king's plan and will. For when the martyrdom of the venerable pontiff was announced, such confusion seized his mind, such sadness disturbed him, such unheard-of horror of the deed at the same time swallowed him up and possessed him, that no words can describe it. He tried to determine, since he was ignorant, whether in fact he might have called them back to thwart their purpose, either by custody in prison or any other method. But sometimes God's providence, using evil men for good, thereby honors his beloved one more highly, whence human malice believes in this humility. In fact human talent and skill are useless against the purpose of the Divinity. Surely it pleased the Savior to snatch from this misery, by martyrdom, one whom fullness of faith had made worthy of martyrdom.

Therefore the said persons, no knights but miserable wretches, as soon as they landed summoned the king's officials, whom the archbishop had excommunicated, and by lyingly declaring that they were acting on the king's orders and in his name they got together a band of followers. They then collected in a body, ready for any impious deed, and on the fifth day after the Nativity of Christ, that is on the day after the festival of the Holy Innocents, gathered together against the innocent. The hour of dinner being over, the saint had departed with some of his household from the crowd into an inner room, to transact some business, leaving a crowd waiting in the hall outside. The four knights with one attendant entered. They were received with respect as the servants of the king and well known; and those who had waited on the archbishop being now themselves at dinner invited them to table. They scorned the food, thirsting rather for blood. By their order the archbishop was informed that four men had arrived from the king and wished to speak with him. He consented and they entered. They sat for a long time in silence and did not salute the archbishop or speak to him. Nor did the man of wise counsel salute them immediately when they came in, that according to the Scripture, "By thy words thou shalt be justified," he might discover their intentions from their questions. After awhile, however, he turned to them, and carefully scanning the face of each one he greeted them in a friendly manner, but the wretches, who had made a treaty with death, answered his greeting with curses, and ironically prayed that God might help him. At this speech of bitterness and malice the man of God colored deeply, now seeing that they had come for his hurt. Whereupon Fitz Urse, who seemed to be the chief and the most eager for crime among them, breathing fury, broke out in these words, "We have somewhat to say to thee by the king's command: say if thou wilt that we tell it here before all." But the archbishop knew what they were going to say, and replied, "These things should not be spoken in private or in the chamber, but in public." Now these wretches so burned for the slaughter of the archbishop that if the door-keeper had not called back the clerks — for the archbishop had ordered them all to go out — they would have killed him, as they afterwards confessed, with the shaft of his cross which stood by. When those who had gone out returned, he, who had before thus reviled the archbishop, said, "The king, when peace was made between you and all disputes were ended, sent you back free to your own see [that is, the bishop's area of jurisdiction], as you demanded: but you on the other hand adding insult to your former injuries have broken the peace and wrought evil in yourself against your lord. For those by whose ministry the king's son was crowned and invested with the honors of sovereignty, you, with obstinate pride, have condemned by sentence of suspension, and you have also bound with the chain of anathema those servants of the king by whose prudent counsels the business of the kingdom is transacted: from which it is manifest that you would take away the crown from the king's son if you were able. Now your plots and schemes you have laid to carry out your designs against the king are known to all. Say, therefore, are you ready to answer in the king's presence for these things: for therefore are we sent." To whom answered the archbishop, "Never was it my wish, God is my witness, to take away the crown from my lord the king's son, or diminish his power; rather would I wish him three crowns, and would aid him to obtain the greatest realms of the earth with right and equity. But it is not just for my lord the king to be offended because my people accompany me through the cities and towns, and come out to meet me, when they have for seven years been deprived of the consolation of my presence; and even now I am ready to satisfy him wherever my lord pleases, if in anything I have done amiss; but he has forbade me with threats to enter any of his cities and towns, or even villages. Moreover, not by me, but by the lord pope, were the prelates suspended from their office." "It was through you," said the madmen, "that they were suspended. Absolve them." "I do not deny," he answered, "that it was through me, but it is beyond my power, and utterly incompatible with my position that I should absolve those whom the pope has bound. Let them go to him, on whom redounds the contempt they have shown towards me and their mother the church of Christ at Canterbury."

"Now," said these butchers, "this is the king's command that you depart with all your men from the kingdom, and the land which lies under his sway: for from this day can there be no peace with you, or any of yours, for you have broken the peace." Then said he, "Let your threats cease and your wranglings be stilled. I trust in the King of heaven, who for His own suffered on the Cross: for from this day no one shall see the sea between me and my church. I came not to fly; here he who wants me shall find me. And it does not befit the king so to command; sufficient are the insults which I and mine have received from the king's servants, without further threats." "Thus did the king command," they replied, "and we will make it good, for whereas you ought to have shown respect to the king's majesty, and submitted your vengeance to his justice, you have followed the impulse of your passion and basely thrust from the church his ministers and servants." At these words Christ's champion, rising in fervor of spirit against his accusers, exclaimed, "Whoso shall presume to violate the decrees of the sacred Roman see or the laws of Christ's church, and shall refuse to make satisfaction, whosoever he be I will not spare him, nor will I delay to inflict ecclesiastical censures on the delinquents."

Confounded at these words the knights sprang up, for they could bear his firmness no longer, and coming close to him they said, "We declare to you that you have spoken in peril of your head." "Do you come to kill me?" he answered, "I have committed my cause to the judge of all; wherefore I am not moved by threats, nor are your swords more ready to strike than is my soul for martyrdom. Seek him who flees from you; me you will find foot to foot in the battle of the Lord." As they went out with tumult and insults, he who was fitly surnamed Ursus [that is, "bear"], called out in a brutal way, "In the king's name we order you, both clerk and monk, that ye take and hold that man, lest he escape by flight ere the king have full justice on his body." As they went out with these words, the man of God followed them to the door and exclaimed, "Here, here shall ye find me"; putting his hand over his neck as though show-ing the place where they were to strike. He returned then to the place where he had sat before, and consoled his clerks, and exhorted them not to fear; and, as it seemed to us who were present, waited as unperturbed — though him alone did they seek to slay — as though they had come to invite him to a bridal. Ere long back came the butchers with swords and axes and falchions and other weapons fit for the crime which their minds were set on. When they found the doors barred and they were not opened to their knocking, they turned aside by a private way through the orchard to a wooden partition which they cut and hacked till they broke it down. At this terrible noise were the servants and clerks horribly affrighted, and, like sheep before the wolf, dis-persed hither and thither. Those who remained called out that he should flee to the church, but he did not forget his promise not to flee from his murderers through fear of death, and refused to go; for in such case it were not meet to flee from city to city, but rather to give example to those beneath that everyone should rather fall by the sword than see the divine law set at naught and the sacred canons subverted. He who had long sighed for martyrdom now saw that as it seemed the occasion was now come, and feared lest he should delay it or put it away altogether if he went into the church. But the monks were instant with him, declaring that it were not fit he were absent from vespers which were at that moment being performed. He remained immoveable in that place of less reverence, for he had now in his mind caught a sight of the hour of happy consummation for which he had sighed so long, and he feared lest the reverence of the sacred place should deter even the impious from their purpose, and cheat him of his heart's desire. For, certain that he would depart in martyrdom from this misery, he had said after his return from exile in the hearing of many, "You have here one beloved of God and a true and holy martyr; another will the divine compassion send you; He will not delay." O pure and trustful was the conscience of that good shepherd, who in defending the cause of his flock would not delay his own death when he was able, nor shun the tormentor, that the fury of the wolves, glutted with the blood of the shepherd, might spare the sheep. But when he would not be persuaded by argument or prayer to take refuge in the church the monks caught hold of him in spite of his resistance, and pulled, dragged, and pushed him, not heeding his clamors to be let go, and brought him to the church.

But the door, through which was the way into the monk's cloister, had been carefully secured some days before, and as the tormentors were now at hand, it seemed to take away all hope of escape; but one of them, running forward, caught hold of the lock, and, to the surprise of all, unfastened it with as much ease as if it had been glued to the door.

When the monks had entered the church, already the four knights followed behind with rapid strides. With them was a certain subdeacon, armed with malice like their own, Hugh, fitly surnamed for his wickedness Mauclerc, who showed no reverence for God or the saints, as the result showed. When the holy archbishop entered the church, the monks stopped vespers which they had begun and ran to him, glorifying God that they saw their father, whom they had heard was dead, alive and safe. They hastened, by bolting the doors of the church, to protect their shepherd from the slaughter. But the champion, turning to them, ordered the church doors to be thrown open, saying, "It is not meet to make a fortress of the house of prayer, the church of Christ: though it be not shut up it is able to protect its own; and we shall triumph over the enemy rather in suffering than in fighting, for we came to suffer, not to resist." And straightway, they entered the house of peace and reconciliation with swords sacrilegiously drawn, causing horror to the beholders by their very looks and the clanging of their arms.

All who were present were in tumult and fright, for those who had been singing vespers now ran hither to the dreadful sight.

Inspired by fury the knights called out, "Where is Thomas Becket, traitor to the king and realm?" As he answered not they cried out the more furiously, "Where is the archbishop?" At this, intrepid and fearless, as it is written, "The just, like a bold lion, shall be without fear," he descended from the stair where he had been dragged by the monks in fear of the knights, and in a clear voice answered "I am here, no traitor to the king, but a priest. Why do ye seek me?" And whereas he had already said that he feared them not, he added, "So I am ready to suffer in His name, Who redeemed me by His Blood: be it far from me to flee from your swords, or to depart from justice." Having thus said, he turned to the right, under a pillar, having on one side the altar of the blessed Mother of God and ever Virgin Mary, on the other that of St. Benedict the Confessor: by whose example and prayers, having crucified the world with its lusts, he bore all that the murderers could do with such constancy of soul as if he had been no longer in the flesh. The murderers followed him; "Absolve," they cried, "and restore to communion those whom you have excommunicated, and restore their powers to those whom you have suspended." He answered: "There has been no satisfaction, and I will not absolve them." "Then you shall die," they cried, "and receive what you deserve." "I am ready," he replied, "to die for my Lord, that in my blood the church may obtain liberty and peace. But in the name of Almighty God, I forbid you to hurt my people whether clerk or lay." Thus piously and thoughtfully, did the noble martyr provide that no one near him should be hurt or the innocent be brought to death, whereby his glory should be dimmed as he hastened to Christ. Thus did it become the martyr-knight to follow in the footsteps of his Captain and Savior, Who when the wicked sought Him said: "If ye seek Me, let these go their way." Then they laid sacrilegious hands on him, pulling and dragging him that they might kill him outside the church, or carry him away a prisoner, as they afterwards confessed. But when he could not be forced away from the pillar, one of them pressed on him and clung to him more closely. Him he pushed off calling him "pander," and saying, "Touch me not, Reginald; you owe me fealty and subjection; you and your accomplices act like madmen." The knight, fired with terrible rage at this severe repulse, waved his sword over the sacred head. "No faith," he cried, "nor subjection do I owe you against my fealty to my lord the king." Then the unconquered martyr, seeing the hour at hand which should put an end to this miserable life and give him straightway the crown of immortality promised by the Lord, inclined his neck as one who prays and joining his hands he lifted them up, and commended his cause and that of the church to God, to St. Mary, and to the blessed martyr Denys. Scarce had he said the words than the wicked knight, fearing lest he should be rescued by the people and escape alive, leapt upon him suddenly and wounded this lamb who was sacrificed to God on the head, cutting off the top of the crown which the sacred unction of the chrism had dedicated to God; and by the same blow he wounded the arm of him who tells this. For he, when the others, both monks and clerks, fled, stuck close to the sainted archbishop and held him in his arms till the one he interposed was almost severed. Behold the simplicity of the dove, the wisdom of the serpent, in the martyr who opposed his body to those who struck that he might preserve his head, that is his soul and the church, unharmed, nor would he use any forethought against those who destroyed the body whereby he might escape. O worthy shepherd, who gave himself so boldly to the wolves that his flock might not be torn. Because he had rejected the world, the world in wishing to crush him unknowingly exalted him. Then he received a second blow on the head but still stood firm. At the third blow he fell on his knees and elbows, offering himself a living victim, and saying in a low voice, "For the Name of Jesus and the protection of the church I am ready to embrace death." Then the third knight inflicted a terrible wound as he lay, by which the sword was broken against the pavement, and the crown which was large was separated from the head; so that the blood white with the brain and the brain red with blood, dyed the surface of the virgin mother church with the life and death of the confessor and martyr in the colors of the lily and the rose. The fourth knight prevented any from interfering so that the others might freely perpetrate the murder. As to the fifth, no knight but that clerk who had entered with the knights, that a fifth blow might not be wanting to the martyr who was in other things like to Christ, he put his foot on the neck of the holy priest and precious martyr, and, horrible to say, scattered his brains and blood over the pavement, calling out to the others, "Let us away, knights, he will rise no more."

Miracles of St. Thomas, by William of Canterbury

Of an armed man whom Brother Honorius saw in his sleep

Three days after the suffering of the glorious martyr Thomas, Honorius, a monk of Canterbury, a man of veracity, in his sleep saw himself entering the monastery. And behold, before the altar of the Lord our Savior a youth of beautiful glowing appearance stood with unsheathed sword. When Honorius approached nearer and with timid voice said, "Who are you, master? It is not fitting for an armed man to be seen in this holy and religious place in this way," he replied, "Do not fear; the custody of this place has been appointed to me, who was given the belt of a knight on the day that Thomas was promoted to the archbishopric to rule the church."

Of a matron who on the seventh day spoke with the martyr in her sleep

Seven days had passed since the death of the martyr. A certain freeborn woman, wife of one Ralph, a man of honor according to this world, was resting on her bed at home. This woman, hearing of the death of the martyr, began to be somewhat sad, mourning as a good sheep for the death of a kind shepherd, for the dishonor to the church and the wickedness of the crime. Because of this sorrow she obtained the honor of seeing a vision in her sleep. On entering her place of prayer she found a man standing before the altar, wearing a hood and clad in white, as though he were performing the divine service. When he saw her he seated himself near the southern part of the room, nodding familiarly to her as if seeking to ask that she draw nearer. She asked what she could do to gain salvation for her soul. He replied, "Every week the sixth day must be observed as a fast day by you, and when you have passed a year in this way come to me." Then he added, "Do you know who it is with whom you are conversing?" "You are the one," she answered, "whom those four wicked men presumed to murder with such insolent boldness."

Of a townsman whom the martyr suddenly snatched from this world, because he had snatched a poor woman's sheep

A rich man named Ralph, of the town of Nottingham, detained some few sheep of a poor woman. This latter begged to be permitted to buy them back, saying, "Grant this kindness, I beg, my master, to your handmaid, that I may receive my sheep as the others, provided I pay eight pieces of silver for each one." He refused, since he wished to transfer to his own possession those sheep which she owned. Hear what happened, in order that you may not be enticed to become rich from the goods of another. He was riding along seated on his pacer, snapping a switch which he was carrying in his hand. The woman pressed him that she might have the property which was really hers by paying for it. "Do not hinder my journey, my master," said she; "I have planned to go to the holy martyr Thomas; I have destined the wool of my sheep to pay my expenses on the way. Show mercy to me, that the martyr may do the same to you." Hearing this he looked down at her, calling out in terrible tones, "Depart, you low and worthless slave, I shall do nothing for you." She kept urging him, adding prayers to her money; but seeing that she gained nothing either from prayers or money, she ended with a curse. "May the curse of God and of the martyr Thomas fall on this man who has offered violence to me concerning my own property." At this word the rich man, struck by the divine hand, fell heavily forward on the pommel of his saddle, where, groaning, he moaned, "I die"; for the blow had stopped his breath.

Of a girl who had sunk in some water

Thanks be to God, he glorifies his martyr Thomas everywhere. In Normandy there was a little girl, Hawisia, daughter of a peasant of the village of Grochet, who, as she was wandering along in her thoughtless childish way, fell into a pond. She was only two years and three months old. When she was not found by her mother the next day or the day following that, she was sought for and found in the pool. The mother, crying out, ran to her, while the father hastened to her all dripping as she was, and, seizing her, held her by the feet. The neighbors came running up and she was pronounced dead. But at the advice of a priest she was dedicated to the holy martyr Thomas, and life was restored the instant the vow was made.

Of a young leper

The venerable queen Eleanor, finding a little boy who had been cast out into the streets and deprived of a mother's love, ordered that he be brought up in the monastery of Abingdon. After living there many years and learning much, he was seized with a virulent form of leprosy, separated from the other scholars, and removed from the monastery at the command of the bishop, Geoffrey of St. Asaph, who was in charge there. His face became blotched, from his eyes streamed water, his eyebrows thinned out, sores covered his arms and limbs, reaching to the bone; all these things produced nausea. His voice became rough and almost inaudible, even to those standing near; cloths had to be changed every day or every other day on account of the bloody matter which came from the sores. These things kept him from dwelling with others or holding any social intercourse with them.

But this youth, trusting in the mercy and merits of the blessed Thomas, whom heavenly love glorified in all ways, departed to Canterbury, and even on the journey felt the beginning of his cure within. Returning home, after two days, from the tomb of St. Thomas, he brought with him merely traces of his healed disease. One day he seized the bishop by his clothing as he was taking a walk, and said to him that he had been cleansed through the merits of St. Thomas of Canterbury. The bishop, however, did not know him, so changed was he, and asked his name and position. He told his name, and by the same reply indicated his position, at the same time rendering speechless the man whom he was addressing. The bishop carefully considered the case and thought over the length of the disease, which had been running for two years. Nevertheless, after physicians had been consulted, he could no longer refuse to believe them, assuring him of the cure, nor could he refuse longer to believe the evidence of his own eyes, so he finally recalled this man to the life of the monastery and the daily intercourse. And he himself came to pray at the tomb of the martyr with the healed man.

Of a ship on the Mediterranean which stuck on some rocks

Certain pilgrims were voyaging on the Mediterranean Sea when their vessel struck on a rock and began to be in danger. The danger was of this kind: the stern and keel stuck fast on the rocks, while the prow, hanging down, touched the waters nearby. The canvas had been torn from the mast, and, saturated with water, was pulling on the sailyard so that the mast would be dragged into the water. Certain of the sailors were climbing on the rigging, others anxious over their sins were offering vows, and all were calling on the name of the martyr Thomas. Then a clearly manifest and wonderful sign was given: the ship rose at the prow and settled at the stern, so that no one doubted but that the martyr had placed his hand under the prow.

Of a dead man thrown into the sea

A certain German pilgrim who had devoted himself to the service of this martyr, while on his way to Jerusalem to offer up prayers, became ill and died, while on a vessel on the Mediterranean Sea. The sailors, in accordance with their custom, cast him into the sea on the same day, stripped of his clothing. The ship, borne on, continued on the journey which it had begun. The thing which I am about to relate is wonderful, yet I am not stretching the truth. Late in the night, behold, the man who had been cast overboard rose above the waters and entered the ship from the stern. The helmsman of the ship, who was seated near the stern, watching the winds and stars, was much astonished at this apparition, and asked whether he were propitious or otherwise, to which he replied: "I am the dead man whom you cast into the sea; the blessed Thomas has restored me to life and to this vessel. Restore to me the place which I hired and my clothes, for I am very cold." All were filled with astonishment and delight over this thing which had happened. This occurrence, received from the helmsman himself, was reported to us by a clerk of Canterbury. A certain man of Brindisi, a fellow-citizen and neighbor of the helmsman of this boat, told us the same thing in the same way.

Of a woman's cow, which the martyr rescued from the pestilence

A woman by the name of Beatrice lived in the coast regions near where the marsh separates Kent and Sussex. When she saw that a pestilence was carrying off the cattle, and by this sudden outbreak the pastures were being stripped of their flocks, she made a vow, saying, "Preserve, O martyr, this one cow of mine, that it be not carried off by this pestilence. I promise you its calf or the value thereof." She prayed and her prayer was answered, for although the rest of the animals were carried off, the murrain did not touch her property.

Questions: How did Becket's death come about? What was his own role in it? How did contemporaries view him, before and after his death? What is Edward Grim's attitude toward the archbishop and toward the king? What do the miracle stories tell us about medieval life and beliefs?

21. ASSIZES OF HENRY II

Henry II issued a number of sets of laws and customs known as "assizes," the closest thing to legislation in this era; two of these are printed in their entirety here. The Assize of Clarendon in 1166 dealt with law and order issues and the treatment of criminals; one of its most important features is its establishment of inquest juries. Also significant is the implicit recognition that the old Germanic "ordeal" was not a satisfactory way of determining guilt. The Assize of the Forest is a brief summary of the laws that had pertained to the royal forest since the Norman Conquest; "forest" meant not woodland specifically but all the areas set aside as the king's hunting preserves and therefore falling under special and arbitrary royal control. In the twelfth century the royal forest may have covered more than a quarter of all the land in the kingdom — hence the importance of forest law.

Source: Assize of Clarendon, trans. E.P. Cheyney, *Translations and Reprints from the Original Sources of European History*, series 1, vol. 1 (Philadelphia: University of Pennsylvania Department of History, 1902), no. 6, pp. 22-26, revised; Assize of the Forest, trans. J.J. Bagley and P.B. Rowley, *A Documentary History of England, 1066-1540* (Harmondsworth: Penguin Books Ltd., 1966), pp. 70-73.

Assize of Clarendon

Here begins the Assize of Clarendon, made by King Henry II with the assent of the archbishops, bishops, abbots, earls, and barons of all England.

1. In the first place, the aforesaid King Henry, with the consent of all his barons, for the preservation of the peace and the keeping of justice, has enacted that inquiry should be made through the several counties and through the several hundreds, by twelve of the most legal men of the hundred and by four of the most legal men of each manor, upon their oath that they will tell the truth, whether there is, in their hundred or in their manor, any man who has been accused or publicly suspected of himself being a robber, or murderer, or thief, or of being a receiver of robbers, or murderers, or thieves, since the lord king has been king. And let the justices make this inquiry before themselves, and the sheriffs before themselves.

2. And let anyone who has been found by the oath of the aforesaid to have been accused or publicly suspected of having been a robber, or murderer, or thief, or a receiver of them, since the lord king has been king, be arrested and go to the ordeal of water and let him swear that he has not been a robber, or murderer, or thief, or receiver of them, since the lord king has been king, to the value of five shillings, so far as he knows.

3. And if the lord of the man who has been arrested or his steward or his men shall have claimed him, with a pledge, within the third day after he has been seized, let him be given up and his chattels until he himself makes his law.

4. And when a robber, or murderer, or thief, or receiver of them shall have

been seized through the above-mentioned oath, if the justices are not to come very soon into that county where they have been arrested, let the sheriffs send word to the nearest justice by some intelligent man that they have arrested such men, and the justices will send back word to the sheriffs where they wish that these should be brought before them; and the sheriffs shall bring them before the justices; and along with these they shall bring, from the hundred and the manor where they have been arrested, two legal men to carry the record of the county and of the hundred as to why they were seized, and there before the justice let them make their law.

5. And in the case of those who have been arrested through the aforesaid oath of this assize, no one shall have court, or judgment, or chattels, except the lord king in his court before his justices, and the lord king shall have all their chattels. In the case of those, however, who have been arrested, otherwise than through this oath, let it be as it has been accustomed and ought to be.

6. And the sheriffs who have arrested them shall bring such before the justice without any other summons than they have from him. And when robbers, or murderers, or thieves, or receivers of them, who have been arrested through the oath or otherwise, are handed over to the sheriffs they also must receive them immediately without delay.

7. And in the several counties where there are no jails, let such be made in a borough or in some castle of the king, from the money of the king and from his forest, if one shall be near, or from some other neighboring forest, on the view of the servants of the king; in order that in them the sheriffs may be able to detain those who have been seized by the officials who are accustomed to do this or by their servants.

8. And the lord king, moreover, wills that all should come to the county court, to make this oath, so that no one shall remain behind because of any franchise which he has or court or jurisdiction which he has, but that they should come to the making of this oath.

9. And there is to be no one within a castle or without a castle or even in the honor of Wallingford, who may forbid the sheriffs to enter into his court or his land for seeing to the frankpledges and that all are under pledges; and let them be sent before the sherifs under a free pledge.

10. And in cities and boroughs, let no one have men or receive them in his house or in his land or his soc [that is, where he has jurisdiction], whom he does not undertake to produce before the justice if they shall be required, or else let them be under a frankpledge.

11. And let there be none within a city or borough or within a castle or without, or even in the honor of Wallingford, who shall forbid the sheriffs to enter into his land or his jurisdiction to arrest those who have been charged or publicly suspected of being robbers or murderers or thieves or receivers of

them, or outlaws, or persons charged concerning the forest; but he requires that they should aid them to capture these.

12. And if anyone is captured who has in his possession the fruits of robbery or theft, if he is of bad reputation and has an evil testimony from the public, and has not a warrant, let him not have law. And if he shall not have been accused on account of the possession which he has, let him go to the [ordeal of] water.

13. And if anyone shall have acknowledged robbery or murder or theft or the reception of them in the presence of legal men or of the hundred, and afterwards shall wish to deny it, he shall not have law.

14. The lord king wills, moreover, that those who make their law and shall be absolved by the law, if they are of very bad testimony, and publicly and disgracefully spoken ill of by the testimony of many and legal men, shall abjure the lands of the king, so that within eight days they shall go over the sea, unless the wind shall have detained them; and with the first wind which they shall have afterward they shall go over the sea, and they shall not afterward return into England, except on the permission of the lord king; and then let them be outlawed if they return, and if they return they shall be seized as outlaws.

15. And the lord king forbids any vagabond, that is a wandering or an unknown man, to be sheltered anywhere except in a borough, and even there he shall be sheltered only one night, unless he shall be sick there, or his horse, so that he is able to show an evident excuse.

16. And if he shall have been there more than one night, let him be arrested and held until his lord shall come to give securities for him, or until he himself shall have secured pledges; and let him likewise be arrested who has sheltered him.

17. And if any sheriff shall have sent word to any other sheriff that men have fled from his county into another county, on account of robbery or murder or theft, or the reception of them, or for outlawry, or for a charge concerning the forest of the king, let him arrest them. And even if he knows of himself or through others that such men have fled into his county, let him arrest them and hold them until he shall have secured pledges from them.

18. And let all sheriffs cause a list to be made of all fugitives who have fled from their counties; and let them do this in the presence of their county courts, and they will carry the written names of these before the justices when they come first before these, so that they may be sought through all England, and their chattels may be seized for the use of the king.

19. And the lord king wills that, from the time when the sheriffs have received the summons of the justices in eyre to appear before them with their county courts, they shall gather together their county courts and make inquiry for all who have recently come into their counties since this assize, and that

they should send them away with pledges that they will be before the justices, or else keep them in custody until the justices come to them, and then they shall have them before the justices.

20. The lord king, moreover, prohibits monks and canons and all religious houses from receiving any one of the lesser people as a monk or canon or brother, until it is known of what reputation he is, unless he shall be sick unto death.

21. The lord king, moreover, forbids anyone in all England to receive in his land or his jurisdiction or in a house under him any one of the sect of those renegades who have been excommunicated and branded at Oxford. And if anyone shall have received them, he will be at the mercy of the lord king, and the house in which they have been shall be carried outside the village and burned. And each sheriff will take this oath that he will hold this, and will make all his servants swear this, and the stewards of the barons, and all knights and free tenants of the counties.

22. And the lord king wills that this assize shall be held in his kingdom so long as it shall please him.

Assize of the Forest

This is the English assize of the Lord King Henry, son of Matilda, which he has made for the protection of his forest and forest game, with the advice and approval of the archbishops and bishops, and of the barons, earls, and nobles of England, at Woodstock.

1. In the first place, he forbids anyone to offend against him in any particular touching his forests or his forest game; and he desires that no one shall place confidence in the fact that he has hitherto been moderate in his punishment of offenders against his forests and forest game, and has taken from them only their chattels in satisfaction for their offenses. For if anyone offends against him in the future and is convicted for his offense, the king will have from him the full measure of justice which was exacted in the time of King Henry, his grandfather.

2. He forbids that anyone shall have bows, arrows, hounds, or harriers in his forests, except by licence from the king or other duly authorized person.

3. He forbids any owner of a wood within King Henry's forest to sell or give away anything out of the wood to its wasting or destruction: but he allows that they may take freely from their woods to satisfy their own needs, provided that they do so without wasting, and under the supervision of the king's forester.

4. The king has commanded that all owners of woods within the boundaries of a royal forest shall appoint suitable foresters to their woods and go

surety for them, or else find other suitable sureties capable of making satisfaction for any offenses which the foresters may commit in matters that concern the lord king. The owners of woods which are outside the forest regard [that is, a triennial survey by twelve knights] but in which the king's game is protected shall only have such men as foresters or keepers of their woods as have sworn to uphold the lord king's assize and to protect his game.

5. The lord king commands his foresters to keep a watchful eye upon the forest holdings of knights and other owners of woods inside the boundaries of a royal forest, to make sure that these woods are not destroyed. If, despite their surveillance, the woods are destroyed, the owners of the woods may be well assured that satisfaction will be taken from no one else, but from their own persons or estates.

6. The lord king has commanded that all his foresters shall take an oath to uphold to the letter, and to the full extent of their powers, this assize which he has made for the protection of his forests, and not to obstruct the knights and other worthy owners when they seek to exercise within their own woods those rights which the king has allowed them.

7. The king has commanded that in every county where he has game, twelve knights shall be appointed as custodians of his game and of his vert [that is, greenwood] and generally to survey the forest; and that four knights shall be appointed to agist [that is, oversee the pasturing of cattle in] his woods and to control and receive the dues from pannage [that is, the feeding of swine]. The king forbids anyone to allow cattle to be pastured in his own woods, where these lie within the boundaries of a forest, before the agisting of the lord king's woods, which takes place during the fifteen days before and the fifteen days after Michaelmas [15 September–14 October].

8. The king has commanded that where any of the demesne woods of the lord king are destroyed and the forester in charge of them is unable to account satisfactorily for their destruction, he shall not be fined, but shall answer with his own body [that is, be imprisoned and maybe mutilated].

9. The king forbids any clerk in holy orders to offend against him in respect of his forests or of his forest game. He has given strict instructions to his foresters that they shall not hesitate to lay hands upon such persons, if they find them offending, in order to restrain them and secure their arrest; and he will cover them fully in their actions by his personal warrant.

10. The king has commanded that surveys shall be made of old and new assarts [that is, forest clearings] and of purprestures [that is, encroachments] and of forest damage generally, and that each item of damage shall be separately recorded.

11. The king has commanded that earls, barons, knights, freeholders, and all men shall come when summoned by his master forester to hear the pleas of the

lord king concerning his forests and to conduct his other business in the county court. If they fail to attend, they will be at the lord king's mercy [that is, they will be fined].

12. At Woodstock, the king commanded that for a first and second forest offense a man shall give safe pledges [for his future good conduct], but that for a third offense no further pledges shall be taken from him, nor shall he be allowed any other manner of satisfaction, but he shall answer with his own body.

13. The king commands that all males over twelve years of age who live within an area where game is protected shall take an oath for the protection of the game. Clerks in holy orders with lay holdings within the area shall not be exempt from taking the oath.

14. The king commands that wherever his wild animals are protected, or have customarily enjoyed protection, mastiffs shall be lawed [that is, have the claws and three toes of their forefeet cut to prevent their being used for hunting].

15. The king commands that no tanner or bleacher of hides shall be resident in his forests, except in a borough.

16. The king absolutely forbids that anyone in future shall hunt wild animals by night, with a view to their capture, in areas where his wild animals are protected or outside these areas in places where they are often to be found or where protection was formerly applied, on penalty of one year's imprisonment or the payment of a fine and ransom at the king's pleasure; or that anyone, at the risk of incurring this same penalty, shall set traps for the king's wild animals, using dead or living animals as bait, anywhere within the king's forests and woods, or within areas which used to form part of a forest, but were later disafforested by the king or his progenitors.

Questions: What issues of law and order are dealt with in the Assize of Clarendon, and how? Which of these may be left over from the civil war of Stephen's reign? What crimes are considered most serious? How does the inquest jury work? What is the perceived problem with the ordeal? What kinds of land fell within the royal forest? How was land used there? What were the king's priorities there?

22. GLANVILL'S TREATISE ON THE LAWS AND CUSTOMS OF THE KINGDOM OF ENGLAND

In the 1180s a treatise describing English civil law was written by someone familiar with the procedures of the royal courts and with Henry II's reforms; the name of the then justiciar, Ranulf Glanville, has traditionally been attached to this work, though there is little evidence supporting his authorship. By far the greatest concern of the civil law was title to land. The excerpts below describe some traditional aspects of land law (dower and inheritance customs) and some of Henry II's innovations (the Grand Assize). The sample writs which the author includes in the treatise have been omitted here.

Source: trans. J. Beames, *A Translation of Glanville*, ed. J.H. Beale (Washington: John Byrne & Co., 1900), pp. 31, 35-37, 39-42, 44-46, 48-55, 91-105, 113-116, 124-128, 133-136, 138-147, 149-150; revised.

Book 2. ... Of Those Things which Appertain to the Duel or Grand Assize

3. ... The demand and claim of the demandant being thus made, it shall be at the election of the tenant, either to defend himself against the demandant by the duel, or to put himself upon the king's Grand Assize, and require a recognition to ascertain, which of the two have the greater right to the land in dispute.

... But here we should observe, that after the tenant has once waged the duel he must abide by his choice, and cannot afterwards put himself upon the Assize.... All the delays which can with propriety be resorted to having expired, it is requisite, before the duel can take place, that the demandant should appear in court, accompanied by his champion armed for the contest. Nor will it suffice, if he then produce any other champion than one of those upon whom he put the proof of his claim: neither, indeed, can any other contend for him, after the duel has been once waged....

The duel being finished, a fine of sixty shillings shall be imposed upon the party conquered, in the name of "recreantise" [that is, acknowledgment of defeat], and besides which he shall lose his law; and if the champion of the tenant should be conquered, his principal shall lose the land in question, with all the fruits and produce found upon it at the time of the seisin of the fee, and never again shall be heard in court concerning the same land. For those matters which have been once determined in the king's court by duel remain for ever after unalterable. Upon the determination of the suit, let the sheriff be commanded by the following writ to give possession of the land to the successful party....

6. But, if the tenant should prefer putting himself upon the king's Grand Assize, the demandant must either adopt the same course, or decline it. If the demandant has once conceded in court that he would put himself upon the Assize, and has so expressed himself before the Justices of the Common Pleas, he cannot afterwards retract, but ought either to stand or fall by the Assize.

If he object to put himself upon the Grand Assize, he ought in such case to show some cause, why the Assize should not proceed between them....

7. The Grand Assize is a certain royal benefit bestowed upon the people, and emanating from the clemency of the prince, with the advice of his nobles. So effectually does this proceeding preserve the lives and civil condition of men, that every one may now possess his right in safety, at the same time that he avoids the doubtful event of the duel. Nor is this all: the severe punishment of an unexpected and premature death is evaded, or at least the opprobrium of a lasting infamy, of that dreadful and ignominious word that so disgracefully resounds from the mouth of the conquered champion.

This legal institution flows from the most profound equity. For that justice, which after many and long delays is scarcely, if ever, elicited by the duel, is more advantageously and expeditiously attained through the benefit of this institution. This Assize, indeed, allows not so many delays as the duel, as will be seen in the sequel. And by this course of proceeding, both the labor of men and the expenses of the poor are saved. Besides, by so much as the testimony of many credible witnesses, in judicial proceedings, preponderates over that of one only, by so much greater equity is this institution regulated than that of the duel. For since the duel proceeds upon the testimony [that is, the combat] of one juror, this constitution requires the oaths of twelve lawful men at least.

These are the proceedings which lead to the Assize. The party who puts himself upon the Assize should, from the first, ... sue out a writ for keeping the peace....

10. By means of such writs, the tenant may protect himself, and may put himself upon the Assize, until his adversary, appearing in court, pray another writ, in order that four lawful knights of the county, and of the neighborhood, might elect twelve lawful knights from the same neighborhood, who should say, upon their oaths, which of the litigating parties have the greater right to the land in question....

12. ... [Because of the large number of possible delays,] a certain just constitution has been passed, under which the court is authorized to expedite the suit, upon the four knights appearing in court on the day appointed them, and being prepared to proceed to the election of the twelve knights.... But, if the tenant himself be present in court, he may possibly have a just cause of exception against one or more of the twelve, and concerning this he should be heard in court. It is usual, indeed, for the purpose of satisfying the absent party, not to

confine the number to be elected to twelve, but to comprise as many more as may incontrovertibly satisfy such absent party, when he return to court....

Indeed, if the object be to expedite the proceedings, it will more avail to follow the direction of the court, than to observe the accustomed course of the law. It is, therefore, committed to the discretion and judgment of the king or his justices, so to temper the proceeding as to render it more beneficial and equitable....

14. The election of the twelve knights having been made, they should be summoned to appear in court, prepared upon their oaths to declare, which of them, namely, the tenant or the demandant, possess the greater right to the property in question. Let the summons be made by the following writ....

16. On the day fixed for the attendance of the twelve knights to take the recognition, whether the tenant appear, or absent himself, the recognition shall proceed without delay....

17. When the Assize proceeds to make recognition, the right will be well known either to all the jurors, or some may know it and some not, or all may be alike ignorant concerning it. If none of them are acquainted with the truth of the matter, and this be testified upon their oaths in court, recourse must be had to others, until such can be found who do know the truth of it. Should it, however, happen that some of them know the truth of the matter, and some not, the latter are to be rejected, and others summoned to court, until twelve, at least, can be found who are unanimous. But, if some of the jurors should decide for one party, and some of them for the other, then others must be added, until twelve, at least, can be obtained who agree in favor of one side. Each of the knights summoned for this purpose ought to swear that he will neither utter that which is false, nor knowingly conceal the truth. With respect to the knowledge requisite on the part of those sworn, they should be acquainted with the merits of the cause, either from what they have personally seen and heard, or from the declarations of their fathers, and from other sources equally entitled to credit, as if falling within their own immediate knowledge.

18. When the twelve knights ... entertain no doubt about the truth of the thing, then the Assize must proceed to ascertain whether the demandant or the tenant have the greater right to the subject in dispute.

But if they decide in favor of the tenant, or make any other declaration by which it should sufficiently appear to the king or his justices that the tenant has greater right to the subject in dispute, then, by the judgment of the court, he shall be ... for ever released from the claim of the demandant, who shall never again be heard in court with effect concerning the matter. For those questions which have once been lawfully determined by the king's Grand Assize shall upon no subsequent occasion be with proriety revived. But if by this Assize it be decided in court in favor of the demandant, then his adversary shall lose the land in question, which shall be restored to the demandant, together with all the fruits and produce found upon the land at the time of seisin....

Book 6. Of Dower

1. The term dower is used in two senses. Dower, in the sense in which it is commonly used, means that which any free man, at the time of his being affianced, gives to his bride at the church door. For every man is bound as well by the ecclesiastical law, as by the secular, to endow his bride, at the time of his being affianced to her. When a man endows his bride, he either names the dower, or not. In the latter case, the third part of all the husband's freehold land is understood to be the wife's dower; and the third part of all such freehold lands as her husband held, at the time of affiancing, and of which he was seised in his demesne, is termed a woman's reasonable dower. If, however, the man names the dower, and mentions more than a third part, such designation shall not avail, as far as it applies to the quantity. It shall be reduced by apportionment to the third part; because a man may endow a woman of less, but cannot of more than a third part of his land.

2. Should it happen, as it sometimes does, that a man endows a woman, having but a small freehold at the time of his being affianced, he may afterwards enlarge her dower to the third part or less of the lands he may have purchased.

But if upon the assignment of dower, no mention was made concerning purchases, even admitting that at the time of affiancing he possessed but a small estate, and that he afterwards much increased it, the wife cannot claim as dower more than a third part of such land as her husband held at the time of being affianced, and when he endowed her. The same rule prevails if a man, not being possessed of any land, should endow his wife with his chattels, and other things, or even with money. Should he afterwards make considerable purchases in land and tenements, the wife cannot claim any part of such property so acquired by purchase; it being, with respect to the quantity or quality of the dower assigned to any woman, a general principle, that if she is satisfied to the extent of her endowment at the door of the church, she can never afterwards claim as dower any thing beyond it.

3. It is understood that a woman cannot, during the lifetime of her husband, make any disposition of her dower. For since the wife herself is in a legal sense under the absolute power of her husband, it is not singular, if the dower, as well as the woman herself and all things belonging to her, should be considered to be fully at the disposal of the husband....

4. Upon the death of the husband of a woman, her dower, if it has been named, will either be vacant or not.

In the former case, the woman may, with the consent of the heir, enter upon her dower, and retain the possession of it. If, however, the dower be not vacant, either the whole will be so circumstanced, or some part will be vacant, and some not. If a certain part be vacant, and a certain part not, she may pursue the course we have described, and enter into the part which is vacant; and for the residue, she shall have a writ of right, directed to her warrantor [that is, her husband's heir], in order to compel him to do complete justice concerning the land which she claims as appertaining to her reasonable dower....

6. The plea shall be discussed in the court of the warrantor by virtue of this writ, until it be proved that such court has failed in doing justice.... Upon proof of this, the suit shall be removed into the county court, through the medium of which, the suit may, at the pleasure of the king or his chief justiciary, be lawfully transferred to the king's court....

8. Pleas of this description, as, indeed, some others, may be transferred from the county court to the supreme court of the king for a variety of causes: as, on account of any doubt which may arise in the county court concerning the plea itself, and which that court is unable to decide.... Upon the day appointed in court, either both parties will be absent, or only one will be so, or both will appear.... If both be present in court, the woman shall set forth her claim against her adversary in the following words. "I demand such land, as appertaining to such land, which was named to me in dower, and of which my husband endowed me at the door of the church, the day he espoused me, as that of which he was invested and seised at the time when he endowed me."

Various are the answers which the adverse party usually gives to a claim of this kind; in substance, however, he will either deny that she was so endowed, or concede it.

But, whatever he may allege, the suit ought not to proceed, without the heir of the woman's husband. He shall, therefore, be summoned to appear in court to hear the suit, by the following writ....

Should the heir, after having been summoned, neither appear, nor essoin himself [that is, give a legal excuse for not appearing], on the first, second, nor third day; or if, after having cast the usual essoins, he should on the fourth day neither appear nor send his attorney, it may be a question, by what means he ought or can be distrained, consistently with the law and custom of the realm. In the opinion of some, his appearance in court shall be compelled by distraining his fee. And [they think] that, therefore, by the direction of the court so much of his fee shall be taken into the king's hands as may be necessary to distrain him to appear in court to show whether he ought to warrant [that is, guarantee to the woman] the land in question or not. Whilst others think that his appearance in court for such purpose may be obtained by attaching him with pledges.

11. When, at last, the heir of the husband of the woman, the complainant, appear in court, either he will affirm the fact, and concede that the land in

question appertains to the dower of the woman, ... or he will deny it. If the heir admit this in court, he shall then be bound to recover the land against the tenant, if [the tenant] be disposed to dispute the matter, and then deliver it to the woman; and thus the contest will be changed into one between the tenant and the heir.

If, however, the heir be unwilling to contest the point, he shall be bound to give to the woman a competent equivalent; because the woman herself shall not afterwards sustain any loss. But, if the heir himself neither admit nor concede to the woman that which she alleges against the tenant, then the suit may proceed between the woman and the heir... [and] the matter may be decided by the duel, provided the woman produce in court those who heard and saw the endowment, or any proper witness who may have heard and seen the fact of her being endowed by the ancestor of the heir at the church door, at the time of the espousals, and be ready to prove such fact against him.

Should the woman prevail against the heir in the duel, then the heir shall be bound to deliver the land in question to the woman, or to give her an adequate recompense.

Book 7. Of Lawful Heirs ...
and of the Custody and Privilege of Minors...

1. The ... portion which is given to a man with a woman is ... what is usually called marriage-hood [or dowry]. Every free man possessed of land may give a certain part of it with his daughter, or with any other woman, in [dowry]…. Though it is thus, generally speaking, lawful for a man, in his lifetime, freely to dispose of the reasonable part of his land, in such manner as he may feel inclined, yet the same permission is not allowed to anyone on his death-bed; because the distribution of the inheritance would probably then be highly imprudent, were such an indulgence to be conceded to men, who, in the glow of a sudden impulse, not unfrequently lose both their memory and reason.

Hence it is to be presumed that if a man laboring under a mortal disease should then for the first time set about making a disposition of his land, a thing never thought of by him in the hour of health, that the act is rather the result of the mind's insanity than of its deliberation. But yet a gift of this description, if made to anyone by the last will, shall be valid, if done with the consent of the heir, and confirmed by his acquiescence in it.... [And] if he has many sons born in wedlock, he cannot, correctly speaking, without the consent of the heir, give any part of his inheritance to a younger son; because, if this were permitted, it would then frequently happen that the eldest son would be disinherited, owing to the greater affection which parents often feel towards their younger children....

3. Of heirs, some are nearest, others more remote. A man's nearest heirs are those of his body, as a son, or a daughter. Upon the failure of these, the more remote heirs are called, namely, the grandson, or grand-daughter, descending in a right line from the son or daughter, infinitely. Then the brother and sister, and those descending from them in a transverse line. After these, the uncle, as well on the part of the father, as of the mother, and in like manner the aunt, and their descendants....

When, therefore, a man possessed of an inheritance dies, leaving one son only his heir, it is unquestionably true that such son shall succeed entirely to his father. If, however, he leaves more sons, then a distinction must be made, whether the deceased was a knight, or one holding by military tenure, or whether he was a free socman [that is, holding land by non-military tenure]. Because, if he were a knight, or holding by military tenure, then, according to the law of the English realm, his eldest son shall succeed to the whole inheritance, so that none of his brothers can by right claim any part of it. But, if the parent were a free socman, then, indeed, the inheritance shall be equally divided amongst all the sons, however numerous, provided such socage land has been anciently divisable, reserving, however, to the eldest son as a mark of respect to his seniority, the chief dwelling, upon his making a compensation to the others equal to its value. If, however, the estate was not anciently divisable, then the eldest son shall, according to some customs, take the whole inheritance, whilst, according to other customs, the younger son shall succeed as heir. In like manner, should any person leave one daughter only, his heir, then what we have laid down with respect to a son shall unquestionably prevail. If, however, he leave more daughters, then the inheritance shall, without distinction, be divided between them, whether their father was a knight or a socman, reserving to the eldest daughter the chief dwelling, under the conditions before mentioned....

5. Heirs are bound to observe the testaments of their fathers, and of their other ancestors — of such, I mean, to whom they are heirs — and to discharge their debts. For every freeman, not involved in debt beyond his circumstances, may on his death-bed make a reasonable division of his effects, under this form, as prescribed by the custom of certain places. In the first place, he should remember his lord, by the gift of the best and chief thing he possesses; then the church, and afterwards other persons at his pleasure. But, whatever the custom of different places inculcate with reference to this point, yet, according to the law of the realm, no man is bound to leave any thing by will to any person in particular, unless it be his inclination; for every man's last will is said to be free, according to the spirit of these laws, as well as others.

A woman, indeed, when at her own disposal, may make a testament; but, if married, she cannot, without the authority of her husband, make any will of

the effects of her husband. Yet it would be a mark of affection and highly cred-
itable to the husband, if he concede a reasonable portion of his effects to his
wife; in other words, a third part, which, indeed, she would be entitled to,
should she outlive him, as will be more fully seen hereafter. Husbands, indeed,
much to their honor, frequently grant to their wives this indulgence.

When, therefore, anyone being indisposed wishes to make his will, if he be
not involved in debt, all his moveables should be divided into three parts; of
which one belongs to his heir, another to his wife, and the third is reserved to
himself. Of this third, he has the free power of disposing. But, if he dies without leaving any wife, the half is reserved to him. But of his inheritance [that is,
land], he cannot by his last will make any disposition, as before observed.

9. This leads us to observe that some heirs are evidently of age, some as
clearly not of full age.... But, if it be evident that the heir is under full age, and
he hold by military service, he is considered to be in the custody of his lord,
until he attains his full age.

The full age of an heir, if the son of a knight, or of anyone holding by military service, is when he has completed his twenty-first year. But if the heir be
the son of a socman, he is esteemed to be of full age when he has completed
his fifteenth year. If he is the son of a burgess, he is understood to have attained
his full age when he has discretion to count money and measure cloth, and in
like manner to manage his father's other concerns.

Lords have the custody of the sons and heirs of their vassals and of their fee,
in so extensive a sense that they, for example, exercise an absolute control with
respect to presenting [clergy] to churches in their custody, in marrying females
(if they fall into wardship), and in regulating other matters, in the same manner
as if they were their own. The law, however, does not permit the lords to make
an absolute disposition of the inheritance. In the meantime, the lord should
maintain the heir in a manner suitable to his dignity and the extent of his
inheritance, and should discharge the debts of the deceased, so far as the estate
and the length of the custody will admit.... Those persons who have the custody are bound to restore the inheritance to the heirs in good condition, and
discharged from debts, in proportion to the duration of the custody, and the
extent of the inheritance....

11. The heirs of socmen upon the death of their ancestors shall be in the
custody of their nearest kindred, with this distinction, that if the inheritance
itself descended from the paternal side, the custody shall be conferred upon the
kindred [who are] the descendants on the maternal side; but, if the inheritance
descend on the part of the mother, then the custody belongs to the kindred on
the father's side. For the custody of a person shall never by law be committed
to another of whom a suspicion can be entertained, that he either could or
might wish to claim any right in the inheritance itself.

12. But if the heirs are females, they shall remain in the custody of their lords. If they are minors, they shall continue in custody until they are of full age, at which period the lord is bound to find them a marriage, delivering to each of them her reasonable portion. But if they were of full age, then also they shall remain in the custody of their lord, until with his advice and disposal they are married; because without the disposal or assent of her lord no female, the heir to land, can by the law and custom of the realm be married.

... The reason is simply this — that as the husband of an heiress is bound to do homage to the lord for her estate, the approbation and consent of the lord is requisite for such purpose; lest he should be compelled to receive from his enemy, or from some other improper person, the homage due in respect of his fee. But if anyone demands of his lord a license to marry his daughter and heir to another, the lord is bound either to consent, or to show some just cause, why he refuses; otherwise the woman may, with the advice and approbation of her father, be married, even contrary to the lord's inclination...

[And a widow with dower] is bound to obtain the consent of her warrantor [that is, her husband's heir] to her marriage, or she shall lose her dower, unless, indeed, she holds other land in [dowry] or by inheritance; for then it suffices if she has obtained the consent of the chief lord....

If female heirs, during such time as they are in custody, are guilty of incontinence, and this be proved, then those who have thus erred shall be excluded from the inheritance; and their portion shall accrue to the others, who are free from the same stain. But if, in this manner, all of them should err, then, the whole inheritance shall devolve upon the lord, as an escheat [that is, land that reverts to the lord in the absence of an heir]. Yet, if such female heirs are once lawfully married, and afterwards become widows, they shall not again be under the custody of their lords; although they are, for the reason formerly explained, bound to ask his consent to their marriage. Nor, in such case, shall they forfeit their inheritance, if guilty of incontinence.

But the assertion which is generally made, that incontinence is no forfeiture of the inheritance, is to be understood of the crime of the mother; because, that son is the lawful heir, whom marriage proves to be such....

15. Upon this subject it has been made a question whether if anyone was begotten or born before his father married the mother, such son is the lawful heir, if the father afterwards married the mother? Although, indeed, the canons and the Roman laws consider such a son as the lawful heir, yet, according to the law and custom of this realm, he shall in no measure be supported as heir in his claim upon the inheritance; nor can he demand the inheritance, by the law of the realm. But yet if a question should arise, whether such a son was begotten or born before marriage, or after, it should, as we have observed, be discussed before the ecclesiastical judge; and of his decision he shall inform the

king, or his justices. And thus, according to the judgment of the court Christian concerning the marriage, namely, whether the claimant was born or begotten before marriage contracted, or after, the king's court shall supply that
which is necessary, in adjudging or refusing the inheritance respecting which
the dispute is; so that by its decision the claimant shall either obtain such inheritance, or lose his claim.

Questions: What checks and balances regarding the power of lords are described here?
What options are available for settling a land dispute? What were the advantages and
disadvantages of widowhood? Can you deduce the reasons for laws regarding wills and
heirs? What do these laws reveal about roles and attitudes within the family? About the
legal status of women?

23. JOCELIN OF BRAKELOND'S ACCOUNT OF HENRY OF ESSEX

Henry of Essex was a locally important baron and, in the 1150s, a royal constable. While
we know a fair amount about him from record sources, this narrative account of his life,
found in a monastic chronicle, is unusual for a layman. Though short, it sheds light on
many aspects of medieval life. The duel in this story represents the normal method of
deciding a judicial dispute between two vassals in their lord's court — in this case two
barons in the court of their lord, the king. It is perhaps relevant that Robert de Montfort
had a claim to Henry's inheritance.

Source: trans. L.C. Jane, *The Chronicle of Jocelin of Brakelond, Monk of St. Edmundsbury: A Picture of
Monastic and Social Life in the XIIth Century* (London: Chatto and Windus, 1907), pp. 108-112;
revised.

When the abbot had come to Reading, and we with him, we were rightly
received by the monks of that place. And among them was Henry of Essex as a
professed monk, who, when he had a chance to speak to the abbot and to those
who were present, told us how he had been conquered in a trial by battle, and
how and why St. Edmund confounded him, in the very hour of conflict. But I
wrote down his tale by command of the lord abbot, and I wrote it also in these
words.

Inasmuch as it is impossible to avoid unknown evil, we have thought it well
to commit to writing the acts and crimes of Henry of Essex, that they may be
a warning, and not an example. Stories often convey a useful and salutary
warning.

The said Henry, then, while he enjoyed great prosperity, had the reputation
of a great man among the nobles of the realm, and he was renowned by birth,

noted for his deeds of arms, the standard-bearer of the king, and feared by all men owing to his might. And when others who lived near him enriched the church of the blessed king and martyr Edmund [that is, the monastery at Bury St. Edmunds] with goods and rents, he on the contrary not only shut his eyes to this fact, but further violently, and wrongfully, and by injuries took away the annual rent of five shillings, and converted it to his own use.

In the course of time, moreover, when a case arose in the court of St. Edmund concerning a wrong done to a certain maiden, the same Henry came thither, and protested and declared that the trial ought to be held in his court because the place where the said maiden was born was within his lordship of Lailand. With the excuse of this affair, he dared to trouble the court of St. Edmund for a long while with journeyings and countless charges.

But fortune, which had assisted his wishes in these and other like matters, brought upon him a cause for lasting grief, and after mocking him with a happy beginning, planned a sad conclusion for him; for it is the custom of fortune to smile, that she may rage; to flatter, that she may deceive; and to raise up only that she may cast down. For presently there rose against him Robert de Montfort, his relative, and a man not unequal to him in birth and power, and slandered him in the presence of the princes of the land, accusing him of treason to the king. For he asserted that Henry, in the course of the Welsh war [in 1157], in the difficult pass of Coleshill, had treacherously cast down the standard of the lord king, and proclaimed his death in a loud voice; and that he had induced those who were coming to the help of the king to turn in flight. As a matter of fact, the said Henry of Essex believed that the renowned king Henry the Second, who had been caught in an ambush by the Welsh, had been slain, and this would have been the truth, had not Roger, earl of Clare, a man renowned in birth and more renowned for his deeds of arms, hastened up quickly with his men of Clare, and raised the standard of the lord king, which revived the strength and courage of the whole army.

Then Henry resisted the said Robert in the council, and utterly denied the charge, so that after a little while, the matter came [in 1163] to a trial by battle. Then when they met at Reading to fight on an island somewhat near the abbey, there gathered there also a multitude of persons, to see how the affair would end. And it came to pass, that when Robert manfully made his armor ring again with hard and frequent blows, and his bold beginning promised the fruit of victory, Henry's strength began to fail him a little. And as he looked round about, behold! on the edge of land and water, he saw the glorious king and martyr Edmund, armed and as it were flying in the air, and looking towards him with an angry countenance, often shaking his head in a threatening manner, and showing himself full of wrath. And Henry also saw with the saint another knight, Gilbert de Cereville, who appeared not only less than the saint in point of dignity, but also head and shoulders shorter; and he looked on him with accusing and angry glances. This Gilbert, by order of the said Henry, afflicted with bonds and tortures, had died, as the result of an accusation brought against him by the wife of Henry, who cast the penalty for her own ill-doing on an innocent man, and said that she could not endure the evil suggestions of the said Gilbert.

When he saw these sights, then, Henry grew alarmed and fearful, and called to mind that an old crime brings new shame. And now, giving up all hope, and abandoning skillful fighting for a blind rush, he took the part of one who attacks rather than that of one who defends himself. And when he gave hard blows, he received harder; and while he fought manfully, he was more manfully resisted. In a word, he fell conquered.

And as he was thought to be dead, in accordance with the earnest request of the magnates of England, the relatives of the said Henry, the monks of that place were allowed to give burial to his corpse. But he afterwards revived, and when he had regained the blessing of health, under the regular habit, he wiped out the stain of his former life, and taking care to purify the long week of his dissolute past with at least one sabbath, he cultivated the study of the virtues, to bring forth the fruit of happiness.

Questions: What were Henry's "crimes"? How does the monastic context shape the story of Henry's life? From a non-religious perspective, what brought about Henry's downfall? What forces shaped his fate?

24. BOROUGH CHARTERS

Perhaps nothing had as wide-ranging an influence on twelfth-century society and culture as the growth of towns and cities, the result of a booming economy and growing population. One aspect of this was the granting of charters which guaranteed specific rights and freedoms to urban populations. Charters were granted by the king or by a lord who had rights over the town; the latter could be either a noble or a bishop.

Source: charter of Henry I, trans. W.d.G. Birch, *The Historical Charters and Constitutional Documents of the City of London* (London, 1884), reprinted in *Source-Book of English History: Leading Documents*, ed. G.C. Lee (New York: Henry Holt and Company, 1900), pp. 127-128, revised; charters of Henry II and Thurstan, trans. E.P. Cheyney, *Translations and Reprints from the Original Sources of European History*, series 1, vol. 2 (Philadelphia: University of Pennsylvania Department of History, 1895), no. 1, pp. 7-11, revised.

Henry I to London

Henry, by the grace of God, king of England, to the archbishop of Canterbury, and to the bishops and abbots, earls and barons, justices and sheriffs, and to all his faithful subjects of England, French and English, greeting.

Know that I have granted to my citizens of London, to hold Middlesex to farm for three hundred pounds, upon account to them and their heirs; so that the said citizens shall appoint as sheriff whom they wish for themselves; and shall appoint whomsoever, or such a one as they wish for themselves, for keeping of the pleas of the crown, and of the pleadings of the same, and none other shall be justice over the same men of London; and the citizens of London shall not plead outside the walls of London for any plea. And they shall be free from scot and lot and danegeld [that is, customary royal taxes], and of all murder [fines]; and none of them shall [have to] wage battle. And if any one of the citizens shall be impleaded concerning the pleas of the crown, the man of London shall discharge himself by his oath, which shall be adjudged within the city; and none shall lodge within the walls, neither of my household, nor any other, nor lodging taken by force.

And all the men of London shall be quit and free, and all their goods, throughout England, and the ports of the sea, of and from all toll and passage and lestage [that is, charges for goods put on a ship], also all other customs; and the churches and barons and citizens shall and may peaceably and quietly have and hold their sokes [that is, jurisdictions] with all their customs; so that the strangers that shall be lodged in the sokes shall give custom to none but to him to whom the soke appertains, or to his officer, whom he shall there put. And a man of London shall not be adjudged in amercements of more than one hundred shillings (I speak of the pleas which appertain to money); and further there shall be no more [penalties for] miskenning [that is, procedural errors] in the hustings [that is, London's civil court], nor in the folkmote [that is, assembly], nor in other pleas within the city; and the hustings may sit once in a week, that is to say, on Monday. And I will cause my citizens to have their lands, promises, bonds, and debts, within the city and without; and I will do them right by the law of the city, of the lands of which they shall complain to me.

And if any shall take toll or custom from any citizen of London, the citizens of London in the city shall take from the borough or town, where toll or custom was so taken, as much as the man of London gave for toll, and as he received damage thereby. And all debtors who owe debts to the citizens of London, shall pay them in London, or else discharge themselves in London, that they owe none; but if they will not pay the same, nor come to clear themselves that they owe none, the citizens of London, to whom the debts shall be due, may take their goods in the city of London, from the borough or town, or from the county wherein he remains who shall owe the debt. And all citizens of London may have their chases to hunt, as well and fully as their ancestors have had, that is to say, in Chiltre, and in Middlesex and Surrey.

Witness the bishop of Winchester, and Robert son of Richier, and Hugh Bigod, and Alured of Toteneys, and William of Alba Spina and Hubert, the king's chamberlain, and William de Montfichet, and Hangulf de Taney, and John Bellet, and Robert son of Siward. At Westminster.

Archbishop Thurstan of York to Beverly

Thurstan, by the grace of God, archbishop of York, to all the faithful in Christ as well present as to come, greeting and God's benediction and his own. Let it be known to you that I have given and conceded, and by the advice of the chapter of York and of Beverly and by the advice of my barons have confirmed by my charter to the men of Beverly all their liberties with the same laws which those of York have in their city. Moreover let it not be hidden from you that lord Henry our king has conceded to us the power of doing this of his own good will, and by his charter has confirmed our statutes and our laws according to the form of the laws of the burgesses of York, saving the dignity and honor of God and Saint John, and of us and of the canons, in order that he might thus increase the benefactions of his predecessors, and promote them by all these free customs.

I will that my burgesses of Beverly shall have their guildhall, which I give to them and concede in order that they may there determine upon their statutes to the honor of God and of St. John, and of the canons, and to the advantage of the whole body of citizens, being enfranchised by the same law as those of York in their hanse house. I give up to them, moreover, their toll forever for eighteen marks a year; besides in those feasts in which toll belongs to us and to the canons, that is to say, in the feast of St. John the Confessor, on May [6], in the feast of the translation of St. John [of Beverly, on October 25], and on the day of the birth of St. John the Baptist [June 24]; and on these festivals I have made all the burgesses of Beverly free and quit from all toll. By the testimony of this charter, moreover, I have conceded to the same burgesses as free entrance and departure within and without the town, in plain and wood and marsh, in roads and byways, and in other suitable places, except in meadows and grainfields, as anyone can ever concede and confirm them most freely and broadly; and know that they are as free and quit from all toll through the whole of Yorkshire, as those of York are. And I will that whosoever opposes this may be accursed, as the custom of the church of St. John asserts and as it has been decreed in the church of St. John.

These are witness: Geoffrey Murdoc, Nigel Fossard, Alan de Percy, Walter Spec, Eustace son of John, Thomas the reeve, Thurstan the archdeacon; Herbert the chamberlain; William son of Toole, and William of Bath, in the presence of the whole household of the archbishop, clerical and lay, in York.

Henry II to Lincoln

Henry, by the grace of God, king of England, duke of Normandy and Aquitaine, count of Anjou, to the bishop of Lincoln, justiciars, sheriffs, barons, officers, and all his faithful, French and English, of Lincoln, greeting. Know that I have conceded to my citizens of Lincoln all their liberties and customs and laws, which they had in the time of Edward and William and Henry, kings of England; and their guild merchant of the men of the city and of other merchants of the county, just as they had it in the time of our aforesaid predecessors, kings of England, best and most freely. And all men who dwell within the four divisions of the city and attend the market are to be at the guilds and customs and assizes of the city as they have been best in the time of Edward, William and Henry, kings of England. I grant to them moreover, that if anyone shall buy any land within the city, of the burgage of Lincoln, and shall have held it for a year and a day without any claim, and he who has bought it is able to show that the claimant has been in the land of England within the year and has not claimed it, for the future as before he shall hold it well and in peace, and without any prosecution. I confirm also to them, that if anyone shall have remained in the city of Lincoln for a year and a day without claim on the part of any claimant, and has given the customs, and is able to show by the laws and customs of the city that the claimant has been in existence in the land of England and has not made a claim against him, for the future as in the past he shall remain in peace, in my city of Lincoln, as my citizen. Witnesses, E., bishop of Lisieux; Thomas, chancellor; H., constable; Henry of Essex, constable. At Nottingham.

Henry II to Wallingford

Henry, by the grace of God, king of England, duke of Normandy and Aquitaine, and count of Anjou... I command you that my burgesses of Wallingford shall have my secure peace through my whole land of England and Normandy, wherever they may be. And know that I have given and conceded to them forever all their liberties and laws and customs well and honorably, just as they had them best and most honorably in the time of King Edward, and in the time of my great grandfather King William, and of his son the second King William, and in the time of King Henry, my grandfather; that is to say, that they should have freely the guild merchant with all its customs and laws, so that neither my bailiff nor any justice of mine should meddle with their guild; but only their own alderman and officer. And if my officers or any justice shall have brought suit against them in any plea or for any occasion or shall have wished to lead them into a suit, I forbid it, and require that they should not make defense in any manner, except in their own proper portmote. And if the reeve himself shall implead them on any occasion without an accuser, they shall not respond, and if on account of any transgression, or by a right judgment any one of them shall have made forfeiture by a right consideration of the burgesses, to the reeve shall he pay it. I forbid, moreover, and require that there shall be no market in Crowmarsh [near Wallingford], nor any merchant, unless he is in the guild of the merchants; and if anyone goes out from the borough of Wallingford and lives from the merchandise of the same Wallingford, I command that he should join the guild of the merchants with the same burgesses, wherever he may be, within the borough or without. Know moreover, that I have given and conceded forever to all the men of Wallingford full quittance from my yearly rent, which they were accustomed to pay from the borough of Wallingford; that is to say, from that which pertains to me in the borough. All these laws and customs and liberties and quittances I give to them and concede forever, and all others which they are able to show that their ancestors had, freely, quietly, and honorably, just as my citizens of Winchester ever had them at the best; and this on account of the great service and labor which they sustained for me in the acquisition of my hereditary right in England. I concede to them, moreover, that wherever they shall go in their journeys as merchants, through my whole land of England and Normandy, Aquitaine and Anjou, "by water and by strand, by wood and by land," they shall be free from toll and passage fees, and from all customs and exactions; nor are they to be troubled in this respect by anyone, under a penalty of £10. I forbid, moreover, and require under the same penalty, that the reeve of Wallingford shall not make any fine of scotale or New Year's gift from anyone, and that he shall not establish any custom in Wallingford which shall injure the burgesses of the town. Of this grant and concession, the witnesses are Theobald, archbishop of Canterbury and others. Given at Oxford, the first day before the Ides of January.

Questions: What rights and freedoms do the towns want? Why? What do we learn about life in the towns from these documents? What economic ideas are evident in the charters? Which town is most privileged? Why do the lords grant these privileges?

25. WILLIAM FITZSTEPHEN'S DESCRIPTION OF LONDON

In his biography of his master Thomas Becket, the clerk William fitz Stephen included a famous description of the saint's birthplace, London. The passage gives us a rare eyewitness view of a twelfth-century city.

Source: trans. H.E. Butler, *Norman London: An Essay*, by F.M. Stenton (London: The Historical Association, 1934), pp. 26-32.

Among the noble cities of the world that are celebrated by fame, the city of London, seat of the monarchy of England, is one that spreads its fame wider, sends its wealth and wares further, and lifts its head higher than all others. It is blest in the wholesomeness of its air, in its reverence for the Christian faith, in the strength of its bulwarks, the nature of its situation, the honor of its citizens, and the chastity of its matrons. It is likewise most merry in its sports and fruitful of noble men. Of these things it is my pleasure to treat, each in its own place.

There "the mild sky doth soften the hearts of men," not that they may be "weak slaves of lust," but that they may not be savage and like unto beasts, nay, rather, that they may be of a kindly and liberal temper.

In the church of St. Paul is the episcopal see. Once it was the metropolitan [that is, the seat of an archbishop], and it is thought that it will be so again, if the citizens return to the island, unless perchance the archiepiscopal title of the Blessed Martyr Thomas and the presence of his body preserve that honor for all time at Canterbury, where it now resides. But since St. Thomas has adorned both these cities, London by his rising and Canterbury by his setting, each city has, in respect of the saint himself, something further that it may urge, not without justice, one against the other. Also as concerns Christian worship, there are both in London and the suburbs thirteen greater conventual churches, and a hundred and twenty-six lesser parochial.

On the east stands the palatine citadel, exceeding great and strong, whose walls and bailey rise from very deep foundations, their mortar being mixed with the blood of beasts. On the west are two strongly fortified castles, while thence there runs continuously a great wall and high, with seven double gates, and with towers along the north at intervals. On the south, London was once walled and towered in like fashion, but the Thames, that mighty river, teeming with fish, which runs on that side with the sea's ebb and flow, has in course of time washed away those bulwarks, undermined and cast them down. Also upstream to the west the royal palace rises high above the river, a building beyond compare, with an outwork and bastions, two miles from the city and joined thereto by a populous suburb.

On all sides, beyond the houses, lie the gardens of the citizens that dwell in the suburbs, planted with trees, spacious and fair, adjoining one another.

On the north are pasture lands and a pleasant space of flat meadows, intersected by running waters, which turn revolving mill-wheels with merry din. Hard by there stretches a great forest with wooded glades and lairs of wild beasts, deer both red and fallow, wild boars and bulls. The corn-fields are not of barren gravel, but rich Asian plains such as "make glad the crops" and fill the barns of their farmers "with sheaves of Ceres' stalk."

There are also round about London in the suburbs most excellent wells, whose waters are sweet, wholesome and clear, and whose "runnels ripple amid pebbles bright." Among these Holywell, Clerkenwell and St. Clement's Well are most famous and are visited by thicker throngs and greater multitudes of students from the schools and of the young men of the city, who go out on summer evenings to take the air. In truth a good City when it has a good Lord!

This city wins honor by its men and glory by its arms and has a multitude of inhabitants, so that at the time of the calamitous wars of King Stephen's reign the men going forth from it to be mustered were reckoned twenty thousand armed horsemen and sixty thousand foot-soldiers. The citizens of London are everywhere regarded as illustrious and renowned beyond those of all other cities for the elegance of their fine manner, raiment, and table. The inhabitants of other towns are called citizens, but of this they are called barons. And with them a solemn oath ends all strife.

The matrons of London are very Sabines [that is, legendary women in the early history of Rome].

In London the three principal churches, to wit the episcopal see of the church of St. Paul, the church of the Holy Trinity, and the church of St. Martin, have famous schools by privilege and in virtue of their ancient dignity. But through the personal favor of some one or more of those learned men who are known and eminent in the study of philosophy there are other schools licensed by special grace and permission. On holy days the masters of the schools assemble their scholars at the churches whose feast-day it is. The scholars dispute, some in demonstrative rhetoric, others in dialectic. Some "hurtle enthymemes," others with greater skill employ perfect syllogisms. Some are exercised in disputation for the purpose of display, which is but a wrestling bout of wit, but others that they may establish the truth for the sake of perfection. Sophists who produce fictitious arguments are accounted happy in the profusion and deluge of their words, others seek to trick their opponents by the use of fallacies. Some orators from time to time in rhetorical harangues seek to carry persuasion, taking pains to observe the precepts of their art and to omit naught that appertains thereto. Boys of different schools strive one against another in verse or contend concerning the principles of the art of grammar or the rules governing the use of past or future. There are others who employ the old wit of the cross-roads in epigrams, rhymes and metre; with "Fescennine License" [that is, bawdy verses], they lacerate their comrades outspokenly, though mentioning no names; they hurl "abuse and gibes," they touch the foibles of their comrades, perchance even of their elders with Socratic wit, not to say "bite more keenly even than Theon's tooth," in their "bold dithyrambs." Their hearers "ready to laugh their fill," "with wrinkling nose repeat the loud guffaw."

Those that ply their several trades, the vendors of each several thing, the hirers out of their several sorts of labor are found every morning each in their separate quarters and each engaged upon his own peculiar task. Moreover there is in London upon the river's bank, amid the wine that is sold from ships and wine-cellars, a public cook-shop. There daily, according to the season, you may find viands, dishes roast, fried and boiled, fish great and small, the coarser flesh for the poor, the more delicate for the rich, such as venison and birds both big and little. If friends, weary with travel, should of a sudden come to any of the citizens, and it is not their pleasure to wait fasting till fresh food is bought and cooked and "till servants bring water for hands and bread," they hasten to the river bank, and there all things desirable are ready to their hand. However great the infinitude of knights or foreigners that enter the city or are about to leave it, at whatever hour of night or day, that the former may not fast too long nor the latter depart without their dinner, they turn aside thither, if it so please them, and refresh themselves, each after his own manner. Those who desire to fare delicately, need not search to find sturgeon or "Guinea-fowl" or "Ionian francolin," since all the dainties that are found there are set forth before their eyes. Now this is a public cook-shop, appropriate to a city and pertaining to the art of civic life. Hence that saying which we read in the *Gorgias* of Plato, to wit, that the art of cookery is a counterfeit of medicine and a flattery of the fourth part of the art of civic life.

In the suburb immediately outside one of the gates there is a smooth field, both in fact and in name. On every sixth day of the week, unless it be a major feast-day on which solemn rites are prescribed, there is a much frequented show of fine horses for sale. Thither come all the earls, barons and knights who are in the city, and with them many of the citizens, whether to look on or buy. It is a joy to see the ambling palfreys, their skin full of juice, their coats a-glisten, as they pace softly, in alternation raising and putting down the feet on one side together; next to see the horses that best befit esquires, moving more roughly, yet nimbly, as they raise and set down the opposite feet, fore and hind, first on one side and then on the other; then the younger colts of high breeding, unbroken and "high-stepping with elastic tread," and after them the costly destriers of graceful form and goodly stature, "with quivering ears, high necks and plump buttocks." As these show their paces, the buyers watch first their gentler gait, then that swifter motion, wherein their fore feet are thrown out and back together, and the hind feet also, as it were, counterclockwise. When a race between such trampling steeds is about to begin, or perchance between others which are likewise, after their kind, strong to carry, swift to run, a shout is raised, and horses of the baser sort are bidden to turn aside. Three boys riding these fleet-foot steeds, or at times two as may be agreed, prepare themselves for the contest. Skilled to command their horses, they "curb their untamed mouths with jagged bits," and their chief anxiety is that their rival shall not gain the lead. The horses likewise after their fashion lift up their spirits for the race; "their limbs tremble; impatient of delay, they cannot stand still." When the signal is given, they stretch forth their limbs, they gallop away, they rush on with obstinate speed. The riders, passionate for renown, hoping for victory, vie with one another in spurring their swift horses and lashing them forward with their switches no less than they excite them by their cries. You would believe that "all things are in motion," as Heraclitus maintained, and that the belief of Zeno was wholly false, when he claimed that motion was impossible and that no man could ever reach the finish of a race.

In another place apart stand the wares of country-folk, instruments of agriculture, long-flanked swine, cows with swollen udders, and "woolly flocks and bodies huge of kine." Mares stand there, meet for plows, sledges and two-horsed carts; the bellies of some are big with young; round others move their offspring, new-born, sprightly foals, inseparable followers.

To this city, from every nation that is under heaven, merchants rejoice to bring their trade in ships.

> Gold from Arabia, from Sabaea spice
> And incense; from the Scythians arms of steel
> Well-tempered; oil from the rich groves of palm
> That spring from the fat lands of Babylon;
> Fine gems from Nile, from China crimson silks;
> French wines; and sable, vair and miniver
> From the far lands where Russ and Norseman dwell.

London, as the chroniclers have shown, is far older than Rome. For, owing its birth to the same Trojan ancestors, it was founded by Brutus before Rome was founded by Romulus and Remus. Wherefore they both still use the ancient laws and like institutions. London like Rome is divided into wards. In place of consuls it has sheriffs every year; its senatorial order and lesser magistrates; sewers and conduits in its streets, and for the pleading of diverse causes, demonstrative, deliberative, and judicial, it has its proper places, its separate courts. It has also its assemblies on appointed days. I do not think there is any city deserving greater approval for its custom in respect of church-going, honor paid to the ordinances of God, keeping of feast-days, giving of alms, entertainment of strangers, ratifying of betrothals, contracts of marriage, celebration of nuptials, furnishing of banquets, cheering of guests, and likewise for their care in regard to the rites of funeral and the burial of the dead. The only plagues of London are the immoderate drinking of fools and the frequency of fires.

To that which I have said this also must be added, that almost all bishops, abbots and magnates of England are, as it were, citizens and freemen of the city of London, having lordly habitations there, whither they repair and wherein they make lavish outlay, when summoned to the city by our lord the king or by his metropolitan to councils and great assemblies, or drawn thither by their own affairs.

Furthermore let us consider also the sports of the city, since it is not meet that a city should only be useful and sober, unless it also be pleasant and merry. Wherefore on the seals of the high pontiffs down to the time when Leo was pope, on the one side of the signet Peter the fisherman was engraved and over him a key stretched forth from heaven as it were by the hand of God, and around it the verse, "For me thou left'st the ship; take thou the key." And on the other side was engraved a city with this devise, "Golden Rome." Also it was said in praise of Caesar Augustus and Rome,

> All night it rains; with dawn the shows return.
> Caesar, thou shar'st thine empery with Jove.

London in place of shows in the theatre and stage-plays has holier plays wherein are shown forth the miracles wrought by holy confessors or the sufferings which glorified the constancy of martyrs.

Moreover, each year upon the day called Carnival — to begin with the sports of boys (for we were all boys once) — boys from the schools bring fighting-cocks to their master, and the whole forenoon is given up to boyish sport; for they have a holiday in the schools that they may watch their cocks do battle. After dinner all the youth of the city goes out into the fields to a much-frequented game of ball. The scholars of each school have their own ball, and almost all the workers of each trade have theirs also in their hands. Elder men and fathers and rich citizens come on horse-back to watch the contests of their juniors, and after their fashion are young again with the young; and it seems that the motion of their natural heat is kindled by the contemplation of such violent motion and by their partaking in the joys of untrammeled youth.

Every Sunday in Lent after dinner a "fresh swarm of young gentles" goes forth on war-horses, "steeds skilled in the contest," of which each is "apt and schooled to wheel in circles round." From the gates burst forth in throngs the lay sons of citizens, armed with lance and shield, the younger with shafts forked at the end, but with steel point removed. "They wake war's semblance" and in mimic contest exercise their skill at arms. Many courtiers come too, when the king is in residence; and from the households of earls and barons come young men not yet invested with the belt of knighthood, that they may there contend together. Each one of them is on fire with hope of victory. The fierce horses neigh, "their limbs tremble; they champ the bit; impatient of delay they cannot stand still." When at length "the hoof of trampling steeds careers along," the youthful riders divide their hosts; some pursue those that fly before, and cannot overtake them; others unhorse their comrades and speed by.

At the feast of Easter they make sport with naval tourneys, as it were. For a shield being strongly bound to a stout pole in mid-stream, a small vessel, swiftly driven on by many an oar and by the river's flow, carries a youth standing at the prow, who is to strike the shield with his lance. If he break the lance by striking the shield and keep his feet unshaken, he has achieved his purpose and fulfilled his desire. If, however, he strike it strongly without splintering his lance, he is thrown into the rushing river, and the boat of its own speed passes him by. But there are on each side of the shield two vessels moored, and in them are many youths to snatch up the striker who has been sucked down by the stream, as soon as he emerges into sight or "once more bubbles on the topmost wave." On the bridge and the galleries above the river are spectators of the sport "ready to laugh their fill."

On feast-days throughout the summer the youths exercise themselves in leaping, archery and wrestling, putting the stone, and throwing the thonged javelin beyond a mark, and fighting with sword and buckler. "Cytherea leads the dance of maidens and the earth is smitten with free foot at moonrise."

In winter on almost every feast-day before dinner either foaming boars and hogs, armed with "tusks lightning-swift," themselves soon to be bacon, fight for their lives, or fat bulls with butting horns, or huge bears, do combat to the death against hounds let loose upon them.

When the great marsh that washes the northern walls of the city is frozen, dense throngs of youths go forth to disport themselves upon the ice. Some gathering speed by a run, glide sidelong, with feet set well apart, over a vast space of ice. Others make themselves seats of ice like millstones and are dragged along by a number who run before them holding hands. Sometimes they slip owing to the greatness of their speed and fall, every one of them, upon their faces. Others there are, more skilled to sport upon the ice, who fit to their feet the shinbones of beasts, lashing them beneath their ankles, and with iron-shod poles in their hands they strike ever and anon against the ice and are borne along swift as a bird in flight or a bolt shot from a mangonel. But sometimes two by agreement run one against the other from a great distance and, raising their poles, strike one another. One or both fall, not without bodily hurt, since on falling they are borne a long way in opposite directions by the force of their own motion; and wherever the ice touches the head, it scrapes and skins it entirely. Often he that falls breaks shin or arm, if he fall upon it. But youth is an age greedy of renown, yearning for victory, and exercises itself in mimic battles that it may bear itself more boldly in true combats.

Many of the citizens delight in taking their sport with birds of the air, merlins and falcons and the like, and with dogs that wage warfare in the woods. The citizens have the special privilege of hunting in Middlesex, Hertfordshire, and all Chiltern, and in Kent as far as the river Cray. The Londoners, who are called Trinobantes, repulsed Gaius Julius Caesar, who "rejoiced to make no way save with the spilth of blood." Whence Lucan writes, "To the Britons whom he sought, he showed his coward back."

The city of London has brought forth not a few men who subdued many nations and the Roman Empire to their sway, and many others whom valor has "raised to the Gods as lords of earth," as had been promised to Brutus by the oracle of Apollo.

> Brutus, past Gaul beneath the set of sun,
> There lies an isle in Ocean ringed with waters.
> This seek; for there shall be thine age-long home.
> Here for thy sons shall rise a second Troy,
> Here from thy blood shall monarchs spring, to whom
> All earth subdued shall its obeisance make.

And in Christian times she brought forth the great Emperor Constantine who gave the city of Rome and all the insignia of empire to God and the Blessed Peter and Silvester the Roman pope, to whom he rendered the office of a groom, and rejoiced no longer to be called emperor, but rather the defender of the holy Roman church. And that the peace of the lord pope might not be shaken with the tumult of the noise of this world by reason of his presence, he himself departed altogether from the city which he had conferred on the Lord Pope, and built for himself the city of Byzantium. And in modern times also she has produced monarchs renowned and magnificent, the Empress Matilda, King Henry III [that is, Henry II's eldest son], and Blessed Thomas, the archbishop, Christ's glorious martyr, "than whom she bore no whiter soul nor one more dear" to all good men in the Latin world.

Questions: What was twelfth-century London like? Which of London's features does the author find particularly impressive? How does he compare London to Rome? How are the author's own professional interests evident in his description of the city? How does his work show the influence of the "twelfth-century renaissance"?

26. THE LIFE OF ST. WILLIAM OF NORWICH BY THOMAS OF MONMOUTH

From the eleventh century onward, Jewish communities could be found in most larger English towns, and outright persecution of this minority occurred from time to time (see doc. 38). The story excerpted here may be the earliest example of the myth of Jews ritually slaughtering Christian children; in later years many other towns developed their own child martyr stories in imitation of this one. There is no factual basis for this Christian myth, but the story is significant for what it tells us about Christian attitudes toward Jews, and for its incidental details about urban life.

Source: trans. A. Jessopp and M.R. James, *The Life and Miracles of St. William of Norwich* (Cambridge: Cambridge University Press, 1896), pp. 10, 12-23, 35-37, 41-48; revised.

Book 1

1. ... The mercy of the divine goodness desiring to display itself to the parts about Norwich, or rather to the whole of England, and to give it in these new times a new patron, granted that a boy should be conceived in his mother's womb without her knowing that he was to be numbered among illustrious martyrs and worthy to be honored among all the army of the saints, and moreover brought it about that he should grow up little by little as a fragrant rose from the thorns.

His father was a certain Wenstan by name. His mother was called Elviva, and they passed their lives as honest people in the country, being somewhat well supplied with the necessaries of life and something more. Let it not seem absurd to any that a boy of such sanctity and destined for such honor should by God's will be born from lowly parents, when it is certain that He Himself was pleased to be born from among the poor....

2. Concerning his birth and infancy.

Some time having elapsed and the day having arrived for his bringing forth, a son was born to the woman, and his name was called William. But he was born on the day of the Purification of the Blessed Virgin Mary, that is on Candlemas [February 2]. Peradventure too by this is indicated how great the purity and sanctity of the child would be, and that he would greatly love candles and the brightness of them. But one circumstance, which I subsequently learnt from his mother and his brothers and the priest who had baptized him, I have judged ought not to be passed over, but inserted here. On the day of his weaning, when his father Wenstan was entertaining his kindred who had been invited to the feast, a man who was undergoing penance, with iron bands upon his arms, presented himself to the guests as if begging for alms; who after the dinner waxing merry, while he held the child in his hands as if admiring him, and the baby, in the innocence of childhood wondering at the iron fetters, began to handle them; suddenly the bonds broke and shivered into pieces. The guests, amazed at the sight, were greatly astonished, and attributed what had occurred to the merits of the child. Wherefore the penitent, set free by divine favor, went his way, giving thanks, and the priest aforesaid, who was present among the guests, collecting the broken rings, placed them in his church at Haveringland and deposited them in a conspicuous place, as well for keeping up the memory of those living as for a record to such as should come after; and he was careful that they should be safely preserved.

The mother, as she loved her child exceedingly, so did she educate him with exceeding care, and by carefully educating she brought him up from his infancy to the years of intelligent boyhood. When he was but seven years old — as I learnt from the mother's narrative — he became so devoted to abstinence that, though his elder brothers did not fast, he himself fasted on three days of the week — to wit the second, fourth and sixth days — and also celebrated the vigils of the apostles and of other saints that were given notice of to the people by devout fasting. And his zeal going on increasing, he used to pass many days content with nothing but bread and water; and his whole inner man overflowing with piety, whatever he could save from his own portion of food or extort from his mother by his entreaties, he used to bestow upon the poor, sometimes openly and sometimes secretly. But while acting thus he conducted himself so dutifully, kindly and prudently, that as far as possible he at once benefitted the poor and did not cause his parents any annoyance. He was a most joyful attendant at church; he used to learn his letters and the psalms and prayers, and all the things of God he treated with the greatest reverence....

3. How he was accustomed to resort to the Jews, and having been rebuked by his own people for so doing, how he withdrew himself from them.

When therefore he was flourishing in this blessed boyhood of his, and had attained to his eighth year, he was entrusted to the skinners to be taught their craft. Gifted with a teachable disposition and bringing industry to bear upon it, in a short time he far surpassed lads of his own age in the craft aforesaid, and he equaled some who had been his teachers. So leaving the country, by the drawing of a divine attraction he went to the city and lodged with a very famous master of that craft, and some time passed away. He was seldom in the country, but was occupied in the city and sedulously gave himself to the practice of his craft, and thus reached his twelfth year.

Now, while he was staying in Norwich, the Jews who were settled there and required their cloaks or their robes or other garments (whether pledged to them, or their own property) to be repaired, preferred him before all other skinners. For they esteemed him to be especially fit for their work, either because they had learnt that he was guileless and skilful, or because attracted to him by their avarice they thought they could bargain with him for a lower price. Or, as I rather believe, because by the ordering of divine providence he had been predestined to martyrdom from the beginning of time, and gradually step by step was drawn on, and chosen to be made a mock of and to be put to death by the Jews, in scorn of the Lord's passion, as one of little foresight, and so the more fit for them. For I have learnt from certain Jews, who were afterwards converted to the Christian faith, how that at that time they had planned to do this very thing with some Christian, and in order to carry out their malignant purpose, at the beginning of Lent they had made choice of the boy William, being twelve years of age and a boy of unusual innocence. So it came to pass that when the holy boy, ignorant of the treachery that had been planned, had frequent dealings with the Jews, he was taken to task by Godwin the priest, who had the boy's aunt as his wife, and by a certain Wulward with whom he lodged, and he was prohibited from going in and out among them any more. But the Jews, annoyed at the thwarting of their designs, tried with all their might to patch up a new scheme of wickedness, and all the more vehemently as the day for carrying out the crime they had determined upon drew near, and the victim which they had thought they had already secured had slipped out of their wicked hands. Accordingly, collecting all the cunning of their crafty plots, they found — I am not sure whether he was a Christian or a Jew — a man who was a most treacherous fellow and just the fitting person for carrying out their execrable crime, and with all haste — for their Passover was coming on in three days — they sent him to find out and bring back with him the victim, which, as I said before, had slipped out of their hands.

4. How he was seduced by the Jews' messenger.

At the dawn of day, on the Monday after Palm Sunday, that detestable messenger of the Jews set out to execute the business that was committed to him, and at last the boy William, after being searched for with very great care, was found. When he was found, he got round him with cunning wordy tricks, and so deceived him with his lying promises. For he pretended that he was the cook of William, archdeacon of Norwich, and that he wished to have him as a helper in the kitchen, where if he should continue steadily with him he would get many advantages in his situation. The simple boy was deceived, and trusted himself to the man; but, wishing to have his mother's favorable consent — for his father had died by this time — he started with the fellow to find her. When they had come to where she was, the boy told her the cause of his errand, and the traitor according to the tenor of his previous offer cast the net of his treachery. So that son of perdition by many promises easily prevailed upon the boy's mind by his tempting offers. Yet at first he could not at all gain the mother's consent; but when the scoundrel persisted the innocent boy agreed though his mother, moved by presentiment, resisted, and in her motherly affection [felt] some fear for her son....

So the traitor took three shillings from his purse with intent to get the better of the mother's fancy and to bend the fickle stubbornness of a fickle woman, seduced by the glitter of money to the lust of gain. Thus the money was offered as the price of the innocent's service, or rather in truth as the price of his blood. But not even yet was the mother's devotion appeased, nor the presentiment of a coming evil easily removed. The wrangling still went on: on one side with prayers, and on the other with the pieces of silver, if so be that, though he could not prevail upon her stubbornness by his continual offers, the brightness of the coins that smiled at her might serve as a lure to her avarice. So the mother's mind was cruelly vanquished by these, even though the maternal affection only slowly gave way under the temptation and, seduced at last by the shining pieces of silver, she was the victim of her covetousness, ... and the boy William was given up to the betrayer.

5. How on his going to the Jews he was taken, mocked, and slain.

In the morning accordingly that traitor, the imitator in almost everything of the traitor Judas, returns to Norwich with the boy, and as he was passing by the house of the boy's aunt he went in with him and said that the mother had entrusted the boy to himself, and then he went out again hastily. But the boy's aunt said quickly to her daughter, "Follow them at once, and take care you find out where that man is leading off the boy to." Thus the girl ran out to explore the way they were going; and she followed them at a distance as they turned about through some private alleys, and at last she saw them entering cautiously into the house of a certain Jew, and immediately she heard the door shut. When she saw this, she went back to her mother and told her what she had seen.

Then the boy, like an innocent lamb, was led to the slaughter. He was treated kindly by the Jews at first, and, ignorant of what was being prepared for him, he was kept till the morrow. But on the next day, which in that year was the Passover for them, after the singing of the hymns appointed for the day in the synagogue, the chiefs of the Jews assembled in the house of the Jew aforesaid suddenly seized hold of the boy William as he was having his dinner and in no fear of any treachery, and illtreated him in various horrible ways. For while some of them held him behind, others opened his mouth and introduced an instrument of torture which is called a teazle, and, fixing it by straps through both jaws to the back of his neck, they fastened it with a knot as tightly as it could be drawn. After that, taking a short piece of rope of about the thickness of one's little finger and tying three knots in it at certain distances marked out, they bound round that innocent head with it from the forehead to the back, forcing the middle knot into his forehead and the two others into his temples, the two ends of the rope being most tightly stretched at the back of his head and fastened in a very tight knot. The ends of the rope were then passed round his neck and carried round his throat under his chin, and there they finished off this dreadful engine of torture in a fifth knot.

But not even yet could the cruelty of the torturers be satisfied without adding even more severe pain. Having shaved his head, they stabbed it with countless thorn-points, and made the blood come horribly from the wounds they made. And cruel were they and so eager to inflict pain that it was difficult to say whether they were more cruel or more ingenious in their tortures. For their skill in torturing kept up the strength of their cruelty and ministered arms thereto. And thus, while these enemies of the Christian name were rioting in the spirit of malignity around the boy, some of those present adjudged him to be fixed to a cross in mockery of the Lord's passion, as though they would say, "Even as we condemned the Christ to a shameful death, so let us also condemn the Christian, so that, uniting the lord and his servant in a like punishment, we may retort upon themselves the pain of that reproach which they impute to us."

Conspiring, therefore, to accomplish the crime of this great and detestable malice, they next laid their blood-stained hands upon the innocent victim, and having lifted him from the ground and fastened him upon the cross, they vied with one another in their efforts to make an end of him. And we, after enquiring into the matter very diligently, did both find the house, and discovered some most certain marks in it of what had been done there. For report goes that there was there instead of a cross a post set up between two other posts, and a beam stretched across the midmost post and attached to the other on either side. And as we afterwards discovered, from the marks of the wounds and of the bands, the right hand and foot had been tightly bound and fastened with cords, but the left hand and foot were pierced with two nails: so in fact the deed was done by design that, in case at any time he should be found, when the fastenings of the nails were discovered it might not be supposed that he had been killed by Jews rather than by Christians. But while in doing these things they were adding pang to pang and wound to wound, and yet were not able to satisfy their heartless cruelty and their inborn hatred of the Christian name, lo! after all these many and great tortures, they inflicted a frightful wound in his left side, reaching even to his inmost heart, and as though to make an end of all they extinguished his mortal life so far as it was in their power. And since many streams of blood were running down from all parts of his body, then, to stop the blood and to wash and close the wounds, they poured boiling water over him.

Thus then the glorious boy and martyr of Christ, William, dying the death of time in reproach of the Lord's death, but crowned with the blood of a glorious martyrdom, entered into the kingdom of glory on high to live for ever. Whose soul rejoiceth blissfully in heaven among the bright hosts of the saints, and whose body by the omnipotence of the divine mercy worketh miracles upon earth. [The murderers then dumped William's body in the woods on Good Friday and bribed the sheriff to keep their secret, but the body was found with miraculous assistance. The finders did not immediately bury it.]

12. How he was buried in the wood.

So the business of burying him was put off. But in the meantime by one man after another telling others their several versions of the story the rumor got spread in all directions, and when it reached the city it struck the heart of all who heard it with exceeding horror. The city was stirred with a strange excitement, the streets were crowded with people making disturbance: and already it was asserted by the greater part of them that it could only have been the Jews who would have wrought such a deed, especially at such a time. And so some were standing about as if amazed by the new and extraordinary affair; many were running hither and thither, but especially the boys and the young men; and, a divine impulse drawing them on, they rushed in crowds to the wood to see the sight. What they sought they found; and, on detecting the marks of the torture in the body, and carefully looking into the method of the act, some suspected that the Jews were not guiltless of the deed; but some, led on by what was really a divine discernment, protested that it was so. When these returned, they who had stayed at home got together in groups, and when they heard how the case stood, they too hurried to the sight, and on their return they bore their testimony to the same effect. And thus all through the Saturday and all through Easter day all the city everywhere was occupied in going backwards and forwards time after time, and everybody was in excitement and astonishment at the extraordinary event.

And so the earnestness of their devout fervor was urging all to destroy the Jews, and they would there and then have laid hands upon them but that restrained by fear of the sheriff John they kept quiet for awhile....

But this fact I think ought to be mentioned, that while the body was being carried by the hands of those who were going to bury it, suddenly such a fragrant perfume filled the nostrils of the bystanders as if there had been growing there a great mass of sweet-smelling herbs and flowers. And I do not think that it was without the divine disposal that the burial happened to take place there, to the intent that afterwards the body might be removed for greater veneration, and though he was [later reburied elsewhere], yet in this place too the divine favor wished to make him illustrious by many tokens of his virtues....

15. Concerning the lamentations of the Mother.

Just at this time as the report was spreading, the story of her son's murder came to the ears of his mother who, naturally overwhelmed by the sad tidings, straightway swooned away as if she were dead. After a while, however, recovering herself she without delay hastened to Norwich to enquire into the truth of the matter. But when she learnt by the relation of many people that her son was dead and was buried in the wood immediately with torn hair and clapping of hands she ran from one to another weeping and wailing through the streets like a mad woman. At last going to the house of her sister whom I mentioned before and enquiring now of the priest Godwin, now of her sister, she could learn no more about the circumstances and the truth than that he had been slain in an extraordinary way. But from many probable indications and conclusions she was convinced that they were not Christians but Jews who had dared to do the deed. With a woman's readiness of belief she easily gave credence to these conjectures. Whereupon she at once burst forth into denouncing the Jews with words of contumely and indignation. Sometimes she behaved like a mother moved by all a mother's love, sometimes she bore herself like a woman with all a woman's passionate rashness. And so, assuming everything to be certain which she suspected and asserting it to be a fact, as though it had actually been seen — she went through the streets and open places and, carried along by her motherly distress, she kept calling upon everybody with dreadful screams, protesting that the Jews had seduced and stolen away from her her son and killed him. This conduct very greatly worked upon the minds of the populace to accept the truth, and so everybody began to cry out with one voice that all the Jews ought to be utterly destroyed as constant enemies of the Christian name and the Christian religion.

16. How the priest Godwin accused the Jews and offered to prove by ordeal that they were guilty of the death of the boy William.

When some days had passed, the day for holding the synod drew near, and according to custom Bishop Eborard presided. The sermon having been preached, the aforesaid priest, Godwin, rose, saying that he was about to bring to the ears of the Bishop and his brother priests a distressing complaint and one which had not been heard of in the present time. Wherefore, silence having been enjoined upon all, he began in the manner following:

"Very Reverend Lord and father and Bishop — May that goodness of yours which has been so notorious hitherto, and which I trust may continue to be so esteemed for all time, vouchsafe to incline your ears graciously to the words of our complaint. May the reverend assembly also of my brethren and fellow priests, whom I see before me attending at the present Synod, vouchsafe with a patient hearing to receive the utterance of my sad complaint, and receive it with no indifference. In sooth I have come forward to plead not so much a private or domestic cause as to make known to you an outrage which has been done to the whole Christian community. Indeed I think it is not unknown to your fathership, very reverend prelate, nor do I think it is a secret to most of you, my dear brethren, that a certain boy — a very little boy — and a harmless innocent too — was treated in the most horrible manner in Passion Week, was found in a wood, and up to this time has been without Christian burial. He was indeed a cousin of my own children, and because of the tie of kindred which united us he was very dear to me. Wherefore, when I lay my complaint before you all concerning his death, I can hardly restrain my eyes from weeping. To begin with, from any complicity in so execrable a murder I hold all Christians excused as guiltless. But, in the second place, I accuse the Jews, the enemies of the Christian name, as the doers of this deed, and as the shedders of innocent blood. Thirdly, I am ready to prove the truth of my words at such time and place and by such proof as is allowed me by Christian law...."

Accordingly, while all were amazed and disturbed at what had occurred, they report that the Prelate, very much moved at the atrocity of the deed, and actuated by his zeal for justice, replied as follows:

"Forasmuch as that which you affirm to be certain is so far clearly uncertain to us, we shall at any rate take care to arrive at a certain knowledge of this business. And if indeed it shall be established to be so, as you maintain, be assured that the rigor of our justice shall in no wise be found wanting. But since it is not seemly that a just judge should pronounce upon those who are absent and unheard, let the Jews be summoned and have a hearing on the morrow; if they be convicted, let them receive the punishment that they deserve."

Thus the dealing with this business being put off till next day, and the business of the synod having been dealt with in part, all dispersed intending to return next morning. But by order of the bishop the dean of Norwich on the same day summoned the Jews to appear, and ordered them to attend to answer on the morrow before the synod regarding so important a matter.

The Jews were greatly disturbed and ran to the sheriff, John, as their only refuge, seeking help and counsel in so difficult a cause, inasmuch as by trusting to his patronage they had often escaped many dangers. So John, having taken counsel and being one who was not ignorant of the truth, did not allow the Jews to come to the synod on the morrow, and indeed he gave notice by his servants to the bishop that he had nothing to do with the Jews, and that in the absence of the king the Jews should make no answer to such inventions of the Christians....

Accordingly it was determined by common consent that notice should be given to John that he should not protect the Jews against God, and to the Jews that peremptory sentence would be passed upon them, and that unless they at once came to purge themselves they must understand that without doubt they would be exterminated.

Of course John moved by these words came without delay, and the Jews with him.... The Jews by the advice of the sheriff denied the charge brought against them; but as to the ordeal proposed, they asked for some small delay for deliberating.... After seeking some way of compromise, with a great deal of discussion, and after dealing with each alternative on its merits, they found no safe escape out of so great a difficulty except only by obtaining some truce and delay. If they could obtain that, they hoped they could easily extort from the king the favor which might be bought for money, of getting a chance of arguing the cause, and so utterly put an end to the rumor of the crime laid to their charge.

When the greatest part of the day had been spent in this kind of disputing, at last they sent to the bishop asking that a respite of some sort should be allowed them. Which being peremptorily denied them, the sheriff with the Jews, without asking for leave to depart as the usual custom is, went their way. But because it was not safe for them to remain outside, the sheriff protected them within the defenses of the castle until, their security having been assured to them by a royal edict, they might be safe for the future and out of harm's way....

Questions: What elements of Christian attitudes toward Jews can be distinguished here? Why were the Jews vulnerable to such charges? Given that the ritual slaughter itself is a fabrication, what are the possible facts of the case? How are the various authorities portrayed? What was the sheriff's role? How are William's relatives depicted?

27. THE LIFE OF ST. GODRIC OF FINCHALE BY REGINALD OF DURHAM

Medieval hagiographies, or "saints' lives," exhibit very strong similarities across the genre, and many of these typical elements are present in the life of St. William of Norwich (above). But the biography of Godric of Finchale (c.1065-1170), written by a close associate and excerpted here, recounts a life rather different from that of the typical medieval saint, and does so in an unusual way, being full of circumstantial and lively detail about Godric's life as a merchant before his religious conversion.

Source: trans. G.G. Coulton, *Social Life in Britain from the Conquest to the Reformation* (Cambridge: Cambridge University Press, 1918), pp. 415-420; additional material trans. H. Waddell, *Beasts and Saints* (London: Constable and Company Ltd., 1934), pp. 84-89.

This holy man's father was named Ailward, and his mother Edwenna; both of slender rank and wealth, but abundant in righteousness and virtue. They were born in Norfolk, and had long lived in the township called Walpole.... When the boy had passed his childish years quietly at home, then, as he began to grow to manhood, he began to follow more prudent ways of life, and to learn carefully and persistently the teachings of worldly forethought. Wherefore he chose not to follow the life of a farmer, but rather to study, learn, and exercise the rudiments of more subtle conceptions. For this reason, aspiring to the merchant's trade, he began to follow the chapman's way of life, first learning how to gain in small bargains and things of insignificant price; and thence, while yet a youth, his mind advanced little by little to buy and sell and gain from things of greater expense. For, in his beginnings, he was wont to wander with small wares around the villages and farmsteads of his own neighborhood; but, in process of time, he gradually associated himself by compact with city merchants. Hence, within a brief space of time, the youth who had trudged for many weary hours from village to village, from farm to farm, did so profit by his increase of age and wisdom as to travel with associates of his own age through towns and boroughs, fortresses, and cities, to fairs and to all the various booths of the market-place, in pursuit of his public bargaining. He went along the highway, neither puffed up by the good testimony of his conscience nor downcast in the nobler part of his soul by the reproach of poverty....

Seeing that he then dwelt by the sea-shore, he went down one day to the strand to seek for some means of livelihood.... The place is called Wellstream, hard by the town of Spalding; there, when the tide was out, the country-folk were wont to scour and explore the stretches of sand, discovering and converting to their own use whatever wreckage or drift the sea might have brought to shore; for hence they sometimes get wealth, since they are free to seize there upon whatsoever goods or commodities they may find by the shore. The saint, then, inspired by such hopes, roamed one day over these stretches of foreshore; and, finding nothing at first, he followed on and on to a distance of three miles, where he found three porpoises lying high and dry, either cast upon the sands by the waves or left there by the ebb-tide. Two were still alive and struggling: the third, in the midst, was dead or dying. Moved with pity, he left the living untouched, cut a portion from the dead fish, and began carrying this away upon his back. But the tide soon began to flow; and Godric, halting under his burden, was overtaken by the waves; first they wet his feet, then his legs; then his upper body was compassed about by the deep; at length the waters went even over his head; yet Godric, strong in faith, bare his burden onwards even under the waves, until, by God's help, he struggled out upon the very shore from which he had gone forth. Then, bringing the fish to his parents, he told them the whole tale, and exhorted them to declare the glory of God.

Yet in all things he walked with simplicity; and, in so far as he yet knew how, it was ever his pleasure to follow in the footsteps of the truth. For, having learned the Lord's Prayer and the Creed from his very cradle, he oftentimes turned them over in his mind, even as he went alone on his longer journeys; and, in so far as the truth was revealed to his mind, he clung thereunto most devoutly in all his thoughts concerning God. At first, he lived as a chapman for four years in Lincolnshire, going on foot and carrying the smallest wares; then he traveled abroad, first to St. Andrews in Scotland and then for the first time to Rome. On his return, having formed a familiar friendship with certain other young men who were eager for merchandise, he began to launch upon bolder courses, and to go frequently by sea to the foreign lands that lay around him. Thus, sailing often to and fro between Scotland and Britain, he traded in many diverse wares and, amid these occupations, learned much worldly wisdom.... Thus aspiring ever higher and higher, and yearning upward with his whole heart, at length his great labors and cares bore much fruit of worldly gain. For he labored not only as a merchant but also as a shipman ... to Denmark and Flanders and Scotland; in all which lands he found certain rare, and therefore more precious, wares, which he carried to other parts wherein he knew them to be least familiar, and coveted by the inhabitants beyond the price of gold itself; wherefore he exchanged these wares for others coveted by men of other lands; and thus he bargained most freely and assiduously. Hence he made great profit in all his bargains, and gathered much wealth in the sweat of his brow; for he sold dear in one place the wares which he had bought elsewhere at a small price.

Then he purchased the half of a merchant-ship with certain of his partners in the trade; and again by his prudence he bought the fourth part of another ship. At length, by his skill in navigation, wherein he excelled all his fellows, he earned promotion to the post of steersman.... He knew, from the aspect of sea and stars, how to foretell fair or foul weather. In his various voyages he visited many saints' shrines, to whose protection he was wont most devoutly to commend himself, more especially the church of St. Andrew in Scotland, where he most frequently made and paid his vows. On the way thither, he oftentimes touched at the island of Lindisfarne, wherein St. Cuthbert had been bishop, and at the Isle of Farne, where that saint had lived as an anchoret, and where St. Godric (as he himself would tell afterwards) would meditate on the saint's life with abundant tears. Thence he began to yearn for solitude, and to hold his merchandise in less esteem than heretofore....

And now he had lived sixteen years as a merchant, and began to think of spending on charity, to God's honor and service, the goods which he had so laboriously acquired. He therefore took the cross as a pilgrim to Jerusalem, and, having visited the Holy Sepulcher, came back to England by way of St. James [of Compostella]. Not long afterwards he became steward to a certain rich man of his own country, with the care of his whole house and household. But certain of the younger household were men of iniquity, who stole their neighbors' cattle and thus held luxurious feasts, whereat Godric, in his ignorance, was sometimes present. Afterwards, discovering the truth, he rebuked and admonished them to cease; but they made no account of his warnings; wherefore he concealed not their iniquity, but disclosed it to the lord of the household, who, however, slighted his advice. Wherefore he begged to be dismissed and went on a pilgrimage, first to St. Gilles and thence to Rome, the abode of the apostles, that thus he might knowingly pay the penalty for those misdeeds wherein he had ignorantly partaken. I have often seen him, even in his old age, weeping for this unknowing transgression....

On his return from Rome, he abode awhile in his father's house, until, inflamed again with holy zeal, he purposed to revisit the abode of the apostles and made his desire known unto his parents. Not only did they approve his purpose, but his mother besought his leave to bear him company on this pilgrimage; which he gladly granted, and willingly paid her every filial service that was her due. They came therefore to London; and they had scarcely departed from thence when his mother took off her shoes, going thus barefooted to Rome and back to London. Godric, humbly serving his parent, was wont to bear her on his shoulders....

Godric, when he had restored his mother safe to his father's arms, abode but a brief while at home; for he was now already firmly purposed to give himself entirely to God's service. Wherefore, that he might follow Christ the more freely, he sold all his possessions and distributed them among the poor. Then, telling his parents of this purpose and receiving their blessing, he went forth to no certain abode, but whithersoever the Lord should deign to lead him; for above all things he coveted the life of a hermit.... [Eventually he settled at Finchale and gained renown as a hermit.]

It was the serene and joyous weather of high summer, and the turning of the year brought nigh the solemn feast of St. John the Baptist [on June 24 or August 29]. And because the man of God had begged it, and it was the familiar custom, two brothers from the monastery [of St. Cuthbert] at Durham were sent out to him to celebrate the divine office with all due honor. The office reverently said, and this most solemn mass ended, the folk who had come for the feast made their way home; and the brethren came to him to ask his blessing, and leave to return to their monastery.

"Ye may have God's blessing," said he, "but when St. Cuthbert's sons have come to visit me, they must not go home without their dinner." And, calling his serving-man, "Quick, beloved," said he, "and set up the table, for these brethren are to eat with us this day."

The table was set up, and oat cake laid upon it, such as he had, and bowls of good milk. Yet when he looked at the feast, it seemed to him but poor, and he bade the serving-man bring fish as well.

"Master," said he in amaze, "where should we get fish at a time like this, in all this heat and drought, when we can see the very bottom of the river? We can cross dry shod where we used to spread the seine and the nets." But he answered, "Go quickly and spread my seine in the same dry pool." The man went out and did as he was told; but with no hope of any sort of catch.

He came back, declaring that the pool had dried up till the very sands of it were parched; and his master bade him make haste to fill the cauldron with water, and set it on the hearth to heat, and this was done. After a little while he bade his man go to the bank and bring back his catch; the man went and looked, and came back empty-handed; he did it again a second time; and then in disgust, refused to go any more. For a little while the man of God held his peace, and then spoke. "Now go this time," said he, "for this very hour the fish has come into the net, that St. John the Baptist promised me; for never could he break a promise by not doing what he said, although our sluggish faith deserved it little. And look you," said he, "but that salmon that is now caught in the seine is a marvelous fine one." So in the end his man went off, and found even as he had been told; and drawing it out of the net he brought the fish alive to where his master sat in the oratory, and laid it at his feet. Then as he was bidden, he cut it into pieces and put it into the pot now boiling on the hearth, and cooked it well, and brought it and set it before the brethren at table, and well were they fed and mightily amazed. For they marvelled how a fish could come swimming up a river of which the very sands were dry; and, above all, how the man of God, talking with them and sitting in the oratory could have seen, by the revelation of the spirit, the very hour when the fish entered the meshes of the net. To which he made reply, "St. John the Baptist never deserts his own, but sheds the blessing of his great kindness on those that trust in him." And so he sent them home, well fed and uplifted at so amazing a miracle; praising and glorifying God, Who alone doeth marvels, for all that they had seen and heard.

... For in winter when all about was frozen stiff in the cold, he would go out barefoot, and if he lighted on any animal helpless with misery of the cold, he would set it under his armpit or in his bosom to warm it. Many a time would the kind soul go spying under the thick hedges or tangled patches of briars, and if haply he found a creature that had lost its way, or cowed with the harshness of the weather, or tired, or half dead, he would recover it with all the healing art he had....

And if anyone in his service had caught a bird or little beast in a snare or a trap or a noose, as soon as he found it he would snatch it from their hands and let it go free in the fields or the glades of the wood. So that many a time they would hide their captive spoils under a corn measure or a basket or some more secret hiding-place still; but even so they could never deceive him or keep it hidden. For without telling, and indeed with his serving-man disavowing and protesting, he would go straight to the place where the creatures had been hidden; and while the man would stand by crimson with fear and confusion, he would lift them out and set them free. So, too, hares and other beasts fleeing from the huntsmen he would take in, and house them in his hut; and when the ravagers, their hope frustrated, would be gone, he would send them away to their familiar haunts. Many a time the dumb creatures of the wood would swerve aside from where the huntsmen lay in wait, and take shelter in the safety of his hut; for it may be that by some divine instinct they knew that a sure refuge abided their coming....

Questions: What does the Life of Godric tell us about economic life in the twelfth century? What are the stages of Godric's spiritual development? Compare his vocation with that of Henry of Essex (doc. 23). Are there surprising aspects of Godric's life as a hermit? Compare the hermit's life with that described in the thirteenth-century Ancrene Wisse (doc. 40).

28. THE BURNING AND REPAIR OF THE CHURCH OF CANTERBURY, BY GERVASE OF CANTERBURY

Canterbury Cathedral was not only the seat of the head of the English church but also the site of the martyrdom and shrine of St. Thomas Becket; as such, it became England's foremost place of pilgrimage. The twelfth century also saw the development, in France, of a new architectural style, known today as gothic, and this style came to Canterbury as the result of a disaster. In the unusual passages excerpted here, a monk of Canterbury describes that disaster and its aftermath.

Source: trans. R. Willis, *The Architectural History of the Church of Canterbury* (London: Longman & Co., 1845), pp. 32-36, 48-56, 58, 61-62; revised.

1. The conflagration

In the year of grace 1174, by the just but secret judgment of God, the church of Christ at Canterbury was consumed by fire, in the forty-fourth year from its dedication, that glorious choir, to wit, which had been so magnificently completed by the care and industry of Prior Conrad.

Now the manner of the burning and repair was as follows. In the aforesaid year, on the nones of September [Sept. 5], at about the ninth hour [between 3 and 4 p.m.] and during an extraordinarily violent south wind, a fire broke out before the gate of the church, and outside the walls of the monastery, by which three cottages were half destroyed. From thence, while the citizens were assembling and subduing the fire, cinders and sparks carried aloft by the high wind were deposited upon the church, and being driven by the fury of the wind between the joints of the lead, remained there amongst the half rotten planks, and shortly glowing with increasing heat, set fire to the rotten rafters; from these the fire was communicated to the larger beams and their braces, no one yet perceiving or helping. For the well-painted ceiling below, and the sheet-lead covering above, concealed between them the fire that had arisen within.

Meantime the three cottages, whence the mischief had arisen, being destroyed, and the popular excitement having subsided, everybody went home again, while the neglected church was consuming with internal fire unknown to all. But beams and braces burning, the flames arose to the slopes of the roof; and the sheets of lead yielded to the increasing heat and began to melt. Thus the raging wind, finding a freer entrance, increased the fury of the fire; and the flames beginning to show themselves, a cry arose in the churchyard: "See! see! the church is on fire."

The people and the monks assemble in haste, they draw water, they brandish their hatchets, they run up the stairs, full of eagerness to save the church

Fig. 25: The Corona, Canterbury Cathedral This chapel at the far eastern end of Canterbury Cathedral shows the early Gothic style of the late twelfth and early thirteenth century, as described in Gervase of Canterbury's account of the rebuilding of the cathedral after the fire of 1174. This is a nineteenth-century engraving of the chapel.

already, alas! beyond their help. But when they reach the roof and perceive the black smoke and scorching flames that pervade it throughout, they abandon the attempt in despair, and thinking only of their own safety, make all haste to descend.

And now that the fire had loosened the beams from the pegs that bound them together, the half-burnt timbers fell into the choir below upon the seats of the monks; the seats, consisting of a great mass of woodwork, caught fire, and thus the mischief grew worse and worse. And it was marvelous, though sad, to behold how that glorious choir itself fed and assisted the fire that was destroying it. For the flames multiplied by this mass of timber, and extending upwards full fifteen cubits, scorched and burnt the walls, and more especially injured the columns of the church.

And now the people ran to the ornaments of the church, and began to tear down the vestments and curtains, some that they might save, but some to steal them. The reliquary chests were thrown down from the high beam and thus broken, and their contents scattered; but the monks collected them and carefully preserved them from the fire. Some there were, who, inflamed with a wicked and diabolical cupidity, feared not to appropriate to themselves the things of the church, which they had saved from the fire.

In this manner the house of God, hitherto delightful as a paradise of pleasures, was now made a despicable heap of ashes, reduced to a dreary wilderness, and laid open to all the injuries of weather.

The people were astonished that the Almighty should suffer such things, and maddened with excess of grief and perplexity, they tore their hair and beat the walls and pavement of the church with their heads and hands, blaspheming the Lord and his saints, the patrons of the church; and many, both of laity and monks, would rather have laid down their lives than that the church should have so miserably perished.

For not only was the choir consumed in the fire, but also the infirmary, with the chapel of St. Mary, and several other offices in the court; moreover many ornaments and goods of the church were reduced to ashes.

2. The operations of the first year

Bethink thee now what mighty grief oppressed the hearts of the sons of the church under this great tribulation; I verily believe the afflictions of Canterbury were no less than those of Jerusalem of old, and their wailings were as the lamentations of Jeremiah; neither can mind conceive, or words express, or writing teach, their grief and anguish. Truly that they might alleviate their miseries with a little consolation, they put together as well as they could, an altar and station in the nave of the church, where they might wail and howl, rather than sing, the diurnal and nocturnal services. Meanwhile the patron saints of the church, St. Dunstan and St. Elfege, had their resting-place in that wilderness. Lest, therefore, they should suffer even the slightest injury from the rains and storms, the monks, weeping and lamenting with incredible grief and anguish, opened the tombs of the saints and extricated them in their coffins from the choir, but with the greatest difficulty and labor, as if the saints themselves resisted the change.

They disposed them as decently as they could at the altar of the Holy Cross in the nave. Thus, like as the children of Israel were ejected from the land of promise, … so the brethren remained in grief and sorrow for five years in the nave of the church, separated from the people only by a low wall.

Meantime the brotherhood sought counsel as to how and in what manner the burnt church might be repaired, but without success; for the columns of the church, commonly termed the pillars, were exceedingly weakened by the heat of the fire, and were scaling in pieces and hardly able to stand, so that they frightened even the wisest out of their wits.

French and English artificers were therefore summoned, but even these differed in opinion. On the one hand, some undertook to repair the aforesaid columns without mischief to the walls above. On the other hand, there were some who asserted that the whole church must be pulled down if the monks wished to exist in safety. This opinion, true as it was, excruciated the monks with grief, and no wonder, for how could they hope that so great a work should be completed in their days by any human ingenuity?

However, amongst the other workmen there had come a certain William of Sens, a man active and ready, and as a workman most skillful both in wood and stone. Him, therefore, they retained, on account of his lively genius and good reputation, and dismissed the others. And to him and to the providence of God was the execution of the work committed.

And he, residing many days with the monks and carefully surveying the burnt walls in their upper and lower parts, within and without, did yet for some time conceal what he found necessary to be done, lest the truth should kill them in their present state of pusillanimity.

But he went on preparing all things that were needful for the work, either of himself or by the agency of others. And when he found that the monks began to be somewhat comforted, he ventured to confess that the pillars rent with the fire and all that they supported must be destroyed if the monks wished to have a safe and excellent building. At length they agreed, being convinced by reason and wishing to have the work as good as he promised, and above all things to live in security; thus they consented patiently, if not willingly, to the destruction of the choir.

And now he addressed himself to the procuring of stone from beyond the sea. He constructed ingenious machines for loading and unloading ships, and for drawing cement and stone. He delivered molds for shaping the stones to the sculptors who were assembled, and diligently prepared other things of the same kind. The choir thus condemned to destruction was pulled down, and nothing else was done in this year.

5. Operations of the first five years

... In the following year [1175-6], that is after the feast of St. Bertin [Sept. 5] before the winter, he erected four pillars, that is, two on each side, and after the winter two more were placed, so that on each side were three in order, upon which and upon the exterior wall of the aisles he framed seemly arches and a vault.... With these works the second year was occupied.

In the third year [1176-7] he placed two pillars on each side, the two extreme ones of which he decorated with marble columns placed around them, and because at that place the choir and crosses were to meet, he constituted these principal pillars. To which, having added the key-stones and the vault, he intermingled the lower triforium from the great tower to the aforesaid pillars, that is, as far as the cross, with many marble columns. Over which he adjusted another triforium of the other materials, and also the upper windows. And in the next place, three bays of the great vault, from the tower, namely, as far as the crosses. All which things appeared to us, and to all who saw them, incomparable and most worthy of praise. And at so glorious a beginning we rejoiced and conceived good hopes to the end, and provided for the acceleration of the work with diligence and spirit. Thus was the third year occupied and the beginning of the fourth.

In the summer of which [1178], commencing from the cross, he erected ten pillars, that is, on each side five. The first two were ornamented with marble columns to correspond with the other two principal ones. Upon these ten he placed the arches and vaults. And having, in the next place, completed on both sides the triforia and upper windows, he was, at the beginning of the fifth year, in the act of preparing with machines for the turning of the great vault, when suddenly the beams broke under his feet, and he fell to the ground, stones and timbers accompanying his fall from the height of the capitals of the upper vault, that is to say, of fifty feet. Thus sorely bruised by the blows from the beams and stones, he was rendered helpless alike to himself and for the work, but no other than himself was in the least injured. Against the master only was this vengeance of God or spite of the devil directed.

The master, thus hurt, remained in his bed for some time under medical care in expectation of recovering, but was deceived in this hope, for his health amended not. Nevertheless, as the winter approached, and it was necessary to finish the upper vault, he gave the charge of the work to a certain ingenious and industrious monk, who was the overseer of the masons; an appointment whence much envy and malice arose, because it made this young man appear more skillful than richer and more powerful ones. But the master reclining in bed commanded all things that should be done in order. And thus was completed the bay between the four principal pillars. In the keystone of this bay the choir and transept seem as it were to meet. Two bays on each side were formed before the winter, when the heavy rains beginning stopped the work. In these operations the fourth year was occupied and the beginning of the fifth....

And the master, perceiving that he derived no benefit from the physicians, gave up the work, and crossing the sea, returned to his home in France. And another succeeded him in charge of the works; William by name, English by nation, small in body, but in workmanship of many kinds acute and honest. In the summer of the fifth year [1179] he finished the transept on each side, that is, the south and the north, and turned the vault which is above the great altar, which the rains of the previous year had hindered, although all was prepared. Moreover, he laid the foundation for the enlargement of the church at the eastern part, because a chapel of St. Thomas was to be built there. For this was the place assigned to [St. Thomas], namely the chapel of the Holy Trinity, where he celebrated his first mass, where he was wont to prostrate himself with tears and prayers, under whose crypt for so many years he was buried, where God for his merits had performed so many miracles, where poor and rich, kings and princes, had worshiped him, and whence the sound of his praises had gone forth into all lands.

The master William began, on account of these foundations, to dig in the cemetery of the monks, from whence he was compelled to disturb the bones of many holy monks. These were carefully collected and deposited in a large trench, in that corner which is between the chapel and the south side of the infirmary house. Having, therefore, formed a most substantial foundation for the exterior wall with stone and cement, he erected the wall of the crypt as high as the bases of the windows.

Thus was the fifth year employed and the beginning of the sixth.

6. The entry into the new choir

In the beginning of the sixth year [1180] from the fire, and at the time when the works were resumed, the monks were seized with a violent longing to prepare the choir, so that they might enter into it at the coming Easter. And the master, perceiving their desires, set himself manfully to work, to satisfy the wishes of the convent. He constructed, with all diligence, the wall which encloses the choir and presbytery. He erected the three altars of the presbytery. He carefully prepared a resting-place for St. Dunstan and St. Elphege. A wooden wall to keep out the weather was set up transversely between the penultimate pillars at the eastern part, and had three glass windows in it.

The choir, thus hardly completed even with the greatest labor and diligence, the monks were resolved to enter on Easter Eve with the new fire [to light the Paschal Candle]. As all that was required could not be fully performed on the Saturday because of the solemnities of that sacred day, it became necessary that our holy fathers and patrons, St. Dunstan and St. Elphege, the co-exiles of the monks, should be transferred to the new choir beforehand. Prior Alan, therefore, taking with him nine of the brethren of the church in whom he could trust, went by night to the tombs of the saints, that he might not be incommoded by a crowd, and having locked the doors of the church, he commanded the stone-work that enclosed them to be taken down.

The monks and servants of the church therefore, in obedience to the prior's commands, took the structure to pieces, opened the stone coffins of the saints, and bore their relics to the vestry. Then, having removed the cloths in which they had been wrapped, and which were half consumed from age and rottenness, they covered them with other and more handsome palls, and bound them with linen bands. They bore the saints, thus prepared, to their altars, and deposited them in wooden chests, covered within and without with lead; which chests, thus lead-covered, and strongly bound with iron, were enclosed in stone-work that was consolidated with melted lead.... On the morrow, however, when this translation of the saints became known to the whole convent, they were exceedingly astonished and indignant that it should have been done without their consent, for they had intended that the translation of the fathers should have been performed with great and devout solemnity.

They cited the prior and those who were with him, before the venerable Archbishop Richard, to answer for the slight thus presumptuously cast upon themselves and the holy patrons of the church, and endeavored to compel the prior and his assistants to renounce their offices. But by the intervention of the archbishop and other men of authority, and after due apology and repentence, the convent was appeased; and harmony being thus restored, the service of Holy Saturday was performed in the chapter-house, because the station of the monks and the altar which had been in the nave of the church were removed to prepare for the solemnities of the following Easter Sunday. About the sixth hour the archbishop in cope and miter, and the convent in albs, according to the custom of the church, went in procession to the new fire, and having consecrated it, proceeded towards the new choir with the appointed hymn.... The remainder of the offices that appertain to the day were devoutly celebrated. And then the pontiff, standing at the altar and vested with the chasuble, began the *Te Deum laudamus*; and the bells ringing, the convent took up the song with great joy, and shedding sweet tears, they praised God with voice and heart for all his benefits....

7. Remaining operations of the sixth year

... Moreover, in the same summer, that is of the sixth year [1180], the outer wall round the chapel of St. Thomas, begun before the winter, was elevated as far as the turning of the vault. But the master had begun a tower at the eastern part outside the circuit of the wall as it were, the lower vault of which was completed before the winter.

The chapel of the Holy Trinity above mentioned was then leveled to the ground; this had hitherto remained untouched out of reverence to St. Thomas, who was buried in the crypt. But the saints who reposed in the upper part of the chapel were translated elsewhere.... The translation of these Fathers having been thus effected, the chapel, together with its crypt, was destroyed to the very ground; only that the translation of St. Thomas was reserved until the completion of his chapel. For it was fitting and manifest that such a translation should be most solemn and public. In the meantime, therefore, a wooden chapel, sufficiently decent for the place and occasion, was prepared around and above his tomb. Outside of this a foundation was laid of stones and cement, upon which eight pillars of the new crypt, with their capitals, were completed. The master also carefully opened an entrance from the old to the new crypt. And thus the sixth year was employed, and part of the seventh....

9. Operations of the seventh, eighth, and tenth years

Now let us carefully examine what were the works of our mason in this seventh year [1181] from the fire, which, in short, included the completion of the new and handsome crypt, and above the crypt the exterior walls of the aisles up to their marble capitals. The windows, however, the master was neither willing nor able to turn, on account of the approaching rains. Neither did he erect the interior pillars. Thus was the seventh year finished, and the eighth begun.

In this eighth year [1182] the master erected eight interior pillars ... and turned the arches and the vault with the windows in the circuit. He also raised the tower up to the bases of the highest windows under the vault. In the ninth year [1183] no work was done for want of funds. In the tenth year [1184] the upper windows of the tower, together with the vault, were finished. Upon the pillars was placed a lower and an upper triforium, with windows and the great vault. Also was made the upper roof where the cross stands aloft, and the roof of the aisles as far as the laying of the lead. The tower was covered in, and many other things done this year....

Questions: What was important to the monks about their church? How did the church building express their religion? Why did the work go so slowly? What kinds of tensions within the monastic community are revealed in this work?

29. JOHN OF SALISBURY'S *POLICRATICUS*

John of Salisbury, a Paris-trained scholar who eventually became bishop of Chartres, was English by birth and a close associate of Thomas Becket, to whom he dedicated the Policraticus, *his treatise on government, politics, and power. The extracts below mention some of the classical sources on which John, one of the great twelfth-century humanists, drew in composing what some consider the earliest book of medieval political theory.*

Source: trans. D.C. Douglas and G.W. Greenaway, eds., *English Historical Documents, vol. II, 1042-1189* (New York: Oxford University Press, 1953), pp. 784-789.

The nature of the State, according to Plutarch, and what takes the place therein of the soul and the members of the body.

Headings of the same political construction follow in the little book entitled *The Institutes of Trajan*, which I have in part thought fit to make use of in this present work. But this I have done by reproducing its views in outline rather than by using its actual words.

First of all it is laid down that the prince should judge everything for himself and diligently consider what place he occupies in the whole body-politic. Moreover, in Plutarch's view, the State is a kind of organism, whose life is a gift of God, controlled by the motions of divine equity and ruled by the governing force of reason. But the powers which establish and implant in us the practices of religion and hand down to us the ceremonies of God — I may not speak of the gods, as Plutarch doth — in the body-politic take the place of the soul. Those, indeed, who preside over the practice of religious duties, ought to be upheld and reverenced as being the soul of the body. For who doubts that the ministers of God's holiness are his vicars? Furthermore, like as the soul hath the pre-eminence over the whole body, so also those whom God calls to be officials of religion are set over the whole body.... The prince, indeed, in the state occupies the position of the head, being subject to the one true God and his representatives on earth, like as in the human body the head is both animated and ruled by the spirit. The senate takes the place of the heart, whence spring the impulses to good and evil deeds. The judges and provincial governors appropriate the functions of the eyes, ears and tongue, the officials and soldiers correspond to the hands, the courtiers to the sides, the treasurers and financial experts — I am not referring to those put in charge of prisons, but to the custodians of private interests — represent the stomach and intestines. These, if they become clogged through excessive indulgence of appetite and remain stubbornly constipated, engender manifold and incurable disorders and bring ruin upon the whole body. The husbandmen correspond to the feet, ever cleaving to the ground, for which the foresight of the head is the more necessary as they find occasion for stumbling, when they tread the earth in obedience to the dictates of the body. Wherefore they should properly be well shod, for they support the weight of the whole body, keep it erect and enable it to move. Take away the support of the feet from a healthy body and it will be unable to walk in its own strength, but will either crawl on its hands, shamefully, helplessly and with great difficulty, or be propelled with the assistance of the animal creation....

The function of the secular arm

The sacred history of the Gospel bears witness that two swords suffice for the Christian empire; the others all belong to those who come out with swords and staves to take Christ captive, and desire to blot out His name. What kind of soldiers are they who, despite their oaths, do not conform to the law, but think that the glory of their warfare consists in showing contempt for the priesthood, in disparaging the authority of the church, in expanding man's empire in such a way as to contract the dominion of Christ, in singing their own praises and flattering and exalting themselves by false proclamations, aping the famous warrior amidst the derision of their hearers? The courage of such men is most evident when they wound the clergy, the defenseless soldiery, either with weapons or with their tongues. What then is the true function of the professional soldier? To protect the church, to fight against treachery, to reverence the priesthood, to ward off injuries from the poor, to ensure peace throughout the provinces and (as taught by a true understanding of the Sacrament) to shed his blood and, if need be, to lay down his life for his brethren. "Let the praises of God be in their mouth and a two-edged sword in their hands, to be avenged of the heathen and to rebuke the people, to bind their kings in chains and their nobles with links of iron." But to what end? That they may become the slaves of passion, vanity and avarice, or their own lusts? By no means; but rather that they may execute thereby the decrees of the judges; wherein each man follows not his own judgment but that of the angels of God and of men from the dictates of equity and the public weal. I say to execute the decrees for, as it is the office of the judges to pronounce sentence, in like manner also it is the duty of these men to execute it: as it is written, "Such honor have all his saints." For the soldiers who do these things are just as much saints and loyal to their prince in proportion as they preserve the faith of God; and they promote the glory of their virtue more effectively inasmuch as they faithfully seek in everything the glory of God....

On tyrants and tyrannicide

That it is lawful to flatter one whom it is also lawful to slay; and that the tyrant is a public enemy.

... In profane letters there is contained a warning that life should be carried on in one way with a friend and in the opposite way with a tyrant. One should certainly not indulge in servile flattery of a friend, but it is permissible to soothe the ears of a tyrant. For it is permissible to flatter one whom it is lawful to slay. Moreover, not only is it lawful to slay the tyrant, but it is likewise just and equitable to do so. For he that takes the sword deserves to perish by the sword. But taking the sword is to be understood of him who seizes it for his own fell purpose, not of him who receives power to wield it from the Lord. He that receives power from God complies with the laws and is the servant of right and justice. But he who seizes power oppresses the rights of men and subordinates the laws to his own will. Therefore the law is justly armed against the man who would disarm the laws, and the authority of the State strikes heavily against him who strives to weaken its power. And though there are many treasonable offenses, none is more serious than this which is practised against the body of the laws themselves. Tyranny therefore is not only a public crime, but, if it be possible, it is an even greater one. For if treason admits the accusations of all men, how much more does the crime of suppressing the laws which should govern the rulers themselves? Assuredly no man takes private vengeance upon a public enemy, but whoso does not bring an accusation against him fails in his duty towards himself and towards the whole body-politic....

Wherein the tyrant differs from the prince, and of the tyranny of priests

The distinction between the prince and the tyrant has been stated above, when we were turning over the pages of Plutarch's *Institutes of Trajan*. Similarly the functions of the prince and the members of the body-politic have been carefully explained. From this may easily and briefly be set down what should be said on the opposite side about the tyrant.

The tyrant then, as the philosophers have depicted him, is one who oppresses the people by violent and despotic rule, even as the prince governs by the laws. Moreover the law is the gift of God, the model of equity, the pattern of justice, the image of the divine will, the guardian of security, the force unifying and consolidating the people, the rule of conduct for officials, the exclusion and extermination of vices, the penalty for violence and all wrong-doing. The law may be assailed either by force or by cunning; it may be, as it were, ravaged by the cruelty of the lion or lured into the lair of the dragon. By whatever means this occurs, it is clear that divine grace is attacked and that God is in some measure provoked to battle. The prince fights for the laws and the liberty of the people; the tyrant reckons that naught has been accomplished unless he has made the laws of none effect and enticed the people into servi-tude. The prince bears the stamp of divinity, while the tyrant's image is that of a perverted strength and satanic wickedness, in that he copies Lucifer who for-sook virtue and strove to place his seat in the north part of heaven and become like unto the most High....

As the image of the deity the prince is worthy of love, reverence and wor-ship; the tyrant, being the image of wickedness, for the most part merits assassi-nation. The tyrant has his roots in iniquity, and from a poisoned root a tree brings forth evil and deadly fruits and should be felled with the axe. For if wickedness and injustice, the destroyer of love, had not engendered the tyrant, his people had enjoyed firm peace and perpetual tranquility, and no one would have contemplated the extension of its territories.... Kings indeed are not the only ones to practise tyranny.... For many are found in the ranks of the clergy who act thus from overweening ambition and avail themselves of every artifice to play the tyrant under cover of their office. For the ungodly State also has head and members and strives, as it were, by civil institutions to conform to the pattern of the lawful State. Its head, the tyrant, is the devil's image; heretical, schismatic, and sacrilegious priests and, to employ Plutarch's term, the officers of religion, who impugn God's law, represent the soul; evil counsellors or, so to speak, a senate of iniquity represent the heart; the eyes, ears, tongue and hands, when unarmed, are represented by the judges and their laws, unjust officials; when armed the hands are the violent soldiery whom Cicero designates rob-bers; the feet are those who in their lowlier transactions act contrary to the precepts of the Lord and lawful institutions. All these similes can indeed be very easily comprehended from what has been written above. But the clergy should not be angry with me if I admit that tyrants can also be found in their ranks....

... Despite the Lord's interdiction the house of prayer has become a house of merchandise, and the temple built on him as corner-stone is turned into a cave of robbers. For the church is verily given over to pillage, some laying open hands on her possessions, others acquiring them by secret usurpation; and in a case where there are no possessions to be alienated the church itself is seized. For it is very rare to find a man who will gird his sword upon his thigh to restrain the presumption of ambition. The ambitious man devises many different stratagems in order to take the church by storm when there is none to defend her. One man, trusting in his noble birth or in the weight of his authority, bursts headlong into the holy places, and if perchance he be repulsed at the door, he is not afraid to undermine the walls or the threshold. For he will stir up rebellion against Moses, offer strange fire in the Lord's temple and defile the vessels of the sanctuary. Another, trusting in the multitude of his riches, enters in with Simon Magus as his guide and finds none therein to bid him and his money depart to perdition. Another fears to approach Peter openly with gifts, but creeps into the church's lap secretly and adulterously, like Jupiter entering through the roof and stealing into Danae in a shower of gold. Another sidles up obsequiously, as if with no thought of offering a gift, or as though his complaisance matched the extent of his present, whereas in reality there is no greater gift offered than when a man devotes himself to the service of his fellows.

... On the other side are ranged many who by no means conceal their purpose, but by blowing their own trumpet, as we say, mock at the tardiness in their ambition shown by those whom we have considered above, which they liken to that of soldiers who dare not openly acknowledge the decorations they have won in war. Of these former — impure as they are, and unwilling to amend their own way of life and ignorant how to instruct that of others — it is said that they break into the Holy of Holies with unclean feet and bear in their polluted hands the shewbread of the Lord and the Flesh of the immaculate Lamb consumed by the fire of his Passion on the Cross. Albeit unworthy to approach the outer doors, yet they incontinently thrust themselves into the priesthood, rush into the sanctuary and, repulsing others, take possession of the sacred altars in such wise that Holy Orders would now appear to have been instituted, not for the purpose of offering a pattern and example to the laity, but to afford an opportunity to live in plenty and security. It might be supposed that the priesthood is not an office subject to the stern judgment of God but some administrative post secure and above dispute....

The majority of them feel themselves secured by a papal privilege or a royal mandate from the need to conform to the decrees of the judges or to execute justice or to subject themselves to the law of God. I do not blame the leniency of the apostolic see for this, but I do not consider that such indulgence is expedient for the church. We read of none such in existence among that glorious band of Christ's followers, although there was strife among them as to which of them should be the greater. We have no mention of any dispensation of this kind having been made by the apostles, although we have read that Paul and Barnabas parted from each other. We believe there is no ground for opposition in that celestial city which is our mother above, nor ought there to be here on earth, except when the most urgent reason demands it. For in these matters —

if I may speak with the leave of the mob and of those who favor this abuse —
I will write as I feel, lest I abate anything of the truth or what is worthy of
credit. I declare then my firm belief that those who, carried away by their own
pride, seek dispensations of this kind, would, if it were possible, shake off the
yoke of Christ and his Divine Father. Nay! I go even further and say that to the
best of their ability they are casting off and willfully breaking the ordinance of
God.... This gives rise to a grave scandal in religion and the Christian faith,
because the priesthood and the ministry are undertaken more from the motive
of ambition and to curry favor than from merit. So run they all, but when they
have reached the goal, one receiveth the prize, namely he that hath proved
himself swifter than others in the race of ambition and hath even outrun Peter
and every other disciple of Christ. For such a one has attained his ambition and
forestalled the utmost speed of a rapid summons....

*Questions: What kinds of analogies does John use to explain the state and society?
What kinds of sources does he purport to use? What is the proper relationship between
the secular government and the church? What does he criticize in society? How should
people react to a tyrant? What are the risks of recommending tyrannicide? What modern
political theories are anticipated here? What ideas are distinctly medieval?*

30. THE HISTORY OF WILLIAM MARSHAL

*William Marshal's contemporaries admired him enormously, for his military prowess and
dashing reputation as a young man, for his successful career in royal politics which earned
him a earldom (through marriage to the heiress of Pembroke), and for his wisdom and
integrity as an elder statesman during the troubled reign of King John (1199-1216) and
the minority of his son, Henry III. After William's death his son commissioned an
unusual and very long verse biography of him in French; the section translated here
recounts episodes from William's early life as a bachelor knight. (The surname "Marshal" derives from the family's hereditary position as royal marshals.)*

Source: trans. L. Algazi from *Histoire de Guillaume le Maréchal, comte de Striguil et de Pembroke, régent
d'Angleterre*, ed. P. Meyer (Paris: Librairie Renouard, 1891-1901), pp. 44-56.

> Everywhere the news was heard
> That between Saint-Jame and Valennes
> A tournament would soon be held.
> Each knight sought to do his best
> To prepare to journey there,
> Doing all he needed to do.
> And two weeks prior it was announced

That those from Anjou and from Maine,
From Poitou and from Brittany,
Would challenge Frenchmen, Englishmen,
And Normans on that glorious day
Without deception or dispute.
The news was spread so far and wide
That it came as far as Tancarville.
The chamberlain equipped himself
And prepared himself with pleasure
To bear arms in the contest.
The knights' hall filled with men
Preparing to go to the tournament,
But the marshal had no means to go;
He sat and thought about his plight.
His lord came over and spoke to him:
"What are you thinking, Sir Marshal, pray?"
"My lord, I have no mount to ride,
And thus I am unfit to go."
"Good Sir Marshal, be at ease;
You need no longer be concerned,
For a fine horse you shall have."
The marshal thanked his sovereign lord,
Trusting in his given word.
All night the knights who would attend
Had chain mail rolled and trousers cleaned,
Adjusting all their suits of mail,
Their neckpieces and coverings,
Saddles, bridles, breast-pieces,
Saddle-girths, stirrups and saddle-straps.
The others tried their helmets on,
In case they might have need of them.
This one said: "I shall carry my shield;
I see that the strap fits me well
And its grip, I also see,
Fits my arm most comfortably;
All here is as it should be."
On every side could then be seen
Knights donning caps and helmet mail,
And putting them among their gear.
Many worked to equip themselves
To the best of their abilities.

All night long they toiled away,
With many awake and few asleep;
The next morn they rushed to meet
In a group on the main square.

The chamberlain had fine horses brought
To give to all his faithful knights.
When the horses all were gone
The marshal still did not have one:
He saw quite well what had transpired,
And never said a single word
But this: "The horses have all gone,
But I have not been given one."
Then replied the chamberlain:
"Sir Marshal, it were wrong indeed
That you were not the first to mount,
But you shall have a battle horse,
A fine and fair one, no matter the cost;
For no reason shall you be left behind."
Someone pointed out to him
That there was one horse that remained
Very well made and strong and fine,
Lively, swift and spirited.
When the horse was brought to him,
A fine, well-bred and valuable steed,
Except for one unfortunate trait
That greatly decreased his worth:
He was so difficult to tame
That none could put his bridle on.
The marshal mounted in a trice:
With no effort nor help from his arm,
He nudged the horse on with his spurs,
And the horse flew like a bird,
Jumped off and galloped away.
When it was time to slow him down,
No other horse was stubborn as he;
No matter how expert his rider be,
If he held him back with fifteen bits
The horse would never stop for him.
The marshal perceived this trait,
And he conceived the perfect trick:

He lengthened the horse's reins
By three fingers' width, with a firm hand,
And this loosened the marshal's grip
So that the bit in the horse's mouth
Came down and settled on his teeth,
So that the horse no longer felt
The bit bearing down on his mouth.
For no gold and no amount of wealth
Would the horse have stopped himself.
But with this the horse was well content
And was so changed by the marshal's grip
That he consented to trot around
A half an acre of open land
Like the sweetest animal in the land.

The day of the tourney, the knights all came;
In front of their refuge they remained
Until they were well and truly armed
And ready as they were supposed to be;
Then they rode forth in small groups
Bunched together in an orderly way;
And know ye that, before the joust-yard,
Such tournaments did not have rules,
Nor did one dispute or discuss,
Except to lose or win it all.
The chamberlain stood back and watched;
Forty or more stalwart knights
Were fighting under his banner;
Such well-equipped knights had never been seen.
Many rode in dignity
To join the contest on that day.
The king of Scotland was present too
And rode his horse like a gentleman;
Many decorated knights rode with him,
Too many to easily count.
But why bore you with the details?
Sir Philip of Valognes
Was so elegantly equipped
And in his bearing quite refined
And more handsome than all the rest,
So much more alert than any bird,

That he was by others much admired.
The marshal studied him carefully:
Forthwith he left the gathering,
He spurred on his horse Blancart,
Between them he raced with all his might
And took Philip's mount by the reins.
Philip tried valiantly to resist,
But against the marshal 'twas all in vain:
By sheer strength the marshal pulled his horse
Out of the midst of the tournament;
The marshal asked for Philip's word
And trusted him to stay outside
So the marshal could continue to fight.
And when he had left his prisoner
He threw himself back into the fray;
Soon he took another knight
With a lance which he retrieved,
And with the remains of the lance
He fought so well that the knight submitted
And said he was his prisoner.
So two wealthy hostages had he,
With no injuries and no cause for shame;
He put his hand to taking a third;
He did so well and fought so hard
That this knight also yielded his sword;
And another knight then came to him,
As his prisoner was dismounting,
And said: "Since I fought at your side,
We should split the price of this horse."
"Very well," said the marshal to him;
"Whenever you wish to depart,
We'll split the spoils before you leave."
After speaking, he regretted his words,
But he never went back on his word.

Good sirs, it is true indeed
That God is wise and courteous:
He comes quickly to render aid
To all who have true faith in him.
That morning, the marshal had been poor
With no money and no horse to ride,
And now he had four and a half

Fine and fair horses, thanks be to God!
Thus he had palfreys and draft horses
And pack-horses and fine harnesses.
The tournament came to an end
And the chamberlain took his leave,
He and the knights who rode with him.
The marshal was esteemed by all
And many looked on him favorably,
Much more so than they had before.
Thus is proven the old saying:
"The more you have, the more you're liked."

Soon afterward was heard the news
That between Saint-Brice and Bouëre
There would be a tournament.
Whoever wished to increase his fame
And demonstrate his skill at arms
Could come and show his prowess there.
The chamberlain was preparing to go,
But then either illness or bad advice
Changed his mind and turned his head
So that he did not go after all.
But the marshal, in any case,
Prepared to travel to the tournament
Because he wanted to compete.
He asked permission of his lord,
Who told him without delay:
"I'm sure you shan't arrive in time,
For it will take at least three days
For you to get from here to there;
Thus will you not make it in time."
The marshal, who did not hesitate,
Said: "If it pleases God, I shall;
Do not worry on my account."
"Go, then, and may God go with you!
I shan't be the one to hold you back."

The marshal took his leave and left
For always he goes willingly
To wherever his fancy leads.
He rode hard both day and night
Through the fields and over hills

So that he arrived in time
To see the knights preparing their arms.
Most were armed and ready to fight.
He dismounted hurriedly
And armed himself most handily,
Then mounted on his handsome steed
Of whom he was really quite fond.
Already the knights could be seen:
Some rode in total disarray
And others came in an orderly way,
Arranging themselves in battle ranks;
And he pursued his business there
As he so well knew how to do.
Thus at the outset did he fight
And triumph over a valiant knight.
He had hardly had a moment's rest
When he saw charging straight at him
Five knights; they seized his horse's reins,
But no matter how hard they tried
They could not take him prisoner,
For he gave them too much to do.
They were anxious to capture him,
But more anxious still to defend themselves:
They hit him hard and many times,
And he was not averse to the idea
Of returning the favor in kind.
He soon lost count of all the blows:
Some wanted to pull him from his horse,
Others tried to remove his helmet,
Still others tried to pull him down
Over the hind end of his mount;
Some struck him, others hit him,
And when he had escaped them all
He struck them hard upon the head,
Giving them their just reward.
No matter how many blows he received,
No one could ever unhorse him.
So many of them tried his mettle
That they renounced this fruitless battle,
And he fought them so fiercely
That he escaped in spite of them;

But they so badly battered him
That they turned his helmet 'round
So that the front was facing his back;
No matter how he tried to pull
Or take it off, it would not budge
And he could only take it off
By breaking one of the laces off,
And mangling his hands in the process.

With much effort and much pain
He pulled the helmet from his head;
Thus he could finally get some air.
Two important knights, methinks,
Who had seen him tourneying
Were passing by that very spot,
Sir Bon-Abbé de Rougé
and Sir Jean de Subligni.
Sir Jean recognized him,
But Bon-Abbé knew him not,
But he praised him, saying then:
"Sir Jean, who is that worthy knight
Who knows so well how to fight?
I have not heard tell of him.
See how weary is his mount!"
"Sir William Marshal is his name,"
Said Sir Jean to Bon-Abbé;
"Methinks that there has never been
A more able and honest man.
His arms are from Tancarville."
Then Sir Bon-Abbé replied:
"Any army led by that knight
Must be the better for it, both
In merit and in bravery."

The marshal heard their every word,
And he rejoiced within his heart.
'Tis true that joy and happiness
Enhance good sense and prowess.
Then he put his helmet back on.
Though he was not eager to fight,
He re-entered the tournament.

He behaved so valiantly
That all were very much impressed
By the strength and competence
With which he made his way through the throng.
None pushed in too close to him,
Thus they left him a clear path.
On both sides the crowd was abuzz.
By blows both given and received
He so increased his own renown
That he was granted by acclaim
All the prizes of the day.

But he did not wish to take them all;
Quickly he held out his hand
To a horse from Lombardy,
But this horse had never been tamed
And had never let anyone mount;
Nor did he want to be harnessed,
So the horse dropped to the ground.
The marshal took the horse by the bit,
Who wished that he would leave him be;
Thus he took him from the crowd,
And gave him to his squire to hold.
But I shall not bore you any more.

Questions: What are the knights in this poem interested in? How does the poem express chivalric values? What obstacles does William overcome? What are his rewards?

31. RICHARD OF DEVIZES' CHRONICLE OF THE THIRD CRUSADE

King Richard I (1189-99) is better known as Richard the Lionheart, the famed warrior. He visited England only twice during his reign, preferring to use its rich resources to fund his wars on the continent and his crusade to the Middle East. The latter is described here by a chronicler who was not an eyewitness but was well informed.

Source: trans. J.A. Giles, *Chronicles of the Crusades, Being Contemporary Narratives...*, ed. H.G. Bohn (London: Henry G. Bohn, 1848), pp. 55-56, 60-64; revised.

86. Richard, the king of the English, had already spent two years in conquering the region around Jerusalem, and during all that time no aid had been sent to him from any of his realms. Nor yet were his only and uterine brother, John,

count of Mortain, nor his justiciars, nor his other nobles, observed to take any care to send him any part of his revenues, and they did not even think of his return. However, the church prayed to God for him without ceasing. The king's army shrank daily in the Promised Land, and besides those who were slain by the sword, many thousands of people perished every month by the too sudden extremities of the nightly cold and the daily heat. When it appeared that they would all have to die there, every one had to choose whether he would die as a coward or in battle.

On the other side, the strength of the infidels greatly increased, and their confidence was strengthened by the misfortunes of the Christians; their army was relieved at certain times by fresh troops; the weather was natural to them; the place was their native country; their labor, health; their frugality, medicine. Amongst us, on the contrary, that which brought gain to our adversaries became a disadvantage. For if our people had too little to eat even once in a week, they were rendered less effective for seven weeks after. The mingled nation of French and English fared sumptuously every day, at whatever cost, while their treasure lasted; and (no offense to the French) they ate until they were sick. The well-known custom of the English was continually kept up even under the clarions and the clangor of the trumpet or horn: with due devotion they drained their wine-cups to the dregs. The merchants of the country, who brought the victuals to the camp, were astonished at their wonderful and extraordinary habits, and could scarcely believe even what they saw to be true, that one people, and that small in number, consumed three times more bread and a hundred times more wine than that on which many nations of the infidels had been sustained, and some of those nations innumerable. And the hand of the Lord was deservedly laid upon them according to their merits. Such great lack of food followed their great gluttony, that their teeth scarcely spared their fingers, as their hands presented to their mouths less than their usual allowance. To these and other calamities, which were severe and many, a much greater one was added by the sickness of the king.

87. The king was extremely sick, and confined to his bed; his fever continued without intermission; the physicians whispered that it was an acute semitertian fever. And as they despaired of his recovery even from the beginning, terrible dismay was spread from the king's abode through the camp. There were few among the many thousands who did not consider fleeing, and the utmost confusion of dispersion or surrender would have followed, had not Hubert Walter, bishop of Salisbury, immediately assembled the council. By strenuous argument he won this concession: that the army should not break up until a truce was requested from Saladin. All the armed men stood in array more steadily than usual, and with a threatening look concealing the reluctance of their mind, they feigned a desire for battle. No one spoke of the king's illness, lest the

secret of their intense sorrow should be disclosed to the enemy; for it was well known that Saladin feared the charge of the whole army less than that of the king alone; and if he should know that he was sick in bed, he would instantly pelt the French with cow-dung, and intoxicate the best of the English drunkards with a dose which should make them tremble....

[The Saracens eventually proposed a truce in these terms:] If it pleased King Richard, for the space of three years, three months, three weeks, three days, and three hours, such a truce would be observed between the Christians and the infidels, that whatever either one party or the other in any way possessed, he would possess without molestation to the end. During the interval the Christians would be permitted at their pleasure to fortify Acre only, and the infidels Jerusalem. All contracts, all commerce, every act and every thing would be mutually carried on by all in peace. [Saladin's brother] Saffadin himself was dispatched to the English as the bearer of this offer.

94. While King Richard was sick at Jaffa, word was brought to him that the duke of Burgundy was taken dangerously ill at Acre. It was the day for the king's fever to take its turn, and through his delight at this report, it left him. The king immediately with uplifted hands imprecated a curse upon the duke, saying, "May God destroy him, for he would not destroy the enemies of our faith with me, although he had long served in my pay." ... [Eventually,] having resumed his strength of body more by the greatness of his mind than by repose or nourishment, he issued a command for the whole coast from Tyre to Ascalon, that all who were able to serve in the wars should come to fight at the king's expense. A countless multitude assembled before him, the greater part of whom were on foot. Having rejected them as useless, he mustered the cavalry, and found scarcely five hundred knights and two thousand shield-bearers whose lords had perished. And not discouraged by their small number, he, being a most excellent orator, strengthened the minds of the fearful with a timely speech. He commanded that it be proclaimed through the companies that on the third day they must follow the king to battle, either to die as martyrs or to take Jerusalem by storm. This was the sum of his project, because as yet he knew nothing of the truce. For there was no one who dared even hint to him, when he had so unexpectedly recovered, that which they had undertaken without his knowledge, through fear of his death. However, Hubert Walter, bishop of Salisbury, took counsel with Count Henry concerning the truce, and obtained his ready concurrence in his wishes. So having deliberated together how they might safely hinder such a hazardous engagement, they conceived of the one stratagem out of a thousand, namely, to try to dissuade the people from the enterprise. And the matter turned out most favorably; the spirit of those who were going to fight had so greatly failed even without dis-

suasion, that on the appointed day, when the king, according to his custom leading the van, marshaled his army, of all the knights and shield-bearers no more than 900 were found. On account of which defection, the king, greatly enraged, even raving, and gnawing the pine rod which he held in his hand, at length opened his indignant lips as follows: "O God!" said he, "O God, my God, why hast thou forsaken me? For whom have we foolish Christians, for whom have we English come hither from the furthest parts of the earth to bear our arms? Is it not for the God of the Christians? O fie! How good art thou to us thy people, who now are for thy name given up to the sword; we shall become a portion for foxes. O how unwilling should I be to forsake thee in so forlorn and dreadful a position, were I thy lord and advocate as thou art mine! In sooth, my standards will in future be despised, not through my fault but through thine; in sooth, not through any cowardice of my warfare, art thou thyself, my King and my God, conquered this day, and not Richard thy vassal."

98. He spoke, and returned to the camp extremely dejected; and as a fit occasion now offered, Bishop Hubert and Henry, count of Champagne, approaching him with unwonted familiarity, as if nothing had yet been arranged, begged under diverse pretexts the king's consent for making such overtures to the infidels as were necessary. And thus the king answered them: "Since a troubled mind is usually more likely to thwart than to afford sound judgment — I, who am greatly troubled in mind, authorize you, whom I see to be calm of mind, to arrange what you shall think most proper for the good of peace." Having gained their desires, they chose messengers to send to Saffadin upon these matters; Saffadin, who had returned from Jerusalem, was suddenly announced to be at hand. The count and the bishop went to meet him, and being assured by him of the truce, they instructed him how he must speak with the lord their king. Being admitted to an interview with the king as one who previously had been his friend, Saffadin could scarcely prevail upon the king not to destroy himself but to consent to the truce. For so great were the man's strength of body, mental courage, and entire trust in Christ, that he could hardly be prevailed upon not to undertake in his own person a single combat with a thousand of the choicest infidels, as he was destitute of soldiers. And as he was not permitted to attack, he chose this evasion, that, after a truce of seven weeks, the stipulations of the compact being preserved, it should remain for him to choose whether it were better to fight or to forbear. The two parties put their right hands to the final agreement, that they would faithfully observe it; and Saffadin, more honored than burdened with the king's present, went back again to his brother, to return at the expiration of the term for the final conclusion or breaking of the above truce.

99. Richard, king of England, held a council at Acre, and there prudently regulating the government of that state, he appointed his nephew, Henry, count of Champagne, on whom he had formerly conferred Tyre, to be captain and lord of the whole Promised Land. But he thought it proper to defer his consecration as king till he might perhaps be crowned at Jerusalem. King Richard, now thinking to return home, with the assistance of Count Henry appointed men for all the strongholds in his territories and found Ascalon alone without garrison or inhabitants, for lack of people. Wherefore, taking precaution that it might not become a receptacle of the infidels, he caused the ramparts and fortifications of the castle to be cast down.

The seventh day of the seventh week appeared, and behold Saffadin, with many emirs who desired to see the face of the king, drew near. The truce was confirmed on both sides by oath, with this provision being added to what had been previously agreed, that during the continuance of the truce no one, whether Christian or infidel, should inhabit Ascalon, and that all the fields pertaining to the town should still belong to the Christians. Hubert, bishop of Salisbury, and Henry, captain of Judea, together with a numerous band, went up to Jerusalem to worship in the place where the feet of Christ had stood. And there was woeful misery to be seen — captive confessors of the Christian name, wearing out a hard and constant martyrdom; chained together in gangs, their feet blistered, their shoulders raw, their backsides goaded, their backs wealed, they carried materials to the hands of the masons and stone-layers to make Jerusalem impregnable against the Christians. When the captain and bishop had returned from the sacred places, they endeavored to persuade the king to go up; but the worthy indignation of his great heart could not consent to receive by the courtesy of the infidels that which he could not obtain by the gift of God.

Questions: How do Richard's values and concerns manifest themselves in this account? What does the author think of the king? How do the Europeans see the Muslims of the Middle East? What divisions exist among the crusaders?

32. A SONG OF RICHARD I

Richard was also a product and practitioner of the southern French troubadour culture;
tradition holds that he wrote the following song himself while being held for ransom in
Germany. He had been captured by an enemy on his way home from the crusade, and
the raising of the king's ransom, supervised by his mother Eleanor of Aquitaine, was an
additional strain on the kingdom which had already paid heavily for Richard's cam-
paigning in the East.

Source: trans. J.J. Wilhelm, *Medieval Song: An Anthology of Hymns and Lyrics* (New York: E.P. Dutton & Co, Inc., 1971), pp. 263-4.

A man imprisoned can never speak his mind
As cleverly as those who do not suffer,
But through his song he can some comfort find.
I have a host of friends, poor the gifts they offer.
Shame on them if this ransoming should trail
      Into a second year in jail!

This they know well, my barons and my men,
English, Norman, Gascon, and Poitevin,
What I'd leave of my property in prison!
O I'm not saying this to cast derision,
      But I'm still here in jail!

Here is a truth I know that can be told:
Dead men and prisoners have neither parents nor friends,
No one to offer up his silver and gold.
It matters to me, but much more to my men,
For after my death, they'll be bitterly assailed
      Because I'm so long in jail!

No wonder if I have a grieving heart
When I see my land torn by its lord asunder:
If he'll recall the pact in which we took part
And remember the pledges we vowed we'd both live under,
Truly within the year, without a fail,
      I'd be out of jail!

This they know, the Angevins and Tourains,
Those bachelors there who are strong and own a lot,
While I'm encumbered here in another's hands;

They loved me lots, but now they don't love a jot;
Over the plains I don't see a piece of mail
    Although I'm still in jail!

I've loved and I love still my companions true,
The men of Cahiu and the men of Porcherain,
But tell me, song, if they still love me too,
For never to them was I double-faced or vain:
They're villains if my lands they now assail —
    Since I am here in jail!

Questions: What is the tone of this work? How does it accord with the portrait of King Richard in the chronicle by Richard of Devizes, and with the values expressed in the History of William Marshal? How does it appeal to Richard's barons?

CHAPTER THREE

THE THIRTEENTH CENTURY

33. LETTERS OF INNOCENT III
AND KING JOHN

Threatened with the papal appointment of Stephen Langton, an unwanted archbishop of Canterbury, King John (1199-1216) stood up for the traditional relative independence of the English church — and the English king — from papal intervention; the quarrel resulted in a papal interdict which shut down most church functions in England for seven years. In the first letter below, the pope explains details of the interdict to the English clergy. In the others, John makes his ultimate submission to the pope, thus making possible the lifting of the penalty.

Source: trans. H. Gee and W.G. Hardy, *Documents Illustrative of the History of the English Church* (London: Macmillan, 1910), pp. 73-77.

Answer of Innocent III concerning the Interdict, 1208

Innocent the bishop, etc., to the Bishops of London, Ely, and Worcester, greeting and apostolic blessing. We reply to your inquiries, that whereas by reason of the interdict new chrism cannot be consecrated on Maundy Thursday, old must be used in the baptism of infants, and, if necessity demand, oil must be mixed by hand of the bishop, or else the priest, with the chrism, that it fail not. And although the viaticum seem to be meet on the repentance of the dying, yet, if it cannot be had, we who read it believe that the principle holds good in this case, "believe and thou hast eaten," when actual need, and not contempt of religion, excludes the sacrament, and the actual need is expected soon to cease. Let neither gospel nor the church hours be observed in the accustomed place, nor any other, though the people assemble in the same. Let religious men, whose monasteries people have been wont to visit for the sake of prayer, admit pilgrims inside the church for prayer, not by the greater door, but by a more secret place. Let church doors remain shut save at the chief festival of the church, when the parishioners and others may be admitted for prayer into the church with open doors. Let baptism be celebrated in the usual manner with old chrism and oil inside the church with shut doors, no lay person being admitted save the godparents; and if need demand, new oil must be mixed. Penance is to be inflicted as well on the whole as the sick; for in the midst of life we are in death. Those who have confessed in a suit, or have been convicted of some crime, are to be sent to the bishop or his penitentiary, and, if need be, are to be forced to this by church censure. Priests may say their own hours and prayers in private. Priests may on Sunday bless water in the churchyard and sprinkle it; and can make and distribute the bread when blessed, and announce feasts and fasts and preach a sermon to the people. A woman after childbirth may come to church, and perform her purification outside the church walls. Priests shall visit the sick, and hear confessions, and let them perform the commendation of souls in the accustomed manner, but they shall not follow the corpses of the dead, because they will not have church burial. Priests shall, on the day of the Passion, place the cross outside the church, without ceremony, so that the parishioners may adore it with the customary devotion.

John's surrender of the kingdom to the pope, 1213

John, by grace of God king of England, lord of Ireland, duke of Normandy and Aquitaine, earl of Anjou, to all the faithful in Christ who shall inspect this present charter, greeting. We will it to be known by all of you by this our charter, confirmed by our seal, that we, having offended God and our mother the holy church in many things, and being on that account known to need the Divine mercy, and unable to make any worthy offering for the performance of due satisfaction to God and the church, unless we humble ourselves and our realms — we, willing to humble ourselves for Him who humbled Himself for us even to death, by the inspiration of the Holy Spirit's grace, under no compulsion of force or fear, but of our good and free will, and by the common consent of our barons, offer and freely grant to God and His holy apostles Peter and Paul, and the holy Roman church, our mother, and to our lord the pope Innocent and his catholic successors, the whole realm of England and the whole realm of Ireland with all their rights and appurtenances, for the remission of our sins and those of all our race, as well quick as dead; and from now receiving back and holding these, as a feudal dependent, from God and the Roman church, in the presence of the prudent man Pandulf, subdeacon and familiar of the lord the pope, do swear fealty for them to the aforesaid our lord the pope Innocent and his catholic successors and the Roman church, according to the form written below, and will do liege homage to the same lord the pope in his presence if we shall be able to be present before him; binding our successors and heirs by our wife, for ever, that in like manner to the supreme pontiff for the time being, and to the Roman church, they should pay fealty and acknowledge homage without contradiction. Moreover, in proof of this our perpetual obligation and grant, we will and establish that from the proper and special revenues of our realms aforesaid, for all service and custom that we should render for ourselves, saving in all respects the penny of blessed Peter, the Roman church receive 1000 marks sterling each year, to wit at the feast of St. Michael 500 marks, and at Easter 500 marks; 700 to wit for the realm of England, and 300 for Ireland; saving to us and our heirs, our rights, liberties, and royalties. All which, as aforesaid, we willing them to be perpetually ratified and confirmed, bind ourselves and our successors not to contravene. And if we or any of our successors shall presume to attempt this, whoever he be, unless he come to amendment after due admonition, let him forfeit right to the kingdom, and let this charter of obligation and grant on our part remain in force for ever.

The Oath of Fealty

I, John, by grace of God king of England and lord of Ireland, from this hour forward will be faithful to God and the blessed Peter and the Roman church, and my lord the pope Innocent and his successors following in the catholic manner: I will not be party in deed, word, consent, or counsel, to their losing life or limb or being unjustly imprisoned. Their damage, if I am aware of it, I will prevent, and will have removed if I can; or else, as soon as I can, I will signify it, or will tell such persons as I shall believe will tell them certainly. Any counsel they entrust to me, immediately or by their messengers or letter, I will keep secret, and will consciously disclose to no one to their damage. The patrimony of blessed Peter, and specially the realm of England and the realm of Ireland, I will aid to hold and defend against all men to my ability. So help me God and these holy gospels. Witness myself at the house of the Knights of the Temple near Dover, in the presence of the lord H., archbishop of Dublin; the lord J., bishop of Norwich; G. FitzPeter, earl of Essex, our justiciar; W., earl of Salisbury, our brother; W. Marshall, earl of Pembroke; R., count of Boulogne; W., earl of Warenne; S., earl of Winchester; W., earl of Arundel; W., earl of Ferrers; W. Brewer; Peter son of Herbert; Warren son of Gerald. The 15th day of May in the 14th year of our reign.

34. ROGER OF WENDOVER'S ACCOUNT OF THE REBELLION AGAINST KING JOHN

John's troubles were far from over with the lifting of the interdict. Early in his reign he had also lost most of his French territories to the French king, Philip II. Having made his peace with the pope, he launched a final effort to reclaim those lands, but in 1214 he was soundly defeated at Bouvines in Normandy. The English barons, chafing under the oppressive and expensive government of a militarily unsuccessful king, now saw their hopes of regaining their French inheritances disappear. The most dissatisfied of them now resolved to try at least to improve John's treatment of them at home.

Source: trans. J.A. Giles, *Roger of Wendover's Flowers of History* (London: Henry G. Bohn, 1859), vol. II, pp. 304–309; revised.

Of the demands made by the barons of England for their rights

A.D. 1215; which was the seventeenth year of the reign of King John; he held his court at Winchester at Christmas for one day, after which he hurried to London, and took up his abode at the New Temple; and at that place the above-mentioned nobles came to him in gay military array, and demanded the confirmation of the liberties and laws of King Edward [the Confessor], with other liberties granted to them and to the kingdom and church of England, as were contained in the charter and above-mentioned laws of Henry I; they also asserted that, at the time of the king's absolution [by the pope's representatives] at Winchester, he had promised to restore those laws and ancient liberties, and was bound by his own oath to observe them. The king, hearing the bold tone of the barons in making this demand, much feared an attack from them, as he saw that they were prepared for battle; he however made answer that their demands were a matter of importance and difficulty, and he therefore asked a truce till the end of Easter, so that he might, after due deliberation, be able to satisfy them as well as the dignity of his crown. After much discussion on both sides, the king at length, although unwillingly, procured the archbishop of Canterbury, the bishop of Ely, and William Marshall as his sureties that on the day pre-agreed on he would, in all reason, satisfy them all, upon which the nobles returned to their homes. The king, however, wishing to take precautions against the future, caused all the nobles throughout England to swear fealty to him alone against all men, and to renew their homage to him; and, the better to take care of himself, on the day of St. Mary's Purification [February 2] he assumed the cross of our Lord [that is, he vowed to go on crusade], being induced to this more by fear than devotion. In the same year Eustace bishop of Ely, a man well skilled in divine as well as human knowledge, died at Reading.

Of the principal persons who compelled the king to grant the laws
and liberties

In Easter week of this same year, the above-mentioned nobles assembled at
Stamford, with horses and arms; for they had now induced almost all the nobility of the whole kingdom to join them, and constituted a very large army; for
in their army there were computed to be two thousand knights, besides horse
soldiers, attendants, and foot soldiers, who were variously equipped. The chief
promoters of this pestilence were Robert fitzWalter, Eustace de Vescy, Richard
de Percy, Robert de Roos, Peter de Bruis, Nicholas de Stuteville, Saher earl of
Winchester, R. Earl Clare, H. Earl Clare, Earl Roger Bigod, William de Mowbray, Roger de Cressi, Ralph fitzRobert, Robert de Vere, Fulk fitzWarin,
William Malet, William de Montacute, William de Beauchamp, S. de Kyme,
William Marshal the younger, [24 more named men], and many others; all of
these, being united by oath, were supported by the concurrence of Stephen
archbishop of Canterbury, who was at their head. The king at this time was
awaiting the arrival of his nobles at Oxford. On the Monday next after the
octaves of Easter, the said barons assembled in the town of Brackley; and when
the king learned this, he sent the archbishop of Canterbury and William Marshal, earl of Pembroke, with some other prudent men, to them to inquire what
the laws and liberties were which they demanded. The barons then delivered
to the messengers a document containing in great measure the laws and
ancient customs of the kingdom, and declared that, unless the king immediately granted them and confirmed them under his own seal, they would, by
taking possession of his fortresses, force him to give them sufficient satisfaction
as to their before-named demands. The archbishop with his fellow messengers
then carried the document to the king, and read to him the heads of the document one by one throughout. The king, when he heard the purport of these
heads, derisively said, with the greatest indignation, "Amongst these unjust
demands, why didn't the barons ask for my kingdom too? Their demands are
vain and visionary, and are unsupported by any plea of reason whatever." And
at length he angrily declared with an oath that he would never grant them
such liberties as would render him their slave....

The castle of Northampton besieged by the barons

As the archbishop and William Marshal could not by any persuasions induce
the king to agree to their demands, they returned by the king's orders to the
barons, and duly reported all they had heard from the king to them; and when
the nobles heard what John said, they appointed Robert fitzWalter commander
of their soldiers, giving him the title of "Marshal of the army of God and the

holy church," and then, one and all flying to arms, they directed their forces towards Northampton. On their arrival there they at once laid siege to the castle, but after having stayed there for fifteen days, and having gained little or no advantage, they determined to move their camp; for having come without *petrariae* [that is, stone-throwers] and other engines of war, they, without accomplishing their purpose, proceeded in confusion to to the castle of Bedford. At that siege the standard-bearer of Robert fitzWalter, amongst others slain, was pierced through the head with an arrow from a cross-bow and died, to the grief of many.

How the city of London was given up to the barons

When the army of the barons arrived at Bedford, they were received with all respect by William de Beauchamp. There also came to them there messengers from the city of London, secretly telling them, if they wished to get into that city, to come there immediately. The barons, encouraged by the arrival of this agreeable message, immediately moved their camp and arrived at Ware; after this they marched the whole night, and arrived early in the morning at the city of London, and, finding the gates open, they, on the 24th of May, which was the Sunday next before our Lord's ascension, entered the city without any tumult whilst the inhabitants were performing divine service; for the rich citizens were favorable to the barons, and the poor ones were afraid to murmur against them. The barons, having thus got into the city, placed their own guards in charge of each of the gates, and then arranged all matters in the city at will. They then took sureties from the citizens, and sent letters throughout England to those earls, barons, and knights who appeared to be still faithful to the king, though they only pretended to be so, and advised them with threats, as they regarded the safety of all their property and possessions, to abandon a king who was perjured and who warred against his barons, and together with them to stand firm and fight against the king for their rights and for peace; and that, if they refused to do this, they, the barons, would make war against them all, as against open enemies, and would destroy their castles, burn their houses and other buildings, and destroy their warrens, parks, and orchards. The names of some of those who had not as yet sworn to strive for these liberties were William Marshal, earl of Pembroke; Ralph, earl of Chester; William, earl of Salisbury; William, earl of Warrenne; William, earl of Albermarle; H., earl of Cornwall; [and 16 other named individuals]; the majority of these, on receiving the message of the barons, set out to London and joined them, abandoning the king entirely. The pleas of the exchequer and of the sheriffs' courts ceased throughout England, because there was no one to make a valuation for the king or to obey him in anything.

The conference between the king and the barons

King John, when he saw that he was deserted by almost all, so that out of his regal superabundance of followers he scarcely retained seven knights, was much alarmed lest the barons would attack his castles and reduce them without difficulty, as they would find no obstacle to their so doing; and he deceitfully pretended to make peace for a time with the aforesaid barons, and sent William Marshal earl of Pembroke, with several other trustworthy messengers, to them, and told them that, for the sake of peace, and for the exaltation and honor of the kingdom, he would willingly grant them the laws and liberties they required; he also sent word to the barons by these same messengers, to appoint a fitting day and place to meet and carry all these matters into effect. The king's messengers then came in all haste to London, and without deceit reported to the barons all that had been deceitfully imposed on them; they in their great joy appointed the 15th of June for the king to meet them, at a field lying between Staines and Windsor. Accordingly, at the time and place pre-agreed on, the king and nobles came to the appointed conference, and when each party had stationed themselves apart from the other, they began a long discussion about terms of peace and the aforesaid liberties. There were present, on behalf of the king, the archbishops, Stephen of Canterbury and J. of Dublin; the bishops [of London, Winchester, Lincoln, Bath, Worcester, Coventry, and Rochester]; Master Pandulph, [papal legate,] familiar of our lord the pope; brother Almeric, master of the Knights Templar in England; the nobles, William Marshal earl of Pembroke, the earl of Salisbury, Earl Warrenne, the earl of Arundel, Alan de Galwey, W. fitzGerald, Peter fitzHerbert, Alan Basset, Matthew fitzHerbert, Thomas Basset, Hugh de Neville, Hubert de Burgh, seneschal of Poitou, Robert de Ropely, John Marshal, and Philip d'Aubigny. Those who were on behalf of the barons it is not necessary to enumerate, since the whole nobility of England were now assembled together in numbers not to be computed. At length, after various points on both sides had been discussed, King John, seeing that he was inferior in strength to the barons, without raising any difficulty, granted the underwritten laws and liberties, and confirmed them by his charter....

Questions: What do the barons' grievances appear to be? What is the king's position? Where do the chronicler's sympathies lie? Who is still loyal to the king? What roles do military strength and military action play in the political situation?

35. MAGNA CARTA

The popular reputation of Magna Carta ("the great charter") as a revolutionary document which is the foundation of modern freedom and democracy has no foundation in the document itself. The content of the text was hardly innovative: the barons were securing the rights to which they felt they were already entitled by custom; the king was agreeing to fulfill his traditional role by acting with the advice and assent of his greater subjects. Nor was the idea of a charter promising good royal behavior new; every twelfth-century ruler had issued such a document at his coronation. What is new and remarkable about Magna Carta is that the barons forced the king to acknowledge his misdeeds and his obligations in writing, and the impact it had as a symbol of that victory and a guarantee for the future.

Source: trans. E.P. Cheney, *Translations and Reprints from the Original Sources of European History*, series 1, vol. 1 (Philadelphia: University of Pennsylvania Department of History, 1902), no. 6, pp. 6-17; revised.

John, by the grace of God, king of England, lord of Ireland, duke of Normandy and Aquitaine, count of Anjou, to the archbishops, bishops, abbots, earls, barons, justiciars, foresters, sheriffs, reeves, servants, and all bailiffs and his faithful people, greeting. Know that by the suggestion of God and for the good of our soul and those of all our predecessors and of our heirs, to the honor of God and the exaltation of holy church, and the improvement of our kingdom, by the advice of our venerable fathers Stephen, archbishop of Canterbury, primate of all England and cardinal of the holy Roman church, Henry, archbishop of Dublin, William of London, Peter of Winchester, Jocelyn of Bath and Glastonbury, Hugh of Lincoln, Walter of Worcester, William of Coventry, and Benedict of Rochester, bishops; of Master Pandulf, subdeacon and companion of the lord pope; of Brother Aymeric, master of the Knights of the Temple in England; and of the noblemen William Marshal, earl of Pembroke, William, earl of Salisbury, William, earl of Warren, William, earl of Arundel, Alan of Galloway, constable of Scotland, Warin fitzGerald, Peter fitzHerbert, Hubert de Burgh, steward of Poitou, Hugh de Neville, Matthew fitzHerbert, Thomas Bassett, Alan Bassett, Philip d'Albini, Robert de Roppelay, John Marshal, John fitzHugh, and others of our faithful.

1. In the first place we have granted to God, and by this our present charter confirmed, for us and our heirs forever, that the English church shall be free, and shall hold its rights entire and its liberties uninjured; and we will that it thus be observed; which is shown by this, that the freedom of elections, which is considered to be most important and especially necessary to the English church, we, of our pure and spontaneous will, granted, and by our charter confirmed, before the contest between us and our barons had arisen; and obtained a confirmation of it by the lord pope Innocent III; which we will observe and

which we will shall be observed in good faith by our heirs forever.

We have granted moreover to all free men of our kingdom for us and our heirs forever all the liberties written below, to be had and held by themselves and their heirs from us and our heirs.

2. If any of our earls or barons, or others holding from us in chief by military service shall have died, and when he has died his heir shall be of full age and owe relief, he shall have his inheritance by the ancient relief; that is to say, the heir or heirs of an earl for the whole barony of an earl a hundred pounds; the heir or heirs of a baron for a whole barony a hundred pounds; the heir or heirs of a knight, for a whole knight's fee, a hundred shillings at most; and who owes less let him give less according to the ancient custom of fiefs.

3. If moreover the heir of any one of such shall be under age, and shall be in wardship, when he comes of age he shall have his inheritance without relief [that is, inheritance tax] and without a fine.

4. The custodian of the land of such a minor heir shall not take from the land of the heir any except reasonable products, reasonable customary payments, and reasonable services, and this without destruction or waste of men or of property; and if we shall have committed the custody of the land of any such a one to the sheriff or to any other who is to be responsible to us for its proceeds, and that man shall have caused destruction or waste from his custody we will recover damages from him, and the land shall be committed to two legal and discreet men of that fief, who shall be responsible for its proceeds to us or to him to whom we have assigned them; and if we shall have given or sold to anyone the custody of any such land, and he has caused destruction or waste there, he shall lose that custody, and it shall be handed over to two legal and discreet men of that fief who shall be in like manner responsible to us as is said above.

5. The custodian moreover, so long as he shall have the custody of the land, must keep up the houses, parks, warrens, fish ponds, mills, and other things pertaining to the land, from the proceeds of the land itself; and he must return to the heir, when he has come to full age, all his land, furnished with plows and implements of husbandry according as the time of cultivation requires and as the proceeds of the land are able reasonably to sustain.

6. Heirs shall be married without disparity, but so that before the marriage is contracted, it shall be announced to the heir's blood relatives.

7. A widow, after the death of her husband, shall have her marriage portion and her inheritance immediately and without obstruction, nor shall she give anything for her dowry or for her marriage portion, or for her inheritance which inheritance her husband and she held on the day of the death of her husband; and she may remain in the house of her husband for forty days after his death, within which time her dowry shall be assigned to her.

8. No widow shall be compelled to marry so long as she prefers to live

without a husband, provided she gives security that she will not marry without our consent, if she holds from us, or without the consent of her lord from whom she holds, if she holds from another.

9. Neither we nor our bailiffs will seize any land or rent, for any debt, so long as the chattels of the debtor are sufficient for the payment of the debt; nor shall the pledges of a debtor be distrained so long as the principal debtor himself has enough for the payment of the debt; and if the principal debtor fails in the payment of the debt, not having the wherewithal to pay it, the pledges shall be responsible for the debt and if they wish, they shall have the lands and the rents of the debtor until they shall have been satisfied for the debt which they have before paid for him, unless the principal debtor shall have shown himself to be quit in that respect towards those pledges.

10. If anyone has taken anything from the Jews, by way of a loan, more or less, and dies before that debt is paid, the debt shall not draw interest so long as the heir is under age, from whomsoever he holds; and if that debt falls into our hands, we will take nothing except the chattel contained in the agreement.

11. And if anyone dies leaving a debt owing to the Jews, his wife shall have her dower, and shall pay nothing of that debt; and if there remain minor children of the dead man, necessaries shall be provided for them corresponding to the holding of the dead man; and from the remainder shall be paid the debt, the service of the lords being retained. In the same way debts are to be treated which are owed to others than the Jews.

12. No scutage or aid shall be imposed in our kingdom except by the common council of our kingdom, except for the ransoming of our body, for the making of our oldest son a knight, and for once marrying our oldest daughter, and for these purposes it shall be only a reasonable aid; in the same way it shall be done concerning the aids of the city of London.

13. And the city of London shall have all its ancient liberties and free customs, as well by land as by water. Moreover, we will and grant that all other cities and boroughs and villages and ports shall have all their liberties and free customs.

14. And for holding a common council of the kingdom concerning the assessment of an aid otherwise than in the three cases mentioned above, or concerning the assessment of a scutage [that is, payment by a vassal in lieu of military service], we shall cause to be summoned the archbishops, bishops, abbots, earls, and greater barons by our letters under seal; and besides we shall cause to be summoned generally, by our sheriffs and bailiffs, all those who hold from us in chief, for a certain day, that is at the end of forty days at least, and for a certain place; and in all the letters of that summons, we will express the cause of the summons, and when the summons has thus been given the business shall proceed on the appointed day, on the advice of those who shall be present, even if not all of those who were summoned have come.

15. We will not grant to anyone, moreover, that he shall take an aid from his free men, except for ransoming his body, for making his oldest son a knight, and for once marrying his oldest daughter; and for these purposes only a reasonable aid shall be taken.

16. No one shall be compelled to perform any greater service for a knight's fee, or for any other free tenement, than is owed from it.

17. The common pleas shall not follow our court, but shall be held in some certain place.

18. The recognitions of *novel disseisin, mort d'ancestor,* and *darrein presentment* [that is, the common law procedures determining temporary possession of disputed land] shall be held only in their own counties and in this manner: we, or, if we are outside of the kingdom, our principal justiciar, will send two justiciars through each county four times a year, who with four knights of each county, elected by the county, shall hold in the county and on the day and in the place of the county court, the aforesaid assizes of the county.

19. And if the aforesaid assizes cannot be held within the day of the county court, a sufficient number of knights and free-holders shall remain from those who were present at the county court on that day to give the judgments, according as the business is more or less.

20. A free man shall not be fined for a small offense, except in proportion to the measure of the offense; and for a great offense he shall be fined in proportion to the magnitude of the offense, saving his freehold; and a merchant in the same way, saving his merchandise; and the villein shall be fined in the same way, saving his tools of cultivation, if he shall be at our mercy; and none of the above fines shall be imposed except by the oaths of honest men of the neighborhood.

21. Earls and barons shall only be fined by their peers, and only in proportion to their offense.

22. A clergyman shall be fined, like those before mentioned, only in proportion to his lay holding, and not according to the extent of his ecclesiastical benefice.

23. No manor or man shall be compelled to make bridges over the rivers except those which ought to do it of old and rightfully.

24. No sheriff, constable, coroners, or other bailiffs of ours shall hold pleas of our crown.

25. All counties, hundreds, wapentakes, and tithings [that is, small traditional units of land] shall be at the ancient rents and without any increase, excepting our demesne manors.

26. If any person holding a lay fief from us shall die, and our sheriff or bailiff shall show our letters-patent of our summons concerning a debt which the deceased owed to us, it shall be lawful for our sheriff or bailiff to attach and levy on the chattels of the deceased found on his lay fief, to the value of that debt, in the view of legal men, but in such a way that nothing be removed

thence until the clear debt to us shall be paid; and the remainder shall be left to the executors for the fulfilment of the will of the deceased; and if nothing is owed to us by him, all the chattels shall go to the deceased, saving to his wife and children their reasonable shares.

27. If any free man dies intestate, his chattels shall be distributed by the hands of his near relatives and friends, under the oversight of the church, saving to each one the debts which the deceased owed to him.

28. No constable or other bailiff of ours shall take anyone's grain or other chattels, without immediately paying for them in money, unless he is able to obtain a postponement at the good-will of the seller.

29. No constable shall require any knight to give money in place of his ward of a castle if he is willing to furnish that ward in his own person or through another honest man, if he himself is not able to do it for a reasonable cause; and if we shall lead or send him into the army he shall be free from ward in proportion to the amount of time by which he has been in the army for us.

30. No sheriff or bailiff of ours or anyone else shall take horses or wagons of any free man for carrying purposes except on the permission of that free man.

31. Neither we nor our bailiffs will take the wood of another man for castles, or for anything else which we are doing, except by the permission of him to whom the wood belongs.

32. We will not hold the lands of those convicted of a felony for more than a year and a day, after which the lands shall be returned to the lords of the fiefs.

33. All the fish-weirs in the Thames and the Medway, and throughout all England, shall be done away with, except those on the coast.

34. The writ which is called *praecipe* shall not be given for the future to anyone concerning any tenement by which a free man can lose his court.

35. There shall be one measure of wine throughout our whole kingdom, and one measure of ale, and one measure of grain, that is the London quarter, and one width of dyed cloth and of russets and of halbergets, that is two ells within the selvages; of weights, moreover, it shall be as of measures.

36. Nothing shall henceforth be given or taken for a writ of inquisition concerning life or limbs, but it shall be given freely and not denied.

37. If anyone holds from us by fee farm or by non-military tenure or by urban tenure, and from another he holds land by military service, we will not have the guardianship of the heir of his land which is of the fief of another, on account of that fee farm, or soccage, or burgage; nor will we have the custody of that fee farm, or soccage, or burgage, unless that fee farm itself owes military service. We will not have the guardianship of the heir or of the land of anyone, which he holds from another by military service on account of any petty serjeanty which he holds from us by the service of paying to us knives or arrows, or things of that kind.

38. No bailiff for the future shall place anyone to his law on his simple affirmation, without credible witnesses brought for this purpose.

39. No free man shall be taken or imprisoned or dispossessed, or outlawed, or banished, or in any way destroyed, nor will we go upon him, nor send upon him, except by the legal judgment of his peers or by the law of the land.

40. To no one will we sell, to no one will we deny or delay, right or justice.

41. All merchants shall be safe and secure in going out from England and coming into England and in remaining and going through England, as well by land as by water, for buying and selling, free from all evil tolls, by the ancient and rightful customs, except in time of war; and if they are of a land at war with us, and if such are found in our land at the beginning of war, they shall be attached without injury to their bodies or goods, until it shall be known from us or from our principal justiciar in what way the merchants of our land are treated who shall be then found in the country which is at war with us; and if ours are safe there, the others shall be safe in our land.

42. It is allowed henceforth to anyone to go out from our kingdom, and to return, safely and securely, by land and by water, saving their fidelity to us, except in time of war for some short time, for the common good of the kingdom; excepting persons imprisoned and outlawed according to the law of the realm, and people of a land at war with us, and merchants, of whom it shall be done as is before said.

43. If anyone holds from any escheat [that is, a fief reverting to the lord in the absence of an heir], as from the honor of Wallingford, or Nottingham, or Boulogne, or Lancaster, or from other escheats which are in our hands and are baronies, and he dies, his heir shall not give any other relief, nor do to us any other service than he would do to the baron, if that barony was in the hands of the baron; and we will hold it in the same way as the baron held it.

44. Men who dwell outside the forest shall not henceforth come before our justiciars of the forest, on common summons, unless they are in a plea of the forest, or are pledges for any person or persons who are arrested on account of the forest.

45. We will not make justiciars, constables, sheriffs or bailiffs except of such as know the law of the realm and are well inclined to observe it.

46. All barons who have founded abbeys for which they have charters of kings of England, or ancient tenure, shall have their custody when they have become vacant, as they ought to have.

47. All forests which have been afforested in our time shall be disafforested immediately; and so it shall be concerning river banks which in our time have been fenced in.

48. All the bad customs concerning forests and warrens and concerning foresters and warreners, sheriffs and their servants, river banks and their guardians shall be inquired into immediately in each county by twelve sworn

knights of the same county, who shall be elected by the honest men of the same county, and within forty days after the inquisition has been made, they shall be entirely destroyed by them, never to be restored, provided that we be first informed of it, or our justiciar, if we are not in England.

49. We will give back immediately all hostages and charters which have been delivered to us by Englishmen as security for peace or for faithful service.

50. We will remove absolutely from their bailiwicks the relatives of Gerard de Athyes, so that for the future they shall have no bailiwick in England; Engelard de Cygony, Andrew, Peter and Gyon de Chancelles, Gyon de Cygony, Geoffrey de Martin and his brothers, Philip Mark and his brothers, and Geoffrey his nephew and their whole retinue.

51. And immediately after the re-establishment of peace we will remove from the kingdom all foreign-born soldiers, cross-bow men, servants, and mercenaries who have come with horses and arms for the injury of the realm.

52. If anyone shall have been dispossessed or removed by us without legal judgment of his peers, from his lands, castles, franchises, or his right we will restore them to him immediately; and if contention arises about this, then it shall be done according to the judgment of the twenty-five barons, of whom mention is made below concerning the security of the peace. Concerning all those things, however, from which anyone has been removed or of which he has been deprived without legal judgment of his peers by King Henry our father, or by King Richard our brother, which we have in our hand, or which others hold, and which is our duty to guarantee, we shall have respite till the usual term of crusaders; excepting those things about which the suit has been begun or the inquisition made by our writ before our assumption of the cross; when, however, we shall return from our journey, or if by chance we desist from the journey, we will immediately show full justice in regard to them.

53. We shall, moreover, have the same respite, in the same manner, about doing justice in regard to the forests which are to be disafforested or to remain forests, which Henry our father or Richard our brother made into forests; and concerning the custody of lands which are in the fief of another, custody of which we have until now had on account of a fief which anyone has held from us by military service; and concerning the abbeys which have been founded in fiefs of others than ourselves, in which the lord of the fee has asserted for himself a right; and when we return or if we should desist from our journey we will immediately show full justice to those complaining in regard to them.

54. No one shall be seized nor imprisoned on the appeal of a woman concerning the death of anyone except her husband.

55. All fines which have been imposed unjustly and against the law of the land, and all penalties imposed unjustly and against the law of the land are altogether excused, or will be on the judgment of the twenty-five barons of whom

mention is made below in connection with the security of the peace, or on the judgment of the majority of them, along with the aforesaid Stephen, archbishop of Canterbury, if he is able to be present, and others whom he may wish to call for this purpose along with him. And if he should not be able to be present, nevertheless the business shall go on without him, provided that if any one or more of the aforesaid twenty-five barons are in a similar suit they should be removed as far as this particular judgment goes, and others who shall be chosen and put upon oath by the remainder of the twenty-five shall be substituted for them for this purpose.

56. If we have dispossessed or removed any Welshmen from their lands, or franchises, or other things, without legal judgment of their peers, in England, or in Wales, they shall be immediately returned to them; and if a dispute shall have arisen over this, then it shall be settled in the borderland by judgment of their peers, concerning holdings of England according to the law of England, concerning holdings of Wales according to the law of Wales, and concerning holdings of the borderland according to the law of the borderland. The Welsh shall do the same to us and ours.

57. Concerning all those things, however, from which any one of the Welsh shall have been removed or dispossessed without legal judgment of his peers, by King Henry our father, or King Richard our brother, which we hold in our hands, or which others hold, and we are bound to warrant to them, we shall have respite till the usual period of crusaders, except those about which suit was begun or inquisition made by our command before our assumption of the cross. When, however, we shall return or if by chance we shall desist from our journey, we will show full justice to them immediately, according to the laws of the Welsh and the aforesaid parts.

58. We will give back the son of Llewellyn immediately, and all the hostages from Wales and the charters which had been delivered to us as a security for peace.

59. We will act toward Alexander, king of the Scots, concerning the return of his sisters and his hostages, and concerning his franchises and his right, according to the manner in which we shall act toward our other barons of England, unless it ought to be otherwise by the charters which we hold from William his father, formerly king of the Scots, and this shall be by the judgment of his peers in our court.

60. Moreover, all those customs and franchises mentioned above which we have conceded in our kingdom, and which are to be fulfilled, as far as pertains to us, in respect to our men, all men of our kingdom shall observe as far as pertains to them, clergy as well as laymen, in respect to their men.

61. Since, moreover, for the sake of God, and for the improvement of our kingdom, and for the better quieting of the hostility sprung up lately between

us and our barons, we have made all these concessions; wishing them to enjoy these in a complete and firm stability forever, we make and concede to them the security described below; that is to say, that they shall elect twenty-five barons of the kingdom, whom they will, who ought with all their power to observe, hold, and cause to be observed, the peace and liberties which we have conceded to them, and by this our present charter confirmed to them; in this manner, that if we or our justiciar, or our bailiffs, or any one of our servants shall have done wrong in any way toward anyone, or shall have transgressed any of the articles of peace or security; and the wrong shall have been shown to four barons of the aforesaid twenty-five barons, let those four barons come to us or to our justiciar, if we are out of the kingdom, laying before us the transgression, and let them ask that we cause that transgression to be corrected without delay. And if we shall not have corrected the transgression, or if we shall be out of the kingdom, if our justiciar shall not have corrected it within a period of forty days, counting from the time in which it has been shown to us or to our justiciar, if we are out of the kingdom; the aforesaid four barons shall refer the matter to the remainder of the twenty-five barons, and let these twenty-five barons with the whole community of the country distress and injure us in every way they can; that is to say by the seizure of our castles, lands, possessions, and in such other ways as they can until it shall have been corrected according to their judgment, saving our person and that of our queen, and those of our children; and when the correction has been made, let them devote themselves to us as they did before. And let whoever in the country wishes take an oath that in all the above-mentioned measures he will obey the orders of the aforesaid twenty-five barons, and that he will injure us as far as he is able with them, and we give permission to swear publicly and freely to each one who wishes to swear, and no one will we ever forbid to swear. All those, moreover, in the country who of themselves and their own will are unwilling to take an oath to the twenty-five barons as to distressing and injuring us along with them, we will compel to take the oath by our mandate, as before said. And if any one of the twenty-five barons shall have died or departed from the land or shall in any other way be prevented from taking the above-mentioned action, let the remainder of the aforesaid twenty-five barons choose another in his place, according to their judgment, who shall take an oath in the same way as the others. In all those things, moreover, which are committed to those five and twenty barons to carry out, if perhaps the twenty-five are present, and some disagreement arises among them about something, or if any of them when they have been summoned are not willing or are not able to be present, let that be considered valid and firm which the greater part of those who are present arrange or command, just as if the whole twenty-five had agreed in this; and let the aforesaid twenty-five swear that they will observe faithfully all the things which are said above, and with all their ability cause them to be observed. And we will obtain nothing from anyone, either by ourselves or by another by which any of these concessions and liberties shall be revoked or diminished; and if any such thing shall have been obtained, let it be invalid and void, and we will never use it by ourselves or by another.

62. And all ill-will, grudges, and anger sprung up between us and our men, clergy and laymen, from the time of the dispute, we have fully renounced and pardoned to all. Moreover, all transgressions committed on account of this dispute, from Easter in the sixteenth year of our reign till the restoration of peace, we have fully remitted to all, clergy and laymen, and as far as pertains to us, fully pardoned. And moreover we have caused to be made for them testimonial letters-patent of lord Stephen, archbishop of Canterbury, lord Henry, archbishop of Dublin, and of the aforesaid bishops and of master Pandulf, in respect to that security and the concession named above.

63. Wherefore we will and firmly command that the church of England shall be free, and that the men of our kingdom shall have and hold all the aforesaid liberties, rights and concessions, well and peacefully, freely and quietly, fully and completely, for themselves and their heirs, from us and our heirs, in all things and places, forever, as before said. It has been sworn, moreover, as well on our part as on the part of the barons, that all these things spoken of above shall be observed in good faith and without any evil intent. Witness the above named and many others. Given by our hand in the meadow which is called Runnymede, between Windsor and Staines, on the fifteenth day of June, in the seventeenth year of our reign.

Questions: What indications are there in the text of the political events surrounding the making of the charter? What unpopular practices are forbidden? What rights are secured for the barons? What indications are there of other groups in society, and of their status and interests? How does Magna Carta compare with Henry I's coronation charter? How do the barons attempt to ensure the enforcement of the charter? Are such measures likely to work?

36. LETTERS OF QUEEN ISABELLA OF ANGOULÊME

King John died shortly after issuing Magna Carta, to be succeeded by his nine-year-old son, Henry III (1216-72). The young king's newly widowed mother was a southern French noblewoman who had been betrothed to a neighboring Frenchman, Hugh de Lusignan the elder, before King John managed to marry her instead. She was unpopular at the English royal court and was excluded from her son's regency government, to her chagrin. At the time she wrote these letters, she had returned to France, where her young daughter Joanna, sister of the little king, was betrothed to Hugh de Lusignan the younger, son of Isabella's former fiancé.

Source: trans. A. Crawford, *Letters of the Queens of England, 1100-1547* (Dover, NH: Alan Sutton Publishing, 1994), pp. 51-3.

Isabella, queen of England, to her son, Henry III, c. 1218-19

To her dearest son, Henry, by the grace of God, the illustrious king of England, lord of Ireland, duke of Normandy and Aquitaine, count of Anjou, I Isabella, by the same grace of God, his humble mother, queen of England, always pray for your safety and good fortune.

Your Grace knows how often we have begged you that you should give us help and advice in our affairs, but so far you have done nothing. Therefore we attentively ask you again to despatch your advice quickly to us, but do not just gratify us with words. You can see that without your help and advice, we cannot rule over or defend our land. And if the truces made with the king of France were to be broken, this part of the country has much to fear. Even if we had nothing to fear from the king himself, we do indeed have such neighbors who are as much to be feared as the said king of France. So without delay you must formulate such a plan which will benefit this part of the country which is yours and ours; it is necessary that you do this to ensure that neither you nor we should lose our land through your failure to give any advice or help. We even beg you to act on our behalf, that we can have for the time being some part of those lands which our husband, your father, bequeathed to us. You know truly how much we owe him, but even if our husband had bequeathed nothing to us, you ought by right to give us aid from your resources, so that we can defend our land, on this your honor and advantage depend.

Wherefore we are sending over to you Sir Geoffrey de Bodeville and Sir Waleran, entrusting to them many matters which cannot be set down in writing to you, and you can trust them in what they say to you on our behalf concerning the benefit to you and us.

Isabella, queen of England, to Pandulph, bishop-elect of Norwich, c. June 1219

Dearest father and lord Pandulph, by the grace of God, bishop-elect of Norwich, chamberlain of our lord the pope and legate of the apostolic see, I Isabella, by the same grace, queen of England, lady of Ireland, duchess of Normandy and Aquitaine, and countess of Anjou, greetings.

You will know that we have offered to restore to Bartholomew de Podio, at the entreaty of our son, the king of England, and of his Council, in entirety all his land, his possessions and the rents he received before we came hither, with the exception of our castles, and also all his hostages, save for his two sons, whom we desire to hold in fair and fitting custody until we are without fear that he will seek to do us wrong, as he once sought to wrong the count of Augi and the other barons of the land to our despite. If he refused this offer of ours, we offered him the sure judgment of our court, but he totally rejected all this. We are very surprised that our son's Council should have instructed Sir Hugh de Lusignan and Sir Geoffrey Neville, seneschal of Poitou, to support the said Bartholomew against us. Granted that the king our son, or his Council, does not order that we be attacked, nevertheless we know many who will trouble us on Bartholomew's behalf, and our son's Council should be aware lest it issues any instructions as a consequence of which we are driven away from our son's Council and affairs. It will be very serious if we are to be removed from our son's Council. You should know that we have been reliably informed that the aforesaid Bartholomew came into the presence of the king of France and made it known to him that our land was part of his fief; he asked that the king order us to reinstate him in his lands. I certainly think he does not regard our son the king of England very highly, in as much as Bartholomew himself, running hither and thither, is working to do harm to the king and his people. You should know that Sir Hugh de Lusignan and the seneschal are more eager to carry out this order which is against us, than they would be if ordered to help us. For if indeed they have been so ordered, until now they have done very little. So we ask you to have orders given, by a letter from the king our son, to Sir Hugh de Lusignan and the seneschal of Poitou to help us and to take counsel for our land and the land of our lord the king; please write back to us what your will is.

Isabella, queen of England, countess of March and Angoulême, to her son, Henry III, 1220

To her dearest son, Henry, by the grace of God, king of England, lord of Ireland, duke of Normandy and Aquitaine, count of Anjou, Isabella, by the same grace, queen of England, lady of Ireland, duchess of Normandy and Aquitaine, countess of Anjou and Angoulême, sends health and her maternal benediction.

We hereby signify to you that when the counts of March and Eu departed this life, the lord Hugh de Lusignan remained alone and without heirs in Poitou, and his friends would not permit that our daughter should be united to him in marriage, because her age is so tender, but counseled him to take a wife from whom he might speedily hope for an heir; and it was proposed that he should take a wife in France, which if he had done, all your land in Poitou and Gascony would be lost. We, therefore, seeing the great peril that might accrue if that marriage should take place, when our counselors could give us no advice, ourselves married the said Hugh, count of March; and God knows that we did this rather for your benefit than our own. Wherefore we entreat you, as our dear son, that this thing may be pleasing to you, seeing it conduces greatly to the profit of you and yours; and we earnestly pray you that you will restore to him his lawful right, that is, Niort, the castles of Exeter and Rockingham, and 3500 marks, which your father, our former husband, bequeathed to us; and so, if it please you, deal with him, who is so powerful, that he may not remain against you, since he can serve you well — for he is well-disposed to serve you faithfully with all his power; and we are certain and undertake that he shall serve you well if you restore to him his rights, and, therefore, we advise that you take opportune counsel on these matters; and when it shall please you, you may send for our daughter, your sister, by a trusty messenger and your letters patent, and we will send her to you.

Questions: What concerns does Isabella express in these letters? How politically active does she seem to have been? What were her goals? What cards did she hold? How do you explain her surprising course of action as described in the final letter?

37. BRACTON'S NOTEBOOK

One of the works of Henry de Bracton, a prolific thirteenth-century legal writer, is a col-lection of summaries of cases from the royal courts. The cases printed here, all from the year 1230, have been selected to show women as plaintiffs and defendants in civil cases in the royal courts. They can usefully be read in conjunction with the twelfth-century legal treatise by "Glanvill" (doc. 22).

Source: trans. E. Amt from *Bracton's Note-Book*, ed. F.W. Maitland (London: C.J. Clay & Sons, 1887), vol. II, pp. 312, 314–316, 318–319, 325, 331–332.

377. Christiana, who was the wife of Walter Malesoures, through her attorney seeks, versus Robert Grunbant, the manor of Thorp with its appurtenances as her dower, with which the said Walter specifically endowed her etc., because the said Walter, the day he married her, endowed her with one third of all the lands and tenements which he then had, so that if Alicia, mother of the said Walter, who then held the aforesaid manor in dower, were to die during the lifetime of the same Christiana, then Christiana would have that manner in dower for her one third, and if not, then she would have one third of the whole, and she produces sufficient witnesses that she was so endowed, etc.

And Robert comes and does not declare that she was not so endowed, but says that he does not know whether she was so endowed or not.

And because the said Christiana produced sufficient witnesses that she had been so endowed, it has been decided that the said Christiana should recover her seisin and that Robert should be in mercy.

380. And Maria de Valoinis comes seeking one third of a certain advowson [that is, the right to appoint a clergyman to a certain church], by reason of the tenement which she holds in a certain vill as dower. And because she did not wish to agree to the clerk who had been appointed to two thirds of that church, and because that advowson had not been divided before, it has been decided that the possessor of the two thirds should recover the advowson and the power of appointment to the whole church.

381. Alicia de Frowe seeks from the abbot of Flaxley ten marks, which he owes her and unjustly retained, etc., about which she says that a certain John de Kay bought from the said abbot four sacks of wool, and John on his deathbed left those sacks to the same Alicia and John his son, so that when they sought those sacks from the executors of the will of that John de Kay, the same abbot made a fine [that is, an agreement] with them for those sacks for ten marks.

And the abbot through his attorney comes and says that he was not obliged to respond here, because this complaint concerns a will and belongs in ecclesiastical court, and he says moreover that he has satisfied the executors of the will of the said John de Kay concerning all the debts in which he ever owed to the said John, by writing of the said executors which testified to that. And since the said Alicia cannot declare that the complaint did not involve a will, it has been ordered that she pursue her complaint in the court Christian against the executors if she wishes....

382. Muriel, who was the wife of William de Ros, presented herself on the fourth day versus John Marshal concerning a plea to be heard about one third of 60 acres with appurtenances in Wilton, and one third of the pasture of Stanhale, and one third of 16 acres of meadow with appurtenances in the same vill of Wilton, and one third of 4 acres of land and three dwellings with appurtenances in the same vill of Wilton, which thirds she claims versus John Marshal, and she calls to warrant Hugh de Ros, who responds that he is not obliged to warrant that land and meadow to her, because his father William de Ros, by whose gift she claims that land, died and a jury was impaneled previously by assent of the same John and Hugh concerning the 7 virgates [that is, one-quarter of a hide, a variable unit] of land with appurtenances in Wilton, to review whether the said William died seised [that is, in possession] of that land or not.

And the jurors said that the same William died seised of the 7 virgates with appurtenances, by which she recovered seisin of one third of the said 7 virgates with appurtenances as her dower. And because no mention was then made in the oath of the said jurors of the aforementioned 60 acres of land nor of the pasture nor of the meadow nor of the 4 acres, and this was omitted by the forgetfulness of the clerks of the bench, provision was made that the said jurors would be resummoned to certify whether the said William died seised of the aforesaid 60 acres, the meadow, and the pasture, like the 7 virgates of land concerning which they previously swore. The jurors say that the said William died seised of them, just as of the said 7 virgates. And therefore it was decided that Muriel should recover her seisin and John should be in mercy. And be it known that John did not come and had a day at the bench after the jury was resummoned, and therefore a jury was impaneled for his default, just as in the principal plea.

388. Geva Basset and Henry of Prestwood and Margery his wife were attached to respond to William of Bromley as to how they made waste and ruin in the woodland of Bromwich and Northcote and Oseley, against the prohibition of the lord king, etc. Concerning which, the same William de Bromley, guardian of Richard fitzWilliam, who is under age and in his custody, complains that the said Geva, Henry, and Margery, who do not have any right to the said Richard's inheritance except in dower, made waste and ruin of seven oak trees, whereby he has been damaged and despoiled to the value of 100s., and he produces witnesses of this.

And Geva, Henry, and Margery through their attorneys come and maintain that they have made not waste or destruction. And therefore the sheriff has been instructed that the said Geva, Henry, and Margery being present with twelve knights or other free, law-worthy, and discreet persons of the same neighborhood, he himself should go personally to the said woodland and by their oath diligently inquire what waste and how much destruction the said Geva and the others made in the said woodland....

389. Geoffrey fitzJohn and Odierna his wife, through the attorney of the same Geoffrey, seek, versus William of Seven Fountains, three shillings' rent with appurtenances in Westminster, as the right of the same Odierna, but into which she has no entry except by Ralph her father, to whom Ralph Parmenter the late husband of the same Odierna let it go, which she could not prevent, etc.

And William through his attorney comes and says that he does not hold that rent but rather his mother holds it in dower. And Geoffrey and Odierna say that the said William holds the rent, and they agree that if he does not hold it, they will lose their claim. And William through his attorney agrees that if his mother does not hold it he himself will give the rent to them. Afterwards Agnes, who holds the dwelling from which the rent is owed, comes and says that she pays the rent to the said William. And therefore it has been decided that Geoffrey and Odierna should recover their seisin, and William is in mercy.

395. Matilda, abbess of Romsey, was summoned to respond to Roger Wascelin as to how she prevented the same Roger from appointing a suitable clergyman for the church of Stokes, which was vacant, etc., and the right of appointment belongs to the said Roger because the same abbess has granted and handed over to Roger the manor of Stokes with all its appurtenances, except certain things which were specifically excepted in her charter, for a term of seven years.

And the abbess, through Richard the clerk, her attorney by the king's writ, ... comes and acknowledges her charter and that she granted the said manor to him to farm for the said term, with all its appurtenances except aids and tallages of men, and except that no one holding on that manor could marry his daughter outside the fief without first making a fine with the same abbess, and except fines and reliefs of free men, which she withholds for herself with certain other things, no mention being made of the advowson, and [she acknowledges] that the advowson belongs to that manor. And therefore it has been decided that Roger should recover his right of presentation to the same church as tenant, and the abbess is in mercy, and Roger should have a writ of *non obstante* [that is, a writ defending his right] to the officer of the bishop of Winchester.

403. Alicia countess of Eu seeks versus Emma de Belfou two carrucates [that is, a plowland, a variable unit] of land with appurtenances in Gunthorpe and in Judham as her right, of which a certain Beatrice her ancestor was seised in her demesne by fee and inheritance, in the time of King Henry, grandfather of the lord king, in the year and on the day when he was alive and dead, ... and the right to that land descended from Beatrice to a certain Henry as son and heir, and from the said Henry to a certain John as son and heir, and from the said John to a certain Henry as son [and heir], and from the said Henry to the same Alicia as daughter and heir....

And Emma comes and defends her right now in all times and places, and she says that she does not have to respond to this writ because at another time the plea about this land was in the lord king's court, so that a fine was made between Hubert de Burgh, earl of Kent and justiciar of England, plaintiff, and the same Emma, by a cirograph [that is, an agreement written in duplicate], and that neither she nor anyone on her behalf has made a claim, etc.

And the countess comes and says that this ought not to disadvantage her, because she was then overseas, so that she could not make her claim. And Emma cannot deny this. And therefore it has been decided that she should respond.

And Emma says that she holds this land only for her lifetime, and that this land ought to revert to the said Hubert de Burgh after her death, by the charter made between them, and that this is attested both by the cirograph between them in the lord king's court and by the charter of the lord king which testifies to this, and she calls the same Hubert de Burgh to warrant this for her.

The same countess through her words and by the same right seeks versus Oliva de Montbegon two carrucates of land with appurtenances in Tuckford as her right, [by descent from the same Beatrice.]

And Oliva comes and defends her right now etc., and she says that she does not have to answer, because the same countess seeks two carrucates of land with their appurtenances, and the advowson of the church of the same vill is among the appurtenances, and the same countess makes no exception of the advowson, and therefore she does not want to answer this writ, unless the court so decides.

And the countess says that she claims nothing in that advowson, and she did not put it in her writ, and her ancestors were enfeoffed with 7 carrucates in the same vill without the advowson because those who enfeoffed her ancestors kept that advowson for themselves, and therefore it seems to her that she ought to be answered. Afterwards they made an agreement, saving the right of the lord king, if it please the lord king, without whom no agreement can stand. The agreement is that the said Oliva and her heirs will hold the said land with appurtenances from the said countess, etc., for that same service which she previously did for it to the lord king, and both of them will do all in their power to keep the accord.

Questions: What kinds of land tenure are claimed or enforced in these proceedings? What standards of proof are maintained in these cases? What is the role of the jury in the fourth case here? What use did women make of the courts? How active do women appear to have been in these proceedings? How do these cases fit with Henry II's assizes and Glanville's treatise (docs. 21-22)?

38. PERSECUTIONS OF JEWS

Hostility toward the Jewish minority, already evident in the twelfth century, became more active in the thirteenth. The following chronicle extracts and royal documents show the official and unofficial actions that the Jews suffered, culminating in their expulsion from England in 1290. The focus on those Jews who were money-lenders is obvious and clearly contributed to anti-Semitism, but it is important to note that Christians too practiced and profited from usury, even though it was forbidden by canon law.

Source: Howden trans. C.W. Colby, *Selections from the Sources of English History* (New York: Longmans, Green and Co., 1913), pp. 67-68, revised; royal documents trans. A.E. Bland, P.A. Brown, and R.H. Tawney, *English Economic History: Select Documents* (London: G. Bell and Sons, Ltd., 1914), pp. 44-46, 50-51; Trokelowe trans. E.P. Cheyney, *Readings in English History Drawn from the Original Sources* (Boston: Ginn & Company, 1922), pp. 230-31.

Roger of Howden's Chronicle

In the same month of March [1190], ... the Jews of the city of York, in number five hundred men, besides women and children, shut themselves up in the tower of York, with the consent of the sheriff, in consequence of their dread of the Christians; but when the sheriff and the constable sought to regain possession of it, the Jews refused to deliver it up. In consequence of this, the people of the said city, and the strangers who had come within the jurisdiction thereof, at the exhortation of the sheriff and the constable, with one consent made an attack upon the Jews.

After they had made assaults upon the tower day and night, the Jews offered the people a large sum of money to allow them to depart with their lives; but this the others refused to receive. Upon this, one skilled in their laws arose and said, "Men of Israel, listen to my advice. It is better that we should kill one another, than fall into the hands of the enemies of our law." Accordingly, all the Jews, both men and women, gave their assent to his advice, and each master of a family, beginning with the chief persons of his household, with a sharp knife first cut the throats of his wife and sons and daughters, and then of all his servants, and lastly his own. Some of them also threw their slain over the walls among the people; while others shut up their slain in the king's house and burned them, as well as the king's houses. Those who had slain the others were afterwards killed by the people. In the meantime, some of the Christians set fire to the Jews' houses, and plundered them; and thus all the Jews in the city of York were destroyed, and all acknowledgments of debts due to them were burnt.

Charter of King John to the Jews, 1201

John by the grace of God, etc. Know ye that we have granted to all Jews of England and Normandy that they may freely and honorably reside in our land, and hold of us all things that they held of King Henry, our father's grandfather, and all things that they now hold reasonably in their lands and fees and pawns and purchases, and that they may have all their liberties and customs as well and peaceably and honorably as they had them in the time of the aforesaid King Henry, our father's grandfather.

And if a plaint shall have arisen between Christian and Jew, he who shall have appealed the other shall have witnesses for the deraignment of his plaint, to wit, a lawful Christian and a lawful Jew. And if the Jew shall have a writ touching his plaint, his writ shall be his witness; and if a Christian shall have a plaint against a Jew, it shall be judged by the Jew's peers.

And when a Jew be dead, his body shall not be detained above ground, but his heir shall have his money and his debts; so that he be not disturbed thereon, if he have an heir who will answer for him and do right touching his debts and his forfeit.

And it shall be lawful for Jews without hindrance to receive and buy all things which shall be brought to them, except those which are of the church and except cloth stained with blood. And if a Jew be appealed by any man without witness, he shall be quit of that appeal by his bare oath upon his Book. And in like manner he shall be quit of an appeal touching those things which pertain to our crown, by his bare oath upon his Roll.

And if there shall be a dispute between Christian and Jew touching the loan of any money, the Jew shall prove his principal and the Christian the interest.

And it shall be lawful for the Jew peaceably to sell his pawn after it shall be certain that he has held it for a whole year and a day.

And Jews shall not enter into a plea save before us or before those who guard our castles, in whose bailiwicks Jews dwell.

And wherever there be Jews, it shall be lawful for them to go whithersoever they will with all their chattels, as our own goods, and it shall be unlawful for any to retain them or to forbid them this freedom.

And we order that they be quit throughout all England and Normandy of all customs and tolls and prisage of wine, as our own chattel. And we command and order you that you guard and defend and maintain them.

And we forbid any man to implead them touching these things aforesaid against this charter, on pain of forfeiture to us, as the charter of King Henry, our father, reasonably testifies....

Ordinances of Henry III, 1253

The king has provided and decreed ... that no Jew dwell in England unless he do the king service, and that as soon as a Jew shall be born, whether male or female, in some way he shall serve the king. And that there be no communities of the Jews in England save in those places wherein such communities were in the time of the lord King John, the king's father. And that in their synagogues the Jews, one and all, worship in subdued tones according to their rite, so that Christians hear it not. And that all Jews answer to the rector of the parish in which they dwell for all parochial dues belonging to their houses. And that no Christian nurse hereafter suckle or nourish the male child of any Jew, and that no Christian man or woman serve any Jew or Jewess, nor eat with them, nor dwell in their house. And that no Jew or Jewess eat or buy meat in Lent. And that no Jew disparage the Christian faith, nor publicly dispute touching the same. And that no Jew have secret intercourse with any Christian woman, nor any Christian man with a Jewess. And that every Jew wear on his breast a conspicuous badge. And that no Jew enter any church or any chapel save in passing through, nor stay therein to the dishonor of Christ. And that no Jew in any wise hinder another Jew willing to be converted to the Christian faith. And that no Jew be received in any town without the special licence of the king, save in those towns wherein Jews have been wont to dwell.

And the justices appointed to the guardianship of the Jews are commanded to cause these provisions to be carried into effect and straitly kept on pain of forfeiture of the goods of the Jews aforesaid. Witness the king at Westminster on the 31st day of January. By the king and council.

John of Trokelowe's Chronicle

At this time [in 1290] there were Jews dwelling among the Christians in every city and famous town in England. King Edward, with the advice of his nobles, ordered them to leave the country, and to depart without fail on one day, and this was the decree: that whatever Jew should be found in England after the first warning should either be plunged in the baptismal font and thus faithfully acknowledge Christ, the son of God, or should have his head cut off. Immediately the Jews, struck with the fear of death, left England, carrying with them all their possessions. When their vessels had set sail and been carried out to sea, storms arose, severe winds blew, their ships were shattered, and many were drowned. Certain ones driven upon the shores of France, by the judgment of God, perished miserably. At length the king of France was touched with pity, although these were enemies to God, and since they were God's creatures, although ungrateful ones, he permitted them to dwell for a short length of time in his kingdom, and to settle in Amiens. When this was reported in Rome, and had come to the ears of the highest pontiff, burning with rage he bitterly denounced the king.

Edward I's Order, 1290

Edward ... to the treasurer and barons of the exchequer, greeting. Whereas formerly in our Parliament at Westminster on the quinzaine of St. Michael in the third year of our reign, to the honor of God and the profit of the people of our realm, we ordained and decreed that no Jew thenceforth should lend anything at usury to any Christian on lands, rents or other things, but that they should live by their commerce and labor; and the same Jews, afterwards maliciously deliberating among themselves, contriving a worse sort of usury which they called courtesy, have depressed our people aforesaid on all sides under color thereof, the last offense doubling the first; whereby, for their crimes and to the honor of the Crucified, we have caused those Jews to go forth from our realm as traitors: We, wishing to swerve not from our former choice, but rather to follow it, do make totally null and void all manner of penalties and usuries and every sort thereof, which could be demanded by actions by reason of the Jewry from any Christians of our realm for any times whatsoever; wishing that nothing be in any wise demanded from the Christians aforesaid by reason of the debts aforesaid, save only the principal sums which they received from the Jews aforesaid; the amount of which debts we will that the Christians aforesaid verify before you by the oath of three good and lawful men by whom the truth of the matter may the better be known, and thereafter pay the same to us at terms convenient to them to be fixed by you. And therefore we command you that you cause our said grace so piously granted to be read in the aforesaid exchequer, and to be enrolled on the rolls of the same exchequer, and to be straitly kept, according to the form above noted....

Questions: What seem to be Christian concerns about Jews? What evidence is there here of a shift in Christian attitudes and the situation of the English Jews over time? Are there points of resonance with the story of St. William of Norwich, or with Magna Carta? Are there any hints of sympathy with the Jews?

39. DEEDS OF THE ABBOTS OF ST. ALBANS, BY MATTHEW PARIS

Matthew Paris, one of the most respected medieval English historians, wrote among other works a history of his own monastery at St. Albans. The section on the abbacy of William of Trumpington (1214-35) includes an interesting account of a monastic election, as well as both praise and criticism of an abbot who was clearly not the choice of many of the monks. The excerpt below begins after the death of the previous abbot. (The title "Dom," an abbreviation for dominus *or "lord," is used here for the monks themselves.)*

Source: trans. R. Vaughan, *Chronicles of Matthew Paris: Monastic Life in the Thirteenth Century* (Gloucester: Alan Sutton, 1986), pp. 32-33, 35-38, 41-42, 53-55.

Since the king was abroad at that time in Poitou, two of the brothers were sent to ask him for the customary licence to proceed to an election, namely Dom Robert of Britwell and Dom William of Trumpington. When they reached him and he heard their request he did not accede to it, knowing that the guardianship of the abbey was lucrative to him, but he put the matter off until his return to England, which was on the fourteenth of the kalends of November [October 19]. Meanwhile a certain William of Trumpington unknown to and without the consent of Dom William of Trumpington, did his best to see that this Dom William was created abbot through his efforts. This William, who was a knight of Trumpington and seneschal of Earl Saher [de Quincy of Winchester], claimed to be a relative of Dom William of Trumpington, and so he petitioned the king on William's part to accept him, and no one else [as abbot]. When this became known to the convent, the monks decided to try to avoid a refusal from the king lest the abbot-elect be embarrassed by being turned down and the church suffer harm and the convent be thrown into confusion. So those who had been sent to ask for the licence went to the king, whom they found at London and, more definitely informed of the king's wishes, they returned with the licence they had asked for. Without delay those who were to act as the abbot's electors were chosen, namely twelve monks who were fully instructed on all these points. Now there was at that time an outrageous custom in the church, namely that none of those twelve electors could be elected or created abbot. They therefore unwillingly arranged that this William was not one of the electors so that he could be elected without the slightest contradiction of that custom, which would remain unviolated....

Abbot William who, as has been said, was elected and installed on [November 20,] the day of St. Edmund, king and martyr, succeeded [the previous abbot]. He was solemnly consecrated at the great altar as is customary by Eustace the bishop of Ely on [November 30,] St. Andrew's day, which was the first Sunday in Advent, and received benediction. Immediately after his appointment, spurning the friendly society of the cloister monks, he associated with laymen, living a worldly life, with dining and much conversation. Those who had elected him could not believe this, neither did any monk of this church: they thought that they had known him perfectly. On this matter Prior Reimund and Master Walter of Rheims, Alexander of Langley and Alexander of Appleton, the sub-prior Fabian, Amalric, Hubert Ridet, John Scot, and several others conferred together: "We deserve to suffer this for our sins, in fearing the king rather than the law in our election." And [then] one of the electors, Master Walter of Rheims, said: "When the abbot-elect, Dom William of Trumpington, was presented to the king in London, the king inquired in a low voice 'Who is your abbot-elect and what is his name?' and he was told 'Dom William of Trumpington.' 'Aha!' said the king, 'Exactly the person I wanted! it was prudent of you to elect him, to avoid being frustrated of another. He is a relative of that most distinguished knight William of Trumpington whose footsteps I believe he will follow.' And having inquired who and what sort of a person he was, he received him happily with an embrace. From these words, it is evident that this election was not proceeded with solely according to the will of God. But we must suffer this now with patience and correct his excesses first in a spirit of lenience, if indeed they can thus be corrected. If not, we must progress to severer methods."

The next day, when the abbot entered the chapter, he was severely criticised and firmly reprimanded about the above-mentioned excesses, and for infringing the charter [against banishment of monks to cells] made under the previous abbot, in which outrageous crime he had shamelessly blemished the constancy of his words and the integrity of his faith. Giving the prior a sidelong glance with bitterness in his heart, the abbot then turned to the whole convent, concealing his anger behind a serene countenance, and said openly: "Brothers and friends, if any transgression has occurred through negligence amends will be made in full according to your wishes without any hint of dispute, for such is God's will." Then Alexander of Langley, getting to his feet among the brothers, publicly said, "You speak very well, lord, in your kindness. We all in general appeal to the liberties of the convent as set out in the recent charter, discussed by us at first, then drawn up in writing and confirmed." The abbot replied, "What is this Dom Alexander? Have you any doubts about it? Surely I played an important part, taking the utmost trouble, in the making of that charter? Far be it from me to be found against it. You may rest assured; there is no need for any further complaint about this." And so the chapter broke up peacefully that day, with an appearance of submission [on the part of the abbot].

Lo and behold! Scarcely a month later the abbot exiled a certain monk of this church to one of the cells, against his will, although he wept and lamented and with bended knees and hands clasped together mournfully implored for mercy, that is, to be allowed to remain at home. When this was not forthcoming, he lodged an appeal with the prior and senior monks. But, because the abbot was away and absent from the chapter, this monk left and went to the cell he was ordered to by the abbot, never to return; for he died there in mental anguish. After a few days another was exiled in the same way, that is without the consent of the convent. Moreover, the abbot did not deign to amend the faults which he had promised to correct. So there was a considerable uproar in the convent; but then another vexation occurred, worse and greater than the first one.

When the abbot arrived in chapter one day he was criticized much more bitterly for his many excesses as well as for his contempt of the convent and the manifest breaking of his promises, and especially for infringing the above-mentioned charter, of which he had been the principal procurer and was now the audacious violator. The abbot, gnashing his teeth as usual and with the color of his face changed and his whole body bent and quivering, replied fast and furiously, going to the point without any beating about the bush. "It is true that I drew up the charter you are referring to and blaming me for [not observing], and I took the trouble to have it done diligently and efficiently; but I did not appreciate what I was doing. For that reason I can undo what I have done, and what has been confirmed by me can be annulled by me. The things I formerly believed in stand no longer, for I know now what I did not know before." On this Dom Amalric muttered under his breath, "That's true, for now you know you are abbot, which you didn't know before." The abbot heard this and was not pleased. When many spoke against the abbot and the uproar increased he calmed their excitement by saying "We shall take advice about this." This statement had the same effect as pouring a cup of cold water into a boiling cauldron: and so the chapter ended that day.

Shortly after this, on the prudent and secret instigation of the abbot, Nicholas, then papal legate in England, a monk of the Cistercian order, having been fully informed about all this, came to St. Albans and said that he wanted to appear in the chapter with the convent to discuss the affairs of the church. So the legate came to the chapter and, among other things, spoke as follows: "I hear that a certain new charter has been made in this monastery; I request that a copy be submitted to me for my inspection." When it was reluctantly handed to him, he inspected it and read it, exclaiming derisively when he had finished, "Oh how much and what kind of abuse is contained here! What is this, brothers? Are you insane? Do you want to renounce the obedience you have vowed to God?" With these words, bombastically pronounced, he tore the charter into pieces with his front teeth and, smashing the seal attached to it, threw it onto the floor. Then he added, "What villains you are to plot such things in a convent!" On this the satirical and vain braggings of Amalric ceased; the eloquent arguments of Alexander of Langley were silenced; the threats of Walter of Standon, who had anger in his breath, came to an end; the artful pride of John of Shelford was overthrown; and all the abbot's opponents were repelled in confusion. And so the chapter came to a close and the legate went away entreating the abbot to summon him if anyone criticized him about this, so that he could subdue the rebels more effectively. From this time on, therefore, the abbot, transformed from a king into a tyrant, though he was only a young man, behaved in all things like an old man and, although he was criticized again by some people, he made it clear, not without heat, that he had behaved correctly. In order that he could rule on his own, and lest he should experience any offense or hear any contradiction, he exiled his prior, Reimund, the most distinguished monk in the order in our times, knowing that if he subdued the greater person the rest, afraid, would be silent the more. Having deposed the prior and despoiled him by force of his books, which he had made with great care, and of other precious objects necessary to him now that he was old, and which he was entitled to enjoy during his lifetime, he sent him against his will and in a confused state of mind to the cell of Tynemouth, which was the usual place of exile for our monks. After that, all those who had opposed the abbot and confronted him remained silent in his presence, not daring to murmur against him. And the abbot prospered as much as he could desire, joyful and secure in his position. At the beginning of his abbacy he visited the cell at Tynemouth and elsewhere with much honor and magnificence and a large company, for he traveled surrounded by numerous relatives who had ignored him up to then; and he enjoyed every wordly and spiritual happiness....

What was done when [the abbot] returned home
When Abbot William arrived home [from a trip to Rome] the convent went out in procession to meet him. He was joyfully embraced by each of the brothers dressed in albs, which is the customary mode of reception whenever the abbot comes from overseas. And this should be done either in the doorway of the chapter house or of the cloister, on the way to the church, reverently and joyfully, after he has accepted some small favors.

Incidentally, it occurs to me that I ought to say what happens when the abbot comes from Tynemouth. When the abbot comes from Tynemouth he should be escorted by six squires from the lands of St. Albans who are enfeoffed on this account in a most generous and honorable way from the abbey's possessions. That is to say, one from the fief which William de Aete, knight, once held; another from the fief once held by Thomas de Wauz, knight; another from the fief which was once held by William de Wyka; another from the fief which Robert de Thebrugge once held; another from the fief once held by Nicholas Dispensator; and another from the fief which was once held by William de Ockersse.

These six ought to go and return at the abbot's expense but on their own horses, which should be powerful, and suitable for carrying, usually, one monk's clothes if this is necessary, on the squire's crupper. If, however, the horse of any one of the above-mentioned squires dies on the journey, the abbot must pay him seven shillings to make good his loss. And it should be made clear that, as often as he wishes to go to Tynemouth, the abbot must obtain permission from the king to enable him to travel to such a remote part of the kingdom border-ing on the kingdom of Scotland. When he arrives there he should behave in a restrained manner, having corrected the community, not being tyrannical nor dissipating the provisions and stock of the house, as Abbot Simon did, who was laudable indeed, but not at all in this matter. For when he had snatched away everything, the oxen with the plow were led to him and he was tearfully told, "Everything has been devoured, but these our plow-oxen remain, and these we now present to you for eating." Then the abbot, deservedly perplexed, said to his people, "Saddle your horses, let's leave here." And he left the house despoiled of all that year's produce, to his eternal opprobrium.

The abbot should rather consider carefully for what purpose he has gone [to a cell]; namely to reform behavior and the monastic order and lest there be any defect in spiritual or temporal necessities; and to visit the flock under his care in a paternal way, like a good shepherd. But it is frequently otherwise, for abbots arrive and stay far too long in order to be fed instead of supporting oth-ers; and the Lord allows us, by a just judgment, to be similarly oppressed by our superiors....

Concerning the house in London which [the abbot] bought

To the perpetuation of his memory with blessings, this Abbot William, having paid out no small amount of money, bought a house in London which was as large as a palace, providing for himself and his successors as well as for those monks of our convent who go there to stay. For he and all his successors, and any monks who wished, could stay there in comfort and privacy. To this house, which he acquired for us, belonged a chapel, several bedrooms, an orchard, sta-bles, a kitchen, a courtyard, a garden and a well; also the rents from some adjoining houses bordering the street, by which the courtyard was more securely enclosed. Abbot William had prudently built these houses after he had bought the principal house, and he assigned one of them in perpetuity to someone to serve the mansion itself.

Concerning the house at Yarmouth

Having purchased this house in London for 100 marks and made additions which were estimated at 50 marks, the said Abbot William bought a house at Yarmouth for 50 marks in which to store fish, especially herrings, which had been bought at an opportune time, to the inestimable benefit and honor of the house of St. Alban. To this house too he made a costly addition.

Concerning some wooden cloisters which the same abbot constructed
He also constructed various cloisters, one between the chapter house and St. Cuthbert's chapel, lest those crossing from one to the other be molested by water dripping onto them. Another cloister was three-sided; one side went from the kitchen to the door of the monks' cloister, which he assigned to the care of the cooks. Another extended from the doorway of the aforesaid cloister to the entrance to the guest-house which used to be the guest-house of visiting Benedictine monks, and it was assigned to the care of the guest-master. Another side of this cloister, that is the third, extended from the above-mentioned entrance to the doorway which leads to the tailor's workroom; and it was assigned to the chamberlain's care. The way to the infirmary led through another cloister, four-sided, which he commited to the infirmarer's care. All these he constructed soundly and competently of oak, with beams and rafters, and he roofed them with oak shingles. The three-sided cloister which extended from the kitchen to the doorway leading to the tailor's workshop he strengthened with a wicker fence so that free access to the space enclosed in the middle, which was a small shrubbery, should not be offered to all. He decided that this shrubbery should belong to the guest-master.

Concerning the cross of Jehoshaphat
Abbot William acquired for us the cross which Dom Laurence, who was English and a monk of St. Mary's church in the Valley of Jehoshaphat in the Holy Land near Jerusalem…, brought to England in the following way. When the aforesaid monk Laurence, according to his abbot's instructions, took over unhindered the deeds which had been deposited here for a long time unharmed, he promised that, if his plan of obtaining the manor and the church of Britwell, where he hoped to be prior, did not materialize and he had to return home to Jehoshaphat with his business unfinished, he would give this cross, the authenticity and sanctity of which is evident to us, in perpetuity to us in return for the traveling expenses we had given him, so that he could not be accused of ingratitude for so great a benefit. The outcome of this affair is fully set out in a detailed narrative at the end of this book.

Concerning the arm of St. Jerome
Abbot William also acquired for us from the above-mentioned monk an arm of St. Jerome, which he enclosed in superbly-made goldsmith's work embell-

ished with gems. This was carried round at special festivities, and certain other relics were added, namely part of the clothing and staff of St. Jerome and relics of the Holy Innocents.

Questions: How was an abbot chosen, in theory and in practice? What kind of abbot did William of Trumpington turn out to be? What tensions existed between the abbots and monks at St. Albans? Who was right? What kinds of actions won praise for the abbot?

40. THE ANCRENE WISSE

The monastic life was not the only way to dedicate oneself to religion; many men and even more women became anchorites and anchoresses, or hermits. While early Christian hermits had usually dwelt in near total isolation and very harsh conditions, the hermits of medieval England lived rather different lives. The following excerpts come from a set of guidelines produced for a small group of anchoresses, sometime in the first half of the thirteenth century.

Source: trans. J. Morton, *The Nun's Rule, Being the Ancren Riwle Modernised* (London: De La More Press, 1905), pp. 164-165, 237-244, 278-281, 312-321, 323-324; revised.

2. [Temptations] ... An anchoress thinks that she shall be most strongly tempted in the first twelve months after she shall have begun her monastic life, and in the next twelve thereafter; and when, after many years, she feels them so strong, she is greatly amazed, and is afraid lest God may have quite forgotten her, and cast her off. Nay! it is not so. In the first years, it is nothing but ball-play; but now, observe well, by a comparison, how it fares. When a man has brought a new wife home, he, with great gentleness, observes her manners. Though he sees in her some thing that he does not approve, yet he takes no notice of it, and puts on a cheerful countenance toward her, and carefully uses every means to make her love him, affectionately in her heart; and when he is well assured that her love is truly fixed upon him, he may then, with safety, openly correct her faults, which he previously bore with as if he knew them not: he becomes right stern, and assumes a severe countenance, in order still to test whether her love toward him might give way. At last when he perceives that she is completely instructed — that for nothing that he does to her does she love him less, but more and more, if possible, from day to day, then he shows her that he loves her sweetly, and does whatsoever she desires, as to one whom he loves and knows — then is all that sorrow become joy. If Jesu Christ, your Spouse, does thus to you, my dear sisters, let it not seem strange to you. For in the beginning it is only courtship, to draw you into love; but as soon as

he perceives that he is on a footing of affectionate familiarity with you, he will now have less forbearance with you; but after the trial — in the end — then is the great joy. Just in the same way, when he wished to lead his people out of bondage — out of the power of Pharaoh — out of Egypt, he did for them all that they desired — miracles many and fair. He dried the Red Sea and made them a free way through it; and they went there dry-footed where Pharaoh and all their foes were drowned. Moreover, in the desert, when he had led them far within the wilderness, he let them suffer distress enough — hunger and thirst, and much toil, and great and numerous wars. In the end, he gave them rest, and all wealth and joy — all their desire, with bodily ease and abundance. Thus our Lord spares at first the young and feeble, and draws them out of this world gently, and with subtlety. But as soon as he sees them inured to hardships, he lets war arise and be stirred up, and teaches them to fight and to suffer want. In the end, after long toil, he gives them sweet rest, here, I say, in this world, before they go to heaven; and then the rest seems so good after the labor; and the great plenty after the great want seems so very sweet....

3. Confession shall be complete, that is, all said to one man, from childhood. When the poor widow would cleanse her house, she gathers into a heap, first of all, all the largest sweepings, and then shovels it out; after this she comes again and heaps together all that was left before, and shovels it out also; again, upon the small dust, if it is very dusty, she sprinkles water, and sweeps it quite away after all the rest. In like manner must he that confesses himself, after the great sins, shovel out the small, and if the dust of light thoughts fly up too much, sprinkle tears on them, and they will not, then, blind the eyes of the heart. Whoever hides anything has told nothing; for, be he ever so faultless, yet he is like the man who hath upon him many deadly wounds, and shows them all but one to the physician, and lets them all be healed but one, of which he dies. He is also like men in a ship that has many leaks, into which the water makes its way in, and they stop them all but one, by means of which they are every one of them drowned. We are told of a holy man who lay in his death-sickness, and was unwilling to confess a particular sin of his childhood, and his abbot urged him by all means to confess it. He answered and said that it was not necessary, because he was a little child when he did it. Reluctantly, however, at last, through the searching exhortations of the abbot, he told it, and died soon thereafter. After his death, he came one night and appeared to his abbot in snow-white garments, as one who was saved; and said that if he had not fully confessed that particular thing which he did in childhood, he should certainly have been condemned among those who are lost. We are told also of another man who was very nearly condemned because he once compelled a man to drink, and died unshriven of it. Likewise, of a lady because she had lent one of her garments to a woman to go to a wake. But if anyone has searched

diligently all the recesses of his heart, and can discover nothing more, if there still lurks anything unobserved, it is, I hope, thrust out with the rest, since there was no negligence about it; and if he had been conscious of more guilt, he would willingly have confessed it. "If the consciousness is wanting, the punishment makes up for it," says Augustine.

4. Confession must also be candid, that is, made without any concealment, and not palliated by comparisons, nor gently touched upon. But the words should be spoken plainly according to the deeds. It is a sign of hatred when men reprehend severely a thing that is greatly hated. If you hate your sin, why do you speak of it in gentle terms? Why do you hide its foulness? Speak out its shame reproachfully, and rebuke it very sharply, if you would indeed confound the devil. "Sir," says the woman, "I have had a lover;" or, "I have been foolish concerning myself." This is not plain confession. Put no cloak over it. Take away the accessories, that is, the circumstances. Uncover yourself and say, "Sir, the mercy of God, and thine! I am a foul stud mare: a stinking whore." Give your enemy a foul name, and call your sin by its name without disguise, that is, conceal nothing at all that is connected with it. Yet what is too foul may not be spoken. The foul deed need not be named by its own foul name. It is sufficient to speak of it in such a manner that the father confessor may clearly understand what you would express. There are six things about sin which conceal it; in Latin, circumstances; in English, they may be called adjuncts — person, place, time, manner, number, cause.

Person — she that committed the sin, or with whom it was committed. Lay it open, and say, "Sir, I am a woman, and ought rightly to have been more modest than to speak as I have spoken, or to do as I have done; and, therefore, my sin is greater than if a man had done it, for it became me worse. I am an anchoress, a nun, a wedded wife, a maiden, a woman in whom such confidence is put, and one that had before been burnt with the same thing, and ought to have been more on my guard. Sir, it was with such a man;" and then name him — "a monk, a priest, or clerk, and of such an order, a married man, an innocent creature, a woman, as I am." Thus far as to the person.

Also concerning the place: "Sir, I played or spoke thus in the church; went to the play in the churchyard; looked on at this, or at the wrestling, and other foolish sports; spoke thus, or played, in the presence of secular men, or of religious men, in a house of anchorites, and at a different window than I ought; and near something sacred; I kissed him there; I touched him with my hand in such a place; or being alone in the church I thought thus; I looked upon him at the altar."

In like manner as to the time: "Sir, I was of such an age that I ought indeed to have kept myself more wisely. Sir, I did it in Lent, during the fast days, the holidays, when others were at church. Sir, I was soon overcome, and therefore the sin is greater than if I had been overcome by force, and by much violence. Sir, it was my fault, at first, that this thing went forward, through my coming into such a place, and at such a time. Before I ever did it, I reflected well how evil it were to do it, and did it nevertheless."

The manner likewise must be told, which is the fourth circumstance: "Sir, this sin I did thus, and in this manner; thus I first learned it, and thus I came first into it, and thus I went on to do it; and in so many ways; so fully, so shamefully; thus I sought pleasure; how I might give the most satisfaction to my inflamed desires;" and search out all the ways.

Number is the fifth circumstance — to tell the whole, how often it has been done: "Sir, I have done this so often; been accustomed to speak thus, and to listen to such speeches, and to think such thoughts, to neglect and forget things; to laugh, eat, drink, less or more than was needful. I have been so often angry since I last confessed, and for such a thing, and it lasted so long. I have so often spoken falsely, so often, and this, and this. I have done this so many times, and in so many ways, and to so many persons."

Cause is the sixth circumstance. Cause is, why you did it, or helped to do it, or through what means it began: "Sir, I did it for pleasure, and for guilty love, and for gain, through fear, through flattery. Sir, I did it for evil, though no evil came of it. Sir, my light answer, or my light behavior enticed him toward me. Sir, of this word came another; of this action, anger and evil words. Sir, the reason why the evil still continues is this: my heart was so weak." Let everyone, according to what he is, tell the circumstances — man, as relates to him; woman, as it concerns her: for I have not said anything here, but to remind man or woman of that which happens to them, by what is here said in a desultory manner. Thus strip your sin of these six coverings. Make it stark naked in your confession, as Jeremiah teaches, "Pour out thy heart as water." For, if oil be poured out of a vessel, yet there will be left in it somewhat of the liquor; and if milk be poured out, the color will remain; and if wine be poured, the smell remains; but water goes completely out at once. In such a manner, pour out your heart; that is, all the evil that is in your heart. And, if you do not, behold how terribly God threatens you by the prophet Nahum: "Behold, I am against thee," saith the Lord, "and I will show the nations thy nakedness, and the kingdoms thy shame. And I will cast abominations upon thee." You would not uncloak yourself to the priest in confession, and I will show quite nakedly your wickedness to all people, and your shameful sins to all kingdoms — to the kingdom of earth, and to the kingdom of heaven, and to the kingdom of hell; and I will bind up all your vileness upon your own neck, as is done to a thief when he is brought to be judged; and thus, with all that ignominy packed upon you, you shall be hurled headlong into hell....

Part 6. Of Penance

… Let not anyone handle herself too gently, lest she deceive herself. She will not be able, for her life, to keep herself pure, nor to maintain herself aright in chastity without two things, as Saint Ailred wrote to his sister. The one is, giving pain to the flesh by fasting, by watching, by flagellations, by wearing coarse garments, by a hard bed, with sickness, with much labor. The other thing is the moral qualities of the heart, as devotion, compassion, mercy, pity, charity, humility, and other virtues of this kind. "Sir," you answer me, "does God sell his grace? Is not grace a free gift?" My dear sisters, although purity is not bought from God, but is given freely, ingratitude resists it, and renders those unworthy to possess so excellent a thing who will not cheerfully submit to labor for it. Amidst pleasures and ease, and carnal abundance, who was ever chaste? Who ever carried fire within her that did not burn? Shall not a pot that boils rapidly be emptied of some of the water, or have cold water cast into it, and the burning fuel withdrawn? The pot of the belly that is always boiling with food, and especially with drink, is such a near neighbor to that ill-disciplined member that it imparts to it the fire of its heat. Yet many anchoresses, more is the harm, are of such fleshly wisdom, and so exceedingly afraid lest their head ache, and lest their body should be too much enfeebled, and are so careful of their health, that the spirit is weakened and sickens in sin, and they who ought alone to heal their soul, with contrition of heart and mortification of the flesh, become physicians and healers of the body. Did Saint Agatha do so? who answered and said to our Lord's messenger who brought her salve to heal her breasts, "Fleshly medicine I never applied to myself." And have you never heard the story of the three holy men, of whom one was wont, for his cold stomach, to use hot spices, and was more interested in meat and drink than the other two, who, even if they were sick, took no heed of what was wholesome and what was unwholesome to eat or to drink, but always took directly whatever God sent them, nor ever made much ado about ginger, or valerian, or cloves? One day, when the three had fallen asleep, and the third, of whom I spoke above, lay between these two, the Queen of Heaven came, and two maidens with her, one of whom bore what seemed a medicine, the other bore a spoon of good gold. Our Lady took some of it with the spoon, and put it into the mouth of one, and the maidens passed on to the middlemost. "Nay," said our Lady, "he is his own physician, go over to the third." A holy man stood not far off and beheld all this. When a sick man hath at hand any thing that will do him good, he may piously use it; but to be so anxious about it is not pleasing to God, and especially for one of such a religious profession to be anxious is not pleasing to God. God and his disciples speak of the art of healing the soul; Hippocrates and Galen of the health of the body. He who was the most learned of the disciples of Jesus Christ, says that "the wisdom of the flesh is the death of the soul." "We smell the battle afar off," as Job says. Thus we often dread a bodily disease before it comes. The soul disease attacks us and we bear it, to escape from the bodily disease, as if it were better to endure the fire of lust than headache, or the grumbling of a disordered stomach. And which of these two is better, in sickness to be a free child of God, or in bodily health to be a bond-servant under sin? And I do not say this as if wisdom and discretion were not always joined. Wisdom is the mother and the nurse of all virtues; but we often call that wisdom which is not wisdom. For it is true wisdom to prefer the health of the soul to that of the body; and when we cannot have them both together, to choose bodily hurt rather than, by too powerful temptations, the destruction of the soul. We are told that Nicodemus brought for the anointing of our Lord a hundred pounds of myrrh and of aloes, which are bitter spices, and betoken toilsome labor, and mortification of the flesh. A hundred is a complete number and denotes perfection, that is, a complete work, to signify that we ought to perfect the mortification of the flesh as far as may reasonably be endured. By the weight is signified discretion and wisdom — that every man should weigh with wisdom what he is able to do, and not be so exceed-ingly spiritual as to neglect the body, nor, on the other hand, so indulgent to the body that it might become disorderly, and make the spirit its servant....

Part 8. Of Domestic Matters

I said before, at the commencement, that you ought not, like unwise people, to promise to keep any of the external rules. I say the same still; nor do I write them for any but you alone. I say this in order that other anchoresses may not say that I, by my own authority, make new rules for them. Nor do I command that they observe them, and you may even change them, whenever you will, for better ones. In regard to things of this kind that have been in use before, it matters little.

Of sight, and of speech, and of the other senses enough was said. Now this last part, as I promised you at the commencement, is divided and separated into seven small sections.

Men esteem a thing as less dainty when they have it often, and therefore you should be, as lay brethren are, partakers of the holy communion only fifteen times a year: at midwinter [December 25]; Candlemas [February 2]; Twelfth-day [January 6]; on Sunday halfway between that and Easter, or our Lady's day [March 25], if it is near the Sunday, because of its being a holiday; Easter day; the third Sunday thereafter; Holy Thursday [that is, Ascension Day, forty days after Easter]; Whitsunday [that is, Pentecost, six weeks after Easter]; and midsummer day [June 24]; St. Mary Magdalen's day [July 22]; the Assump-tion [August 15]; the Nativity [of the Virgin Mary, September 8]; St. Michael's day [September 29]; All Saints' day [November 1]; St. Andrew's day [November

30]. And before all these days, see that you make a full confession and undergo discipline; but never from any man, only from yourselves. And forego your pittance for one day. And if any thing happens out of the usual order, so that you may not have received the sacrament at these set times, you may make up for it the Sunday next following, or if the other set time is near, you may wait till then.

You shall eat twice every day from Easter until the later Holyrood day [September 14], which is in harvest, except on Fridays, and ember days [that is, days of fasting and prayer in each season of the year], and procession days and vigils. In those days, and in the Advent, you shall not eat any thing white, except when necessity requires it. The other half year you shall fast always, except only on Sundays.

You shall eat no flesh nor lard except in great sickness; or whosoever is infirm may eat potage without scruple; and accustom yourselves to little drink. Nevertheless, dear sisters, your meat and your drink have seemed to me less than I would have it. Fast no day upon bread and water, unless you have permission. There are anchoresses who make their meals with their friends outside the convent. That is too much friendship, because, of all orders, this is most ungenial, and most contrary to the order of an anchoress, who is quite dead to the world. We have often heard it said that dead men speak with living men; but that they eat with living men, I have never yet found. Make no banquetings, nor encourage any strange vagabond fellows to come to the gate; though no other evil come of it but their immoderate talking, it might sometimes prevent heavenly thoughts.

It is not fit that an anchoress should be liberal with other men's alms. Would we not laugh loud to scorn a beggar who should invite men to a feast? Mary and Martha were two sisters, but their lives were different. You anchorites have taken to yourselves Mary's part, whom our Lord himself commended. "Mary hath chosen the best part. Martha, Martha," said he, "thou art much cumbered. Mary hath chosen better, and nothing shall take her part from her." Housewifery is Martha's part, and Mary's part is quietness and rest from all the world's din, that nothing may hinder her from hearing the voice of God. And observe what God saith, "that nothing shall take away this part from you." Martha has her office; let her alone, and sit with Mary stone-still at God's feet, and listen to him alone. Martha's office is to feed and clothe poor men, as the mistress of a house. Mary ought not to intermeddle in it, and if anyone blame her, God himself supreme defends her for it, as holy writ bears witness. On the other hand, an anchoress ought to take sparingly only that which is necessary for her. Whereof, then, may she make herself liberal? She must live upon alms, as frugally as ever she can, and not gather that she may give it away afterwards. She is not a housewife, but a church anchoress. If she can spare any fragments for the poor, let her send them quite privately out of her dwelling. Sin is oft concealed under the semblance of goodness. And how shall those rich anchoresses that are tillers of the ground, or have fixed rents, do their alms privately to poor neighbors? Desire not to have the reputation of bountiful anchoresses, nor, in order to give much, be too eager to possess more. Greediness is the root of bitterness: all the boughs that spring from it are bitter. To beg in order to give away is not the part of an anchoress. From the courtesy of an anchoress, and from her liberality, sin and shame have often come in the end.

Make women and children who have labored for you to eat whatever food you can spare from your own meals; but let no man eat in your presence, except he be in great need; nor invite him to drink any thing. Nor do I desire that you should be told that you are courteous anchoresses. From a good friend take whatever you have need of when she offers it to you; but for no invitation take anything without need, lest you get the name of gathering anchoresses. Of a man whom you distrust, receive neither less nor more — not so much as a race of ginger. It must be great need that shall drive you to ask any thing; yet humbly show your distress to your dearest friend.

You shall not possess any beast, my dear sisters, except only a cat. An anchoress that hath cattle appears as Martha was, a better housewife than anchoress; nor can she in any wise be Mary, with peacefulness of heart. For then she must think of the cow's fodder, and of the herdsman's hire, flatter the hayward, defend herself when her cattle is shut up in the pinfold, and moreover pay the damage. Christ knows, it is an odious thing when people in the town complain of anchoresses' cattle. If, however, anyone must needs have a cow, let her take care that she neither annoy nor harm anyone, and that her own thoughts be not fixed thereon. An anchoress ought not to have anything that draws her heart outward. Carry on no business. An anchoress that is a buyer and seller sells her soul to the chapman of hell. Do not take charge of other men's property in your house, nor of their cattle, nor their clothes, neither receive under your care the church vestments, nor the chalice, unless force compel you, or great fear, for oftentimes much harm has come from such caretaking. Let no man sleep within your walls. If, however, great necessity should cause your house to be used, see that, as long as it is used, you have therein with you a woman of unspotted life day and night.

Because no man sees you, nor do you see any man, you may be well content with your clothes, be they white, be they black; only see that they be plain, and warm, and well made — skins well tawed; and have as many as you need, for bed and also for back.

Next to your flesh you shall wear no flaxen cloth, except it be of hard and coarse canvas.... You shall sleep in a garment and belted. Wear no iron, nor haircloth, nor hedgehog-skins; and do not beat yourselves therewith, nor with a scourge of leather thongs, nor leaded; and do not with holly nor with briars cause yourselves to bleed without leave of your confessor; and do not, at one time, use too many flagellations. Let your shoes be thick and warm. In summer you are at liberty to go and to sit barefoot, and to wear hose without vamps, and whoever likes may sleep in them.... She who wishes to be seen, it is no great wonder that she adorn herself; but, in the eyes of God, she is more lovely who is unadorned outwardly for his sake. Have neither ring, nor brooch, nor ornamented girdle, nor gloves, nor any such thing that is not proper for you to have.

I am always the more gratified, the coarser the works are that you do. Make no purses, to gain friends therewith...; but shape, and sew, and mend church vestments, and poor people's clothes. You shall give nothing away without leave from your father confessor. Assist with your own labor, as far as you are able, to clothe yourselves and your domestics, as St. Jerome teaches. Be never idle; for the fiend immediately offers his work to her who is not diligent in God's work, and he begins directly to talk to her.... An anchoress must not become a schoolmistress, nor turn her anchoress-house into a school for children. Her maiden may, however, teach any little girl concerning whom it might be doubtful whether she should learn among boys, but an anchoress ought to give her thoughts to God only.

You shall not send, nor receive, nor write letters without leave. You shall have your hair cut four times a year to unburden your head; and be bled as oft, and oftener if it is necessary; but if anyone can dispense with this, I may well suffer it. When you are bled, you ought to do nothing that may be irksome to you for three days; but talk with your maidens, and divert yourselves together with instructive tales. You may often do so when you feel dispirited, or are grieved about some worldly matter, or sick. Thus wisely take care of yourselves when you are bled, and keep yourselves in such rest that long thereafter you may labor the more vigorously in God's service, and also when you feel any sickness, for it is great folly, for the sake of one day, to lose ten or twelve. Wash yourselves wheresoever it is necessary, as often as you please.

When an anchoress does not have her food at hand, let two women be employed, one who stays always at home, another who goes out when necessary; and let her be very plain, or of sufficient age.... Let neither of the women either carry to her mistress or bring from her any idle tales, or new tidings, nor sing to one another, nor speak any worldly speeches, nor laugh, nor play, so that any man who saw it might turn it to evil.... No servant of an anchoress ought, properly, to ask stated wages, except food and clothing, with which, and with God's mercy, she may do well enough.... Whoever has any hope of so high a reward will gladly serve, and easily endure all grief and all pain. With ease and abundance men do not arrive at heaven....

Questions: How are these guidelines similar to and different from monastic rules like Lanfranc's Constitutions? How hermit-like are the anchoresses? Which aspects of the Ancrene Wisse would be relevant to ordinary lay people? Which are specific to female anchoresses? What was the appeal of this life? Why might it appeal more to women than to men?

41. THE COMING OF THE FRIARS MINOR TO ENGLAND, BY THOMAS OF ECCLESTON

The religious ferment of the High Middle Ages gave rise to many new religious orders, including the mendicant or "begging" orders, the Dominicans and Franciscans, in the early thirteenth century. In the extracts below, the Franciscan Brother Thomas, later called "of Eccleston," tells of the arrival of the order in England.

Source: trans. H. Rothwell, *English Historical Documents Vol. III, 1189-1327* (New York: Oxford University Press, 1975), pp. 680-683.

Of the first coming of the friars minor to England

In A.D. 1224, in the time of the lord pope Honorius, in the same year, that is, in which he confirmed the Rule of the blessed Francis, the eighth year of the reign of the lord king Henry, son of John, on [September 10,] the Tuesday after the feast of the nativity of the Blessed Virgin, which in that year fell on a Sunday, the friars minor first arrived in England at Dover, being four clerks and five laymen.

The clerks were these: first, brother Agnellus of Pisa, in orders a deacon, in age about thirty, who at the last chapter general had been designated by the blessed Francis as minister provincial for England: he had been custodian at Paris and had borne himself so discreetly as to win the highest favor among the brethren and lay folk alike by reason of his renowned holiness.

The second was brother Richard of Ingworth, an Englishman by birth, a priest and preacher, and an older man. He was the first of the order to preach to people north of the Alps. In course of time, under brother John Parenti of happy memory, he was sent to Ireland to be minister provincial; he had been brother Agnellus's vicar in England while Agnellus himself went to the chapter general in which the translation was effected of the remains of St. Francis and had set a notable example of exceeding holiness. When he had fulfilled a ministry faithful and well-pleasing to God, he was absolved in chapter general by brother Albert of happy memory from all office among the brethren, and fired by zeal for the faith, set out for Syria and there, making a good death, fell on sleep.

The third was brother Richard of Devon, also an Englishman by birth, in orders an acolyte, in age a youth; he left us many examples of long-suffering and obedience. For after he had traveled through diverse provinces under obedience, he lived though frequently worn out by quartan fevers for eleven whole years at the place [that is, a small Franciscan house] at Romney.

The fourth was brother William of Ashby, still a novice wearing the hood of a probationer, likewise English by birth, young in years and in standing. He for a long time endured various offices in praiseworthy fashion, the spirit of Jesus Christ aiding him, and he showed us examples of humility and poverty, love and gentleness, obedience and patience and every perfection. For when brother Gregory, minister in France, enquired of him if he willed to go to England, he replied that he did not know. And when the minister marveled at this reply, brother William at length said the reason he did not know what he willed was that his will was not his own but the minister's. Wherefore he willed whatsoever the minister willed him to will. Brother William of Nottingham testified of him that he was perfect in obedience, for when he offered him the choice of the place where he would live, he said that that place best pleased him which it pleased the brother to appoint for him. And because he was specially gifted with charm and a most prepossessing gentleness, he called forth the goodwill of many layfolk towards the order. Moreover, he brought into the way of salvation many meet persons of diverse positions, ages and ranks, and in many ways he gave convincing proof that sweet Jesus knew how to do marvelous things.... He at a time of fleshly temptation mutilated himself in his zeal for chastity. After which he sought the pope, who, though severely reproving him, granted him a dispensation so that he might celebrate the divine offices. This same William after many years died peacefully in London.

Now the laymen were these: first, brother Henry of Treviso, a Lombard by birth, who by reason of his saintliness and notable sagacity was afterward made guardian at London. When he had fulfilled the course of his labor in England, the number of the brethren having already increased, he returned to his own country. The second was brother Lawrence of Beauvais, who at first worked at his trade as the Rule decreed and afterwards he returned to the blessed Francis and earned the privilege of seeing him often and being consoled by converse with him. Finally the holy father most generously bestowed on him his own tunic and sent him back to England gladdened by his most sweet blessing. This Lawrence, after many toils and, as I think, through the merits of that same father, reached the haven of rest, London, where now, sick beyond recovery, he awaits the end of his long and exhausting labors. The third was brother William of Florence, who after the brethren had been received returned speedily to France. The fourth was brother Melioratus. The fifth was brother James from the other side of the Alps, still a novice in a probationer's hood.

These nine were out of charity conveyed across to England and courteously provided for in their need by the monks of Fecamp. When they reached Canterbury, they stayed for two days at the priory of the Holy Trinity, then without delay four of them set off to London, namely brother Richard of Ingworth, brother Richard of Devon, brother Henry and brother Melioratus. The other five went to the priests' hospital, where they remained until they had found themselves somewhere to live. In fact a small room was soon afterwards granted them underneath the schoolhouse, where they sat all day as if they were enclosed. But when the scholars returned home in the evening they went into the schoolhouse in which they had sat and there made themselves a fire and sat beside it. And sometimes they set on the fire a little pot containing dregs of beer when it was time to drink at the evening collation, and they put a dish in the pot and drank in turn, and one by one they spake some word of edification. And one who was their associate in this unfeigned simplicity and holy poverty, and merited to be a partaker thereof, bore witness that their drink was sometimes so thick that when it had to be heated they put water in and so drank it joyfully…

Of the first separation of the brethren
Now the four brethren already named, when they reached London, betook them to the Friars Preachers [that is, the Dominicans], and were by them graciously received. They remained with them for fifteen days, eating and drinking what was set before them quite as if they were members of the house. After this they hired a house for themselves in Cornhill and made cells for themselves in it stuffing grasses into gaps in the cells. And they remained in that simple state until the following summer, with no chapel, for they had not yet been granted the privilege of setting up altars and celebrating the divine offices in their own places.

And without delay, before the feast of All Saints [November 1], and even before brother Agnellus came to London, brother Richard of Ingworth and brother Richard of Devon set out for Oxford and there were similarly received in the friendliest manner by the Friars Preachers; they ate in their refectory and slept in their dormitory like members of their house for eight days. After that they hired a house for themselves in the parish of St. Ebbe's, and there remained without a chapel until the following summer. There sweet Jesus sowed a grain of mustard-seed that afterward became greater than all herbs. From there brother Richard of Ingworth and brother Richard of Devon set out for Northampton and were taken in at the Hospital. Afterward they hired a house for themselves in the parish of St. Giles, where the first guardian was brother Peter the Spaniard, he who wore an iron corselet next to his skin and gave many other examples of perfection.

The first guardian at Oxford was brother William of Ashby, until then a novice; howbeit, the habit of his profession was granted him. The first guardian at Cambridge was brother Thomas of Spain, the first at Lincoln was brother Henry Misericorde, a layman: under whom brother John of Yarmouth was then a member of the house, a man of great holiness, who afterward died at Nottingham and is buried among the canons of Shelford.

Sir John Travers first received the brethren in Cornhill and hired them a house, and a certain Lombard, a layman, Henry by name, was made guardian. He then for the first time learnt to read, by night, in the church of St. Peter, Cornhill. Afterward he was made vicar of the English province while brother Agnellus was going to the chapter general. In the vicariate he had, however, as coadjutor brother Richard of Ingworth. But he did not support such a high state of happiness unto the end, rather growing luxurious in these honors and estranged from his true self, and he apostatised from the order in pitiable fashion.

It is worthy of record that in the second year of the administration of brother Peter, the fifth minister in England, in the thirty-second year, to wit, from the coming of the brethren to England, the brethren living in England in forty-nine places were numbered at twelve hundred and forty-two.

Questions: How was the Franciscan mission organized? What role does divine intervention play in the story? What do we learn of the organization of the order in general? What characteristics are valued in the Franciscan brothers? What signs are there of the "absolute poverty" promoted by the order?

42. THE SONG OF LEWES

Despite his early re-affirmation of Magna Carta, King Henry III (1216-72) found his reign plagued by clashes with his barons, which eventually broke out into civil war. The main issue was the barons' insistence that the king should be guided by their advice rather than that of his "foreign favorites" — a problem foreshadowed in Magna Carta. Earl Simon de Montfort, formerly a close friend of the king, emerged as the leader of the rebellious barons in the 1260s, and he led them to an important victory over the king at the Battle of Lewes in 1264. A number of political songs supporting the baronial cause survive from this era; the excerpts below come from such a poem, written shortly after the battle.

Source: trans. T. Wright, *The Political Songs of England, from the Reign of John to that of Edward II* (London: The Camden Society, 1839), pp. 71-121; revised.

Write quickly, O pen of mine, for, writing such things as follow, I bless and praise with my tongue thee, O right hand of God the Father, Lord of virtues, who givest prosperity at thy nod to thine own, whenever it is thy will. Let all those people now learn to put their trust in thee, whom they, who are now scattered, wished to destroy — they of whom the head is now taken, and the members are in captivity; the proud people is fallen; the faithful are filled with joy. Now England breathes in the hope of liberty; may the grace of God grant this land prosperity! The English were despised like dogs; but now they have raised their head over their vanquished enemies.

In the year of grace one thousand two hundred and sixty-four, and on [May 14,] the Wednesday after the festival of St. Pancras, the army of the English bore the brunt of a great battle at the castle of Lewes: for reasoning yielded to rage, and life to the sword. They met on the fourteenth of May, and began the battle of this terrible strife; which was fought in the county of Sussex, and in the bishopric of Chichester. The sword was powerful; many fell; truth prevailed; and the false men fled. For the Lord of valor resisted the perjured men, and defended those who were pure with the shield of truth....

May the Lord bless Simon de Montfort! and also his sons and his army! who, exposing themselves magnanimously to death, fought valiantly, condoling the lamentable lot of the English who, trodden under foot in a manner scarcely to be described, and almost deprived of all their liberties, nay, of their lives, had languished under hard rulers, like the people of Israel under Pharaoh, groaning under a tyrannical devastation. But God, seeing this suffering of the people, gives at last a new Matathias, and he, with his sons, zealous after the zeal of the law, yields neither to the insults nor to the fury of the king.

They call Simon a seductor and a traitor; but his deeds lay him open and prove him to be a true man. Traitors fall off in time of need; they who do not fly from death are those who stand for the truth. But says his insidious enemy now, whose evil eye is the disturber of peace, "If you praise the constancy and the fidelity, which does not fly at the approach of death or punishment, they shall equally be called constant who, in the same manner, go to the combat fighting on the opposite side, in the same manner exposing themselves to the chance of war, and subjecting themselves to a hard appellation." But in our war in which we are now engaged, let us see what is the state of the case.

The earl had few men used to arms; the royal party was numerous, having assembled the disciplined and greatest warriors in England, such as were called the flower of the army of the kingdom; those who were prepared with arms from among the Londoners were three hundred set before several thousands; whence they were contemptible to those, and were detested by those who were experienced. Much of the earl's army was raw; fresh in arms, they knew little of war. The tender youth, only now girt with a sword, stands in the morning in battle accustoming himself to arms; what wonder if such an unpractised tyro fear, and if the powerless lamb dread the wolf? Thus those who fight for England are inferior in military discipline, and they are much fewer than the strong men, who boasted in their own valor, because they thought they would safely, and without danger, swallow up, as it were, all whom the earl had to help him. Moreover, of those whom the earl had brought to the battle, and from whom he hoped for no little help, many soon withdrew from fear, and took to flight as though they were amazed; and of three parts, one deserted. The earl with a few faithful men never yielded....

Lo! we are touching the root of the perturbation of the kingdom of which we are speaking, and of the dissension of the parties who fought the said battle. The objects at which these two parties aimed were different. The king, with his, wished thus to be free: and so [it was urged on his side] he ought to be; and they said he would cease to be king, deprived of the rights of a king, unless he could do whatever he pleased; they said it was no part of the duty of the magnates of the kingdom to determine whom he should prefer to his earldoms, or on whom he should confer the custody of castles, or whom he would have to administer justice to the people, and to be chancellor and treasurer of the kingdom. He wanted to have every one at his own will, and counsellors from whatever nation he chose, and all ministers at his own discretion; while the barons of England are not to interfere with the king's actions, the command of the prince having the force of law, and what he may dictate binding upon every body at his pleasure. For [they argued that] every earl also is thus his own master, giving to every one of his own men both as much as he will, and to whom he will; he commits castles, lands, revenues, to whom he will; and although he be a subject, the king permits it all. Which, if he do well, is profitable to the doer; if not, he must himself see to it; the king will not hinder him from injuring himself. Why is the prince worse in condition, [they asked,] when the affairs of the baron, the knight, and the freeman are thus managed? Therefore, [the king's supporters argued,] they who wish to diminish the king's power aim at making the king a slave, taking away his dignity of a prince; they wish by sedition to make the royal power captive and reduce it into guardianship and subjection, and to disinherit the king, that he shall be unable to reign so fully as the kings who preceded him have hitherto done, who were in no respect subjected to their people, but administered their own affairs at their will, and conferred what they had to confer according to their own pleasure. This is the king's argument, which has an appearance of fairness, and this is alleged in defense of the right of the kingdom.

But now let my pen turn to the other side: let me describe the object at which the barons aim; and when both sides have been heard, let the arguments be compared, and then let us come to a final judgment, so that it may be clear which side is the truest. The people is more prone to obey the truer party. Let therefore the party of the barons speak for itself, and proclaim in order by what zeal it is led. This party in the first place protests openly that it has no designs against the kingly honor; nay, it seeks the contrary, and studies to reform and magnify the kingly condition, just as if the kingdom were ravaged by enemies, for then it would not be reformed without the barons, who would be the capable and proper persons for this purpose; and should anyone then hang back, the law would punish him as one guilty of perjury, a traitor to the king, who owes to his lord, when he is in danger, all the aid he can give to support the king's honor, when the kingdom is, as it were, near its end by devastation.

The real adversaries of the king are [foreign] enemies who make war upon him, and counsellors who flatter the king, who seduce their prince with deceitful words, and who lead him into error by their double tongues: these are adversaries worse than those who are perverse; it is these who pretend to be good while they are seducers, and procurers of their own advancement; they deceive the incautious, whom they render less on their guard by means of things that please them, whereby they are not provided against, but are considered as prudent advisers. Such men can deceive more than those who act openly, as they are able to make an outward appearance of being not hostile. What if such wretches, and such liars, should haunt the prince, capable of all malice, of fraud, of falsehood, excited by the spurs of envy, and should seek to do that extreme wickedness, by which they should sacrifice the privileges of the kingdom to their own ostentation, and they should contrive all kinds of hard reasons, which by degrees should confound the commonalty, should bruise and impoverish the mass of the people, and should subvert and infatuate the kingdom, so that no one could obtain justice, except he who would encourage the pride of such men as these by large supplies of money? Who could submit to the establishment of such an injury? And if such, by their conduct, should change the state of the kingdom; if they should banish justice to put injustice in its place; if they should call in strangers and trample upon the natives; and if they should subdue the kingdom to foreigners; if they should not care for the magnates and nobles of the land, and should place contemptible persons over them; and if they should overthrow and humiliate the great; if they should pervert and turn upside-down the order of things; if they should leave the measures that are best, to advance those which are worst — do not those who act thus devastate the kingdom? Although they do not make war upon it with arms from abroad, yet they fight with diabolical arms, and they violate, in a lamentable manner, the constitution of the kingdom; although not in the same manner [as a foreign enemy], yet they do no less damage....

Thus, in order that none of the aforesaid things may happen, which may hinder the form of peace and good customs, but that the zeal of the experienced men may find what is most expedient for the utility of the many, why is a reform not admitted, with which no corruption shall be mixed? For the king's clemency and the king's majesty ought to approve the endeavors, which so amend grievous laws that they be milder, and that they be, while less onerous, more pleasing to God. For the oppression of the commons pleaseth not

God, but rather [he is pleased by] the compassion whereby the commons may have time to think upon God. Pharaoh, who so afflicted the people of God, that they could with difficulty repair to the oracle which he had appointed to Moses, was afterwards so punished, that he was obliged to dismiss Israel against his will; and when he thought to catch them after they were dismissed, he was drowned whilst he thought to run through the deep. Solomon was unwilling to bruise Israel, nor would he reduce to servitude any one of the race, because he knew that it was God's people over whom he reigned; and he feared to hurt the imprint of God; and he praises mercy more than judgment, and the peace of a true father more than execution.

Since it is clear that the barons have a right of doing all this, it remains to answer the king's arguments. The king wishes to be free by the removal of his guardians, and he wishes not to be subject to his inferiors, but to be placed over them; he wishes to command his subjects and not be commanded; he wishes to be humiliated neither to himself nor to those who are his officers. For the officers are not set over the king; but on the contrary they are rather the noble men who support the law. Otherwise there would not be one king of one state, but they to whom the king was subject would reign equally. Yet this inconvenience also, though it seems so great, is easily solved with the assistance of God: for we believe that God wills truth, through whom we dissolve this doubt as follows. He by whom the universe is ruled in pure majesty is said to be, and is in truth, one king alone, who wants neither help whereby he may reign, nor even counsel, in as much as he cannot err. Therefore, all-powerful and all-knowing, he excels in infinite glory all those whom he has appointed to rule and, as it were, to reign under him over his people, who may fail, and who may err, and who cannot avail by their own independent strength, and vanquish their enemies by their own valor, nor govern kingdoms by their own wisdom, but in an evil manner wander in the track of error. They want help which should assist them, and counsel which should set them right. Says the king, "I agree to thy reasoning; but the choice of these must be left to my option; I will associate with myself whom I will, by whose support I will govern all things; and if my ministers should be insufficient, if they want sense or power, or if they harbor evil designs, or are not faithful, but are perhaps traitors, I desire that you will explain, why I ought to be confined to certain persons, when I might succeed in obtaining better assistance?" The reason of this is quickly declared, if it be considered what the constraint on the king is: all constraint does not deprive of liberty, nor does every restriction take away power. Princes desire free power; those who reign decline miserable servitude. To what will a free law bind kings? — to prevent them from being stained by an adulterated law. And this constraint is not one of slavery, but is rather an enlarging of the kingly faculty....

It is hard to love one who does not love us; it is hard not to despise one who despises us; it is hard not to resist one who ruins us; we naturally applaud him who favors us. It is not the part of a prince to bruise, but to protect; neither is it the part of a prince to oppress, but rather to deserve the favor of his people by numerous benefits conferred upon them, as Christ by his grace has deserved the love of all. If a prince love his subjects, he will necessarily be repaid with love; if he reign justly, he will of necessity be honored; if the prince err, he ought to be recalled by those whom his unjust denial may have grieved, unless he be willing to be corrected; if he is willing to make amends, he ought to be both raised up and aided by these same persons. Let a prince maintain such a rule of reigning, that it may never be necessary for him to avoid depending on his own people. The ignorant princes who confound their subjects will find that those who are unconquered will not thus be tamed. If a prince should think that he alone has more truth, more knowledge, and more intelligence than the whole people, that he abounds more in grace and the gifts of God, if it be not presumption, but it be truly so, then his instruction will visit the true hearts of his subjects with light, and will instruct his people with moderation....

Therefore let the community of the kingdom advise; and let it be known what the generality thinks to whom their own laws are best known. Nor are all those of the country so uninstructed, as not to know better than strangers the customs of their own kingdom, which have been bequeathed from father to son. They who are ruled by the laws know those laws best; they who experience them are best acquainted with them; and since it is their own affairs which are at stake, they will take more care, and will act with an eye to their own peace. They who want experience can know little; they will profit little the kingdom who are not steadfast. Hence it may be concluded, that it concerns the community to see what sort of men ought justly to be chosen for the utility of the kingdom; they who are willing and know how, and are able to profit it, such should be made the councillors and coadjutors of the king, to whom are known the various customs of their country, who feel that they suffer themselves when the kingdom suffers; and who guard the kingdom, lest, if hurt be done to the whole, the parts have reason to grieve while they suffer along with it; who rejoice, when it has cause to rejoice, if they love it. Let us call attention to the noble judgment of King Solomon: she who did not feel horror at the cruelty of dividing the infant, because she did not feel for it, and lacked maternal love, showed, as the king testified, that she was not its mother. Therefore let a prince seek such [councillors] as may condole with the community, who have a motherly fear lest the kingdom should undergo any sufferings. But if anyone be not moved by the ruin of the many ... he is not fitted to rule over the many, since he is entirely devoted to his own interest, and to none other. A man who feels for others is agreeable to the community; but a man who does not feel for others, who possesses a hard heart, cares not if misfortunes fall upon the many — such walls are no defense against misfortunes. Therefore, if the king has not wisdom to choose by himself those who are capable of advising him, it is clear, from what has been said, what ought then to be done. For it is a thing which concerns the community to see that miserable wretches be not made the leaders of the royal dignity, but the best and chosen men, and the most approved that can be found. For since the governance of the kingdom is either the safety or perdition of all, it is of great consequence who they are that have the custody of the kingdom, just as it is in a ship: all things are thrown into confusion if unskilful people guide it; if any one of the passengers belonging to it who is placed in the ship abuse the rudder, it matters not whether the ship be governed prosperously or not. So those who ought to rule the kingdom, let the care be given to them, if any one of the kingdom does not govern himself rightly; he goes on a wrong path which perhaps he has himself chosen. The affairs of the generality are best managed if the kingdom is directed in the way of truth. And, moreover, if the subjects labor to dissipate their property, those who are set over them may restrain their folly and temerity, lest by the presumption and imbecility of fools, the power of the kingdom be weakened, and courage be given to enemies against the kingdom. For whatever member of the body be destroyed, the strength of the body is diminished thereby. So if it be allowed even that men may abuse what belongs to themselves, when it be injurious to the kingdom, many others, immediately repeating the injurious liberty, will so multiply the wildness of error, that they will ruin the whole. Nor ought it properly to be named liberty, which permits fools to govern unwisely; but liberty is limited by the bounds of the law; and when those bounds are despised, it should be known as error. Otherwise you will call a raving madman free, although he be at enmity with everything like prosperity. Therefore the king's argument concerning his subjects, who are ruled at their own choice by whom they will, is by this sufficiently answered and overthrown; since every one who is subject is ruled by one who is greater. For we say that no man is permitted all that he will, but that everyone has a lord who may correct him when erring, and aid him when doing well, and who sometimes raises him up when he is falling. We give the first place to the community: we say also that the law rules over the king's dignity; for we believe that the law is the light, without which we conclude that he who rules will wander from the right path.... If the king lacks this law, he will wander from the right track; if he does not hold it, he will err foully; its presence gives the power of reigning rightly, and its absence overturns the kingdom. This law speaks thus, "Kings reign through me; through me justice is shown to those who make laws." No king shall alter this firm law; but by it he shall make himself stable when he is variable. If he conform to this law, he will stand; and if he disagree with it, he will waver. It is said commonly, "As the king wills, so goes the law," but the truth is otherwise, for the law stands, but the king falls. Truth and charity and the zeal of salvation, this is the integrity of the law, the regimen of virtue: truth, light, charity, warmth, zeal.... Whatever the king may ordain, let it be consonant with these; for if it be otherwise, the commonalty will be made sorrowful; the people will be confounded, if either the king's eye lacks truth, or the prince's heart lacks charity, or he does not always moderately fulfill his zeal with severity.

These three things being supposed, whatever pleases the king may be done; but by their opposites the king resists the law. However, kicking against it does not hurt the spur; thus the instruction which was sent from heaven to Paul teaches us. Thus the king is deprived of no inherited right, if there be made a provision in concordance with just law. For dissimulation shall not change the law, whose stable reason will stand without end. Wherefore if anything that is useful has been long put off, it is not to be criticized when adopted late. And let the king never set his private interest before that of the community, as if the salvation of all yields to him alone. For he is not set over them in order to live for himself; but that his people who is subject to him may be in safety.... Therefore if the prince will be warm with charity as much as possible towards the community, if he shall be solicitous to govern it well, and shall never be rejoiced at its destruction; wherefore if the king will love the magnates of the kingdom, although he should know alone, like a great prophet, whatever is needful for the ruling of the kingdom, whatever is becoming in him, whatever ought to be done, truly he will not conceal what he will decree from those without whom he cannot effect that which he will ordain. He will therefore negotiate with his people about bringing into effect the things which he will not think of doing by himself. Why will he not communicate his councils to those whose aid he will ask supplicatingly? Whatever draws his people to benignity, and makes friends and cherishes unity, it is fit the royal prudence should indicate it to those who can augment his glory. Our Lord laid open all things to his disciples, dividing from the servants those whom he made his friends; and as though he were ignorant, he often inquired of his people what was their opinion on matters which he knew perfectly. Oh! if princes sought the honor of God, they would rule their kingdoms rightly, and without error. If princes had the knowledge of God, they would exhibit their justice to all. Ignorant of the Lord, as though they were blind, they seek the praises of men, delighted only with vanity. He who does not know how to rule himself will be a bad ruler over others; if anyone will look at the Psalms, he will read the same.... David in the innocence of his heart and by his intelligence fed Israel. From all that has been said, it may be evident that it becomes a king to see together with his nobles what things are convenient for the government of the kingdom, and what are expedient for the preservation of peace; and t. the king have natives for his companions, not foreigners or favorites for his councillors or for the great nobles of the kingdom, who supplant others and abolish good customs. For such discord is a stepmother to peace, and produces battles, and plots treason. For as the envy of the devil introduced death, so hatred separates the troop. The king shall hold the natives in their rank, and by this governance he will have joy in reigning. But if he study to degrade his own people, if he pervert their rank, it is in vain for him to ask why thus deranged they do not obey him; in fact they would be fools if they did.

Questions: How does the account of the battle, early in the poem, support the rightness of the barons' cause? What does the baronial party want? What are the king's arguments, and how does the poet refute them? How is religion used to legitimize the baronial position? How does this argument compare with that in the twelfth-century Policraticus *(doc. 29)?*

43. SUMMONSES TO PARLIAMENT

During the turmoil of Henry III's reign (1216-72), the formal royal council, consisting of the barons and the higher clergy, was gradually enlarged to include representative knights, townsmen, and lower clergy. At the same time it came to be known by a new name, "Parliament." By the end of the century it was customary for all these groups to be included when the general business of the kingdom was to be discussed — though more selective groups might be summoned to advise the king on more specific items. The following writs from 1295 are typical parliamentary summonses issued by Edward I (1272-1307).

Source: trans. E.P. Cheyney, *Translations and Reprints from the Original Sources of European History*, series 1, vol. 1 (Philadelphia: University of Pennsylvania Department of History, 1902), no. 6, pp. 33-35; revised.

Summons of a bishop

The king to the venerable father in Christ, Robert, by the same grace archbishop of Canterbury, primate of all England, greeting. As a most just law, established by the careful providence of sacred princes, exhorts and decrees that what affects all, by all should be approved, so also, very evidently should common danger be met by means provided in common. You know sufficiently well, and it is now, as we believe, divulged through all regions of the world, how the king of France fraudulently and craftily deprives us of our land of Gascony, by withholding it unjustly from us. Now, however, not satisfied with the before-mentioned fraud and injustice, having gathered together for the conquest of our kingdom a very great fleet, and an abounding multitude of

ich he has made a hostile attack on our kingdom and the
ame kingdom, he now proposes to destroy the English lan-
rom the earth, if his power should correspond to the
on of the contemplated injustice, which God forbid.
arts seen beforehand do less injury, and your interest espe-
, as that of the rest of the citizens of the same realm, is concerned in this
affair, we command you, strictly enjoining you in the fidelity and love in which
you are bound to us, that on [November 13,] the Lord's day next after the feast
of St. Martin, in the approaching winter, you be present in person at Westminster, citing beforehand the dean and chapter of your church, the archdeacons
and all the clergy of your diocese, causing the same dean and archdeacons in
their own persons, and the said chapter by one suitable proctor, and the said
clergy by two, to be present along with you, having full and sufficient power
from the same chapter and clergy, to consider, ordain and provide, along with
us and with the rest of the prelates and principal men and other inhabitants of
our kingdom, how the dangers and threatened evils of this kind are to be met.
Witness the king at Wangham, the thirtieth day of September.

Summons of a baron

The king to his beloved and faithful relative, Edmund, Earl of Cornwall, greeting. Because we wish to have a consultation and meeting with you and with
the rest of the principal men of our kingdom, as to provision for remedies
against the dangers which in these days are threatening our whole kingdom,
we command you, strictly enjoining you in the fidelity and love in which you
are bound to us, that on [November 13,] the Lord's day next after the feast of
St. Martin, in the approaching winter, you be present in person at Westminster,
for considering, ordaining and doing along with us and with the prelates, and
the rest of the principal men and other inhabitants of our kingdom, as may be
necessary for meeting dangers of this kind. Witness the king at Canterbury, the
first of October.

Summons of representatives of shires and towns

The king to the sheriff of Northamptonshire. Since we intend to have a consultation and meeting with the earls, barons and other principal men of our
kingdom with regard to providing remedies against the dangers which are in
these days threatening the same kingdom; and on that account have commanded them to be with us on [November 13,] the Lord's day next after the
feast of St. Martin in the approaching winter, at Westminster, to consider,
ordain, and do as may be necessary for the avoidance of these dangers; we

strictly require you to cause two knights from the aforesaid county, two citizens from each city in the same county, and two burgesses from each borough, of those who are especially discreet and capable of laboring, to be elected without delay, and to cause them to come to us at the aforesaid time and place.

Moreover, the said knights are to have full and sufficient power for themselves and for the community of the aforesaid county, and the said citizens and burgesses for themselves and the communities of the aforesaid cities and boroughs separately, then and there for doing what shall then be ordained according to the common counsel in the premises; so that the aforesaid business shall not remain unfinished in any way for defect of this power. And you shall have there the names of the knights, citizens and burgesses and this writ. Witness the king at Canterbury on the third day of October.

Questions: What is the purpose of this Parliament? How will representatives of the clergy, knights, and townspeople be selected? How does this parliament compare with what Magna Carta (doc. 35) called the "common council of the kingdom"? Why has it changed?

44. CONFIRMATION OF CHARTERS, 1297

Edward I (1272-1307) called frequent parliaments and considered them a tool of royal government. Generally a strong and successful king, he faced a crisis in the 1290s in which he needed Parliament's support, and this led him to grant the following confirmation of the Magna Carta, with some new concessions.

Source: trans. G.C. Lee, *Source-Book of English History: Leading Documents* (New York: Henry Holt and Company, 1900), pp. 184-185; revised.

1. Edward, by the grace of God king of England, lord of Ireland, and duke of Aquitaine, to all those that shall hear or see these present letters, greeting: Know ye, that we to the honor of God and of the holy church, and to the profit of our realm, have granted for us and our heirs that the Charter of Liberties and the Charter of the Forest, which were made by common assent of all the realm, in the time of King Henry our father, shall be kept in every point without breach. And we will that the same charters shall be sent under our seal as well to our justices of the forest as to others, and to all sheriffs of shires, and to all other officers and to all our cities throughout the realm, together with our writs, in which it shall be contained that they cause the aforesaid charters to be published, and declare to the people that we have confirmed them in all points, and that our justices, sheriffs, mayors, and other officials, which under us

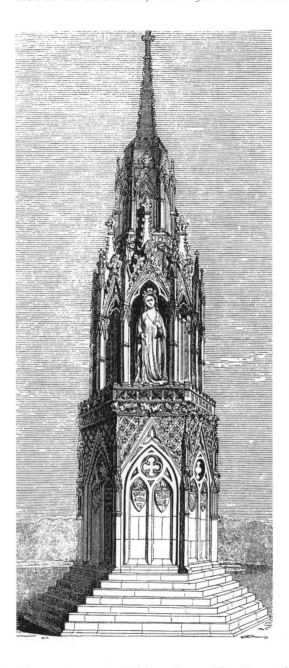

Fig. 26: The Eleanor Cross near Waltham, Essex When Queen Eleanor, wife of Edward I, died in 1291, her husband commemorated her with a series of stone monuments built along the route of her funeral procession. Three of them survive today; this one is shown in a nineteenth-century engraving.

have the laws of our land to guide, shall allow the said charters pleaded before them in judgment in all their points; that is to wit, the Great Charter as the common law and the Charter of the Forest according to the assize of the forest, for the welfare of our realm.

2. And we will that if any judgment be given from henceforth, contrary to the points of the charter aforesaid, by the justices or by any other of our officials that hold pleas before them, it shall be null and void.

3. And we will that the same charters shall be sent under our seal to cathedral churches throughout our realm, there to remain, and shall be read before the people twice yearly.

4. And that all archbishops and bishops shall pronounce the sentence of greater excommunication against all those that by word, deed, or counsel, do contrary to the aforesaid charters, or that in any point break or undo them. And that the said courses be twice a year denounced and published by the prelates aforesaid. And if the same prelates or any of them be remiss in the denunciation of the said sentences, the archbishops of Canterbury and York for the time being, as is fitting, shall compel and distrain them to make that denunciation in form aforesaid.

5. And because diverse people of our realm are in fear that the aids and tasks which they have given to us beforetime towards our wars and other business, of their own grant and good-will, howsoever they were made, might turn to a bondage to them and their heirs, because they might be at another time found in the rolls, and so likewise the prises taken [that is, confiscations made] throughout the realm by our ministers; we have granted for us and our heirs, that we shall not draw such aids, tasks, nor prises, into a custom, because of anything that has been done heretofore, be it by roll or any other precedent that may be found.

6. Moreover, we have granted for us and our heirs, as well to archbishops, bishops, abbots, priors, and other folk of holy church, as also to earls, barons, and to all the commonalty of the land, that for no business from henceforth will we take such manner of aids, tasks, nor prises, but by the common consent of the realm, and for the common profit thereof, saving the ancient aids and prises due and accustomed.

7. And for as much as the more part of the commonalty of the realm find themselves sore grieved with the maletote of wools, that is to wit, a toll of forty shillings for every sack of wool, and have made petition to us to release the same, we, at their requests, have clearly released it, and have granted for us and our heirs that we shall not take such thing or any other without their common assent and good will, saving to us and our heirs the custom of wools, skins, and leather granted before by the commonalty aforesaid. In witness of which things we have caused these our letters to be made patent. Witness Edward,

our son, at London, the tenth day of October, the five and twentieth year of our reign.

And be it remembered that this same charter in the same terms, word for word, was sealed in Flanders under the king's great seal, that is to say at Ghent, the fifth day of November in the twenty-fifth year of the reign of our aforesaid lord the king, and sent into England.

Questions: Clauses 5 and 6 are considered the most important parts of this document. What do they promise? What are the implications of such a promise? How does the document show that Magna Carta was still politically important?

45. LONDON CORONERS' ROLLS

From the thirteenth century on, all sudden or unexpected deaths had to be investigated by the local coroner, and the testimony recorded in these cases gives us some of our most vivid glimpses into the daily activities of common folk.

Source: trans. H.T. Riley, *Memorials of London and London Life in the XIIIth, XIVth, and XVth Centuries* (London: Longmans, Green, and Co., 1868), pp. 1–19; revised.

On Thursday [March 19], the morrow of St. Edward the king and martyr, ... in [1276,] the fourth year of the reign of King Edward [I], Gregory de Rokesle, the chamberlain, and the sheriffs of the city of London were given to understand that one John Fuatard was lying dead, by another death than his rightful death, in the house of John de Blecchinggele, in the parish of St. Michael Candlewick Street, in the ward of Thomas de Basinge. Upon hearing which, the said chamberlain and sheriffs went there, and calling together the good men of that ward, and of the ward of John Horn, made diligent inquisition how this happened.

These men say, on the fealty in which they are bound to our lord the king, that on [March 8,] the Sunday next before the feast of St. Gregory in this year, while the said John Fuatard and one John le Clerk were playing together [a game of] tiles in the churchyard of St. Mary in Southwark, the aforesaid John, who was clerk of St. Mary Magdalen in Southwark, when throwing the tile in his turn, and quite against his own will, struck the said John Fuatard with his tile on the right side of the head, making a wound two inches in length, and penetrating to the brain: languishing from the effects whereof, he lived from the Sunday aforesaid until St. Edward's Day [March 18], when, by reason of the said wound, he died. And the body was viewed, upon which no other wound, hurt, or bruise appeared. Being asked what became of the said John after so doing, they say that he went forthwith to the church of St. Mary Magdalen in Suthwark, but has never since been seen in the city. Being asked about his chattels, they say that goods or chattels he had none.

And John de Blecchingele was attached [that is, asked to provide two sureties for his cooperation], and Sarria, his wife, by two sureties; and John de Langmeuede, who dwelt in the same house, by two sureties. And the first neighbor, Henry de Lyre, fishmonger, the second, Robert de Long, fishmonger, the third, Roger de Bedewelle, skinner, and the fourth, Alan of Enfield Well, were attached, each by two sureties.

On [May 18, the] Monday next after our Lord's Ascension in the year aforesaid, the said chamberlain and sheriffs were given to understand that one Gervase le Noreys was lying dead in the king's highway in the parish of Barking Church, in the ward of William de Hadestoke. Upon hearing which, the said chamberlain and sheriffs went there, and by good and lawful men diligent inquisition was made how this happened.

These men say that on the Sunday before, at the hour of Vespers, there arose a dispute between the said Gervase and one William de Lindeseye; whereupon, the said William feloniously assaulted Gervase with a knife, giving him a wound in the left side of the back, two inches in length and one inch deep, and penetrating to the heart; and another wound, under the right breast, two inches long, one inch wide, and two inches deep; from the effect of which wounds he immediately died. After which, the said William forthwith fled to the church, that is to say, the chapel of St. Mary Barking Church. Being asked if they think that anyone else is guilty of causing that death, they say they do not. Being asked about the goods and chattels of the said William, they say that for goods, he had one tabard, of the value of ten pence, one hatchet, one bow with three arrows, value two pence, and one sheet, valued at four pence; beyond which, he had no goods or chattels, as they understand.

And the four nearest neighbors were attached, by sureties.

On the Wednesday following, the said William, acknowledging before the chamberlain and sheriffs, and other good and trusty men, within the church aforesaid, that he had committed the felony before-mentioned, in their presence abjured the realm [that is, he swore to leave sanctuary and go into exile overseas]. And the port of Dover was assigned to him, to set sail within three days therefrom. He had no chattels, save only those above-mentioned.

On [June 14, the] Sunday next before the feast of St. Botolph in the year aforesaid, the said chamberlain and sheriffs were given to understand that one Henry Grene, water-carrier, was lying drowned in the river Thames, in the ward of Castle Baynard, in the parish of St. Andrew, and at the hithe [that is, a small harbor] of Castle Baynard. Upon hearing which, they went there, and having called together the good men of that ward, and of the ward of Simon de Hadestok, diligent inquisition was made how this happened.

These men say that on the preceding Thursday, the said Henry, having come to St. Paul's Wharf with a tub, and intending to take up water with the tub, attempted to place it upon the wharf; after which, it so happened that, from the weight of the water in the tub, as he was standing upon the board of the boat aforesaid, the boat moved away from the wharf, and he fell between it and the quay into the water, and so by mischance was drowned. Being asked if they believe anyone else to be guilty or suspected of that death, or otherwise, they say that it was no other than a misadventure, as before stated. And the body was viewed; upon which no wound, hurt or bruise appeared. And the boat was appraised, with the whole of its tackle, and the tub, at 5s. 6d.

And the two neighbors nearest to the place where the mischance took place were attached; and the two nearest neighbors to the place where the body was found.

On [September 30, the] Wednesday next after the feast of St. Michael in the year aforesaid, the said chamberlain and sheriffs were given to understand that one John le Hancrete was lying dead, by another death than his rightful death, in the house of William the Cooper in the ward of Anketil de Auvergne, in the parish of St. Brigid. Upon hearing which, the said chamberlain and sheriffs went there, and upon the oath of the good men of that ward diligent inquisition was made thereon.

These men say that the said John came from a certain feast that had been held in the city of London to the house of William before-named, being very drunk, that is to say, on the Monday before, at the hour of Vespers, where he had hired his bed by the day; and that then, intending to lie down upon it, he took a lighted candle for the purpose of making his bed; which done, he left the candle burning, and fell asleep thereon. And the candle being thus left without anyone to look after it, the flame of it caught the straw of the bed upon which the said John was lying; and accordingly, he, as well as the bed and the straw aforesaid, was burnt, through the flame of the candle so spreading, at about the hour of midnight. And so, languishing from the effects thereof, he lived until the Tuesday following, at the hour of matins, on which day and hour he died from the burning aforesaid. Being asked if they hold anyone suspected of the death of the said John, they say they do not. And the body was viewed; upon which no wound or hurt appeared, save only the burning aforesaid.

And the two nearest neighbors were attached, by sureties. And William the Cooper was attached, in whose house he was burnt; and Fynea, the wife of the same William, was attached; as also Remund, the son of William.

On Sunday the feast of St. Lucy [December 13] in the year above-mentioned, the said chamberlain and sheriffs were given to understand that one Roger

Canny, charcoal-seller, was lying dead in the king's highway, opposite to the house of Sir William le Maceler. Upon hearing which, the said chamberlain and sheriffs went there, and calling together the good men of the ward of the Cheap and the ward of Henry le Waleys, diligent inquisition was made how this happened.

These men say that the said Roger was sitting in the tavern of Robert Box on the preceding Saturday, and drinking there to the hour of curfew; and that afterwards, on leaving, he went towards the house where he used to lodge, but when he had come opposite the house of William before-mentioned, he was struck with the falling sickness [that is, epilepsy] in the king's highway, from which he had frequently suffered; and so by reason of that disease, and through his own drunkenness and extreme cold, he died there by misadventure. They hold no one suspected thereof. And the body was viewed, upon which no wound, hurt, or bruise appeared.

And the two nearest neighbors were attached.

On [February 12, 1277,] the Friday next after Ash Wednesday, in the fifth year of the reign of King Edward, the said chamberlain and sheriffs were given to understand that one Matilda, wife of Henry le Coffeur, was lying dead, by another death than her rightful death, in the house of the said Henry, in the parish of St. Nicholas Shambles, in the ward of Anketil de Auvergne. On hearing which, the said chamberlain and sheriffs went there, and having called together the good men of that ward, and of the ward of John de Blakethorn, diligent inquisition was made thereon.

These men say that as the said Matilda was coming from West Cheap towards the hospice [or church guest hall], being drunk, she fell upon the pavement opposite the church of St. Martin, and so broke her right arm, upon the Sunday, namely, before our Lord's Nativity, and immediately after the hour of curfew. Upon being carried from that place to the house of the said Henry, her husband, she survived in a languishing state from that day until the Monday before Ash Wednesday next ensuing; on which day she died. They hold no one suspected. The body was viewed, upon which no injury appeared, except the arm broken, as aforesaid.

And the two nearest neighbors were attached, each by two sureties. And the said Henry was attached, in whose house she died, by two sureties.

On Monday [April 5, 1277,] the morrow of the close of Easter, in the fifth year of King Edward, the said chamberlain and sheriffs were given to understand that one Symon de Winton, taverner, was lying dead etc., in the parish of St. Martin, in Ironmonger Lane in the ward of Cheap, in a house belonging to Robert le Surgeon, of Friday Street; in which house the said Symon kept a tavern. On hearing which, the said chamberlain and sheriffs went there, and calling together the good men of that ward and of Bassishaw, and of the ward of Henry de Frowke, diligent inquisition was made how this had happened.

The jurors say that on [December 5, 1276,] the eve of St. Nicholas…, a dispute arose between the said Symon and a certain man who said that he was called "Roger of Westminster," and who was Symon's servant. And on the next day also, they were seen by the neighbors in the same house and tavern, abusing each other and quarreling, by reason of the same dispute; and on the same night they slept there, in the same room together. But as soon as this Roger saw that the said Symon was sound asleep, he seized a knife, and with it cut the throat of Symon quite through, so that the head was entirely severed from the body. After which, he dragged the body out, and put it in a certain secret spot, a dark and narrow place, situated between two walls in the same house, where coals were usually kept; such a place being somewhat long, and not quite two feet wide. And on the following day, the same Roger, as was his custom, set out the bench of the tavern, and sold wine there. And as the said Symon had not been seen by the neighbors all that day, they asked Roger what had become of his master; whereupon he made answer that he had gone to Westminster, to recover some debts that were owing to him there; and on the second day and third he gave the same answer. At twilight however on the third day, he departed by the outer door, locking it with the key, and carrying off with him a silver cup, a robe, and some bedclothes, which had belonged to the same Symon. Afterwards he returned, and threw the key into the house of one Hamon Cook, a near neighbor, telling him that he was going to seek the said Symon, his master, and asking him to give him the key, in case he should come back. And from that day the house remained closed and empty until [December 31,] the eve of our Lord's circumcision following; upon which day John Doget, a taverner, taking with him Gilbert of Colchester, went to the house aforesaid to recover a debt which the said Symon owed to him for wines. But when he found the door closed and locked, he enquired after the key, of the neighbors who were standing about: upon hearing of which, the said Hamon gave him up the key forthwith. Upon entering the tavern with Gilbert aforesaid, he found there one tun full of wine, and another half full, which he himself had sold to Symon for 50 shillings; and this he at once ordered to be taken out by the porters … and put in a cart … and taken to his own house, for the debt so due to him; together with some small tables, canvas cloths, gallons, and wooden potels, two shillings in value. This being done, the said John Doget shut the door of the house, carrying away with him the key thereof; from which time the house was empty, no one having entered it until [March 16,] the Tuesday before Palm Sunday. Upon which day, Master Robert aforesaid, to whom the house belonged, came and broke open the door for want of a key, and so entering it, immediately put Michael le Oynter in possession of it; which Michael, on [April 3,] the Saturday in Easter week, went there alone, to examine all the offices belonging thereto, and see which of them required to be cleansed of filth and dust. But when he came to the narrow and dark place aforesaid, he there found the headless body, upon seeing which, he sent word to the said chamberlain and sheriffs.

Being asked if anyone else dwelt in the house, save and except those two persons, or if anyone else had been seen or heard in that house with them on the night the felony was committed, or if any other person had had frequent or especial access to the house by day or night, from which mischief might have arisen, they say not beyond the usual resort that all persons have to a tavern. Being asked if the said Roger had any well-known or especial [friend] in the city, or without, to whose house he was accustomed to resort, they say they understand that he had not, seeing that he was a stranger, and had been in the service of this Symon hardly a fortnight. Being asked therefore where he had taken the goods he had carried off, they say that, seeing that the house was near to the Jewry, they believe that he took them to the Jewry; but to whose house they know not. Being asked what became of the head so cut off, they say they know not, nor can they ascertain anything as to the same. They say also that the said Roger escaped by stealth, and has not since been seen. Chattels he had none.

And the four nearest neighbors were attached, by sureties, and all the persons whose names are above-mentioned.

On Friday [January 21, 1278], the morrow of Sts. Fabian and Sebastian, in the sixth year of the reign of King Edward, son of King Henry, Gregory de Rokesle, chamberlain of London, and John Adrien and Walter le Engleys, sheriffs of the same city, were given to understand that one William le Pannere, skinner, was lying dead in the market of West Cheap, near the Conduit in the ward of Cheap. On hearing which, the said chamberlain and sheriffs went there; and calling together the good men of that ward, and of the ward of Henry de Frowyk, where he dwelt, diligent inquisition was made how this happened.

These men say that while the said William, on the Friday before-mentioned, was passing through the middle of West Cheap, and had reached the place where he was now lying dead, being greatly weakened through having been bled on Thursday, the feast before-mentioned, and having had too much blood taken from him through such excessive bleeding, he fell upon the pavement, and suddenly died. They hold no one suspected of the death of the said William, his death being thus sudden. And the body being viewed, there was no wound or hurt found thereon.

And Joanna, the wife of the dead man, was attached, by two sureties. The two neighbors were also attached, who dwelt next to him; also, the two neighbors who lived nearest to the Conduit, where he was found dead.

[In May, 1278,] the said chamberlain and sheriffs were given to understand that one Henry de Lanfare was lying dead in the house of Sibil le Feron, in the ward of Cheap, in the parish of Colcherche. Upon hearing which... and having called together the good men of that ward, and of the ward of John de Blakethorn, and the ward of Henry de Frowyk, diligent inquisition was made thereon.

These men say that one Richard de Codesfold having fled to the church of St. Mary Staining Lane in London, by reason of a certain robbery being imputed to him by one William of London, cutler, and the same William pursuing him on his flight thereto; it so happened that on the night [of May 5], in the present year, there being many persons watching about the church aforesaid, to take him, in case he should come out, a certain Henry de Lanfare, ironmonger, one of the persons on the watch, hearing a noise in the church, and thence fearing that the same Richard was about to get out by another part of the church, and so escape through a breach that there was in a certain glass window therein, went to examine it. The said Richard and one Thomas, the then clerk of that church, perceiving this, the said Thomas, seizing a lance, without an iron head, struck at Henry before-mentioned through the hole in the window, and wounded him between the nose and the eye, penetrating almost to the brain. From the effects of which wound he languished until the Day of St. Dunstan [May 19], when he died, at about the third hour. They say also that both the said Richard and Thomas before-mentioned are guilty of that felony, seeing that Richard was consenting thereto.

And the said Thomas was taken, and imprisoned in Newgate, and afterwards delivered before Hamon Haweteyn, justiciar of Newgate. And the said Richard still keeps himself within the church before-named. Being asked if they hold any more persons suspected as to that death, they say they do not. [The suspects] have no lands or chattels. And the body was viewed, upon which no other injury or wound was found, save only the wound aforesaid.

And the two neighbors nearest to the spot where he was wounded were attached; and the two neighbors nearest to the place where he died; and the said Sibil was attached, in whose house he died.

On Thursday [August 11, 1278], the morrow of St. Laurence the martyr, in the sixth year of the reign of King Edward, the chamberlain of our lord the king in the same city, and the sheriffs, were given to understand that a certain man, William Cole by name, a citizen of London, was lying dead, by another death than his rightful death, in the ward of William de Hadestoke, and the parish of St. Dunstan, near the Tower of London. On hearing which, the said chamberlain and sheriffs went there, and calling together the good men of the ward and of the two nearest wards, those, namely, of Wolmar de Essex and Nicholas de Winton, diligent inquisition was made how this had happened.

These men say that on [July 27,] the Wednesday next after the feast of St. James the Apostle, the said William was in the fields of the village of Stratford [near London], getting in his corn; and that one John, parish-clerk of the same village, as to whose surname they are ignorant, came into the same fields on that day, and secrely took and carried off certain sheaves belonging to the said William, and certain neighbors of his. Whereupon it so happened that the said William met this same John, and rebuked him for so carrying off the sheaves, and took them away from him; upon which, the said John went to one Richard, chaplain to the prioress of Stratford, but as to whose surname they are ignorant, and also to one John de Scheld, and made grievous complaint to them that the said William had taken away from him the sheaves before-mentioned; upon which, being greatly moved thereat, they went to the fields aforesaid, and finding the said William there, suddenly rushed upon him and threw him on the ground, beating him with sticks both behind and before, all over the body, from his neck down to the soles of his feet; and then left him in the said fields for dead. Afterwards, he was carried to the village of Stratford aforesaid, where he lay languishing from the effects of the blows before-mentioned, down to [August 6,] the Saturday next before the feast of St. Laurence; upon which day he was carried in a cart to London, and still lived on from that day to Thursday [August 11,] the morrow of St. Laurence; early in the morning of which he died, from the blows before-mentioned. And the body was viewed, which was black and blue all over, and quite crushed by excessive and most grievous blows, from the neck down to the soles of the feet, as before-mentioned. Being asked what became of them, after committing the felony aforesaid, they say that they fled forthwith to the parish church of the same village, and afterwards secretly escaped therefrom, and have never since been found. Being asked if they hold anyone else suspected of his death, they say they do not, but only the before-named Richard the chaplain, and John de Scheld; who on hearing the complaint of John the clerk before-mentioned, went off in haste to the fields to avenge him. But whether the same John was present when the said William was so slain, or whether he gave any blow, they cannot ascertain. Being asked about the goods and chattels of those felons, they say that they know nothing thereof, because they are foreigners [that is, not Londoners].

And the four nearest neighbors were attached, by sureties.

Question: What procedures are followed in these cases? What are the standards of evidence? How do these compare to modern courtroom standards? In what situation did a person who committed homicide find himself or herself? What do these records tell us about everyday life in thirteenth-century London? What role did drink and drunkenness play in everyday life and death there?

46. HUNDRED ROLLS

In 1279 the royal government launched a census of land tenures in a large number of English counties, organized by hundreds (subdivisions of shires). The resulting records, known as the Hundred Rolls, are like the Domesday Book in giving us a remarkably detailed picture of the conditions on individual manors, including the terms on which named individual peasants farmed their land. Here are the results from the manor of Alwalton in Huntingdonshire.

Source: trans. E.P. Cheyney, *Translations and Reprints from the Original Sources of European History*, series 1, vol. 3 (Philadelphia: University of Pennsylvania Department of History, n.d.) no. 5, pp. 4-7.

The abbot of Peterborough holds the manor of Alwalton and vill from the lord king directly; which manor and vill with its appurtenances the lord Edward, formerly king of England, gave to the said abbot and convent of that place in free, pure, and perpetual alms. And the court of the said manor with its garden contains one-half an acre. And to the whole of the said vill of Alwalton belong 5 hides and a half and 1 virgate of land and a half; of which each hide contains 5 virgates of land and each virgate contains 25 acres. Of these hides the said abbot has in demesne 1 hide and a half of land and half a virgate, which contain as above. Likewise he has there 8 acres of meadow. Also he has there separable pasture which contains 1 acre. Likewise he has there 3 water mills. Likewise he has there a common fish pond with a fish-weir on the bank of the Nene, which begins at Wildlake and extends to the mill of Newton and contains in length 2 leagues. Likewise he has there a ferry with a boat.

Free Tenants. Thomas le Boteler holds a messuage with a court yard which contains 1 rood [that is, a quarter acre], and 3 acres of land, by charter, paying thence yearly to the said abbot 14s.

Likewise the rector of the church of Alwalton holds 1 virgate of land with its appurtenances, with which the said church was anciently endowed. Likewise the said rector has a holding the tenant of which holds 1 rood of ground by paying to the said rector yearly 1d.

And the abbot of Peterborough is patron of the church.

Villeins. Hugh Miller holds 1 virgate of land in villeinage by paying thence to the said abbot 3s. 1d. Likewise the same Hugh works through the whole year except 1 week at Christmas, 1 week at Easter, and 1 at Whitsuntide [that is, Pentecost, forty days after Easter], that is in each week 3 days, each day with 1 man, and in autumn each day with 2 men, performing the said works at the will of the said abbot as in plowing and other work. Likewise he gives 1 bushel of wheat for benseed and 18 sheaves of oats for foddercorn. Likewise he gives 3 hens and 1 cock yearly and 5 eggs at Easter. Likewise he does carrying to

Peterborough and to Jakele and nowhere else, at the will of the said abbot. Likewise if he sells a brood mare in his court yard for 10s. or more, he shall give to the said abbot 4d., and if for less he shall give nothing to the aforesaid. He gives also merchet [that is, a payment upon his daughter's marriage] and heriot [that is, a death tax], and is tallaged at the feast of St. Michael [September 29], at the will of the said abbot. There are also there 27 other villeins, viz. John of Ganesoupe, Robert son of Walter, Ralph son of the reeve, Emma at Pertre, William son of Reginald, Thomas son of Gunnilda, Eda widow of Ralph, Ralph Reeve, William Reeve, William son of William Reeve, Thomas Flegg, Henry Abbot, William Hereward, Serle son of William Reeve, Walter Palmer, William Abbot, Henry Serle; each of whom holds 1 virgate of land in villeinage, paying and doing in all things, each for himself, to the said abbot yearly just as the said Hugh Miller. There are also 5 other villeins, viz. Simon Mariot, Robert of Hastone, Thomas Smith, John Mustard, and William Carter, each of whom holds half a virgate of land by paying and doing in all things half of the whole service which Hugh Miller pays and does.

Cotters. Henry, son of the miller, holds a cottage with a croft which contains 1 rood, paying thence yearly to the said abbot 2s. Likewise he works for 3 days in carrying hay and in other works at the will of the said abbot, each day with 1 man, and in autumn 1 day in cutting grain with 1 man.

Likewise Ralph Miller holds a cottage with a croft which contains a rood, paying to the said abbot 2s.; and he works just as the said Henry.

Likewise William Arnold holds a cottage with a croft which contains half a rood, paying to the abbot 2d.; and he works just as the said Henry.

Likewise Hugh Day holds a cottage with a croft which contains 1 rood, paying to the abbot 8d.; and he works just as the said Henry.

Likewise Sara, widow of Matthew Miller, holds a cottage and a croft which contains half a rood, paying to the said abbot 4d.; and she works just as the said Henry.

Likewise Sara, widow of William Miller, holds a cottage and a croft which contains half a rood, paying to the abbot 4d.; and she works just as the said Henry.

Likewise William Kendale holds a cottage and a croft which contains 1 rood, paying to the abbot 8d.; and he works just as the said Henry.... [Here ten other cottars are named, their holdings, varying from a half rood to an acre, specified, and their payments and services indicated.]

Likewise William Drake holds a cottage with a croft which contains half a rood, paying to the abbot 6d.; and he works just as the said Henry.

There are there also 6 other cotters, viz. William Drake Jr., Amycia the widow, Alice the widow, Robert son of Eda, William Pepper, William Coleman, each of whom holds a cottage with a croft which contains half a rood, paying and doing in all things, each for himself, just as the said William Drake.

Likewise William Russel holds a cottage with a croft which contains half a rood, paying to the abbot 8d.; and he works in all things just as the said Henry Miller.

There are moreover there 5 other cotters, viz. Walter Pestel, Ralph Shepherd, Henry Abbot, Matilda Tut, Jordan Mustard, each of whom holds a cottage with a croft which contains half a rood, paying thence and doing in all things to the said abbot just as the said William Russel.

Likewise Beatrice of Hampton holds a cottage and a croft which contains 1 rood, paying to the abbot 12d.; and she works in all things just as the said Henry.

Likewise Hugh Miller holds 3 acres of land, paying to the abbot 42d.

Likewise Thomas, son of Richard, holds a cottage with a croft which contains half a rood, and 3 acres of land, paying to the abbot 4s.; and he works just as the said Henry.

Likewise Ralph Reeve holds a cottage with a croft which contains 1 rood, and 1 acre of land, paying to the abbot 2s.; and he works just as the said Henry.

Likewise each of the said cottagers, except the widows, gives yearly after Christmas a penny which is called head-penny.

Questions: What is the population of the manor? What obligations do the peasants have to their lord? What goods does the manor produce? How does the position of individual peasants vary? What do we learn about women from this document?

47. MERTON COLLEGE STATUTES

Scholars had gathered in the city of Oxford by the mid-twelfth century; in the early thirteenth century such academic communities in a number of European cities organized themselves into the new universities, which would continue to grow in the centuries to come. Oxford's university was made up of small colleges and halls of scholars, such as Merton College, founded in 1274 by the document which is excerpted below.

Source: trans. A.F. Leach, *Educational Charters and Documents, 598 to 1909* (Cambridge: Cambridge University Press, 1911), pp. 181-187; revised.

1. Of the grant of the manors of Maldon and Farleigh.

In the name of the most glorious and undivided Trinity, Father, and Son, and Holy Ghost. Amen.

I, Walter of Merton, clerk, formerly chancellor of the illustrious lord the king of England, trusting in the goodness of the Great Maker of property and possessions, confidently relying on the grace of him who disposes the desires of men to good and directs them at his will, and after anxiously turning over in my mind what I can contribute to the honor of his name in return for those things which he has abundantly contributed to me in my life, before the disturbances that lately arose in England founded and established a house, which I wished and directed should be entitled or called "of the Scholars of Merton," in my own property acquired by my own labors at Maldon in the county of Surrey, for the perpetual maintenance of scholars studying in the schools, for the health of my soul…, [and] now when the peace of England has been reestablished and the former disturbances have been quieted, with stable mind I approve, establish and confirm, and grant and assign to them the place of their habitation and house at Oxford, where a university of students flourishes, on my own land adjoining St. John's church; which I will shall be called "the House of the Scholars of Merton" and in it I decree the scholars shall dwell forever. And to this house, or to the scholars for ever dwelling in the same, by the grant of the Highest, I have transferred my manors of Maldon and Farleigh with their appurtenances, which I gave in the time of disturbance, for the perpetual maintenance of the same scholars and the ministers of the altar who shall reside therein, and now, when the peace of the realm has been restored, grant and approve and with deliberate judgment ratify and confirm the same transfer of my own free will. And I decree that these manors with other property acquired or to be acquired by me for them shall always remain with the same scholars and brethren in the form and on the conditions underwritten to be continually observed in time to come, the Lord willing, as regards the persons as well as their rule of life.

2. Of the lawyers and scholars living in the house.

This form then I constitute and decree to be for ever observed, that in this house, called the House of the Scholars of Merton, there shall be forever scholars devoted to learning, and bound to devote their time to the study of arts, philosophy, canon law or theology. And the greater part of them shall devote themselves to the study of the liberal arts and philosophy, until at the will of the warden and fellows, as being persons who have been laudably proficient in them, they transfer themselves to the study of theology. But four or five of them shall be allowed by the provision of their superior, he declaring that they are able and apt for this, to study canon law. And the same superior may dispense them for a time to hear lectures in civil law if it shall appear expedient. There shall be also in the assembly a grammarian who shall devote his whole time to a grammar school, and books and other necessaries shall be provided for him from the possessions of the house; and he shall have the care of those who are applying themselves to the study of grammar; and even the seniors, if they have any doubts in their own faculties, shall have resort to him without blushing; and under his mastership the scholars themselves, if and when it shall seem to be for the benefit of their own readiness, shall speak Latin or the vulgar idiom [French], and he shall be bound to instruct each of them faithfully to the utmost of his capacity....

7. Of the deans' duties, etc.

Some of the more discreet of the aforesaid scholars shall be elected to take charge, under the warden and as his assistants, of the less advanced as to their progress in learning and conduct. So that over every twenty, or ten, if necessary, there shall be a president, and more ample provision as appears proper shall be made for them while they diligently fulfil their charge of the rest. Also in each chamber in which the aforesaid scholars live there shall be one more mature than the rest, who shall superintend his fellows, and shall report to the warden of the house himself and the rest of the prepositors having charge and to the assembly of scholars itself, if necessary, on their progress in morals and studies.

8. Of the scholars' table.

Moreover, the scholars studying in the house shall have a common table under the warden and other prepositors, the twenty-men and deans, and also as far as possible a uniform dress.

40. Of the education of the boys, etc.

But whereas I have exchanged the succession to which my heirs and kindred were entitled in my freehold property by the custom of the realm for this charity, under the eye of God, as is aforesaid, I will and decree that if any little ones of the kindred aforesaid becoming orphans or otherwise through their parents' poverty lack support while they are receiving primary instruction in the rudiments, then the warden shall have them educated up to thirteen in number in the house aforesaid, until they can become proficient in the university, if they shall be found to be of ability for it; and from them, those who are found able and fit shall be taken to fill the places of the scholars, as above set out.

And lest there should break out in the said house or society, the plague which through the temptations of the flesh so often vexes the incautious, all service in the said house, at least in the court of the house of the scholars and of the manor of Maldon and elsewhere, as far as may be, shall always be done by males....

Questions: What are Walter's reasons for founding the college? Who will the students and teachers be? What do we learn of the curriculum? How will the college be organized? In the last paragraph, is he referring to a literal plague?

48. THE SPHERE OF SACROBOSCO

Astronomy, one of the seven liberal arts taught in medieval European universities, was widely taught from this early thirteenth-century textbook by the English scholar John Holywood, or Sacrobosco in Latin.

Source: trans. L. Thorndike, *The Sphere of Sacrobosco and Its Commentators* (Chicago: University of Chicago Press, 1949), pp. 118-122, 141-142.

Proemium. Contents of the Four Chapters

The treatise on the sphere we divide into four chapters, telling, first, what a sphere is, what its center is, what the axis of a sphere is, what the pole of the world is, how many spheres there are, and what the shape of the world is. In the second we give information concerning the circles of which this material sphere is composed and that supercelestial one, of which this is the image, is understood to be composed. In the third we talk about the rising and setting of the signs, and the diversity of days and nights which happens to those inhabiting diverse localities, and the division into climes. In the fourth the matter concerns the circles and motions of the planets, and the causes of eclipses.

1. Sphere Defined.

A sphere is thus described by Euclid. A sphere is the transit of the circumference of a half-circle upon a fixed diameter until it revolves back to its original position. That is, a sphere is such a round and solid body as is described by the revolution of a semicircular arc.

By Theodosius a sphere is described thus: A sphere is a solid body contained within a single surface, in the middle of which there is a point from which all straight lines drawn to the circumference are equal, and that point is called the "center of the sphere." Moreover, a straight line passing through the center of the sphere, with its ends touching the circumference in opposite directions, is called the "axis of the sphere." And the two ends of the axis are called the "poles of the world."

Sphere Divided.

The sphere is divided in two ways, by substance and by accident. By substance it is divided into the ninth sphere, which is called the "first moved" or the *primum mobile*; and the sphere of the fixed stars, which is named the "firmament"; and the seven spheres of the seven planets, of which some are larger, some smaller, according as they the more approach, or recede from, the firmament. Wherefore, among them the sphere of Saturn is the largest, the sphere of the moon the smallest, as is shown in the accompanying figure.

By accident the sphere is divided into the sphere right and the sphere oblique. For those are said to have the sphere right who dwell at the equator, if anyone can live there. And it is called "right" because neither pole is elevated more for them than the other, or because their horizon intersects the equinoctial circle and is intersected by it at spherical right angles. Those are said to have the sphere oblique who live this side of the equator or beyond it. For to them one pole is always raised above the horizon, and the other is always depressed below it. Or it is because their artificial horizon intersects the equinoctial at oblique and unequal angles.

The Four Elements.

The machine of the universe is divided into two, the ethereal and the elementary region. The elementary region, existing subject to continual alteration, is divided into four. For there is earth, placed, as it were, as the center in the middle of all, about which is water, about water air, about air fire, which is pure and not turbid there and reaches to the sphere of the moon, as Aristotle says in his book of *Meteorology*. For so God, the glorious and sublime, disposed. And these are called the "four elements" which are in turn by themselves altered, corrupted and regenerated. The elements are also simple bodies which cannot be subdivided into parts of diverse forms and from whose commixture are produced various species of generated things. Three of them, in turn, surround the earth on all sides spherically, except in so far as the dry land stays the sea's tide to protect the life of animate beings. All, too, are mobile except earth, which, as the center of the world, by its weight in every direction equally avoiding the great motion of the extremes, as a round body occupies the middle of the sphere.

The Heavens.

Around the elementary region revolves with continuous circular motion the ethereal, which is lucid and immune from all variation in its immutable essence. And it is called "Fifth Essence" by the philosophers. Of which there are nine spheres, as we have just said: namely, of the moon, Mercury, Venus, the sun, Mars, Jupiter, Saturn, the fixed stars, and the last heaven. Each of these spheres incloses its inferior spherically.

Their Movements.

And of these there are two movements. One is of the last heaven on the two extremities of its axis, the Arctic and Antarctic poles, from east through west to east again, which the equinoctial circle divides through the middle. Then there is another movement, oblique to this and in the opposite direction, of the inferior spheres on their axes, distant from the former by 23 degrees. But the first movement carries all the others with it in its rush about the earth once within a day and night, although they strive against it, as in the case of the eighth sphere one degree in a hundred years. This second movement is divided through the middle by the zodiac, under which each of the seven planets has its own sphere, in which it is borne by its own motion, contrary to the movement of the sky, and completes it in varying spaces of time — in the case of Saturn in thirty years, Jupiter in twelve years, Mars in two, the sun in three hundred and sixty-five days and six hours, Venus and Mercury about the same, the moon in twenty-seven days and eight hours.

Revolution of the Heavens from East to West.

That the sky revolves from east to west is signified by the fact that the stars, which rise in the east, mount gradually and successively until they reach mid-sky and are always at the same distance apart, and, thus maintaining their relative positions, they move toward their setting continuously and uniformly. Another indication is that the stars near the North Pole, which never set for us, move continuously and uniformly, describing their circles about the pole, and are always equally near or far from one another. Wherefore, from those two continuous movements of the stars, both those that set and those which do not, it is clear that the firmament is moved from east to west.

The Heavens Spherical.

There are three reasons why the sky is round: likeness, convenience, and necessity. Likeness, because the sensible world is made in the likeness of the archetype, in which there is neither end nor beginning; wherefore, in likeness to it the sensible world has a round shape, in which beginning or end cannot be distinguished. Convenience, because of all isoperimetric bodies the sphere is the largest and of all shapes the round is most capacious. Since largest and round, therefore the most capacious. Wherefore, since the world is all-containing, this shape was useful and convenient for it. Necessity, because if the world were of other form than round — say, trilateral, quadrilateral, or many-sided — it would follow that some space would be vacant and some body without a place, both of which are false, as is clear in the case of angles projecting and revolved.

A Further Proof.

Also, as Alfraganus says, if the sky were flat, one part of it would be nearer to us than another, namely, that which is directly overhead. So when a star was there, it would be closer to us than when rising or setting. But those things which are closer to us seem larger. So the sun when in mid-sky should look larger than when rising or setting, whereas the opposite is the case; for the sun or another star looks bigger in the east or west than in mid-sky. But, since this is not really so, the reason for its seeming so is that in winter and the rainy season vapors rise between us and the sun or other star. And, since those vapors are diaphanous, they scatter our visual rays so that they do not apprehend the object in its true size, just as is the case with a penny dropped into a depth of limpid water, which appears larger than it actually is because of a like diffusion of rays.

The Earth a Sphere.

That the earth, too, is round is shown thus. The signs and stars do not rise and set the same for all men everywhere but rise and set sooner for those in the east than for those in the west; and of this there is no other cause than the bulge of the earth. Moreover, celestial phenomena evidence that they rise sooner for orientals than for westerners. For one and the same eclipse of the moon which appears to us in the first hour of the night appears to orientals about the third hour of the night, which proves that they had night and sunset before we did, of which setting the bulge of the earth is the cause.

Further Proofs of This.

That the earth also has a bulge from north to south and vice versa is shown thus: To those living toward the north, certain stars are always visible, namely, those near the North Pole, while others which are near the South Pole are always concealed from them. If, then, anyone should proceed from the north southward, he might go so far that the stars which formerly were always visible to him now would tend toward their setting. And the farther south he went, the more they would be moved toward their setting. Again, that same man now could see stars which formerly had always been hidden from him. And the reverse would happen to anyone going from the south northward. The cause of this is simply the bulge of the earth. Again, if the earth were flat from east to west, the stars would rise as soon for westerners as for orientals, which is false. Also, if the earth were flat from north to south and vice versa, the stars which were always visible to anyone would continue to be so wherever he went, which is false. But it seems flat to human sight because it is so extensive.

Surface of the Sea Spherical.

That the water has a bulge and is approximately round is shown thus: Let a signal be set up on the seacoast and a ship leave port and sail away so far that the eye of a person standing at the foot of the mast can no longer discern the signal. Yet if the ship is stopped, the eye of the same person, if he has climbed to the top of the mast, will see the signal clearly. Yet the eye of a person at the bottom of the mast ought to see the signal better than he who is at the top, as is shown by drawing straight lines from both to the signal. And there is no other explanation of this thing than the bulge of the water. For all other impediments are excluded, such as clouds and rising vapors.

Also, since water is a homogeneous body, the whole will act the same as its parts. But parts of water, as happens in the case of little drops and dew on herbs, naturally seek a round shape. Therefore, the whole, of which they are parts, will do so.

The Earth Central.

That the earth is in the middle of the firmament is shown thus. To persons on the earth's surface the stars appear of the same size whether they are in mid-sky or just rising or about to set, and this is because the earth is equally distant from them. For if the earth were nearer to the firmament in one direction than in another, a person at that point of the earth's surface which was nearer to the firmament would not see half of the heavens. But this is contrary to Ptolemy and all the philosophers, who say that, wherever man lives, six signs rise and six signs set, and half of the heavens is always visible and half hid from him....

The Earth Immobile.

That the earth is held immobile in the midst of all, although it is the heaviest, seems explicable thus. Every heavy thing tends toward the center. Now the center is a point in the middle of the firmament. Therefore, the earth, since it is heaviest, naturally tends toward that point. Also, whatever is moved from the middle toward the circumference ascends. Therefore, if the earth were moved from the middle toward the circumference, it would be ascending, which is impossible....

4. ...Of the Other Planets: Equant, Deferent, and Epicycle.

Every planet except the sun has three circles, namely, equant, deferent, and epicycle. The equant of the moon is a circle concentric with the earth and in the plane of the ecliptic. Its deferent is an eccentric circle not in the plane of the ecliptic — nay, one half of it slants toward the north and the other toward the south — and the deferent intersects the equant in two places, and the figure of that intersection is called the "dragon" because it is wide in the middle and narrow toward the ends. That intersection, then, through which the moon is moved from south to north is called the "head of the dragon," while the other intersection through which it is moved from north to south is called the "tail of the dragon." ...

Cause of Lunar Eclipse.

Since the sun is larger than the earth, it is necessary that half the sphere of earth be always illuminated by the sun and that the shadow of the earth, extended into the air like a cone, diminish in circumference until it ends in the plane of the circle of the signs inseparable from the nadir of the sun. The nadir is a point in the firmament directly opposite to the sun. Hence, when the moon at full is in the head or tail of the dragon beneath the nadir of the sun, then the earth is interposed between sun and moon, and the cone of the earth's shadow falls on the body of the moon. Wherefore, since the moon has no light except from the sun, it actually is deprived of light and there is a general eclipse, if it is in the head or tail of the dragon directly but partial if it is almost within the bounds determined for eclipse. And it always happens at full moon or thereabouts. But, since in every opposition — that is, at full moon — the moon is not in the head or tail of the dragon or beneath the nadir of the sun, it is not necessary that the moon suffer eclipse at every full moon.

Cause of Solar Eclipse.

When the moon is in the head or tail of the dragon or nearly within the limits and in conjunction with the sun, then the body of the moon is interposed between our sight and the body of the sun. Hence it will obscure the brightness of the sun for us, and so the sun will suffer eclipse — not that it ceases to shine but that it fails us because of the interposition of the moon between our sight and the sun. From these it is clear that a solar eclipse should always occur at the time of conjunction or new moon. And it is to be noted that when there is an eclipse of the moon, it is visible everywhere on earth. But when there is an eclipse of the sun, that is by no means so. Nay, it may be visible in one clime and not in another, which happens because of the different point of view in different climes. Whence Virgil most aptly and concisely expresses the nature of either eclipse:

Varied defects of the moon, and of the sun travails.

Eclipse during the Passion Miraculous.

From the aforesaid it is also evident that, when the sun was eclipsed during the Passion and the same Passion occurred at full moon, that eclipse was not natural — nay, it was miraculous and contrary to nature, since a solar eclipse ought to occur at new moon or thereabouts. On which account Dionysius the Areopagite is reported to have said during the same Passion, "Either the God of nature suffers, or the mechanism of the universe is dissolved."

Questions: How does this picture of the universe differ from the modern one? What aspects of the universe interest the author? What sources and proofs does he use? How does he reason?

49. ROGER BACON'S THIRD OPUS

As a Franciscan friar at a time of official concern about unorthodox teachings and writings within the order, the great English scholar Roger Bacon was bound by a general ban on Franciscans disseminating their work. But in 1266 the pope, impressed by Bacon's reputation, wrote to him requesting a summary of his work. In response, Bacon produced three books in less than two years. The excerpts below describe his reaction to the papal order and various aspects of his academic career.

Source: trans. G.G. Coulton, *Social Life in Britain from the Conquest to the Reformation* (Cambridge: Cambridge University Press, 1918), pp. 130-136; revised.

To the most holy father and lord Pope Clement, supreme pontiff by the grace of God, your servant writes as follows, kissing in spirit the blessed feet of your holiness....

I recall how for ten years I have now been an exile from that fame which I formerly won in the schools; and I recognize mine own littleness, my manifold ignorance, my stammering speech and scratching pen. With all this I wonder at your wisdom, which now deigns to demand works of philosophy from me who am now unheard of all men, even as a man already buried and eaten up by oblivion.... The head of the church has made request of the unworthy sole of the church's foot; the vicar of Christ and governor of the whole world deigns to solicit me, who am scarcely to be reckoned among the atoms of the universe!... My gratitude is not small; nay, it behooves me to be the most grateful of all men, since your holiness has requested of me that very thing which I have yearned for with burning desire, which I have toiled for with bitter sweat, which I have pushed forward at great expense of money. Nevertheless the foundations are not yet laid — the very stones and timber — until I shall have diligently investigated the mastery of sciences and languages, and other things requisite for building the edifice of wisdom. For the marvels of arts and sciences are subject to so many difficulties (and especially in these times of ours, when we are waiting for the days of Antichrist and his followers, on whose behalf the Devil is full of fury, that he may in diverse manners confound the study of wisdom, as I shall make plain in later pages of my book) that remedy will never be applied unless through the prudence of the pope. But, where so great an authority as his stands over us, there can be no difficulty; for his power penetrates the heavens, looses the bonds of purgatory, treads hell under foot, and holds the whole world in subjection....

But this delay was necessary, and against my own will, who grieved then and grieve still thereat. For, when you last wrote, the things which you believed me to have written had not yet been composed. In truth, before I became a friar, I composed no philosophical book; nor, since I came into this order, have I ever been asked to do so by those who are set in authority over me. Nay, a grievous constitution has even been made to the contrary, under pain of loss of our book and of several days' fasting on bread and water, if any writing done in a friary be communicated to others. But I could not get it copied in a fair hand save by scribes who are not friars; and such scribes would then make copies for themselves or for other folk, whether I would or not, even as things are so frequently published at Paris through the copyists' frauds. Certainly, if I had been able to communicate my writings freely, I would have composed many books for my brother who is a student, and for others of my friends. But when I saw no hope of publication I neglected to write. Wherefore, when I offered myself to your highness as ready, you must know that this meant for future writing of books not yet written; therefore Raymond de Laon, your clerk, was altogether deceived when he recommended me to you. For although I had sometimes hurriedly written a few chapters on diverse matters, at the instance of my friends, here is no notable writing worthy to be offered to your wisdom; for they are things of which even I take no account, wherein is nothing continuous or complete. Nevertheless the greatness and authority of your reverence kept me long idle, since I knew not at first what I could offer worthy of your attention. Then, considering that nothing should be presented to your highness but such as was magnificent, to your blessedness nothing but what was excellent, to your wisdom nothing save of the fairest, it is no wonder that I delayed in setting to work.... For the treatise on optics alone, which I here send you, could not be written by any other in less than a year..., nay, nor in ten. For, howsoever well he knew the matter, he would need to make many experiments of these things, and to practise an almost infinite number of described figures, which demand much time, and to write it all out five or six times until he had one tried and trustworthy book. I say nothing here of other and greater subjects, until a more convenient time.

To this add other and far more grievous causes of delay, which oftentimes drove me almost to despair. Truly, an hundred times I thought of breaking off my work; and, had it not been for the reverence due to the vicar of Christ, and the profit of mankind which could be procured through him alone, I would not have gone through with these impediments in this business — nay, not for all the churchmen in the world, howsoever they might have besought me and insisted.

The first impediment came through those who are set over me. Since you wrote nothing to them in my excuse, and since I could not nor should not reveal unto them your secret, they lay hard upon me, with unspeakable violence, that I, like the rest, should obey their will; which I could not do, bound as I was by your command to proceed with your work, notwithstanding any contrary command of my prelates. Know therefore that, not being excused by you, I was involved in more and more grievous hindrances than I can tell; yet perchance I may explain in another place certain particulars of these hindrances, writing with mine own hand for the weightiness of the secret which I have to tell.

Another kind of hindrance, which alone was enough to ruin the whole project, was my lack of money. For I had to spend more than sixty pounds in Parisian money in this matter; whereof I will give full and sufficient account in its own place. I marvel not that you had no thought of these expenses, seeing that you, sitting aloft over the whole world, must needs think of so many weighty affairs that no man can measure the cogitations of your heart. But the mediators who bore the letters were careless, in that they said naught of the expenses; and they themselves would not lay out a single penny, albeit I said to them that I would keep an exact account, and that each should have his own restored unto him. I myself, as you know, neither have money nor can have money; nor, by consequence, can I borrow, since I have no means of repaying. I sent therefore to my rich brother in our own country; but he, having taken the king's part [in the barons' wars], was driven from his home together with my mother and brethren and the whole family; nay, he was oftentimes taken by the enemy and put to ransom. Wherefore he was too impoverished and ruined to succor me, nor have I had any answer from him even unto this present day.

Considering therefore your Reverence's command, I solicited many great folk — some of whom you know well by face, but not their inward mind — saying that I had to transact a certain business for you in France (which business I unfolded not) which could not be performed without great expense. But no tongue can tell how many of these men called me shameless, how many repelled me, how many lured me with false hopes, and what confusion I suffered in mine own person. Nay, not even my friends would believe me, seeing that I was unable to unfold this business to them; wherefore this way was debarred unto me. At last, therefore, in greater anguish than I can express, I compelled succor, as it were, from poor men who were my familiar friends, constraining them to spend all their substance, and to sell much and set the rest to pledge, even oftentimes at usury; and I promised them that I would render you a full and faithful account of the expense, and pledged my faith to procure full payment on your part. Yet these folk were so poor that I oftentimes broke off this work, and despaired, and ceased to labor further; wherefore, had I not known that you had forgotten to take these expenses into account, for all the world I would never have proceeded; rather would I have given mine own body to prison. For all these causes therefore has this delay come to pass, for which I am vehemently grieved; for not only is your Clemency now sick with hope deferred, but I also have sustained grievous loss, as you may well think from what I have already said, and as shall be more certainly and clearly set forth below....

My fourth reason [for thus insisting] is on my own account; for I have labored in many ways at science from my youth up, and at languages, and at all the aforesaid branches of learning; whereby I have collected much profitable learning and have also ordered other folk in that way. For I have sought the friendship of all wise men in this western world, and have caused young men to be instructed in tongues and figures and numbers and tables and instruments and many necessary things. And I have examined all things that are requisite hereunto, and know now how we must proceed, and by what means, and in the face of what hindrances; but how to proceed I know not, for lack of the aforesaid monies.

Yet, if any man would expend as much as I myself have already expended in my life, certainly a great part of the work might be completed. For during those twenty years wherein I labored especially in the study of wisdom, neglecting the opinions of the common sort, I expended more than £2000 sterling on these things — on secret books, and various experiments, and languages and instruments and tables and such like matters; and also in seeking the friendship of wise men and in teaching others who should help me in languages, in figures, in numbers, in tables, in instruments, and in many other things. Nor is it my intention to bestir your Clemency that the multitude or their leaders may be corrected by violence, nor that I should contend with them; but I only insist upon these things by reason of the aforesaid four causes. And, if it pleased your wisdom that [my writings] should be published, copies would be given first of all to such as are wise, and then little by little to all who wish, that no man may be coerced. And yet I know that all would wish for copies; but all are not worthy of all sciences....

Nevertheless, since your wisdom has so long been busied in church affairs and in various cares for the state, and since no man on the throne of the apostles can find much time for studies, and these things whereof I write are of great difficulty and foreign to the sense of many men — therefore I was more solicitous to find a fit mediator for presentation to your reverence, than for the words of my own writings.... Wherefore I set my thoughts on a certain poor youth whom, some five or six years ago, I caused to be instructed in languages and mathematics and optics, wherein is the whole difficulty of the things which I now send. Moreover, I taught him freely by word of mouth, after receiving your command, since I felt that I could find none other at present who knew my mind so well. Wherefore I thought to send him to you, as a ready mediator if your wisdom should deign to make use of him; and, if not, he could none the less bear my writings to your majesty.... He came to me in poverty, and a mere boy; I caused him to be nourished and taught for the love of God, especially since I had found no other youth so able both for study and for [practical] life. And he has profited so far that he might earn all that he needs in great abundance, and better than any other scholar of Paris, although his age be only twenty years or twenty-one at most....

Nor is it only for that cause that I send this messenger; but also that you may see how nothing is difficult to a man of diligence and confidence, though a negligent or craven-spirited scholar shuts himself from all that is good. For this youth came to me at the age of fifteen, and in poverty, having neither livelihood nor sufficient masters nor patron to take pity on his destitution; nor did he learn for as long as a single year, since he must needs work as servant to those who gave him the necessities of life; nor in his studies did he find for two whole years any man who would teach him a single word; notwithstanding all which impediment, he now knows many great matters by reason of his own confidence and diligence.... Wherefore I am fully persuaded that there is no difficulty of youth or of learning which may not be surmounted, if men have the will to learn, and confidence, and diligence. Nor is there any such difficulty in languages or sciences, but only in the teachers themselves, who will not or cannot teach. For, from our youth up, we find no profitable teachers; and therefore we languish our whole lives long, and know very little in the end. But, if we had capable teachers, I doubt not that we should learn more in one year than we now learn in twenty — all which I am ready to prove in practice; and I will stake my head on its success.

I have labored much in sciences and languages. For forty years have I now labored since first I learned the alphabet; and I was always studious; and for all but two years of those forty I have been always at the university; and I have spent much money, as others commonly spend much. Yet I am assured that within a quarter of a year, or half a year at most, I would teach with mine own mouth all that I know to a resolved and confident man; provided only that I had first written a compendious manual thereof. Yet it is well known that no man has labored in so many languages and sciences as I, nor has labored so hard therein; for, before I became a friar, men marveled that I could live through such excessive labor; yet afterwards I have been as studious as before; not indeed that I have labored so hard, for it was no longer necessary, by reason of my exercise in wisdom.

Questions: What obstacles has Bacon faced in his scholarly career? How has he overcome them? Of what is he particularly proud? What are his present worries?

CHAPTER FOUR

THE FOURTEENTH CENTURY

Fig. 27: Coins of Richard II During the early Middle Ages and through the twelfth century, the only coins minted in England were silver pennies. Larger denominations were first introduced in the thirteenth century and became standard in the fourteenth. The groat was worth four pence; half-groats and gold coins worth 6s. 8d. (that is, half a mark) were also used. These coins of Richard II, shown in nineteenth-century engravings, have the usual portrait of the current king on the front; the inscripton on the back identifies the town or city where the coin was minted. The smallest is a penny minted at York; the others are a half-groat and groat minted at London.

50. CORRESPONDENCE OF THE QUEEN WITH LONDON

The records of London include transcripts of many letters received, such as this one from Queen Isabel in 1312, announcing the birth of the future Edward III. The records also describe the celebrations that resulted.

Source: trans. H.T. Riley, *Memorials of London and London Life in the XIIIth, XIVth, and XVth Centuries* (London: Longmans, Green, and Co., 1868), pp. 105-7; revised.

"Isabel, by the grace of God, queen of England, lady of Ireland, and duchess of Aquitaine, to our well beloved, the mayor, and aldermen, and the commonalty of London, greeting. Forasmuch as we believe that you would willingly hear good tidings of us, we do make known unto you that our Lord, of his grace, has delivered us of a son on the 13th day of November, with safety to ourselves, and to the child. May our Lord preserve you. Given at Windsor, on the day above-named."

The bearer of this letter was John de Falaise, tailor to the queen; and he came on [November 14,] the Tuesday next after the feast of St. Martin, in the 6th year of the reign of King Edward [II], son of King Edward. But as the news had been brought by Robert Oliver on the Monday before, the mayor and the aldermen, and great part of the commonalty, assembled in the guildhall at time of Vespers, and danced, and showed great joy thereat; and so passed through the city with great glare of torches, and with trumpets and other minstrelsies.

And on the Tuesday next, early in the morning, cry was made throughout all the city to the effect that there was to be no work, labor, or business in shop, on that day; but that every one was to apparel himself in the most becoming manner that he could, and come to the guildhall at the hour of Prime [that is, about six in the morning]; ready to go with the mayor, together with the [other] good folks, to St. Paul's, there to make praise and offering, to the honor of God, who had shown them such favor on earth, and to show respect for this child that had been born. And after this, they were to return all together to the guildhall, to do whatever might be enjoined.

And the mayor and the aldermen assembled at the guildhall, together with the good folks of the commonalty; and from thence they went to St. Paul's, where the bishop, on the same day, chanted mass with great solemnity; and there they made their offering. And after mass, they led carols in the church of St. Paul, to the sound of trumpets, and then returned each to his house.

On the Wednesday following, the mayor, by assent of the aldermen, and of others of the commonalty, gave to the said John de Falaise, bearer of the letter aforesaid, ten pounds sterling and a cup of silver, four marks in weight. And on the morrow, this same John de Falaise sent back the present aforesaid, because it seemed to him too little.

On the Monday following, the mayor was richly costumed, and the alder-men arrayed in like suits of robes; and the drapers, mercers, and vintners were in costume; and they rode on horseback from thence to Westminster, and there made offering, and then returned to the guildhall, which was excellently well tapestried and dressed out, and there they dined. And after dinner, they went in carols thoughout the city all the rest of the day, and great part of the night. And on the same day, the Conduit in Cheap ran with nothing but wine, for all those who chose to drink there. And at the cross just by the church of St. Michael in West Cheap, there was a pavilion extended in the middle of the street, in which was set a tun of wine, for all passers-by to drink of, who might wish for any.

On [February 5, 1313,] the Sunday next after Candlemas ..., the fish-mongers of London were costumed very richly, and they caused a boat to be fitted out in the guise of a great ship, with all manner of tackle that belongs to a ship; and it sailed through Cheap as far as Westminster, where the fishmon-gers came, well mounted, and presented the same ship unto the queen. And on the same day, the queen took her route for Canterbury, on pilgrimage thither; whereupon, the fishmongers, all thus costumed, escorted her through the city.

Questions: What kinds of activities are part of the celebrations? In what other ways is the city's joy expressed? How are the people of London organized? Why is the celebra-tion so big? Was it spontaneous or orchestrated?

51. THE MANNER OF HOLDING PARLIAMENT

This treatise, which appeared in the first quarter of the fourteenth century, is an interest-ing but not entirely accurate description of how Parliament operated. Though well informed on the details of procedure, the anonymous author portrays Parliament as more standardized than it was in practice, and the first paragraph, on the origins of this thir-teenth-century institution, is entirely fictitious. In an age when custom often had the force of law, claiming antiquity for current (or favored) practices was an effective way of pro-moting them. This author reveals himself as a supporter of broad representation and the power of Parliament as opposed to that of the king.

Source: trans. T.D. Hardy, *Modus Tenendi Parliamentum; An Ancient Treatise on the Mode of Holding the Parliament in England* (London: Eyre & Spottiswood, 1846), pp. 2–46; revised.

Here is described the way the Parliament of the king of England and his Eng-lishmen used to be held in the time of King Edward [the Confessor], the son of King Etheldred; which method was recited by the more select men of the kingdom before William duke of Normandy, both conqueror and king of England, the Conqueror himself commanding it, and it was approved by him and used in his own times, and also in the times of his successors, kings of England.

The Summoning of the Parliament

The summoning of the Parliament ought to precede the first day of the Parliament by forty days.

Each and every archbishop, bishop, abbot, and prior ought to be summoned and come to the Parliament by reason of their tenure; and the other chief clergy who hold by county or barony by reason of such tenure; and none of inferior order, unless their presence and coming is required, otherwise than in respect of their tenures, because they are members of the king's council, or their presence is deemed necessary or useful to the Parliament, and to them the king is bound to furnish their costs and expenses in coming to and tarrying at the Parliament; nor ought such inferior clergy to be summoned to the Parliament, but the king used to issue his writs to such persons in this way, enjoining them to be present at his Parliament.

Also the king used to issue his summonses to the archbishops, bishops, and other exempt persons such as abbots, priors, deans, and other ecclesiastical persons who have jurisdictions by such exemptions and privileges, separately, that they, for each deanery and archdeaconry of England, should cause to be elected, by the deaneries and archdeaconries themselves, two experienced and fit procurators from their own archdeaconry to come and be present at the Parliament, to undertake, allege, and do the same which each and every person of those deaneries and archdeaconries would do if they were personally present there.

And that such procurators shall come with their duplicate warrants, sealed with the seals of their superiors, that they are the clergy sent to such procuratorship; one of which warrants shall be delivered to the clerks of the Parliament to be enrolled, and the other shall remain in possession of the procurators themselves, and thus under these two classes the whole clergy ought to be summoned to the Parliament.

Concerning the Laity

Also there ought to be summoned and come each and every earl and baron and their peers, that is, those who have lands and rents to the value of a county or entire barony, to wit, twenty knights' fees, each fee being computed at twenty pounds, which make four hundred pounds in the whole; or to the value of an entire barony, that is, thirteen knights' fees and the third part of one knight's fee, each fee being computed at twenty pounds, which make four hundred marks in the whole; and none of the inferior laymen ought to be summoned or come to the Parliament in respect of their tenure, unless their presence for other causes is useful or necessary to the Parliament, and then it shall be done concerning them as it has been said concerning the inferior clergy, who by virtue of their tenure are in no way bound to come to the Parliament.

Concerning the Port Barons

Also the king is bound to send his writs to the warden of the Cinque Ports, that he cause two fit and experienced barons to be elected from each port, by the port itself, to come and be present at his Parlianaent, to answer, undertake, allege, and do the same which their baronies would do, as if each and every person of those baronies were there personally present; and that such barons come with their duplicate warrants, sealed with the common seals of their ports, that they are duly elected and attorned for this purpose, and sent for those baronies, one of which warrants shall be delivered to the clerks of the Parliament, and the other shall remain in the possession of the barons themselves. And when such port barons, with permission, had departed from the Parliament, then they used to have a writ under the Great Seal directed to the warden of the Cinque Ports, that he should cause such barons to have from the commonalty of the port their reasonable costs and expenses from the first day they came to the Parliament till the day they were permitted to return home, express mention being also made in that writ of how long they had stayed at the Parliament, of the day on which they came there, and of that on which they had leave to return; and sometimes mention used to be made in the writ how much such barons ought to receive by the day from those commonalties, some, to wit, more, some less, according to the means, rank, and respect of the persons, nor was it customary for more than twenty shillings a day to be expended on those two barons, regard being had to their stay, labors, and expenses; nor are such expenses certainly to be allowed by the court to any persons so elected and sent for the commonalties, unless those persons had conducted themselves well and honorably in the Parliament.

Concerning the Knights of the Shires

Also the king used to send his writs to all the sheriffs of England, that each of them for his own county should cause two fit, honorable, and experienced knights to be elected, by the county itself, to come to his Parliament just as it has been said of the Port Barons, and of their warrants it is the same, but for the expenses of the two knights the payment from one county used to be not more than one mark a day.

Concerning the Citizens

In the same manner it used to be commanded to the mayor and sheriffs of London, and the mayor and bailiffs or the mayor and citizens of York and other cities, that they for the commonalty of their city should elect two fit, honorable, and experienced citizens to come and be present at the Parliament in the same manner as it has been said concerning the barons of the Cinque Ports and the knights of shires; and the citizens used to be on a par and equality with the knights of the shires in the expenses of coming, tarrying, and returning.

Concerning the Burgesses

In the same manner also it used and ought to be commanded to the bailiffs and good men of boroughs that they should elect two fit, honorable, and experienced burgesses from among themselves and for themselves to come and be present at the Parliament in the same manner as it has been said of citizens, but the two burgesses used not to receive for their expenses more than ten shillings for one day, and sometimes not more than half a mark, and this used to be taxed by the court according to the greatness and power of the borough and according to the credit of the persons sent.

Concerning the Principal Clerks of the Parliament

Also the two principal clerks of the Parliament, who shall enroll all the pleas and transactions of the Parliament, shall sit in the midst of the justices.

And be it known that those two clerks are not subject to any of the justices, nor is any justice of England done in the parliament, nor do the justices have the privilege of making records in the Parliament, except so far as a new power is assigned or given to them in the Parliament by the king and peers of Parliament, as when they are assigned with others to hear the suitors of the Parliament and determine diverse petitions and complaints laid before the Parliament. And these two clerks are answerable directly to the king and his parliament in common, unless perchance one or two justices are assigned to examine and amend their rolls, and when peers of the Parliament are assigned specially by themselves to hear and examine any petitions. Then when those peers shall be unanimous and agreed in rendering their judgments on such petitions, they shall explain the proceeding had therein, and shall render their judgments in full Parliament, so that those two clerks may enroll principally all pleas and all judgments in the principal roll of Parliament, and deliver those rolls to the king's treasurer before the Parliament is permitted to break up, so that those rolls are definitely in the treasury before the recess of Parliament; but the same clerks may have the transcript or counter-roll thereof if they wish. These two clerks, unless they are in some other office under the king and take fees from him on which they can live respectably, shall receive from the king one mark a day for their expenses by equal portions, unless they eat at the lord king's table; then they shall take, beside their board, half a mark per day by equal portions, during the whole Parliament.

Concerning the Five Clerks

Also the king shall assign five skillful and approved clerks, the first of whom shall assist and attend the bishops, the second the procurators of the clergy, the third the earls and barons, the fourth the knights of shires, the fifth the citizens and burgesses; and each of them, unless he is under the king, and receives from him a fee or wages on which he can respectably live, shall receive from the king two shillings a day, unless he eats at the lord king's table; then he shall receive twelve pence a day. These clerks shall write their questions and the answers which they make to the king and Parliament, and shall be present at their council whenever they wish to have them, and when they are unemployed they shall assist the principal clerks to write the rolls.

Concerning Difficult Cases and Judgments

When any dispute, question, or difficult case, whether of peace or war, shall arise in or out of the kingdom, the case shall be related and recited in writing in full Parliament, and be dealt with and debated on there among the peers of the Parliament, and if it be necessary it shall been joined by the king, or on his behalf if he is not present, to each rank of peers, that each rank proceed by itself, and the case shall be delivered in writing to its clerk, and in an appointed place they shall cause him to recite the case before them, so that they may order and consider among themselves how it may be better and more justly proceeded in as they shall be willing to answer before God for the king's person and their own persons, and for the persons of those whom they represent; and they shall report their answers and advice in writing, so that, all their answers, counsel, and advice being heard on all sides, it may be proceeded in according to the best and soundest counsel, and where at least the major part of Parliament agrees. And if the peace of the kingdom is disturbed, or the people or country troubled, by disagreement between them and the king and any nobles, or perchance between the nobles themselves, so that it seems to the king and his council that it is expedient that this business be treated of and amended by the consideration of all the peers of his kingdom, or if the king and kingdom be troubled by war, or if a difficult case arises before the chancellor of England, or a difficult judgment is to be rendered before the justices, in such cases, and if perchance in such deliberations all or at least the greater part cannot agree, then the earl steward, the earl constable, and the earl marshal, or two of them, shall elect twenty-five persons out of all the peers of the realm, that is, two bishops and three procurators for the whole clergy, two earls and three barons, five knights of shires, five citizens, and [five] burgesses, which make twenty-five. And these twenty-five may select twelve from among themselves, and reduce themselves to that number, and these twelve may reduce themselves to six, and those six may still further reduce themselves to three, but those three cannot reduce themselves to a less number unless license be obtained from our lord the king; and should the king give his consent, then those three may reduce themselves to two, and one of those two may delegate his power to the other, and thus, finally, his ordinance will stand superior in authority to the whole Parliament; and so by reduction from twenty-five persons to one individual person (unless the greater number be able to come to agreement and give judgment), in the end, one single individual, as it is said, who cannot disagree with himself, shall ordain for all — reserving to our lord king and his council the power of examining and amending such ordinances after they have been written, if they know how and wish so to do, so that it then be done there in full Parliament, and with the consent of Parliament, and not otherwise.

Concerning the Business of the Parliament

The business for which the Parliament is held ought to be deliberated on according to the calendar of Parliament, and according to the order of petitions delivered and filed, without respect to persons, but who first proposes shall first act. In the calendar of Parliament all business of the Parliament ought to be regarded in the following order: first, concerning war, if there be war, and other affairs touching the persons of the king and queen and their children; secondly, concerning the common affairs of the kingdom, such as making laws against the defects of original laws, judicial and executorial, after judgments rendered, which are chiefly common affairs; thirdly, private business ought to be considered, and this according to the order of the filing of petitions as is aforesaid.

Concerning the Days and Hours of Parliament

The Parliament ought not to be held on Sundays, but it may be held on all other days, except three, namely All Saints [November 1], All Souls [November 2], and the nativity of St. John the Baptist [June 24]. And it ought to begin at midprime on each day, at which hour the king is bound to be present at the Parliament, and all the peers of the realm; and the Parliament ought to be held in a public and not in a private or obscure place. On festival days the Parliament ought to begin at prime hour on account of divine service.

Concerning the Ranks of Peers

The king is the head, beginning, and end of Parliament, and so he has no peer in his rank, and so the first rank consists of the king alone; the second rank is that of the archbishops, bishops, abbots, and priors holding by barony; the third rank is of the procurators of the clergy; the fourth is of the earls, barons, and other magnates and nobles, holding land to the value of a county or barony, as is aforesaid under the head of the laity; the fifth is of the knights of shires; the sixth is of the citizens and burgesses. And so Parliament is composed of six ranks. But it must be known that even if any of the said ranks, below the king, is absent, if they have been summoned by reasonable summonses of Parliament, the Parliament shall nevertheless be considered complete.

Concerning the Manner of Parliament

Having first shown how, to whom, and at what time the summons of the Parliament ought to be issued, and who ought to come by summons, and who not, we will now relate, secondly, who they are who ought to come by virtue of their offices, without summons, and are bound to be present during the whole Parliament. Thus it is to be observed that the two principal clerks of Parliament chosen by the king and his council, and the other secondary clerks (about whom and their offices we will give more details hereafter), and the chief crier of England with his under-criers, and the chief usher of England (which two offices, that is, of crier and usher, used to belong to one and the same) — these officers are bound to be present on the first day. The chancellor of England, the treasurer, the chamberlain, and barons of the exchequer, the justices, all clerks and knights of the king, together with the king's sergeants at pleas, who are of the king's council, are bound to be present on the second day, unless they have reasonable excuses that they cannot be present, and then they ought to send good excuses.

Concerning the Opening of the Parliament

The lord king shall sit in the middle of the larger bench, and is bound to be present at prime, on the sixth day of the Parliament. And the chancellor, treasurer, barons of the exchequer, and justices are accustomed to record defaults made in Parliament in the following order: on the first day the burgesses and citizens of all England shall be called over, on which day if they do not come, a borough shall be amerced a hundred marks and a city a hundred pounds; on the second day the knights of shires of all England shall be called, on which day if they do not come, their county shall be amerced a hundred pounds; on the third day of the Parliament the barons of the Cinque Ports shall be called, and afterwards the barons, and afterwards the earls, when, if the barons of the Cinque Ports do not come, the barony whence they were sent shall be amerced a hundred marks; in the same manner a baron by himself shall be amerced a hundred marks, and an earl a hundred pounds; in like manner shall be done with those who are peers of earls and barons, that is, those who have lands and rents to the value of a county or a barony, as is aforesaid under the title of "Summons"; on the fourth day the procurators of the clergy shall be called, on which day if they do not come, their bishops shall be amerced a hundred marks for every archdeaconry making default; on the fifth day the deans, priors, abbots, bishops, and lastly the archbishops, shall be called, who, if they do not come, shall be amerced each archbishop a hundred pounds, a bishop holding an entire barony a hundred marks, and in like manner with respect to the abbots, priors, and others. On the first day proclamation ought to be made, first in the hall or monastery, or other public place where the Parliament is held, and afterwards publicly in the town or village, that all who wish to deliver petitions and complaints to the Parliament may deliver them from the first day of the Parliament for the five next following days.

Concerning the Preaching before the Parliament

An archbishop, or bishop, or eminent, discreet, and eloquent clerk, selected by the archbishop in whose province the Parliament is held, ought to preach on one of the first five days of the Parliament in full Parliament, and in the presence of the king, and this when the Parliament for the greater part is assembled and congregated, and in his discourse he ought in due order to enjoin the Parliament that they with him should humbly beseech God and implore him for the peace and tranquillity of the king and kingdom, as will be more specially treated of in the following section concerning the declaration to the Parliament.

Concerning the Declaration in Parliament

After the preaching the chancellor of England, or the chief justice of England, that is, he who holds pleas before the king, or some fit, honorable, and eloquent justice or clerk elected by the chancellor and chief justice, ought to declare the causes of the Parliament, first generally, and afterwards specially, standing. And it is to be observed that all in Parliament, whoever they are, shall stand while they speak, except the king, so that all in Parliament may be able to hear him who speaks. And if he speaks obscurely or low he shall speak over again and louder, or another shall speak for him.

Concerning the King's Speech after the Declaration

The king, after the declaration for the Parliament, ought to entreat the clergy and laity, naming all their degrees, that is, the archbishops, bishops, abbots, priors, archdeacons, procurators, and others of the clergy, the earls, barons, knights, citizens, burgesses, and other laymen, that they diligently, studiously, and cordially will labor to deal with and deliberate on the affairs of Parliament as they shall think and perceive how this may best and principally be done according to God's will in the first place, and afterwards for the king's and their own honor and welfare.

Concerning the King's Absence from Parliament

The king is bound by all means to be personally present in Parliament, unless hindered by bodily infirmity, and then he can keep to his chamber, as long as he does not lie out of the manor or at least the town where Parliament is holden, and then he ought to send for twelve of the greater and better persons who are summoned to Parliament, that is, two bishops, two earls, two barons, two knights of shires, two citizens, and two burgesses to visit him and testify about his condition, and in their presence he ought to commission the archbishop of the province, the steward, and the chief justice jointly and severally to begin and continue the Parliament in his name, making express mention in that commission of the cause of his absence, which should satisfy and advise the rest of the nobles and magnates of Parliament, together with the evident testimony of their said twelve peers. The reason is that clamor and murmurs used to be in Parliament on account of the king's absence, because it is a hurtful and dangerous thing for the whole commonalty of Parliament, and also for the realm, when the king is absent from the Parliament, nor ought he nor can he absent himself, except in the abovesaid case.

Concerning the Place and Sittings in the Parliament

First, as is aforesaid, the king shall sit in the middle place of the greater bench, and on his right hand shall sit the archbishop of Canterbury, and on his left hand the archbishop of York, and immediately after them the bishops, abbots, and priors in rows, with the ranks and places always so arranged that each one sits among his peers; and the steward of England is bound to attend to this, unless the king appoint another person. At the king's right foot shall sit the chancellor of England and the chief justice of England, and his associates, and their clerks who are of Parliament, and at his left foot shall sit the treasurer, chamberlain, barons of the Exchequer, justices of the bench, and their clerks who are of Parliament.

Concerning the Doorkeeper of the Parliament

The chief usher of Parliament shall stand within the great door of the monastery, hall, or other place where the Parliament is held, and shall keep the door so that no one may enter the Parliament except him who owes suit and appearance at the Parliament, or shall be called on account of the business which he is prosecuting in the Parliament. It is necessary that the doorkeeper have knowledge of the persons who ought to enter, so that entrance be denied to none who ought to be present at the Parliament; and the doorkeeper may and ought, if necessary, to have many doorkeepers under him.

Concerning the Crier of the Parliament

The crier of Parliament shall stand outside the door of the Parliament, and the doorkeeper shall announce to him what he shall proclaim. The king used to send his sergeants at arms to stand amid the great space outside the door of Parliament to keep the door, so that none should make assaults or tumults about the doors, by which the Parliament might be disturbed, under pain of imprisonment, because by right the door of Parliament ought not to be shut, but guarded by the doorkeepers and king's sergeants at arms.

Concerning the Station of the Persons Speaking

All the peers of Parliament shall sit, and no one shall stand except when speaking, and he shall speak so that everyone in the Parliament may hear him. No one shall enter Parliament, nor go out of the Parliament, except by one door, and whoever speaks anything that ought to be deliberated on by the Parliament, while he speaks he and all who speak shall stand; the reason is that he may be heard by the peers, because all peers are judges and justices.

Concerning the King's Aid

The king is not accustomed to ask aid from his kingdom except for approaching war, or making his sons knights, or marrying his daughters, and then such aids ought to be asked in full Parliament, and delivered in writing to each rank of peers of the Parliament, and answered in writing. And be it known that if such aids are to be granted it is needful that all the peers of the Parliament consent; and be it understood that the two knights who come to the Parliament for a shire have a greater voice in Parliament in agreeing or dissenting than an earl of England who is greater than they are, and in like manner the procurators of the clergy of a single bishopric have a greater voice in Parliament, if they all agree, than the bishop himself, and this is so in all things which ought to be granted, refused, or done by Parliament. And by this it is evident that the king can hold a Parliament with the commons of his kingdom without bishops, earls, and barons, provided they have been summoned to Parliament, even if no bishop, earl, or baron obeys the summons, because formerly there was neither bishop, nor earl, nor baron, yet then kings held their Parliaments. Yet, on the other hand, if the commons — the clergy and laity — are summoned to Parliament, as of right they ought to be, and for any cause will not come, pretending, for instance, that the lord king does not govern them as he ought, and specifying cases in which he has not governed them, then there is no Parliament at all, even though the archbishops, bishops, earls, and barons, and all their peers, are present with the king; and therefore it is needful that all things which ought to be affirmed or abrogated, granted or refused, or done by the Parliament ought to be done by the commons of the Parliament, which is composed of three ranks or orders of Parliament, namely the procurators of the clergy, the knights of shires, and the citizens and burgesses, who represent the whole commons of England, and not by the nobles, because every one of them is in the Parliament for his own proper person and for none other.

Concerning the Breaking Up of the Parliament

The Parliament ought not to disband as long as any petition remains which has not been discussed, or at least to which the answer is not determined on, and if the king permits the contrary he is perjured. And no single one alone of the peers of the Parliament can or ought to retire from the Parliament without having obtained the permission of the king and all his peers, and this in full Parliament, and of this permission record shall be made in the roll of the Parliament. And if any one of the peers is sick during the Parliament, so that he cannot come to the Parliament, then for three days he shall send excusers to the Parliament. And if he does not come on the third day, two of his peers shall be sent to see and testify to his sickness, and if there be any suspicion those two peers shall be sworn that they will speak the truth; and if it be found that he has feigned he shall be amerced as if for default, and if he has not feigned then he shall attorn some sufficient person before them to be present at the Parliament for him. Nor can any sane person be excused if he is of sane memory.

The separation of the Parliament used to be in this manner: it ought first to be asked and publicly proclaimed in the Parliament, and within the palace of the Parliament, if there be anyone who shall have delivered a petition to the Parliament to which no answer has yet been given, or at least been answered as far as can be rightly done, and if no one shall answer, it is to be supposed that remedy has been afforded to everyone, and then, that is, when no one who at that time has exhibited his petition shall answer, [the king shall say,] "We will release our Parliament."

Concerning Transcripts of Records in Parliament

The clerks of the Parliament shall not refuse to anyone a copy of his proceeding, but shall deliver it to everyone who requests it, and shall always take for ten lines one penny, unless oath be made of inability to pay, in which case they shall take nothing. The rolls of Parliament shall be ten inches wide. The Parliament shall be held in whatever place in the kingdom the king shall choose.

Here ends the Manner of Holding Parliament.

Questions: Is the section on the summoning of Parliament an accurate description of that process in 1295? Where are the emphases in this document? What political beliefs and sympathies underlie this description of Parliament? What is the balance of power between Parliament and the king? Between the different groups that make up Parliament? What practical matters are dealt with here? What role does religion play?

52. CHRONICLE ACCOUNT OF THE GREAT FAMINE

In the early fourteenth century a terrible natural disaster overtook northern Europe when several years of inordinately rainy weather led to repeated massive crop failures and widespread famine. Marginal farmland had to be abandoned, animals could not be fed, many people starved, and a long period of population growth came to an end. In these brief extracts from the anonymous Life of Edward the Second, *the chronicler pauses in his account of wars and politics to comment several times on the catastrophe and its effects.*

Source: trans. N. Denholm-Young, *The Life of Edward the Second by the So-called Monk of Malmesbury* (London: Thomas Nelson and Sons Ltd., 1957), pp. 59, 64, 69–70, 90.

Then at the Purification of the Blessed Mary [February 2, 1315] the earls and all the barons met at London, ... and [the meeting] dragged on almost to the end of Lent [in the middle of March].

In this parliament, because merchants going about the country selling victuals charged excessively, the earls and barons, looking to the welfare of the state, appointed a remedy for this malady; they ordained a fixed price for oxen, pigs and sheep, for fowls, chickens, and pigeons, and for other common foods.... These matters were published throughout the land, and publicly proclaimed in shire courts and boroughs....

By certain portents the hand of God appears to be raised against us. For in the past year there was such plentiful rain that men could scarcely harvest the corn or bring it safely to the barn. In the present year worse has happened. For the floods of rain have rotted almost all the seed, so that the prophecy of Isaiah might seem now to be fulfilled; for he says that "ten acres of vineyard shall yield one little measure and thirty bushels of seed shall yield three bushels": and in many places the hay lay so long under water that it could neither be mown nor gathered. Sheep generally died and other animals were killed in a sudden plague. It is greatly to be feared that if the Lord finds us incorrigible after these visitations, he will destroy at once both men and beasts; and I firmly believe that unless the English church had interceded for us, we should have perished long ago....

After the feast of Easter [in 1316] the dearth of corn was much increased. Such a scarcity has not been seen in our time in England, nor heard of for a hundred years. For the measure of wheat sold in London and the neighboring places for forty pence, and in other less thickly populated parts of the country thirty pence was a common price. Indeed during this time of scarcity a great famine appeared, and after the famine came a severe pestilence, of which many thousands died in many places. I have even heard it said by some, that in Northumbria dogs and horses and other unclean things were eaten. For there, on account of the frequent raids of the Scots, work is more irksome, as the accursed Scots despoil the people daily of their food. Alas, poor England! You who once helped other lands from your abundance, now poor and needy are forced to beg. Fruitful land is turned into a salt-marsh; the inclemency of the weather destroys the fatness of the land; corn is sown and tares are brought forth. All this comes from the wickedness of the inhabitants. Spare, O Lord, spare thy people! For we are a scorn and a derision to them who are around us. Yet those who are wise in astrology say that these storms in the heavens have happened naturally; for Saturn, cold and heedless, brings rough weather that is useless to the seed; in the ascendant now for three years he has completed his course, and mild Jupiter duly succeeds him. Under Jupiter these floods of rain will cease, the valleys will grow rich in corn, and the fields will be filled with abundance. For the Lord shall give that which is good and our land shall yield her increase....

[In 1318] the dearth that had so long plagued us ceased, and England became fruitful with a manifold abundance of good things. A measure of wheat, which the year before was sold for forty pence, was now freely offered to the buyer for sixpence....

Questions: What explanations for the disaster are offered here? What were the effects of the poor weather? What attempts were made to limit the damage? After weather conditions returned to normal in 1318, might there have been any long term effects for individuals and for society?

53. THE ROYAL RESPONSE TO THE FAMINE

As indicated in the previous piece, price controls were the government's response to the inflation caused by the scarcity of food.

Source: trans. C.W. Colby, *Selections from the Sources of English History* (New York: Longmans, Green and Co., 1913), pp. 92-93.

Edward, by the grace of God, king of England, lord of Ireland, and duke of Aquitaine, to the mayor and sheriffs of London, greeting. We have received a complaint of the archbishops, bishops, earls, barons, and others of the commonalty of our kingdom, presented before us and our council, that there is now a great and intolerable dearth of oxen, cows, sheep, hogs, geese, hens, capons, chickens, pigeons and eggs, to the no small damage and grievance of them and all others living within the said kingdom. Wherefore, they have pressingly besought us, that we should take care to provide a fit remedy thereof. We therefore, for the common benefit of the people of the said kingdom, assenting to the aforesaid supplication, as seemed meet, have ordained, by the advice and assent of the prelates, earls, barons, and others, being of our council, in our last parliament held at Westminster, that a good saleable fat live ox, not fed with grain, be henceforth sold for 16s. and no more; and if he have been fed with corn, and be fat, then he may be sold for 24s. at the most; and a good fat live cow for 12s. A fat hog of two years of age for 40d. A fat sheep with the wool for 20d. A fat sheep shorn for 14d. A fat goose in our city aforesaid for 3d. A good and fat capon for 2d., ... and three pigeons for 1d., and twenty eggs for 1d. And that if it happen that any person or persons be found that will not sell the said saleable goods at the settled price aforesaid, then let the foresaid saleable goods be forfeited to us. And forasmuch as we will that the foresaid ordinance be henceforth firmly and inviolably kept in our said city and the suburbs thereof, we strictly order and command you, that you cause the fore-said ordinance to be proclaimed publicly and distinctly in our foresaid city and the suburbs thereof, where you shall think meet, and to be henceforth invio-lably kept, in all and singular its articles, throughout your whole liberty, under the foresaid forfeiture; and by no means fail herein, as you are minded to avoid our indignation, and to save yourselves harmless. Witness ourself at Westmin-ster, the 14th day of March, in the eighth year of our reign.

Questions: What are the king's reasons for making this proclamation? What specific effects of the poor weather are cited in this document? What provisions are made for the enforcement of the order? How severe are the proposed penalties?

54. MANOR COURT ROLLS

On every manor in England, the manor court enforced the lord's rights over his tenants, dealt with disputes between residents, and tried minor criminal cases; thus the records kept of these sessions during the later Middle Ages provide a window onto manorial affairs. The extracts below come from Great Cressingham in Norfolk, in the years 1328-29.

Source: trans. H.P. Chandler, *Five court rolls of Great Cressingham, in the county of Norfolk* (privately printed, 1885), reprinted in *Translations and Reprints from the Original Sources of European History*, series 1, vol. 3 (Philadelphia: University of Pennsylvania Department of History, n.d.), no. 5, ed. E.P. Cheyney, pp. 20-24; revised.

A Court in [Great Cressingham], on [September 12, the] Monday next after the feast of the nativity of the Blessed Mary in the year of the reign of King Edward above mentioned [1328].

Excuse. William of Glosbridge, attorney of Sir Robert de Aspale by the common excuse through W. Prat. (He came afterwards.)

Order. It was ordered, as before, to distrain [that is, seize some of his property in order to compel] master Firmin to show by what right, etc., concerning the tenement Walwayn. Likewise to distrain Sir John Walwayn for fealty.

Amercement [that is, a monetary penalty], 3d. From Petronilla of Mintling for leave to agree with William Attewent, concerning a plea of trespass.

Order. It was ordered to distrain Peter the Cooper for 15d. which he owed to Roger the Miller, at the suit of William Attestreet, who proved against him four shillings in court.

Fine [that is, payment to settle a dispute], 12d. From Walter Orengil for his term of four years to hold in 6 acres of land rented from Gilbert Cloveleek, for which grant the said Walter is to pay annually, at the feast of All Saints [November 1], to the said Gilbert four quarters and four bushels of barley, during the said term. Pledges Nally and John Buteneleyn.

Amercement, 2d. From John Brichtmer because he was summoned to do one boon-work [that is, work owed to the lord by an unfree peasant] in autumn and did not come. Therefore he is to be amerced.

Amercement, 2d. From Alice, wife of Richard of Glosbridge, for the same.

Amercement, 2d. From William Robin for the same.

Order. From Walter Page and Margaret his wife, because they cannot deny that they are keeping back from John of Enston 3d.; and therefore it was ordered that the said 3d. should be levied from the said Walter to the use of the said John. (Reversed, because he is poor.)

Fine, 4d. Martin the son of Basil and Alice his wife having been examined by the bailiff, surrendered into the lord's hand one rood of land with a cottage thereon, to the use of Isabel daughter of John Fayrsay and their heirs, to hold in villeinage at the will of the lord, doing etc., all rights being saved [that is, not making any change in basic status and obligations]. And she gives, etc.

Fine, 4d. Isabel Fayrsay surrendered into the lord's hands one rood and one quarter of a rood of land and one rood of meadow and half of a cottage to the use of Martin Basil's son and Alice his wife and their heirs, to hold in villeinage at the will of the lord, doing etc. All rights being saved. And he gives to the lord [etc.].

Fine, 4d. From John Pye for his term of five years to hold in three roods of land rented from Hugh Holer. The term begins at the feast of St. Michael [September 29].

Fine, £4. It is to be remembered that the lord out of his seisin delivered and gave to Vincent of Lakenham one messuage [that is, dwelling], 7 acres 2 roods of land of the villeinage of the lord, which had been taken into the lord's hand after the death of William the son of Hugh because the aforesaid William was a bastard son and died without heirs, to hold of him to the aforesaid Vincent and his heirs, in villeinage at the will of the lord, doing thence the services and customs due. All rights being saved. And he gives to the lord for his entry. And saving to Alice who was the wife of Hugh the son of Lawrence half of the said tenements to hold in dower for the term of her life.

Note, 1 beast; price 10s. The jury says John Bassisson has died seized of one messuage, 16 acres and 1 rood of land of villeinage, and that John his son is his next heir, and is of the age of nine years. And because the said heir has not come, therefore it is ordered that seisin be in the whole villeinage until, etc.

Order. To distrain the tenants of the tenement Sowle for one boon-work withheld in autumn.

Fine, 40s. All the jury says that Thomas Ode has died seised of a cottage and 5 acres and one rood of land of the villeinage of the lord, and that they know him to have no surviving heir, and therefore the whole tenement was taken into the lord's hand. And the lord out of his seisin delivered and gave the whole of the said tenement to a certain Simon Maning of Walton and his heirs to hold in villeinage at the will of the lord, doing therefor the service and customs due. Saving all kinds of rights. And he gives to the lord to have entry.

Order. Ordered to distrain Henry Cook, John Maggard, chaplain, and John Ingel, because they withhold from the lord 3d. rent now for five years for the parcel tenement Merchant.

Likewise to distrain Richard of the River for fealty for the tenement formerly of Reyner Attechurch.

Election. The whole homage elect the tenement of Geoffrey Attechurchgate for the office of reeve this year, and the tenants are Nally, Buteneleyn, Martin, Bassisson, and others. And the said Alexander [sic] was sworn.

Likewise the tenement of Lawrence Smith for the next year.

Likewise the tenement Ernald for the office of reaper: and the tenants are W. Macurneys, Buteneleyn, W. Pawe, and T. Attenewhouse. And the said W. Pawe was sworn and afterward excused. And Prat performs the office for him.

Order. It was ordered to distrain Alan son of William Attehallgate and John his brother, for fealty for the tenement which belonged to master Roger de Snettisham of the fee of the lord.

Likewise to distrain John Pye to show by what right, etc., and for fealty.

Likewise to retain the pledges taken from the men of Hilborough until they have made satisfaction for damages done in the common.

Amercement, 12d. From William Hubbard for damage in the lord's meadows.

Amercement, 6d. From John Aylmer for damage in the fields in autumn.

Amercement, 2d. From Hugh Holer because he did not do his boon-work in autumn, as he was summoned to do.

12d. From Isabel Syapping for license to have a fold of her own sheep.

Memorandum. Of 4 bushels of barley taken from Roger the miller, etc., by the reaper; and let them be handed over to Thomas Pawe for a debt recovered against the said Roger.

Total £6 4s. 11d., besides a heriot [that is, death tax] valued at 10s.

Total of all the courts for the whole year, £8 16s. 8d.

Cressingham. A court and leet there on [July 3, 1329, the] Monday next after the feast of the apostles Peter and Paul, in the third year of the reign of King Edward, the third from the Conquest....

Fine, 18d. Gilbert de Sedgeford surrendered into the hands of the bailiff, in the presence of the whole homage, a cottage to the use of John Putneys and his heirs, to hold in villeinage at the will of the lord, doing thence the services and customs due; saving rights of all kinds. And he gives for entry, etc.

Order. It was ordered to retain in the lord's hand one messuage and one acre of land of which John Belesson was seized when he died, because it is not known of what condition he was; and therefore the rolls of the 34th and 32nd [years] of King Edward are being examined.

Amercement, 3d. From Alice, daughter of Geoffrey Attenewhouse, for marrying without leave.

Amercement, 4d. From John, son of Martin, for the same.

Postponement. A suit between Thomas Attetunsend, plaintiff, and Adam Attewater, defendant, concerning a plea of agreement, was postponed till the next court by consent of the parties on account of arbitration.

Postponement. A distraint taken from John Maggard and Henry Cook for arrears of rent was postponed till the next court. And it was ordered to distrain John Ingel, their joint-tenant, etc.

Chief Pledges: John Buteneleyn, John Hardy, William Robin, Thomas Hardy, Henry Pawe, Nicholas, son of Roger, Laurence Smith, Roger Attehallgate, Roger Gumay, William le Warde, William Attestreet, Robert Gemming. These were sworn and say:

Fine, 3d. From William Hubbard for license to put his grain, growing in the lord's villeinage, out of villeinage.

Amercement. From Silvester Smith, for blood drawn from John Marschal. [Erased.] Because he was elsewhere.

Amercement, 6d. From John Barun for the same from William, son of Sabina.

Amercement, 3d. From Margaret Millote for the same from Agnes, daughter of Martin Skinner.

Amercement, 6d. From the rector for an encroachment on the common at Greenholm, 12 perches long and 2 feet wide.

Amercement, 6d. From the same rector for an encroachment made at Caldwell, 20 perches long and 11 foot wide.

Amercement, 3d. From Roger of Drayton because he made an encroachment at the Strete 3 perches long and 1 foot wide....

Amercement, 6d. From Hugh Reff and Hugh Holer for license to resign the office of ale-taster.

Election. Alan Cook and Alan Spicer were elected to the office of ale-taster, and sworn.

Amercement, 2d. From Christiana Punt because she has sold ale and bread contrary to the assize.

Amercement, 2d. From William, son of Clarissa, because he broke into the house of John son of Geoffrey Brichtmer.

Amercement, 2d. From Adam son of Matilda Thomas because he is not in the tithing.

Amercement, 2d. From John son of Thomas Brun for the same.

Amercement, 6d. From Peter Miller for a hue and cry justly raised against him by the wife of William Fuller.

Questions: What evidence is there here of different ranks of people and their occupations? How do women figure in these records? What laws and legal obligations are mentioned? What kinds of disputes are brought to the court?

55. LONDON CRAFT GUILD ORDINANCES

In towns, the practitioners of each craft or industry banded together in craft guilds which regulated their businesses, set quality standards and prices, and determined who was eligible to work in the craft.

Source: trans. H.T. Riley, *Memorials of London and London Life in the XIIIth, XIVth, and XVth Centuries* (London: Longmans, Green, and Co., 1868), pp. 120-121, 216-217, 226-228, 232-234, 292-294, 372-373, 400-401, 405-407; revised.

Ordinances of the Pepperers of Soper Lane (1316)

These are the points which the good folks of Soper Lane, of the trade of Pepperers, with the assent of Sir Stephen de Abyndone, mayor of London, John de Gisors, Nicholas of Faringdon, and other aldermen, have made for the common profit of all the people of the land…, on [May 5,] the Wednesday next after the feast of St. Philip and St. James, in the 9th year of the reign of King Edward.

In the first place, that no one of the trade, or other person in his name or for him, shall mix any manner of wares, that is to say, shall put old things with new, or new things with old, by reason whereof the good thing may be impaired by the old; nor yet things of one price, or of one sort, with other things of another price, or of another sort.

Also, that no person shall dub any manner of wares; that is to say, by putting in a thing that was in another bale, and then dressing the bale up again in another manner than the form in which it was first bought, so as to make the ends of the bale contain better things than the remainder within the bale, by reason whereof the buyer may be deceived, and so lose his goods.

Also, that no one shall moisten any manner of merchandise, such as saffron, alum, ginger, cloves, and such manner of things as may admit of being moistened; that is to say, by steeping the ginger, or turning the saffron out of the sack and then anointing it, or bathing it in water, by reason whereof any manner of weight may be increased, or any deterioration arise to the merchandise.

Also, that every vendor shall give to his buyer the thing that is on sale by the hundredweight of 112 pounds to the hundred, 15 ounces to every pound; save only, things that are confected, or things powdered. And such things confected and powdered are to be sold by the 12 ounces, the same as always has been the custom.

Also, that all their weights shall agree, the one with the other.

Articles of the Girdlers (1344)

Unto the mayor, aldermen, and chamberlain, of the city of London, pray the good folks, the girdlers [that is, beltmakers] of the same city, that certain defaults which they find in their trade may be amended, and by certain folks of the trade be regulated; the same persons before you to be sworn to do the same.

In the first place, that no man of the trade shall work any manner of tissue of silk, or of wool, or of linen thread, if the tissue be not of such length and assize as was wont to be used heretofor, that is to say, 6 quarters.

Also, that no man of the said trade shall garnish, or cause to be garnished, girdles or garters, with any but pure metal, such as latten [that is, a copper alloy], or else with iron or steel....

Also, that no tissue of silk or wool, or of thread or leather, that is in breadth of sixth size, fifth, third, or double size, shall be garnished, unless it have a double point in the buckle, and in the tongue; as also, the bars with a double point down to the rowel below; that is to say, as well with reference to close-harness, as other [work]....

Also, that no man of the trade shall take an apprentice, unless he be free of the city; and if he be free, that he shall take no one for less than seven years.

Also, that no strange man shall be admitted to work in the trade, if he will not be an apprentice in the trade, or buy his freedom.

Also, that no man of the trade shall work on Saturday, or on the eve of a double feast, after None has been rung.

Also, that no man of the trade shall work in such trade at either roset or tirlet [that is, types of straps].

Also, that no man of the trade shall keep his shop open on Sundays, or on double feasts, to sell his wares. But if any strange person, passing by chance through the city upon any feast day, shall have occasion in a hurry to buy anything touching the said trade, it shall be fully lawful for a man of the same trade, whosoever he may be, to sell to him within his own house whatever he shall wish to buy; but without opening his shop.

Also, that no one of the trade shall set any woman to work, other than his wedded wife or his daughter.

Also, that no one of the said trade shall dare to work by night at the said trade, on pain hereafter written.

Also, that no man from henceforth shall make a girdle of any worse leather than ox leather.

And hereupon, it is ordained by the mayor and aldermen, with the assent of all the good folks of the said trade, that if anyone of the trade shall be found by the men so sworn acting against the ordinances aforesaid, or any one point of them, the first time, he shall be amerced in 40 pence, the second time half a mark, the third time 10 shillings, the fourth time one mark, and the fifth time 20 shillings, to the use of the chamber. And such girdles as shall be found to have been falsely made, against the points aforesaid, by the sworn men before mentioned, shall be burnt.

Articles of the Spurriers (1345)

In the first place, that no one of the trade of spurriers shall work longer than from the beginning of the day until curfew rung out at the church of St. Sepulcher, outside Newgate, by reason that no man can work so neatly by night as by day. And many persons of the said trade, who compass how to practice deception in their work, desire to work by night rather than by day: and then they introduce false iron, and iron that has been cracked, for tin, and also, they put gilt on false copper, and cracked. And further, many of the said trade are wandering about all day, without working at all at their trade; and then, when they have become drunk and frantic, they take to their work, to the annoyance of the sick and of all their neighborhood, as well by reason of the broils that arise between them and the strange folks who are dwelling among them. And then they blow up their fires so vigorously, that their forges begin all at once to blaze, to the great peril of themselves and of all the neighborhood around. And then too, all the neighbors are much in dread of the sparks, which so vigorously issue forth in all directions from the mouths of the chimneys in their forges. By reason whereof, it seems unto them that working by night [should be ended,] in order to avoid such false work and such perils; and therefore, the mayor and aldermen do will, by assent of the good folks of the said trade, and for the common profit, that from henceforth such time for working, and such false work made in the trade, shall be forbidden. And if any person shall be found in the said trade to do to the contrary hereof, let him be amerced, the first time in 40d., one half thereof to go to the use of the chamber of the guildhall of London, and the other half to the use of the said trade; the second time, in half a mark, and the third time, in 10s., to the use of the same chamber and trade; and the fourth time, let him forswear the trade forever.

Also, that no one of the said trade shall keep a house or shop to carry on his business, unless he is free of the city; and that no one shall cause to be sold, or exposed for sale, any manner of old spurs for new ones; or shall garnish them, or change them for new ones.

Also, that no one of the said trade shall take an apprentice for a term of less than seven years; and such apprentice shall be enrolled, according to the usages of the said city....

Also, that no one of the said trade shall receive the apprentice, serving-man, or journeyman of another in the same trade, during the term agreed between his master and him, on the pain aforesaid.

Also, that no alien of another country, or foreigner of this country, shall follow or use the said trade, unless he is enfranchised before the mayor, aldermen, and chamberlain; and that, by witness and surety of the good folks of the said trade, who will undertake for him as to his loyalty and his good behavior.

Also, that no one of the said trade shall work on Saturdays, after Nones has been rung out in the city; and not from that hour until the Monday morning following.

Ordinances of the White Tawyers (1346)

In honor of God, of Our Lady, and of all saints, and for the nurture of tranquility and peace among the good folks the megucers, called "white tawyers," [that is, processors of animal hides] the folks of the same trade have, by assent of Richard Lacer, mayor, and of the aldermen, ordained the points under-written.

In the first place, they have ordained that they will find a wax candle, to burn before Our Lady in the church of All Hallows, near London Wall.

Also, that each person of the said trade shall put in the box such sum as he shall think fit, in aid of maintaining the candle.

Also, if by chance anyone of the said trade shall fall into poverty, whether through old age, or because he cannot labor or work, and have nothing with which to help himself, he shall have every week from the said box 7d. for his support, if he be a man of good repute. And after his decease, if he have a wife, a woman of good repute, she shall have weekly for her support 7d. from the said box, so long as she shall behave herself well, and keep single.

And that no stranger shall work in the said trade, or keep house [for the same] in the city, if he be not an apprentice, or a man admitted to the franchise of the said city.

And that no one shall take the serving-man of another to work with him, during his term, unless it be with the permission of his master.

And if anyone of the said trade shall have work in his house that he cannot complete, or if for want of assistance such work shall be in danger of being lost, those of the said trade shall aid him, that so the said work shall be not lost.

And if anyone of the said trade shall depart this life, and have not where-withal to be buried, he shall be buried at the expense of their common box; and when anyone of the said trade shall die, all those of the said trade shall go to the vigil, and make offering on the morrow.

And if any serving-man shall conduct himself in any other manner than properly towards his master, and act rebelliously towards him, no one of the said trade shall set him to work, until he shall have made amends before the mayor and aldermen; and before them such contempt shall be redressed.

And that no one of the said trade shall behave himself the more thought-lessly, in the way of speaking or acting amiss, by reason of the points aforesaid; and if anyone shall do to the contrary thereof, he shall not follow the said trade until he shall have reasonably made amends.

And if anyone of the said trade shall do to the contrary of any point of the ordinances aforesaid, and be convicted thereof by good men of the said trade, he shall pay to the chamber of the guildhall of London, the first time 2s., the second time 40d., the third time half a mark, and the fourth time 10s., and shall forswear the trade.

[Ordinances added in 1376:]

Also, that the good folks of the same trade shall once in the year be assembled in a certain place, convenient thereto, there to choose two men of the most loyal and befitting of the said trade, to be overseers of work and all other things touching the trade, for that year. These persons shall be presented to the mayor and aldermen for the time being, and sworn before them diligently to enquire and make search, and loyally to present to the said mayor and aldermen such defaults as they shall find touching the said trade, without sparing anyone for friendship or for hatred, or in any other manner. And if anyone of the said trade shall be found rebellious against the said overseers, so as not to let them properly make their search and assay, as they ought to do, or if he shall absent himself from the meeting aforesaid, without reasonable cause, after due warn-ing by the said overseers, he shall pay to the chamber, upon the first default, 40d., and on the second like default, half a mark; and on the third, one mark; and on the fourth, 20s., and shall forswear the trade for ever.

Also, that if the overseers shall be found lax and negligent about their duty, or partial to any person, for gift or for friendship, maintaining him or voluntarily permitting him [to continue] in his default, and shall not present him to the mayor and aldermen, as before stated, they are to incur the penalty aforesaid.

… And if it shall be found that through laxity or negligence of the said governors such assemblies are not held, each of the said overseers is to incur the said penalty.

Also, that all skins falsely and deceitfully wrought in their trade, which the said overseers shall find on sale in the hands of any person, citizen or foreigner, within the franchise, shall be forfeited to the said chamber, and the worker thereof amerced in manner aforesaid.

Also, that no one who has not been an apprentice, and has not finished his term of apprenticeship in the said trade, shall be made free of the same trade; unless it be attested by the overseers for the time being, or by four persons of the said trade, that such person is able, and sufficiently skilled to be made free of the same.

Also, that no one of the said trade shall induce the servant of another to work with him in the same trade, until he has made a proper fine with his first master, at the discretion of the said overseers, or of four reputable men of the said trade.…

Also, that no one shall take for working in the said trade more than they were wont heretofore; that is to say, for [tawing] ten Scottish stags, half a mark; for ten Irish stags, half a mark; for ten Spanish stags, 10s.; for the hundred of goatskins, 20s.; the hundred of roe-leather, 16s.; for the hundred skins of young female deer, 8s.; and for the hundred of kidskins, 8s.

Ordinances of the Farriers (1356)

… To Henry Pycard, mayor, and the aldermen of the city of London, the good folks, the master farriers of the same city, show that whereas many offenses and great damages had been committed, against the persons of the court and the commonalty of the same city and of all the realm, by people not wise therein, who kept forges in the said city, and intermeddled with works of farriery, which they did not understand how to bring to good end, by reason whereof, many horses had been lost, to the great damage of the people: … therefore, the said mayor doth will and doth grant, by assent of the good folks of the said trade, that all those who shall be found or proved to be making false work in shoes or nails, or works of fase metal, shall pay 40 pence, the first time, to the chamber of the guildhall; the second time, half a mark; the third time, 13s. 4d.; the fourth time, they shall forswear the said trade within the city for ever. And that no one from henceforth shall take any forge in the said city, until he shall have been admitted by the masters of the said trade, so as to be known as able and skilled in his trade, to the profit of the commonalty of the said city, and of all the realm.

And also, it is agreed between the said masters and the good folks of the said trade, that they will well and loyally advise all those who shall ask counsel of them, as well in the purchase of horses as in their cure; and that this they will not fail to do for any brokerage or gifts, whereby the said trade may be scandalized....

And that no one of the said trade shall commence or undertake any great cure, if he does not reasonably see at the beginning that the same cure will be brought to good end. And that if any person shall undertake any great cure, and shall fear in his conscience that the same will take a disastrous turn, then, in such case, he shall come before the masters and other wise men of the said trade, to ask their counsel and aid, for the saving of the horse, and for the profit of him to whom the horse belongs, and the honor of the trade. And if the contrary thereof shall in any manner be found, or it shall be proved against any person, that through conceit, or through negligence, he has let the same horse perish, then he shall be accused thereof before the mayor and aldermen, and be punished at their discretion, in the way of making restitution for the same horse to the person to whom the same belongs.

And also, it is agreed between the said masters and the good folks of the said trade, that they shall not take from henceforth more than they were wont to take before the time of the pestilence; that is to say, for a shoe of 6 nails 1d.; for a shoe of 8 nails 2d.; and for taking off a shoe of 6 nails or 8 nails, one halfpenny; for putting on the shoe of a courser, 2d.; the shoe of a charger, 3d.; and for taking off the shoe of a courser or charger, one penny; which points aforesaid the said masters and good folks of the said trade agree well and lawfully to keep and perform, to the best of their power, and have sworn thereto on the Holy Evangelists.

And also, it is agreed between the said masters and the good folks of the said trade, that no one of them shall commence or follow the trade or work of a smith, or any other than the trade which they follow, and by which they live, that is to say, horse-shoeing and farriery of horses. And further, that no one of them shall withdraw, take, or set to work, any smith, or any servants of smiths, or any serving-man of any other trade, if he be not a skilful man, and well versed in horse-shoeing and farriery; whereby the said trade might be slandered, and the commonalty deceived or damaged....

Ordinances of the Court-hand Writers, or Scriveners (1373)

Unto the honorable lords, the mayor and aldermen of the city of London, the writers of court-hand of the same city pray that, whereas their craft is very much in request in the same city, and as it is especially requisite that it should be ruled and followed lawfully and wisely and by persons instructed therein, and seeing that, for want of good rule, many mischiefs and defaults are, and have been oftentimes, committed in the said craft, by those who resort from diverse countries unto the said city, both chaplains and others, who have no knowledge of the customs, franchises, and usages of the city, and who cause themselves to be called "scriveners," and undertake to make wills, deeds, and all other things touching the said craft; the fact being that they are foreigners and unknown, and also are less skilled than the aforesaid scriveners who are free of the said city, and who for long have been versed in their craft, and have largely given of their means for their instruction and freedom therein: to the great damage and disinheritance of many persons, as well of the said city as of many countries of the realm, and to the great damage and scandal of all the good and lawful men of the said craft — therefore the good scriveners pray that it may please your honorable and discreet lordships, to grant unto them, and to establish for the common profit of the said city, and of many other countries, and for the well-being and amendment of their condition, that they, and their successors for all time, may be ruled and may enjoy their franchise in their degree in manner as other folks of diverse trades of the said city are ruled and do enjoy their franchise, in their degree; according to the points that follow.

In the first place, they pray that no person shall be suffered to keep shop of the said craft in the city, or in the suburb thereof, if he be not free of the city, made free in the same craft, and that, by men of the craft.

Also, that no one shall be admitted to such freedom, if he be not first examined and found able by those of the same craft who shall, for the time being, by you and your successors be assigned and deputed to do the same, and to be wardens of the said craft.

Also, that every scrivener of the said city, and of the suburb thereof, shall put his name to the deeds which he makes, that it may be known who has made the same.

Also, that every one who shall act against this ordinance and enactment, shall pay to the chamber the first time 40d.; the second time, half a mark; and the third time, 10s.

Also, that these articles shall be enrolled in the said chamber, as being firm and established for ever.

Ordinances of the Fullers (1376)

To the honorable lords, and gracious, the mayor and aldermen of the city of London, pray very humbly, and with all their heart, John Oliscompe, Geoffrey Suttone, and John Swift, for themselves and all other fullers, and all other good folks of the same trade, in the city of London, that whereas the said trade has for a long time past used urine in the fulling of cloths, by reason whereof the said trade has been and is always being reproved by many folks of the said city, and certain persons of the trade of dyers say that no cloth can be either properly fulled or dyed, when such urine is put thereupon in fulling: and the said trade of fullers is of good desire that no urine shall be put upon any cloth in fulling, that so they may avoid reproach and for the profit of all the commonalty: may it please your very gracious lordships, that the said point be accepted before you, and enrolled: that no one of the said trade of fullers shall dare to allow urine any longer to be used henceforth in their trade, on pain of paying 100s. to the chamber of the guildhall.

And that it be ordained, that no one in the said trade of fullers shall be allowed from henceforth to work within the city, if he be not free of the same.

Also, the said fullers do pray, that, whereas the hurers [that is, makers of shaggy fur caps] of the said city are wont to full their caps in the mills at Wandsworth, Old Ford, Stratford, and Enfield, where the said fullers full their cloths, it may please your very benign lordships, that the said hurers shall not be allowed from henceforth to full in the said mills; having regard that the said fullers cannot there full their cloths, by reason that when the caps are mixed with their cloths in fulling, such caps crush and tear the cloths, to the great damage and loss, as well of the said fullers, as of all the community.

Ordinances of the Cheesemongers (1377)

To the honorable lords, the mayor, recorder, and aldermen of London, pray the cheesemongers of London, that whereas our said lord the mayor has told them heretofore to devise and ordain how the price of cheese and of butter may be amended, the said cheesemongers therefore, by their common assent, have well considered how the said price may be well amended; if our said lord the mayor, and his good council, will put their hand to, confirm, and enroll the points underwritten.

First, that foreigners who come to the city with cheese and butter for sale, in carts and upon horses, shall be charged to bring their wares into the market of the Ledenhall, or the market between St. Nicholas Shambles and Newgate, and nowhere else, before noon rung at such place where the purchase shall be made: and shall be charged that they shall not put away in houses or in rooms, privily or openly, either after noon rung or before, any cheese or butter, on pain of forfeiting the same that shall be so put away.

Also, whereas those who carry or bring cheese or butter to the city by water, do sell it in secret to hucksters and to others, against the ancient usage…: they do pray that from henceforth all such dealers shall be charged to bring such cheese or butter to the markets aforesaid, and there sell the same; on pain of forfeiting the thing to be sold, and also on pain of imprisonment and of making fine at the will and ordinance of our said lord the mayor.

Also, diverse hucksters of cheese, from Ham, Hackney, and the suburbs of London, are wont to go to diverse markets, and to buy up such wares in order to make a profit, when the wares ought to come to the hands of the working-men in London; and such hucksters then bring the same into London, and go about through diverse streets in the said city, and sell it, to the great damage of the commonalty, saying and affirming that it is the produce of their own cattle, and of their own making; they do pray therefore that from henceforth such forestallers, regrators, and hucksters, and all other vendors of cheese or of butter, foreigners or freemen, shall be charged to sell the same at one of the said markets, on the pain aforesaid.

Also, whereas strangers do come and bring to the city cheese of Wales, called "talgar," and house the same in Fleet Street and in Holborn, and other places, both within the city and without, and there sell it in secret, against the ancient custom, in manner aforesaid;... [the cheesemongers ask] that they may be charged to bring their wares to the said markets, in form and on the pain aforesaid....

Also, that the good folks of the said trade shall be charged every year, at the feast of St. Michael [September 29], to choose two of the most able men to oversee as to the points aforesaid, that they are well kept and observed in manner before stated. And that the persons so chosen shall have power to seize such manner of merchandise, so forfeitable, and to present the same before the mayor; in amendment of the price aforesaid, to the great profit of the commonalty in time to come....

Questions: What goods and services were available in London? What were the functions of the craft guilds? How did the crafts present themselves? What problems did the members of the guilds anticipate? What sanctions could a guild apply to its members? How do the guilds differ from each other? How had economic conditions changed recently?

56. URBAN ENVIRONMENTAL PROBLEMS AND REGULATIONS

Environmental problems have existed throughout human history; the medieval town was a place where the concentration of human and industrial wastes caused persistent trouble for the inhabitants and authorities, who had to balance economic, safety, and quality-of-life concerns through legislation, litigation, and other means.

Source: trans. H.T. Riley, *Memorials of London and London Life in the XIIIth, XIVth, and XVth Centuries* (London: Longmans, Green, and Co., 1868), pp. 77-78, 107, 171-172, 225-226, 295-296, 339-340, 355-356, 366-367, 374-375; revised.

Oath made by the Keeper of the Conduit in Cheap (1310)

William Hardy came on Saturday [October 3,] the eve of All Hallows..., before Sir Richer de Refham, the mayor, and other aldermen, and made oath that he will well and trustily, with the greatest diligence, cause the conduit in Cheap to be kept, so that neither brewers nor fishmongers shall waste the water thereof: nor will he sell the water thereof to anyone, by night or day, on peril of losing his freedom, etc.

Receivers sworn, of moneys to be taken for the use of the Conduit in Cheap (1312)

Be it remembered, that on [November 27,] the Monday next before the feast of St. Andrew the apostle, in the 6th year of the reign of King Edward II..., at the husting of common pleas, Roger de Paris, Ranulph Balle, and William Hardi were sworn before the mayor and aldermen to receive from the brewers, cooks, and fishmongers the moneys which, at their discretion, they shall assess upon such brewers, cooks, and fishmongers, for the easement which they have from the water of the conduit in Cheap. And such moneys they will trustily expend on the repair and maintenance thereof, and, on being requested, will give a faithful account thereof.

Unlawful nets condemned to be burnt (1329)

...[On April 19], in the 3rd year of the reign of King Edward III, there came Estmar Coker and John Wychard, citizens of London, together with Ralph Bourghard, serjeant of the chamber of guildhall, and brought before the mayor and aldermen, at the guildhall, John Jacob of Rith [and seven other] fishermen, because they had been found fishing in the water of Thames with twelve nets which are known as "tromkeresnet," and are a kind of kidel: the meshes of which nets — which are called "mascles" — ought to be one inch and a half in size, whereas they were hardly half an inch; and with which nets the said fishermen caught every fish, and every little fish even, that entered such nets. By reason whereof, the small fish, which are called "fry," were unable to escape or get out of the said nets; to the great damage of all the people of the city, and also, of others unto the same city resorting.

And the said John Jacob and others, being questioned as to this, did not deny it, nor could they deny that they had done as before stated.... It was therefore ordered by the mayor and aldermen that the said nets should be burnt at the cross in Cheap, and the said fishermen committed to prison, until they should have made fine.... And they were accordingly delivered to the sheriff ... and taken to Newgate.

Afterwards, on [May 19], they were brought to the guildhall, before the mayor and aldermen, and by especial favor and for charity's sake, seeing that they were but poor men, the fines were remitted to them for the present, on the understanding that they should behave themselves well for the future, and no longer presume to fish with such nets.

Ordinance that Brewers shall not waste the water of the Conduit in Cheap (1345)

At a husting [that is, court session] of pleas of land, held on [July 20] in the 19th year of the reign of King Edward III... it was shown by William de Iford, the common serjeant, on behalf of the commonalty, that whereas of old a certain conduit was built in the midst of the city of London, that so the rich and middling persons therein might have water for preparing their food, and the poor for their drink; the water aforesaid was now so wasted by brewers, and persons keeping brewhouses, and making malt, that in these modern times it will no longer suffice for the rich and middling, or for the poor, to the common loss of the whole community.

And for avoiding such common loss, it was by the mayor and aldermen agreed, with the assent of the commonalty thereto, that such brewers, or persons keeping brewhouses, or making malt, shall in future no longer presume to brew or make malt with the water of the conduit. And if anyone shall hereafter presume to make ale with the water of the conduit, or to make malt with the same, he is to lose the tankard or tyne with which he shall have carried the water from the conduit, and 40d., the first time, to the use of the commonalty; the tankard or tyne, and half a mark, the second time; and the third time, he is to lose the tankard or tyne, and 10s., and further, he is to be committed to prison, at the discretion of the mayor and aldermen there to remain.

It was also agreed at the same husting, that the fishmongers at the stocks, who wash their fish [with that water], shall incur the same penalty.

Royal order for cleansing the streets of the city, and the banks of the Thames (1357)

The king to the mayor and sheriffs of our city of London, greeting. Considering how the streets, and lanes, and other places in the city aforesaid, and the suburbs thereof, in the times of our forefathers and our own, were accustomed to be cleansed from dung, refuse heaps, and other filth, and ... to be protected from the corruption arising therefrom, from the which no little honor did accrue unto the said city, and those dwelling therein; and whereas now, when passing along the water of the Thames, we have beheld dung, and refuse heaps, and other filth, accumulated in diverse places in the said city, upon the bank of the river aforesaid, and have also perceived the fumes and other abominable stenches arising therefrom; from the corruption of which, if tolerated, great peril, both to the persons dwelling within the said city and to the nobles and others passing along the said river, will, it is feared, ensue, unless indeed some fitting remedy be speedily provided for the same —

We, wishing to take due precaution against such perils, and to preserve the honor and decency of the same city, in so far as we may, do command you, that you cause both the banks of the said river, and the streets and lanes of the same city, and the suburbs thereof, to be cleansed of dung, refuse heaps, and other filth, without delay, and the same when cleansed so to be kept; and public proclamation to be made in the city aforesaid and the suburbs thereof, and it to be strictly forbidden on our behalf, that anyone shall, on pain of heavy forfeiture unto us, place or cause to be placed dung or other filth to be accumulated in the same. And if you find any persons doing to the contrary hereof, after proclamation and prohibition are so made, then you are to cause them so to be chastised and punished, that such penalty and chastisement may cause fear and dread unto others of perpetrating the like....

Royal order for the removal of Butchers' Bridge and the prevention of the slaughtering of beasts at St. Nicholas Shambles (1369)

Edward, by the grace of God etc., to the mayor, recorder, aldermen, and sheriffs of London, greeting. Whereas of late, upon the grievous complaint of diverse prelates, nobles, and other persons of the city aforesaid, who have houses and buildings in the streets, lanes, and other places, between the Shambles of the butchers of St. Nicholas, near to the mansion of the friars minor of London, and the banks of the water of Thames near to Baynard's Castle, in the same city, shown by their petition before us and our council in our last Parliament, held at Westminster, we had heard that by reason of the slaughtering of beasts in the said shambles, and the carrying of the entrails and offal of the said beasts through the streets, lanes, and places aforesaid, to the said banks of the river, at the place called "Butchers' Bridge," where the same entrails and offal are thrown into the water aforesaid, and the dropping of the blood of such beasts between the said shambles and the waterside aforesaid, the same running along the midst of the said streets and lanes, grievous corruption and filth have been generated, both in the water and in the streets, lanes, and places aforesaid, and the parts adjacent, in the said city; so that no one, by reason of such corruption and filth, could hardly venture to abide in his house there: and we ... had determined, with the assent of all our Parliament aforesaid, that the said bridge should, before [August 1] last past, be pulled down and wholly removed,... and did accordingly give you our commands, that ... you would cause some more fitting place to be ordained outside the said city, where such slaughtering might to the least nuisance and grievance of the city aforesaid be done,... of the which you have not hitherto cared to do anything, in manifest contempt of ourselves, ... and to the no small damage and grievance of the same prelates, nobles, and people of the city aforesaid, by which we are greatly moved —

We do therefore again command you, as distinctly as we may, and do enjoin, that you will cause some certain place outside the said city to be ordained, where the slaughtering of such beasts, to the least nuisance and grievance of the commonalty of the city aforesaid, may be done, by [August 15] next ensuing, and the bridge aforesaid in the meantime to be pulled down and wholly removed; or else that you will signify unto us why you have not obeyed our command aforesaid.... And this, on pain of paying one hundred pounds, you must in no manner omit....

Complaint as to a melting-furnace leased by plumbers in East Cheap, and decision given thereon (1371)

"To the honorable men, and wise, the mayor, recorder, and aldermen of the city of London: John Walkot, Richard Scut, Thomas Clenche, and all the other good folks of Candlewick Street and of St. Clement's Lane in East Cheap, together with other neighbors of other parishes, make complaint, that whereas certain plumbers, namely, Robert Belcampe and Richard Diche, do intend to melt their solder in a vacant place called 'Wodhawe,' in the parish of St. Clement (which place one Richard Godchild rented to William de Campdene, carpenter, who has sublet it to the said plumbers), to the great damage and peril of death of all who shall smell the smoke from such melting — as may be proved by some of the same trade, and other good folks, and trustworthy, who bear witness that whosoever has smelt the smoke from the furnace has never escaped without mischief — may it please your honorable and rightful lordships, at the request of the said good folks, and for the saving of human life, to ordain a befitting remedy, as a work of charity, in such manner that such perilous work may not be done within the city, commanding, most honorable sir, if so it please you, the said Richard and William not to let the said place to the plumbers aforesaid, for doing such work there."

By reason of which petition, an order was given to John Chamberlain, serjeant, to summon here, on [September 7] then next ensuing, the aforesaid Robert Beauchampe and Richard atte Diche, to make answer as to the matters aforesaid, and further, to do as the court should direct. Upon which Thursday the parties appeared..., and the said Robert and Richard asked to hear the said petition; which being read and heard, they said that they had hired the said vacant place, which had a furnace therein, for doing their melting and following their trade there, as had been accustomed for about the last forty years to be done there; and they said that the said vacant place was not so noxious as the said John Walcot and the others above alleged, and this they were ready to prove, so far as the court should think proper..., and they asked that they might follow their trade, and do their melting in that place, in manner as before they had been there accustomed.... And the said John Walcot and the others said that the shaft of the furnace was too low, and that the smell of smoke issuing from it at the time of melting their lead was rendered all the more offensive thereby, to the nuisance [of those nearby]. And they asked that the mayor and aldermen should find a remedy for the same.

And afterwards, conference being held by the mayor and aldermen thereupon, it having been testified unto them that the place aforesaid had for many years past been let to men of the trade of plumbers, and for melting and doing other things pertaining to such trade, as they now do, and that the place was not so prejudicial as the same John Walcot and others alleged, it was agreed and granted by the mayor and aldermen that the same Robert Beauchampe and Richard atte Dyche, and others of their trade, might follow their trade at the place and furnace aforesaid, and do their melting in manner as theretofore they had been accustomed to do, provided however, that the shaft of the said furnace should be heightened, for the benefit of the neighbors there.

Ordinance for the cleansing of Smithfield (1372)

On [July 20], in the 46th year [of the reign of Edward III], the reputable men, the horse-dealers and drovers, came here, and delivered unto the mayor and aldermen a certain petition, in these words:

"To the mayor, recorder, and aldermen of the city of London, the dealers of Smithfield show that … they have granted and assented among them that, for the term of three years next ensuing after the date of this petition, for every horse sold in the said field there shall be paid one penny, for every ox and cow one half-penny, for every eight sheep one penny, and for every four swine one penny, by the seller, and the same by the purchaser, who buys the same for resale. Wherefore they pray that this ordinance may be enrolled in the chamber of the guildhall, to be in force for three years only, according to the good discretion of the said good lords; the same ordinance beginning to hold good and be in force at the feast of St. James the Apostle [July 25], in the 46th year of our lord the king now reigning."

And conference being held between the mayor and aldermen hereupon, it was agreed and granted by them, with the assent of the same dealers and drovers, that the said pennies be levied for such three years in form aforesaid, for cleansing the field of Smithfield by the aid thereof....

Inundation in the vicinity of St. Mary's Hospital outside Bishopsgate, from a defective watercourse (1373)

It was presented, upon the oath of twelve reputable men of the Ward of Bishopsgate, at the Wardmote held before Jon Lytle, alderman of the same Ward, on [December 6], in the 47th year [of Edward III], that after great rains the waters coming down from the fields of the Lord Bishop of London into Berward's Lane, and from the street outside Bishopsgate, used to and rightly ought to have their course through an arched passage beneath a certain tenement belonging to Nicholas de Altone, which Thomas de Leuesham, skinner, then held, opposite to the Berward's Lane aforesaid, towards the Moor of London; which watercourse was then choked up: by reason whereof, in winter-time every year, water, a foot or more in depth, overflowed and rose in the church of the Hospital of St. Mary outside Bishopsgate, and in many of the houses there, and also in many houses and gardens of the whole vicinity of Berward's Lane; whereby very many walls and partitions, throughout the whole vicinity, were oftentimes thrown down or torn up; so much so that Sir Thomas, the then prior of the Hospital aforesaid, and the convent of that place, and all the men of the vicinity, were in doubt whether the greatest damage and peril might not shortly befall them and their tenements, unless the said watercourse should be speedily repaired. Therefore the said Thomas was warned to be here on [February 5], to show if he had anything to say for himself, why he ought not to clear out and cleanse the passage aforesaid, that the water might have its course there, as it was accustomed to have....

Questions: What environmental problems and concerns did fourteenth-century London-ers have? How did they respond to these problems? Who had the authority to order changes and on what grounds? What attitudes and assumptions about the urban envi-ronment underlie their actions? How do these conditions and responses compare with modern ones?

57. JEAN FROISSART'S CHRONICLE: ON THE BATTLE OF CRÉCY

Under Edward III (1327-77), England became involved in the Hundred Years' War, a protracted but intermittent conflict with France, over a range of issues including English claims to lands in France, the succession to the French throne, and Flemish politics. In 1346 the two sides fought at Crécy; the story of the battle is told by the great French chronicler Froissart in his long chronicle of the war.

Source: trans. T. Johnes, *Froissart's Chronicles* (London, 1803); reprinted in F.A. Ogg, *A Source Book of Mediaeval History: Documents Illustrative of European Life and Institutions from the German Invasions to the Renaissance* (New York: American Book Company, 1908), pp. 428-436; revised.

The king of England, as I have mentioned before, encamped this Friday in the plain [east of the village of Crécy], for he found the country abounding in pro-visions; but if they should have failed, he had an abundance in the carriages which attended him. The army set about furbishing and repairing their armor; and the king gave a supper that evening to the earls and barons of his army, where they made good cheer. On their taking leave, the king remained alone with the lord of his bed-chamber. He retired into his oratory and, falling on his knees before the altar, prayed to God, that if he should fight his enemies on the morrow he might come off with honor. About midnight he went to his bed and, rising early the next day, he and the prince of Wales [Edward, the Black Prince] heard Mass and took communion. The greater part of his army did the same, confessed, and made proper preparations.

After Mass the king ordered his men to arm themselves and assemble on the ground he had before fixed on. He had enclosed a large park near a wood, on the rear of his army, in which he placed all his baggage-wagons and horses; and this park had but one entrance. His men-at-arms and archers remained on foot. The king afterwards ordered, through his constable and his two marshals, that the army should be divided into three battalions....

The king then mounted a small palfrey, having a white wand in his hand, and, attended by his two marshals on each side of him, he rode through all the ranks, encouraging and entreating the army, that they should guard his honor. He spoke this so gently, and with such a cheerful countenance, that all who had been dejected were immediately comforted by seeing and hearing him.

When he had thus visited all the battalions, it was near ten o'clock. He retired to his own division and ordered them all to eat heartily afterwards and drink a glass. They ate and drank at their ease; and, having packed up pots, barrels, etc., in the carts, they returned to their battalions, according to the marshals' orders, and seated themselves on the ground, placing their helmets and bows before them, that they might be the fresher when their enemies should arrive.

That same Saturday, the king of France arose betimes and heard Mass in the monastery of St. Peter's in Abbeville, where he was lodged. Having ordered his army to do the same, he left that town after sunrise. When he had marched about two leagues from Abbeville and was approaching the enemy, he was advised to form his army in order of battle, and to let those on foot march forward, that they might not be trampled on by the horses. The king, upon this, sent off four knights — the lord Moyne of Bastleberg, the lord of Noyers, the lord of Beaujeu, and the lord of Aubigny — who rode so near to the English that they could clearly distinguish their position. The English plainly perceived that they were come to reconnoitre. However, they took no notice of it, but suffered them to return unmolested. When the king of France saw them coming back, he halted his army, and the knights, pushing through the crowds, came near the king, who said to them, "My lords, what news?" They looked at each other, without opening their mouths; for no one chose to speak first. At last the king addressed himself to the lord Moyne, who was attached to the king of Bohemia, and had performed very many gallant deeds, so that he was esteemed one of the most valiant knights in Christendom. The lord Moyne said, "Sir, I will speak, since it pleases you to order me, but with the asssistance of my companions. We have advanced far enough to reconnoitre your enemies. Know, then, that they are drawn up in three battalions and are awaiting you. I would advise, for my part (submitting, however, to better counsel), that you halt your army here and quarter them for the night; for before the rear shall come up and the army be properly drawn out, it will be very late. Your men will be tired and in disorder, while they will find your enemies fresh and properly arrayed. On the morrow, you may draw up your army more at your ease and may reconnoitre at leisure on what part it will be most advantageous to begin the attack; for, be assured, they will wait for you."

The king commanded that it should be so done; and the two marshals rode, one towards the front, and the other to the rear, crying out, "Halt banners, in the name of God and St. Denis." Those that were in the front halted; but those behind said they would not halt until they were as far forward as the front. When the front perceived the rear pushing on, they pushed forward; and neither the king nor the marshals could stop them, but they marched on without any order until they came in sight of their enemies. As soon as the foremost rank saw them, they fell back at once in great disorder, which alarmed those in the rear, who thought they had been fighting. There was then space and room enough for them to have passed forward, had they been willing to do so. Some did so, but others remained behind.

All the roads between Abbeville and Crécy were covered with common people, who, when they had come within three leagues of their enemies, drew their swords, crying out, "Kill, kill"; and with them were many great lords who were eager to make show of their courage. There is no man, unless he had been present, who can imagine, or describe truly, the confusion of that day, especially the bad management and disorder of the French, whose troops were beyond number.

The English, who were drawn up in three divisions and seated on the ground, on seeing their enemies advance, arose boldly and fell into their ranks. That of the prince was the first to do so, whose archers were formed in the manner of a portcullis, or harrow, and the men-at-arms in the rear. The earls of Northampton and Arundel, who commanded the second division, had posted themselves in good order on his wing to assist and succor the prince, if necessary.

You must know that these kings, dukes, earls, barons, and lords of France did not advance in any regular order, but one after the other, or in any way most pleasing to themselves. As soon as the king of France came in sight of the English his blood began to boil, and he cried out to his marshals, "Order the Genoese forward, and begin the battle, in the name of God and St. Denis."

There were about fifteen thousand Genoese cross-bowmen; but they were quite fatigued, having marched on foot that day six leagues, completely armed, and with their cross-bows. They told the constable that they were not in a fit condition to do any great things that day in battle. The earl of Alençon, hearing this, said, "This is what one gets by employing such scoundrels, who fail when there is any need for them."

During this time a heavy rain fell, accompanied by thunder and a very terrible eclipse of the sun; and before this rain a great flight of crows hovered in the air over all those battalions, making a loud noise. Shortly afterwards it cleared up and the sun shone very brightly; but the Frenchmen had it in their faces, and the English at their backs.

When the Genoese were somewhat in order they approached the English and set up a loud shout in order to frighten them; but the latter remained quite still and did not seem to hear it. They then set up a second shout and advanced a little forward; but the English did not move. They hooted a third time, advancing with their cross-bows presented, and began to shoot. The English archers then advanced one step forward and shot their arrows with such force and quickness that it seemed as if it snowed.

When the Genoese felt these arrows, which pierced their arms, heads, and through their armor, some of them cut the strings of their cross-bows, others flung them on the ground, and all turned about and retreated, quite discomfited. The French had a large body of men-at-arms on horseback, richly dressed, to support the Genoese. The king of France, seeing them fall back, cried out, "Kill me those scoundrels; for they stop up our road, without any reason." You would then have seen the above-mentioned men-at-arms lay about them, killing all that they could of these runaways.

The English continued shooting as vigorously and quickly as before. Some of their arrows fell among the horsemen, who were sumptuously equipped, and, killing and wounding many, made them caper and fall among the Genoese, so that they were in such confusion they could never rally again. In the English army there were some Cornish and Welshmen on foot who had armed themselves with large knives. These, advancing through the ranks of the men-at-arms and archers, who made way for them, came upon the French when they were in this danger and, falling upon earls, barons, knights and squires, slew many, at which the king of England was afterwards much exasperated.

The valiant king of Bohemia was slain there. He was called Charles of Luxemburg, for he was the son of the gallant king and emperor, Henry of Luxemburg. Having heard the order of the battle, he inquired where his son, the lord Charles, was. His attendants answered that they did not know, but believed that he was fighting. The king said to them: "Sirs, you are all my people, my friends and brethren at arms this day; therefore, as I am blind, I request of you to lead me so far into the engagement that I may strike one stroke with my sword." The knights replied that they would lead him forward immediately; and, in order that they might not lose him in the crowd, they fastened the reins of all their horses together, and put the king at their head, that he might gratify his wish, and advanced towards the enemy. The king rode in among the enemy, and made good use of his sword; for he and his companions fought most gallantly. They advanced so far that they were all slain; and on the morrow they were found on the ground, with their horses all tied together.

Early in the day, some French, Germans, and Savoyards had broken through the archers of the prince's battalion, and had engaged with the men-at-arms, upon which the second battalion came to his aid; and it was time, for otherwise he would have been hard pressed. The first division, seeing the danger they were in, sent a knight [Sir Thomas Norwich] in great haste to the king of England, who was posted upon an eminence, near a windmill. On the knight's arrival, he said, "Sir, the earl of Warwick, the lord Stafford, the lord Reginald Cobham, and the others who are about your son are vigorously attacked by the

French; and they entreat that you come to their assistance with your battalion for, if the the number of the French should increase, they fear he will have too much to do."

The king replied, "Is my son dead, unhorsed, or so badly wounded that he cannot support himself?" "Nothing of the sort, thank God," rejoined the knight; "but he is in so hot an engagement that he has great need of your help." The king answered, "Now, Sir Thomas, return to those who sent you and tell them from me not to send again for me this day, or expect that I shall come, let what will happen, as long as my son has life; and say that I command them to let the boy win his spurs; for I am determined, if it please God, that all the glory and honor of this day shall be given to him, and to those into whose care I have entrusted him." The knight returned to his lords and related the king's answer, which greatly encouraged them and made them regret that they had ever sent such a message.

Late after vespers, the king of France had not more about him than sixty men, every one included. Sir John of Hainault, who was of the number, had once remounted the king; for the latter's horse had been killed under him by an arrow. He said to the king, "Sir, retreat while you have an opportunity, and do not expose yourself so needlessly. If you have lost this battle, another time you will be the conqueror." After he had said this, he took the bridle of the king's horse and led him off by force; for he had before entreated him to retire.

The king rode on until he came to the castle of La Broyes, where he found the gates shut, for it was very dark. The king ordered the governor of it to be summoned. He came upon the battlements and asked who it was that called at such an hour. The king answered, "Open, open, governor; it is the fortune of France." The governor, hearing the king's voice, immediately descended, opened the gate, and let down the bridge. The king and his company entered the castle; but he had with him only five barons — Sir John Hainault, the lord Charles of Montmorency, the lord of Beaujeu, the lord of Aubigny, and the lord of Montfort. The king would not bury himself in such a place as that, but, having taken some refreshments, set out again with his attendants about midnight, and rode on, under the direction of guides who were well acquainted with the country, until, about daybreak, he came to Amiens, where he halted.

This Saturday the English never quitted their ranks in pursuit of anyone, but remained on the field, guarding their positions and defending themselves against all who attacked them. The battle was ended at the hour of vespers. When, on this Saturday night, the English heard no more hooting or shouting, nor any more crying out to particular lords, or their banners, they looked upon the field as their own and their enemies as beaten.

They made great fires and lighted torches because of the darkness of the night. King Edward then came down from his post, who all that day had not put on his helmet, and, with his whole battalion, advanced to the prince of

Wales, whom he embraced in his arms and kissed, and said, "Sweet son, God give you good preference. You are my son, for most loyally have you acquitted yourself this day. You are worthy to be a sovereign." The prince bowed down very low and humbled himself, giving all honor to the king his father.

The English, during the night, made frequent thanksgivings to the Lord for the happy outcome of the day, and without rioting; for the king had forbidden all riot or noise.

Questions: Edward III and his contemporaries actively promoted chivalric values; how is that interest evident in this text? What is the author's attitude toward the two sides? Why do the English win?

58. THE BLACK PRINCE'S LETTER ANNOUNCING VICTORY AT POITIERS

Ten years after Crécy, the prince of Wales again proved his mettle by leading the English army to a similar victory over the French at the battle of Poitiers. Here he writes to the city of London, telling the citizens of his success.

Source: trans. H.T. Riley, *Memorials of London and London Life in the XIIIth, XIVth, and XVth Centuries* (London: Longmans, Green, and Co., 1868), pp. 285-288; revised.

Very dear and very much beloved. As concerning news in the parts where we are, know that since the time when we informed our most dread lord and father, the king, that it was our purpose to ride forth against the enemies in the parts of France, we took our road through the country of Périgueux and of Limousin, and straight on towards Bourges in Vienne, where we expected to have found the [French] king's son, the count of Poitiers; and the sovereign cause for our going towards these parts was that we expected to have had news of our said lord and father, the king, as to his passage; and seeing that we did not find the said count there, or any other great force, we turned towards [the river] Loire, and commanded our people to ride forth and reconnoitre if we could find a passage anywhere: the which people met the enemy, and had to enter into conflict, so that some of the said enemies were killed or taken; and the prisoners so taken said that the king of France had sent Grismoutoun, who was in that company, to obtain for him certain news of us, and of our force; and the said king, for the same purpose, had sent in another direction the sieur de Creon, Messire Bursigaud, the mareschal de Clermont, and other. And the same prisoners declared that the king had made up his mind for certain to fight with us, at whatever time we should be on the road towards Tours, he meeting us in the direction of Orléans.

And on the morrow, where we were posted, there came news that the said sieur de Craon and Bursigaud were in a castle very near to our quarters; and we determined to go there, and so came and took up our quarters around them; and we agreed to assault the said place, the which was gained by us by force, and was quite full of their people, both prisoners and slain, and also some of ours were killed there; but the said sieurs de Craon and Bursigaud withdrew themselves into a strong tower which was there, and which occupied us five days before it was taken; and there they surrendered. And there we were assured that all the bridges upon the Loire were broken down, and that we could nowhere find a passage; whereupon, we took our road straight towards Tours; and there we remained four days before the city, in which were the count of Anjou and the Mareschal de Clermont, with a great force of troops. And upon our departing from thence, we took the road so as to pass certain dangers by water, and with the intention of meeting with our most dear cousin, the duke of Lancaster, of whom we had certain news, that he would make haste to draw towards us. At which time the cardinal de Perigord came to us at Montbazon, three leagues from Tours, where he spoke to us fully as to matters touching a truce and peace. Upon which parley we made answer to him, that peace we had no power to make, and that we would not intermeddle therewith, without the command and the wishes of the king, our most dear lord and father; nor yet as to a truce were we at that time of opinion that it would be the best thing for us to assent thereto, for there we were more fully assured that the [French] king had prepared in every way to fight with us.

Whereupon, we withdrew ourselves from thence towards Chastel Heraud, by passage over the stream of the Vienne; where we remained four days, waiting to know for greater certainty of him. And the king came with his force to Chauvigny, five leagues from us, to pass the same river, in the direction of Poitiers. And thereupon, we determined to hasten towards him, upon the road along which he would have to pass, so as to have a fight with him; but his battalions had passed before we had come to the place where we intended to meet him, save a part only of their people, about 700 men-at-arms, who engaged with ours; and there were taken the counts de Sousseire and de Junhy, the sieur de Castillon, a great number of others being both taken and slain, both on their side and ours. And then our people pursued them as far as Chauvigny, full three leagues further; for which reason we were obliged that day to take up our quarters as near to that place as we could, that we might collect our men. And on the morrow we took our road straight towards the king, and sent out our scouts, who found him with his army; [and he] set himself in battle array at one league from Poitiers, in the fields; and we went as near to him as we could take up our post, we ourselves on foot and in battle array, and ready to fight with him.

Where came the said cardinal, requesting very earnestly for a little respite, that so there might parley together certain persons of either side, and so attempt to bring about an understanding and good peace; the which he undertook that he would bring about to a good end. Whereupon, we took counsel, and granted him his request; upon which, there were ordered certain persons of the one side and the other, to treat upon this matter; which treating was of no effect. And then the said cardinal wished to obtain a truce, by way of putting off the battle at his pleasure; to which truce we would not assent. And the French asked that certain knights on the one side and the other should take equal shares, so that the battle might not in any manner fail: and in such manner was that day delayed; and the battalions on the one side and the other remained all night, each one in its place, and until the morrow, about half Prime; and as to some troops that were between the said main armies, neither would give any advantage in commencing the attack upon the other. And for default of victuals, as well as for other reasons, it was agreed that we should take our way, flanking them, in such manner that if they wished for battle or to draw towards us, in a place that was not very much to our disadvantage, we should be the first; and so forthwith it was done. Whereupon battle was joined, on [September 19,] the eve of the day before St. Matthew; and, God be praised for it, the enemy was dicomfited, and the king was taken, and his son; and a great number of other great people were both taken and slain; as our very dear bachelor Messire Neele Lorraine, our chamberlain, the bearer hereof, who has very full knowledge thereon, will know how to inform and show you more fully, as we are not able to write to you; to him you should give full faith and credence; and may our Lord have you in his keeping. Given under our privy seal, at Bordeaux, the 22nd day of October.

Questions: Compare this narrative with Froissart's account of Crécy: how do they differ in tone, emphasis, and viewpoint? Why would the prince have written to London?

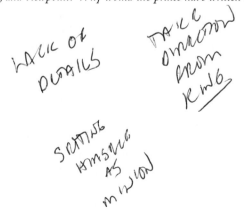

59. ACCOUNTS OF THE BLACK DEATH AND ITS EFFECTS

While the Great Famine had already stopped the population boom, it was the Black Death that had the truly catastrophic long-term impact demographically and in many other ways. The bubonic plague arrived in southern Europe from the east in 1347 and quickly spread northward; by the end of 1349, according to modern estimates, about one third of Europe's population had died from it. Excerpted below are two chronicle accounts from England, one with a national and one with a local focus, and two accounts from manorial records of new arrangements made after the devastation of the workforce.

Source: trans. R. Horrox, *The Black Death* (Manchester: Manchester University Press, 1994), pp. 68-69, 76-80, 285-287.

Henry Knighton's Chronicle

In that year and the following year there was a universal mortality of men throughout the world. It began first in India, then in Tarsus, then it reached the Saracens and finally the Christians and Jews....

On a single day 1,312 people died in Avignon, according to a calculation made in the pope's presence. On another day more than 400 died. 358 of the Dominicans in Provence died during Lent. At Montpellier only seven friars survived out of 140. At Magdalen seven survived out of 160, which is quite enough. From 140 Minorites at Marseilles not one remained to carry the news to the rest.... At the same time the plague raged in England. It began in the autumn in various places and after racing across the country it ended at the same time in the following year....

Then the most lamentable plague penetrated the coast through Southampton and came to Bristol, and virtually the whole town was wiped out. It was as if sudden death had marked them down beforehand, for few lay sick for more than 2 or 3 days, or even for half a day. Cruel death took just two days to burst out all over a town. At Leicester, in the little parish of St. Leonard, more than 380 died; in the parish of Holy Cross more than 400; in the parish of St. Margaret 700; and a great multitude in every parish. The bishop of Lincoln sent word through the whole diocese, giving general power to every priest (among the regular as well as the secular clergy) to hear confession and grant absolution with full and complete authority except only in cases of debt. In such cases the penitent, if it lay within his power, ought to make satisfaction while he lived, but certainly others should do it from his goods after his death. Similarly the pope granted plenary remission of all sins to those at the point of death, the absolution to be for one time only, and the right to each person to choose his confessor as he wished. This concession was to last until the following Easter.

In the same year there was a great murrain of sheep throughout the realm, so much so that in one place more than 5,000 sheep died in a single pasture, and their bodies were so corrupt that no animal or bird would touch them. And because of the fear of death everything fetched a low price. For there were very few people who cared for riches, or indeed for anything else. A man could have a horse previously valued at 40s. for half a mark, a good fat ox for 4s., a cow for 12d., a bullock for 6d., a fat sheep for 4d., a ewe for 3d., a lamb for 2d., a large pig for 5d., a stone of wool for 9d. And sheep and cattle roamed unchecked through the fields and through the standing corn, and there was no one to chase them and round them up. For want of watching animals died in uncountable numbers in the fields and in bye-ways and hedges throughout the whole country; for there was so great a shortage of servants and laborers that there was no one who knew what needed to be done. There was no memory of so inexorable and fierce a mortality since the time of Vortigern, king of the Britons, in whose time, as Bede testifies in his *De gestis Anglorum*, there were not enough living to bury the dead. In the following autumn it was not possible to hire a reaper for less than 8d. and his food, or a mower for 12d. with his food. For which reason many crops rotted unharvested in the fields; but in the year of the pestilence, as mentioned above, there was so great an abundance of all types of grain that no one cared.

The Scots, hearing of the cruel plague of the English, declared that it had befallen them through the revenging hand of God, and they took to swearing "by the foul death of England" — or so the common report resounded in the ears of the English. And thus the Scots, believing that the English were overwhelmed by the terrible vengeance of God, gathered in the forest of Selkirk with the intention of invading the whole realm of England. The fierce mortality came upon them, and the sudden cruelty of a monstrous death winnowed the Scots. Within a short space of time around 5,000 died, and the rest, weak and strong alike, decided to retreat to their own country. But the English, following, surprised them and killed many of them.

Master Thomas Bradwardine was consecrated as archbishop of Canterbury by the pope, and on his return to England he went to London, where he died within two days. He was renowned above all other clerks in Christendom, especially in theology but also in the other liberal arts. At that time there was such a great shortage of priests everywhere that many churches were widowed and lacked the divine offices, masses, matins, vespers, and the sacraments and sacramentals. A man could scarcely get a chaplain for less than £10 or 10 marks to minister to any church, and whereas before the pestilence there had been a glut of priests, and a man could get a chaplain for 4 or 5 marks, or for 2 marks with board and lodging, in this time there was scarcely anyone who would accept a vicarage at £20 or 20 marks. But within a short time a great crowd of men whose wives had died in the pestilence rushed into priestly orders. Many of them were illiterate, no better than laymen — for even if they could read, they did not understand what they read.

The hide of an ox was priced at a mere 12d., a pair of shoes at 10d., 12d. or 14d., a pair of boots at 3s. or 4s. Meanwhile the king sent commands into every county that reapers and other workers should not take more than they were accustomed to take, under penalties laid down by the statute which he had introduced to this end. But the workers were so above themselves and so bloody-minded that they took no notice of the king's command. If anyone wished to hire them he had to submit to their demands, for either his fruit and standing corn would be lost or he had to pander to the arrogance and greed of the workers. When it was brought to the king's attention that people were not obeying his orders, but were giving higher wages to the workers, he levied heavy fines on abbots, priors, greater and lesser knights, and on others, of both greater and lesser standing, in the country; taking 100s. from some, 40s. or 20s. from others, depending on their ability to pay. And he took 20s. from each plowland nationwide, and in this way raised as much as a fifteenth [that is, a customary tax]. Then the king had numerous workers arrested and sent to prison, and many of these escaped and took to the woods and if they were captured they were heavily fined. And most took oaths that they would not take more than their old daily wages, and thereby secured their release from prison. The same was done to artisans in boroughs and towns.

In the same year, on 25 October, the body of St. Thomas of Hereford was translated [that is, moved to a new tomb]. After the aforesaid pestilence many buildings of all sizes in every city fell into total ruin for want of inhabitants. Likewise, many villages and hamlets were deserted, with no house remaining in them, because everyone who had lived there was dead, and indeed many of these villages were never inhabited again. In the following winter there was such a lack of workers in all areas of activity that it was thought that there had hardly ever been such a shortage before; for a man's farm animals and other livestock wandered about without a shepherd and all his possessions were left unguarded. And as a result all essentials were so expensive that something which had previously cost 1d. was now worth 4d. or 5d. Confronted by this shortage of workers and the scarcity of goods the great men of the realm, and the lesser landowners who had tenants, remitted part of the rent so that their tenants did not leave. Some remitted half the rent, some more and some less; some remitted it for two years, some for three and some for one — whatever they could agree with their tenants. Likewise those whose tenants held by the year, by the performance of labor services (as is customary in the case of serfs), found that they had to release and remit such works, and either pardon rents completely or levy them on easier terms, otherwise houses would be irretrievably ruined and land left uncultivated. And all victuals and other necessities were extremely dear.

Meaux Abbey Chronicle, by Thomas Burton

When Abbot Hugh had ruled the monastery for 9 years, 11 months and 11 days (at which time there were 42 monks and 7 lay brothers, not counting himself), he died in the great pestilence, along with 32 monks and lay brothers. This pestilence grew so strong in our monastery, as it did in other places, that within the month of August the abbot, 22 monks and 6 lay brothers died; of whom the abbot and 5 monks were buried together on a single day. Other deaths followed, so that when the pestilence ceased only 10 monks and no lay brothers were left alive out of the 50 monks and lay brothers. From this time the rents and goods of the monastery began to dwindle, largely because the majority of our tenants had died, and because after the abbot, prior, cellarer, bursar and other experienced men and officials had died, the survivors made misguided grants of the goods and possessions of the monastery.

The abbot died on 12 August 1349 and was buried in the lay brothers' choir before the crucifix which he had had put up. In addition he left the house a debt of more than £500 and the monastery unprovided with any supplies of grain.

At the beginning of 1349, during Lent on [March 27,] the Friday before Passion Sunday, an earthquake was felt throughout England. Our monks of Meaux were at vespers and had come to the verse "He hath put down the mighty" in the Magnificat, when they were thrown from their stalls by the earthquake and sent sprawling on the ground. The earthquake was quickly followed in this part of the country by the pestilence.

In 1349 there befell that great and universal pestilence. The pope accordingly sent to England a general absolution, to last for 3 months from its publication, for all who died of the pestilence within those three months. He instituted a new mass for assuaging the plague, and within the papal curia he took part in person in solemn processions of the clergy and people. In addition he had a beautiful silver statue made in honor of the Blessed Virgin Mary and had it carried in these processions, until the pestilence was laid to rest in the curia by the merits of the Blessed Virgin.

It was said that the pestilence had first broken out strongly among the infidel. As a result the Saracens who survived, believing that the judgment of God had blasted them because they had not adopted the Christian faith, were inclined to believe in Christ. They sent men into Christendom to investigate whether the pestilence was as strong there as it was among them, but when the messengers returned and announced that there was the same general pestilence among the Christians as among the Saracens, they again refused to believe in Christ.

This pestilence held such sway in England at that time that there were hardly enough people left alive to bury the dead, or enough burial grounds to hold them. During that time two closes or crofts were consecrated for the burial of the dead in London, and two monasteries were afterwards founded in them, one of the Cistercian order, the other of the Carthusians. The pestilence grew so strong that men and women dropped dead while walking in the streets, and in innumerable households and many villages not one person was left alive. However, God's providence ensured that, in most places, chaplains survived unharmed until the end of the pestilence in order to perform the exequies of those who died. But, after the funerals of the laymen, chaplains were swallowed by death in great numbers, as others had been before.

Valuation of the manor of Wood Eaton, Oxfordshire

Walter Dolle, virgater, holds a messuage, 18 acres of arable and 2 acres of meadow. He used to pay ... 5s. rent; perform one plowing (with the lord providing a meal); give one hen; give eggs at Easter; render pannage [that is, payment to pasture pigs in woodland]; harrow for one day (which shall consist of harrowing 3 roods of land); weed for one day with another man; cart hay for a day; and perform three bedereaps [or boon-works, that is, days of work at the lord's request] with three men in autumn, without food, and a fourth with the same number of men with a meal provided by the lord.

When, however, it was not at farm he used to work for five days a week from Michaelmas [September 29] to Martinmas [November 11]; and for four days a week from Martinmas to the feast of St. John the Baptist [June 24]; and perform carrying service as far as Eynsham on Sundays should it be necessary. He also rendered pannage, aid, and toll if he brewed for resale. He could not sell an ox or a male foal, or give his daughter in marriage without the lord's licence. A day's work was defined as follows: when threshing, he threshed one measure of wheat (four measures making one bushel), two measures of barley, three of oats or one of beans and peas; when ditching he dug one perch [that is, 5 yards], two armslength deep; when hedging he did two perches.

If it was at farm without labor services, he collected nuts for one day in the lord's wood, and took two loads of wood or four faggots [that is, bundles of sticks] to court for Christmas.

At the time of the mortality or pestilence, which occurred in 1349, scarcely two tenants remained in the manor, and they expressed their intention of leaving unless Brother Nicholas de Upton, then abbot and lord of the manor, made a new agreement with them and other incoming tenants. And he made an agreement with them as follows: that Walter and other tenants of the same standing would pay an entry fine to the lord whenever they took possession of a tenement; they would attend every court; they would give their best animal as heriot [that is, a death tax]; they would not sell an ox or male foal, or give their daughters in marriage without the lord's licence. They would perform three boon-works or plowings at the two sowings, with a meal provided by the lord for those using their own plows; perform three bedereaps [that is, days of harvesting] with two men without a meal, and a fourth with the same number of men with a meal provided by the lord; reap the lord's hay or corn for 12 days without a meal; and render 13s. 4d.rent each year as long as it pleases the lord — and would that it might please the lord for ever, since the aforesaid services were not worth so much. However, lords in future must do as seems best to them.

Manor Court Rolls from Aldham, Sussex

As the result of a plea from various unfree tenants on various manors of the lord John de Vere, Earl of Oxford, concerning the waiving of part of the labor services and customs which they used to perform before the pestilence, and which now (as everyone knows) they lack the power to perform in their entirety, the said earl wrote to me, Thomas de Chabham (steward of all his estates) about the complaint of all the unfree tenants, authorising me, in my capacity as steward, to use my discretion in coming to an agreement with all the unfree tenants wherever it seemed to me that the lord's interests made it necessary, and, as a special favor on the part of the said earl, to release part of the works and customs which they used to perform before the pestilence. And since I have been given to understand by the earl's unfree tenants on his manor of Aldham that they cannot hold their land by performing all the works and customs which they used to perform before the pestilence, as has been very clearly demonstrated to the earl and his council, be it known to the steward, the auditors of the account, the tenants holding land there, the bailiffs, reeves and all the lord's officials that I, the said Thomas de Chabbam, by virtue of the authority vested in me by the said letters, have, as a special favor, come to an agreement with the unfree tenants of the earl's manor of Aldham concerning part of their labor service and customs from the feast of the Purification last past [2 February] for the following three years.

At this court I have granted to all the unfree tenants who hold 15-acreware tenements in the said manor that a third part of their customary plowing works and all their carrying services shall be waived annually during the said term. Item, I have granted to all the tenants of 8-acreware tenements in the said manor that a third part of their plowing service and all their carrying services be waived during the same period. Item, I have granted to Nicholas Aylwyne,

Nicholas Skelman and John Crembel, cottars, who each owes 80 works a year, that 20 of the works and all the carrying services shall be waived annually during the same period. Item, I have granted to John Aylwyne who holds a two-acreware tenement and owes 40 works and carrying service, that 10 works and all his carrying service shall be waived during the same period. I have released the works and carrying services for the specified period because, according to the terms of the authority vested in me by the earl, it seems to me that the concession is necessary.

Questions: What were the effects of the plague? How can apparently contradictory economic effects be explained? How did lords explain the new agreements they had made? What attitudes did the elite hold toward laboring people?

60. WAGE AND PRICE REGULATIONS

As working people found themselves in demand and able to earn higher wages, as they moved around and negotiated for better terms of employment, and as land became a glut on the market and rents fell, the response of the authorities was to try to legislate their way back to pre-plague conditions.

Source: Ordinance of Laborers trans. G.C. Lee, *Source-Book of English History: Leading Documents* (New York: Henry Holt and Company, 1900), pp. 206-208, revised; London regulations trans. H.T. Riley, *Memorials of London and London Life in the XIIIth, XIVth, and XVth Centuries* (London: Longmans, Green, and Co., 1868), pp. 250-251, 253-258, revised.

The Ordinance of Laborers, 1349

Because a great part of the people, and especially of workmen and servants, have lately died in the pestilence, many, seeing the necessities of masters and great scarcity of servants, will not serve unless they may receive excessive wages, and others preferring to beg in idleness rather than by labor to get their living; we, considering the grievous incommodities which may hereafter come from the lack, especially of plowmen and such laborers, have upon deliberation and treaty with the prelates and the nobles and learned men assisting us, with their unanimous counsel ordained:

That every man and woman of our realm of England, of whatever condition he be, free or bond, able in body, and within the age of sixty years, not living in merchandise, nor exercising any craft, nor having of his own whereof he may live, nor land of his own about whose tillage he may occupy himself, and not serving any other, if he be required to serve in suitable service, his estate considered, he shall be bound to serve him which shall so require him; and take only the wages, livery, meed, or salary which were accustomed to be given in the places where he is obliged to serve, during the twentieth year of our reign of England, or five or six other common years next before. Provided always, that the lords be preferred before others in their bondmen or their land tenants, so in their service to be retained; so that, nevertheless, the said lords shall retain no more than be necessary for them. And if any such man or woman being so required to serve will not do the same, and that be proved by two true men before the sheriff, bailiff, lord, or constable of the town where the same shall happen to be done, he shall immediately be taken by them or any of them, and committed to the next jail, there to remain under strait keeping, till he find surety to serve in the form aforesaid.

If any reaper, mower, other workman or servant, of whatever estate or condition he be, retained in any man's service, do depart from the said service without reasonable cause or license, before the term agreed, he shall have pain of imprisonment; and no one, under the same penalty, shall presume to receive or retain such a one in his service.

No one, moreover, shall pay or promise to pay to anyone more wages, liveries, meed, or salary than was accustomed, as is before said; nor shall anyone in any other manner demand or receive them, upon pain of doubling of that which shall have been so paid, promised, required or received, to him who thereof shall feel himself aggrieved; and if none such will sue, then the same shall be applied to any of the people that will sue; and such suit shall be in the court of the lord of the place where such case shall happen.

And if lords of towns or manors presume in any point to come against this present ordinance, either by them or by their servants, then suit shall be made against them in the form aforesaid, in the counties, wapentakes, and tithings, or such courts of ours, for the penalty of treble that so paid or promised by them or their servants. And if any before this present ordinance hath covenanted with any so to serve for more wages, he shall not be bound, by reason of the said covenant, to pay more than at another time was wont to be paid to such a person; nor, under the same penalty, shall presume to pay more.

Also, saddlers, skinners, white tawyers, cordwainers, tailors, smiths, carpenters, masons, tilers, shipwrights, carters, and all other artificers and workmen, shall not take for their labor and workmanship more than was wont to be paid to such persons the said twentieth year, and other common years next preceding, as before is said, in the place where they shall happen to work; and if any man take more he shall be committed to the next jail, in manner as before is said.

Also, that butchers, fishmongers, innkeepers, brewers, bakers, poulterers, and all other sellers of all manner of victuals shall be bound to sell the same victuals for a reasonable price, having respect to the price that such victuals be sold at in the places adjoining, so that the same sellers have moderate gains, and not excessive, reasonably to be required according to the distance of the place from which the said victuals be carried; and if any sell such victuals in any other manner, and thereof be convicted, in the manner and form aforesaid, he shall pay the double of the same that he so received to the party injured, or in default of him, to any other that will sue in this behalf. And the mayors and bailiffs of cities, boroughs, merchant towns, and others, and of the ports and maritime places, shall have power to inquire of all and singular, which shall in any thing offend against this, and to levy the said penalty to the use of them at whose suit such offenders shall be convicted. And if the same mayors and bailiffs be negligent in carrying out these provisions, and are convicted of such before our justices, to be assigned by us, then the same mayors and bailiffs shall be compelled by the same justices to pay the treble of the thing so sold to the party injured, or to any other that will sue in his place; and nevertheless toward us they shall be grievously punished.

And because many strong beggars, as long as they may live by begging, do refuse to labor, giving themselves to idleness and vice, and sometimes to theft and other abomination; none, upon the said pain of imprisonment, shall, under the color of pity or alms, give anything to such, which may labor, or presume to favor them in their idleness, so that thereby they may be compelled to labor for their necessary living.

London Wage and Price Regulations, 1350

To amend and redress the damages and grievances which the good folks of the city, rich and poor, have suffered and received within the past year, by reason of masons, carpenters, plasterers, tilers, and all manner of laborers, who take immeasurably more than they have been wont to take, by assent of Walter Turk, mayor, the aldermen, and all the commonalty of the city, the points under-written are ordained, to be held and firmly observed for ever; that is to say:

In the first place, that the masons, between the feasts of Easter and St. Michael [September 29], shall take no more by the working-day than 6d., without victuals or drink; and from the feast of St. Michael to Easter, for the working-day, 5d. And upon feast days, when they do not work, they shall take nothing. And for the making or mending of their implements they shall take nothing.

Also, that the carpenters shall take, for the same time, in the same manner.

Also, that the plasterers shall take the same as the masons and carpenters take.

Also, that the tilers shall take for the working-day, from the Feast of Easter to St. Michael 5½d., and from the feast of St. Michael 4½d.

Also, that the laborers shall take in the first half year 3½d., and in the other half 3d.

Also, that the master daubers shall take between the feasts of Easter and St. Michael 5d., and in the other half year 4d.; and their laborers are to take the same as the laborers of the tilers.

Also, that the sawyers shall take in the same manner as the masons and carpenters take.

Also, that no one shall pay more to the workmen aforesaid, on pain of paying 40s. to the commonalty, without any release therefrom; and he who shall take more than the above, shall go to prison for 40 days.

Also, that the thousand of tiles shall be sold for 5s., at the very highest.

Also, that the hundred of lime shall be sold at 5s., at the very highest.

Also, that a cart with sand, and with clay, that comes from Aldgate as far as the Conduit, shall take 3d. for its hire; and if the cart shall pass the Conduit, let it take 3½d. And in the same manner, let the carts from Cripplegate to Cheap take 3d.; and if they pass that place, 3½d. And if the cart with sand shall not enter the city, but only bring it to serve folks who live in the suburbs outside the gates, let it take 2d.: and let the carts be of capacity of one quarter, well heaped up, as they used to be.

Also, that carters, called "waterleaders," shall take for the cart, from Dovegate to Cheap, 1½d.; and from Castle Baynard to Cheap, in the same manner; and if they pass beyond Cheap, they are to take one penny [more]; and if they do not come as far as Cheap, 1¼d.

Also, that carts which bring wares coming from beyond the sea shall take, from Woolwharf to Cheap, 4d.

Also, that the cart which brings [long pieces of] firewood ... shall take for the hundred, at Cripplegate, 6d., and for the hundred of faggots [that is, short pieces] 4d.

Also, that the tailors shall take for making a gown, garnished with fine cloth and silk, 18d.

Also, for a man's gown, garnished with linen thread and with buckram, 14d.

Also, for a cote and hood, 10d.

Also, for a long gown for a woman, garnished with fine cloth or with silk, 2s. 6d.

Also, for a pair of sleeves, to change, 4d.

Also, that the porters of the city shall not take more for their labor than they used to take in olden time, on pain of imprisonment.

Also, that no vintner shall be so daring as to sell the gallon of wine of Vernaccia for more than 2s., and wine of Crete, wine of the River, Piement, and Clare, and Malveisin, at 16d.

Also, that one person of every company may see that the vessel into which their wine is drawn is clean, and from what tun their wine is drawn; on pain of imprisonment, and of paying to the Chamber, for the first time, half a mark; for the second time, one mark; for the third time, 20s.; and every other time that a person shall be found in like default, let his fine be increased by half a mark.

Also, that the measures shall be standing upright, and sealed with the seal of the alderman of the ward; and he who shall sell by other measures, let him go to prison, and further, be amerced in half a mark.

Also, that the skinners shall make their furs according to the ancient ordinances, of olden time ordained, and according to the purport of their charter; on pain of forfeiture and punishment for the same, as of old ordained.

Also, that no one shall go to meet those who are bringing victuals or other wares by land or by water to the city for sale, for the purpose of buying them or bargaining for them, before that they shall have come to certain places assigned thereto, where they ought to be sold; on pain of forfeiture of the victuals and other wares, and of their bodies being committed to prison, until they have been sufficiently punished, at the discretion of the mayor and aldermen.

Also, that the wheat and barley which come towards the city by land or by water, for sale, shall come wholly into the markets, and shall there be sold to all folks by the hands of those who bring the same, for the support and sustenance of their households, and to the bakers for serving the people. And that no hosteler shall demand to have any victuals, if they be not solely for the sustenance of his hostel, and that, for his money down, as other folks do.

Also, that the men of the serjeants who take cartage shall not take more carts or more horses than there is need, and then from the cart-hirers, and from such horses as are let on hire; and not those of poor folks who bring victuals and other wares to the city, while they spare the carts and horses that are on hire.

Also, that hostelers of the city shall be good folks, proper, and sufficient, as regards serving their guests well and lawfully; that so every one who is lodged [with them] may be sure both as to body and to chattels.

Also, if any man or woman shall be dwelling in any ward, who is notoriously known or convicted of being of bad repute, let the alderman of the ward be warned forthwith to remove the same.

Also, that a pair of shoes of cordovan shall be sold for 6d., and a pair of shoes of cow-leather for 6d., and a pair of boots of cordovan and of cow-leather for 3s. 6d.

Also, that a pair of spurs shall be sold for 6d., and a better pair for 8d., and the best at 10d. or 12d., at the very highest.

Also, that a pair of gloves of sheepskin shall be sold for one penny, and a better pair at 1½d., and a pair at 2d., so going on to the very highest.

Also, that the shearmen shall not take more than they were wont to take; that is to say, for [shearing] a short cloth 12d., and for [shearing] a long cloth 2s.; and for a cloth of striped serge, for getting rid of the stripes, and shearing the same, 2s.

Also, that the farriers shall not take more than they were wont to take before the time of the pestilence, on pain of imprisonment and heavy ransom; that is to say, for a horse-shoe of six nails 1½d., and for a horse-shoe of eight nails 2d.; and for taking off a horse-shoe of six nails or of eight, one halfpenny; and for the shoe of a courser 2½d., and the shoe of a charger 3d.; and for taking off the shoe of a courser or charger, one penny.

Also, if any workman or laborer will not work or labor as is above ordained, let him be taken and kept in prison until he shall have found good surety, and have been sworn to do that which is so ordained. And if anyone shall absent himself, or go out of the city, because he does not wish to work and labor, as is before mentioned, and afterwards by chance be found within the city, let him have imprisonment for a quarter of the year, and forfeit his chattels which he has in the city, and then let him find surety, and make oath, as is before stated. And if he will not do this, let him forswear the city for ever.

Also, that the servants in the houses of good folks shall not take more than they were wont to take before the time of the pestilence; on pain of imprisonment and heavy ransom, and of paying to the city double that which they shall have taken in excess. And he who shall pay more than he used to pay before the time above-mentioned, shall pay to the city treble what he shall have so paid in excess.

Also, that no cook shall take more for putting a capon or rabbit in a pasty than one penny, on pain of imprisonment.

Also, that a quart of bran shall be sold according to the value of a pound of wheat.

Also, that no cordovan or bazen shall be carried out of the city, on pain of forfeiture thereof; and he who can spy out the same shall have half the thing so forfeited.

Also, that four good men, or two, of every ward, shall be chosen to keep all these points; and if victuals or other wares coming towards the city by land or by water shall be sold in any other manner than is before mentioned, let the same be forfeited by award of the mayor [and] aldermen; and let one part thereof be delivered to the chamberlain, to the use of the commonalty, and a second part to the sheriffs, if they or their officers are ready in aid of the wardens in seizing the said things; and the wardens shall have the third part for their trouble; saving always to the sheriffs what shall appertain to their farm [that is, the royal revenues], according to the purport of the charters and liberties of the city. And he who shall contravene any article above written, where no punishment has been before ordained thereon, shall pay to the commonalty 40 shillings. And it shall be fully lawful for the mayor, aldermen, and good folks of the wards sworn, or others in their places, if any of them have been taken by God unto himself, to increase or diminish, or make amendment in, the articles aforesaid, for the common profit, according as the times shall shape themselves.

Questions: Whose attitudes are expressed in these regulations? What attitudes towards laborers and craftspeople are expressed here? What do different parties think about economic conditions? How were these regulations to be enforced? How are these regulations different from those of 1315?

61. MEDICAL DOCUMENTS

Like many other London records, these show the members of a profession acting to regulate and control their area of expertise.

Source: trans. H.T. Riley, *Memorials of London and London Life in the XIIIth, XIVth, and XVth Centuries* (London: Longmans, Green, and Co., 1868), pp. 273–274, 365, 464–466, 519–520; revised.

Inquisition by Surgeons as to the treatment of a wound (1354)

Be it remembered, that on [March 3,] the Monday after the feast of St. Matthias the apostle, the prior of Hogges, Master Paschal, Master Adam de la Poletrie, and Master David of Westmoreland, surgeons, were sworn before the mayor, aldermen, and sheriffs, to inform them as to a certain enormous and horrible hurt, appearing on the right side of the jaw of Thomas de Shene; whether or not such injury was curable at the time when John le Spicer of Cornhill took the same Thomas under his care, to heal the wound aforesaid.

These men say, upon their oath, that if the aforesaid John le Spicer, at the time when he took the said Thomas under his care, had been expert in his craft or art, or had called in counsel and assistance to his aid, he might have cured the injury aforesaid; and they further say that, through want of skill on part of the said John le Spicer, the said injury under his care has become apparently incurable.

Punishment of the Pillory, for pretending to be a Physician (1382)

Roger Clerk, of Wandsworth, on the 13th day of May ... was attached in the chamber of the guildhall of London, before the mayor and aldermen, to make answer, both to the mayor and commonalty of the city of London, and to Roger atte Hacche, in a plea of deceit and falsehood: as to which, the same Roger [atte Hacche] said, that whereas no physician or surgeon should intermeddle with any medicines or cures within the liberty of the city aforesaid, but those who are experienced in the said arts, and approved therein, the said Roger Clerk, who knew nothing of either of the arts aforesaid, being neither experienced nor approved therein, nor understood anything of letters, came to the house of him, Roger atte Hacche, in the parish of St. Martin, in Ironmongers Lane, in London, on Thursday, the morrow of Ash Wednesday, in the 5th year etc.; and there saw one Johanna, the wife of the aforesaid Roger atte Hacche, who was then lying ill with certain bodily infirmities, and gave the said Roger, her husband, to understand that he was experienced and skilled in the art of medicine, and could cure the same Johanna of her maladies, if her husband desired it.

Whereupon, the said Roger atte Hacche, trusting in his words, gave him 12 pence, in part payment of a larger sum which he was to pay him, if the said Johanna should be healed. And upon this, the same Roger Clerk then and there gave to the said Roger atte Hacche an old parchment, cut or scratched across, being the leaf of a certain book, and rolled it up in a piece of cloth of gold, asserting that it would be very good for the fever and ailments of her neck, but in no way did it profit her; and so, falsely and maliciously, he deceived the same Roger atte Hacche. And he produced the said parchment here in court, wrapped up in the same cloth, in proof of the matters aforesaid.

And the said Roger Clerk personally appeared, and the said parchment was shown to him by the Court, and he was asked what the virtue of this piece of parchment was; whereupon, he said that upon it was written a good charm for fevers. Upon being further asked by the Court what were the words of this charm of his, he said, "Anima Christi, sanctifica me; corpus Christi, salva me; sanguis Christi, inebria me; cum bonus Christus tu, lava me." And the parchment being then examined, not one of those words was found written thereon. And he was then further told by the court, that a straw beneath his foot would be of just as much avail for fevers, as this said charm of his was; whereupon, he fully granted that it would be so. And because the same Roger Clerk was in no way a literate man, and seeing that on the examinations aforesaid, as well as others afterwards made, he was found to be an infidel, and altogether ignorant of the art of physic or of surgery, and to the end that the people might not be deceived and aggrieved by such ignorant persons, etc., it was adjudged that the same Roger Clerk should be led through the middle of the city, with trumpets and pipes, he riding on a horse without a saddle, the said parchment and a whetstone, for his lies, being hung about his neck, a urinal also being hung before him, and another urinal on his back.

Admission and Oath of Master Surgeons of the City (1390)

On Monday, the 10th day of April ... Master John Hynstok, Master Geoffrey Grace, Master John Brademore, and Master Henry Suttone, surgeons, were admitted, in the Chamber of the Guildhall of London, before William Venour, mayor, and the aldermen, and sworn, as Master Surgeons of the city aforesaid, well and faithfully to serve the people in undertaking their cures, taking reasonably from them etc.; and faithfully to follow their calling, and faithful scrutiny to make of others, both men and women, undertaking cures, or practising the art of surgery; and to present their defaults, as well in their practice as in their medicine, to the aforesaid mayor and aldermen, so often as need shall be; and further, that they will be ready, so often as they shall be warned thereto, to examine persons hurt or wounded, and other etc.; and to give faithful information to the officers of the city aforesaid as to such persons hurt, or wounded, and others, whether they are in peril of death or not; and all other things touching their calling faithfully to do.

Questions: How was the medical profession organized and regulated in London? What do we learn about medical treatment from these documents? How do these documents compare with the craft regulations (doc. 55) above?

62. CHRONICLE ACCOUNTS OF THE PEASANTS' REVOLT

The rising expectations of ordinary people in post-plague England, and the repressive actions of their lords and employers, led to escalating tensions. In 1381 these broke out in the Peasants' Revolt, the first rebellion of English commoners. The specific event that sparked it was a poll tax, a flat tax on every "poll" or head, which was burdensome to many (although many exemptions were also given out) and the collection of which involved some notoriously ill-behaved officials. But the accounts of the rebellion, including those excerpted below, reveal more deep-seated and wide-ranging grievances. (Knighton's dating of the revolt is somewhat confused.)

Source: trans. E.P. Cheyney, *Readings in English History Drawn from the Original Sources* (Boston: Ginn and Company, 1922), pp. 260–265; revised.

Froissart's Account of a Sermon by John Ball

Of this imagination was a foolish priest in the county of Kent called John Ball, who, for his foolish words, had been three times in the archbishop of Canterbury's prison; for this priest used oftentimes, on the Sundays after mass, when the people were going out of the minster, to go into the cloister and preach, and made the people to assemble about him, and would say thus, "Ah, ye good people, things are not going well in England, nor shall they do so till everything be common, and till there be no villeins nor gentlemen, but we be all united together, and the lords be no greater masters than we be. What have we deserved, or why should we be kept thus in serfdom? We be all come from one father and one mother, Adam and Eve; whereby can they say or show that they be greater lords than we be, except that they cause us to earn and labor for what they spend? They are clothed in velvet and camlet furred with grise, and we be vestured with poor cloth; they have their wines, spices, and good bread, and we have the drawing out of the chaff and drink water; they dwell in fair houses and we have the pain and travail, rain and wind in the fields; and by what cometh of our labors they keep and maintain their estates: we be called their bondmen, and unless we readily do them service, we be beaten; and we have no sovereign to whom we may complain, nor that will hear us and do us right. Let us go to the king — he is young — and show him what serfage we be in, and show him how we will have it otherwise, or else we will provide us with some remedy, either by fairness or otherwise." Thus John Ball said on Sundays, when the people issued out of the churches in the villages; wherefore many of the lowly people loved him, and such as intended to no goodness said how he said truth; and so they would murmur one with another in the fields and in the ways as they went together, affirming how John Ball spoke the truth.

Henry Knighton's Chronicle

In the year 1381, the second of the reign of King Richard II, during the month of May, ... that impious band began to assemble from Kent, from Surrey, and from many other surrounding places. Apprentices also, leaving their masters, rushed to join these. And so they gathered on Blackheath, where, forgetting themselves in their multitude, and neither contented with their former cause nor appeased by smaller crimes, they unmercifully planned greater and worse evils and determined not to desist from their wicked undertaking until they should have entirely extirpated the nobles and great men of the kingdom.

So at first they directed their course of iniquity to a certain town of the archbishop of Canterbury called Maidstone, in which there was a jail of the said archbishop, and in the said jail was a certain John Ball, a chaplain who was considered among the laity to be a very famous preacher; many times in the past he had foolishly spread abroad the word of God, by mixing tares with wheat, too pleasing to the laity and extremely dangerous to the liberty of ecclesiastical law and order, execrably introducing into the church of Christ many errors among the clergy and laymen. For this reason he had been tried as a clerk and convicted in accordance with the law, being seized and assigned to this same jail for his permanent abiding place. On [June 12,] the Wednesday before the feast of the Consecration, they came into Surrey to the jail of the king at Marshalsea, where they broke the jail without delay, forcing all imprisoned there to come with them to help them; and whomsoever they met, whether pilgrims or others of whatever condition, they forced to go with them.

On [June 14,] the Friday following the feast of the Consecration, they came over the bridge to London; here no one resisted them, although, as was said, the citizens of London knew of their advance a long time before; and so they directed their way to the Tower where the king was surrounded by a great throng of knights, esquires, and others. It was said that there were in the Tower about one hundred and fifty knights together with one hundred and eighty others, with the mother of the king, the duchess of Britanny, and many other ladies; and there was present, also, Henry, earl of Derby, son of John, duke of Lancaster, who was still a youth; so, too, Simon of Sudbury, archbishop of Canterbury and chancellor of England, and brother Robert de Hales, prior of the Hospital of England and treasurer of the king.

John Leg and a certain John, a Minorite, a man active in warlike deeds, skilled in natural sciences, an intimate friend of Lord John, duke of Lancaster, hastened with three others to the Tower for refuge, intending to hide themselves under the wings of the king. The people had determined to kill the archbishop and the others above mentioned with him; for this reason they came to this place, and afterwards they fulfilled their vows. The king, however, desired to free the archbishop and his friends from the jaws of the wolves, so he sent to the people a command to assemble outside the city, at a place called Mile End, in order to speak with the king and to treat with him concerning their designs. The soldiers who were to go forward, consumed with folly, lost heart, and gave up, on the way, their boldness of purpose. Nor did they dare to advance, but, unfortunately, struck as they were by fear, like women, kept themselves within the Tower.

But the king advanced to the assigned place, while many of the wicked mob kept following him…. More, however, remained where they were. When the others had come to the king they complained that they had been seriously oppressed by many hardships and that their condition of servitude was unbearable, and that they neither could nor would endure it longer. The king, for the sake of peace, and on account of the violence of the times, yielding to their petition, granted to them a charter with the great seal, to the effect that all men in the kingdom of England should be free and of free condition, and should remain both for themselves and their heirs free from all kinds of servitude and villeinage forever. This charter was rejected and decided to be null and void by the king and the great men of the kingdom in the parliament held at Westminster in the same year, after the feast of St. Michael [September 29].

While these things were going on, behold those degenerate sons, who still remained, summoned their father the archbishop with his above-mentioned friends without any force or attack, without sword or arrow, or any other form of compulsion, but only with force of threats and excited outcries, inviting those men to death. But they did not cry out against it for themselves, nor resist, but, as sheep before the shearers, going forth barefooted with uncovered heads, ungirt, they offered themselves freely to an undeserved death, just as if they had deserved this punishment for some murder or theft. And so, alas! before the king returned, seven were killed at Tower Hill, two of them lights of the kingdom, the worthy with the unworthy. John Leg and his three associates were the cause of this irreparable loss. Their heads were fastened on spears and sticks in order that they might be told from the rest....

Whatever representatives of the law they found or whatever men served the kingdom in a judicial capacity, these they slew without delay.

On the following day, which was Saturday, they gathered in Smithfield, where there came to them in the morning the king, who although only a youth in years yet was in wisdom already well versed. Their leader, whose real name was Wat Tyler, approached him; already they were calling him by the other name of Jack Straw. He kept close to the king, addressing him for the rest. He carried in his hand an unsheathed weapon which they call a dagger, and, as if in childish play, kept tossing it from one hand to the other in order that he might seize the opportunity, if the king should refuse his requests, to strike the king suddenly (as was commonly believed); and from this thing the greatest fear arose among those about the king as to what might be the outcome.

They begged from the king that all the warrens, and as well waters as park and wood, should be common to all, so that a poor man as well as a rich should be able freely to hunt animals everywhere in the kingdom — in the streams, in the fish ponds, in the woods, and in the forest; and that he might be free to chase the hare in the fields, and that he might do these things and others like them without objection. When the king hesitated about granting this concession Jack Straw came nearer, and, speaking threatening words, seized with his hand the bridle of the horse of the king very daringly. When John de Walworth, a citizen of London, saw this, thinking that death threatened the king, he seized a sword and pierced Jack Straw in the neck. Seeing this, another soldier, by name Radulf Standyche, pierced his side with another sword. He sank back, slowly letting go with his hands and feet, and then died. A great cry and much mourning arose: "Our leader is slain." When this dead man had been meanly dragged along by the hands and feet into the church of St. Bartholomew, which was near by, many withdrew from the band, and, vanishing, betook themselves to flight, to the number it is believed of ten thousand....

After these things had happened and quiet had been restored, the time came when the king caused the offenders to be punished. So Lord Robert Tresillian, one of the judges, was sent by order of the king to inquire into the uprisings against the peace and to punish the guilty. Wherever he came he spared no one, but caused great slaughter. And just as those evil doers plotted in hostile manner against the judges, Lord John de Candishe and any others they could find, by bringing them to capital punishment, and against all those skilled in the laws of the country whom they could reach, and not sparing any one of them, but punishing them by capital punishment, just so this judge spared no one, but demanded misfortune for misfortune. For whoever was accused before him in this said cause, whether justly or as a matter of spite, he immediately passed upon him the sentence of death. He ordered some to be beheaded, others to be hanged, still others to be dragged through the city and hanged in four different parts thereof; others to be disemboweled, and the entrails to be burned before them while they were still alive, and afterwards to be decapitated, quartered, and hanged in four parts of the city according to the greatness of the crime and its desert. John Ball was captured at Coventry and led to St. Albans, where, by order of the king, he was drawn and hanged, then quartered, and his quarters sent to four different places.

Questions: Who were the rebels? What did they want, and why? What was the attitude of the authorities toward the rebel demands? Can you detect anything of lasting significance in these events?

63. PEASANTS' REVOLT TRIALS

After the failure of the Peasants' Revolt, there were severe retaliations not only against those suspected of involvement, but also of those suspected of sympathizing with the rebels. Two of the many existing trial transcripts are printed below.

Source: trans. A.E. Bland, P.A. Brown, and R.H. Tawney, *English Economic History: Select Documents* (London: G. Bell and Sons, Ltd, 1914), pp. 108–110.

Ely. Adam Clymme was taken as an insurgent traitorously against his allegiance, and because on [June 15, the] Saturday next after the feast of Corpus Christi in the 4th year of the reign of King Richard the second after the conquest, he traitorously with others made insurrection at Ely, feloniously broke and entered the close of Thomas Somenour and there took and carried away diverse rolls, estreats of the green wax of the lord the king and the bishop of Ely, and other muniments touching the court of the lord the king, and forthwith caused them to be burned there to the prejudice of the crown of the lord the king.

Further that the same Adam on Sunday and Monday next following caused to be proclaimed there that no man of law or other officer in the execution of duty should escape without beheading.

Further that the same Adam the day and year aforesaid at the time of the insurrection was always wandering armed with arms displayed, bearing a standard, to assemble insurgents, commanding that no man of whatsoever condition he were, free or bond, should obey his lord to do any services or customs, under pain of beheading, otherwise than he should declare to them on behalf of the Great Fellowship. And so he traitorously took upon him royal power. And he came, brought by the sheriff, and was charged before the aforesaid justices touching the premises, in what manner he would acquit himself thereof. And he says that he is not guilty of the premises imputed to him or of any of the premises, and hereof puts himself on the country, etc. And forthwith a jury is made thereon for the lord the king by twelve [good and lawful men] etc., who being chosen hereto, tried and sworn, say on their oath that the aforesaid Adam is guilty of all the articles. By the discretion of the justices the same Adam is drawn and hanged, etc. And it was found there that the same Adam has in the town aforesaid chattels to the value of 32s., which Ralph atte Wyk, escheator of the lord the king, seized forthwith and made further execution for the lord the king, etc.

Cambridge. John Shirle of the county of Nottingham was taken because it was found that he was a vagabond in diverse counties the whole time of the disturbance, insurrection and tumult, carrying lies and worthless talk from district to district whereby the peace of the lord the king could be speedily broken and the people disquieted and disturbed; and among other dangerous words, to wit, after the proclamation of the peace of the lord the king made the day and year aforesaid, the [justices assigned by] the lord the king being in the town and sitting, he said, in a tavern in Bridge Street, Cambridge, where many were assembled to listen to his news and worthless talk, that the stewards of the lord the king, the justices and many other officers and ministers of the king were more worthy to be drawn and hanged and to suffer other lawful pains and torments, than John Ball, chaplain, a traitor and felon lawfully convicted; for he said that [John Ball] was condemned to death falsely, unjustly and for envy by the said ministers with the king's assent, because he was a true and good man, prophesying things useful to the commons of the realm and telling of wrongs and oppressions done to the people by the king and the ministers aforesaid; and his death shall not go unpunished but within a short space he would well reward both the king and his officers and ministers aforesaid; which sayings and threats redound to the prejudice of the crown of the lord the king and the contempt and manifest disquiet of the people. And hereupon the aforesaid John Shirle was brought forthwith by the sheriff before the aforesaid [justices] in Cambridge castle, and was charged touching the premises and diligently examined as well touching his conversation as touching his tarrying and his estate, and the same being acknowledged by him before the aforesaid assigns, his evil behavior and condition is plainly manifest and clear. And hereupon trustworthy witnesses at that time in his presence, when the aforesaid lies, evil words, threats and worthless talk were spoken by him, were asked for, and they being sworn to speak the truth in this behalf, testify that all the aforesaid words imputed to him were truly spoken by him; and he, again examined, did not deny the premises imputed to him. Therefore by the discretion of the said assigns he was hanged; and order was made to the escheator to enquire diligently of his lands and tenements, goods and chattels, and to make due execution thereof for the lord the king.

Questions: What are the defendants charged with? What evidence is brought against them? What is the penalty? What do these texts tell us about reactions to the Peasants' Revolt?

64. ROYAL PROCLAMATIONS ON THE PEASANTS' REVOLT

The peasant rebels had put their trust in the young king, Richard II (1377-99), who granted their demands at first. But then the authorities gained the upper hand, and the royal response changed dramatically, as the following royal proclamations show.

Source: trans. E.P. Cheyney, *Translations and Reprints from the Original Sources of European History*, series 1, vol. 2 (Philadelphia: University of Pennsylvania Department of History, 1895), no. 5, pp. 19-20; revised.

Charter of Manumission and Pardon to the Rebels of Hertfordshire

Richard, by the grace of God, king of England and France, and lord of Ireland, to all his bailiffs and faithful ones, to whom these present letters shall come, greeting. Know that of our special grace, we have manumitted all of our lieges and each of our subjects and others of the county of Hertford; and have made them and each of them free from all bondage, and by these presents make them quit. And moreover we pardon our same lieges and subjects for all kinds of felonies, treasons, transgressions and extortions, however done or perpetrated by them or any of them, and also outlawry, if any shall have been promulgated on this account against them or any of them; and our most complete peace to them and each of them we concede in these matters. In testimony of which thing we have caused these our letters to be made patent. Witness, myself, at London, on the fifteenth day of June, in the fourth year of our reign.

Withdrawal of Manumissions

It is ordained that all manner of manumissions, obligations, releases, and other bonds made by compulsion, duress and threat, in the time of this last rumor and riot against the laws of the land and good faith shall be wholly quashed, annulled and held void; and they which have caused to be made or do yet withhold such manumissions, obligations, releases, bonds and other deeds, so made by duress, shall be sent before the king and his council, there to answer of their deed; and further, shall be constrained to make delivery and restitution of the said deeds to them that made the same against their good will, with the copies of the same, if perchance they have thereof made any before in order to use or renew the effect of the same another time, if they may. And likewise, it is accorded that all entries made in lands or tenements, and also all feoffments made in the time of the same rumor by compulsion and menace, or otherwise with force of people, against the law, shall be void and held for none. And the king straitly forbiddeth to all manner of people, upon pain of as much as they are able to forfeit to him in body and goods, that none from henceforth make nor begin again, in any manner, such riot and rumor, nor other like them. And if any do the same, and this be duly proved, it shall be done concerning him as of a traitor to the king and to his said realm.

Pardon of the King to the Lords

Our sovereign lord the king, perceiving that many lords and gentlemen of his realm, and others with them in the rumor and insurrection of villeins, and of other offenders, which now of late did traitorously rise by assemblies in outrageous numbers in diverse parts of the realm, against God, good faith, and reason, and against the dignity of our sovereign lord the king and his crown, and the laws of his land, made diverse punishments upon the said villains and other traitors, without due process of the law, and otherwise than the laws and usages of the realm required, although they did it of no malice propense, but only to appease and cease the evident mischief, and considering the great diligence and loyalty of the lords and gentlemen in this behalf, who were not knowledgeable about the said laws and usages (and if at that time they had been knowledgeable, a man might not have been able to delay as long as the law required before administering those punishments), and perceiving that they did this with good intent, according to their own best judgment, and being willing therefore to do them grace, according as they have greatly deserved the same, of the assent aforesaid I have both pardoned and released the said lords and gentlemen, and all others who aided them in the same deed, and every one of them, of whatever pertains to him, or may pertain to him and to his heirs; so that hereafter for whatever was done by them in administering the said punishments in resistance, they shall never be impeached nor grieved in body, goods, nor their inheritances and possessions, in any way, by our sovereign lord the king, his heirs or ministers, nor anyone else in time to come, but utterly shall be quit thereof forever by this grant and statute without having any other special charter or pardon.

Questions: What does each of the documents do? How does the king justify the second proclamation? For what do the lords need pardoning? How does the king justify the third proclamation?

65. ORDINANCES OF THE GUILD OF ST. KATHARINE AT NORWICH

Guilds or societies for mutual assistance had existed since Anglo-Saxon times, but they were especially characteristic of late medieval towns.

Source: trans. T. Smith, *English Guilds: The Original Ordinances of More than One Hundred English Guilds*, ed. L.T. Smith (London, 1870), reprinted in *Translations and Reprints from the Original Sources of European History*, series 1, vol. 2 (Philadelphia: University of Pennsylvania Department of History, 1895), no. 1, ed. E.P. Cheyney, pp. 34–35; revised.

To the most excellent prince and lord, our lord Richard, by the grace of God, king of England and France, and to his council in his chancery, his humble lieges, the guardians of a certain fraternity of St. Katharine the virgin and martyr, in the church of St. Simon and St. Jude in Norwich, all subjection and reverence and honor. By virtue of a certain proclamation recently made according to royal command by the sheriff of the county of Norfolk at Norwich, we certify to your excellency according to the form of the aforesaid proclamation, that our aforesaid fraternity was founded in the year 1307, by certain parishioners of the said church, and by others devoted to God, to the honor of the Holy Trinity, and of the blessed Virgin Mary, and of St. Katharine the virgin and martyr, and of all saints, and for keeping up an increase of light in the said church, under certain ordinances made and issued with common consent of the brothers and sisters of the aforesaid fraternity. The tenor of these ordinances follows in these words.

In the first place with one assent it is ordained that all the brethren and sisters of this guild shall come together to the parish church of St. Simon and St. Jude, in Norwich, on the day of St. Katharine [November 25], to go in the procession with their candle, which is borne before them, and to hear the mass of St. Katharine in the aforesaid church; and at that mass every brother and sister shall offer a half-penny.

And also it is ordained that whatever brother or sister shall be absent at the procession aforesaid, or at mass, or at offering, he shall pay to the chattels of the guild two pounds of wax, but they may be excused reasonably.

And also it is ordained, that where a brother or a sister is dead, every brother and sister shall come to the dirge and to mass; and at the mass, each shall offer a half-penny, and give a half-penny to alms; and for a mass to be sung for the soul of the dead, a penny. And at the dirge, every brother and sister that is lettered shall say, for the soul of the dead, the office of the dead and the dirge, in the place where they shall come together; and every brother and sister that is not lettered shall say for the soul of the dead, twenty times, the Paternoster, with the *ave Maria*; and from the chattels of the guild shall there be two candles of wax, of sixteen pounds weight, about the body of the dead.

And also it is ordained, that if any brother or sister die out of the city of Norwich, within eight miles, six of the brethren that have the chattels of the guild in keeping shall go to that brother or sister that is dead; and if it be lawful, they shall carry it to Norwich, or else it be buried there; and if the body be buried out of Norwich all the brethren and sisters shall be warned to come to the foresaid church of St. Simon and St. Jude, and there shall be done for the soul of the dead all service, light and offering as if the body were there present. And what brother or sister be absent at office of the dead and the dirge, or at mass, he shall pay two pounds of wax to the chattels of the guild, unless he be reasonably excused. And nevertheless he shall do for the dead as it is said before.

And also it is ordained that, on the morrow after the guild day all the brethren and sisters shall come to the aforesaid church, and there sing a mass of requiem for the souls of the brethren and sisters of this guild, and for all Christian souls, and each offer there 9 farthings. And whoever is absent shall pay a pound of wax.

And also it is ordained that if any brother or sister fall into poverty, through adventure of the world, his estate shall be helped by every brother and sister of the guild, with a farthing each week.

And also it is ordained by common assent that if there be any discord between brothers and sisters, that discord shall be first shown to other brothers and sisters of the guild, and by them shall accord be made, if it may be skilfully. And if they cannot be so brought to accord, it shall be lawful to them to go to the common law, without any maintenance. And whoso does against this ordinance, he shall pay two pounds of wax to the light.

Also it is ordained, by common assent, that if any brother of this guild be chosen into office and refuse it, he shall pay two pounds of wax to the light of St. Katharine.

Also it is ordained, by common assent, that the brethren and sisters of this guild, in the worship of St. Katharine, shall have a livery of hoods in suit, and eat together in their guild day, at their common cost; and whoso fails, he shall pay two pounds of wax to the light.

Also it is ordained, by common assent, that no brother or sister shall be received into this guild but by the alderman and twelve brethren of the guild.

And as to the goods and chattels of the said fraternity, we make known to your excellency, likewise, that we the aforesaid guardians have in our custody, for the use of the said fraternity, twenty shillings of silver.

Questions: What is the purpose of the guild? What specific benefits can its members expect? What are the members' obligations? What concerns of medieval society are evident in this text?

66. A PREACHER'S HANDBOOK

The extracts below come from a book called "Bundle of Morals," a collection of useful material for sermons, organized by moral topics. This sort of writing reflects the late medieval emphasis on preaching as a tool of moral reform, also evident in the popularity of the Dominicans and other preaching orders.

Source: trans. S. Wenzel, *Fasciculus Morum: A Fourteenth-Century Preacher's Manual* (University Park and London: Pennsylvania State University Press, 1989), pp. 135–141, 143, 317–321.

The Need for Patience

In order to know when patience is necessary, through which we shall fulfill God's will even to the point of becoming his imitators, notice that we need this virtue particularly in four situations: in the adversity we suffer from our enemies, in correction from our superiors, in the loss of our goods, and in bearing various kinds of infirmity.

If we patiently endure adversity from our enemies who inflict on us hard words and harder strokes, we will be like those who in time of war put up cushions or straw or anything soft of this kind against the battering rams, so that their walls and towers may not be broken down; Proverbs 12: "A soft

Fig. 28: Friar Preaching In this nineteenth-century copy of a manuscript illustration, men and women listen to a sermon preached by a barefoot friar, who speaks from a simple pulpit that is apparently portable. The growth of towns in the high middle ages was one of the stimuli to the growth of the thirteenth-century preaching orders, the Franciscans (or Friars Minor; see doc. 41) and the Dominicans.

answer breaks wrath." The more a nut-tree is beaten and shaken in one year, the more fruit it bears the next; thus a person who is truly patient under insults bears more fruit in bringing forth virtues, as can be seen in the children of Israel: the more they were oppressed, the more numerous they grew. Therefore the truly patient person can be compared to gold: the more it is beaten, the wider it spreads; thus a man who is worn thin and beaten in his injuries grows greater in his patience; as the Psalm says: "When I was in distress, you have enlarged me." To a knight it is the greatest honor if his sword breaks in battle, his horse is felled and killed, and yet he himself has won and is not overcome; and wretched is the knight who gets beaten too much and is handed over to the enemy without striking a single blow. Thus an impatient person who cannot endure any injuries but at once breaks into anger does not deserve to receive any reward from God. Therefore it is said in Proverbs: "You shall be crowned if you suffer patiently." And you have to endure injuries. But whenever you suffer any adversity or injury from an enemy, ask yourself within if you have any fault or not; if so, you complain unjustly, for you may have deserved more than you actually suffer; but if not, then behold what Christ says in Matthew: "Blessed are they who suffer persecution on account of justice." And so, a story is told about a philosopher who was cursed by his wife and highly annoyed by her words; when she saw that he would not answer her a single word, she poured a pot of water over his head; whereupon he said with all patience: "I knew well that normally after a storm comes rain."

In the second place patience is necessary when we are corrected by our superiors. As an ox that always pulls in the direction in which he is driven, thus a patient person humbly directs his steps after the goading of his superior and bends his will under his superior's correction. Therefore he may be compared to the snail which, if you touch it, at once pulls in its horns and hides; thus also a patient and humble person, when he is touched by his superior through fatherly corrections, bows his head and withdraws and hides his horns of pride and impatience; Genesis 1: "I heard your voice, Lord, and hid myself."

In the third place patience is necessary when we lose temporal goods, as Job did, of whom we read that when he lost all his belongings he said patiently: "The Lord has given, the Lord has taken away; as it has pleased the Lord," etc. Hence we read in *The Lives of the Fathers* of a hermit from whom a thief took his donkey, giving him a blow in the face. The hermit endured this patiently, offered him the other cheek, and gave him the bridle so that he could lead the donkey away more easily. Whereupon a demon went out of the robber with a loud cry and said: "By patience alone have I been overcome." Such a patient person can be compared to a diamond. According to Isidore, it is harder than any other material, such as iron, cannot be broken by fire, and never heats up; whence it is called *adamas* in Greek, *uis indomita*, "untamed power" in Latin. But while it thus resists iron or fire unabated, it yet becomes weakened by the blood of a goat. Similarly, a patient person cannot be broken or dissolved by the iron or fire of injuries, and yet out of love for the blood of Jesus Christ he will grow soft in compassion; Romans 12: "Be not overcome by evil, but overcome evil with good."

In the fourth place patience is necessary in sickness, which is the fetter of Christ with which he binds those whom he loves. As an anxious mother restrains her child whom she sees nearing water or fire where some danger might threaten, so does the Heavenly Father sometimes tie down a son he loves through some sickness, so that he may be held back from the fire or water of sin. Hence the Lord does to them what boys do to birds they have caught: to prevent them from flying away, they pull out part of their feathers. The feathers with which many people would fly away from Christ's will if they could are wealth and power; and these Christ takes away, the first through poverty, the second through sickness. If the king of France took some castle from the king of England, and the latter besieged him because of this loss and made war on him until he had regained the castle — would it not show that he loves that castle very much if he did not raze its walls? By the king of France I understand the devil, who has taken the castle of our soul from Christ, that is, our king of England; but in order not to lose that soul, Christ, out of the deep love he has for her, does not at once raze the walls of the body in death, but wins her by sending sickness. Therefore, we must not grumble against sickness, for we see that a boy who weeps when he is chastised provokes his teacher to even harder punishment; the same is true of Christ. Whence Isidore says in his *Soliloquy*: "He who grumbles when he is punished stirs God even more against himself." Blessed Paul had this in mind when he wrote: "Gladly will I glory in my infirmities."

Listen to the reason why, as I think, Christ justly sends sickness to the body, and especially of those whom he loves. I set the case that has often happened among merchants in these large cities, such as London and Coventry, that two partners share equally in their profit and loss. Now, if they owe someone a debt which they could not pay, and one of them wanted to disappear secretly and leave his partner in the lurch, if in this case the mayor of the city were to notice this and were to detain him until he paid his debt together with his partner — would this not be a sign of great faithfulness and love toward the other merchant? Yes, indeed. Now, since body and soul are partners in delights and sins, we see that the flesh, if it could, would like to steal away without punishment and leave all his debt with the soul. This would be quite unjust. Therefore, our mayor, Christ, out of his love for our soul, takes the body and restrains it and sends it infirmities, and thus he forces it to pay the part of the debt which belongs to it. And therefore says Gregory, "Pay your debt before your time is up, lest you be bound for it." We also observe that sometimes the nearest person who has given security is punished for someone else's debt for which he had given his pledge, so that for that debt sometimes his security is taken from him and sometimes he is put in jail, which would not happen if the real debtor were paying up. To the point: out of necessity the soul will be punished or tormented for the debt of the body unless the body pays its debt for its sins here, which it does when it is afflicted with infirmities. And it is better that the flesh, the handmaiden, be punished here a little than that the soul, its mistress, be damned in eternity. Therefore we must not grumble against Christ on account of infirmities by which God, as it were, tries us, for the wise man says: "Blessed is the man who endures temptation, for when he has been proved," etc.

But I fear that with some people it goes as it does with sailors who in calm weather play dice and have no thought of danger, but when a storm comes call to God and the saints and offer vows; yet when they are out of danger, they forget all about these things. In the same way, some people fail to make good their promises when their sickness is over. There is a story about a Welshman who, in danger at sea, promised the Blessed Virgin a candle as tall as the mast of his ship; but when he had escaped the danger, he said that on his account she would not get anything bigger than a bedside candle.

And notice that sickness sent by God has the following good effects. First, it strengthens one's hope in God, according to Job 13: "Even if he should kill me, I will hope in him." For which we read in *The Lives of the Fathers* that a hermit was frequently ill, and that one year it happened that he did not fall ill; whereupon he burst out weeping and said: "Now God has forsaken me and has not visited me."

Second, it causes man to scorn these worldly values and desire heavenly ones, just as a boy in school who is flogged desires more intently to go home than he who is totally left to his own will. Whence Gregory says: "The saints consider temporal affliction a gain, for through it they hope to go free of future and eternal pain." ...

Third, sickness cools down lustful people. As a teacher who takes an insolent student by his ears, lashes his hand with a switch, and finally gives him a flogging so that he may pay more attention, so does Christ our teacher....

The Properties of Avarice...

Speaking of the clergy, we see them striving so much for temporal goods that in order to acquire these, a wretched person of whatever social rank can, to the very end of his life, lie in falsehood and other forms of wretchedness, such as lechery, simony, and the like, who by right should be firmly reproved and corrected by the clergy in true wisdom. But speaking of the lay people, and particularly of such leaders of the country as lawyers and judges and the like, who should rule the people in all wisdom and truth, I believe that here, too, the world is going backwards. It should be marching straight with wisdom in the direction of truth; but nowadays it goes astray through avarice and covetousness in the direction of falsehood and injustice.

Therefore it is patently true that the world has taken away wisdom. This is borne out by the following story. In order to help a poor man in his just cause, a certain judge is said to have accepted a cart in payment, perhaps because the man had no money. Then the poor man's adversary came and gave the same judge a yoke of oxen of much greater value, in order to further his unjust cause. As they came together to hear the case, the judge, for worldly gain, decided against the poor man. Then the latter said: "My lord, the cart is running poorly." And the judge replied: "No wonder. The oxen are so strong that they have pulled it from the right road." To such people the words of Isaiah 59 may well apply: "Justice has stood far off, because truth has fallen down in the street." And about such men the saying of Wisdom 9 has come true: "Error was kept as a law." For they err most shamefully when they unceasingly and with such effort collect the goods of poor people as if in agreement with a true law and invent some crime, they whose task it is to correct the crimes of the wicked through true knowledge and the established law, knowing that "for the just there is no law" according to the laws.

These people behave like some small children who cannot in any way pronounce the letter r but instead say l as a rule. If they should say "Roger," they pronounce it "Logel," and so forth. To the case in point: all the laws require that judges and advocates and the like always correct failings with true wisdom. But alas, like little children they turn r into l when they pretend to *correct* failings and never cease in their greed to *collect* worldly goods. Of them is said in Baruch 1: "They made a collection of money according to every man's power." And thus they allow the wicked to continue with impunity in their crimes, for according to the Psalm "their right hand is filled with gifts," for "all things obey money" and gifts.

To them also applies a joke we read about a vicar. When he was censured by his bishop for giving burial to his ass, he answered: "Dear lord, do you not know how much my ass has left for you in his will?" As the bishop replied, "No," the vicar said: "Forty shillings, to be sure." At which the bishop answered: "May he rest in peace!" Thus it is evident how the world, that is, the goods of the world, has taken away wisdom.

This is the strongest reason why the second pronouncement also has come true, namely that "the country's peace is lost," as can be clearly seen. Because once true wisdom and teaching are gone, no real peace is found in city or realm, family or house, not even — what is worse — between father and son, mother and daughter, for indeed each one desires the other's death in order to gain his temporal goods. No wonder, then, that after the just judgment of God this realm is falling, as we have seen, now by the sword, now by hunger, and now by fire.

Let these people therefore pay attention to what is reported of a Parisian lawyer of this kind. As was his habit, he once planned to take the stand falsely against innocent and religious people for the gifts he had received. His name was John or William Malemorte. It happened that one day he entered his chamber to prepare ruses and arguments contrary to the truth in order to convict them. As on the following day he was called to appear and could not be found, his companions broke the door of his chamber, and behold, they found him strangled by a demon and his body totally reduced to dust, from whose stench many people died when they came near. One of his companions who was literate then said in verse:

Both evil death and evil life
Are felled at once in sudden death....

To whom the other responded in verse as follows:

Avoid such life that thou not end
Like he in such a death!

And remember the story of the false judge called Gayus, who finally was caught by demons and cried out horribly and said:

Alas, alas, what pain! I'm judged as I have judged!

as if he were saying: as I have falsely sentenced the innocent for gifts, so am I now rightly sentenced by God, who says through the Psalmist: "When I shall take the time, I shall judge justices."

Questions: What points is the author trying to make in these excerpts? What efforts does he make to reach his intended audience? How does he address a range of experiences? What techniques does he employ to convey his message? From what sources and what aspects of everyday life does he draw his examples?

67. ROBERT MANNING OF BRUNNE'S *HANDLYNG SYNNE*

This early fourteenth-century poem, composed in English by a monk who based much of it on a similar French work, takes a different approach to moral instruction but a similarly orthodox stance. The extracts below deal with concrete examples of problem situations: tournaments, miracle plays, the care of a congregation, and the raising of children. (The mention of Eli at the end of this selection refers to the story of "Sir Eli and his Wicked Sons," recounted earlier in the poem.)

Source: Modernized from *Robert of Brunne's "Handlyng Synne,"* ed. F.J. Furnivall (London: Early English Text Society, 1901), vol. I, pp. 153-155, 160-163.

Of tournaments that are forbade
in holy church, as men do read,
of tournaments I shall prove therein,
seven points of deadly sin:
first is pride, as thou well know'st,
vanity, pomp, and many a boast;
of rich attire there is great flaunting,

spurring her horse with much vaunting.
Know you well this is envy
when one sees another do mastery,
some in words, some in deeds;
envy most of all him leads.
Ire and wrath cannot be late;
oft are tournaments made for hate.
If all knights loved each other well,
tournaments would never be held;
And of course they fall into slothfulness,
they love it more than God or Mass;
And truly, there can be no doubt,
they spend more gold thereabout —
that is, they give it all to folly —
than on any deed of mercy.
And yet be very careful lest
you forget Dame Covetousness,
for she shall be foolish, in all ways,
to win a horse and some harness.
And a man shall also do robbery,
or beguile his host where he shall stay.
Gluttony also is them among,
delicious meats do make him strong;
and gladly he drinks wine untold,
with gluttony to make him bold.
Also is there Dame Lechery;
from here comes all her mastery.
Many times, for women's sake,
knights these tournaments do make;
and when he goes to the tournament
she sends him some secret present,
and bids him do, if he loves her best,
all that he can at her behest,
for which he gets so much the worst,
that he may not sit upon his horse,
and that peradventure, in all his life,
shall he never after thrive.
Consider whether such tournaments
should more truly be called torments? ...

It is forbidden him, in the decree,
miracle plays for to make or see,

for, miracles if thou begin,
it is a gathering, a site of sin.
He may in the church, through this reason,
portray the resurrection —
that is to say, how God rose,
God and man in strength and loss —
to make men hold to belief good,
that he rose with flesh and blood;
and he may play, without danger,
how God was born in the manger,
to make men to believe steadfastly
that he came to us through the Virgin Mary....

A parson is slothful in holy church
who on his sheep will not work
how they should heed his own word
and please the church and their Lord.
The high Shepherd shall him blame,
for how he lets them go to shame.
If he should see in anything
that they have a lack of chastising,
unless he teach them and chastise so
that they from henceforth better do,
for them he shall, at God's assize,
be punished before the high Justice.
Also it behooves him to pray
that God, of grace, show him the way....

Man or woman that has a child
that with bad manners grows too wild,
that will both mis-say and -do,
chastisement behooves them too;
But chastise them with all your might,
Otherwise you'll be in their plight.
Better were the child unborn
than lack chastising, and thus be forlorn.
Thus says the wise king Solomon
to men and women every one,
"If you want your children to be good,
give them the smart end of the rod;"
and teach them good manners each one;
but take care that you break no bone....

Everywhere I see this custom:
that rich men have shrews for sons —
shrews in speech and in act —
Why? They hold no one in respect.
In his youth shall he mis-say
and scorn others by the way;
then says the father, "This child's story
doesn't hang together — sorry!"
And if he learns guilefulness,
false words and deceitful looks,
his father shouldn't acquit him then;
his sly wit will be his only friend.
If he injures foes in rages,
then says his father, "He shall be courageous,
he shall be hardy, and no man dread,
he begins early to be doughty in deed."
But right so shall it him befall
as it did with Eli's bad sons all....

*Questions: What moral points does the poet make? How well acquainted does he seem
to be with secular life? Who was the intended audience? Which do you think would be
more effective in reaching its audience, this poem or a preacher following the manual
above (doc. 66)?*

68. THE LOLLARD CONCLUSIONS

*The ideas of an Oxford theologian named John Wycliff (d. 1384) gave rise to a heretical
movement known as Lollardy. Though his writings were condemned as unorthodox,
Wycliff himself was protected by powerful friends and died a natural death, but many of
his followers, in later years, were executed as heretics. Their beliefs were anticlerical, chal-
lenging the need for priests as intermediaries between God and the individual believer,
and in many other ways, too, they anticipated the ideas that would one day give rise to
the Protestant Reformation. In 1394 a group of Lollards presented to Parliament the following summary of their beliefs.*

Source: trans. H. Gee and W.G. Hardy, *Documents Illustrative of the History of the English Church*
(London: Macmillan, 1910), pp. 126-132.

1. That when the church of England began to go mad after temporalities [that
is, worldly wealth and power], like its great step-mother the Roman church,
and churches were authorized by appropriation in diverse places, faith, hope,
and charity began to flee from our church, because pride, with its doleful

progeny of mortal sins, claimed this under title of truth. This conclusion is general, and proved by experience, custom, and manner or fashion, as you shall afterwards hear.

2. That our usual priesthood which began in Rome, pretended to be of power more lofty than the angels, is not that priesthood which Christ ordained for his apostles. This conclusion is proved because the Roman priesthood is bestowed with signs, rites, and pontifical blessings, of small virtue, nowhere exemplified in Holy Scripture, because the bishop's ordinal and the New Testament scarcely agree, and we cannot see that the Holy Spirit, by reason of any such signs, confers the gift, for he and all his excellent gifts cannot consist in anyone with mortal sin. A corollary to this is that it is a grievous play for wise men to see bishops trifle with the Holy Spirit in the bestowal of orders, because they give the tonsure in outward appearance in the place of white hearts; and this is the unrestrained introduction of antichrist into the church to give color to idleness.

3. That the law of continence enjoined to priests, which was first ordained to the prejudice of women, brings sodomy into all the holy church, but we excuse ourselves by the Bible because the decree says that we should not mention it, though suspected. Reason and experience prove this conclusion: reason, because the good living of ecclesiastics must have a natural outlet or worse; experience, because the secret proof of such men is that they find delight in women, and when thou hast proved such a man mark him well, because he is one of them. A corollary to this is that private religions and the originators of beginning of this sin would be specially worthy of being checked, but God of his power with regard to secret sin sends open vengeance in his church.

4. That the pretended miracle of the sacrament of bread drives all men, but a few, to idolatry, because they think that the body of Christ which is never away from heaven could by power of the priest's word be enclosed essentially in a little bread which they show the people; but God grant that they might be willing to believe what the evangelical doctor says in his Trialogus, that the bread of the altar is habitually the body of Christ, for we take it that in this way any faithful man and woman can by God's law perform the sacrament of that bread without any such miracle. A final corollary is that although the body of Christ has been granted eternal joy, the service of Corpus Christi, instituted by Brother Thomas [Aquinas], is not true but is fictitious and full of false miracles. It is no wonder; because Brother Thomas, at that time holding with the pope, would have been willing to perform a miracle with a hen's egg; and we know well that any falsehood openly preached turns to the disgrace of him who is always true and without any defect.

5. That exorcisms and blessings performed over wine, bread, water and oil, salt, wax, and incense, the stones of the altar, and church walls, over clothing,

mitre, cross, and pilgrims' staves, are the genuine performance of necromancy rather than of sacred theology. This conclusion is proved as follows, because by such exorcisms creatures are honored as being of higher virtue than they are in their own nature, and we do not see any change in any creature which is so exorcized, save by false faith which is the principal characteristic of the devil's art. A corollary: that if the book of exorcizing holy water, read in church, were entirely trustworthy we think truly that the holy water used in church would be the best medicine for all kinds of illnesses — sores, for instance; whereas we experience the contrary day by day.

6. That king and bishop in one person, prelate and judge in temporal causes, curate and officer in secular office, puts any kingdom beyond good rule. This conclusion is clearly proved because the temporal and spiritual are two halves of the entire holy church. And so he who has applied himself to one should not meddle with the other, for no one can serve two masters. It seems that hermaphrodite or ambidexter would be good names for such men of double estate. A corollary is that we, the procurators of God in this behalf, do petition before parliament that all curates, as well superior as inferior, be fully excused and should occupy themselves with their own charge and no other.

7. That special prayers for the souls of the dead offered in our church, preferring one before another in name, are a false foundation of alms, and for that reason all houses of alms in England have been wrongly founded. This conclusion is proved by two reasons: the one is that meritorious prayer, and of any effect, ought to be a work proceeding from deep charity, and perfect charity leaves out no one, for "Thou shalt love thy neighbor as thyself." And so it is clear to us that the gift of temporal good bestowed on the priesthood and houses of alms is a special incentive to private prayer which is not far from simony. For another reason is that special prayer made for men condemned is very displeasing to God. And although it be doubtful, it is probable to faithful Christian people that founders of a house of alms have for their poisonous endowment passed over for the most part to the broad road. The corollary is: effectual prayer springing from perfect love would in general embrace all whom God would have saved, and would do away with that well-worn way or merchandise in special prayers made for the possessionary mendicants and other hired priests, who are a people of great burden to the whole realm, kept in idleness: for it has been proved in one book, which the king had, that a hundred houses of alms would suffice in all the realm, and from this would rather accrue possible profit to the temporal estate.

8. That pilgrimages, prayers, and offerings made to blind crosses or roods, and to deaf images of wood or stone, are pretty well akin to idolatry and far from alms, and although those be forbidden and imaginary, a book of error to the lay folk, still the customary image of the Trinity is specially abominable.

This conclusion God clearly proves, bidding alms to be done to the needy man because they are the image of God, and more like than wood and stone; for God did not say, "let us make wood or stone in our likeness and image," but man; because the supreme honor which clerks call *latria* appertains to the Godhead only; and the lower honor which clerks call *dulia* appertains to man and angel and to no inferior creature. A corollary is that the service of the cross, performed twice in any year in our church, is full of idolatry, for if that should, so might the nails and lance be so highly honored; then would the lips of Judas be relics indeed if any were able to possess them. But we ask you, pilgrim, to tell us when you offer to the bones of saints placed in a shrine in any spot, whether you relieve the saint who is in joy, or that almshouse which is so well endowed and for which men have been canonized, God knows how. And to speak more plainly, a faithful Christian supposes that the wounds of that noble man, whom men call St. Thomas [Becket], were not a case of martyrdom.

9. That auricular confession which is said to be so necessary to the salvation of a man, with its pretended power of absolution, exalts the arrogance of priests and gives them opportunity of other secret colloquies which we will not speak of; for both lords and ladies attest that, for fear of their confessors, they dare not speak the truth. And at the time of confession there is a ready occasion for assignation that is for "wooing," and other secret understandings leading to mortal sins. [Confessors] themselves say that they are God's representatives to judge of every sin, to pardon and cleanse whomsoever they please. They say that they have the keys of heaven and of hell, and can excommunicate and bless, bind and loose, at their will, so much so that for a drink, or twelve pence, they will sell the blessing of heaven with charter and close warrant sealed with the common seal. This conclusion is so notorious that it needs not any proof. It is a corollary that the pope of Rome, who has given himself out as treasurer of the whole church, having in charge that worthy jewel of Christ's passion together with the merits of all saints in heaven, whereby he grants pretended indulgence from penalty and guilt, is a treasurer almost devoid of charity, in that he can set free all that are prisoners in hell at his will and cause that they should never come to that place. But in this any Christian can well see there is much secret falsehood hidden away in our church.

10. That manslaughter in war, or by pretended law of justice for a temporal cause, without spiritual revelation, is expressly contrary to the New Testament, which indeed is the law of grace and full of mercies. This conclusion is openly proved by the examples of Christ's preaching here on earth, for he specially taught a man to love his enemies, and to show them pity, and not to slay them. The reason is this, that for the most part, when men fight, after the first blow, charity is broken. And whoever dies without charity goes the straight road to hell. And beyond this we know well that no clergyman can by Scripture or

lawful reason remit the punishment of death for one mortal sin and not for another; but the law of mercy, which is the New Testament, prohibits all manner of manslaughter, for in the Gospel: "It was said unto them of old time, 'Thou shalt not kill.'" The corollary is that it is indeed robbery of poor folk when lords get indulgences from punishment and guilt for those who aid their army to kill a Christian people in distant lands for temporal gain, just as we too have seen soldiers who run into heathendom to get them a name for the slaughter of men; much more do they deserve ill thanks from the King of Peace, for by our humility and patience was the faith multiplied, and Christ Jesus hates and threatens men who fight and kill, when He says: "He who smites with the sword shall perish by the sword."

11. That the vow of continence made in our church by women, who are frail and imperfect in nature, is the cause of bringing in the gravest horrible sins possible to human nature, because, although the killing of abortive children before they are baptized and the destruction of nature by drugs are vile sins, yet connection with themselves or brute beasts or any creature not having life surpasses them in foulness to such an extent as that they should be punished with the pains of hell. The corollary is that, widows and such as take the veil and the ring, being delicately fed, we could wish that they were given in marriage, because we cannot excuse them from secret sins.

12. That the abundance of unnecessary arts practised in our realm nourishes much sin in waste, profusion, and disguise. This, experience and reason prove in some measure, because nature is sufficient for a man's necessity with few arts. The corollary is that since St. Paul says: "having food and raiment, let us be therewith content," it seems to us that goldsmiths and armorers and all kinds of arts not necessary for a man, according to the apostle, should be destroyed for the increase of virtue; because although these two said arts were exceedingly necessary in the old law, the New Testament abolishes them and many others.

This is our embassy, which Christ has bidden us fulfill, very necessary for this time for several reasons. And although these matters are briefly noted here they are however set forth at large in another book, and many others besides, at length in our own language, and we wish that these were accessible to all Christian peole. We ask God then of his supreme goodness to reform our church, as being entirely out of joint, to the perfectness of its first beginning.

Questions: What are the bases for Lollard beliefs? What views of human nature are expressed here? What view of women is taken here? What typical practices of the medieval church are objected to? Why? How did the Lollards' beliefs threaten the status quo?

69. THE DEPOSITION OF RICHARD II

In 1327 Edward II had become the first king of England to be deposed; his great-grand-son Richard II met a similar fate in 1399, after a determined effort by his cousin Henry of Lancaster (soon to be Henry IV) to force him from the throne. The following account is taken from the Parliamentary rolls.

Source: trans. A.R. Myers, *English Historical Documents IV, 1327-1485* (New York: Oxford University Press, 1969), pp. 407-414.

Memorandum that on Monday, the feast of St. Michael the Archangel [September 29], in the 23rd year of King Richard II, the lords spiritual and temporal and other notable persons [16 names follow] deputed for the following act, came into the presence of the said king Richard, being within the Tower of London, at nine o'clock. And the Earl of Northumberland recited before the king on behalf of the aforesaid deputation, how the same king at Conway in North Wales, being still at liberty, promised to the lord Thomas Archbishop of Canterbury and to the Earl of Northumberland that he was willing to cede and renounce the crown of England and France and his royal majesty, because of the inability and insufficiency to which the same king confessed, and to do this in the best manner and form which could be done as might be best devised by the counsel of experienced men. The king in the presence of the lords and others named above benignly replied that he was willing to give effect to what he had formerly promised; he desired however to have speech with Henry of Lancaster and the archbishop (Arundel) his kinsmen, before he fulfilled his promise. He asked for a copy of the resignation to be made by him to be given to him, so that he might in the meantime deliberate on it; this copy was given to him, and the lords and the others returned to their lodgings. Afterwards on the same day after dinner the king greatly desiring the arrival of the duke of Lancaster, who tarried for a long time, at last the duke, the lords and persons named above and also the Archbishop of Canterbury, came into the king's presence in the Tower, the lords Roos, Willoughby, and Abergavenny and many others being present. And after the king had spoken apart with the duke and the archbishop, looking from one to the other with a cheerful countenance, as it seemed to the bystanders, at last the king, calling all those present to him, declared publicly in their presence, that he was ready to make the renunciation and resignation according to his promise. And although, to save the labor of such a lengthy reading, he might, as he was told, have had the resignation and renunciation, which was drawn up in a certain parchment schedule, read by a deputy, the king willingly, as it seemed, and with a cheerful countenance, holding the same schedule in his hand, said that he would read it him-

self, and he did read it distinctly. And he absolved his lieges and made renunciation and cession, and swore this … and he signed it with his own hand….

And immediately he added to the aforesaid renunciation and cession, in his
own words, that if it were in his power the duke of Lancaster should succeed
him in the realm. But because this was in no wise in his power, as he said, he
asked the archbishop of York and bishop of Hereford, whom he appointed as
his proctors to declare and intimate his renunciation and cession to all the
estates of the realm, to declare his intention and wish in this matter to the people. And as a token of his intention and wish in this matter, he took off his
finger the gold ring with his signet, and put it on the duke's finger, desiring the
same, as he affirmed, to be known to all the estates of the realm. And when this
was done, all said farewell to him and left the Tower to return to their lodgings.

On the morrow, Tuesday, the feast of St. Jerome [September 30], in the great
hall at Westminster, in the place honorably prepared for holding parliament, the
archbishops of Canterbury and York and the duke of Lancaster, and other
dukes, and lords both spiritual and temporal, whose names are written below,
and a great multitude of the people of the realm being gathered there on
account of parliament, the duke of Lancaster occupying his usual and proper
place, and the royal throne, solemnly prepared with cloth of gold being vacant,
without any president, the archbishop of York and the bishop of Hereford
according to the king's injunction publicly declared the cession and renunciation to have been made by him, with the delivery of the seal, and the royal sig-
nature, and they caused the cession and renunciation to be read, first in Latin
and then in English. And at once the archbishop of Canterbury, to whom pertains by reason of the dignity and prerogative of the metropolitan church of
Canterbury to have the first voice amongst the prelates and magnates of the
realm, asked the estate of the people then present, whether they wished to
accept the renunciation and cession for their interests and the good of the
realm. The estates and people considering, for the reasons specified by the king
himself in his renunciation and cession, that it would be very expedient, each
one singly, and then in common with the people, unanimously and cordially
gave his consent. After this acceptance it was publicly set forth that besides the
cession and renunciation which had been accepted, it would in many ways be
expedient and advantageous for the kingdom, to avoid all scruple and evil suspicion, that the many crimes and defects frequently committed by the king in
the bad government of the realm — on account of which, as he himself had
asserted in his abdication, he was worthy to be deposed — should by means of
articles which had been drawn up in writing be publicly read, that they might
be declared to the people. And so a large part of these articles was then publicly read, of which article the tenor is as follows…

1. In the first place the king is indicted on account of his evil rule, that is, he has given the goods and possessions which belong to the crown to unworthy persons and otherwise dissipated them indiscreetly, and therefore has imposed collections and other grave and insupportable burdens on his people without cause. And he has perpetrated innumerable other evils. By his assent and command certain prelates and other lords temporal were chosen and assigned by the whole parliament to govern the realm; and they faithfully labored with their whole strength for the just government of the realm. Nevertheless the king made a conventicle with his accomplices and proposed to accuse of high treason the lords spiritual and temporal who were occupied for the good of the realm; and in order to strengthen his evil design he violently forced the justices of the realm by fear of death and torture of body to destroy the said lords.

2. Also the king caused the greater part of his justices to come before him and his adherents secretly at Shrewsbury, and he induced, made and compelled them to reply singly to certain questions put to them on behalf of the king, touching the laws of the realm. This was contrary to their wishes, and other than what they would have replied if they had been free and not under compulsion. By color of these replies the king proposed to proceed later to the destruction of the duke of Gloucester, the earls of Arundel and Warwick and other lords, against whom the king was extremely indignant because they wished the king to be under good rule. But with divine help and the resistance and power of the said lords opposing him, the king could not bring his scheme into effect....

7. Also, after many of these people had made fines and redemptions, they sought from the king letters patent of general pardon, concerning the above; but they could secure no advantage from these letters of pardon until they had paid new fines and redemptions to save their lives; by this they were much impoverished. On account of this the royal name and estate were brought into great disrepute....

10. Also, although the crown of England and the rights of the crown, and the same realm, have been so free for all time past that neither the lord high pontiff nor anyone else outside the kingdom ought to intermeddle with the same, yet the king, in order to strengthen his erroneous statutes, begged the lord pope to confirm the statutes ordained in the last parliament. On which the king sought for apostolic letters, in which grave censures were threatened against all who presumed to contravene the statutes in any way....

16. Also, the king refused to keep and defend the just laws and customs of the realm, but according to the whim of his desire he wanted to do whatever appealed to his wishes. Sometimes — and often when the laws of the realm had been declared and expressed to him by the justices and others of his council and he should have done justice to those who sought it according to those

laws — he said expressly, with harsh and determined looks, that the laws were in his own mouth, sometimes he said that they were in his breast, and that he alone could change or establish the laws of his realm. And deceived by this idea, he would not allow justice to be done to many of his lieges, but compelled very many persons to desist from suing for common justice by threats and fear.

17. Also, after certain statutes were established in his parliament, which should always bind until they should be especially repealed by the authority of another parliament the king, desiring to enjoy such liberty that no statutes should bind him subtly procured that such a petition should be put forward in parliament on behalf of the community of the realm, and to be granted to him in general, that he might be as free as any of his predecessors were before him. By color of this petition and concession the king frequently did and ordered many things contrary to such statutes which had never been repealed, acting expressly and knowingly against his oath made in his coronation....

19. Also, although by statute and custom of the realm, upon the summons of parliament the people of each shire ought to be free to choose and depute knights for the shire to be present in parliament to set forth their grievances, and sue for remedy as might seem to them expedient; yet the king, that he might be the more free to carry out in parliament his rash designs, directed his mandates frequently to his sheriffs, to see that certain persons nominated by himself should come to parliament as knights of the shire. The knights thus favorable to him he could induce, as he frequently did, sometimes by fear and various threats, sometimes by gifts, to agree to measures prejudicial to the realm and extremely burdensome to the people; and especially he induced them to concede to the king the subsidy of wools for the term of his life, and another subsidy for a term of years, oppressing his people too much....

21. Also, the king, wishing to crush the people under his feet and craftily acquire their goods, that he might have a superabundance of riches, induced the people of seventeen shires to make their submission to the king as traitors, by letters under their seals; by color of which he obtained great sums of money conceded by the clergy and people of the shires, to be taken at the king's pleasure. And although to please the people the king caused those forced letters to be restored to them, yet the king caused the proctors of the people, who had full powers conceded to them to bind themselves and their heirs to the king, to give undertakings to him under their seals in the name of the people. Thus he deceived his people, and craftily extorted their goods from them....

23. Also, in many great councils of the king, when the lords of the realm, the justices, and others were charged faithfully to counsel the king in matters touching the estate of himself and the realm, often the lords, justices and others when they were giving their advice according to their discretion were sud-

denly and sharply rebuked and censured by him, so that they did not dare to speak the truth about the state of the king and the kingdom in giving their advice....

26. Also, although the lands and tenements, goods and chattels of every freeman, according to the laws of the realm used through all past times, ought not to be seized unless they have been lawfully forfeited; nevertheless the king, proposing and determining to undo such laws, declared and affirmed in the presence of very many lords and others of the community of the realm that the lives of every one of his lieges and their lands, tenements, goods, and chattels are his at his pleasure, without any forfeiture, which is entirely against the laws and customs of the realm....

It seemed to all the estates who were interrogated thereupon, singly and in common, that those accusations of crime and defaults were sufficient and notorious enough for the deposition of the king; and they also considered his confession of inadequacy and other matters contained in the renunciation and cession, publicly announced; whereupon all the estates unanimously agreed that there was abundant reason for proceeding to deposition, for the greater security and tranquillity of the realm and the good of the kingdom. Therefore the estates and communities unanimously and cordially constituted and publicly deputed certain commissioners, i.e. the bishop of St. Asaph, the abbot of Glastonbury, the earl of Gloucester, Lord Berkeley, Sir Thomas Erpingham, Sir Thomas Grey, and William Thirnyng, justice, to carry out this sentence of deposition and to depose King Richard from all his royal dignity, majesty, and honor, on behalf of, in the name of, and by authority of all the estates, as has been observed in similar cases by the ancient custom of the realm. And soon the commissioners assuming the burden of the commission, and sitting before the royal seat as a tribunal, had some discussion on these matters and reduced the sentence of deposition to writing; and by the wish and authority of the commission the sentence was read and recited by the bishop of St. Asaph....

And at once, it being manifest from the foregoing transactions and by reason of them that the realm of England with its appurtenances was vacant, Henry, duke of Lancaster, rising in his place, and standing erect so that he might be seen by the people, and humbly making the sign of the cross on his forehead and his breast, and invoking the name of Christ, claimed the realm of England, vacant as aforesaid, along with the crown and all its members and appurtenances, in his mother tongue in the following words:

In the name of the Father, Son, and Holy Ghost, I, Henry of Lancaster, challenge this realm of England and the crown with all its members and appurtenances, as I am descended by right line of the blood coming from the good lord, King Henry III, and through that right that God of his grace has sent me, with the help of my kindred and my friends to recover it; the which realm was on the point of being undone for default of governance and undoing of good laws....

When [the archbishop's] sermon was finished, the lord king Henry, in order to set at rest the minds of his subjects declared publicly in these words:

Sires, I thank God and you lords spiritual and temporal and all the estates of the land; and let you know that it is not my will that any man should think that by way of conquest I would disinherit any man of his heritage, franchise, or other rights that he ought to have, nor put him out of what he has and has had by the good laws and customs of the realm; except those persons who have been against the good purpose and the common profit of the realm....

On Monday [October 13], the day of St. Edward, king and confessor, King Henry was crowned at Westminster, with all the solemnity and honor that was fitting; and certain lords and others did severally their services to King Henry according to their tenures, in the accustomed manner at the time of such a coronation.

Questions: How do the main characters conduct themselves? How does the king face his deposition? What is the role of Parliament? What charges are made against Richard? Which of these ideas about kingship have been encountered in earlier documents?

CHAPTER FIVE

THE FIFTEENTH CENTURY

Fig. 29: Warfare around a town A nineteenth-century copy of a fifteenth-century manuscript illustration showing troops storming a town. Among the weapons depicted are swords, crossbows, longbows, and a small cannon in the foreground. On the left are the tents of the attackers.

70. CHRONICLE OF THE REIGN OF HENRY V

Henry V (1413-22), called "Harry" in this vernacular chronicle, revived the Hundred Years' War and won a famous victory at Agincourt. He followed this up with further military successes and a favorable treaty, but died before he could enjoy his defeat of France.

Source: modernized from *An English Chronicle of the Reigns of Richard II, Henry IV, Henry V, and Henry VI,* ed. J.S. Davies (London: The Camden Society, 1856), pp. 39-52.

Of King Harry V, the son of King Harry IV after the Conquest

After the death of King Harry IV reigned his son, King Harry V, who was born at Monmouth in Wales and crowned at Westminster on Passion Sunday [April 9].

And immediately, the first year of his reign, for the great and tender love that he had for King Richard [II], he translated his body from Langley to Westminster, and buried him beside Queen Anne his first wife, as his desire was....

And this same year were captured certain Lollards and heretics, who had intended through their false treason to slay the king and the lords spiritual and temporal, and to destroy all the clergy of the realm. But the king, as God willed, was warned of their false purpose and plan, and fought at Ficketts field, and with him Master Thomas Arundel, archbishop of Canterbury, and kept the roads around London secure. And many of them were captured, and drawn and hanged and burnt on the gallows in St. Giles' field. And a knight called Sir Roger of Acton was taken for Lollardy and for treason, and drawn and hanged and burnt in St. Giles' field.

The second year of his reign, he held a parliament at Westminster of all the lords of the realm, who discussed and spoke of his title that he had to Normandy, Gascony, and Guienne, that were his inheritance, which the king of France withheld wrongfully and unrightfully. And so advised by his council, he sent ambassadors to the king of France and his council, requiring them to yield up unto him his said inheritance, or else he would get it by the sword with the help of Jesus. The dauphin of France answered our ambassadors, and said that our king was too young and too tender of age to be a good warrior, and not likely to make such a conquest over them. Our ambassadors, hearing this scornful answer, returned to England again, notifying the king and his council of the answer of the dauphin and of the council of France.

Then the king made ready his ordnance necessary for the war, commanding all men that would go with him to be ready at Southampton, at Lammas [August 1] next following, the third year of his reign. On which day, when the king was ready to take his passage, it was there published and openly known that three lords, that is to say, Sir Richard, earl of Cambridge, brother of the duke of York, Lord Scrope, treasurer of England, and Sir Thomas Grey, knight, had received a huge sum of money, that is to say, a million gold coins, to betray the king and his brethren to the Frenchmen, wherefore their heads were smitten off, outside the north gate at Southampton.

When this was done, the king sailed forth into Normandy with 1500 ships, and landed [near Harfleur], on [August 14,] the day before the Assumption of our Lady, and from thence he went to Harfleur, and besieged it by land and by water, and commanded [the leader there] to deliver the town, and he said he would not. Wherefore the king commanded his gunners to beat down the walls on every side, and immediately the people of the town sent out to the king asking him for eight days' respite in hope of rescue, and if none would come, they would deliver the town: and so they did. And then the king made his uncle, the earl of Dorset, captain thereof, and commanded him to put out all the French people, man, woman, and child, and fill the town with English people.

When this was done, the king went toward Calais by land in order to come to England, but the Frenchmen had broken all the bridges he would pass over, wherefore he had to seek his way far upstream, and so he went over the water of the Somme, and came down into Picardy to a place called Agincourt, where all the power of France was gathered ready to block his way, and gave him battle.

The king, seeing the great multitude and number of people of his enemies, prayed to God Almighty for help and succor, and comforted his people, and told every man to make himself ready for battle; and with such people as he had, not fully 8000, he arranged them for battle, and granted to the duke of York the forward position, as he desired. And then the duke commanded every man to provide himself with a wooden stake sharpened at both ends, so that the stake might be stuck in the earth slantwise before them, and the Frenchmen should not override them, for that was fully their purpose. And all night before the battle, the Frenchmen made much revel and much crying, and played at dice for our men, an archer for a *blanc* [that is, a small coin of poor silver], as it was said.

On the morrow, when all was ready, the king asked what time of the day it was, and they said, "Prime." Then said the king, "Now is good time, for all England prayeth for us, and therefore be of good cheer, and let us go to our journey." And right then every English man kneeled down, and put a little portion of the earth in his mouth. And then said the king with a loud voice, "In the name of almighty God, and of St. George, forward banners! And St. George be this day thy help!" Then the two armies met together and fought sore and a long time, but almighty God and St. George fought that day for us, and granted our king the victory: and this was on the Friday, [October 25,] the day of Sts. Crispin and Crispinian, in the year of our Lord 1415 in a field called Agincourt in Picardy. And there were slain that day more than 11,000 of the Frenchmen in the field of Agincourt: and there were numbered of them in the field 120,000.

Then came tidings to our king, that there was another host of Frenchmen ordained ready to fight against him; and immediately he commanded every man to slay his prisoner, and when they saw that, they withdrew and went their way.

And there were slain in the field on the French part the duke of Berry, the duke of Alençon, the duke of Brabant, the earl of Narbonne, the chief constable of France, eight other earls, the archbishop of Sens, more than 100 barons, and 1500 other worthy knights and men in coat-armor. And of Englishmen that were dead that day, the duke of York, the earl of Suffolk, and not more than 26 others.

And there were taken prisoners of the French part the duke of Orléans, the duke of Bourbon, the earl of Vendôme, the earl of Eu, the earl of Richmond, Sir Bursigaund, marshal of France, and other worthy men.

And after this, the king came to Calais, and so to England, with all his prisoners, and was received with much joy and worship.

This same year came Sigismund, the emperor of Germany, to England to speak with King Harry, to negotiate about certain things regarding the peace of England and France, and also for the welfare and unity of all holy church. And the king and his lords met with him at St. Thomas Watering, outside Southwark, and received him with great reverence and worship, and brought him to London, and from thence to Westminster, and there he was lodged in the palace at the king's cost; and that same time the king gave him the livery of the garter.

And soon after came the duke of Holland to England, to speak with the emperor and with the king; and he was lodged in the bishop's inn at Ely, at the king's cost.

And while this was going on in England, the Frenchmen thought they would be avenged, and with a great army besieged the town of Harfleur, both by water and by land, and had gotten and hired great carracks [that is, armed merchant ships] of Genoa, and other small vessels, to lie and guard the mouth of the River Seine, so that no victuals nor other help should come up to the town; of this army the earl of Armagnac was captain.

Then the earl of Dorset, captain of Harfleur, sent messengers to the king notifying him of all this, and what scarcity and penury of victuals was within the town; and immediately the king sent his brother John, duke of Bedford, to break the siege by water: and he came with a notable force and fought with the aforesaid great carracks, and took four of them and many other French vessels.

And one of the greatest carracks of all escaped and fled away, but she was so shot up with holes in her sides in the said battle, that soon after it was drowned. And the noble earl of Dorset rescued the said town by land, and discomfited and slew many of the Frenchmen, and had a gracious victory over them.

When this was done, the said duke with his prizes and prisoners returned to England again, and for as much as this was done on [August 14,] the vigil of the Assumption of our Lady, the king commanded that his chaplain should say, every day while he lived, an anthem with the versicle and collect in remembrance of our Lady.

And when the emperor had been in this land as long as it pleased him at the king's cost, he took his leave of the king; and the king brought him to Calais, and tarried there to have an answer from the French party, about such things as the emperor and the king had sent to them for; and at last it came, and it pleased them not at all; and then the emperor went his way, and the king came to England again.

And right after this, the king sent ambassadors to the general council of Constance for the union and peace of all the holy church, and to redress and cease the schism and strife that was at that time in the church of Rome between three popes. And at that same time, by assent of all nations, it was ordered in this council that England should be called a nation, and be counted one of the five nations that owe obedience to the pope of Rome, which before that time was under the nation of Germany.

And this same year, the earl Douglas of Scotland came to England, and was sworn to the king to be his true man; but afterward he broke his oath, and was slain by Englishmen at the battle of Verneuil.

How King Harry went the second time into Normandy, and of the getting of Calais, and of the siege of Rouen

The fifth year of his reign, he made ready his ordnance and his retinue to sail to Normandy again, and commanded all men that would go with him to be ready at Southampton, in the Whitsuntide next following [that is, around May 30]. And then he made John his brother, the duke of Bedford, lieutenant of England; and then he sailed to Normandy with a notable force and great ordnance, and landed at Touques on Lammas Day [August 1]; and there he made 48 knights, at his landing.

Then came tidings to the king that there was a great navy of enemies upon the sea, that is to say, nine great carracks, hulks, galleys, and other ships to destroy his navy: and immediately he sent the earl of March with a sufficient force to keep the sea, and he took many of the said navy, and put the remnant to flight; and some were drowned with tempest. And one of the carracks was driven near Southampton, and its mast was thrown over the town walls; and this was on St. Bartholomew's day [August 24].

Then the king sent to the captain of Touques, commanding him to deliver the town, and so he did. And the king made Sir John Kiley captain thereof, and commanded him to put out all the French people.

And then was Louviers yielded to the earl marshal, and the king made him captain thereof.

And then the king went his way to Caen and besieged it on every side, and sent to the captain to deliver it, but he would not, wherefore they assaulted the town; and the duke of Clarence beat down the walls with guns on his side, and first entered into the town, and cried, "À Clarence! à Clarence! à St. George!" and so was the town captured. And the king entered and commanded the captain of the castle to deliver it unto him; and he asked for 14 days' respite in hope of rescue, and if none came, [he promised] to deliver the castle to him. And under this agreement were included the town and castle of Baons with other towns, fortresses, and villages, to the number of fourteen. And at the end of 14 days came no rescue, wherefore the castle of Caen and the other 14 towns were delivered unto the king; and he made the duke of Clarence captain of the town of Caen and of Baons and of the other towns also; and there the king held St. George's feast [on April 23] and made fifteen knights of the bath...

And at this same time came the duke of Brittany unto King Harry and became his man.

And the king sent Humphrey his brother, duke of Gloucester, to Cherbourg, and Richard, earl of Warwick, to Domfront, the which towns soon afterward were yielded unto them.

In the meantime, the earl of March, whom the king had sent to keep the sea, after many storms and great tempests landed at La Hague in Normandy, and so went forth unto the king.

Then the king took Argentan, Cessy, Alençon, Bellême, Verneuil in Perche, and all the towns and castles and strongholds unto Pont de l'Arche, and from thence unto the city of Rouen.

And this same year, Sir John Oldcastle, knight, Lord Cobham, was arrested for Lollardy, and put into the Tower of London, and right afterwards he broke out thereof, and fled into Wales and stayed there a long time, and at last the Lord Powys took him, but he made a great defense and was sore wounded before he could be taken; and then he was brought in a horsedrawn litter to Westminster, and there he was judged to be drawn unto St. Giles' field, and there he was hanged and burnt on the gallows for his false opinions.

The sixth year of King Harry, he sent his uncle Sir Thomas Beaufort to the gates of Rouen, and there he displayed the king's banner, and sent heralds to the town and bade them yield it to the king of England, and they said shortly that they would not. And then the said Beaufort collected good information about the ground all around, and returned to the king at Pont de l'Arche; and immediately after, the people of Rouen cast down their suburbs that stood around the city, so that the king should have no succor there.

And the Sunday before Lammas Day [August 1] then next following, the king with his host besieged the city of Rouen round about, and did make over the water of the Seine, at Pont de l'Arche, a strong and a mighty chain of iron, and put it through great piles of wood driven deep in the ground, and it went over the water of the Seine so that no vessel might pass that way; and above that chain the king had a bridge made over the river Seine so that man and horse and all other carriages might pass to and fro, when there was need.

Then came the earl of Warwick from Domfront, and the king sent him to Caudebec, and they of the town came out and negotiated with the earl to be under agreement to do as Rouen did; and it was granted on this condition, that the king's navy with his ordnance might pass upstream safely without any hindrance or disturbance; and to this agreement they set their seals. And then came up 100 ships and cast there their anchors, and then was Rouen besieged both by water and by land; and when this was done, the earl of Warwick went again to the king at the siege of Rouen; and the duke of Gloucester came thither also from the capturing of Cherbourg.

Then came tidings that the king of France, the dauphin, the duke of Burgundy, and all the power of France would come down to rescue the city of Rouen, and break the siege; but they came not.

And at the first coming of the king unto Rouen, there were numbered in the city, by heralds, 300,000 men, women, and children; and this siege endured 20 weeks; and ever they of the town hoped to be rescued, but it would not be: and many hundreds died for hunger, for they had eaten all their cats, horses, hounds, rats, mice, and all that might be eaten; and ofttimes the men of arms drove the poor people out of the gates of the city for spending of victuals, and right away our men drove them in again; and young children lay dead in the streets, hanging on their dead mothers' breasts, which was piteous to see. And when the captain of the town saw this great mischief and hunger, he sent to the king, beseeching him of his mercy and grace, and brought the keys, and delivered the town to him, and all the soldiers left the town with their horses and harness, and the commons of the town abode still in the town, paying 20,000 marks yearly to the king for all manner of customs, fee farms, and quatrymes. When the king had entered the town, and rested himself in the castle till the town was set in rule and governance, then Caudebec and other garrisons nearby were yielded under the same agreement.

Then the dauphin's ambassadors, as it was before agreed, with full power to do all things as if he were there himself, came to the king at Rouen; and after much negotiation, thus it was agreed that at a certain day set, the dauphin should come to the town of Dreux, and King Harry to Avranches; and there they would choose a meeting place, by the assent of them both, where they might peaceably negotiate the peace; to which appointment truly to be kept, the king and the said ambassadors set their seals. At the appointed day the king came, but the dauphin came not, wherefore the peace was broken at that time.

In the meantime John, duke of Burgundy, who had the rule and governance of the king of France because of his sickness, by letters and ambassadors sought King Harry's grace. And the king sent ambassadors again to King Charles of France and to the said duke of Burgundy in Provence, of which ambassadors Richard, earl of Warwick, was the chief; and in the way he was to go lay a great ambush of Frenchmen to capture him and obstruct his purpose; but he slew and captured the greater part of them, and went forth to Provence, and set out on his embassy and message.

And there it was thus agreed and appointed that King Harry of England and Charles of France with the queen his wife and the duke of Burgundy should come to a meeting place to negotiate a peace, and to deliver this message the earl of Saint-Pol and the son and heir of the duke of Burgundy came to our king as ambassadors.

Then King Harry, knowing all the background of the matter by relation of ambassadors of both parties, agreed with his enemies in this way: that at a certain day he would come to Mantes, and Charles of France and the duke of Burgundy to Pontoise, to choose there a meeting place to negotiate a peace, which meeting place for this treaty should be Meulan upon Seine; to the which place neither party should come with more than 2,500 men, and in the meantime a truce should be on both parties. This meeting place was afterward arrayed between two villages, and limited and marked between two great ditches, wherein no man should come except such as should negotiate peace; and there the king's tents were royally pitched and set up, and the king of France's tents also. And King Harry had two tents set up between two ditches, wherein both kings might talk apart with their secret council, and the estate of both kings be observed and kept; and a stake was driven in the middle of an open space, to which, and no further, each king should come to the other.

At the day appointed King Harry came to Mantes, and King Charles because of his accustomed sickness came not, but the queen his wife and the duke of Burgundy with other noble princes of their alliance and with 2500 men came to Pontoise, and afterward to the meeting place. Then King Harry first kissed the queen of France, and then Dame Katherine her daughter, for that time he saw her first; and then King Harry, the queen of France and her daughter, the duke of Burgundy, and others went into a tent, to negotiate a peace, where they were almost three days; but it came to no end at that time.

Meanwhile, the dauphin with letters and abassadors stirred up the duke of Burgundy, that neither he nor any of his men should assent to the peace. And on [August 1,] the fifth of the nones of August, when the said kings should have assembled, neither the king of France, the queen, the duke of Burgundy, nor any of them came; wherefore it was openly known that the French party was the reason that the peace was not concluded at that time.

Then went the king to Pontoise and captured it, and sent his brother the duke of Clarence with a notable force to Paris, and he captured it, and returned again to the king; and then the king captured Bokende Villers.

And while this was going on, the duke of Burgundy, who first had sought King Harry's grace, went under safe conduct to the dauphin at Montereau; and there he was traitorously and unmanfully slain by the said dauphin, and cast into a pit; and as soon as Philip his son and heir learned of this, he became King Harry's man.

At the same time came certain ambassadors of King Charles, of the duke of Burgundy, and of the citizens of Paris to King Harry at Mantes, to negotiate peace, but because King Harry was busily occupied in his wars, and also because he supposed that the Frenchmen were not fully inclined to the peace then, no treaty was concluded at that time, but afterward at Rouen it was fully concluded.

And afterward while King Harry held his Christmas at Rouen, the ambassadors of King Charles and of the duke of Burgundy came thither unto him, to whom King Harry sent again Richard, earl of Warwick, with other wise men and a notable force of men of arms, with full power and authorization to conclude the peace. And after many wise negotiations on both sides, peace was concluded by the affinity and wedlock of King Harry and Dame Katherine, King Charles' daughter. But because certain things were necessary for which the presence of both kings must needs be had, for setting to of their seals, and for the making of the marriage, and also because Charles was so enfeebled with age and ofttimes vexed with his usual sickness, it was between them thus agreed, that King Harry should come at a day specified, under truce, with such forces as he liked, to Nogent upon the Seine, to perform finally all things that were needful to the peace, and if he came not, all things should be null and void. After this agreement thus made, the earl returned to the king, notifying him in writing of the whole import of his embassy.

The king from thence went to Nogent; and there the duke of Burgundy met with him with a great company of men of arms. And after many and diverse negotiations, [on May 26,] the seventh of the kalends of June, the fortieth year of King Charles' reign, in the cathedral church of Nogent, King Harry with the duke of Clarence his brother and other princes and nobles, and Isabelle queen of France with the duke of Burgundy, being there for King Charles, who was then laboring in his aforementioned sickness, and in their own names also, and the three estates of France, peace between the two realms of England and of France was made, and with certain conditions approved. And King Charles charged all his liege men on pain of forfeiture of their allegiances to keep the said peace; and thereto they made their oath, and pledged their faith to King Harry. And then Queen Isabelle of France, and Philip duke of Burgundy, in the name of King Charles, swore upon the holy Gospels, to keep the said peace so concluded for them and for their heirs and successors without fraud and ill will for evermore; and Queen Isabelle, and the duke of Burgundy, and the three estates of France made this same oath to King Harry, to his heirs and successors. And on the ninth of the kalends of June, before Queen Isabelle and King Charles' council, before the parliament and the three estates of France, and other English princes and lords, contract of matrimony by present words was there made and solemnized between King Harry and Dame Katherine, King Charles of France's daughter.

And as soon as all this was enacted in writing as it was agreed, King Harry, King Charles, the two queens Isabelle and Katherine, and the duke of Burgundy went unto Senlis and captured it, and from thence unto Meulan and besieged it, and that siege lasted from July until November in much duress; and at last, for lack of victuals, the town was yielded. Then the two kings, the two queens, and the duke of Burgundy with their hosts went to Paris, and the citizens of Paris met with them in full noble array.

And the next January King Harry and Queen Katherine went to England, and left at Paris Thomas duke of Exeter, governor, and Thomas his brother, duke of Clarence, regent of Normandy; and the duke of Clarence was slain there with the Scots on Easter eve, while the king was in England. And on Sunday the [23rd] day of February, in the eighth year of King Harry, Dame Katherine was crowned at Westminster.

At the following midsummer, the king left the queen in England, and went again to France, and took certain garrisons that were in rebellion, and besieged the town of Meaux, at which siege tidings came to the king that the queen was delivered [of a child]; and after her purification she went again to France.

When Meaux was yielded, King Harry went to Paris, making plans to besiege the town of Cosne; and then a sore and burning malady assailed him, and from day to day grievously vexed him, till he died in the castle of Vincennes, the last day of August, when he had reigned nine years, five months, three weeks, and three days, and he is buried at Westminster: on whose soul almighty God have mercy. Amen.

Questions: What English domestic matters are of interest to the chronicler? How was warfare conducted under Henry? Are there similarities between Crécy, Poitiers, and Agincourt? What difficulties did he face in negotiations with the French? What was the significance of his marriage to Katherine?

71. THE AGINCOURT CAROL

This short and simple song in English spread the news of Agincourt among England's people. The Latin refrain, which would have at least sounded familiar to a church-going populace, means "England, give thanks to God for victory."

Source: modernized by A.R. Myers, *English Historical Documents IV, 1327-1485* (New York: Oxford University Press, 1969), pp. 214-215.

Deo gracias, anglia,
redde pro victoria.
Our king went forth to Normandy,
With grace and might of chivalry;
There God for him wrought marvelously,
Wherefore England may call and cry,
Deo gracias!

He set a siege, the sooth for to say,
To Harfleur town with royal array;
That town he won and made affray,
That France shall rue until Domésday,
Deo gracias!

Then went our king with all his host
Through France, for all the hostile host,
He spared no dread of least or most,
Until he came to Agincourt coast,
Deo gracias!

Then forsooth that knight comely
In Agincourt field he fought manly;
Through grace of God most mighty
He had both the field and victory.
Deo gracias!

There dukes and earls, lord and baron
were taken and slain, and that well soon;
And some were led into London
With joy and mirth and great renown
Deo gracias!

May gracious God now save our king
His people and his well-willing;
Give him good life and good ending,
That we with mirth may safely sing,
Deo gracias!

Questions: To whom would such a song appeal, and how? What is the difference between "field" and "victory" in the fourth stanza? Is there nascent nationalism evident in the Carol?

72. LIBEL OF ENGLISH POLICY

"Libel" here is from the Latin libellus, *or "little book" — this is, in fact, a polemical poem setting out the case for a more aggressive English naval and commercial policy. The anonymous work was composed in 1436.*

Source: modernized from T. Wright, ed., *Political Poems and Songs Relating to English History* (London: Longman, Green, Longman, and Roberts, 1861), pp. 157-159, 178-180, 201-202.

Here begins the prologue of the process of the Little Book of English Policy, exhorting all England to guard the sea around it, and namely the narrow sea [that is, the English Channel], showing what profit comes from it, and also respect and security to England and all Englishmen.

The true purpose of English policy:
To keep this realm from foreign attack at rest,
That of our England no man may deny
Or say, in truth, it's not one of the best;
That he who sails south, north, east or west,
Keep merchandise safe and guard the admiralty,
And we be masters of the narrow sea.

For Sigismond, the great emperor,
Who reigneth yet, when he was in this land,
With King Henry the Fifth, prince of honor,
Much glory here, as he thought, he found;
A mighty land, which had taken in hand
To war with France and cause mortality,
And which evermore kept watch upon the sea.

And to the king thus he said: "My brother,"
When he perceived two towns, Calais and Dover,
"Of all your towns, choose this one and the other,
To guard the sea, and soon you may go over
To make war abroad and your realm to recover;
Guard these two towns, sire, and your majesty,
As your two eyes to watch the narrow sea."

For if this sea be guarded, in time of war,
Who can pass here without danger and woe,
Who may escape, who may mischief offer?
What merchandise could past us go?
For we could get a truce from every foe,
Flanders, and Spain, and others too — trust me —
Else they'd be trapped within the narrow sea.

Therefore I start me on a little writing
To show all eyes this my conclusion,
For conscience and my own acquitting
Before God, and against abusing,
And cowardice, to our enemy's confusion;
Four things our noble shows to me:
King, ship, and sword, and power on the sea.

Where are our ships? What have our swords become?
Our enemies value our ship as but a sheep!
Alas! our rule halteth, it is all gone.
Who dares to say that power a watch must keep?
I will attempt, though my heart begins to weep,
To do this work, so we might able be,
For very shame, to rule upon the sea.

Shall any prince, whatever be his name,
Who has nobles much like ours,
Be lord of the sea, and Flemings, to our blame,
Stop us, take us, and so make fade the flowers
Of English state, and disdain our honors?
For cowardice, alas, it so should be!
Therefore I begin to write now of the sea....

7. ...Now the principal matter:
Why should we go to such expensive lengths
In their countries, while in our English lands
They do not so, but have more liberty
Than we ourselves? ...
I wish men would of presents take no heed
That harm our public business for to speed;
For this we see for certain every day,
Gifts and feasts can stop our policy.
Now see that fools are either they or we,
But ever we have the worse in this country.
Therefore let them have expenses here,
Or let's be just as free when over there
In their country; and if it will not be,
Force them to pay their costs, and you shall see
Advantages and much profit arise,
Much more than I can write in any wise.
Of our charge and discharge at their markets:

Know well that English men at markets
Are charged for all their crafts and arts,
In the Brabant, for all their merchandise
And wares in fourteen days, and then
In the same two weeks are charged again;
And if they stay there longer all is gone:
Soon they will forfeit all their goods
And merchandise — that's how it goes.
And off to markets of Brabant are we
With English cloth, full good and fair to see,
Where we are taxed not only as clothiers,
But also as haberdashers and grocers.
To which markets, that Englishmen call fairs,
Many a foreign traveler repairs:
English and French, Lombards, Genoese,
Catalans, thither they take their ways,
Scots, Spaniards, Irishmen all come along,
Bringing salt hides in a great throng.
And I here say, while we in Brabant lie,
And Flanders and Zeeland, we buy more merchandise
In common use, than do all other nations;
This I have heard by merchants' own relations.

And if the English are not at the fair,
The market is feeble, as if no one were there;
For they buy more, and from their purse shell out,
More merchandise than the rest of the crowd.
If the sea were guarded, ships wouldn't bring and fetch,
And even big ships would not thither stretch;
And the state of their markets would evil be,
If we manfully guarded the sea.

Fig. 30: Warships   A nineteenth-century engraving of English warships, copied from a fifteenth-century manuscript. Such ships would have been used to carry out the measures recommended by the author of the Libel of English Policy (doc. 72), and similar ships would have carried the Celys' wool from England to France (doc. 83).

12. Of unity, showing our guarding of the sea, with a final purpose of peace by authority:

> Now then for love of Christ and of his joys,
> Bring yet England out of trouble and noise,
> Take heart and wit, and set a governance,
> Set many wits without any variance
> To one accord and unanimity,
> Put to good will for to safeguard the sea.
> First for worship and profit also,
> And for rebuke of each ill-willed foe;
> Thus shall riches and worship to us belong;
> Then to the noble shall we do no wrong....
> Thus must Flanders for need have unity
> And peace with us — as you will surely see —
> Within a short time, and ambassadors
> Would be here soon to bargain at our doors.
> This unity is most pleasing to God's ear,
> As is peace after the din of war.
> The end of battle is peace certainly,
> And power causes peace finally.
> Guard then the sea most especially of all,
> Which is of England the encircling wall,
> As though England were likened to a city,
> and the wall around it were the sea....

Questions: What is the author's goal? What tactics does he recommend? What arguments and evidence does he muster? What is his vision of "peace" and "unity"?

73. ORDER OF THE PAGEANTS OF THE YORK CORPUS CHRISTI PLAY

The roots of modern English drama lie in the religious plays of the later Middle Ages, one form of which was the series of short scenes presented on a parade of wagons with which the city of York celebrated Corpus Christi day, a festival in honor of the body of Christ. The city's craft guilds produced these plays; the following list, from 1415, tells us about both the organization of the pageant and the economic life of this northern city.

Source: trans. L.T. Smith, "York Plays," reprinted in *Translations and Reprints from the Original Sources of European History*, series 1, vol. 2 (Philadelphia: University of Pennsylvania Department of History, 1895), no. 1, ed. Edward P. Cheyney, pp. 29–32; revised.

Tanners — God the Father Omnipotent creating and forming the heavens, the angels and archangels, Lucifer and the angels who fell with him into the pit.

Plasterers — God the Father in his substance creating the earth and all things which are therein, in the space of five days.

Wool Cardmakers — God the Father forming Adam from the mud of the earth, and making Eve from Adam's rib, and inspiring them with the breath of life.

Fullers — God forbidding Adam and Eve to eat of the tree of life.

Coopers — Adam and Eve and the tree between them, the serpent deceiving them with apples; God speaking to them and cursing the serpent, and an angel with a sword driving them out of Paradise.

Armorers — Adam and Eve, an angel with a spade and distaff appointing them their labor.

Glovers — Able and Cain sacrificing victims.

Shipwrights — God warning Noah to make an ark out of planed wood.

Fishmongers and Mariners — Noah in the ark with his wife, three sons of Noah with their wives, with various animals.

Parchment-makers and Book-binders — Abraham sacrificing his son Isaac on the altar.

Hosiers — Moses lifting up the serpent in the wilderness, King Pharaoh, eight Jews looking on and wondering.

Spicers — A learned man declaring the sayings of the prophets concerning the future birth of Christ. Mary, the angel saluting her; Mary saluting Elizabeth.

Pewterers and Founders — Mary, Joseph wishing to send her away, the angel telling them to go over to Bethlehem.

Tilers — Mary, Joseph, a nurse, the child born and lying in a manger between an ox and an ass, and an angel speaking to the shepherds, and to the players in the next pageant.

Chandlers — Shepherds speaking to one another, the star in the East, an angel announcing to the shepherds their great joy in the child which has been born.

Goldsmiths, Goldbeaters and Moneyers — Three kings coming from the East, Herod questioning them about the child Jesus, and the son of Herod and two counsellors and a herald. Mary with the child and the star above, and three kings offering gifts.

… Masons — Mary, with the boy, Joseph, Anna; the nurse, with the young doves. Simeon receiving the boy into his arms, and the two sons of Simeon.

Farriers — Mary with the boy and Joseph fleeing into Egypt, at the bidding of the angel.

Girdlers, Nailers, and Sawyers — Herod ordering the male children to be slain, four soldiers with lances, two counsellors of the king, and four women weeping for the death of their sons.

Spurriers and Bit-makers — Learned men, the boy Jesus sitting in the temple in the midst of them, asking them questions and replying to them, four Jews, Mary and Joseph seeking him, and finding him in the temple.

Barbers — Jesus, John the Baptist baptizing him, and two angels attending.

Vintners — Jesus, Mary, bridegroom with the bride, ruler of the feast with his slaves, with six vessels of water in which the water is turned into wine.

Smiths — Jesus on a pinnacle of the temple, and the devil tempting him with stones, and two angels attending, etc.

Leather Curriers — Peter, James, and John; Jesus ascending into a mountain and transfiguring himself before them. Moses and Elias appearing, and the voice of one speaking in a cloud.

Ironmongers — Jesus, and Simon the leper asking Jesus to eat with him; two disciples, Mary Magdalene bathing Jesus' feet with her tears and drying them with her hair.

Plumbers and Pattenmakers — Jesus, two apostles, the woman taken in adultery, four Jews accusing her.

Pouchmakers, Leather Bottle-makers, and Capmakers — Lazarus in the sepulcher, Mary Magdalene and Martha, and two Jews wondering.

Skinners and Vestmakers — Jesus on an ass with its colt, twelve apostles following Jesus, six rich and six poor, eight boys with branches of palm, singing Blessed, etc., and Zaccheus climbing into a sycamore tree.

Cutlers, Bladesmiths, Sheathers, Scalers, Bucklermakers, and Horners — Pilate, Caiaphas, two soldiers, three Jews, Judas selling Jesus.

Bakers — The Passover lamb, the Lord's Supper, twelve apostles, Jesus girded with a towel washing their feet, institution of the sacrament of the body of Christ in the new law, communion of the apostles.

Cordwainers — Pilate, Caiaphas, Annas, fourteen armed soldiers, Malchus, Peter, James, John, Jesus, and Judas kissing and betraying him.

Bow-makers and Arrow-makers — Jesus, Annas, Caiaphas, and four Jews beating and scourging Jesus. Peter, the woman accusing Peter, and Malchus.

Tapestry-makers and Couchers — Jesus, Pilate, Annas, Caiaphas, two counsellors and four Jews accusing Jesus.

Bed-makers — Herod, two counsellors, four soldiers, Jesus, and three Jews.

Cooks and Watercarriers — Pilate, Annas, Caiaphas, two Jews, and Judas bringing back to them the thirty pieces of silver.

Tilemakers, Millers, Furriers, Horsehair-workers, Bowl-makers — Jesus, Pilate, Caiaphas, Annas, six soldiers holding spears with banners and four others leading Jesus away from Herod, asking to have Barabbas released and Jesus crucified, and likewise binding and scourging him, and placing the crown of thorns upon his head; three soldiers casting lots for the clothing of Jesus.

Shearmen — Jesus, stained with blood, bearing the cross to Calvary. Simon of Cyrene, the Jews compelling him to carry the cross; Mary the mother of Jesus; John the apostle then announcing the condemnation and passage of her son to Calvary. Veronica wiping the blood and sweat from the face of Jesus with a veil on which is imprinted the face of Jesus, and other women mourning for Jesus.

Pinmakers, Latenmakers, and Painters — The cross, Jesus stretched upon it on the ground; four Jews scourging Him and binding Him with ropes, and afterwards lifting the cross, and the body of Jesus nailed to the cross on Mount Calvary.

Butchers and Poultry Dealers — The cross, two thieves crucified, Jesus hanging on the cross between them, Mary the mother of Jesus, John, Mary, James, and Salome. A soldier with a lance, a servant with a sponge, Pilate, Annas, Caiaphas, the centurion, Joseph of Arimathea and Nicodemus, placing him in the sepulcher.

Saddlers, Glaziers and Joiners — Jesus conquering hell; twelve spirits, six good, and six evil.

Carpenters — Jesus rising from the sepulcher, four armed soldiers, and the three Marys mourning. Pilate, Caiaphas, and Annas. A young man seated at the sepulcher clothed in white, speaking to the women.

Winedrawers — Jesus, Mary Magdalene with aromatic spices.

Brokers and Woolpackers — Jesus, Luke, and Cleophas in the guise of travelers.

Scriveners, Illuminators, Pardoners and Cloth-furbishers — Jesus, Peter, John, James, Philip, and the other apostles with parts of a baked fish, and a honeycomb; and Thomas the apostle touching the wounds of Jesus.

Tailors — Mary, John the evangelist, the eleven apostles, two angels, Jesus ascending before them, and four angels carrying a cloud.

Potters — Mary, two angels, eleven apostles, and the Holy Spirit descending upon them, and four Jews wondering.

Drapers — Jesus, Mary, Gabriel with two angels, two virgins and three Jews of Mary's acquaintance, eight apostles, and two devils.

Linen-weavers — Four apostles carrying the bier of Mary, and Fergus hanging above the bier, with two other Jews and an angel.

Woolen-weavers — Mary ascending with a throng of angels, eight apostles, and the apostle Thomas preaching in the desert.

Innkeepers — Mary, Jesus crowning her, with a throng of angels singing.

Mercers — Jesus, Mary, the twelve apostles, four angels with trumpets, and four with a crown, a lance, and two whips, four good spirits, and four evil spirits, and six devils.

Questions: What are the religious emphases and message of the pageant? Where does its story begin and end? How many guilds are there? What kinds of goods were manufactured in York? Is there any indication of which guilds were larger or richer? Can the content of certain scenes be associated with the work of the guilds which sponsored them?

74. GYNECOLOGICAL TREATISE

This fifteenth-century treatise in English is one of a number of such manuals which appeared in the fifteenth century, apparently aimed at women who were practicing medicine and were literate but lacked formal training. The unknown author draws on classical writers, earlier medieval treatises in Latin, and practical experience.

Source: trans. B. Rowland, *Medieval Woman's Guide to Health* (Kent, Ohio: The Kent State University Press, 1981), pp. 59–63, 67–69, 75, 77, 123–127, 133–137, 147–149, 163.

Because there are many women who have numerous diverse illnesses — some of them almost fatal — and because they are also ashamed to reveal and tell their distress to any man, I therefore shall write somewhat to cure their illnesses, praying to merciful God to send me grace to write truly to His satisfaction and to the assistance of all women. For charity calls for this: that everyone should work to help his brothers and sisters according to the grace that he has received of God. And although women have various maladies and more terrible sicknesses than any man knows, as I said, they are ashamed for fear of

Fig. 31: Childbirth A fifteenth-century scene of childbirth, as shown in a nineteeth-century copy. The new mother, a wealthy noblewoman, rests in bed, attended by three waiting-women or relatives, while a fifth woman holds the baby near the fireplace. The clothing and household items are typical of the time period.

reproof in times to come and of exposure by discourteous men who love women only for physical pleasure and for evil gratification. And if women are sick, such men despise them and fail to realize how much sickness women have before they bring them into this world. And so, to assist women, I intend to write of how to help their secret maladies so that one woman may aid another in her illness and not divulge her secrets to such discourteous men.

But nevertheless, whoever he be that offends a woman because of the malady that she has by God's command, commits a great sin; for he despises not only women but God who sends such sickness in their best interests. And therefore no one should despise another for the disease that God sends but should have compassion and help if he can.

Therefore, you must understand that women have less heat in their bodies than men and have more moisture because of lack of heat that would dry their moisture and their humors, but nevertheless they have bleeding which makes their bodies clean and whole from sickness. And they have such purgations from the age of twelve to fifty. Even so, some women have purgations for a longer time because they are of a high complexion and are nourished with hot food and drink and live in much ease. And they have this purgation once every month unless they are pregnant or are of a dry complexion and work hard. For women, from the time that they are with child until they are delivered, do not have this purgation, because the child in the womb is nourished with the blood instead. And if they have a purgation at this time, it is a sign that the child refuses the blood and is sick or will die in its mother's womb. Women who are of a high complexion and are prosperous and live in comfort have this purgation more than once a month. And this blood that passes from women at the time of their purgation comes out of the veins that are in the uterus that is called the "mother" and nourishes the children properly conceived there. The "mother" is a skin in which the child is enclosed in his mother's womb. And many of the sicknesses that women have come from the ailments of this "mother" that we call the marice [uterus]....

The first chapter is concerned with the stopping of the blood that women should have in their purgations and be purged of.

Retention of this blood so that they cannot have their purgations at the proper time occurs in various ways and for various reasons: because of the heat or the cold of the uterus or the heat or cold of the humors that are enclosed inside the uterus, or excessive dryness of their complexion, or being awake too much, thinking too much, being too angry or too sad, or eating too little. Signs and general indications of this sickness are these: aching and suffering with physical discomfort and a feeling of weight from the navel down to the privy member. And the ache of their kidneys, backbone, forehead, neck, eyes, and infection of the waters, that is to say, their changing into the wrong color. Also heaviness about the mouth of the stomach, aching around the shoulder blades both in front and behind, and heaviness of thighs, hips, hands, and legs. And such women have, at times, an unreasonable appetite for food not suited to them, such as coal or rinds or shells, and their complexion is a bad color or grows pale. And sometimes at this time they have a desire to consort with men and so they do, and produce children that are lepers or have some other such evil sickness. And long retention of this blood occasionally makes women have dropsy or hemorrhoids; or it harms the heart and lungs and produces heart disease. And sometimes it terrifies the heart so much that it causes women to fall down in a faint as though they had the falling sickness. And they lie in that sickness for a day or two as though dead. And sometimes they have dizziness with great confusion in the brain and think that everything is turned upside down. And if this retention is because of sickness of the blood in the uterus — so that the blood does not flow regularly as it should, the woman's urine at times will be as red as blood. And at the time when she should have her purgation the blood will be dark, the veins will be full of blood, and the colors of her waters, that is, of their changing, will then be bright red....

Cure: To help women in these illnesses there are various remedies, such as blood-letting in other places to get rid of the blood that they cannot be cleansed of, and this is useful in case they may suffer heart disease or dropsy. And useful bleedings are at the veins of the big toe and cuts on the legs below the calf, both in front and behind, and cupping under the nipples and also under the kidneys at the back. Also baths are useful to them, made from herbs able to open the veins of the uterus so that the blood can emerge more quickly. And if the stoppage is due to bile, that is to say, through a humor that is hot and dry, have made a hot bath of seasonal herbs that are aperients, such as polypody, laurel leaves, ivy, savin, madder, origanum, rosemary, cumin, asphodel, fennel, artemisia, calamint, hyssop, wild thyme, catmint, and such other herbs, and let her sit on a hollow stool over these herbs when they are well boiled and hot. And afterward let her drink a draught of wine in which artemisia and polypody are boiled and sometimes cause her to be very unhappy, sometimes very angry, sometimes very merry, and let her use hot and piquant relishes such as garlic, pepper, mustard, cresses, and other such things, and let her bathe in baths made from such herbs as I have just spoken of. And let her walk a great deal, work, eat and drink well, and then she will be easily purged of her blood. And about that time of the moon that women should have their purgation, if they have none, have them bled a considerable quantity of blood at their big toe one day, and another day at their other big toe. And once every week accustom the woman to take a bath in such herbs as I spoke of earlier, and she may be helped even though her sickness has lasted a long time. But if the complaint is of a cold humor, first give her this medicine to make it more possible for her trouble to pass easily away from her.

Take fennel root, parsley, wild carrot, celery, the roots of these and not the leaves, and then take the leaves of artemisia, savin, calamint, origanum — if you don't have all these herbs take what you have — and cook them in vinegar so that they are well boiled; and then clean the mixture, throw into the vinegar half as much honey as there is vinegar, boil the two together for a time over the fire, and afterward, when it is cold, let her use it two or three days mixed with water in which radishes and madder have been boiled. And after that, let her soak and bathe herself in such herbs as I referred to earlier, and when the mixture is cooked let her drink a draught of wine in which savin, artemisia, or madder is boiled in, and mix that wine with water that polypody is boiled in. And if women have no purgation, let them bleed a good quantity of blood, as I said previously. Suppositories are useful medicines for these maladies. And they should be put in a woman's privy member just as a man puts a suppository in his anus in order to cleanse his stomach. But these suppositories for women should be fastened with a thread bound round one of her thighs, in case the suppositories should be drawn completely into the uterus. And it is a good thing to use such suppositories four or five days before the time of the month when women have their purgation, to make it easier. One suppository is this: … take the root of smallage — the size of your finger — all green, and grease it with the root of pellitory of Spain, and afterward put that root in the earth again for a fortnight or for three weeks, then take it up, wipe it clean, and put it into her privy member all day and all night; and afterward take it out, anoint it with oil of laurel or with a suitable oil, put it in again, and let it remain there until she has her purgation. For even if there was a dead child in her womb, it would bring it out….

The second chapter is concerned with excessive flowing of blood at the wrong time; and this sickness weakens a great number of women.

Excessive discharge of blood at the vagina comes in many ways: through the great amount of blood that is in the woman; or through the fierceness of the blood that through its strength destroys veins; or through the thinness of the blood that sweats out through the small pores of the veins and so flows out; or through the blood being undigested and runny and thin as water; or through the weakness of the woman who cannot keep the blood inside her; or through the breaking of some vein that is in the privy member or near to it….

Cure: And if there is a great quantity of blood, dehydrate her with food and drink that produce only a little blood, such as fruit and herbs, and have her bled at the vein of her arm and be cupped under her nipples and about the kidneys and loins, and scarified on her legs to draw the blood away from the uterus.

A powder: take pomegranate, hypocistis, acacia, colophony, and make suppositories of them; or mix all these with the juice of plantain and plaster it both in front of the womb and behind it and even in contact with it. Other medicines that are also good to staunch the bloody flux: take a great root of horseheal — half a pound and 6 ounces, 1 gallon of clean water; boil them [down to half a gallon], strain it, add half a pound of white sugar, boil it again for a while, and let it cool. And let her drink it at all hours, and it will stop the blood within four days; the prior of Bermondesey taught this medicine to a woman who was almost dead from the flux in her womb….

The tenth chapter is concerned with the sicknesses that women have in child-bearing.

Sicknesses that women have bearing children are of two kinds, natural and unnatural. When it is natural, the child comes out in twenty pangs or within those twenty, and the child comes the way it should: first the head, and afterward the neck, and with the arms, shoulders, and other members properly as it should. In the second way, the child comes out unnaturally, and that may be in sixteen ways, as you will find in their proper chapters, and the first is as follows:

When the child's head appears, as it were, head first, and the rest of the child remains inside the uterus. The remedy for this is that the midwife, with her hand anointed with oils, that is, wild thyme oil, pure lily oil, or oil of musk, as is necessary, put her hand in and turn the child properly with her hands from the sides of the uterus. And [see that] the orifice of the womb is so well anointed that the child can come forth in right order.

The second mode of unnatural childbirth occurs when the child comes out with his feet jointly together, only the midwife can never bring the child out when it comes down like this. But when the child begins to come out in this way, the midwife with her hands anointed with oil must put them in and push him up again and so arrange him that he can come forth in the most natural manner, so that he does not flatten his hands in the sides of the uterus.

The third unnatural mode is if the child's head is so bulky and large that he cannot emerge: the midwife should then push him back and anoint the orifice, that is, the mouth of the privy member with fresh May butter or with common oil, and then the midwife's hand, oiled first and then put in and the orifice enlarged, brings the child forth by the head.

In the fourth mode of unnatural childbirth, the woman in labor shall be placed in a short, narrow, high-standing bed, with her head off the bed, and the midwife, with her hand anointed with oil, thrusts her hand in after the child who is in an unnatural position, turns him correctly, and then brings him forth; but the bed that the woman should lie in must be made hard.

The fifth mode of unnatural childbirth is when the child extends his hand first, his head is turned back, and the mouth of the privy member is narrow or shut; then, with the inducement of the hands of the midwife, the orifice should be enlarged, and the child's hand put in again so that the child does not die as the result of the midwife's error. We prescribe that the midwife put her hand in, turning the child's shoulders toward the back and hands properly down at the side. And then take the head of the child; then slowly bring him forth....

The sixteenth mode of unnatural childbirth occurs when there is more than one child, as happens every day, and they all come to the orifice at once; then let the midwife put one back again with her fingers while she brings out one of the children. And then afterward, another, so doing that the uterus is not constricted nor the children brought to grief, as often happens.

In order to deliver a woman of a child and to kill it if it cannot be brought out: take rue, savin, southernwood, and iris, and let her drink them. Also take 2 drachms each of the juice of hyssop, and of dittany, and 2 scruples of quicksilver, and this medicine is proved to be effective. Also take 4 drachms each of the juice of iris and bull's gall, 2 drachms of suitable oil, mix all these together, put it in a pessary, give it to the woman, and this medicine will bring out all the decomposed matter of the womb. And it will deliver a woman of a dead child, and of her secundines, and it brings on menstruation. Again, give to the pregnant woman 2 drachms of asafetida 3 times daily, and let the stomach and back be anointed with oil and gall, and afterward let oil, ox gall, and asafetida be placed in the vulva with a feather.

And the sicknesses that women have in childbearing come sometimes from the sickness of the child, and that may be because the child has grown considerably in his mother's womb before she has caught the dropsy; and this the midwife may well know, and the woman also. And sometimes the sickness comes through the frailty of the woman because she is not strong enough to deliver the child. And this may be in two ways: because of the great sickness that the woman has had and that has greatly weakened her; or because of the great anxiety of the woman, and if this is the first time that she has conceived for twelve years. Sometimes it comes from the blocking of the womb. And that may be due to two reasons: because fatness stops the mouth of the womb and holds back the blood that she should have been purged of before children were conceived; or sometimes it is because the child is dead in its mother's womb. And the signs are as follows: they feel no stirring or movement of the child inside; on the second day of labor the mouth smells evil; they feel much pain and distress about the navel; the face and the entire body waste away; they want things that are harmful to them; they wake a lot and sleep little; they have a great trouble in making water and going to the privy, and also they have great discomfort about the genitals. And if the child does not come out as it should, the midwife can help well enough without any other medicines, as I have previously described. But if her sickness be any of the ones that I have mentioned, make her a bath of mallows, fenugreek, linseed, wormwood, southernwood, pellitory, fennel, and mugwort boiled in water, and let her bathe in it for a good time. And when she comes out of the bath, see that she is anointed from the navel downward to the privy member with butter, deute, and ointment of Aragon, both in front and behind. And afterward make her a fumigation underneath of 1 ounce of spikenard and 1 ounce of roots of costmary. And also when she comes from the bath, if she is a rich woman, give her 1 ounce of the juice of the balsam tree in warm wine; if she is a poor woman, boil roots of costmary and artemisia in wine, add to it 2 ounces of bull's gall, and let her drink the mixture when she comes from the bath. Or mix 2 ounces of borax with wine and give her that to drink; or give her 3 drachms each of the juice of dittany, hyssop, half a scruple of mercury, and this medicament will cast out the child alive or dead, and even more successfully if it is given with a pill of myrrh, according to Rhazes' instruction, take 2 ounces of myrrh, 2 ounces of lupins, 8 drachms each of rue leaves dried with wild mint, thyme, that is, woodruff, mountain willow, asafetida, orchis, juice of panax, galbanum, aromatic gum, and some good malmsey as required. Make pills like small tablets, each weighing 2 drachms. Give her one of them with an infusion of junipers in wine, for these are good for difficult births, to bring out the secundines and destroy the mola of the womb....

The twelfth chapter is on how to make a woman conceive a child if God wills. First, if she is full of menstrual blood, have her cleansed with medicines for the retention and suppression of menstruation, with baths and immersions. Alternatively, take 1 handful each of calamint, catmint, fennel, pellitory, savory, hyssop, artemisia, rue, wormwood, anise, cumin, rosemary, thyme, pennyroyal, and mountain origanum, a gallon of wine, 6 gallons of water, boil them, and have her take this medicine. Take 3 ounces of powder of cloves and 4 yolks of raw eggs, mix the powder and the yolks together, bake on a hot stone, and give to the woman after a four-day fast, and make her abstain from fluids for some time afterwards. Also, for either a man or woman, make a plaster of 4 yolks of raw eggs, half an ounce of powder of cloves, 1 drachm of saffron. First anoint with hot oil of roses on the orifice of the stomach, spread on it some of the powder, make a plaster, and lay it on it.

The thirteenth chapter is concerned with excessive bleeding after childbirth. Women sometimes bleed too much after childbirth, and this makes them very weak. But you should not in this case give her any medicines that are comforting, nor baths nor strong medicated compresses, but other medicines such as were described earlier in the chapter on hemorrhage. Have her bled under the ankle of one foot, and another day under the other ankle. Then give her other medicines as before stated here that we should give, such medicines as were described in the chapter on the retention of blood. And some women have decaying matter when they have a discharge, and sometimes such matter passes from them instead of blood; and sometimes bleeding comes with the blood that they should be purged of. And if they are old women or women that are barren, there is no need to give them medicines. If they are young women, boil watercress, septfoil, cinquefoil, or water parsnips in wine. And let her sit over the smoke of them so that it reaches her privy member.

Alternatively, take wild thyme, make a powder of it, and put it in a bag of sufficient breadth and length to cover both privy members of the woman. And put it on hot and fasten it securely so that it cannot fall off.

... For the pestilence: Take 12 drachms each of myrrh, pimpernel, and fumitory, 6 drachms of Armenian bole, 15 drachms of rue, 6 drachms each of dittany, and tourmaline, 10 drachms each of wood aloes, sandalwood, madder, fleawort, origanum, round birthwort, and laurel berries, and 6 drachms of gentian, and let them be made into a powder. For all sickness of the eyes, take an eightieth part of a tortoise exactly, and 12 handfuls of fennel cooked in half a flagon of water. To prevent vomiting: take seed of sorrel, costmary, barberry, red and white coral, the scrapings of the intestine of a deer, 3 drachms each of pomegranates, sandalwood, oil, and tourmaline, infused with cumin, burnt with anise, and 1 ounce each of mint, madder, galingale, wood aloes, cloves, the inner parts of tree nightshade, cinnamon, and white ginger, 4 drachms each of grains of paradise, tree nightshade, saffron, mace, spikenard, caraway, zedoary, cucumber, long and black pepper, and red roses, finely powdered with 1 pound of white sugar, 12 drachms of quinces, 6 drachms of water of roses, and have an electuary made in the manner of diacitonicon syrup, that is, an electuary of quinces.

Questions: What reasons does the author cite for producing this work? According to this treatise, how do women differ from men? What is the author's general approach to medical treatment? Would any of the treatments described here actually be harmful? Is there any indication of how midwives might deal with an unwanted pregnancy?

75. POEMS ABOUT RAISING CHILDREN

"How the Goodwife Taught Her Daughter" may have appeared in the late fourteenth century, but circulated much more widely in the fifteenth. "How the Wise Man Taught His Son" is apparently imitative of it. Both belong to the late medieval trend of instructional writing about the raising and education of children.

Source: modernized from *The Babees' Book: Medieval Manners for the Young*, ed. Edith Rickert (London: Chatto & Windus, 1908, 1923), pp. 31-42, 43-47.

How the Goodwife Taught Her Daughter

The good wife taught her daughter,
Full many a time and oft,
A full good woman to be;

For said she: "Daughter to me dear,
Something good now must thou hear,
If thou wilt prosper thee.

Daughter, if thou wilt be a wife,
Look wisely that thou work;
Look lovely and in good life,
Love God and Holy Kirk.
Go to church whene'er thou may,
Look thou not miss it for rain,
For best thou farest on that day;
To commune with God be fain.
He must needs well thrive,
That liveth well all his life,
My dear child.

Gladly give thy tithes and thy offerings both,
To the poor and the bed-rid — look thou be not loth.
Give of thine own goods and be not too hard,
For seldom is the house poor where God is steward.
Well is he proved
Who the poor hath loved,
My dear child.

When thou sittest in the church, o'er thy beads bend;
Make thou no jangling with gossip or with friend.
Laugh thou to scorn neither old body nor young,
But be of fair bearing and of good tongue.
Through thy fair bearing
Thy worship hath increasing,
My dear child.

If any man offer thee courtship, and would marry thee,
Look that thou scorn him not, whatsoever he be;
But show it to thy friends and conceal it naught.
Sit not by him nor stand where sin might be wrought,
For a slander raised of ill
Is difficult to still,
My dear child.

The man that shall thee wed before God with a ring,
Love thou him and honor most of earthly thing.
Meekly thou him answer and not as a shrewish being,
So may'st thou slake his mood and be his dear darling.
A fair word and a meek
Doth anger slake,
My dear child.

Fair of speech shalt thou be, glad and of mild mood,
True in word and in deed, and in conscience good.
Keep thee from sin, from villainy and from blame;
And look thou bear thee so that none say of thee shame,
For he that in good life hath run,
Full oft his weal hath won,
My dear child.

Be of seemly semblance, wise, and other good cheer;
Change not thy countenance for anything thou may hear.
Behave not giddily, for naught that may betide.
Laugh thou not too loud nor yawn thou not too wide.
But laugh thou soft and mild,
And be not of cheer too wild,
My dear child.

And when thou goest on thy way, go thou not too fast,
Brandish not with thy head, nor with thy shoulders cast,
Have not too many words, from swearing keep aloof,
For all such manners come to an evil proof.
For he that catcheth to him an evil name,
It is to him a foul fame,
My dear child.

Go thou not into the town, as it were, agaze.
From one house to another, for to seek the maze;
Nor to sell thy cloth, to the market shalt thou go,
And then to the tavern to bring thy credit low.
For they that taverns haunt
From thrift soon come to want,
My dear child.

And if thou be in any place where good ale is aloft,
Whether that thou serve thereof or that thou sit soft,
Moderately take thou thereof, that thou fall in no blame,
For if thou be often drunk, it falleth to thy shame.
For those that be often drunk —
Thrift is from them sunk,
My dear child.

Go not to the wrestling or shooting at the cock,
As it were a strumpet or a giggle-a-lot,
Dwell at home, daughter, and love thy work much,
And so thou shalt, my dear child, wax the sooner rich.
A merry thing 'tis evermore,
A man to be served from his own store,
My dear child.

Acquaint thee not with each man that goeth by the street,
Though any man speak to thee, briefly thou him greet;
By him do not stand, but let him his way depart,
Lest he by his villainy should tempt thy heart.
For all men be not true
That fair words can show,
My dear child.

Also, for covetousness gifts beware to take;
Unless thou know why else, quickly them forsake;
For with gifts may man soon women overcome,
Though they were as true as steel or as stone.
Bound forsooth is she
That of any man takes fee,
My dear child.

And wisely govern thy house, and serving maids and men,
Be thou not too bitter or too easy with them;
But look well what most needs to be done,
And set thy people at it, both quickly and soon.
For ready is at need
A foredone deed,
My dear child.

And if thy husband be from home, let not thy folk do ill,
But look who doeth well and who doeth nil;
And he that doeth well, quit him well his while,
But he that doeth other, serve him as the vile.
A foredone deed
Will another speed,
My dear child.

And if thy time be strait and great be thy need,
Then like a housewife set to work with speed;
Then will they all do better that about thee stand,
For work is sooner done that hath full many a hand.
For many a hand and wight
Makes a heavy work light;
And after thy good service,
Thy name shall arise,
My dear child.

Whate'er thy household doth, about them must thou wend,
And as much as thou mayest, be at that one end,
If thou find any fault, make them soon amend,
As they have time and space, and may them defend.
To compel a deed be done, if there be no space,
It is but tyranny, without temperance and grace,
My dear child.

And look that all things be well when they their work forsake,
Forget thou not the keys into thy ward to take
And beware to whom thou trustest, and for no fancy spare,
For much harm hath fallen to them that be not 'ware.
But, daughter, look thou be wise, and do as I thee teach,
And trust none better than thyself, for no fair speech,
My dear child.

And give your household their hire at their pay-day,
Whether they dwell still with thee, or they wend away.
Do well by them of the goods thou hast in hold,
And then shall they say well of thee, both the young and old.
Thy good name to thy friends
Great joy and gladness lends,
My dear child.

And if thy neighbor's wife hath on rich attire,
Therefore mock not, nor let scorn burn thee as a fire.
But thank thou God in heaven for what he may thee give,
And so shalt thou, my daughter dear, a good life live,
He hath ease in his power,
Who thanks the Lord every hour,
My dear child.

Housewifely thou shalt go on the working day,
For pride, rest, and idleness take thrift away;
But when the Holy Day is come, well clothed shalt thou be,
The Holy Day to honor, and God will cherish thee.
Have in mind to worship God always
For much pride comes of the evil day,
My dear child.

When thou art a wife, a neighbor for to be,
Love then well thy neighbors as God hath commanded thee.
It behoveth thee so for to do,
And to do to them as thou wouldst be done to.
If any discord happen, night or day,
Make it no worse, mend it if thou may,
My dear child.

And if thou art a rich wife, be not then too hard,
But welcome fair thy neighbors that come thee toward
With meat, drink, and honest cheer, such as thou mayest bid.
To each man after his degree, and help the poor at need.
And also for hap that may betide,
Please well thy neighbors that dwell thee beside,
My dear child.

Daughter, look that thou beware, whatsoever thee betide,
Make not thy husband poor with spending or with pride.
A man must spend as he may that hath but modest goods,
For as a wren hath veins, men must let her blood.
His thrift waxeth thin
That spendeth ere he win,
My dear child.

Borrow not too busily, nor take thine hire first,
This may make the more need, and end by being worst.
Nor make thee not to seem rich with other man's store,
Therefore spend thou never a farthing more.
For though thou borrow fast,
It must go home again at last,
My dear child.

And if thy children be rebel and will not bow them low,
If any of them misdo, neither curse them nor blow;
But take a smart rod and beat them in a row,
Till they cry mercy and their guilt well know.
Dear child, by this lore
They will love thee ever more,
My dear child.

And look to thy daughters that none of them be lorn;
From the very time that they are of thee born,
Busy thyself and gather fast for their marriage,
And give them to spousing, as soon as they be of age.
Maidens be fair and amiable,
But in their love full unstable,
My dear child.

Now have I taught thee, daughter, as my mother did me;
Think thereon night and day, that forgotten it not be.
Have measure and lowness, as I have thee taught,
Then whatever man shall wed thee will regret it naught.
Better you were a child unbore
Than untaught in this wise lore,
My dear child.

Now thrift and speed be thine, my sweet bairn (near or far)!
Of all our former fathers that ever were or are,
Of all patriarchs and prophets that ever were alive —
Their blessing may'st thou have, and well may'st thou thrive!
For well it is with that child
That with sin is not defiled,
My dear child.

The blessing of God may'st thou have, and of His mother bright,
Of all angels and archangels and every holy wight!
And may'st thou have grace to wend thy way full right,
To the bliss of heaven, where God sits in His might!
Amen.

How the Wise Man Taught His Son

Listen, lordlings, and ye shall hear how the wise man taught his son.
Take good heed to this matter and learn it if ye can,
For this song was made with good intent to make men true and steadfast,
And a thing well begun makes often a good ending.

There was a wise man taught his son
While he was yet a child of tender years, meek and fair to look upon,
Very eager for learning and with a great desire to all goodness;
And his father taught him well and featly by good example and fair words.

He said: My son, take good heed every morning,
Ere ye do worldly thing, lift up your heart to God,
And pray as devoutly as you can for grace to lead a good life,
And to escape sin both night and day,
And that heaven's bliss may be your meed.

And, my son, wherever you go, be not full of tales;
Beware what you say, for your own tongue may be your foe.
If you say aught, take good heed where and to whom,
For a word spoken today may be repented seven years after.

And, son, whatever manner of man ye be, give yourself not to idleness,
But busy yourself every day according to your estate.
Beware of rest and ease, which things nourish sloth.
Ever to be busy, more or less, is a full good sign of honesty.

And, son, I warn you also not to desire to bear office,
For then you must either displease and hurt your neighbors,
Or else forswear yourself and not do as your office demands;
And get yourself, here and there, a hundredfold more than thanks.

And, son, as far as you may, go on no evil quests,
Nor bear false witness in any man's matter.
It were better for you to be deaf and dumb than to enter wrongfully into a
quest.
Think, son, on the dreadful doom that God shall judge us at the last!

And, son, of another thing I warn you, on my blessing
Take good heed of tavern-haunting, and of the dice, and flee all lechery,
Lest you come to an evil end, for it will lead astray all your wits
And bring you into great mischief.

And, son, sit not up too long at even, or have late suppers,
Though ye be strong and hale, for with such outrage your health shall worsen.
And of late walking comes debate, and of sitting and drinking out of time,
Therefore beware and go to bed betimes and wink.

And, son, if ye would have a wife, take her not for her money,
But inquire wisely of all her life, and give good heed
That she be meek, courteous and prudent, even though she be poor;
And such a one will do you more good service in time of need, than a richer.

And if your wife be meek and good, and serve you well and pleasantly,
Look ye be not so mad as to charge her too grievously,
But rule her with a fair hand and easy, and cherish her for her good deeds.
For a thing unskilfully overdone makes needless grief to grow,

And it is better to have a meal's meat of homely fare with peace and quiet,
Than a hundred dishes with grudging and much care.
And therefore learn this well that if you want a wife to your case,
Take her never the more for the riches she may have,
Though she might endow you with lands.

And ye shall not displease your wife, nor call her by no villainous names,
For it is a shame to you to miscall a woman; and in so doing, ye are not wise,
For if ye defame your own wife, no wonder that another should do so!
Soft and fair will tame alike hart and hind, buck and doe.

On the other hand, be not too hasty to fight or chide,
If thy wife come to you at any time with complaint of man or child;
And be not avenged till you know the truth,
For you might make a stir in the dark, and afterwards it should rue you both.

And, son, if you be well at ease, and sit warm among your neighbors,
Do not get newfangled ideas, or be hasty to change, or to flit;
For if ye do, ye lack wit and are unstable,
And men will speak of it and say: "This fool can bide nowhere!"

And, son, the more goods you have, the rather bear you meekly,
And be humble, and boast not overmuch;
It is wasted, for by their boasting men know fools.

And look you pay well what you owe, and set no great store by other riches,
For death takes both high and low, and then — farewell, all that there is!
And therefore do by my counsel, and take example from other men,
How little their goods avail them when they be buried in their graves;
And one that was not of his kin hath his wife, and all that there is.

Son, keep you from deadly sin, and assay to enter Paradise.
Make amends for your trespasses and deal out of your goods to poor men,
Make friends of your foes, and strive to gain salvation for your soul,
For the world is false and frail, and every day doth worsen.

Son, set naught by this world's weal, for it fares as a ripe cherry.
And death is ever, I trow, the most certain thing that is;
And nothing is so uncertain as to know the time thereof.
Therefore, my son, think on this, on all that I have said,
And may Jesus, who for us bare the crown of thorns, bring us to his bliss.
Amen.

Questions: What instructions do the parents give to their children? What are their greatest concerns? How realistic is the advice? How is the advice similar for the girl and the boy? How is it different?

76. APPRENTICESHIP DOCUMENTS

The typical career of a person in almost any kind of craft or industry began with appren-ticeship, in which the apprentice, typically a child or adolescent, was legally bound to a master or mistress. The apprentice was housed and fed and thoroughly trained in the craft; in return he or she worked exclusively for the master or mistress during the appren-ticeship (often a seven-year term) and handed over any profits earned.

Source: indenture trans. A.E. Bland, P.A. Brown, and R.H. Tawney, *English Economic History: Select Documents* (London: G. Bell and Sons, Ltd, 1914), pp. 147-148, revised; repudiation trans. H.T. Riley, *Memorials of London and London Life in the XIIIth, XIVth, and XVth Centuries* (London: Long-mans, Green, and Co., 1868), pp. 629-630, revised.

Indenture of Apprenticeship (1459)

This indenture, made between John Gibbs of Penzance in the county of Corn-wall, on the one part, and John Goffe, Spaniard, on the other part, witnesses that the aforesaid John Goffe has put himself to the aforesaid John Gibbs to learn the craft of fishing, and to stay with him as apprentice and to serve from the feast of Philip and James [May 1] next to come after the date of these pre-sents until the end of eight years then next ensuing and fully complete; throughout which term the aforesaid John Goffe shall well and faithfully serve the aforesaid John Gibbs and Agnes his wife as his masters and lords, shall keep their secrets, shall everywhere willingly do their lawful and honorable com-mands, shall do his masters no injury nor see injury done to them by others, but prevent the harm as far as he can, shall not waste his masters' goods nor lend them to any man without his special command. And the aforesaid John Gibbs and Agnes his wife shall teach, train and inform or cause the aforesaid John Goffe, their apprentice, to be informed in the craft of fishing in the best way they know, chastising him duly and finding for the same John, their apprentice, sufficient food, clothing linen and woollen, and shoes, as befit such an apprentice to be found, during the term aforesaid. And at the end of the term aforesaid the aforesaid John Goffe shall have from the aforesaid John Gibbs and Agnes his wife 20s. sterling without any fraud. In witness whereof the parties aforesaid have interchangeably set their seals to the parts of this indenture....

Repudiation by a Master of the acts and deeds of a runaway Apprentice (1416)

On the first day of July, in [1416], Nicholas Wottone, the mayor, and the alder-men, were given to understand, by Robert Arnold and other trustworthy persons, that one William Bolecley, son of the late John Bolecley, of Delbury, in the county of Shropshire, who, on the 28th day of March in [1411], had put himself apprentice to the aforesaid Robert, and who, on behalf of the said Robert, his master, had heretofore been on business for trading in diverse parts, both on this side of the sea and beyond, had of late without leave, and without reasonable cause, unlawfully withdrawn himself from the service of his master, and departed; to the no small loss and grievance of his said master.

And whereas the said Robert feared that he might very possibly be held responsible for the deeds of the same William, if he should appear under the pretense of being the factor and attorney of his said master, while so living at large, as he might in the name of such master receive diverse quantities of things and merchandizes, and various sums of money: therefore ... the said Robert Arnold came here, before the mayor and aldermen, and in full court repudiated and renounced whatever the same apprentice should have done, as being his factor and attorney, from the time that he so withdrew himself and departed, or should in any parts whatsoever in future do for him, or in his name.

Questions: What was the purpose of apprenticeship? What was the apprentice's life probably like? What were the hazards of apprenticeship for each party?

77. THE BOOK OF MARGERY KEMPE

Margery Kempe is a most unusual figure — not only a religious misfit who attracted a great deal of attention (most of it unfavorable) in her own time, but also the first author of an autobiography in English. When she decided to dictate the story of her life, it was difficult to find a competent scribe; eventually the writing began in 1436. Her book is full of travel and adventure, but it focuses continually on Margery's spiritual development, her visions, and her expression of her religious experiences, often through what she calls her "cryings." She refers to herself throughout the book as "this creature." The excerpts below describe her first religious conversion and an episode between her and her husband some years later.

Source: Modernized by W. Butler-Bowdon, *The Book of Margery Kempe, 1436* (London: Jonathan Cape, 1936), pp. 23-33, 47-50.

The First Book

1. When this creature was twenty years of age, or some deal more, she was married to a worshipful burgess (of Lynne) and was with child within a short time,

as nature would. And after she had conceived, she was belabored with great accesses till the child was born and then, what with the labor she had in childing, and the sickness going before, she despaired of her life, weening she might not live. And then she sent for her ghostly father [that is, her confessor], for she had a thing on her conscience which she had never shown before that time in all her life. For she was ever hindered by her enemy, the devil, evermore saying to her that whilst she was in good health she needed no confession, but to do penance by herself alone and all should be forgiven, for God is merciful enough. And therefore this creature oftentimes did great penance in fasting on bread and water, and other deeds of alms with devout prayers, save she would not show that in confession.

And when she was at any time sick or diseased, the devil said in her mind that she should be damned because she was not shriven of that default. Wherefore after her child was born, she, not trusting to live, sent for her ghostly father, as is said before, in full will to be shriven of all her lifetime, as near as she could. And when she came to the point for to say that thing which she had so long concealed, her confessor was a little too hasty and began sharply to reprove her, before she had fully said her intent, and so she would no more say for aught he might do. Anon, for the dread she had of damnation on the one side, and his sharp reproving of her on the other side, this creature went out of her mind and was wondrously vexed and labored with spirits for half a year, eight weeks and odd days.

And in this time she saw, as she thought, devils opening their mouths all inflamed with burning waves of fire, as if they would have swallowed her in, sometimes ramping at her, sometimes threatening her, pulling her and hauling her, night and day during the aforesaid time. Also the devils cried upon her with great threatenings, and bade her that she should forsake Christendom, her faith, and deny her God, his Mother and all the saints in heaven, her good works and all good virtues, her father, her mother and all her friends. And so she did. She slandered her husband, her friends and her own self. She said many a wicked word, and many a cruel word; she knew no virtue nor goodness; she desired all wickedness; like as the spirits tempted her to say and do, so she said and did. She would have destroyed herself many a time at their stirrings and have been damned with them in hell, and in witness thereof, she bit her own hand so violently, that the mark was seen all her life after.

And also she rived the skin on her body against her heart with her nails spitefully, for she had no other instruments, and worse she would have done, but that she was bound and kept with strength day and night so that she might not have her will. And when she had long been labored in these and many other temptations, so that men weened she should never have escaped or lived, then on a time as she lay alone and her keepers were from her, our merciful Lord Jesus Christ, ever to be trusted, worshipped be his name, never forsaking his servant in time of need, appeared to his creature who had forsaken him, in the likeness of a man, most seemly, most beauteous and most amiable that ever might be seen with man's eye, clad in a mantle of purple silk, sitting upon her bedside, looking upon her with so blessed a face that she was strengthened in all her spirit, and said to her these words: —

"Daughter, why has thou forsaken me, and I forsook never thee?"

And anon this creature became calmed in her wits and reason, as well as ever she was before, and prayed her husband as soon as he came to her, that she might have the keys of the buttery to take her meat and drink as she had done before. Her maidens and her keepers counselled him that he should deliver her no keys, as they said she would but give away such goods as there were, for she knew not what she said, as they weened.

Nevertheless, her husband ever having tenderness and compassion for her, commanded that they should deliver to her the keys; and she took her meat and drink as her bodily strength would serve her, and knew her friends and her household and all others that came to see how our Lord Jesus Christ had wrought his grace in her, so, blessed may he be, who ever is near in tribulation. When men think he is far from them, he is full near by his grace. Afterwards, this creature did all other occupations as fell to her to do, wisely and soberly enough, save she knew not verily the call of our Lord.

2. When this creature had thus graciously come again to her mind, she thought that she was bound to God and that she would be his servant. Nevertheless, she would not leave her pride or her pompous array, which she had used beforetime, either for her husband, or for any other man's counsel. Yet she knew full well that men said of her full much villainy, for she wore gold pipes on her head, and her hoods, with the tippets, were slashed. Her cloaks also were slashed and laid with diverse colors between the slashes, so that they should be the more staring to men's sight, and herself the more worshipped.

And when her husband spoke to her to leave her pride, she answered shrewdly and shortly, and said that she was come of worthy kindred — he should never have wedded her — for her father was sometime mayor of the town of [Lynne] and afterwards he was alderman of the high guild of the Trinity in [Lynne]. And therefore she would keep the worship of her kindred whatever any man said.

She had full great envy of her neighbors, that they should be as well arrayed as she. All her desire was to be worshipped by the people. She would not take heed of any chastisement, nor be content with the goods that God had sent her, as her husband was, but ever desired more and more.

Then for pure covetousness, and to maintain her pride, she began to brew, and was one of the greatest brewers in the town of [Lynne] for three years or four, till she lost much money, for she had never been used thereto. For, though she had ever such good servants, cunning in brewing, yet it would never succeed with them. For when the ale was as fair standing under barm [that is, forming a foamy yeast on top] as any man might see, suddenly the barm would fall down, so that all the ale was lost, one brewing after another, so that her servants were ashamed and would not dwell with her.

Then this creature thought how God had punished her aforetime — and she could not take heed — and now again, by the loss of her goods. Then she left and brewed no more.

Then she asked her husband's mercy because she would not follow his counsel aforetime, and she said that her pride and sin were the cause of all her punishing, and that she would amend and that she had trespassed with good will.

Yet she left not the world altogether, for she now bethought herself of a new housewifery. She had a horse-mill. She got herself two good horses and a man to grind men's corn, and thus she trusted to get her living. This enterprise lasted not long, for in a short time after, on Corpus Christi eve [in early summer], befell this marvel. This man, being in good health of body, and his two horses sturdy and gentle, had pulled well in the mill beforetime, and now he took one of these horses and put him in the mill as he had done before, and this horse would draw no draught in the mill for anything the man might do. The man was sorry and essayed with all his wits how he should make this horse pull. Sometimes he led him by the head, sometimes he beat him, sometimes he cherished him and all availed not, for he would rather go backward than forward. Then this man set a sharp pair of spurs on his heels and rode on the horse's back to make him pull, and it was never the better. When the man saw it would work in no way, he set up this horse again in the stable, and gave him corn, and he ate well and freshly. And later he took the other horse and put him in the mill, and, like his fellow did, so did he, for he would not draw for anything the man might do. Then the man forsook his service and would no longer remain with the aforesaid creature. Anon, it was noised about the town of [Lynne] that neither man nor beast would serve the said creature.

Then some said she was accursed; some said God took open vengeance on her; some said one thing and some said another. Some wise men, whose minds were more grounded in the love of our Lord, said that it was the high mercy of our Lord Jesus Christ that called her from the pride and vanity of the wretched world.

Then this creature, seeing all these adversities coming on every side, thought they were the scourges of our Lord that would chastise her for her sin. Then she asked God's mercy, and forsook her pride, her covetousness, and the desire that she had for the worship of the world, and did great bodily penance, and began to enter the way of everlasting life as shall be told hereafter.

3. On a night, as this creature lay in her bed with her husband, she heard a sound of melody so sweet and delectable, that she thought she had been in Paradise, and therewith she started out of her bed and said: —

"Alas, that ever I did sin! It is full merry in Heaven."

This melody was so sweet that it surpassed all melody that ever might be heard in this world, without any comparison, and caused her, when she heard any mirth or melody afterwards, to have full plenteous and abundant tears of high devotion, with great sobbings and sighings after the bliss of Heaven, not dreading the shames and the spites of this wretched world. Ever after this inspiration, she had in her mind the mirth and the melody that was in Heaven, so much, that she could not well restrain herself from speaking thereof, for wherever she was in any company she would say oftentimes: — "It is full merry in Heaven."

And they that knew her behavior beforetime, and now heard her speaking so much of the bliss of Heaven, said to her: —

"Why speak ye so of the mirth that is in Heaven? Ye know it not, and ye have not been there, any more than we." And were wroth with her, for she would not hear nor speak of worldly things as they did, and as she did beforetime.

And after this time she had never desired to commune fleshly with her husband, for the debt of matrimony was so abominable to her that she would rather, she thought, have eaten or drunk the ooze and the muck in the gutter than consent to any fleshly communing, save only for obedience.

So she said to her husband: — "I may not deny you my body, but the love of my heart and my affections are withdrawn from all earthly creatures, and set only in God."

He would have his will and she obeyed, with great weeping and sorrowing that she might not live chaste. And oftentimes this creature counseled her husband to live chaste, and said that they often, she knew well, had displeased God by their inordinate love, and the great delectation they each had in using the other, and now it was good that they should, by the common will and consent of them both, punish and chastise themselves wilfully by abstaining from the lust of their bodies. Her husband said it was good to do so, but he might not yet. He would when God willed. And so he used her as he had done before. He would not spare her. And ever she prayed to God that she might live chaste; and three or four years after, when it pleased Our Lord, he made a vow of chastity, as shall be written afterwards, by leave of Jesus.

And also, after this creature heard this heavenly melody, she did great bodily penance. She was shriven sometimes twice or thrice on a day, and specially of that sin she so long had (hid), concealed and covered, as is written in the beginning of the book.

She gave herself up to great fasting and great watching; she rose at two or three of the clock, and went to church, and was there at her prayers unto the time of noon and also all the afternoon. Then she was slandered and reproved by many people, because she kept so strict a life. She got a hair-cloth from a kiln, such as men dry malt on, and laid it in her kirtle as secretly and privily as she might, so that her husband should not espy it. Nor did he, and she lay by him every night in his bed and wore the hair-cloth every day, and bore children in the time.

Then she had three years of great labor with temptations which she bore as meekly as she could, thanking our Lord for all his gifts, and was as merry when she was reproved, scorned and japed for our Lord's love, and much more merry than she was beforetime in the worship of the world. For she knew right well she had sinned greatly against God and was worthy of more shame and sorrow than any man could cause her, and despite of the world was the right way heavenwards, since Christ himself had chosen that way. All his apostles, martyrs, confessors and virgins, and all that ever came to heaven, passed by the way of tribulation, and she, desiring nothing so much as heaven, then was glad in her conscience when she believed that she was entering the way that would lead her to the place she most desired.

And this creature had contrition and great compunction with plenteous tears and many boisterous sobbings for her sins and for her unkindness against her Maker. She repented from her childhood for unkindness, as our Lord would put it in her mind, full many a time. Then, beholding her own wickedness, she could but sorrow and weep and ever pray for mercy and forgiveness. Her weeping was so plenteous and continuing, that many people thought she could weep and leave off, as she liked. And therefore many men said she was a false hypocrite, and wept before the world for succor and worldly goods. Then full many forsook her that loved her before while she was in the world, and would not know her. And ever, she thanked God for all, desiring nothing but mercy and forgiveness of sin....

11. It befell on a Friday on midsummer eve in right hot weather, as this creature was coming from York-ward carrying a bottle with beer in her hand, and her husband a cake in his bosom, that he asked his wife this question:

"Margery, if there came a man with a sword, who would strike off my head, unless I should commune naturally with you as I have done before, tell me on your conscience — for ye say ye will not lie — whether ye would suffer my head to be smitten off, or whether ye would suffer me to meddle with you again, as I did at one time?'

"Alas, sir," said she, "why raise this matter, when we have been chaste these eight weeks?"

"For I will know the truth of your heart."

And then she said with great sorrow: "Forsooth, I would rather see you being slain, than that we should turn again to our uncleanness."

And he replied: "Ye are no good wife."

She then asked her husband what was the cause that he had not meddled with her for eight weeks, since she lay with him every night in his bed. He said he was made so afraid when he would have touched her, that he dare do no more.

"Now, good sir, amend your ways, and ask God's mercy, for I told you nearly three years ago that [your lust] should be slain suddenly, and now is this the third year, and so I hope I shall have my desire. Good sir, I pray you grant me what I ask, and I will pray for you that ye shall be saved through the mercy of Our Lord Jesus Christ, and ye shall have more reward in Heaven than if ye wore a hair-cloth or a habergeon. I pray you, suffer me to make a vow of chastity at what bishop's hand God wills.'"

"Nay," he said, "that I will not grant you, for now may I use you without deadly sin, and then might I not do so."

Then she said to him: "If it be the will of the Holy Ghost to fulfill what I have said, I pray God that ye may consent thereto; and if it be not the will of the Holy Ghost, I pray God ye never consent to it."

Then they went forth towards Bridlington in right hot weather, the creature having great sorrow and dread for her chastity. As they came by a cross, her husband sat down under the cross, calling his wife to him and saying these words unto her: "Margery, grant me my desire, and I shall grant you your desire. My first desire is that we shall still lie together in bed as we have done before; the second, that ye shall pay my debts, ere ye go to Jerusalem; and the third, that ye shall eat and drink with me on the Friday as ye were wont to do."

"Nay, sir," said she, "to break the Friday, I will never grant you whilst I live."

"Well," said he, "then I shall meddle with you again." She prayed him that he would give her leave to say her prayers, and he granted it kindly. Then she knelt down beside a cross in the field and prayed in this manner, with a great abundance of tears:

"Lord God, thou knowest all things. Thou knowest what sorrow I have had to be chaste in my body to thee all these three years, and now might I have my will, and dare not for love of thee. For if I should break that manner of fasting which thou commandest me to keep on the Friday, without meat or drink, I should now have my desire. But, blessed Lord, thou knowest that I will not contravene thy will, and much now is my sorrow unless I find comfort in thee. Now, blessed Jesus, make thy will known to me unworthy, that I may follow it thereafter and fullfil it with all my might."

Then our Lord Jesus Christ with great sweetness, spoke to her, commanding her to go again to her husband, and pray him to grant her what she desired, "And he shall have what he desireth. For, my dearworthy daughter, this was the cause that I bade thee fast, so that thou shouldst the sooner obtain and get thy desire, and now it is granted to thee. I will no longer that thou fast. Therefore I bid thee in the name of Jesus, eat and drink as thy husband doth."

Then this creature thanked our Lord Jesus Christ for his grace and goodness, and rose up and went to her husband, saying to him:

"Sir, if it please you, ye shall grant me my desire, and ye shall have your desire. Grant me that ye will not come into my bed, and I grant you to requite your debts ere I go to Jerusalem. Make my body free to God so that ye never make challenge to me, by asking any debt of matrimony. After this day, whilst ye live, I will eat and drink on the Friday at your bidding."

Then said her husband: "As free may your body be to God, as it hath been to me."

This creature thanked God, greatly rejoicing that she had her desire, praying her husband that they should say three Paternosters in worship of the Trinity for the great grace that he had granted them. And so they did, kneeling under a cross, and afterwards they ate and drank together in great gladness of spirit. This was on a Friday on midsummer's eve. Then went they forth Bridlington-ward and also to many other countries and spoke with God's servants, both anchorites and recluses, and many others of Our Lord's lovers, with many worthy clerks, doctors of divinity and bachelors also, in diverse places. And this creature, to many of them, showed her feelings and her contemplations, as she was commanded to do, to find out if any deceit were in her feelings.

Questions: What kind of a person was Margery? Trace her spiritual journey and compare it to that of Godric of Finchale (doc. 27). What was Margery's husband like? What does this work tell us about a woman's day-to-day life, and about marriage?

78. MONASTIC VISITATIONS

One of the duties of a bishop was the regular inspection of religious communities within his diocese. The documents below consist mainly of the evidence given by the individual monks and nuns during such visitations; in each case the bishop then issued specific injunctions charging that all infractions be rectified, ordering audits of the accounts, and so on, but these are omitted here because they tend to repeat the original testimony.

Source: trans. A.H. Thompson, *Visitations of Religious Houses in the Diocese of Lincoln, Vol. II: Records of Visitations Held by William Alnwick, Bishop of Lincoln A.D. 1436 to A.D. 1449* (Horncastle: The Lincoln Record Society, 1918), pp. 46-50, 52-53, 68-78.

Dorchester Abbey

The Visitation of the monastery of Dorchester, of the order of St. Austin, of the diocese of Lincoln, performed in the chapter-house there on the 27th day of the month of March, in the year of our Lord 1441, by the reverend father in Christ and lord, the Lord William, by the grace of God bishop of Lincoln....

In the first place, as the said reverend father was sitting in his capacity of judge in the beginning of the business of such his visitation, ... the abbot before all else delivered to the said reverend father the certificate of my lord's mandate which had been addressed to him for the business of such visitation.... And when this had been read through, the same abbot showed my lord the title of the confirmation of his election.... And then the abbot, being examined, says these things which follow.

Brother John Clyftone, the abbot, says that, as far as regards the governance of the temporal affairs of the house, while it was in the hands of certain canons of his appointment, the house was in debt in large and heavy sums; and therefore one Marmyone has the direction of such temporal affairs with the consent of the convent. Also he says that, as he believes, the house today is £60 in debt and something more.

Brother John Hakeburne, the prior, says that the abbot does not show the state of the house [to the monks], and makes no reckoning in common of his administration, nor has ever made reckoning. Also he says that secular folk, both male and female, have often passage through the cloister precincts to the church, and this almost of custom.

Brother John Henrethe says that no fixed hour is observed for rising to matins, and this because the prior, albeit he fills the office of the sacristship, takes no care of the clock which this deponent did provide, and therefore it does not strike the hours by day and by night: accordingly they do not rise at a fixed hour, but at the beck of the prior, and the prior has applied the cords which belong to the same [clock] to the church bells.

Also the canons do often go out of the house to the public taverns in the town and do use to drink and eat with secular folk in the same.

Also he says that, although he himself is stricken in years and is therefore almost incapable of tasks out of cloister, nevertheless they have appointed him to the office of kitchener. Notwithstanding it would be disastrous for him to lay down the office before Michaelmas next, by reason of the provisions which he has made in the same office.

Brother Thomas Tewkesbury says all things are well. Brother Thomas Henrethe says that [the] report was that brother John Shrewesbury, a canon, had carnal knowledge of a certain woman, whose name he knows not, in the bell-tower of the church. The man appeared and, on the article being charged against him, denies all crime with such woman since the time of the correction appointed by the abbot, the which was his imprisonment in ward and confinement to cloister and fasting on bread and water. Wherefore he was enjoined to clear himself with three of his brethren; and then of my lord's grace he cleared himself with two of his brethren and was acquitted. The same says that the abbot has shown no entire account before the convent in common since he was elected abbot.

Brother Nicholas Plymmouthe says as above concerning the neglect of the abbot to render an account. Also he says that the tenements of the monastery in the town of Dorchester are not in good repair.

Brother Walter Dorchestre says that all things are well.

Brother John Shrewesbury says that all things are well.

Brother Ralph Calethra says that brother John Wynchestre, late the abbot, receives from the house in meat and drink as much as two canons receive, and seven pounds. Also he says that Marmyone keeps in the same every week sixteen dogs for coursing, for the which he receives two pecks of barley a week besides bran, and five horses that are fed continually at the costs of the house. The same Marmyone has a chamber within the cloister, and, since the doors of the cloister are in that place, they are left open almost the whole night through, so that secular folk do use to run in and out of the cloister all that time....

Brother Henry Yorke says that all things are well.

Brother John Wynchestre, sometime abbot, says of the canons that they eat and drink in the public taverns in the town with lay-folk: he craves therefore that an injunction be made under pain of imprisonment to them that do [so], for this the constitutions of the order require. Also he says that cloister is not kept at the due hours for meditation and reading. Also he says as above of the accounts that they are not rendered by the abbot. Also he says that Marmyone is very burdensome to the house as regards his serving-folk and them that come to visit him, and says that, as it seems to him, it is not very expedient that the same [Marmyone] should have so great governance with respect to the temporal affairs of the house. Also he says that while according to the rule their canons ought not to go out either on foot or on horseback, save in closed cloaks only, now [however] they walk about in the open cloaks which are called quire copes. Also he prays that ordinance be made that the canons ... do go out together for their recreation and return together, and not roam about by themselves, as is their wont, wherefrom there springs exceeding scandal to the house. Also he says that by the custom of the monastery there should be appointed caretakers for the young canons, to lay out their private allowance to their advantage until they be advanced to the priesthood, for now the opposite of this is observed: he prays therefore that an injunction be made in this regard, since hereof follow diverse evils. The same has a hundred shillings for himself and two of his household, and meat and drink even as two canons, and this he has under the common seal [by grant made] during the voidance of the monastery.

The abbot was enjoined in virtue of obedience and under the pains of excommunication and deprivation to grant no corrody, annuity, pension or livery to anyone in perpetuity, for term of life or for a certain time, save with the counsel, consent and licence of the diocesan and patron asked and had.

Brother Walter Dorchestre [is defamed] with Joan Barbour, a married woman. He appeared and denies [his guilt] at any time. He was ordered to clear himself with three of his brethren, and then cleared himself according to the form bidden him. Also with the wife of Thomas Deye, a serving-man in the monastery: then he cleared himself with three of his brethren. He confesses to the impawning of a gilded chalice to Marmyone for four nobles and the alienation of five silver spoons belonging to the infirmary: the spoons were taken away by stealth. The abbot was enjoined to cause these things to be restored out of the same canon's allowance. He confesses the possession of hawks: the possession of such birds was forbidden him. He confesses that he has lain diverse times in the infirmary: he was enjoined not to do this henceforward, unless by reason of bodily weakness and with the abbot's leave; and he abjured the fellowship of the woman.

Nicholas Plymmouthe was taken ... with the tanner's wife..., and in proof of such matter they that took them have their shifts to show. He denies his guilt at any time. He was ordered to clear himself with three of his brethren; but, because he is a defaulter in his purgation, he was declared convicted. He was enjoined to be kept in cloister and [to keep] silence for a week to be appointed by the prior within the next three weeks, and to lay aside his shift on all eves of the blessed Mary until Michaelmas; and he abjured his sin and the fellowship of the woman.

The abbot confesses that he did put in pawn a cover of pure gold for a cup and diverse other jewels of the house, without the knowledge and without asking leave of the convent....

The same abbot commits adultery with (1) Joan Baroun, with whom he was taken in manner suspect in the steward's chamber; (2) the wife of John Forde; (3) the wife of John Roche; (4) the wife of John Prest; (5) the wife of Thomas Fisher; and all these he maintains upon the common goods of the house, and so by pawning, nay more truly, as it is feared, by selling the jewels of the house he dilapidates and wastes all the goods of the house. He comes not to quire for the canonical hours by day or night, nor comes he to chapter to correct transgressions; and by his improvident governance the house is more than £200 in debt.

The canons do not keep cloister any day after breakfast, but some do spend their time in hawking, some in hunting, some in the public taverns, drinking and eating in the same with suspect persons, even with low women, to the great scandal of the house....

Catesby Priory

The Visitation of the priory of the nuns of Catesby, of the order of Citeaux, of the diocese of Lincoln, performed in the chapter-house there on the 17th day of the month of July, in the year of our Lord 1442, by the reverend father in Christ and lord, the Lord William, by the grace of God bishop of Lincoln....

In the first place, as the said reverend father was sitting in his capacity of judge as a tribunal in the business of the said visitation on and in the day and place aforesaid, there appeared before him the prioress and convent of the aforesaid place, in readiness, as was apparent, to undergo such visitation.... And then the same reverend father proceeded to his preparatory inquiry in the following manner.

Sister Margaret Wavere [the prioress] says that sister A[gnes Allesl]ey has six or seven young folk of both sexes that do lie in the dorter [that is, dormitory]. [Also she says] that secular folk have often recourse to the nuns' chambers within the cloister, and talkings and junketings take place there without the knowledge of [the prioress]. [Also] she says that she herself has four nuns in her household, and there are three other households of nuns within the cloister. [Also] she says that divine service is not said at the due hours according to the rule, and she says that silence is not observed in the due places. [Also] the nuns do send out letters and receive [letters] sent to them, without the advice of the prioress. [Also] she says that the secrets of the house are disclosed in the neighborhood by such seculars when they come there. Also the nuns do send out the serving-folk of the priory on their businesses and do also receive the persons for whom they send and with whom they [hold] parleyings and conversations, whereof the prioress is ignorant. Also she says that Isabel Benet is defamed with Sir William Smythe, sometime chaplain in that place, and did conceive of him and bare a child, and that she has not corrected her, because she dared not. Also the said Isabel is not obedient to the prioress. Likewise the other nuns are sometimes obedient, sometimes not; and the nuns do not wear their veils down to their [eye-brows], but do keep their foreheads bare.

Sister Juliane Wolfe says that there should be two lights burning in the upper church and quire in time of divine service. Also she says that the prioress does not show the account of her administration to the sisters. Also she says that the prioress has pawned the jewels of the house, to wit, for a period of ten years a cup for the body of Christ, which still remains in pawn, and also other pieces of silver. Also she says that the prioress did threaten that, if the nuns disclosed aught in the visitation, they should pay for it in prison. Also she says that the prioress is wont to go by herself to the town of Catesby to the gardens with one man alone, a priest, by name William Taylour. Also Isabel Wavere, the prioress's mother, rules almost the whole house together with Joan Coleworthe, the kinswoman of a certain priest, and these two do carry the keys of all the offices. Also when guests come to the house, the prioress sends out the young nuns to make their beds, the which is a scandal to the house and a perilous thing. Also the prioress does not give the nuns satisfaction in the matter of raiment and money for victuals; and she says that touching the premises the prioress is in the nuns' debt for three quarters of a year. Also the buildings and tenements both within and without the priory are dilapidated, and many have fallen to the ground because of default in repairs.

Dame Isabel Benet says that, when the prioress is enraged against any of the nuns, she calls them whores and pulls them by the hair, even in quire. Also she says that the prioress was defamed with Sir William Taylour. The man appeared in person before my lord [bishop] in the church of Brampton, and, the article having been laid to his charge, denies the crime at any time. Wherefore at his own request my lord appointed him the Saturday next after the festival of [St.] Margaret [in July] to clear himself with five chaplains of good report, who have knowledge of his behavior, in the church of Rothwell, etc. The nuns are in ignorance of the receipt and expenses of the house, likewise also of the state of the house, because the prioress has never rendered an account. These ten years the prioress has done no repairs except in one piece of the cloister, and then she sold trees to the amount of twenty shillings, and to another piece of the church, for which she received 26s. 8d. of the bequest of the wife of Brewes of Daventry. The prioress at the time of her entry had a sack and a half of wool and twelve marks of John Catesby to pay debts and do repairs, and for other needful purposes. Also she says that divine service is chanted with so great speed that no pauses are made. Also the prioress is so harsh and headstrong that she may in no wise be appeased. Also the prioress's mother knows well the secrets of the chapter and publishes them in the town. So also does the prioress publish them. Also in the last visitation which was made [by the previous bishop], the prioress said that for a purse and certain monies a clerk of the said bishop made known what every nun disclosed in that visitation.

Sister Agnes Allesley says that the prioress sows discord among the sisters, saying "Thus and thus spake such an one of you," if she to whom she speaks has transgressed in aught. Also she says as above concerning the scandal of the prioress and Sir William Taylour, who is now dwelling at Boughton by Northampton; and she says that the overmuch kindness between them was a cause of scandal, because she did go out of a morning to the offices by herself but for that chaplain; and when the prioress had been told of that scandal, that chaplain after his departure did come to the house thrice within a month. The revenues of the house, thirteen years gone by, were worth sixty pounds a year and now scarce fifty pounds; and this decrease has come to pass from the ill governance of the prioress and Sir William Taylour, and because of neglect in repair of tenements and in obtaining tenants, etc. Also two sheep-folds have stood roofless these two years: therefore the timber is beginning to rot and the lambs born in them have died owing to the wet. Also she says that at the time of the prioress's entry the house was but a little or nothing in debt. Also she found at the same time table-linen meet to serve the king, and a set of twelve silver spoons; and now all has disappeared, and the spoons and the other vessels which are in the house belong to the prioress's mother. Also she says that quire is not kept, inasmuch as the prioress calls out the young nuns to her tasks.

Sister Alice Kempe says that, because the nuns at the last visitation disclosed what should be disclosed, the prioress whipped some of them; and the prioress is too cruel and harsh with the nuns, and loves them not. Also if haply the nuns transgress, she rebukes and reproaches them before secular folk, and even during the divine office, and stints not. Also the prioress discloses the secrets of their religion to secular folk....

Sister Agnes Halewey says that the prioress in quire and without pulls the veils from the nuns' heads, calling them beggars and whores. Also, albeit she is young and would fain learn religious discipline and other things, the prioress sets her to make beds, to sewing and spinning and other tasks....

The prioress denies the article of cruelty as regards calling them whores and beggars; she denies also the violent laying of hands upon the nuns. As to not having rendered an account, she confesses it, and for the reason that she has not a clerk who can write. As to the burden of debt, she refers herself to the account now to be rendered. As to the neglect in repairing the sheepfolds, she refers herself to the visible evidence. As to pawning the cup, she says that the same was done with the consent of the convent for the payment of tithes. As to felling trees, she says that it was turned to the profit of the house, partly with the knowledge and partly without the knowledge of the convent. As to the disclosures in the last visitation and the reproaching of them that made them and the whipping, she denies the article. As to threatening them lest they should make disclosures, she denies the article. As to the publishing of the secrets of their religion, she denies the article. As to her mother and Joan Cole-worthe, she denies the article. As to the bed-making and the other tasks, she denies the article. As to withholding victuals and raiment from the nuns, she confesses it in part. As to the dilapidation of the outer tenements, she says that they are partly in repair and partly not. As to the sowing of discord, she says that she might have done this; she is not certain. As to this, [that] she said that for a purse and money she knew all the disclosures at the last visitation, she flatly denies the article. As to Sir William Taylour, she denies the crime at any time.

She has the morrow for clearing herself, of [the articles] she has denied with four of her sisters, and to receive penance for those she has confessed. At the which term she brought forward no compurgators; therefore she was declared to have made default in purgation, and, having advanced nothing, she was pronounced to be convicted, and forswore the said man and all familiar converse with the same henceforward.

Isabel Benet confesses her crime, but not with Sir William Smythe. Notwithstanding she forswore him and all familiar converse [with him] henceforward, and has the morrow to receive her penance. Thereafter she cleared herself with Juliane Wolfe, Elizabeth Langley, Alice Holewellel, and Alice Kempe.

As to the lights, the prioress says that they shall be provided. As to the chaplains, the prioress says that none can be had; she will do her diligence that they be had.

And then ... [the bishop] ordained that there be two [nuns] receivers, to receive and to pay out [the money to be kept in a chest] under three locks; and that all live in common, leaving off their separate households, and that these things do begin at Michaelmas [September 29] next. And all were warned to remove all secular folk from the dorter on this side the morrow of the Assumption [that is, before August 16]. And all were warned under pain of excommunication that none do reproach another by reason of her disclosures. And the prioress was warned to [shut] and open the doors of the church and cloister at the due times, and to keep the keys with her by night in the dorter....

Dames Isabel Benet and Agnes Halesley, nuns of Catesby, will not obey or hearken to the injunctions of the lord bishop, and especially that concerning giving up their [private] chambers, asserting that they are not subject to the same.

Also the said Dame Isabel on Monday last past did pass the night with the Austin friars at Northampton and did dance and play the lute with them in the same place until midnight, and on the night following she passed the night with the friars preachers at Northampton, luting and dancing in like manner.

Questions: What was life like in these two religious houses? How does the type of source here affect our view of the two communities? What flaws are evident in the visitation process? What variety of opinions and concerns is found among the monks and nuns? Compare the male and female monastic experience.

79. PARLIAMENTARY DEBATES

We know very little about debates in the medieval Parliament — hence the value of the two accounts below, despite their brevity and the relative unimportance of their content. Both are from 1449.

Source: A.R. Myers, ed., *English Historical Documents IV, 1327-1485* (New York: Oxford University Press, 1969), pp. 468-469.

The question is how supplies may be found for the setting forth of the armies into Normandy and Guienne.

Lord Stourton thinks there should be certain commissioners of oyer and terminer [that is, specially designated royal judges] to enquire of murders and riots against the peace. Also of liveries and that every sheriff should certify to the commissioners all the names of knights, squires, and all other men of might within his shire, that they may know whom they may empanel, such as be sufficient.

Lords Sudley and Cromwell think that due justice might be had and a good agreement amongst the lords first.

The bishop of Chichester thinks there are two ways to have goods. One is that all those who have incomes should bind themselves to give the value of that income to defend the land.

Also that those who have grants and annuities of the king's grant give a year's value of the grant and annuity beforehand to help the arms for the defense of that country.

The bishops of Norwich and Chester hold that justice may be had without difference, and that half the shire knights should be sent forth with the grants that are granted for the defense of those parts.

The bishops of Bath and Worcester hold the same. The bishops of Salisbury and Ely hold that the precedents that have been in such matters should be seen. The lord treasurer thinks that the diligence that the lords do for this matter, both for ordnance and for men to be sent forth and to see the ways how goods may be procured for them to be sent forth, should be laid before the commons. And they [ought] to be entreated to consider this great diligence and to put their hands to their good benevolence to see how supplies may be had to perform the purpose of sending forth the said armies.

The lord of Winchester holds that due justice may be had and then to ordain of others of the shire archers.

The lord cardinal and the lord of Suffolk hold to the same opinion. The conclusion of this communication is to take the usual grant of goods for the defense of the land.

Also this day the letter that Sir Francis Le Arragonois [François de Surienne] sent to the duke of Suffolk was read before the lords in the Parliament, the which was thought right notably written.

The question is whether the earl of Arundel in the Parliament held [in the twelfth year of] Henry VI should there be earl by new creation, or else by admission to his old inheritance.

Lord Hastings and Lord Say think it no new creation, but affirm the old title.

Lord Stourton and Lord Dudley affirm according to the same, that my lord of Arundel should have the said earldom by inheritance and by no new creation.

Lord Cromwell thinks the same, that it should be no new creation but admission to his former state.

The abbots of Winchcombe and Peterborough agree with Lord Cromwell.

The abbots of Gloucester and St. Albans agree.

Viscount Beaumont thinks the same.

The earl of Salisbury the same.

The bishops of Bangor, Chester, and Norwich the same.

The bishop of Winchester of the contrary opinion.

The bishops of Bath, Ely, and Salisbury hold the first opinion.

The bishops of Rochester and Carlisle agree with the first opinion.

Questions: Do these accounts bear out the prescriptions of The Manner of Holding Parliament (doc. 51)? Can you see how the clerks managed to record arguments quickly? What do you think of the arguments in the first debate?

80. A LONDON CHRONICLE ON THE WARS OF THE ROSES

Until the fifteenth century, history was written almost exclusively by churchmen, but in the 1400s there was an upsurge in historical writing by laymen. Many of them worked in London, producing a group of chronicles with a distinctly urban outlook. The following extract, covering an eventful period (1457-71) during the dynastic struggles known as the Wars of the Roses, is from such a chronicle. Its system of dating shows this clearly: the author begins each year's entry on October 31, the first day of the term of London's mayor and sheriffs, whose names are entered along with the year of the reigning king. The main characters in this somewhat convoluted story are, on the Lancastrian side, King Henry VI, his wife Queen Margaret, and their son Prince Edward; on the Yorkist side, Duke Richard of York and his sons, including Edward, earl of March (who becomes King Edward IV), George, duke of Clarence, and Richard, earl of Gloucester (later Richard III); and the famous "kingmaker," Richard earl of Warwick.

Source: modernized from *Chronicles of London,* ed. C.L. Kingsford (Oxford: The Clarendon Press, 1905), pp. 168-185.

36 Henry VI [that is, the 36th year of his reign]
Godfrey Boleyn, William Edward, Thomas Reyner

In this year ... the Duke of York and the earls of Warwick and Salisbury were sent to London to the council. And thither came the aforesaid duke, the 25th day of January, with 400 men, and was lodged at Baynard's Castle. And the 15th day of the said month came the earl of Salisbury with 500 men, and was lodged in the herber [that is, garden]. And after came the dukes of Exeter and Somerset with 800 men, and these two dukes lay outside the Temple Gate; and the earl of Northumberland, the Lord Egremont, and Lord Clifford came with 1500 men, who were lodged outside the town. Wherefore the mayor with the sheriffs, constables, and other officers of the city kept great watch, so that as long as these said lords were at this council the mayor rode about the city daily, and made the circuit of Holborn and Fleet Street, accompanied by 5000 men or thereabouts, well and sensibly arrayed, to watch and to see that the king's peace was kept. And the 14th day of February the earl of Warwick came to London from Calais with 600 men, all appareled in red jackets with [the earl's sign of] white ragged staves. And he was lodged at the Grey Friars. And the 7th day of March the king and queen came to London, at which time a concord and unity was made among these aforesaid lords. In token whereof upon our Lady's day next following, which was the 25th day of March, the king and queen and these aforesaid lords went in procession together royally at St. Paul's. And immediately after, the king and all these estates departed.... And on [May 29, the] Monday after Trinity Sunday, certain ships of Calais belonging to the earl of Warwick met with the Spanish fleet, and after a long fight took six of them laden with merchandise, and six others of the said Spanish fleet sank; and the remnant of them to the number of 21 sails fled sore beaten, with many of their men slain and sore hurt. And of the English men were slain about a hundred, and many sore hurt....

38 Henry VI

William Hulyn, John Plumer, John Stokker

Because in the year before at Ludlow field Andrew Trollope, with many of the old soldiers of Calais, went and departed secretly from the duke of York's party unto the king's party, and there revealed the secrets of the duke and his host, therefore the said duke, secretly by counsel with such lords as he had in his party, fled and evacuated, leaving behind upon the field his people to make a show of keeping the field until morning. And the duke, so departed, went toward Wales with his second son, and so through Wales into Ireland, leaving his eldest son [Edward] the earl of March with the earls of Warwick and Salisbury, and these three with three or four other persons rode into Devonshire, where by the aid of one Denham, a squire, they got a ship which cost six score nobles, wherein they sailed into Guernsey and there rested themselves.

And so in the beginning of this year of [Mayor] William Hulyn, [on November 3,] the Friday next following All Hallows' day, the earls of March, Warwick, and Salisbury came to Calais in a whaler, and there kept themselves.... Also in this year began the Parliament at Coventry, where the duke of York, the earls of March, Rutland, Warwick, and Salisbury, with the said duke's wife, and many other knights, squires, and gentlemen, were attainted for high treason, and the acts of the Parliament made at Westminster after the battle of St. Albans were annulled. All this season the earls who were in Calais gathered to them a great company....

And the second day of July the said lords of Calais came to London; and from thence they departed unto Northampton, and the people flocked steadily to them. And at Northampton the king chose to do battle, the which battle was won by the earls of March and Warwick and their company with sore fight. In this battle were slain the duke of Buckingham, the earl of Shrewsbury, Viscount Beaumont, Lord Egremont, and many knights and esquires, with many others. And the king himself was captured upon that field, and so brought unto London the 16th day of July. And immediately after this began a Parliament at Westminster. Also this year, the Friday before St. Edward's day, the duke of York came unto Westminster, his sword borne upright before him, and lodged himself in the king's palace, where also the king was, and so into the Parliament chamber, where the duke took the king's place, claiming it for his right and inheritance, and said that he would keep it to live and die. Wherewith all the lords were sore dismayed; and so the duke abode still at Westminster in the king's palace, and the lords wanted him to speak with the king, but he would not, saying he held of no man but of God. And whereas men deemed the king should have worn his crown upon St. Edward's day [October 13] with the procession, he did not, nor any of his lords, for they were all at the Black Friars at a council for this matter of the duke of York, and so continued till All Hallows' eve [October 31].

39 Henry VI
Richard Lee, Richard Flemyng, John Lumbard
And upon All Hallows' eve, in the beginning of this mayor's year, it was granted and agreed, by all the authority of the Parliament, that the king should enjoy the crown for the term of his natural life, and after the king's death the duke of York was to be king if he then lived, and after them both, the duke's heirs were to be kings. And that also the said duke was to be regent of England and of France during the king's life; and if the king would resign at any time after that, then he should resign to the duke and to no other person, and to his heirs after his days. And then towards evening they came to St. Paul's and heard evensong; and in the morning the king wore his crown, and abode there still in the bishop's palace. And upon the Saturday the 9th day of November the duke was proclaimed through the city heir apparent to the crown, and all his progeny after him. And forasmuch as the queen, the dukes of Buckingham, Exeter, and Somerset, and the earls of Devonshire and Northumberland intended to make war against the king's peace, therefore the duke of York and the earls of Rutland and Salisbury rode northward, the second day of December, to capture them. And the 30th day of December they met with the queen's party at Wakefield, where the duke of York and [his second son] the earl of Rutland and Sir Thomas Neville were slain, and many others. And the earl of Salisbury was captured alive, and John Hardowe, a captain of London, and Hanson of Hull; and these were afterwards brought to Pontefract, and there beheaded, and their heads set upon York's gates.

And all this season was great watch made in the city of London, for it was reported that the queen with the northern men would come down to the city and rob and despoil the city, and destroy it utterly, and all the south country. Wherefore the king and the lords of his council raised all the southern country to go northward against the queen and her party; and at this time [Edward] earl of March, being in Shrewsbury, hearing of the death of his father, requested aid from the town to avenge his father's death. And from thence he went into Wales, where at the following Candelmas [February 2] he fought a battle at Mortimer's Cross against the earls of Pembroke and Wiltshire, where the earl of March had the victory. And the queen with the lords in her party, after they had distressed the duke of York and his company, came southward with a great fellowship and people to come to the king, to reverse such articles and conclusions as were taken by the authority of the Parliament aforesaid. Against their coming the duke of Norfolk and the earl of Warwick with a great host went to St. Albans, and led King Henry with them; and there was fought a great battle upon Shrove Tuesday [February 17] at three o'clock in the morning; and the queen and her party had the victory, and the earl of Warwick with his company fled. And the king was taken, and brought to the queen and his son Prince Edward; and as some said, there the king made him a knight, and diverse others to the number of thirty persons.

And in this season the prickers or fore-riders of the northern men came to London, and would have come in; but the mayor and the commons would not allow them, and many of them went to Westminster and disported there, and three of them were slain at Cripplegate. And the Wednesday before, the duchess of Bedford and Lady Scales, with diverse clerks and curates of the city, went to St. Albans to the king, queen, and prince, to entreat for grace for the city. And the king and his council granted that four knights with 400 men should go to the city, and see the disposition of it, and make an agreement with the mayor and aldermen. Whereupon certain aldermen were appointed to ride to Barnet to fetch in the said knights. And after this certain carts were laden with victuals to go to St. Albans by the queen's command. But when they came to Cripplegate the commons of the city would not let the carts depart. And immediately after this came tidings that the earl of Warwick in support of the earl of March was coming toward London. Wherefore the king, with the queen and the prince, with all their people drew northward, and so into Northumberland. And the following Thursday the earl of March and the earl of Warwick came to London with a great host. And upon the Sunday after, all the host mustered in St. John's field, where were read among the people certain articles and points that King Henry had offended in. And then it was asked of the people whether the said Henry was worthy to reign still; and the people cried, "Nay! Nay!" And then they asked if they would have the earl of March to be their king; and they said, "Yea! Yea!" And then certain captains were sent to the earl of March's place at Baynard's Castle, and told the the earl that the people had chosen him as king; whereof he thanked God and them, and, by the advice of the bishops of Canterbury and of Exeter, and the earl of Warwick and others, he took it upon him. And you shall understand that before King Henry, with the queen and the prince, departed from St. Albans, they beheaded Lord Bonville and Sir Thomas Keryell, who were taken at the battle aforesaid. Then the duchess of York, hearing of the loss of that battle, sent over the sea her two young sons George and Richard, who went to Utrecht....

Then the 4th day of March, by the advice of the lords spiritual and temporal, the earl of March by the right of inheritance as the eldest son of the duke of York, the day aforesaid, which was in the year of our Lord 1460, took possession of the realm of England, after solemn procession made and done at St. Paul's, in the great hall of Westminster; and there, sitting in the king's seat with the scepter in his hand, it was asked of the people again if they would have him king; and they cried, "Yea! Yea!" And there he took his oath; and this done, he went into the abbey, where he was received with procession bearing the scepter royal, and all the lords did homage to him as to their sovereign lord. And on the following day proclamations were made through all the city, Edward the Fourth of that name, and when all these ceremonies were done, and "Te Deum" solemnly sung in the abbey, the king came by water to St. Paul's, and there dined. And after dinner the mayor with his brethren, the aldermen, and certain commoners came to the palace, beseeching the king to be good and gracious to the city, and that they might have their old liberties and franchises granted and confirmed as they had been in his noble progenitors' days, and this was granted to them. And upon the following Saturday the earl of Warwick took his journey northward, with a great people; and the following week, the king's foot people went also northward with the king's standard. And on Friday of the same week, which was the 14th day of March, the king rode through London and so out at Bishopsgate, with a goodly fellowship with him…. And on the following Palm Sunday [March 29] the king met with the northern men, nine miles on this side of York, at a place or village called Sherborne, where he fought and won the battle. In this fight were slain eleven lords with other knights, and about 28,000 men, of which eleven lords follow some of the names: the earl of Northumberland, Lord Clifford, the earl of Westmoreland's brother Sir John Neville, with Andrew Trollope, and many others…. And after Easter the king removed to Durham, before which departing the earl of Devonshire was beheaded, who had been taken before in the battle. And within a while after Easter the earl of Wiltshire was captured, and King Henry with his company fled into Scotland; and soon after this the king [Edward] came to Sheen, and from Sheen to Lambeth, and there lodged. And upon Friday the 26th day of June the mayor of London, with the aldermen and commons, the mayor with his brethren being in scarlet and the commons in green, brought the king from Lambeth to the Tower of London, where he made 28 knights of the Bath. And in the morning he dubbed four knights, before he rode to Westminster. And in the afternoon, on the Saturday, he rode through the city to Westminster. And in the morning on Sunday, which was St. Peter's eve, and the 28th day of June, he was crowned at Westminster, with great solemnity of bishops and other temporal lords. And on next morning the king wore his crown again in Westminster Abbey, in the worship of God and St. Peter. And the next morning he wore his crown also in St. Paul's, in the worship of God and St. Paul. And there the angel came down, and censed him, at which time there was as great a multitude of people in St. Paul's as ever was seen before in any days. And soon after the coronation, the king made his brother George duke of Clarence.... And in harvest the king rode to Canterbury, and so to Sandwich, and so along by the seaside to Southampton, and so into the marches of Wales, and then to Bristol, where he was royally received with great solemnity, and so about in diverse places of the land....

2 Edward IV
Thomas Cook, William Hampton, Barthu. Jamys
In this year, the third day of November, Queen Margaret came out of France into Scotland with a strength of people; and so entered into England and made open war. Then the king went northward with a great host; and the 13th day of November the queen, hearing of his coming with his great host, immediately broke formation and fled. And she fled in a caravel, wherein was the substance of her goods; and as she sailed there came upon her such a tempest that she was glad to leave the caravel and take a fishing boat, and so she went ashore at Berwick; and the caravel and goods were sunk.... And when the king had knowledge of her departure, he intended to pursue her to capture her; but then it happened that he was visited with the sickness of measles, through which his intention was stymied. And on the 12th day of Christmas the Scots came to rescue the castle of Alnwick, but it was yielded to the king also. And the duke of Somerset and Sir Ralph Percy submitted themselves to the king's grace, whom the king admitted to his grace. And about Shrovetide the king came southward. And when the Scots knew of the king's departure they came again to Bamburgh Castle and captured it. Then the king on St. John's day in harvest [August 29] with a great host went again northward toward Scotland; and many ships were supplied in the west country, and at London, and at Sandwich, to go by water with victuals and men by sea.

3 Edward IV
Matthew Philip, Robert Basset, Thomas Muschamp
This year the duke of Somerset, Lord Hungerford, and Lord Roos were captured, with many others, as was King Henry's helmet, richly garnished with two crowns; and his followers were dressed in blue velvet. And forthwith the said duke of Somerset was beheaded with others at Exham. And Lord Hungerford and Lord Roos, with others, were beheaded at Newcastle. And Sir Philip Wentworth and others were beheaded at Middleham. And Sir Thomas Husey with others at York. And immediately after this, at Pontefract, Lord Montagu presented [Edward] the king with King Henry's helmet, and his three followers; but where King Henry was could not be known. And then King Edward,

considering that great feat done by the said Lord Montagu, made him earl of Northumberland; and the following July the earl of Warwick with the aid of the said earl of Northumberland captured again the castle of Bamburgh, wherein was taken Sir Ralph Grey, who was afterwards beheaded and quartered at York. Also in this year, the first day of May, the king wedded Dame Elizabeth Grey, formerly wife of Lord Grey of Groby, and daughter of Lord Rivers....

9 Edward IV
Richard Lee, Richard Gardiner, Robert Drope
This year after All Hallows' eve there were proclamations made in London, that the king had pardoned all the northern men for their rising, and all others both for the death of Lord Rivers and others; and afterward was much to-do about a rising of the people in Lincolnshire, wherefore the king intended to go thitherward; but just then Lord Wells, on whom the guilt was placed, was taken and beheaded. And in February the earl of Warwick came to London, where about that time was much to-do about bills that were set up in diverse places of the city for the duke of Clarence and him [who were turning against King Edward]. And on Shrove Sunday [February 12] the king had intended to go northward, but the same day the duke of Clarence came to London, and therefore the king tarried, as it was said, till the following Tuesday. And that day the king came from Westminster to Baynard's Castle, to his mother, where the duke of Clarence met with him, and from thence he came with the king to St. Paul's, where they prayed. And they took to their horses and rode to Ware the same night, and with him rode also, among other lords, Lord Percy, who was newly made earl of Northumberland. And meanwhile the earl of Warwick was in the town of Warwick, and had raised many people, as it was reported.... In this season was the duke of Clarence gone unto the earl of Warwick to take his side, and the king sent to them willing them to come in, and they would have his forgiveness; and they made a pretended agreement, saying that they would order their people and come; but that same night they broke and fled the land in all haste. And in Easter week Sir Geoffrey Gate and one Clapham, servants of the said earl of Warwick, were taken at Southampton by Lord Howard and his company; and Clapham was beheaded soon after. And then was Lord St. John arrested, but he was in the custody of the bishop of Canterbury a good while; but at last he was sent to the Tower. And about this time the earl of Oxford, hearing of the duke of Clarence and the earl of Warwick being in France, went over to them. And in the beginning of July Lord Fitzhugh made a rising in the north; but as soon as he knew of the king's coming he fled into Scotland. And then the king abode still at York and thereabouts. And in September the duke of Clarence, the earl of Warwick, the earl of Pembroke, the

earl of Oxford, with diverse gentlemen, landed at Dartmouth in Devonshire, to whom flocked many people of every region; and the people of Kent made an insurrection in Kent and came to London, where, in the suburbs of the city and other places such as St. Katherine's and Radcliffe, they robbed and despoiled diverse Dutchmen and their beer houses. And the said duke and his company made, as he came landward, his proclamations in King Henry's name, who at that time was prisoner in the Tower of London. And when they drew toward King Edward, who was then at York, he feared them, and also he had only a small company about him in comparison with the duke and his company. Wherefore, seeing he could not make his party match theirs, and also because some of his own folks around him were not very loyal to him, he with a few horses took the next way over the Wash in Lincolnshire, where some of his company were drowned, and he escaped with great jeopardy. And then the queen, who was in the Tower, hearing of the king's departure, the first day of October just after this, departed thence secretly and went to Westminster [Abbey], where she abode as a sanctuary woman a good while after.... And upon the 12th day of October the Tower was given up by arrangement. And then King Henry was taken from the place where he was imprisoned, and lodged in the king's lodging, where the queen before had been lodged. And on the Saturday after that came in the duke of Clarence, and with him the earl of Warwick, the earl of Shrewsbury, and Lord Stanley. And they rode to the Tower and fetched out King Henry, and brought him to St. Paul's and lodged him in the bishop's palace, where the earl of Warwick also lodged with him....

1 Henry VI; 10 Edward IV
John Stockton, John Croby, John Ward
This year, the third day of November, Prince Edward the son of King Edward IV, his father then being fled into Flanders, was born at Westminster within the sanctuary, and christened in the abbey, whose godfathers were the abbot and prior of Westminster, and Lady Scrope, godmother. Also this year, the 26th day of November, began the Parliament at Westminster, and from thence it was prorogued to St. Paul's and there continued till Christmas.... And during this Parliament King Edward was proclaimed through the city usurper of the crown, and [Richard] the duke of Gloucester his younger brother was proclaimed traitor, and both were attainted by the authority of the said Parliament.... And in the beginning of April King Edward with his brother the duke of Gloucester came ashore in the north country at a place called Ravenscar; and with them came about 500 Englishmen, and as many Dutchmen; and after he was on land he drew toward York, making proclamations as he went in King Henry VI's name. And when he came to York the citizens kept him out till they knew what his intent was; and when he had told them that he came

with no other intent but to claim his inheritance, which was the duchy of York, he was received into the town, and there refreshed himself and his people; and after that more and more people drew unto him. And after he was departed out of the city southward, he saw his strength increased, and that he was past the danger of the lord Marquis Montagu, who lay in that country, and then he made proclamations in his own name as king of the land. And on the Thursday before Easter King Henry rode about the city with diverse lords to gather the people of the city together to keep out King Edward; but notwithstanding, that same afternoon, King Edward came into the city with his company, and was lodged at the palace, where he found King Henry almost alone, for he was a good and spiritual man and set little store by worldly matters. And there King Edward stayed until Easter eve. And in the meantime the duke of Clarence with his affinity gathered their people and were coming toward London. And on Easter eve the king rode through the city toward Barnet. And the duke and his company were at that time at St. Albans. And that night, contrary to the promise and oath he had made to the French king when he was in France, the said duke of Clarence denied the title of King Henry and went unto his brother King Edward with his people, and left the earl of Warwick and all the remainder of the lords. And early in the morning the battle began, at which battle, on the plain outside Barnet town, on one side were King Edward, King Henry VI, the duke of Clarence, the duke of Gloucester, Lord Hastings, and diverse other lords and gentlemen. And on the other side were the earl of Warwick, the lord Marquis Montagu his brother, the duke of Exeter, the earl of Oxford, and many other gentlemen. There was a sore fight, but in conclusion King Edward had the victory. And upon the same Easter day aforesaid, at the same battle, were slain the earl of Warwick, and his brother the lord marquis, with Lord Barneys from the king's party, and many more from both parties, upon whose souls Jesus have mercy.

And the same day in the afternoon the king came riding through the city, and prayed at St. Paul's, and so went unto Westminster; and after him was brought King Henry, riding in a long blue velvet gown, and so to Westminster, and from thence to the Tower, where he remained prisoner as he had done before. And in May Queen Margaret and Prince Edward her son landed; and at Tewkesbury they met [in battle] with King Edward, and there was slain Prince Edward, and his mother was captured and brought to London in a chariot, and afterward sent home to her own country....

Also upon Ascension eve [May 22] King Henry was brought from the Tower though Cheap unto St. Paul's upon a bier; and about the bier were more gloves and staves than torches; and it was said he had been slain by the duke of Clarence; but however he was dead, thither he was brought dead; and in the church the corpse lay all night. And in the morning it was conveyed to

Chertsey, where he was buried. And within two days afterward, the king with a great host rode into Kent, where he appointed his justices, and made inquiries into [a recent uprising], and there were some hanged, and some beheaded, and the heads were set on London Bridge, and one named Spising was set upon Aldgate; and some were grievously fined. And when the king had set the country in peaceable rule, he came again to London upon Whitsun eve.

Questions: Compare the wars described here with previous civil wars: what sense is there of the issues involved? Are there other differences? What indications are there of the loyalties and concerns of London? What role did women play in these events?

81. FORTESCUE: IN PRAISE OF THE LAWS OF ENGLAND

The political theorist John Fortescue was a Lancastrian supporter who dedicated In Praise of the Laws of England, *from which this short selection is taken, to Prince Edward, son of Henry VI, in about 1470.*

Source: trans. R. Mulcaster, 1573, reprinted in G.G. Coulton, *Social Life in Britain from the Conquest to the Reformation* (Cambridge: Cambridge University Press, 1918), pp. 30-33, 35-37; modernized.

For the king of England cannot alter or change the laws of his realm at his pleasure. The reason is, he governs his people by power, not only royal, but also political. If his power over them were royal only, then he might change the laws of his realm, and charge his subjects with tallage and other burdens without their consent, and such is the dominion that the civil laws refer to, when they say, "The Prince's pleasure hath the force of a law." But very different from this is the power of a king whose government over his people is political, for he can neither change laws without the consent of his subjects, nor yet charge them with unaccustomed impositions against their wills. Wherefore his people do frankly and freely enjoy and occupy their own goods, being ruled by such laws as they themselves desire; neither are they plundered either by their own king or by any other. The subjects of a king ruling only by power royal have similar pleasure also and freedom, so long as he falls not into tyranny. Of such a king speaks Aristotle in the third book of his civil philosophy, saying that it is better for a city to be governed by a good king, than by a good law. But forasmuch as a king is not ever such a man, therefore St. Thomas, in the book which he wrote to the king of Cyprus, *Of the Governance of Princes*, wishes the state of a realm to be such, that it may not be in the king's power to oppress his people with tyranny, which thing is performed only while the power royal is restrained by power political. Rejoice therefore, O sovereign Prince, and be glad, that the law of your realm, wherein you shall succeed, is such, for it shall exhibit and minister to you and your people no small security and comfort. With such laws (as St. Thomas says) should all mankind have been governed, if in Paradise they had not transgressed God's commandment; with such laws also was the synagogue ruled, while it served under God only as king, who adopted the same to him for a peculiar kingdom. But at the last, when at their request [the Hebrews] had a human king set over them, they were then, under royal laws only, brought very low. And yet under the same laws, while good kings were their rulers, they lived wealthily; and when willful and tyrannous kings had the government of them, then they continued in great discomfort and misery, as the book of Kings doth more plainly declare....

Now whether the statutes of England be good or not, that only remains to be discussed. For they proceed not only from the prince's pleasure, as do the laws of those kingdoms that are ruled only by regal government, where sometimes the statutes do so procure the sole benefit of the maker, that they redound to the hindrance and damage of his subjects. Sometimes also by the negligence and oversight of such princes, and their slight regard, respecting only their own interests, they are so unadvisedly made, that they are more worthy to have the name of disorders, than of well ordered laws. But statutes cannot thus pass in England, for so much as they are made not only by the prince's pleasure, but also by the assent of the whole realm: so that of necessity they must procure the wealth of the people, and in no wise tend to their hindrance. And it cannot otherwise be thought but that they are full of much wit and wisdom, seeing that they are ordained not by the devising of one man alone or of a hundred wise counsellors only, but of more than three hundred chosen men, very similar in number to the ancient senators of Rome: as they that know the fashion of the Parliament of England, and the order and manner of calling the same together, are able more distinctly to declare. And if perchance these statutes, being devised with such great solemnity and wit, do not fall out so effectually as the intent of the makers did wish, they may be quickly reformed, but not without the assent of the commons and estates of the realm, by whose authority they were first devised....

Call to remembrance, most worthy prince, after what sort you saw the wealthy villages and towns (as regards stores of grain) in the realm of France, while you were there a sojourner, pestered with the king's men at arms and their horses, so that scarcely in any of the great towns there could you get any lodging.... [A description of oppressive conditions in France follows, each instance of which contrasts with the description of England below.] Also, while you were abiding in France, and near to the same kingdom, you heard of other great enormities like unto these, and some much worse than these detestable and damnable, done no otherwise but under the color of that law, to rehearse which here would continue our talk too long a time. Now therefore, let us see what the effect of the law political and royal ... hath wrought in the realm of England; that you, being instructed with the experience of both laws, may by their effects better judge which of them you ought rather to choose, seeing ... that opposites laid together do more clearly reveal themselves.

Within the realm of England, no man sojourns in another man's house, without the love and leave of the good man of the same house: except in common inns, where, before his departure thence, he shall fully satisfy and pay for all his charges there. Neither shall he escape unpunished, whosoever he be, who takes another man's goods without the good will of the owner thereof. Neither is it unlawful for any man in the realm to provide and store salt for himself, and other merchandises or wares, at his own will and pleasure, from any man that sells the same. Howbeit, the king, even if the owners would say no, may through his officers take necessities for his house, at a reasonable price, to be assessed by the discretion of the constables of the towns: nevertheless, he is bound by the laws to pay therefor, either presently in hand, or else at a day to be limited and set by the higher officers of his house: for by his laws he may take away none of his subjects' goods, without due satisfaction for the same. Neither doth the king there, either by himself or by his servants and officers, levy upon his subjects tallages, subsidies, or any other burdens, or alter their laws, or make new laws, without the express consent and agreement of his whole realm in Parliament. Wherefore every inhabiter of that realm uses and enjoys, at his pleasure, all the fruits that his land or cattle bear, with all the profits and commodities which, by his own labor, or by the labor of others, he gains by land or by waters, not hindered by the injury or wrong detainment of any man, unless he shall be allowed a reasonable recompense. And hereby it comes to pass that the men of that land are rich, having abundance of gold and silver, and other things necessary for the maintenance of man's life. They drink no water, unless it be so that some, for devotion and upon a zeal of penance, do abstain from other drinks. They eat plentifully of all kinds of flesh and fish. They wear fine woolen cloth in all their apparel. They have also abundance of bed coverings in their houses, and of all other woolen stuff. They have great store of wares and implements of household. They are plentifully furnished with all instruments of husbandry, and all other things that are requisite to the accomplishment of a quiet and wealthy life, according to their estates and degrees. Neither are they sued in the law, except when before ordinary judges where by the laws of the land they are justly treated. Neither are they arrested or impleaded for their moveables or possessions, or arraigned for any criminal offense, however great and outrageous, except according to the laws of the land and before the judges aforesaid. And these are the fruits which government political and regal conjoined doth bear and bring forth: whereof now appear evidently unto you the experiences of the effects of the law, which some of your progenitors worked to abolish. Before, also, you saw plainly the effects the other law, which they with such earnest endeavor labored to advance and place in stead of this law; so that, by the fruits of them both, you may know what they are: and did not ambition, riot, and wanton lust, which your said progenitors esteemed above the wealth of the realm, move them to this alteration.

Questions: What political ideas does Fortescue emphasize here? How do these compare with the political ideas of other medieval writers and documents you have read (docs. 29, 35, 42, 51, 69)? What comparison does he draw between England and France? How does the work fit into the political situation in 1470?

82. THE PLUMPTON LETTERS

Another type of source material that we encounter for the first time in the fifteenth century is the private family letter collection. One such set is the correspondence preserved by the Plumptons, a northern gentry family. The letters below were written to two successive heads of this family between 1469 and 1499: Sir William Plumpton died in 1480, to be succeeded by his son, Sir Robert Plumpton. Many of the writers are relatives; Robinett (a nickname for Robert) is an illegitimate son, and Edward Plumpton is probably a first cousin of Sir Robert, for whom he acts as attorney.

Source: modernized from T. Stapleton, *Plumpton Correspondence* (London: The Camden Society, 1839), pp. 20-22, 26-29, 36-42, 44, 48-49, 60-66, 72, 74-75, 83-84, 89, 106, 123, 138-144.

[Thomas Billop to William Plumpton, August 21, 1469]
Right worshipful master, I recommend me unto you.... Letting you know also that I have been in the Peake and there I cannot get any money from Harry Fulgiam, nor from John of Tor, nor any other that owes you, unless I take from your cattle, and so I think for to do; for I have no oxen to get your corn with, nor can I get any carried, for every man is so busy with his own: for the weather is so latesome in this country, that men can neither well get corn nor hay.

Letting you know that your tenant Nicholas Bristow has not gotten but twelve fodder of hay, and it is no good, and the cornland is overfloating with water; letting you know that I have gotten the hay in Hesthornmeen that was left after Lammas Day [August 1], as you commanded me to do.

Letting you know that I was at Melton on St. Lawrence's day [August 10] with forty of your sheep to sell, and could sell none of them, unless I had sold twenty of the best of them for thirteen pence apiece, and therefore I sold none.

Letting you know that I sent five pounds unto you with William Plumpton and with William Marley, and also twenty-five shillings which was borrowed from Bryan Smith, which I must pay again, and therefore I do not have money for to get your harvest with.

Also [advising] that you make the malt be winnowed, before it be laid in any store-rooms, for otherwise weevils will breed in it, for I could not get it winnowed before it went to the ship, because I could not get any help, and therefore I upheaped with a quarter, twenty-one quarters for twenty quarters; and also six of your cheeses have two marks that I know are the best of them. No more I write you at this time, but that the holy Trinity have you ever in his keeping. Written in haste by your servant Thomas Billop at Kinalton, the Monday before St. Bartholomew's Day, 9[th year of the reign of] Edward IV.

[Richard, Duke of Gloucester, to William Plumpton, October 13, c. 1472]
To our right trusty and well-beloved Sir William Plumpton, knight, steward of the lordship of Spofford, and to the bailiff of the same, and to either of them, [from] the Duke of Gloucester, Constable and Admiral of England.

R. Gloucester. Right trusty and well-beloved, we greet you well. And whereas at the fresh pursuit of our well-beloved Christopher Stansfield, one Richard of the Burgh, who had taken and led away feloniously certain cows and other livestock belonging to him, was taken and arrested with the said [stock] at Spofford, where they yet remain; wherefore we desire and pray you that upon sufficient surety to be found by the said Christopher to sue against the said felon, as the law wills for that offense, you will make delivery unto him of the said livestock, as is according with right: showing him your good aid, favor, and benevolence, all the more at the instance of this our letters. And our Lord preserve you. From Pontefract, under our signet, the thirteenth of October.

[Henry, Earl of Northumberland, to William Plumpton]
To my right trusty and well-beloved cousin, Sir William Plumpton, knight.

Right trusty and with all my heart my well-beloved cousin, I greet you heartily well, and desire and pray that my well-beloved servant Edmund Cape may have and occupy the office of the bailiffship of Sessay, as his father did before in time past. My trust is in you, that all the more for this mine instance and contemplation, you will fulfill this my desire, and I will be as well inclined to do things for your pleasure. That our Lord knows, who have you in his blessed keeping. Written in my manor of Topcliffe, the seventeenth day of August.
Your cousin,
H. Northumberland

[Henry, Earl of Northumberland, to William Plumpton, September 15, between 1471 and 1476]
To my trusty and well-beloved cousin, Sir William Plumpton, knight.

Right trusty and with all my heart my right well-beloved cousin, I greet you well, and desire and pray you to beseech Sir Richard Aldborough, to cause him to deliver unto my cousin, Dame Isabel Ilderton, such beasts and cattle as he retains and withholds from her: for she has no other means to help herself with, until a determination be had betwen Thomas Ilderton and her, regarding the livelihood that stands in dispute between them. Cousin, as you love me, [I wish] that you will endeavor yourself for the performance of the promises, wherein you shall deserve great thanks from God, and to me right great pleasure. That our Lord knows, who have you, cousin, in his blessed keeping. Written in my manor of Leconfield, the twenty-fifth day of September.

Your cousin,

H. Northumberland

[John Johnson to William Plumpton]

To my right worshipful and reverend master, Sir William Plumpton, knight.

Right worshipful and reverend sir and master, I recommend me unto you. And [may it] please your good mastership to know, there is a clerk at York, who intends to say his first mass the Sunday next after the feast of the nativity of our Lady the Virgin [in September]; and if you would vouchsafe that he might have a morsel of venison for the said Sunday for Robert Manfeld's sake, then truly I shall let [Robert] know both how ye did [a favor] for his kinswoman for her wedding, and now for this said priest; for he is full brother to the said woman, and they are both right near of his kin. I am sure he will thank you full heartily, when I let him know, and that shall be in all the goodly haste that I may, with the grace of God, who increase your good estate to his pleasure. Written in haste at York, the Friday next before the said feast.

Your own servant and beadsman [that is, one who prays for you],

John Johnson of York

[Richard Banks to William Plumpton]

To my reverend and worshipful master, Sir William Plumpton, knight.

To my reverend and worshipful master, I recommend me unto you in the heartiest wise I can. And for as much as a poor widow, called Ellen Helme, who is my son-in-law William Nesfield's tenant, is grievously worried about her sons, I pray you heartily to be their tender and especial master, as I and my said son[-in-law] may have cause to do you service, the which we shall be ready to do, with God's grace, who have you in his blessed keeping. Written at Newton on St. Cuthbert's day [March 20].

By your own,

Richard Banks

[Robinett Plumpton to William Plumpton, April 1, 1476]

To my most reverend and worshipful master Sir William Plumpton, knight, be this delivered.

After all lowly and due recommendations, I lowly recommend me unto your good mastership; notifying your mastership I sent you by one William Atkinson a letter and the copy of the answer of the privy seal, and a box with 6 pieces, 5 sealed and one unsealed; and, sir, the box sealed for your mastership took me no more. First, they took from me 7, and 2 filed together that were of one, the grant of Stuteville and the petition thereon; and they took away the petition, and so I had but 6, which I send your mastership by the said William in the said box sealed; and if it were so, and the letter delivered to you with the copy, I desire you send word....

And as for the suits in the [court of the] King's Bench against them in Brereton, and in the [court of] Common Pleas against William Pulleyne and his sureties, they are in process; and since they be in *exigent*, you shall have the *exigent* sent to you, as soon as it will be sped. And for the day of appearances of Aylmer's wife the month of Easter is set, so that she be here the [fourth day of May]. I would have sent you word before, except that I had not the [writ of] *habeas corpus* against John Esomock and Robert Galaway.... And so I send you now the *habeas corpora* and a copy thereof, and you must ask the sheriff to serve it, if so be that you agree not. And also, sir, [I ask] that you will send word as soon as you can, if the principals were not delivered at York, and what way is had between you and them, and if there be any town or hamlet in Craven that is called Middleton, and that you send word....

Also, sir, I send your mastership the bill of expenses and costs that I have made since I came hither, and may it please you to see it and send money the next term. All other things which you want me to do, I shall do those that I either may or can. I beseech your mastership to recommend me lowly to my lady; and if I dare, sir, the matter between my brother Robert and Mr. Gascoine's sister, I think, is too long in making up, for in long tarryings come great obstacles. And I beseech the blessed Trinity have you in his continual keeping. From London, the first day of April.

Your servant in all,

Robinett Plumpton

[Tenants of the manor of Idle to William Plumpton]

Complaints about your servants of Idle, John Rycroft and William Rycroft. To our master and lord, Sir William Plumpton, knight.

All your tenants and servants of your lordship of Idle beseech your good mastership, except William Rycroft the elder, William Rycroft the younger, John Rycroft, Henry Bycroft, and John Chalner. And may it please your good mastership to hear and consider the great rumor, slander, and full noise of your tenants of your said lordship, that they are untrue people of their hands, taking goods by means of untruth; and for as much as the said William Rycroft the elder, William Rycroft the younger, John Rycroft, Henry Bycroft, and John

Chalner are dwelling within your said lordship, they all not having any cow or calves, or any other goods whereby they might live, nor any other occupations, and fine they look, and well they fare, and at all sports and games they are in our country for the most part, and [have] silver to spend and for gaming, which they have more ready than anyone else within your said lordship; and to the welfare of our sovereign lord the king and you, nothing they will pay, unless your said tenants will fight with them, wherefore they are in arrears for diverse of your debts. And by what means they are in this way, with five persons being in the household, God or some evil angel knows. And as for geese, ... hens, and capons, your said tenants may keep none, without them being stolen away by night to the great hurt of your tenants. And for as much as these persons aforenamed are not laboring in due time, as all other of your tenants are, but live as vagabonds, your said tenants think even worse of them. Wherefore in reverence of God and in way of charity, your said tenants beseech you to call all of them before you, and to set such remedy in these premises as may be to your worship, and great profit to your tenants, and in showing of great unthriftiness, which without you is likely to grow hereafter, and your said tenants shall pray to Almighty God for your welfare and estate.

[Henry, Earl of Northumberland, to Robert Plumpton, September 7, 1480]
To my right well-beloved Robert Plumpton, esquire.

Right well-beloved friend, I greet you well. And whereas the Scots in great number are entered into Northumberland, whose malice with God's help I intend to resist, therefore on the king our sovereign lord's behalf, I charge you, and also on mine as a warden, that you with all such persons as you may make in their most defensible array, be with me at Topcliffe upon Monday by eight o'clock, as my trust is in you. Written in Wressle, the seventh day of September.
Your cousin,
Henry Northumberland

[William Joddopkan to Lady Plumpton, July, c. 1481]
To my old Lady Plumpton be this bill delivered.

Right worshipful and my especial good lady, I recommend me unto your good ladyship, evermore desiring to know of your welfare. And, madam, I pray you to recall how good a preacher I have been to my master, who is gone, and to you. And, madam, there is one duty owing unto me, part of which was taken before my master deceased, on whose soul God have mercy, and the most part of which was taken to yourself since he died — taken by Henry Fox and by Henry of Selay, your servants, of which I send you one bill with Henry Fox. The sum is £19 2s. 9d., whereof I have received from Henry Fox in money £3 and 2 fat oxen, price 36s. The sum that I have received is £4 16s., so there remains behind £14 6s. 9d. Madam, if case be that you will have sent word for Sir John Wixley, that draws £6 6s. 8d., so then there is owing to me £9 1d. And I beseech you, madam, that I might have my money; I have forborne it long. You know well, madam, the great trouble that I was in, and the great cost and charges that I had this last year past; and, madam, you know well I have no living except my buying and selling: and, madam, I pray you send me my money, as you want me to do you service, or else to send me word when I shall have it, for it costs me much money sending for it. And Henry Fox bade me send my reckoning at Ripon, and I should be answered for my money, for Henry received most of the stuff from me; and if you will not answer me for it, Henry must answer for it…. And therefore I beseech you to look if there be anything I may do for your ladyship, or for my master your son; I shall be ready with grace of God, who preserve your ladyship. Written at York, on Friday after St. Peter's day.

By your own,

William Joddopkan

[Edward Plumpton to Robert Plumpton, October 18, 1483]
To the right honorable and worshipful my singular good master, Sir Robert Plumpton, knight, be these delivered.

The most humble and due recommendations premised, [may it] please your mastership to recommend me unto my singular good lady your mother, and my lady your wife; humbly praying your good mastership to take no displeasure with me that I sent not to you before this, as my duty was. People in this country are so troubled, in such commandment as they have in the king's name and otherwise, marvelously, that they know not what to do. My lord Strange goeth forth from Latham [in support of the king] upon Monday next with ten thousand men, where we cannot say. The [rebel] duke of Buckingham has so many men, as it is said here, that he is able to go where he will; but I trust he and all his malice shall be right withstood: and otherwise it would be a great pity. Messengers come daily, both from the king's grace and from the duke, into this country. In short space I trust to see your mastership; such men as I have to do with are as yet occupied with my said lord. Sir, I find my kinsmen all well disposed to me; if your mastership will command me any service, I am ready and ever will be to my life's end, with the grace of Jesu, who ever preserve you. Written at Aldcliffe, upon St. Luke's day.

Your most humble servant,

Edward Plumpton

[Sir Thomas Betanson to Robert Plumpton, December 13, 1485]

To his especial good master, Sir Robert Plumpton, knight, deliver this letter. Sir, if it please your mastership, on the Saturday after our Lady's day [in December], the Parliament was adjourned unto the 27th day of January, and then it begins again. Sir, my lord chancellor published in the Parliament house the same day, that the king's good grace [that is, Henry VII] shall wed my lady Elizabeth [the daughter of Edward IV], and so she is taken as queen; and that at the marriage there shall be great jousting. Also, sir, there are diverse lords and gentlemen attainted [for treason] by the Parliament, which be these; [a list follows.] ... However, there were many gentlemen against it, but it would not be, for it was the king's pleasure. Sir, here is much speech that we shall have [trouble] again, and no man can say from whom, but they think from northern men and Welshmen. And much speech is in the king's house and of his householdmen. Sir, there are no other tidings here as yet. There is much business amongst the lords, but no man knows what it is; it is said it is not well amongst them. Sir, I send your mastership a letter by Roger, Mr. Middleton's man. Sir, if there are any newer things, your mastership will have word, if I can get it carried from London. On the day of St. Lucy the virgin.

Your beadsman,

Sir Thomas Betanson

[The Prior of Newburgh to Robert Plumpton]

To the right worshipful knight, Sir Robert Plumpton.

Right worshipful sir, I commend me to you, and am full sorry that you should be displeased against the writing which came last to you in my name. I commanded the officer to write to you in my name, but I saw not the letter afterwards. Sir, you have always been a good master to our house and I pray you so to continue, and in any thing which you are miscontented with, it shall be amended by the sight of yourself. And I beseech you to be a good master to his bearer, for he is guiltless in this matter. And as for our land, we pay our tithes therefor, and trust in you that you will not seize any thereof, whereby we should have cause to make further labor; for it is not the king's mind to seize any titheable land, and we have no suit land, but it is titheable, as God knows, who preserve you forever.

Your loving friend,

The prior of Newburgh

[Henry, earl of Northumberland, to Robert Plumpton, April 24, 1489]

To my right heartily well-beloved cousin, Sir Robert Plumpton.

Right heartily beloved cousin, I commend me unto you, and for right weighty consideration moving me, concerning the pleasure of the king's highness, on the behalf of his grace, charge you, and on my desire pray you, that you, with such a company, and as many as you may bring with your ease, such as you trust, having bows and arrows, and secretly harnessed, come with my nephew, Sir William Gascougne, so that you be with me next Monday night, in the town of Thirsk; not failing thereof, as my special trust is in you, and as ye love me. Written in my manor of Seamer, the 24th day of April.

Your cousin,

Henry Northumberland

[Abbot Thomas of Kirkstall to Robert Plumpton]

To my right worshipful and entirely beloved gossip, Sir Robert Plumpton, knight.

Right worshipful and my full trusty entirely beloved gossip, after all hearty recommendations as I can think, I pray you heartily to be a good and tender master and lord to Thomas Hirst, my full special friend, in the matter he will bring to you; and the more tender at this my poor prayer and instance, and for the love of [your son] my godson, to whom I beseech Almighty God to give good grace to increase in virtue, and you, with my ladies, your mother and your wife, my comrade, to preserve in worship and favor, unto his pleasure and heart's ease. From Kirkstall in haste, upon Monday next before St. Luke the evangelist [in October].

Your poor gossip and true lover,

Thomas, abbot of Kirkstall

[The Abbot of Lilleshull to Robert Plumpton]

To the worshipful in God Master Plumpton, knight, these letters be delivered in haste.

Right worshipful sir, I commend me to you, being glad to hear of your welfare. Sir, I heartily thank you for my tenants of Arkendale, praying you of good continuance, and also for your writing, the which you send unto me about my lands in Arkendale. Sir, I have sent to you by my servant, Thomas Morton, the copy of my evidence of the nine acres of land, in which they claim an interest for the king. And I trust that I have sent to you such writing as shall discharge that matter. Sir, I pray you that you will see to my matters according to right, and according to your good mind, for I remit all unto your good wisdom. Sir, it is so that I am a young beginner of the world in my office; and sir, for your good will and counsel I will that my officer reward you yearly 6s. 8d. as was rewarded to other men aforetime, praying you of your good continuance, and anything that I can, I will, as God knows, who have you in his blessed keeping. Amen. Written at Lilleshull, the 26th day of May.

Your loving friend,

The abbot of Lilleshull

[The Abbot of Lilleshull to Robert Plumpton]
To Sir Robert Plumpton, knight in Yorkshire, be this letter delivered in good speed.

Right worshipful sir, we recommend us unto you. And so it is that Dame Joyce Percy has showed unto the earl of Shrewsbury, who is our very good lord, and tender lord in all our rightful causes, how you wrong her of certain lands lying in our lordship of Arkendale, where you are our steward; wherein the said lord has made labor unto us for the said Dame Joyce, and desired us that we [see to it that] she be not wronged in her right: and considering how good a lord he has been and still always is unto us, and remembering also that we, being men of the holy church, ought not to permit any wrong to be done to any manner of persons within our lordship, we may do no less but effectually tender the said lord's desire in that behalf. Wherefore we desire you, that you will see the said Dame Joyce to have all that which she of right ought to have within our lordship of Arkendale aforesaid, so as she find herself not grieved, nor have cause to make any more labor to the said lord for her remedy therein. For if she does, we must set some other person in your place, that will not wrong her; for we may in no way abide the displeasure of the said lord. Tendering therefore this our desire, as we trust you; and our Lord have you in his governance. From Lilleshull, the 28th day of May.
Your good loving
Abbot of Lilleshull

[B. Roos to Lady Plumpton]
To my worshipful Lady Plumpton the elder.

Right reverend lady, with due recommendations. I have wonder that you do so unkindly to me; except for great need I would not have sent. I lent to my kinsman 100 marks, and I have it not; they have forfeited 200 marks. And for the lack of it, I send more humbly to you, praying you to send me £3 by this messenger without delay, and then it is but 40s. owing, for the which I shall wait until Easter; and Jesu preserve you. Written at Kirkstall in haste,
by your B. Roos

[Henry, Earl of Northumberland, to Robert Plumpton]
To my right heartily beloved cousin, Sir Robert Plumpton, knight.

Right trusty and well-beloved cousin, I commend me unto you, and desire and pray you that in such things as my right entirely beloved cousin, Mary Gascougne, has to do with you, as touching her right of inheritance, that you will give unto her aid and support, as right law and conscience will, as my special trust is in you, whom God keep. Written in my manor of Seamer, the first day of April.

Your loving cousin,

Henry Northumberland

[Henry, earl of Northumberland, to Robert Plumpton]

To my right heartily beloved cousin, Sir Robert Plumpton, knight.

Right heartily beloved cousin, I commend me unto you, and desire and pray you to cause sure search to be made, what horse and cattle there be, that get into my spring within my park at Spofford; and such as can be found there, I pray you to see them driven and evacuated out thereof: and also henceforth, that you will see neither horse nor cattle get into my said spring, as my special trust is in you, whom God preserve. Written in my manor of Seamer, the second day of April. Over this, cousin, I heartily pray you to see my said park inspected, and that the deer within the same may be easily dealt withal, and what remains within the same I pray you to certify to me, after the said inspection be made.

Your loving cousin,

Henry Northumberland

[Robert Greene to Robert Plumpton]

To the right worshipful master, Sir Robert Plumpton, knight, deliver these.

Right worshipful sir, in the most heartiest wise I recommend me to you, thanking you for your tender mastership shown me in all causes. May it please your mastership to know that I am somewhat in heaviness, for my wife has such sickness, once or twice at least every day, that it puts her in jeopardy of her life with a swooning; so that the next day after the assize I will not leave her. Wherefore, sir, I beseech you to take no displeasure, because I do not see you and my lady at Plumpton either. And because ... your mastership has Robert Ward, clerk, in your ward at Knaresborough, sir, I intend very soon to pursue the law against him in their names whose cattle he heretofore helped to steal: intending to have him expelled from the lordship, if so be that the owners of the same cattle will maintain their suit in their name at my cost. And in the meantime I pray your mastership that this pure woman, the bearer of this letter, beadswoman to your mastership, may have surety of peace from the same Robert, which I trust she will request of your mastership from him. Written at Newby, the Wednesday next after our Lady's day [March 25] in Lent. And as for William Bullock, I shall shortly send him to your mastership to know your good advice and counsel, and all causes concerning me.

Your servant,

Robert Greene

[Edward Plumpton to Robert Plumpton, January 3, 1490]
To the right honorable my especial good master, Sir Robert Plumpton, knight.

After the most humble and due recommendation, may it please your mastership, that in the most lowly wise I may be recommended unto my singular good ladies; praying you to have me excused in that I have sent no wild fowl to you before this time, for in all Lancashire could none be had for any money. The snow and frost was so great, none was in the country, but fled away to sea; and that caused me that I sent not, as I promised.

Sir, Robert, my servant, is a true servant to me; nevertheless he is too large to ride in front of my baggage, and over weighty for my horse; wherefore he heartily desires me to write to your mastership for him. He is a true man of tongue and hands, and a kind and good man. If it please your mastership to take him to your service, I beseech you to be his good master, and the better at the instance of my especial prayer. Sir, I have given to him the black horse that bore him from the field [that is, in a recent battle]; and if there be any service that you will command me, I am ready, and will be to my life's end at your commandment, all other lordship and mastership laid apart. My lord keepeth a great Christmas, as ever was in this country, and is my especial good lord, as I trust in a short time your mastership shall know. My simple bedfellow, your beadswoman and servant, in the most humble wise recommends her unto your mastership, and to my lady's good ladyship, and your servants; as knows Jesu, who preserve you. Written at Latham, the third day of January.
Your most humble servant,
Edward Plumpton, secretary to my lord Strange

[Henry, earl of Northumberland, to Robert Plumpton]
To my right heartily beloved cousin, Sir Robert Plumpton, knight.

Right heartily beloved cousin, I commend me unto you. And for as much as I am destitute of running hounds, I desire and pray you to send me a couple with my servant, the bringer [of this letter]. And of anything similar I have for your pleasure, it shall be ready. Written in my lodging in Spittle in the Street, the 29th day of October. Over this, cousin, I pray you to send me your tame hart, for my deer are dead.
Your cousin,
Henry Northumberland

[Edward Plumpton to Robert Plumpton, March 2, 1497]
To my master, Sir Robert Plumpton, knight.

In my humble and most heartiest wise I recommend me unto your good mastership, and to my singular good lady. Sir, it is so that certain lovers and friends of mine in London hath brought me unto the sight of a gentlewoman,

a widow of the age of 40 years and more, and of good substance; first, she is goodly and beautiful, womanly and wise, as ever I knew any — not to insult any other: of a good stock and worshipful. Her name is Agnes. She has in charge but one gentlewoman to her daughter, of twelve years of age. She has twenty marks of good land within three miles of London, and a royal manor builded thereupon, to give or sell at her pleasure. She has in coin, in old nobles, £100; in royals, £100; in debts, £40; in plate, £110, with other goods of great value; she is called worth £1000 beside her land. Sir, I am bold upon your good mastership, as I have ever been; and if it please God and you that this matter take effect, I shall be able to deserve all things done and past. She and I are agreed in our mind and all one; but her friends, that she is ruled by, desire from me twenty marks jointure more than my lands come to; and thus I answered them, saying that your mastership is so good a master to me, that you gave to my other wife twelve marks for her jointure in Stodley Roger, and now, that it will please your said mastership to endow this woman in some lordship of yours of twenty marks during her life, such as they shall be pleased with: and for this my said friends offer to be bound in £1000. Sir, upon this they intend to know your pleasure and mind privily, I not knowing; wherefore, I humbly beseech your good mastership, as my especial trust is and ever has been above all earthly creatures, now for my great promotion and heart's desire, to answer to your pleasure, and my wealth and poor honesty; and I trust, before it comes to pass, to give you surety to be discharged without any charge; for now, your good and discreet answer may be my making. For, if she and I are fortunate, by God's and your means together, our two goods and substance will make me able to do you good service, the which good service and I are and shall be yours, now and at all times, to jeopardy of my life and them both. Sir, I beseech your good mastership to write to me an answer in all haste possible, and after that you shall hear more, with God's grace, who preserve you and yours in prosperous felicity long time to endure. Written at Furnivall Inn in Holborn, the second day of March 1496.
Your humble servant,
Edward Plumpton

[German Pole to Robert Plumpton, c. 1499]
To his right worshipful father, Sir Robert Plumpton, knight, be these delivered in most godly haste.

Right honorable and worshipful father[-in-law] and mother[-in-law], in the most lowliest wise that I can, I meekly recommend me unto you, desiring to hear of your welfare and prosperity, the which I pray almightly Jesu long to continue to his pleasure, and to your most joy, and comfort, and heart's ease. Also, father, my brother[-in-law] William heartily and meekly recommends himself unto you, and unto my lady my mother, desiring you of your daily blessing. And I also lowly pray you of your daily blessing, the which is as glad unto me, as unto any child that you have, for I have no other father but you, nor any other mother but my lady; for my special trust is in you. Therefore I pray you take me as your poor son, a beadsman, for by my prayer you shall know I live. Sir, if it pleases you to know that on Monday my brother was at Thornton Bridge, and I was; all, blessed be almighty Jesu, in good health. And my sister[-in-law] Margaret, and my wife, and my sister[-in-law] Elinor lowly recommend them unto you and unto my lady, praying you of your daily blessing, the which is better unto them than any worldly goods.

Verily, sir, Master Neville nor Mrs. Neville, neither of them was at home; but his brother was at home, and he made us very great cheer as might be. Also, sir, I am very sorry that the death ceases not at Plumpton, but I trust to almighty Jesu that his great mercy and grace [*some words are missing here*] send to my lady her joy and comfort, and to all your friends, as my daily prayer shall be therefore. Sir, the cause of my writing is but to hear of your good welfare, the which is to me great joy and comfort. And, sir, I lowly pray you and my lady, my mother, to take this letter in good part, for it is written hastily with my own hand, and without the advice of any other body; for I trust you had rather have it of my own hand, than of another body's. Also, sir, John Tynderley recommends him unto you and unto my lady, my mother, gladly willing to hear of your welfare. No more unto you, good father, nor mother, at this time, but pray the holy Trinity to have you in his blessed keeping.
Your good son[-in-law] and beadschild,
German Pole

[Robert Eyre to Robert Plumpton, October 15, 1499]
To my right worshipful brother, Sir Robert Plumpton, knight, be this delivered.

Right worshipful brother, I recommend me unto you, and to my lady, and also to my daughter and yours, with all my other young cousins, desiring heartily to hear of your welfare and theirs both, which I beseech Jesu preserve unto his pleasure and your heart's comfort, ever thanking you, and my lady both, of the great worship and good cheer that I and my friends had at my last being with you. Brother, it is so that your fare-man, Christopher Law, is departed from this world and has left behind him a wife and seven small children, wherefore I heartily pray you to be a good master unto her, so that she might have her farm, and the more so for my prayer. And if it please you, when your servants come over into this country, that they will hear my advice in the letting of the said house; and I trust to take such measures therein, as shall be for your worship and profit both, as Jesu knows, who ever preserve you. At Padley, the Tuesday next before St. Luke's day, in haste.

Your loving brother,

Robert Eyre

[John Pullan to Robert Plumpton, Nov. 21, 1499]

To his especial good master, Sir Robert Plumpton, knight, be these delivered.

Right worshipful sir, I recommend me unto your mastership. Sir, lately I sent writing to my father to convey to you, which I trust has come to your hands before this time; in which writing is contained how the justices of the Common Pleas awarded a new [writ of] *venire facias* between my master, your son, and William Babthorp; and also in a little bill therein is contained the names of such persons as the said William Babthorp intended to have had reckoned in the first *venire facias*. I advise your mastership to make special labor to have one impartial panel of coroners; they must be worked on by some friend of yours. Sir, the process in the action of West goes forward, as fast as the law will serve. Sir, I received two letters from you with 26s. 8d., and all such copies, as was contained in your writing.

Sir, so it was that Perkin Warbeck and three others were arraigned, on Saturday next before the making hereof, before Sir John Sygly, knight marshal, and Sir John Trobilfield; and there they all were attainted [for treason], and judgment given that they should be drawn on hurdles from the Tower, throughout London, to the Tyburn, and there to be hanged, and cut down quick, and their bowels to be taken out and burned: their heads to be struck off, and quartered, their heads and quarters to be disposed at the king's pleasure. And on Monday next afterwards, at the Guildhall in London were the judges, and many other knights, commissioners to inquire and determine all offenses and trespasses; and thither from the Tower were brought eight prisoners, which were indicted, and part of them confessed themselves guilty, and the others were arraigned: and as yet they are not judged. I think they shall have judgment this next Friday. Sir, this present day were new troubles made in Westminster Hall, and thither was brought the earl of Warwick, and arraigned before the earl of Oxford, being the king's grace's commissioner, and before other lords (because he is a peer of the realm), whose names follow.... And there the earl of Warwick confessed the indictments that were laid to his charge, and like judgments were given on him, as is before rehearsed. When these persons shall be put in execution I intend to show to your mastership right shortly; and give credence unto this bearer. From Lincoln's Inn at London, this 21st day of November.

By your servant and beadsman,

John Pullan

[Robert Eyre to Robert Plumpton, February 14, 1499-1500]
To my right worshipful brother, Sir Robert Plumpton, knight, these be delivered.

Right worshipful brother, I recommend me unto you, and to my lady your wife, and to my daughter and to yours, with all my other cousins your children, desiring to hear of your welfare and theirs both, which I beseech Jesu preserve unto your most heart's comfort; evermore thanking you and my good lady, your wife, for the great and worshipful cheer I and my kinsmen had with you. Brother, you remember how the writings of the covenant of marriage of my son and your daughter were not made up by the advice of learned counsel; wherefore, if it please you to appoint any day, and please about the beginning of Lent, when I might wait upon you, I will be glad to wait upon you, and a learned man with me: and all such promise as I have made on my part shall be well and truly performed, with the grace of Jesu, for you shall find me ever one man.

Also, brother, I pray you that you would send me by my servant, William Bewott, the bringer [of this letter], the payment, which I should have had from you at Candlemas last past, for I have put myself unto more charge, since I was with you, than I had before. For I have married another of my daughters, and I have begun to make a wall about my park that I showed you I was minded to do, which, I trust, when you see it, you will like well. Praying you not to fail herein, as my trust is in you, and to give credence to this bringer. No more but Jesu preserve you. Written at Padley on St. Valentine's day [February 14] with the hand of your brother,
Robert Eyre

Questions: What different types of letters are included here? What is revealed about relations between individuals of different ranks? How do the writers seek favors and advancement in their letters? What are the considerations in arranging marriages? What relationships do the Plumptons have with churchmen?

83. THE CELY LETTERS

The Cely correspondence is another goldmine of information. The Celys were wool mer-
chants based in London and doing much business in Flanders. In the following letters,
written by and to the Celys in 1480, 1481, and 1482, we meet, among others, the three
sons of Richard the Elder: Robert, Richard the Younger, and George (George is stationed
mainly in Calais). William Maryon is a family friend and godfather to the younger
Richard; William and John Cely are humble relations. Richard the Younger, as well as
helping to run the family business, is in the service of (his "lord") Sir John Weston, prior
of the order of the Hospitallers in England.

Source: modernized from *The Cely Papers: Selections from the Correspondence and Memoranda of the*
Cely Family, Merchants of the Staple, A.D. 1475-1488, ed. H.E. Malden (London: Longmans, Green,
and Co., 1900), pp. 34-40, 46, 51-52, 57-60, 73-76, 83-86, 101-104, 106, 110-111, 117, 131-132.

[Richard Cely the Younger to George Cely at Calais, 1480]
Right entirely well beloved brother, I recommend me unto you as lovingly as
heart can think, informing you that, at the making of this, our father, mother
and we all were in good health, thanked be God. And the 26th day of this
month I received two letters from you, one to our father, another to myself, the
which I do well understand, and here I send you enclosed in this a bill of Master Richard's hand, from the mayor of the Staple, for the discharge of 23s. 4d.
per sarpler [that is, a sack of wool weighing 2,240 pounds], for seventeen
sarplers, £19 16s. 8d. And I feel, by your letter, that the wool shipped at your
departing from hence was not so good as I wish it had been. Our father was at
the packing thereof himself. I trust to God this wool shall please you better,
and as for middle wool, you have all that belongs to that sort. Sir, I have
received as of yet but 15 of our fells [that is, fleeces], but they are good. I
understand by your writing that you will come into England shortly. I pray
you keep your purpose and we shall be merry by God's grace. My lord commends himself to you and looks daily for the goods that you promised to purvey him, and Gladman prays you to purvey a saddle for him somewhat less than
my lord's shall be. He lies still at Berwick and I think will do all this summer.
Sir, I have received at the day well and truly the £4 sterling from our brother
Robert. And now the ship is here, but our father intends not to ship until
almost Michaelmas, and therefore we will look for you daily. And sir, I pray
you bring with you the reckoning how much I am indebted to you, and we
shall see a way therein by the grace of Jesu, who keep you and bring you to
England soon and in safety. Written at London the last day of June.

Sir, our father has been sick; I trust it be but a temporary attack, but I would
fain that you were here till he be better mended.
By your brother
Richard Cely

[Richard Cely the Younger to George Cely at Calais, 1480]

Right entirely well beloved brother, I recommend me unto you, informing you at the making of this our father is all whole and right merry, thanked be God, as my uncle the bringer of this can inform you. Sir, our father wishes that you be not over-hasty in coming into England, for this cause: he understood well that the wool that was shipped at your departing from London is not of like goodness to that which is of the last year's growth, and therefore he wishes that you would not sell them together, but as for the middle wool that was last shipped, he desires that Jan Van Der Heyden have it, according to your writing. And our father would fain that you might sell the good wool of the first sort as well as you can. He dare not send any more to Calais till he hears of the sale of the aforesaid. Sir, our father understands about our brother Robert's childish dealing, and William Burwell has been with him and me, and he says that Dalton or you have a letter of obligation for £14 Flemish, payable to him at the next St. Baf's [that is, autumn] market, as it had been payable at the Ascension market last, and that made him so bold as he says, but our father wishes that you see the clearance and send us word how it is. No more to you. Written at Bretts [Place, Aveley, Essex], the fifth day of July.

Tomorrow I go with my lord to Gravesend to bring in my Lady Margaret.

By your brother

Richard Cely

[John Cely to George Cely at Calais, 1480]

Right worshipful and well beloved cousin, I recommend me unto you, and also my sister your aunt commends herself unto you as heartily as she can or may, always thanking you for your great labor and business that you did for her now at this time, for the which she hopes to reward you in such wise as you shall be pleased, with the grace of God.

Item, sir, you have been with Master Ylam, and he has promised to pay this £70 6s. 8d. It is ready for her. Also, sir, you shall understand that my sister, your aunt, has made her exchange with John Matthew, mercer of London, for the £91 Flemish, the which is in your hands, and she shall receive here, from the said John Matthew, at such days as they shall agree, £75 16s. 8d. sterling. And hereupon she has delivered to the said John Matthew the bill of your hand, the which money she prays you heartily to pay to the said John or to his attorney and bringer of your said bill, now at this next market, as her very trust is in you, that you will so do.

Furthermore, sir, as for the bills of John Elton that Fethyan asks for, Ingguld says we cannot yet find them, I think, nor never shall. If we can, he shall have them, and so says Fethyan. No more to you at this time, but almighty Jesu have you in keeping. Written at London the sixth day of September, in the year 1480.

By John Cely

[Robert Cely to George Cely at Calais, 1480]

Right reverend and worshipful brother, I heartily recommend me to you. Furthermore please it you to know that at the making of this letter our father and mother were merry and in good health, blessed be God, and so we hope that you be. And as for our brother Richard Cely, he is departed with my lord of St. John's with the ambassadors into France, whereof I suppose you understand right well. And I am at London and have been greatly diseased almost ever since you departed from Aveley, and for the most part have kept to my bed, for I have been so sick and sore that I go with a staff. I thank God I am now daily amended.

Item, brother George, the cause of my writing is this, and I pray you heartily for our good brotherhood, that you will do so much for me, to see that William Burwell, mercer of London, be satisfied for his bill of £14 15s., and what money you lay out for me, I will satisfy you for here. For if I had not had that money from William Burwell at that time, I would have lost all my plate. Wherefore, good brother, remember me, and I shall be good for it, with the grace of God, who have you and all of us in his blessed keeping. Amen. Written at London, the 6th day of September, with great pain.

By your brother,

Robert Cely

[Richard Cely the Younger to George Cely at Calais, 1480]

Right entirely well beloved brother, I recommend me heartily unto you, and I thank you for your great cost and share that you did to me and my fellows at our last being with you at Calais. Sir, we had a fair passage, and the Saturday after our departing we came to the king at Eltham, to whom my lord was right welcome, and there we tarried till the king's daughter was christened, whose name is Bridget. And the same night right late we came to London, and here I found our father, brother Robert, and my godfather Maryon, and they are merry. Our mother is in Essex; I see her not yet. My godfather Maryon told me that he has written letters to you; I understand a part of them. Robin Good told our father that you had five horses, and I told him you had only three, and how you have sold the first Pie to Sir Humfrey Talbot, and he was well content. I told our father of the loss of Twissulton's mule. Sir, our father will not ship until March, and he would fain that the wool were packed. I feel from him that he would not prefer that you come home at Christmas, for he thinks there will be sales about Twelfth Night. There is great death of sheep in England. Sir, I would write more to you, but I depart into Essex this same day to see our mother. No more to you. Written at London the 15th day of November.

By your brother

Richard Cely

If the mule may be gotten, send him to our father, for he would like to have him.

[William Maryon to George Cely at Calais, 1480]

Right reverend sir and my special good friend, I recommend me unto you. Furthermore, may it please you to know that I have received a letter from you written at Calais the 12th day of November, the which letter I have read, and well understand that you have received a letter from me, written at London the 9th day of November, in the which letter I wrote a clause about your horse, the which I understand you took sore at your stomach. Sir, in good faith I am sorry therefore, for if I had known that you would take so sore I would not have written so unto you, not if I would have gotten thereby 20 nobles. But you shall understand what caused me so for to write unto you. Sir, you wrote unto my master that you supposed by likelihood it should be war, and if it so be it should be war, there should be great riding and much ado about Calais, and if you were well horsed I fear me that such soldiers as you are acquainted with should cause you for to put your body in adventure, and if there came anything to you otherwise than good, in good faith a great part of my master's joy in the world would be removed. Sir, this caused me in good faith for to write so unto you as I did, for I know well if you have no good horse they will not desire you out of town. Sir, in good faith, neither my master your father nor my mistress your mother know anything of my writing, and in good faith you shall understand that I wrote not so unto you for no spite, neither for no evil that I have to you, but for great love, for in good faith, saving my master our father and your brother Richard, in good faith there is no man in England I would do so much for, and that you should know, if you had need. And that caused me to be so bold to write to you, the which I would it could be undone, since you take it as you do. No more unto you at this time, but the Trinity have you in his keeping. Written at Aveley the 19th day of November.

By William Maryon

[George Cely to Richard Cely the Elder at London, 1480]

Right reverend and worshipful father, after all due recommendation I recommend me unto you in the most lowliest wise that I can or may. Furthermore, may it please you to understand that I have sold unto Gysbright Van Wijnsberg two sarplers of good cottes. He has taken one of the twenty that is packed, and again another of the other sort, as a bill enclosed herein makes mention, etc. It is so that I have not yet made an end of the packing of your sort. Of twenty sarplers there is eleven packed already. The cause of the delay of the rest is that there was much better wool, and as soon as that can be wound and made ready, it shall be entered into that which is to pack.... Here there are as now but few merchants. There shall be some fete done between Christmas and Candlemas, because of the ordinance, wherefore now I intend to tarry and come not to you until Candlemas. As of any tidings here, I can none write you as yet. There is, but I cannot have the truth thereof. There has been a variance between the duke's men of war and his Germans, and there are many of his Germans slain, and therefore he takes great displeasure, for there are various of his gentlemen stolen away therefore, and some are come to Calais, and one of them is sent to our sovereign lord the king, and some have gone over to the Frenchmen, and the French king has gotten lately various of the best men of war the duke had, whereof he makes him now bold. No more unto you at this time, but Jesu have you and all yours in his keeping. Amen. Written at Calais, the 24th day of November, 1480.

By your son,

George Cely

It is so that I do send Harry my boy to wait upon my brother this Christmas.

[William Cely to George Cely at Bruges, 1481]

Right worshipful sir, after due consideration I lowly recommend me unto your mastership, etc. Furthermore may it please your mastership to understand that I have received a letter from you, the which I have read, and well understood all things therein. And as for your debentures, I have delivered them to William Bentham according to your commandment, and he has promised me as soon as he is furnished with money I shall be paid and satisfied for the exchange of ten shillings of the pound with the first. And as for your warranties of fifteen shillings of the pound, I have spoken to the master lieutenant for them, and he has promised me that at your coming to Calais thay shall be set upon your bills of custom and subsidy, etc.

Also, sir, may it please you to know that on the 12th day of May two Frenchmen chased an English ship in front of Calais, and Fetherston and John Davy and Thomas Overton lay in Calais Road, but themselves were ashore. And as soon as they saw them they got boats and went aboard, and so did the master marshal and Sir Thomas Everingham and Master Messefold with diverse soldiers of Calais, and rescued the English ship and took the Frenchmen and brought one of them into Calais haven. The other was so great she might not come in, but they brought the master and the captain to my lord, and they say there are Scots amongst them. And they say that Fetherston and his fellows are gone with the biggest Frenchman into England, etc.

Also, sir, it is said here that after this day, the 12th day of May, no man shall keep any lodging of guests, strangers, or Englishmen outside the gates of Calais, except two houses assigned, that is, the searcher's house and the water bailiff's house. And any man that has housing outside the gates is warned to remove his house as quickly as he can into the town, and set it there where he please that he has ground, and if he do not so, stand at his own risk at such time that it shall come to be plucked quickly down or else burned for the shorter work. And betwixt this and that time, none of them are so hardy, except the two places aforementioned, to lodge no man over a night, on pain of treason, etc.

Also, sir, may it please you to know that Sir William Chanon, who was lodged with John Fowle, is dead; he was buried last Sunday, and Sir William Stappel, priest, has his benefice granted by my lord, etc. Sir, other tidings have we none, but the Almighty have you in his keeping. Written at Calais, the 13th day of May.
By your servant
William Cely

[Richard Cely the Younger to George Cely at Calais, 1481]
Right entirely well beloved brother, I recommend me heartily unto you, thanking you for all good brotherhood that you have showed to me at all times. Sir, you know well that I have been in the north country, and there I have had great share of my old acquaintance, as the bringer hereof can inform you. And as for my uncle, his executors have promised me and Plumpton by the faith of their bodies to be with our father here on Michaelmas, and to make an end with him. And as I went northward, I met Roger Wigston on this side of Northampton, and he desired me to do so much as drink with his wife at Leicester. And after that I met with William Dalton, and he gave me a token to his mother. And at Leicester I met with Ralph Dalton, and he brought me to his mother, and there I delivered my token, and she prayed me to come to breakfast on the morrow. And so I did, and Plumpton too, and there we had a great welfare, and there was Friar East, and I pray you thank them for me. Sir, if you remember, we talked together in our bed of Dalton's sister, and you feared the conditions of her father and brethren, but you need not. I saw her, and she was at breakfast with her mother and us. She is as goodly a young woman, as fair, as well-bodied, and as serious as I see any this seven years, and a good height. I pray to God that it may be imprinted in your mind to set your heart there. Sir, our father and I talked together in the new

orchard on Friday last, and he asked me many questions of you, and I told him all as it was, and he was right sorry for the death of the child [that is, George's illegitimate child]. And I told him of the good will that the Wigstons and Daltons owe to you, and how I liked the young gentlewoman. And he commanded me to write to you, and he would gladly that it were brought about and that you worked at it betimes. And I have told our father of Chester's daughter, how that I would gladly be there, and our father was right glad of this communication. Dalton's mother commends herself to you and thanks you for the knives that you sent to her. Our father has received a letter from you whereby he understood about the sale of two sarplers and a poke [that is, a smaller bale of wool]. As for the money that is by you, he wishes that it lie by you until Ascension market, and let the mercers Burwell and Palmer have the longer days, and their money according. Sir, I thank you that it pleased you to leave me Joyce, for he has done me good service in this journey, and I have delivered to him ten shillings to bring him to you. My godfather has been sick, but he is well mended, thanked be God. This same day my lord is come to London to ask the king's leave to go to Rhodes, for he is sent for. Sir, I send you by Joyce a purse such as was given me at York, and I pray you buy for Alison Michael a mantel of fine black shanks, for I have money therefor, and she commends herself to you. No more to you at this time. Jesu keep you. Written at London, the 4th day of June.

By your brother

Richard Cely

[Richard Cely the Younger to George Cely at Calais, 1481]

Right well beloved brother, I recommend me unto you with all mine heart, informing you that, at the making of this, our father and mother were well comforted and send you their blessings. It was so that by the means of Brandon, our father and I were indicted for slaying a hart that was driven into Kent, the which we never saw nor knew of. And this day I have been with Master Montgomery and given him the value of a pipe of wine to have us out of the book before it be showed to the king, and so he has promised me, and to be a good master to our father and us in the matter between Brandon and us. John Frost, forester, brought me to his mastership and acquainted me with a gentleman of his whose name is Ramston, that is a close man to Master Montgomery, and so I must inform him of my matters at all times, and he will show them to his master, etc.

    ... Sir, it was so that when [Sheriff William] Wikyng was dead and another was chosen, our father was nearly called upon [to be sheriff], and but that [Richard] Chary was better known, our father would have been sheriff, etc. Our father wishes that you buy 600 sticks more canvas at this market. And I understand that you have sold your great gray horse, and I am right glad thereof, for two is as good as twenty. I understand that you have a fair hawk; I am right glad of her, for I trust God she shall make you and me right great sport. If I were sure at what passage you would send her I would fetch her at Dover and keep her until you come. A great misfortune has befallen your bitch, for she had fourteen fair puppies, and after she had whelped she would never eat meat, and so she is dead and all her puppies, but I trust to get before your coming as fair and as good a dog to please that gentleman. I understand you intend to be with us for Christmas, and whereof am right glad, and we shall make merry whether Brandon wishes or not, by the grace of God. And as for Pie, he is as hearty as ever I saw him and in reasonable good condition and whole. William Cely does his part well in keeping him. And as for our pension in Furnival's Inn, it shall be paid within these four days. Sir, hereafter appear our father's shipping and ships' names and masters:

Item, in the *Mary of London*, William Sordywoll, master: seven packs Cotswold fells bestowed behind the mast. Six are under the deck and a pack lies uppermost upon Dalton's, behind the mast. Total 2,108 fells.

Item, in the *Christopher of Rainham*, Harry Wilkins, master: seven packs and a half Cotswold; they lie behind the mast and no man's above them. Total 3,000 fells.

Item, in the *Thomas of Maidstone*, Harry Lawson, master: six packs Cotswold mixed with summer London fells, marked with O. They lie before the mast under hatches and part behind, even next to the mast in a pile as broad as two fells long. Total 2,003 fells.

Item, in the *Mary Grace of London*, John Lockington, master: six packs of fells, whereof 556 are winter London fells; they are marked with C. And the rest are Cotswold; they lie behind the mast, and Granger's upon them, and reeds between them. Total 2,004 fells.

Item, in the *Michael of Hull*, Andrew Good, master: one pack of fells Cotswold mixed with summer London, marked with O; they lie behind the mast uppermost, and I have paid him his whole freight for that pack of fells. Total 400 fells.

Item, in the *Thomas of New Hythe*, Robert Hevan, master: a pack and 64 fells Cotswold; they lie behind the mast, and Betson's fells lie above them. Total 464 fells....

Item, in the *Mary of Rainham*, John Dangell, master, I shipped four packs and 41 fells of yours and mine; they lie behind the mast. Three packs of them are Cotswold and one pack and 41 fells are Warwickshire; they lie uppermost. I pray you lay them by themselves to avoid hurting the other sort. 1,641 fells.

Item, my godfather has six and a half packs and 57 fells in the same ship, and no man has a fell in that ship but we, my godfather, and I. Total 2,657 summer London fells.

And I have spoken with William Dalton and showed him the clause that you wrote about Leicester in, and he was right glad thereof. I was his guest on Hallows' eve in Old Fish Street at dinner with him and Charles Willers. I pray you thank them at their coming to Calais. Sir, I would gladly hear some good tidings of your matter that Clays De Moll has in hand. No more to you at this time. Jesu keep you. Written at London the fifth day of November.

By your brother

Richard Cely

[John Dalton to George Cely in London, 1482]

Right entirely well beloved brother, after all due recommendation I recommend me unto you as heartily as I can or may. Furthermore, sir, I have received two letters from you, by the which letters I understand about your great heaviness for your father, on whose soul God have mercy. Furthermore, sir, Gysbright Van Wijnsberg has been here since you departed, and he will be here again, he tells me, within 15 days after Candlemas, and see the eleven sarplers Cotswold of yours, on the which I have taken a good penny from him. For also, sir, no Hollanders have come here since you left, except one fellowship of Delft, to which I could sell no fleeces and none since. We have made bills of 13s. 4d. on the sarplers, the which must be sent over into England and there paid at pleasure. Your father's bill at pleasure amounts unto £15 6s. 8d. sterling; your brother Richard's 44s. sterling; and William Maryon's bill £3 10s. 8d. sterling. Also, sir, since it is so as it is of my master your father, in the reverence of God take it patiently and hurt not yourself, for that which God will have done no man may be against. Also, sir, all your fells here do well.... Your horses do well, God save them. Also, sir, whereas we ate the good puddings, the woman [Margery] of the house that made them, as I understand, is with child with my brother that had the Irish dagger from me [that is, George]. Sir, all our household by name recommend themselves unto you and they are right sorry for your heaviness. In good faith, sir, I pray you that I may be recommended unto your brother Richard Cely, and each of you cheer the other in the reverence of our Lady, who preserve you. At Calais the 27th day of January.

Your brother to my power,

John Dalton,

that I can or may.

[Joyce Parmenter to George Cely in London, 1482]

Right worshipful master, I recommend me unto you, letting you know that I have received two letters that came from you, by the which writing I understand my master your father is deceased, on whose soul God have mercy. Letting you know that your wool and fells are in good sort. We lack nothing but only one pelt and fur. We can have none here under twenty pence a dozen. If it please you to send me a thousand with the next shipping that comes between, I would pray you. Also, your brother Dalton has promised me one thousand pelts that he has bought in Flanders; they are not sufficient.

Also, I let you know that Bottrell has broken up a window of the west side of your woolhouse, and there he has cast in horse dung upon your fells. I did make a man with a dung fork in his hand to cast the dung aside. Bottrell came in and took the fork from him and beat him well and unthriftily. I, seeing his uncourteous dealing, prayed John Ekynton, Robert Turney, John Ellyrbek, and William Hill, and others, to breakfast in your chamber for this intent: to see the hurts and harms he did you upon your goods, that they might bear witness another day, whatsoever you would say thereto. Letting you know that there are no Hollanders come unto their day that their bill was made, and then there came one cart.... Also I let you know that Charles has offered £8 Flemish for Bayard your horse. I have granted him for £11, wherefore I pray you to send me word how you wish to be disposed therein. Also, I let you know that where you go and eat puddings, the woman is with child as I understand.... I can [write] no more to you, but I beseech you to recommend me to my good mistress your mother, to all my masters your brethren, and to Hankyn, and that all your household is in safety, blessed be Jesu, who preserve you both body and soul.

At Calais the 30th day of [January.]

By your servant

Joyce Parmenter

[Richard Cely the Younger to George Cely at Calais, 1482]

Right entirely well beloved brother, I recommend me heartily unto you, informing you that, at the making of this, our mother, brother, my godfather, and the household are in good health, thanked be the good Lord. Sir, the same day that I departed into Cotswold I received a letter from you written at Calais the 14th day of April, wherein I find the inventory of such goods that were our father's, and money on that side of the sea. Sir, I have not spoken with the bishop's officers since I received your letter. When I spoke last with them they said that all things should wait for your coming. I understand by your letter that you will make over above £500. I have been in Cotswold this three weeks and packed with William Midwinter 22 sarplers and a poke, whereof four are middle. William Bretten says it is the fairest wool that he saw this year....

Sir, I write to you a process. I pray God send thereof a good end. The same day that I came to Northleach, on a Sunday before Matins, from Burford, William Midwinter welcomed me, and in our communication he asked me if I were in any way of marriage. I told him nay, and he informed me that there was a young gentlewoman whose father's name is Limerick, and her mother is dead, and she shall inherit from her mother £40 a year, as they say in that country. And her father is the greatest ruler and richest man in that country, and there have been great gentlemen to see her, who would like to have her. And before matins were done, William Midwinter had moved this matter to the greatest man serving the gentleman Limerick, and he went and informed the foresaid of all the matter, and the young gentlewoman too. And the Saturday after, William Midwinter went to London.... When I had packed at Camden and William Midwinter parted, I came to Northleach again to make an end of packing, and on Sunday next after, the same man that William Midwinter had talked first with came to me and told me that he had talked to his master according as Midwinter desired him, and he said his master was right well pleased therewith. And the same man said to me, if I would tarry until May Day, I should have a sight of the young gentlewoman, and I said I would tarry with a good will. And the same day her father should have sat [as a justice of the peace] at Northleach for the king, but he sent one of his clerks and rode himself to Winchcombe. And to matins the same day came the young gentlewoman and her stepmother, and I and William Bretten were saying matins when they came into church. And when matins was done, they went to a kinswoman of the young gentlewoman, and I sent to them a half-gallon of white romney [wine], and they took it thankfully, for they had come a mile on foot that morning. And when mass was done, I came and welcomed them and kissed them, and they thanked me for the wine and prayed me to come to dinner with them. And I excused myself, and they made me promise to drink with them after dinner. And I sent them for dinner a gallon of wine, and they sent me a roasted young heron. And after dinner I came and drank with them and took William Bretten with me, and we had a right good communication. And the person pleases me well, as by the first communication. She is young, little, and very well-favored and witty, and the country speaks much good about her. Sir, all this matter waits for the coming of her father to London, that we may understand what sum he will part with [as dowry] and how he likes me. He will be here within three weeks. I pray send me a letter how you think by this matter.

Michael Coke and his wife from York have been with my mother all this while, and my mother and I have made them great cheer. And my mother has given to Michael's wife a crimson gown of her wearing, and she has prayed me to write to you to buy for her some squirrel fur for to trim the same gown, and Coke's wife and she pray you to buy for them ten minks as fine as you can find in the market, and you shall be paid for them. I shall send to Calais by Robert Herrick at this Whitsuntide the bill of 13s. 4d.; it amounts to £15 6s. 8d. and

Fig. 32: Commercial Regulation   King Henry VII took special care to standardize weights and measures for the benefit of English commerce. In this scene, copied in the nineteenth century, royal officials enforce the standards. Such a scene would have been familiar to the Celys in their role as wool merchants.

paid. I understand by William's letter that you have writing from my lord of St. John's. I pray you send me part of your tiding. I sent to you the last that I had. Sir, they begin to ship at London, and all our wool and fell is in Cotswold except four sarplers; therefore we can do nothing at this time. Sir, I think money will be good at this market, for the king has sent to the mercers and let them know he will have three money exchanges, one at Bruges, another at Calais, the third at London. And as I am informed, any merchant of the Staple that sells his wool, he may buy what wares he will again. And they that are nowhere shall bring in their money into the king's exchange at Bruges or Calais and be paid at London at a month day, and the money shall be established at 8s. The mercers are not content therewith. I pray you remember our bows. No more. Written at London the 13th day of May.
By Richard Cely

[Richard Cely the Younger to George Cely at Calais, 1482]
Right well beloved brother, I recommend me heartily unto you, informing you that I have received a letter from you by Robert Herrick, whereby I understand that you will send over a young horse. We shall keep him with grass as well as we can till you come, according to your writing. Sir, it was told Robert Herrick at Calais that our mother would be married or in the way of marriage, so much so that they said our mother would go on procession on Corpus Christi day in a crimson gown, and her household in black. And on my soul, our mother went at that day, but as she went at our father's month's mind [that is, in mourning]. And therefore I would like it to be found out who the bringer of that [rumor] to Calais was.

Sir, we are greatly envied; I trust Jesu we shall be able to withstand our enemies. Sir John is in great trouble, and God knows full wrongfully, and some of them to whom we gave gowns labor most against him. I had rather than a good payment that you were here. No more to you. Written at London the 24th day of June. I pray Jesu send you safe hither. And the son of Robert Herrick was chased by Scots between Calais and Dover; they narrowly escaped.
By Richard Cely

[William Cely to George Cely at London, 1482]
Right worshipful sir, after due recommendation I lowly recommend me unto your mastership.... Furthermore may it please your mastership to be informed that Margery commends herself unto your mastership, and she tells me she should have such raiment as a gown and other things for her churching [after childbirth], as she had the other time, whereof she prays you for an answer. Also, Sir John Dalton desires to have two rooms in your stable, and he would pay for it, and he told me he would write to you for the same, but Joyce told

me that your mastership had granted him the stable and the house at his coming again to Calais for to occupy it, and your mastership to have your room at
your coming, etc. Sir, I pray your mastership for an answer about this, etc. Sir,
as for your other stuff, I shall send it unto your mastership by one of the wool-
ers, etc. No more unto your mastership at this time, but Jesu keep you. Written
at Calais the 13th day of August.
By your servant
William Cely

[William Cely to George Cely at London, 1482]
Right worshipful sir, after due recommendation I lowly recommend me unto
your mastership. Furthermore may it please your mastership to be informed
that Margery's daughter is passed to God. It was buried this same day, on
whose soul Jesu have mercy. Sir, I understand it had a great pang; what sickness
it was I cannot say, etc. Item, sir, Bottrell is departed out of Calais and is in England. And this day his wife goes to him with all her stuff, and they are commanded that they shall not come within the town of Calais as long as my lord
chamberlain is lieutenant of Calais, etc. No more unto your mastership at this
time but Jesu keep you. Written at Calais the 29th day of August.
By your servant
William Cely

*Questions: What do the letters reveal of the personalities of family members and rela-
tions within the family? What are the interests of the Cely brothers? What difficulties
do they cope with, and how? Trace the history of George's love life.*

84. POLYDORE VERGIL'S ACCOUNT OF HENRY VII

*In 1485 the Yorkist king Richard III (1483-5), who had succeeded his brother Edward IV
and nephew Edward V, faced a challenge from Henry Tudor, who defeated him at the
Battle of Bosworth and became Henry VII (1485-1509). The battle and some aspects of
Henry's reign are described by Polydore Vergil, an Italian scholar who came to England
during Henry's reign and first published his history a few years after the king's death.*

Source: *Three Books of Polydore Vergil's English History ... from an Early Translation*, ed. H. Ellis (London: Camden Society, 1844), pp. 221-226, revised; and trans. D. Hay, *The Anglica Historia of Polydore
Vergil, 1485-1537* (London: The Camden Society, 1950), pp. 3-7, 11-13, 127-131.

In the meantime King Richard, hearing that the enemy drew near, came first
to the place of fight, a little beyond Leicester (the name of that village is

Bosworth), and there, pitching his tents, refreshed his soldiers that night from their travail, and with many words exhorted them to the fight to come. It is reported that King Richard had that night a terrible dream; for he thought in his sleep that he saw horrible images, as it were of evil spirits haunting evidently around him, as it were before his eyes, and that they would not let him rest; which vision truly did not so much strike into his breast a sudden fear, as replenish the same with heavy cares: for forthwith after, being troubled in mind, his heart told him from this that the outcome of the battle following would be grievous, and he did not buckle himself to the conflict with such liveliness of courage and countenance as before. So that it should not be said that he showed this heaviness, appalled with fear of his enemies, he reported his dream to many in the morning. But I believe it was no dream but a conscience guilty of heinous offenses, a conscience (I say) so much the more grievous as the offenses were more great, which, thought of at no other time, yet in the last day of our life is accustomed to represent to us the memory of our sins committed, and also to show unto us the pains imminent for the same, that, being upon good cause penitent at that instant for our evilly led life, we may be compelled to go hence in heaviness of heart. Now I return to my purpose. The next day afterwards King Richard, furnished thoroughly with all manner of things, drew his whole host out of their tents, and arrayed his vanguard, stretching it forth in a wondrous length, so fully replenished both with footmen and with horsemen that to the beholders afar off it gave a terror for the multitude, and in the front were placed his archers, like a most strong trench and bulwark; of these archers he made John, duke of Norfolk, the leader. After this long vanguard followed the king himself, with a choice force of soldiers.

In the meantime Henry [Tudor], being departed back from the conference with his friends, began to take better heart, and without any tarrying encamped himself near his enemies, where he rested all night, and very early in the morning commanded the soldiers to arm themselves, sending also to Thomas Stanley, who was now approaching the place of fight, as in the midway between the two forces, asking that he would come to [help Henry instead of Richard] with his forces, to set the soldiers in array. Stanley answered that Henry should set his own folks in order, before he should come to him with his army well appointed. With which answer, given contrary to what was looked for, and to that which the opportunity of time and weight of cause required, though Henry was not a little vexed, and began to be somewhat fearful, yet without lingering he, of necessity, ordered his men in this sort. He made a slender vanguard for the small number of his people; before the same he placed archers, of whom he made John, earl of Oxford, the captain; in the right wing of the vanguard he placed Gilbert Talbot to defend the same; in the left verily he set John Savage; and himself, trusting to the aid of Thomas Stanley, with one troop of horsemen and a few footmen did follow; for the number of all his soldiers, of all kinds, was scarcely five thousand, besides Stanley's men, whereof about three thousand were at the battle, under the conduct of William. The king's forces were twice as many and more. Thus both the vanguards being arrayed, as soon as the soldiers might see one another afar off, they put on their headpieces and prepared for the fight, listening for the alarm with expectant ear. There was a marsh between the two hosts, which Henry on purpose left on the right hand, that it might serve his men instead of a fortress; by doing this he also left the sun upon his back. But when the king saw them across the marsh, he commanded his soldiers to make a charge against them. They, suddenly making great shouts, assaulted the enemy first with arrows; the others were nothing faint to fight but began also to shoot fiercely; but when they came to hand-strokes the matter then was dealt with by blades. In the meantime the earl of Oxford, fearing lest his men in fighting might be surrounded by the multitude, commanded in every rank that no soldiers should go more than ten feet from the standards; which order being known, when all the men had thronged densely together, and paused from fighting, the adversaries were therewith afraid, supposing some trick, and so they all forebore the fight a certain space, and this truly many [of Richard's soldiers] did with right goodwill, for they rather wished the king dead than alive, and therefore fought faintly. Then the earl of Oxford in one part, and others in another part, with the bands of men close to one another, made a fresh charge upon the enemy, and in triangular array vehemently renewed the conflict. While the battle continued thus hot on both sides between the vanguards, King Richard understood, first by spying where Earl Henry was afar off with a small force of soldiers about him, and then afterwards drawing nearer he knew it perfectly by evident signs and tokens that it was Henry; wherefore, all inflamed with ire, he struck his horse with the spurs, and ran out of his own side, ahead of the vanguard, against him. Henry perceived King Richard coming upon him, and because all his hope was then in valor of arms, he received him with great courage. King Richard at the first brunt killed certain men, overthrew Henry's standard together with William Brandon the standard bearer, and fought also with John Cheney, a man of much strength, far exceeding the common sort, who fought with him as he came, but the king with great force drove him to the ground, making way with his weapon on every side. But yet Henry abode the brunt longer than his own soldiers would ever have thought, who were now almost out of hope of victory, when suddenly William Stanley with three thousand men came to the rescue: then truly in a moment the rest all fled, and King Richard alone was killed fighting manfully in the thickest press of his enemies. In the meantime also the earl of Oxford after a little skirmishing put to flight them who fought in the front, whereof a great company were killed in the chase. But many more forbore to fight, who came to the field with King Richard for awe, and for no goodwill, and departed without any danger, as men who desired not the safety but the destruction of that prince whom they hated. There were killed about a thousand men, and amongst them of noble men of war were John, duke of Norfolk; Walter, Lord Ferrers; Robert Brackenbury; Richard Radcliffe; and many more. Two days afterwards, at Leicester, William Catesby, lawyer, and a few who were his fellows, were executed. And of those who took to their feet, Francis Lovell, Humphrey Stafford, with Thomas his brother and much more company, fled into the sanctuary of St. John which is at Colchester, a town by the seaside in Essex. As for the number of captives, it was very great; for when King Richard was killed, all men forthwith threw away their weapons, and freely submitted themselves to Henry's obeisance, whereof the most part would have done the same at the beginning, and had it not been for King Richard's scurriers, scouring to and fro, they might have done so. Amongst them the chief were Henry, earl of Northumberland, and Thomas, earl of Surrey. The earl of Surrey was committed to captivity, where he remained long; the earl of Northumberland as a friend at heart was received into favor. Henry lost in that battle scarcely a hundred soldiers, amongst whom there was one principal man, William Brandon, who bore Earl Henry's standard. The field was fought on [August 22, 1485], and the fight lasted more than two hours.

The report is that King Richard might have sought to save himself by flight; for they who were about him, seeing the soldiers even from the first stroke lift up their weapons feebly and faintly, and some of them depart the field furtively, suspected treason, and exhorted him to flee; and indeed when the matter began manifestly to go against him, they brought him swift horses; but he, who was not unaware that the people hated him, out of hope to have a better situation afterwards, is said to have answered that that very day he would make an end either of war or of life, such great fierceness and such huge force of mind he had; wherefore, knowing certainly that that day would either yield him a peaceable and quiet reign thenceforth or else perpetually bereave him of the same, he came to the field with the crown upon his head, that thereby he might make either a beginning or an end of his reign....

Henry, after the victory was obtained, gave forthwith thanks unto almighty God for the same; then afterwards, replenished with incredible joy, he got himself unto the nearby hill, where, after he had commended his soldiers, and ordered them to care for the wounded, and to bury them that were slain, he gave unto the nobility and gentlemen immortal thanks, promising that he would be mindful of their benefits; all the meanwhile the soldiers cried, "God save King Henry, God save King Henry!" and with heart and hand uttered all the show of joy that might be; and, when Thomas Stanley saw this, he at once set King Richard's crown, which was found among the spoil in the field, upon

his head, as though he had been already by commandment of the people proclaimed king after the manner of his ancestors, and that was the first sign of
prosperity. After that, ordering them to pack up all bag and baggage, Henry
with his victorious army proceeded in the evening to Leicester, where, for
refreshing of his soldiers from their travail and pains, and to prepare for going
to London, he tarried two days. In the meantime the body of King Richard,
naked of all clothing, and laid upon a horse's back, with the arms and legs
hanging down on both sides, was brought to the abbey of Franciscan [friars] at
Leicester — a miserable spectacle in good truth, but not unworthy for the
man's life — and there was buried two days afterwards without any pomp or
solemn funeral....

After Henry had obtained power, from the very start of his reign he then set
about quelling the insurrections. Accordingly, before he left Leicester, he dispatched Robert Willoughby to Yorkshire with instructions to bring back
Edward, the fifteen-year-old earl of Warwick, sole survivor of George, duke of
Clarence, whom [King] Richard had held hitherto in the castle called Sheriff
Hutton. For indeed, Henry, not unaware of the mob's natural tendency always
to seek changes, was fearful lest, if the boy should escape and given any alteration in circumstances, he might stir up civil discord. Having made for the castle without delay, Robert received the boy from the commander of the place
and brought him to London, where the wretch, born to misery, remained in
the Tower until his death.... Henry meanwhile made his way to London like a
triumphing general, and in the places though which he passed was greeted
with the greatest joy by all. Far and wide the people hastened to assemble by
the roadside, saluting him as king and filling the length of his journey with
laden tables and overflowing goblets, so that the weary victors might refresh
themselves. But when he approached the capital, the chief magistrate (whom
they call the "mayor") and all the citizens came forth to meet him and accompanied him ceremoniously as he entered the city: trumpeters went in front
with the spoils of the enemy, thundering forth martial sounds. In this manner
Henry came, after all his toils, to his kingdom, where he was most acceptable to
all. After this he summoned a parliament, as was the custom, in which he
might receive the crown by popular consent. His chief care was to regulate
well affairs of state and, in order that the people of England should not be further torn by rival factions, he publicly proclaimed that (as he had already
promised) he would take for his wife Elizabeth daughter of King Edward [IV]
and that he would give complete pardon and forgiveness to all those who
swore obedience to his name. Then at length, having won the good will of all
men and at the instigation of both nobles and people, he was made king at
Westminster on 31 October and called Henry, seventh of that name....

As soon as he was crowned the king created his uncle Jasper, to whom he was much indebted, duke of Bedford; Thomas Stanley he made earl of Derby, Giles Daubeney Lord Daubeney, Robert Willoughby lord of Broke; and he ennobled many others. To others he restored their ranks and estates. Upon yet others he bestowed public office or further preferment; or enriched them with gifts of money, according to his estimate of their services to him. Furthermore, he recalled home Thomas, marquis of Dorset, and John Bourchier, Lord Feneway, who ... had both been left behind in Paris as sureties or bondsmen for the money which had been advanced there as a loan. Likewise he summoned to his side John Morton, bishop of Ely, from Flanders. To his mother Margaret, a most worthy woman whom no one can extol too much or too often for her sound sense and holiness of life, Henry allotted a share in most of his public and private resources, thus easing her declining years. Henry, moreover, was the first English king to appoint retainers, to the number of about two hundred, to be a bodyguard: these he incorporated in his household so that they should never leave his side; in this he imitated the French kings so that he might thereafter be better protected from treachery. These things having been done, the king, so that he might deserve equally well of both his friends and his enemies, at once granted his pardon for past offenses to all of whatever party who swore allegiance to him. He then took in marriage Elizabeth, daughter of Edward, a woman indeed intelligent above all others, and equally beautiful. It is legitimate to attribute this to divine intervention, for plainly by it all things which nourished the two most ruinous factions were utterly removed, by it the two houses of Lancaster and York were united and from the union the true and established royal line emerged which now reigns....

After Henry had well regulated his affairs in London he set out for York, in order to keep in obedience the folk of the north, savage and more eager than others for upheavals. He halted his journey at Lincoln, where he kept the feast of Easter. While he lingered here, he was informed that Francis, Lord Lovell, together with Humphrey Stafford, had disappeared from sanctuary at Colchester, but no one could say for certain where they had gone. Treating the matter as of small account the king made as he had planned to do for York. But he was no sooner there than the whole town was suddenly filled with the news that Francis Lovell had assembled a large number of troops in Yorkshire itself, a little beyond the castle of Middleham, and was to march on the city itself with hostile intent; and that Humphrey, moreover, was provoking a major rebellion in Gloucestershire. Since the news at first lacked confirmation, the king was not much disturbed, but when he learnt from the dispatches of his own servants that what had at first been rumored was indeed true, he was struck by great fear; for he had neither an army nor arms ready for his supporters, and did not know whence he could gather a reliable force at that time in a town so little devoted to his interests, which hitherto had cherished the name of Richard. But since it was essential to act quickly in order not to give his enemies the opportunity of increasing their numbers, he dispatched against the enemy his whole retinue, including his bodyguard, to the total of 3,000 men, even although they were ill equipped: for the greater part had made armor for themselves from leather. Meanwhile the king assembled soldiers from every possible source. The extemporized forces which had been sent forward advanced hurriedly until they approached the enemy camp, where they immediately announced the royal terms: that the king would voluntarily extend his pardon to those who laid down their arms. This step proved to be the salvation of the king. For Francis, whether because as a result of this offer he had less faith in his troops, or because the irresolute fellow was seized by groundless fear, fled secretly by night with his men. When the flight of their leader was known, they all submitted themselves without delay to the king's authority. Francis, who had not attempted a fight through his feebleness of spirit, betook himself headlong to the district or county of Lancashire and went to Thomas Broughton, a knight of great authority in those parts, with whom he hid for some months. Humphrey, frightened by the flight of Francis, fled from his troops to the sanctuary known as Culham, not far from the place called Abingdon. But because this sanctuary does not protect those who are accused of lèse-majesté, Humphrey was taken out and beheaded; his brother Thomas earned a pardon. [After this Henry put down further attempts to overthrow him.]

Henry, after he had subdued in this way the final conspiracy made against him, and established peaceful relations with all neighboring kings, could now after many anxieties and dangers relax his mind in peace when, while he was enjoying his deserved quiet, he became at once preoccupied by a fresh care. For he began to treat his people with more harshness and severity than had been his custom, in order (as he himself asserted) to ensure they remained more thoroughly and entirely in obedience to him. The people themselves had another explanation for his action, for they considered they were suffering not on account of their own sins but on account of the greed of the monarch. It is not indeed clear whether at the start it was greed; but afterwards greed did become apparent, so irresolute, vacillating, and corrupted are all human purposes. Indeed nothing could certainly be found wanting in King Henry which should be found in the best of princes. But, lest he alone of all men should have been universally blessed, behold, while employing harshness against his people, he gradually laid aside all moderation and sank into a state of avarice, which — since it is itself without limits — torments beyond all bounds those whom it once preoccupies. Evil fortune blighted Henry in this manner so that he, who already excelled other princes in his many virtues, should not also be pre-eminent in subduing all vices. The king wished (as he said) to keep all

Englishmen obedient through fear, and he considered that whenever they gave him offense they were actuated by their great wealth. He began severely to punish all offenders who had committed any crime prohibited and forbidden by the laws of the realm or municipal regulations. All of his subjects who were men of substance, when found guilty of whatever fault, he harshly fined, in order, by a penalty which especially deprived of their fortunes not only the men themselves but even their descendants, to make the population less well able to undertake any upheaval and to discourage at the same time all offenses. This drastic method of inflicting punishment was so rapidly applied that all people, in terror of losing their wealth, at once began to behave themselves and (as the saying goes) to withdraw into their shells. But, lo and behold, no sooner had Henry embarked on this course of action than at once a multitude of informers, a type of creature always most ruinous in any state, converged from all directions on the court. They dangled before the king's eyes ways of making money, and poured into his ears the crimes of many, by which the treasury could be filled with enormous spoils. At first the king, on the urgent advice of his faithful counselors, refused to listen, but later, attracted by the chance of advancing his private interest, he began gradually to pay attention to the informers, and at length to listen to them eagerly. Thus the good prince by degrees lost all sense of moderation and was led into avarice.

The informers, when they saw they could easily approach the king, thereupon indiscriminately and dishonorably entrapped and accused men of all sorts and conditions, and charged them with a variety of crimes. While the informers were thus trying to twist the king's severity into brutality, there then came on the scene two astute lawyers, Richard Empson and Edmund Dudley. They very soon claimed great weight with the monarch and, since they were educated men, he rapidly appointed them as judges to pronounce judicial sentence on wrongdoers. The pair, probably realizing that they had been given the job by the king not so much to administer justice as to strip the population of its wealth, without respite and by every means fair and foul vied with each other in extorting money. Whomsoever, whether a nobleman or a man of the people, the informers charged with the flimsiest or vaguest false accusations, Empson and Dudley condemned and deprived of their property. Every day even laws which had been anciently revoked and invalidated they called into use again, brought into the light of day and at their discretion whom they would they judged to have offended against these old laws. And they proceeded against not the poor but the wealthy, churchmen, rich magnates, even the intimates of the king himself, and any and every individual of fortune — not only the living, but the dying, and those who were long since dead, if by chance they had left property. Moreover they devised many fresh ways of satisfying the king's avarice while they were eagerly serving as the ministers of their own private fortunes. In addition, they dabbled in religious as well as secular matters and considered that everything had its price, so that some were promoted to dignities who were most unworthy of the position. While such methods were in vogue, you could have seen daily in the halls of Empson's and Dudley's houses a host of convicted persons awaiting sentence, to whom wretchedly evasive replies were given, so that they were exhausted by the duration of their anxiety and voluntarily gave up their money. For many preferred to do this, rather than remain longer in that sort of agony. Thus through the agency of these two men, who behaved as if they were plotting to snatch all lay and ecclesiastical wealth, the most savage harshness was made complete.

In the meantime serious men who were unwilling to tolerate this state of affairs urgently entreated the two judges to refrain from plotting damage for wretched mortals and from conspiring their deaths (for many indeed died, stricken by grief at the loss of their possessions). Some important clergymen also publicly preached their disgust at such proceedings and at the same time exposed the king's avarice. But these remonstrances were of no avail. Shortly afterwards the king died and the two extortioners (as we shall presently mention in the life of Henry VIII) were deprived of their lives, just as they had deprived others of their possessions.

While this state of affairs persisted no one dared to complain, at all events openly, but all greatly feared for themselves and their interests, since the king claimed that he tolerated these exactions of set plan, in order thereby to maintain the population in obedience. For the rest, avarice (as we have showed) now so dominated and penetrated into all activities, that it was truly burdensome to his people and brought no profit to the monarch. For although the king was not unaware that, as a result of this ruthless extortion, there were many who rather feared than loved him, his sole interest was to ensure his safety by supervising all details of government; through which preoccupation he at last so wore out his mind and body that his energies gradually declined, he fell into a state of weakness, and from that, not long after, came to his death. Had he been spared to live a little longer, it may be believed that he would have established a more moderate manner of conducting all his affairs. For in the year prior to his death, learning that there was widespread complaint concerning the plundering in which the two judges daily indulged, he is said to have decided to restrain them, to deal more gently with his people and to restore what the two had illegally seized, so that thereafter justice and mercy might flourish throughout his kingdom. But even while he was contemplating this reform death cut him off. When he realized he was not to be allowed to live longer he laid down in his will that all were to be given back such possessions as had been illegally carried off to the treasury by those two most brutal extortioners.

Questions: Why did the Battle of Bosworth turn out as it did? What moral elements does the author find in the story of the battle? What made Henry king, and what steps did he take to secure his throne? Compare this account of Henry's first parliament with that in Sir Thomas Betanson's letter to Robert Plumpton (doc. 82). How does Polydore Vergil judge Henry VII? How was the judicial system subject to abuse and corruption? Who resisted these abuses, and how?

85. AN ITALIAN RELATION OF ENGLAND

The following extracts come from the report of a Venetian official who traveled to England in 1496-97 in the entourage of a Venetian ambassador. While it is not always entirely accurate, the impressions of the foreign visitor are always interesting and at times perceptive, while the wealth of detail and the sweeping generalizations make for good reading.

Source: trans. C.A. Sneyd, *A Relation, or Rather a True Account, of the Island of England* (London: The Camden Society, 1847), pp. 8-12, 20-29, 31-39, 41-46, 54; revised.

A Relation, or Rather a True Account, of the Island of England, with Sundry Particulars of the Customs of these People, and of the Royal Revenues under King Henry the Seventh.

... The climate, as your magnificence knows, is very healthy, and free from many complaints with which [Italy] is afflicted; and, though so far to the north-west, the cold in winter is much less severe than in Italy, and the heat proportionably less in summer. This is owing to the rain, which falls almost every day during the months of June, July, and August; they have never any spring here, according to the report of the islanders. In addition to this equality of temperature, they have, as I have read, and which has been confirmed to me by the inhabitants themselves, a great abundance of large rivers, springs, and streams, in which are found every species of Italian fish, excepting, however, carp, tench, and perch; but on the other hand they have a quantity of salmon, a most delicate fish, which they seem to hold in great estimation, because these people greatly prefer sea-fish; of which, indeed, they have many more than we have. Nor are they without springs of hot water, wholesome and salutary for various disorders. They abound also in every description of tree, though, according to Caesar, they have not the beech, or the fir. They have laurels, and myrtles, and all our fruit trees, with the exception, however, of the olive, and the class of the orange. They are not without vines; and I have eaten ripe grapes from one, and wine might be made in the southern parts, but it would probably be harsh. This natural deficiency of the country is supplied by a great quantity of excellent wines from ... Germany, France, and Spain; besides which, the common people make two beverages from wheat, barley, and oats, one of which is called beer, and the other ale; and these liquors are much liked by them, nor are they disliked by foreigners, after they have drunk them four or six times; they are most agreeable to the palate, when a person is by some chance rather heated.

Agriculture is not practised in this island beyond what is required for the consumption of the people; because were they to plow and sow all the land that was capable of cultivation, they might sell a quantity of grain to the surrounding countries. This negligence is, however, atoned for, by an immense profusion of every comestible animal, such as stags, goats, fallow-deer, hares, rabbits, pigs, and an infinity of oxen.... But above all, they have an enormous number of sheep, which yield them quantities of wool of the best quality. They have no wolves, because they would, immediately, be hunted down by the people; it is said, however, that they still exist in Scotland, as well as in the forest of Caledonia at the extremity of the island, towards the north. Common fowls, pea-fowls, partridges, pheasants, and other small birds abound here above measure, and it is truly a beautiful thing to behold one or two thousand tame swans upon the River Thames, as I, and also your magnificence have seen, which are eaten by the English like ducks and geese. Nor do they dislike what we so much abominate, i.e. crows, rooks, and jackdaws; and the raven may croak at his pleasure, for no one cares for the omen; there is even a penalty attached to destroying them, as they say that they keep the streets of the towns free from all filth.

It is the same case with the kites, which are so tame, that they often take out of the hands of little children the bread smeared with butter, in the Flemish fashion, given to them by their mothers. And although this is general throughout the island, it is more observed in the kingdom of England, than elsewhere.

This island also produces a quantity of iron and silver, and an infinity of lead and tin; of the latter, which is of the purest quality, they make vessels as brilliant as if they were of fine silver; and these are held in great estimation.

A certain shell fish is taken in the sea, called by the inhabitants mussels, in which many, though small, pearls are found; and I myself, dining one morning with the Milanese ambassador, discovered several; but, as I have said, they were very minute, and not round like oriental pearls.

I believe that what has been written concerning the extreme shortness of the nights in summer is true; for many persons of veracity tell me, and assure me that it is a positive fact, that at the farthest extremity of Scotland, at the time of the summer solstice, one may see to read and write at any hour of the night, and that the days in winter are short in the same proportion. But this cannot be the case all over the island, because during the whole winter that I found myself there with your magnificence, I observed the length of the daylight with great attention, and there were never less than seven hours together, in which one could see to read and write. How many hours the sun might be above the horizon, however, I cannot say, for it is so rarely to be seen in the winter, and never but at mid-day: but our Italian merchants say, that in London also, the nights in summer are much shorter than the days in winter; and as London, where your lordship resided, is a place in the south of the island, and more than 600 miles from the highest point of Scotland, the nights there may possibly be much shorter; but English authors never touch upon these subjects.

The form of the island is triangular, as we have said before, and it is divided into three parts, thus: Scotland, Wales, and England....

Although England is mentioned as the third part of the whole island, it alone is larger and richer than both the others, and everything that I find the island produces, is yielded in most abundance there. This third division is all diversified by pleasant undulating hills, and beautiful valleys, with nothing to be seen but agreeable woods, or extensive meadows, or lands in cultivation and the greatest plenty of water springing everywhere....

The English are, for the most part, both men and women of all ages, hand-some and well-proportioned; though not quite so much so, in my opinion, as it had been asserted to me, before your magnificence went to that kingdom; and I have understood from persons acquainted with these countries, that the Scotch are much handsomer; and that the English are great lovers of them-selves, and of everything belonging to them; they think that there are no other men than themselves, and no other world but England; and whenever they see a handsome foreigner, they say that "he looks like an Englishman," and that "it is a great pity that he should not be an Englishman;" and when they partake of any delicacy with a foreigner, they ask him, "whether such a thing is made in *their* country?" They take great pleasure in having a quantity of excellent vict-uals, and also in remaining a long time at table, being very sparing of wine when they drink it at their own expense. And this, it is said, they do in order to induce their other English guests to drink wine in moderation also; not con-sidering it any inconvenience for three or four persons to drink out of the same cup. Few people keep wine in their own houses, but buy it, for the most part, at a tavern; and when they mean to drink a great deal, they go to the tav-ern, and this is done not only by the men, but by ladies of distinction. The deficiency of wine, however, is amply supplied by the abundance of ale and beer, to the use of which these people are become so habituated, that, at an entertainment where there is plenty of wine, they will drink them in prefer-ence to it, and in great quantities. Like discreet people, however, they do not offer them to Italians, unless they should ask for them; and they think that no greater honor can be conferred, or received, than to invite others to eat with them, or to be invited themselves; and they would sooner give five or six ducats to provide an entertainment for a person, than a groat to assist him in any distress.

They all from time immemorial wear very fine clothes, and are extremely polite in their language; which, although it is, like the Flemish, derived from the German, has lost its natural harshness, and is pleasing enough as they pronounce it. In addition to their civil speeches, they have the incredible courtesy of remaining with their heads uncovered, with an admirable grace, whilst they talk to each other. They are gifted with good understandings, and are very quick at everything they apply their minds to; few, however, excepting the clergy, are addicted to the study of letters; and this is the reason why anyone who has learning, though he may be a layman, is called by them a clerk. And yet they have great advantages for study, there being two general universities in the kingdom, Oxford and Cambridge; in which are many colleges founded for the maintenance of poor scholars....

The common people apply themselves to trade, or to fishing, or else they practise navigation; and they are so diligent in mercantile pursuits, that they do not fear to make contracts on usury.

Although they all attend mass every day, and say many Paternosters in public (the women carrying long rosaries in their hands, and any who can read taking the office of our Lady with them, and with some companion reciting it in the church verse by verse, in a low voice, after the manner of churchmen), and they always hear mass on Sunday in their parish church, and give liberal alms, because they may not offer less than a piece of money, of which fourteen are equivalent to a golden ducat, nor do they omit any form incumbent upon good Christians, yet there are, however, many who have various opinions concerning religion.

They have a very high reputation in arms; and from the great fear the French entertain of them, one must believe it to be justly acquired. But I have it on the best information, that when the war is raging most furiously, they will seek for good eating, and all their other comforts, without thinking of what harm might befall them.

They have an antipathy to foreigners, and imagine that they never come into their island, but to make themselves masters of it, and to usurp their goods; neither have they any sincere and solid friendships amongst themselves, insomuch that they do not trust each other to discuss either public or private affairs together, in the confidential manner we do in Italy. And although their dispositions are somewhat licentious, I never have noticed anyone, either at court or amongst the lower orders, to be in love; whence one must necessarily conclude, either that the English are the most discreet lovers in the world, or that they are incapable of love. I say this of the men, for I understand it is quite the contrary with the women, who are very violent in their passions. Howbeit the

English keep a very jealous guard over their wives, though anything may be compensated in the end, by the power of money.

The want of affection in the English is strongly manifested towards their children; for after having kept them at home till they arrive at the age of 7 or 9 years at the utmost, they put them out, both males and females, to hard service in the houses of other people, binding them generally for another 7 or 9 years. And these are called apprentices, and during that time they perform all the most menial offices; and few are born who are exempted from this fate, for everyone, however rich he may be, sends away his children into the houses of others, whilst he, in return, receives those of strangers into his own. And on inquiring their reason for this severity, they answered that they did it in order that their children might learn better manners. But I, for my part, believe that they do it because they like to enjoy all their comforts themselves, and that they are better served by strangers than they would be by their own children. Besides which the English being great epicures, and very avaricious by nature, indulge in the most delicate fare themselves and give their household the coarsest bread, and beer, and cold meat baked on Sunday for the week, which, however, they allow them in great abundance. If they had their own children at home, they would be obliged to give them the same food they made use of for themselves....

Nevertheless, the apprentices for the most part make good fortunes, some by one means and some by another; but, above all, those who happen to be in the good graces of the mistress of the house in which they are domiciled at the time of the death of the master; because, by the ancient custom of the country, every inheritance is divided into three parts; for the church and funeral expenses, for the wife, and for the children. But the lady takes care to secure a good portion for herself in secret, first, and then the residue being divided into three parts as aforesaid, she, being in possession of what she has robbed, of her own third, and that of her children besides (and if she have no children, the two-thirds belong to her by right), usually bestows herself in marriage upon the one of those apprentices living in the house who is most pleasing to her, and who was probably not displeasing to her in the lifetime of her husband; and in his power she places all her own fortune, as well as that of her children, who are sent away as apprentices into other houses. Then, when the boys are of age, their fortunes are restored to them by their mother's husband, who has enjoyed them for many years, but never to the full amount; and these boys in process of time enact to others the same part that their step-fathers performed to them. No Englishman can complain of this corrupt practice, it being universal throughout the kingdom; nor does anyone, arrived at years of discretion, find fault with his mother for marrying again during his childhood, because, from very ancient customs this license has become so sanctioned, that it is not considered any discredit to a woman to marry again every time that she is left a widow, however unsuitable the match may be as to age, rank, and fortune.

I saw, one day, when I was with your magnificence at court, a very handsome young man of about 18 years of age, the brother of the Duke of Suffolk, who, as I understood, had been left very poor, the whole of the paternal inheritance amongst the nobility descending to the eldest son; this youth, I say, was boarded out to a widow of fifty, with a fortune, as I was informed, of 50,000 crowns; and this old woman knew how to play her cards so well, that he was content to become her husband, and patiently to waste the flower of his beauty with her, hoping soon to enjoy her great wealth with some handsome young lady....

Nor must your magnificence imagine that these successions may be of small value, for the riches of England are greater than those of any other country in Europe, as I have been told by the oldest and most experienced merchants, and also as I myself can vouch, from what I have seen. This is owing, in the first place, to the great fertility of the soil, which is such that, with the exception of wine, they import nothing from abroad for their subsistence. Next, the sale of their valuable tin brings in a large sum of money to the kingdom; but still more do they derive from their extraordinary abundance of wool, which bears such a high price and reputation throughout Europe. And in order to keep the gold and silver in the country, when once it has entered, they have made a law, which has been in operation for a long time now, that no money nor gold nor silver plate should be carried out of England, under a very heavy penalty. And everyone who makes a tour in the island will soon become aware of this great wealth, as will have been the case with your magnificence, for there is no small innkeeper, however poor and humble be may be, who does not serve his table with silver dishes and drinking cups; and no one who has not in his house silver plate to the amount of at least £100 sterling, which is equivalent to 500 golden crowns with us, is considered by the English to be a person of any consequence. But above all are their riches displayed in the church treasures; for there is not a parish church in the kingdom so mean as not to possess crucifixes, candlesticks, censers, patens, and cups of silver; nor is there a convent of mendicant friars so poor, as not to have all these same articles in silver, besides many other ornaments worthy of a cathedral church in the same metal. Your magnificence may therefore imagine what the decorations of those enormously rich Benedictine, Carthusian, and Cistercian monasteries must be. These are, indeed, more like baronial palaces than religious houses....

The population of this island does not appear to me to bear any proportion to her fertility and riches. I rode, as your magnificence knows, from Dover to London, and from London to Oxford, a distance of more than 200 Italian miles, and it seemed to me to be very thinly inhabited; but, lest the way I went with your magnificence should have differed from the other parts of the country, I enquired of those who rode to the north of the kingdom, i.e. to the borders of Scotland, and was told that it was the same case there; nor was there any variety in the report of those who went to Bristol and into Cornwall, where there is the promontory that looks to the south-west....

The English, however, could muster a very large army, were they as devoted to their crown as the Scotch are; but from what I understand few of them are very loyal. They generally hate their present, and extol their dead sovereigns. Nevertheless they reject the Caesarean code of laws, and adopt those given to them by their own kings. Nor are proceedings carried on in this country by the deposition of anyone, or by writing, but by the opinion of men, both in criminal and civil causes. And if anyone should claim a certain sum from another, and the debtor denies it, the civil judge would order that each of them should make choice of six arbitrators, and when the twelve are elected, the case they are to judge is propounded to them: after they have heard both parties, they are shut up in a room, without food or fire, or means of sitting down, and there they remain till the greater number have agreed upon their common verdict. But before it is pronounced each of them endeavors to defend the cause of him who named him, whether just or unjust; and those who cannot bear the discomfort, yield to the more determined, for the sake of getting out sooner. And therefore the Italian merchants are gainers by this bad custom every time that they have a dispute with the English; for although the native arbitrators chosen by the English are very anxious to support the cause of their principal, before they are shut up, yet they cannot stand out as the Italians can, who are accustomed to fasting and privations, so that the final judgment is generally given in favor of the latter....

There are three estates in England, the popular, the military, and the ecclesiastical. The people are held in little more esteem than if they were slaves.

The military branch is employed in time of war in mustering troops. The clergy are they who have the supreme sway over the country, both in peace and war. Amongst other things, they have provided that a number of sacred places in the kingdom should serve for the refuge and escape of all delinquents, and no one, were he a traitor to the crown, or had he practised against the king's own person, can be taken out of these by force. And a villain of this kind, who, for some great excess that he has committed, has been obliged to take refuge in one of these sacred places, often goes out of it to brawl in the public streets, and then, returning to it, escapes with impunity for every fresh offense he may have been guilty of. This is no detriment to the purses of the priests, nor to the other perpetual sanctuaries; but every church is a sanctuary for 40 days; and, if a thief or murderer who has taken refuge in one cannot leave it in safety during those 40 days, he gives notice that he wishes to leave England. In which case, being stripped to the shirt by the chief magistrate of the place, and a crucifix placed in his hand, he is conducted along the road to the sea, where, if he finds a passage, he may go with a "God speed you!" But if he should not find one, he walks into the sea up to the throat, and three times asks for a passage; and this is repeated till a ship appears, which comes for him, and so he departs in safety. It is not unamusing to hear, how the women and children lament over the misfortune of these exiles, asking "how they can live so destitute out of England;" adding moreover that "they had better have died than go out of the world," as if England were the whole world!

... But, notwithstanding all these evasions, people are arrested every day by dozens, like birds in a covey, and especially in London; yet, for all this, they never cease to rob and murder in the streets. Perhaps this great prevalence of crime might have been better prevented, had not former kings condensed the criminal jurisdiction under one head, called the chief justice, who has the supreme power over punishment by death. This officer either goes himself, or sends his lieutenants or commissioners, at least twice a year all over the kingdom, but still more frequently to London, to put the unfortunate criminals to death; and it is scarcely possible that one person should suffice for so great an extent of country, though the arrangements are as good as possible, for the kingdom of England, with the principality of Wales, is divided into thirty-six parts, which they call in their language shires; and, for each of these divisions a president is named every year, who is called the sheriff, and he is the administrator of the fiscal concerns, and the executor of all the orders emanating from the king's majesty, or the court, or this chief justice. And if the king should propose to change any old established rule, it would seem to every Englishman as if his life were taken from him; but I think that the present King Henry will do away with a great many, should he live ten years longer.

I dare say that your magnificence will have been surprised, when I stated that there was only one chief justice in the whole kingdom; and will, perhaps, have imagined that I meant to imply that the dukes of Lancaster, York, Suffolk, and many others dispensed justice in their own countries; but these English noblemen are nothing more than rich gentlemen in possession of a great quantity of land belonging to the crown; ... and the jurisdiction, both civil and criminal, and the fortresses remain in the hands of the crown.... In the earliest times of the Norman kings, it was no great matter to give large estates to many gentlemen; for when King William the Bastard conquered England for the crown, all the land that was not fit for cultivation was divided into a number of parts called [fees].... It is computed that there are at present 96,230 of these fees; but the English church is in possession of 28,015 of them; the remainder are the property of the crown, or of the barons of the realm, who, however, pay acknowledgments to the crown for them. There is not a foot of land in all

England, which is not held either under the king or the church.... In former times the titled nobility, though, as I said before, they possessed no fortresses, nor judiciary powers, were extremely profuse in their expenditure, and kept a very great retinue in their houses (which is a thing the English delight in beyond measure); and in this manner they made themselves a multitude of retainers and followers, with whom they afterwards molested the court, and their own countries, and in the end themselves, for at last they were all beheaded. Of these lords, who are called *milites* (knights), there are very few left, and those diminish daily. But the present King Henry has appointed certain military services, to be performed by some of his own dependents and familiars, who he knows can be trusted on any urgent occasion; and can be kept on a much smaller number of fees.... All the lands of the nobility, however, are not in cultivation, for a great portion lies barren and waste; and I am told that there are more than 4000 parks in England, all enclosed with timber fences. And such is the condition of the lords temporal, in this kingdom.

.... There are scarcely any towns of importance in the kingdom, excepting these two: Bristol, a seaport to the west, and Eboracum, otherwise York, which is on the borders of Scotland; besides London to the south.... At present, all the beauty of this island is confined to London; which, although sixty miles distant from the sea, possesses all the advantages to be desired in a maritime town, being situated on the river Thames, which is very much affected by the tide, for many miles (I do not know the exact number) above it: and London is so much benefited by this ebb and flow of the river, that vessels of 100 tons burden can come up to the city, and ships of any size to within five miles of it; yet the water in this river is fresh for twenty miles below London. Although this city has no buildings in the Italian style, but of timber or brick like the French, the Londoners live comfortably, and it appears to me that there are not fewer inhabitants than at Florence or Rome. It abounds with every article of luxury, as well as with the necessaries of life.... In one single street, named the Strand, leading to St. Paul's, there are fifty-two goldsmith's shops, so rich and full of silver vessels, great and small, that in all the shops in Milan, Rome, Venice, and Florence put together, I do not think there would be found so many of the magnificence that are to be seen in London.... These great riches of London are not occasioned by its inhabitants being noblemen or gentlemen; being all, on the contrary, persons of low degree, and artificers who have congregated there from all parts of the island, and from Flanders, and from every other place. No one can be mayor or alderman of London, who has not been an apprentice in his youth; that is, who has not passed the seven or nine years in that hard service described before. Still, the citizens of London are thought quite as highly of there, as the Venetian gentlemen are at Venice, as I think your magnificence may have perceived.

The city is divided into several wards, each of which has six officers; but superior to these are twenty-four gentlemen whom they call aldermen, which in their language signifies old or experienced men; and, of these aldermen, one is elected every year by themselves, to be a magistrate named the mayor, ... and the day on which he enters upon his office, he is obliged to give a sumptuous entertainment to all the principal people in London, as well as to foreigners of distinction; and I, being one of the guests, together with your magnificence, carefully observed every room and hall, and the court where the company were all seated, and was of opinion that there must have been 1000 or more persons at table. This dinner lasted four hours or more; but it is true that the dishes were not served with that assiduity and frequency that is the custom with us in Italy; there being long pauses between each course, the company conversing the while.

... But the diligent watch that is now kept over the Tower of London, was never so before the reign of Henry VII, who keeps there a great store of heavy artillery and band-guns, bombards, arquebuses, and battle-axes; but not in that quantity that I should have supposed; it must be owned, however, that the ammunition of bows, arrows, and cross-bows in the said Tower, is very large and fine....

And in such manner is England ruled and governed.

Questions: What aspects of England impress the author positively? Which aspects does he view negatively? Can you find any inaccuracies in his description? What sources of information does he use? Where has he exaggerated or overgeneralized? How does England, in his view, compare with other parts of Europe?

INDEX

SOURCES

The Author of the book and the Publisher have made every attempt to locate the authors of the copyrighted material or their heirs or assigns, and would be grateful for any information that would allow them to correct any errors or omissions in a subsequent edition of the work.

"Anglo-Saxon Wills." *Anglo-Saxon Wills*. Trans. Dorothy Whitelock. New York: Cambridge University Press, 1930. Reprinted with permission of Cambridge University Press.

"Praise of Queen Emma." *Ecomium Emmae Reginae*. Trans. Alistair Campbell. Camden 3rd Series, 1949. Reprinted with permission of the Royal Historical Association, London.

"The Life of King Edward Who Rests at Westminster" © Frank Barlow 1962, 1992. From *The Life of King Edward who rests at Westminster*, edited and translated with an introduction and notes by Frank Barlow (2nd edition, 1992), reprinted by permission of Oxford University Press.

"Orderic Vitalis's Account of His Life." Reprinted from *The Ecclesiastical History of Orderic Vitalis*, Volume VI, edited and translated by Marjorie Chibnall (1978) by permission of Oxford University Press. © Oxford University Press 1978.

"Assizes of Henry II: Assize of the Forest." *A Documentary History of England*. Vol. I. Trans. J.J. Bagley and P.B. Rowley. London: Penguin, 1966. Copyright © J.J. Bagley and P.B. Rowley, 1966. Reprinted with permission of the publisher.

"William fitzStephen's Description of London." *Norman London*. Ed. F.M. Stenton. Trans. H.E. Butler. London: G. Bell & Sons, 1934. Reprinted with permission of the Historical Association, London.

"The Life of St. William of Norwich by Thomas of Monmouth." *The Life and Miracles of St. William of Norwich by Thomas of Monmouth*. Ed. Augustus Jessop and Montague Rhodes James. Cambridge, UK: Cambridge University Press, 1896. Reprinted with permission of the publisher.

"The Life of St. Godric of Finchale by Reginald of Durham," "Roger Bacon's Third Opus." *Social Life in Britain from the Conquest to the Reformation*. Trans. G.G. Coulton. Cambridge, UK: Cambridge University Press, 1918. Reprinted with permission of the publisher.

"John of Salisbury's *Policraticus*." *English Historical Documents II, 1042-1189*. Trans. David C. Douglas and George W. Greenaway. London: Routledge, 1953. Reprinted with permission of the publisher.

"The History of William Marshall." Trans. Lisa Algazi. Reprinted with permission of the translator.

"Letters of Queen Isabella of Angoulême." *Letters of the Queens of England, 1000-1547.* Trans. Anne Crawford. Stroud, UK: Sutton Publishing, 1994. Reprinted with permission of the publisher.

"Deeds of the Abbots of St. Albans, by Matthew Paris." *Chronicles of Matthew Paris.* Trans. Richard Vaughan. Stroud, UK: Sutton Publishing, 1986. Reprinted with permission of the publisher.

"The Coming of the Friars Minor to England, by Thomas of Eccleston." *English Historical Documents III, 1189-1327.* Trans. Harry Rothwell. London: Routledge, 1975. Reprinted with permission of the publisher.

"The Sphere of Sacrobosco." *The Sphere of Sacroboasco and its Commentators.* Trans. Lynn Thorndike. Chicago, IL: University of Chicago Press, 1949. Reprinted with permission of the publisher.

"Chronicle Account of the Great Famine." *The Life of Edward the Seventh.* Trans. N. Denholm-Young. London: Thomas Nelson & Sons, 1957. Reprinted with permission of the publisher.

"Accounts of the Black Death and its Effects." *The Black Death.* Trans. Rosemary Horrox. Manchester, UK: Manchester University Press, 1994. Reprinted with permission of the publisher.

"A Preacher's Handbook." *Fasciculus Morum: A Fourteenth-Century Preacher's Manual.* Trans. Siegfried Wenzel. University Park: The Pennsylvania State University Press, 1989. Copyright 1989 by The Pennsylvania State University. Reprinted by permission of the publisher.

"The Deposition of Richard II," "The Agincourt Carol," "Parliamentary Debates." *English Historical Documents IV, 1327-1585.* Trans. A.R. Myers. London: Routledge, 1969. Reprinted with permission of the publisher.

"Gynecological Treatise." *Medieval Woman's Guide to Health.* Ed. Beryl Rowland. Kent, OH: Kent State University Press, 1981. Reprinted with permission of The Kent State University Press.